IN THE AFTERMATH of World War II, Prussia—a centuries-old state pivotal to Europe's development—ceased to exist. In their eagerness to erase all traces of the Third Reich from the earth, the Allies believed that Prussia, the very embodiment of German militarism, had to be abolished.

But as Christopher Clark reveals in this pioneering history, Prussia's legacy is far more complex. Though now a fading memory in Europe's heartland, the true story of Prussia offers a remarkable glimpse into the dynamic rise of modern Europe.

What we find is a kingdom that existed nearly half a millennium ago as a patchwork of territorial fragments, with neither significant resources nor a coherent culture. With its capital in Berlin, Prussia grew from being a small, poor, disregarded medieval state into one of the most vigorous and powerful nations in Europe. *Iron Kingdom* traces Prussia's involvement in the continent's foundational religious and political conflagrations: from the devastations of the Thirty Years War through centuries of political machinations to the dissolution of the Holy Roman Empire, from the enlightenment of Frederick the Great to the destructive conquests of Napoleon, and from the "iron and blood" policies of Bismarck to the creation of the German Empire in 1871, with all that implied for the tumultuous twentieth century.

By 1947, Prussia was deemed an intolerable threat to the safety of Europe; what is

Iron Kingdom

CHRISTOPHER CLARK

Iron Kingdom

The Rise and Downfall of Prussia,
1600–1947

The Belknap Press of
Harvard University Press
Cambridge, Massachusetts
2006

For Nina

·

First United Kingdom publication in 2006 by the Penguin Group

Copyright © Christopher Clark, 2006

The moral right of the author has been asserted

A Cataloging-in-Publication Data record for this book
is available through the Library of Congress.

ISBN-13: 978-0-674-02385-7
ISBN-10: 0-674-02385-4

Contents

List of Illustrations and Maps

Maps

Acknowledgements

Between March 1985 and October 1987, I lived and studied in West Berlin, a place that no longer exists. It was a walled city islanded in Communist East Germany, ringed by a palisade of concrete slabs, 'a cage,' as one visiting Italian journalist put it, 'in which one feels free.' No one who lived there will forget the unique atmosphere of this marooned western citadel – a vibrant, multi-ethnic enclave, a haven for youthful refuseniks dodging West German military service, and a symbol of the Cold War in which formal sovereignty still rested with the victorious powers of 1945. There was little in West Berlin to invoke the Prussian past, which seemed as remote as antiquity.

Only when you crossed the political border at Friedrichsstrasse station, passing through turnstiles and metal corridors under the scrutiny of unsmiling guards, did you encounter the heart of the old Prussian city of Berlin – the long line of graceful buildings on Unter den Linden and the breathtaking symmetries of the Forum Fredericianum, where Frederick the Great advertised the cultural pretensions of his kingdom. To cross the border was to travel back into the past, a past only partly obscured by wartime devastation and decades of post-war neglect. A tree had sprouted in the broken dome of the eighteenth-century French Church on the Gendarmenmarkt, its roots reaching deep into the stonework. Berlin Cathedral was still a blackened hulk disfigured by the artillery and rifle fire of 1945. For an Australian from easygoing seaside Sydney, these crossings had an inexhaustible fascination.

Students of the Prussian past can draw on one of the world's most sophisticated and varied historiographies. There is, first of all, the rich and still robust tradition of transatlantic Anglophone writing on Prussia. For readers of German, there is the extraordinary native Prussian canon, which reaches back to the beginnings of history as a modern academic

ix

discipline. The articles and monographs of the classic era of Prussian historiography are still remarkable for the depth and ambition of their scholarship and for the verve and elegance of their writing. The years since 1989 have seen a renewal of interest among younger German scholars and brought wider recognition to those East German historians whose work, notwithstanding the narrow intellectual horizons of the German Democratic Republic, did much to illuminate the evolving textures of Prussian society. One of the chief pleasures of working on this book has been the licence to browse widely in the writings of so many colleagues, alive and dead.

There are also more immediate debts. James Brophy, Karin Friedrich, Andreas Kossert, Benjamin Marschke, Jan Palmowski, Florian Schui and Gareth Stedman Jones shared with me pre-publication versions of their manuscripts. Marcus Clausius sent copies of his transcripts from the archives of the German Colonial Office. I benefited from the advice and conversation of Holger Afflerbach, Margaret Lavinia Anderson, David Barclay, Derek Beales, Stefan Berger, Tim Blanning, Richard Bosworth, Annabel Brett, Clarissa Campbell-Orr, Scott Dixon, Richard Drayton, Philip Dwyer, Richard Evans, Niall Ferguson, Bernhard Fulda, Wolfram Kaiser, Alan Kramer, Michael Ledger-Lomas, Julia Moses, Jonathan Parry, Wolfram Pyta, James Retallack, Torsten Riotte, Emma Rothschild, Ulinka Rublack, Martin Rühl, Hagen Schulze, Hamish Scott, James Sheehan, Brendan Simms, Jonathan Sperber, Thomas Stamm-Kuhlmann, Jonathan Steinberg, Adam Tooze, Maiken Umbach, Helmut Walser-Smith, Peter Wilson, Emma Winter and Wolfgang Mommsen, a frequent visitor to Cambridge, whose unexpected death in August 2004 was such a shock to his friends and colleagues here. Like many historians of Germany now working in the United Kingdom, I learned a great deal from collaborating on 'The Struggle for Mastery in Germany', the Cambridge Specified Subject convened by Tim Blanning and Jonathan Steinberg in the 1980s and early 1990s. I owe much to twenty-five years of spirited conversation with my father-in-law, Rainer Lübbren, a discerning reader of history.

Special thanks are due to those friends who had the generosity and stamina to read and comment on part or all of the manuscript: Chris Bayly, my father Peter Clark, James Mackenzie, Holger Nehring, Hamish Scott, James Simpson, Gareth Stedman Jones, and John A. Thompson. Patrick Higgins dispensed imaginative advice and ran a red line through passages of bombast and irrelevance. Working with the people at Penguin – Chloe Campbell, Richard Duguid and Rebecca Lee – has been another of the pleasures of this project. Simon Winder is the editor's Platonic ideal, endowed with that second sight that sees more clearly than authors themselves the book trapped within the manuscript. Bela Cunha's copy-editing was a vigilante rampage against error, inconsistency and syllogism. Thanks also to Cecilia Mackay for help in resourcing the pictures. With all this able support, the book ought in theory to be faultless – I take full responsibility for the fact that it is not.

How does one thank the most important people of all? Josef and Alexander grew taller during the writing of this book and distracted me in a thousand happy ways. Nina Lübbren bore my selfish obsession with humour and good grace and was the first reader and critic of every paragraph. It is to her that I dedicate this book with much love.

Introduction

On 25 February 1947, representatives of the Allied occupation authorities in Berlin signed a law abolishing the state of Prussia. From this moment onward, Prussia belonged to history.

> The Prussian State, which from early days has been a bearer of militarism and reaction in Germany, has de facto ceased to exist.
> Guided by the interests of preservation of peace and security of peoples, and with the desire to assure further reconstruction of the political life of Germany on a democratic basis, the Control Council enacts as follows:
> ARTICLE I
> The Prussian State together with its central government and all its agencies is abolished.[1]

Law No. 46 of the Allied Control Council was more than an administrative act. In expunging Prussia from the map of Europe, the Allied authorities also passed judgement upon it. Prussia was not just one German territory among others, on a par with Baden, Württemberg, Bavaria or Saxony; it was the very source of the German malaise that had afflicted Europe. It was the reason why Germany had turned from the path of peace and political modernity. 'The core of Germany is Prussia,' Churchill told the British Parliament on 21 September 1943. 'There is the source of the recurring pestilence.'[2] The excision of Prussia from the political map of Europe was thus a symbolic necessity. Its history had become a nightmare that weighed upon the minds of the living.

The burden of that ignominious termination presses on the subject matter of this book. In the nineteenth and early twentieth centuries, the history of Prussia had been painted in mainly positive tones. The Protestant historians of the Prussian School celebrated the Prussian state as a vehicle of rational administration and progress and the liberator of Protestant Germany from the toils of Habsburg Austria and Bonapartist France. They saw in the Prussian-dominated nation-state founded in 1871 the natural, inevitable and best outcome of Germany's historical evolution since the Reformation.

This rosy view of the Prussian tradition faded after 1945, when the criminality of the Nazi regime cast its long shadows over the German past. Nazism, one prominent historian argued, was no accident, but rather 'the acute symptom of a chronic [Prussian] infirmity'; the Austrian Adolf Hitler was an 'elective Prussian' in his mentality.[3] The view gained ground that German history in the modern era had failed to follow the 'normal' (i.e. British, American or west European) route to a relatively liberal and untroubled political maturity. Whereas the power of traditional elites and political institutions had been broken in France, Britain and the Netherlands by 'bourgeois revolutions', so the argument ran, this had never been achieved in Germany. Instead, Germany followed a 'special path' (*Sonderweg*) that culminated in twelve years of Nazi dictatorship.

Prussia played a key role in this scenario of political malformation, for it was here that the classical manifestations of the special path seemed most clearly in evidence. Foremost among these was the unbroken power of the Junkers, the noble landowners of the districts to the east of the river Elbe, whose dominance within government, the military and rural society had survived the age of the European revolutions. The consequences for Prussia and by extension for Germany were, it appeared, disastrous: a political culture marked by illiberalism and intolerance, an inclination to revere power over legally grounded right, and an unbroken tradition of militarism. Central to nearly all diagnoses of the special path was the notion of a lopsided or 'incomplete' process of modernization, in which the evolution of political culture failed to keep pace with innovation and growth in the economic sphere. By this reading, Prussia was the bane of modern German and European history. Imprinting its own peculiar political culture on the nascent German nation-state, it stifled and marginalized the more liberal political cultures of the German south and thus laid the foundations for political extremism and dictatorship. Its habits of authoritarianism, servility and obedience prepared the ground for the collapse of democracy and the advent of dictatorship.[4]

This paradigm shift in historical perceptions met with energetic counterblasts from historians (mainly West German, and mainly of liberal or conservative political orientation) who sought to rehabilitate the reputation of the abolished state. They highlighted its positive achievements – an incorruptible civil service, a tolerant attitude to religious minorities, a law code (from 1794) admired and imitated throughout the German states, a literacy rate (in the nineteenth century) unequalled in Europe and a bureaucracy of exemplary efficiency. They drew attention to the vibrancy of the Prussian enlightenment. They noted the capacity of the Prussian state to transform and reconstitute itself in times of crisis. As a counterpart to the political servility emphasized by the special-path paradigm, they stressed notable episodes of insubordination, most importantly the role played by Prussian officers in the plot to assassinate Hitler in July 1944. The Prussia they depicted was not without flaws, but it had little in common with the racial state created by the Nazis.[5]

The high-water mark for this work of historical evocation was the massive Prussia Exhibition that opened in Berlin in 1981 and was seen by over half a million visitors. Room after room full of objects and tables of text prepared by an international team of scholars allowed the viewer to traverse Prussian history through a succession of scenes and moments. There were military paraphernalia, aristocratic family trees, images of life at court and historic battle paintings, but also rooms organized around the themes of 'tolerance', 'emancipation' and 'revolution'. The aim was not to shed a nostalgic glow over the past (though it was certainly too positive for many critics on the political left), but to alternate light and shadow, and thereby to 'draw the balance' of Prussian history. Commentaries on the exhibition – both in the official catalogues and in the mass media – focused on the meaning of Prussia for contemporary Germans. Much of the discussion centred on the lessons that could or could not be learned from Prussia's troubled journey into modernity. There was talk of the need to honour the 'virtues' – disinterested public service and tolerance, for example – while disassociating oneself from the less appetizing features of the Prussian tradition, such as autocratic habits in politics or a tendency to glorify military achievement.[6]

Prussia remains, more than two decades later, an idea with the power to polarize. The unification of Germany after 1989 and the transfer of the capital from Catholic, 'western' Bonn to Protestant, 'eastern' Berlin gave rise to misgivings about the still unmastered potency of the Prussian past. Would the spirit of 'old Prussia' reawaken to haunt the German Republic? Prussia was extinct, but 'Prussia' re-emerged as a symbolic political token. It has become a slogan for elements of the German right, who see in the 'traditions' of 'old Prussia' a virtuous counterweight to 'disorientation', 'the erosion of values', 'political corruption' and the decline of collective identities in contemporary Germany.[7] Yet for many Germans, 'Prussia' remains synonymous with everything repellent in German history: militarism, conquest, arrogance and illiberality. The controversy over Prussia has tended to flicker back into life whenever the symbolic attributes of the abolished state are brought into play. The re-interment of the remains of Frederick the Great at his palace of Sans Souci in August 1991 was the subject of much fractious discussion and there have been heated public disputes over the plan to reconstruct the Hohenzollern city palace on the Schlossplatz in the heart of Berlin.[8]

In February 2002, Alwin Ziel, an otherwise inconspicuous Social Democratic minister in the Brandenburg state government, achieved instant notoriety when he intervened in a debate over a proposed merger of the city of Berlin with the federal state of Brandenburg. 'Berlin-Brandenburg', he argued, was a cumbersome word; why not name the new territory 'Prussia'? The suggestion set off a new wave of debate. Sceptics warned of a rebirth of Prussia, the issue was discussed on television talk shows across Germany, and the *Frankfurter Allgemeine Zeitung* ran a series of articles under the rubric 'Should there be a Prussia?' (*Darf Preussen sein?*) Among the contributors was Professor Hans-Ulrich Wehler, a leading exponent of the German special path, whose article – a vociferous rejection of Ziel's proposal – bore the title 'Prussia poisons us'.[9]

No attempt to understand the history of Prussia can entirely escape the issues raised by these debates. The question of how exactly Prussia was implicated in the disasters of Germany's twentieth century must be a part of any appraisal of the state's history. But this does not mean that we should read the history of Prussia (or indeed of any state) from the perspective of Hitler's seizure of power alone. Nor does it oblige us to assess the Prussian record in binary ethical categories, dutifully praising light and deploring shadow. The polarized judgements that abound in contemporary debate (and in parts of the historical literature) are problematic, not just because they impoverish the complexity of the

Prussian experience, but also because they compress its history into a national teleology of German guilt. Yet the truth is that Prussia was a European state long before it became a German one. Germany was not Prussia's fulfilment – here I anticipate one of the central arguments of this book – but its undoing.

I have thus made no attempt to tease out the virtue and vice in the Prussian record or to weigh them in the balance. I make no claim to extrapolate 'lessons' or to dispense moral or political advice to present or future generations. The reader of these pages will encounter neither the bleak, warmongering termite-state of some Prussophobe treatises, nor the cosy fireside scenes of the Prussophile tradition. As an Australian historian writing in twenty-first-century Cambridge, I am happily dispensed from the obligation (or temptation) either to lament or to celebrate the Prussian record. Instead, this book aims to understand the forces that made and unmade Prussia.

It has recently become fashionable to emphasize that nations and states are not natural phenomena but contingent, artificial creations. It is said that they are 'edifices' that have to be constructed or invented, with collective identities that are 'forged' by acts of will.[10] No modern state more strikingly vindicates this perspective than Prussia: it was an assemblage of disparate territorial fragments lacking natural boundaries or a distinct national culture, dialect or cuisine. This predicament was amplified by the fact that Prussia's intermittent territorial expansion entailed the periodic incorporation of new populations whose loyalty to the Prussian state could be acquired, if at all, only through arduous processes of assimilation. Making 'Prussians' was a slow and faltering enterprise whose momentum had begun to wane long before Prussian history reached its formal termination. The name 'Prussia' itself had a contrived quality, since it derived not from the northern heartland of the Hohenzollern dynasty (the Mark Brandenburg around the city of Berlin), but from a non-adjacent Baltic duchy that formed the easternmost territory of the Hohenzollern patrimony. It was, as it were, the logo the Electors of Brandenburg adopted after their elevation to royal status in 1701. The core and essence of the Prussian tradition was an absence of tradition. How this desiccated, abstract polity acquired flesh and bones, how it evolved from a block-printed list of princely titles into something coherent and alive, and how it learned to win the voluntary allegiance of its subjects – these questions are at the centre of this book.

The word 'Prussian' stills stands in common parlance for a particular kind of authoritarian orderliness, and it is all too easy to imagine the history of Prussia as the unfolding of a tidy plan by which the Hohenzollerns gradually unfurl the power of the state, integrating their possessions, extending their patrimony and pushing back the provincial nobilities. In this scenario, the state rises out of the confusion and obscurity of the medieval past, severing its bonds with tradition, imposing a rational, all-embracing order. The book aims to unsettle this narrative. It attempts, firstly, to open up the Prussian record in such a way that both order and disorder have their place. The experience of war – the most terrible kind of disorder – runs through the Prussian story, accelerating and retarding the state-building process in complex ways. As for the domestic consolidation of the state, this has to be seen as a haphazard and improvised process that unfolded within a dynamic and sometimes unstable social setting. 'Administration' was sometimes a byword for controlled upheaval. Well into the nineteenth century there were many areas of the Prussian lands where the presence of the state was scarcely perceptible.

Yet this does not mean that we should relegate 'the state' to the margins of the Prussian story. Rather we should understand it as an artefact of political culture, a form of reflexive consciousness. It is one of the remarkable features of Prussia's intellectual formation that the idea of a distinctively Prussian history has always been interwoven with claims about the legitimacy and necessity of the state. The Great Elector, for example, argued in the mid seventeenth century that the concentration of power within the executive structures of the monarchical state was the most reliable surety against external aggression. But this argument – sometimes rehearsed by historians under the rubric of an objective 'primacy of foreign policy' – was itself a part of the story of the state's evolution; it was one of the rhetorical instruments with which the prince underpinned his claim to sovereign power.

To put the same point a different way: the story of the Prussian state is also the story of the story of the Prussian state, for the Prussian state made up its history as it went along, developing an ever more elaborate account of its trajectory in the past and its purposes in the present. In the early nineteenth century, the need to shore up the Prussian administration in the face of the revolutionary challenge from France produced a unique discursive escalation. The Prussian state legitimated itself as the carrier of historical progress in terms so exalted that it became the model of a particular kind of modernity. Yet the authority and sublimity of the state in the minds of educated contemporaries bore little relation to its actual weight in the lives of the great majority of subjects.

There is an intriguing contrast between the modesty of Prussia's ancestral territorial endowment and the eminence of its place in history. Visitors to Brandenburg, the historic core province of the Prussian state, have always been struck by the meagreness of its resources, the sleepy provinciality of its towns. There was little here to suggest, let alone explain, the extraordinary historical career of the Brandenburg polity. 'Someone ought to write a little piece on what is happening at present,' Voltaire wrote at the beginning of the Seven Years War (1756–63), as his friend King Frederick of Prussia struggled to fight off the combined forces of the French, Russians and Austrians. 'It would be of some use to explain how the sandy country of Brandenburg came to wield such power that greater efforts have been marshalled against it than were ever mustered against Louis XIV.'[11] The apparent mismatch between the force wielded by the Prussian state and the domestic resources available to sustain it helps to explain one of the most curious features of Prussia's history as a European power, namely the alternation of moments of precocious strength with moments of perilous weakness. Prussia is bound up in public awareness with the memory of military success: Rossbach, Leuthen, Leipzig, Waterloo, Königgrätz, Sedan. But in the course of its history, Brandenburg-Prussia repeatedly stood on the brink of political extinction: during the Thirty Years War, again during the Seven Years War and once again in 1806, when Napoleon smashed the Prussian army and chased the king across northern Europe to Memel at the easternmost extremity of his kingdom. Periods of armament and military consolidation were interspersed with long periods of contraction and decline. The dark side of Prussia's unexpected success was an abiding sense of vulnerability that left a distinctive imprint on the state's political culture.

This book is about how Prussia was made and unmade. Only through an appreciation of both processes can we understand how a state that once loomed so large in the awareness of so many could so abruptly and comprehensively disappear, unmourned, from the political stage.

A History of Brandenburg–Prussia
in Six Maps

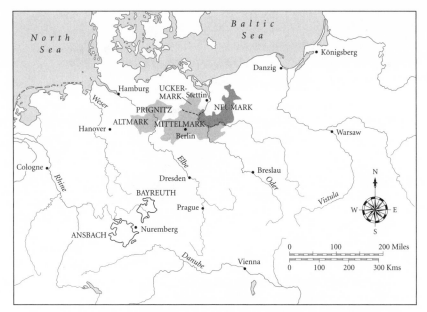

Map 1. The Electorate of Brandenburg at the time of its acquisition by the Hohenzollerns in 1415

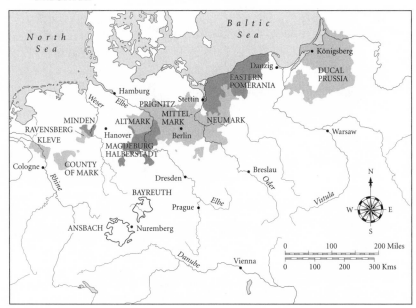

Map 2. Brandenburg–Prussia at the time of the Great Elector (1640–88)

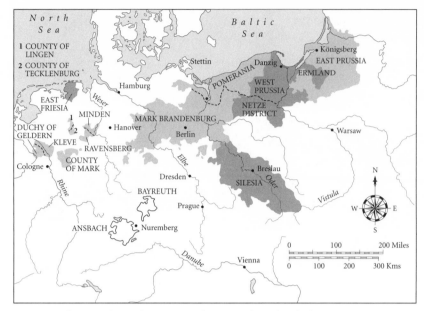

Map 3. The Kingdom of Prussia at the time of Frederick the Great (1740–86)

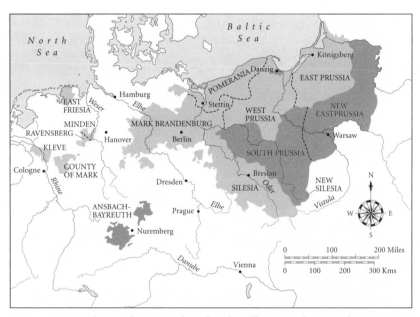

Map 4. Prussia during the reign of Frederick William II, showing the territories taken during the second and third partitions of Poland

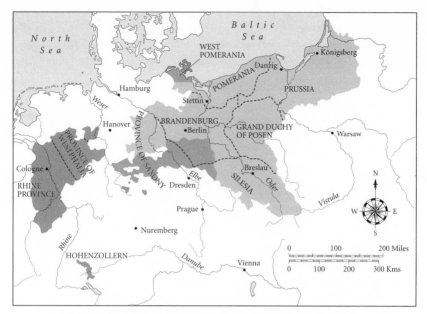

Map 5. *Prussia following the Congress of Vienna (1815)*

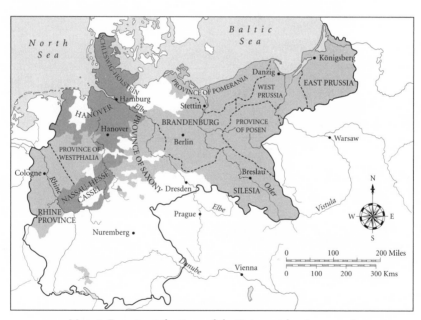

Map 6. *Prussia at the time of the* Kaiserreich *1871–1918*

I

The Hohenzollerns of Brandenburg

HEARTLAND

In the beginning there was only Brandenburg, a territory encompassing some 40,000 square kilometres and centred on the city of Berlin. This was the heartland of the state that would later be known as Prussia. Situated in the midst of the dreary plain that stretches from the Netherlands to northern Poland, the Brandenburg countryside has rarely attracted visitors. It possesses no distinctive landmarks. The rivers that cross it are sluggish meandering streams that lack the grandeur of the Rhine or the Danube. Monotonous forests of birch and fir covered much of its surface. The topographer Nicolaus Leuthinger, author of an early description of Brandenburg, wrote in 1598 of a 'flat land, wooded and for the most part swamp'. 'Sand', flatness, 'bogs' and 'uncultivated areas' were recurring topoi in all the early accounts, even the most panegyric.[1]

The soil across much of Brandenburg was of poor quality. In some areas, especially around Berlin, the ground was so sandy and light that trees would not grow on it. In this respect little had changed by the mid nineteenth century, when an English traveller approaching Berlin from the south at the height of summer described 'vast regions of bare and burning sand; villages, few and far between, and woods of stunted firs, the ground under which is hoar with a thick carpeting of reindeer moss'.[2]

Metternich famously remarked that Italy was a 'geographical expression'. The same could not be said of Brandenburg. It was landlocked and without defensible natural borders of any kind. It was a purely political entity, assembled from the lands seized from pagan Slavs during the Middle Ages and settled by immigrants from France, the

Netherlands, northern Italy and England, as well as the German lands. The Slavic character of the population was gradually erased, although there remained until well into the twentieth century pockets of Slavic-language speakers – known as 'Wends' – in the villages of the Spreewald near Berlin. The frontier character of the region, its identity as the eastward boundary of Christian-German settlement, was semantically conserved in the term 'Mark', or 'March' (as in Welsh Marches), used both for Brandenburg as a whole and for four of its five constituent provinces: the Mittelmark around Berlin, the Altmark to the west, the Uckermark to the north and the Neumark to the east (the fifth was the Prignitz to the north-west).

Transport arrangements were primitive. As Brandenburg had no coast, there was no harbour on the sea. The rivers Elbe and Oder flowed northwards towards the North Sea and the Baltic through the western and eastern flanks of the Mark, but there was no waterway between them, so that the residential cities of Berlin and Potsdam remained without direct access to the transportation arteries of the region. Work had begun in 1548 on a canal that would link the Oder with the river Spree that ran between Berlin and its sister-city Cölln, but the project

proved too costly and was abandoned. Since in this period transport was far more expensive by land routes than by water, the paucity of navigable east–west waterways was a serious structural disadvantage.

Brandenburg lay outside the main German areas of specialized crop-based manufacture (wine, madder, flax, fustian, wool and silk), and was not well endowed with the key mineral resources of the era (silver, copper, iron, zinc and tin).[3] The most important centre of metallurgical activity was the ironworks established in the fortified city of Peitz in the 1550s. A contemporary depiction shows substantial buildings situated among fast-flowing artificial watercourses. A large water-wheel powered the heavy hammers that flattened and shaped the metal. Peitz was of some importance to the Elector, whose garrisons depended upon it for munitions; it was otherwise of little economic significance. The iron produced there was prone to shatter in cold weather. Brandenburg was thus in no position to compete for export custom in regional markets and its nascent metallurgical sector could not have survived without government contracts and import restrictions.[4] It had nothing to compare with the flourishing foundries in the ore-rich electorate of Saxony to the south-east. It did not enjoy the self-sufficiency in armaments that enabled Sweden to assert itself as a regional power in the early seventeenth century.

Early accounts of Brandenburg's agrarian topography convey a mixed impression. The poor quality of the soil across much of the territory meant that agricultural yields in many areas were low. In some places, the soil was so quickly exhausted that it could be sown only every six, nine or twelve years, not to mention sizeable tracts of 'infertile sand' or waterland where nothing could be grown at all.[5] On the other hand, there were also areas – especially in the Altmark and Uckermark and the fertile Havelland to the west of Berlin – with sufficient tracts of arable land to support intensive cereal cultivation, and here there were signs of real economic vitality by 1600. Under the favourable conditions of the long European growth cycle of the sixteenth century, the land-lords of the Brandenburg nobility amassed impressive fortunes by producing grain for export. Evidence of this wealth could be seen in the graceful Renaissance houses – virtually none of which survive – built by the better-off families, a growing readiness to send sons abroad for university education, and a sharp rise in the value of agricultural property. The waves of sixteenth-century German immigrants who came to Brandenburg from Franconia, the Saxon states, Silesia and the Rhineland to settle on unoccupied farms were a further sign of growing prosperity.

Yet there is little to suggest that the profits earned even by the most successful landlords were contributing to productivity gains or longer-term economic growth on a more than local scale.[6] Brandenburg's manorial system did not release enough surplus labour or generate enough purchasing power to stimulate the kind of urban development found in western Europe. The towns of the territory developed as administrative centres accommodating local manufactures and trade, but they remained modest in size. The capital city, a composite settlement then known as Berlin-Cölln, numbered only 10,000 people when the Thirty Years War broke out in 1618 – the core population of the City of London at this time was around 130,000.

DYNASTY

How did this unpromising territory become the heartland of a powerful European state? The key lies partly in the prudence and ambition of the ruling dynasty. The Hohenzollerns were a clan of south-German magnates on the make. In 1417, Frederick Hohenzollern, Burgrave of the small but wealthy territory of Nuremberg, purchased Brandenburg from its then sovereign, Emperor Sigismund, for 400,000 Hungarian gold guilders. The transaction brought prestige as well as land, for Brandenburg was one of the seven Electorates of the Holy Roman Empire, a patchwork quilt of states and statelets that extended across German Europe. In acquiring his new title, Frederick I, Elector of Brandenburg, entered a political universe that has since vanished utterly from the map of Europe. The 'Holy Roman Empire of the German Nation' was essentially a survival from the medieval world of universal Christian monarchy, mixed sovereignty and corporate privilege. It was not an 'empire' in the modern Anglophone sense of a system of rule imposed by one territory upon others, but a loose fabric of constitutional arrangements centred on the imperial court and encompassing over 300 sovereign territorial entities that varied widely in size and legal status.[7] The subjects of the Empire included not only Germans but also French-speaking Walloons, Flemings in the Netherlands and Danes, Czechs, Slovaks, Slovenes, Croats and Italians on the northern and eastern periphery of German Europe. Its chief political organ was the imperial diet, an assembly of envoys representing the territorial principalities, sovereign bishoprics, abbeys, counties and imperial Free Cities (independent mini-states such as Hamburg and Augsburg) that composed the 'estates' of the Empire.

Presiding over this variegated political landscape was the Holy Roman Emperor. His was an elective office – each new emperor had to be chosen in concert by the Electors – so that in theory the post could have been held by a candidate from any eligible dynasty. Yet, from the late Middle Ages until the formal abolition of the Empire in 1806 the choice virtually always fell in practice to the senior male member of the Habsburg family.[8] By the 1520s, following a chain of advantageous marriages and fortunate successions (most importantly to Bohemia and Hungary), the Habsburgs were far and away the wealthiest and most powerful German dynasty. The Bohemian crown lands included the mineral-rich Duchy of Silesia and the margravates of Upper and Lower Lusatia, all major centres of manufacture. The Habsburg court thus controlled an impressive swathe of territories reaching from the western margins of Hungary to the southern borders of Brandenburg.

When they became Electors of Brandenburg, the Franconian Hohenzollerns joined a small elite of German princes – there were only seven in all – with the right to elect the man who would become Holy Roman Emperor of the German Nation. The Electoral title was an asset of enormous significance. It bestowed a symbolic pre-eminence that was given visible expression not only in the sovereign insignia and political rites of the dynasty but also in the elaborate ceremonials that attended all the official functions of the Empire. It placed the sovereigns of Brandenburg in a position periodically to exchange the territory's Electoral vote for political concessions and gifts from the Emperor. Such opportunities arose not only on the occasion of an actual imperial election, but at all those times when a still reigning emperor sought to secure advance support for his successor.

The Hohenzollerns worked hard to consolidate and expand their patrimony. There were small but significant territorial acquisitions in almost every reign until the mid sixteenth century. Unlike several other

German dynasties in the region, the Hohenzollerns also managed to avoid a partition of their lands. The law of succession known as the *Dispositio Achillea* (1473) secured the hereditary unity of Brandenburg. Joachim I (r. 1499–1535) flouted this law when he ordered that his lands be divided at his death between his two sons, but the younger son died without issue in 1571 and the unity of the Mark was restored. In his political testament of 1596, Elector John George (r. 1571–98) once again proposed to partition the Mark among his sons from various marriages. His successor, Elector Joachim Frederick, succeeded in holding the Brandenburg inheritance together, but only thanks to the extinction of the southern, Franconian line of the family, which allowed him to compensate his younger brothers with lands from outside the Brandenburg patrimony. As these examples suggest, the sixteenth-century Hohenzollerns still thought and behaved as clan chiefs rather than as heads of state. Yet, although the temptation to put the family first continued to be felt after 1596, it was never strong enough to prevail against the integrity of the territory. Other dynastic territories of this era fractured over the generations into ever smaller statelets, but Brandenburg remained intact.[9]

The Habsburg Emperor loomed large on the political horizons of the Hohenzollern Electors in Berlin. He was not just a potent European prince, but also the symbolic keystone and guarantor of the Empire itself, whose ancient constitution was the foundation of all sovereignty in German Europe. Respect for his power was intermingled with a deep attachment to the political order he personified. Yet none of this meant that the Habsburg Emperor could control or single-handedly direct affairs within the Empire. There was no imperial central government, no imperial right of taxation and no permanent imperial army or police force. Bending the Empire to his will was always a matter of negotiation, bargaining and manoeuvre. For all its continuities with the medieval past, the Holy Roman Empire was a highly fluid and dynamic system characterized by an unstable balance of power.

REFORMATION

In the 1520s and 1530s, the energies released by the German Reformation agitated this complex system, generating a process of galloping polarization. An influential group of territorial princes adopted the Lutheran confession, along with about two-fifths of the imperial Free Cities. The Habsburg Emperor Charles V, determined both to safeguard the Catholic character of the Roman Empire and to consolidate his own imperial dominion, mustered an anti-Lutheran alliance. These forces won some notable victories in the Schmalkaldic War of 1546–7, but the prospect of further Habsburg advancement sufficed to bring together the dynasty's opponents and rivals within and outside the Empire. By the early 1550s, France, ever anxious to block the machinations of Vienna, had begun to provide military support for the Protestant German territories. The consequence of the resulting stalemate was the compromise settlement agreed at the 1555 Diet of Augsburg. The Peace of Augsburg formally acknowledged the existence of Lutheran territories within the Empire and conceded the right of Lutheran sovereigns to impose confessional conformity upon their own subjects.

Throughout these upheavals, the Hohenzollerns of Brandenburg pursued a policy of neutrality and circumspection. Anxious not to alienate the Emperor, they were slow to commit themselves formally to the Lutheran faith; having done so, they instituted a territorial reformation so cautious and so gradual that it took most of the sixteenth century to accomplish. Elector Joachim I of Brandenburg (1499–1535) wished his sons to remain within the Catholic church, but in 1527 his wife Elizabeth of Denmark took matters into her own hands and converted to Lutheranism before fleeing to Saxony, where she placed herself under the protection of the Lutheran Elector John.[10] The new Elector was still a Catholic when he acceded to the Brandenburg throne as Joachim II (r. 1535–71), but he soon followed his mother's example and converted to the Lutheran faith. Here, as on so many later occasions, dynastic women played a crucial role in the development of Brandenburg's confessional policy.

For all his personal sympathy with the cause of religious reform, Joachim II was slow to attach his territory formally to the new faith. He

1. *Lucas Cranach*, Elector
Joachim II *(1535–71)*,
painted c. *1551*

still loved the old liturgy and the pomp of the Catholic ritual. He was also anxious not to take any step that might damage Brandenburg's standing within the fabric of the still predominantly Catholic Empire. A portrait from around 1551 by Lucas Cranach the Younger captures these two sides of the man. We see an imposing figure who stands with fists clenched before a spreading belly, decked in the bulging, bejewelled court garb of the day. There is watchfulness in the features. Wary eyes look out obliquely from the square face.

In the great political struggles of the Empire, Brandenburg aspired to the role of conciliator and honest broker. The Elector's envoys were involved in various failed attempts to engineer a compromise between the Protestant and Catholic camps. Joachim II kept his distance from the more hawkish Protestant princes and even sent a small contingent of mounted troops to support the Emperor during the Schmalkaldic War. It was not until 1563, in the relative calm that followed the Peace of Augsburg, that Joachim formalized his personal attachment to the new religion through a public confession of faith.

Only in the reign of Elector John George (1571–98), Joachim II's son, did the lands of Brandenburg begin to develop a more firmly Lutheran character: orthodox Lutherans were appointed to professorial posts at the University of Frankfurt/Oder, the Church Regulation of 1540 was thoroughly revised to conform more faithfully with Lutheran principles and two territorial church inspections (1573–81 and 1594) were carried out to ensure that the transition to Lutheranism was accomplished at the provincial and local level. Yet in the sphere of imperial politics, John George remained a loyal supporter of the Habsburg court. Even Elector Joachim Frederick (r. 1598–1608), who as a young man had antagonized the Catholic camp by his open support for the Protestant cause, mellowed when he came to the throne, and kept his distance from the various Protestant combinations attempting to extract religious concessions from the imperial court.[11]

If the Electors of Brandenburg were prudent, they were not without ambition. Marriage was the preferred instrument of policy for a state that lacked defensible frontiers or the resources to achieve its objectives by coercive means. Surveying the Hohenzollern marital alliances of the sixteenth century, one is struck by the scatter-gun approach: in 1502 and again in 1523, there were marriages with the House of Denmark, by which the reigning Elector hoped (in vain) to acquire a claim to parts of the duchies of Schleswig and Holstein and a harbour on the Baltic. In 1530, his daughter was married off to Duke Georg I of Pomerania, in the hope that Brandenburg might one day succeed to the duchy and acquire a stretch of Baltic coast. The King of Poland was another important player in Brandenburg's calculations. He was the feudal overlord of the Duchy of Prussia, a Baltic principality that had been controlled by the Teutonic Order until its secularization in 1525, and was ruled thereafter by Duke Albrecht von Hohenzollern, a cousin of the Elector of Brandenburg.

It was partly in order to get his hands on this attractive territory that Elector Joachim II married Princess Hedwig of Poland in 1535. In 1564, when his wife's brother was on the Polish throne, Joachim succeeded in having his two sons named as secondary heirs to the duchy. Following Duke Albrecht's death four years later, this status was confirmed at the Polish Reichstag in Lublin, opening up the prospect of a Brandenburg succession to the duchy if the new duke, the sixteen-year-old Albrecht Frederick, were to die without male issue. As it happened, the wager paid off: Albrecht Frederick lived, in poor mental but good physical health, for a further fifty years until 1618, when he died, having sired two daughters, but no sons.

In the meanwhile, the Hohenzollerns lost no time in reinforcing their claim to the Duchy of Prussia by every means available. The sons took up where the fathers had left off. In 1603, Elector Joachim Frederick persuaded the Polish king to grant him the powers of regent over the duchy (necessary because of the reigning duke's mental infirmity). His son John Sigismund had further reinforced the link with Ducal Prussia by marrying Duke Albrecht Friedrich's eldest daughter, Anna of Prussia, in 1594, overlooking her mother's candid warning that she was 'not the prettiest'.[12] Then, presumably in order to prevent another family from muscling in on the inheritance, the father, Joachim Frederick, whose first wife had died, married the younger sister of his son's wife. The father was now the brother-in-law of the son, while Anna's younger sister doubled as her mother-in-law.

A direct succession to the Duchy of Prussia thus seemed certain. But the marriage between John Sigismund and Anna also opened up the prospect of a new and rich inheritance in the west. Anna was not only the daughter of the Duke of Prussia, but also the niece of yet another insane German duke, John William of Jülich-Kleve, whose territories encompassed the Rhenish duchies of Jülich, Kleve (Cleves) and Berg and the counties of Mark and Ravensberg. Anna's mother, Maria Eleonora, was the eldest sister of John William. The relationship on her mother's side would have counted for little, had it not been for a pact within the house of Jülich-Kleve that allowed the family's properties and titles to pass down the female line. This unusual arrangement made Anna of Prussia her uncle's heiress, and thus established her husband, John Sigismund of Brandenburg, as a claimant to the lands of Jülich-Kleve.[13] Nothing could better illustrate the serendipitous quality of the marriage market in early modern Europe, with its ruthless trans-generational plotting, and its role in this formative phase of Brandenburg's history.

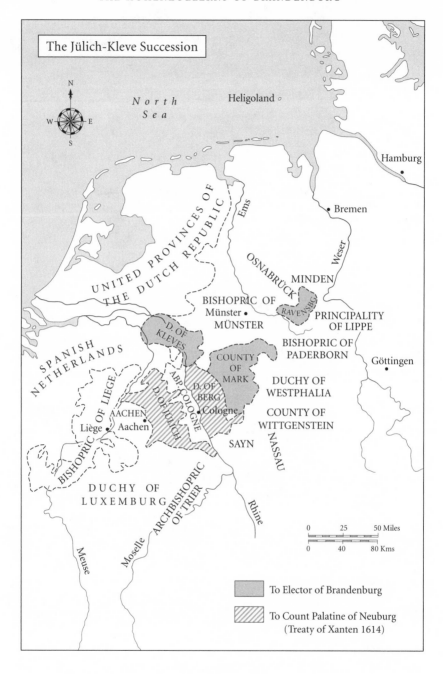

The Jülich-Kleve Succession

North Sea

Heligoland

Hamburg

Bremen

Ems

UNITED PROVINCES OF THE DUTCH REPUBLIC

OSNABRÜCK

Weser

MINDEN

BISHOPRIC OF MÜNSTER
Münster

RAVENSBG.

PRINCIPALITY OF LIPPE

D. OF KLEVES

BISHOPRIC OF PADERBORN

Göttingen

SPANISH NETHERLANDS

COUNTY OF MARK

ABP. COLOGNE

D. OF JÜLICH

D. OF BERG

Cologne

DUCHY OF WESTPHALIA

COUNTY OF WITTGENSTEIN

BISHOPRIC OF LIEGE

AACHEN
Liège   Aachen

SAYN

NASSAU

DUCHY OF LUXEMBURG

ARCHBISHOPRIC OF TRIER

Rhine

Meuse

Moselle

0   25   50 Miles
0   40   80 Kms

To Elector of Brandenburg

To Count Palatine of Neuburg
(Treaty of Xanten 1614)

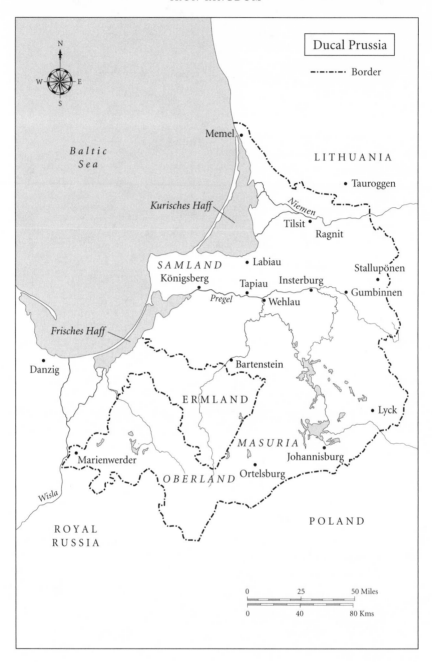

Ducal Prussia

-----·- Border

Baltic Sea

N
W — E
S

Memel

LITHUANIA

• Tauroggen

Kurisches Haff

Niemen

Tilsit
Ragnit

SAMLAND
Königsberg

• Labiau

Tapiau
Pregel
Wehlau
Insterburg

Stallupönen

• Gumbinnen

Frisches Haff

Danzig

• Bartenstein

ERMLAND

Lyck

MASURIA

Marienwerder

Johannisburg

Ortelsburg
OBERLAND

Wisla

POLAND

ROYAL
RUSSIA

| 0 | 25 | 50 Miles |
| 0 | 40 | 80 Kms |

GREAT EXPECTATIONS

By the turn of the seventeenth century, the Electors of Brandenburg stood on the brink of possibilities that were exhilarating, but also troubling. Neither the Duchy of Prussia nor the scattered duchies and counties of the Jülich-Kleve inheritance adjoined the Mark Brandenburg. The latter lay on the western edge of the Holy Roman Empire, cheek by jowl with the Spanish Netherlands and the Dutch Republic. It was a congeries of confessionally mixed territories in one of the most urban and industrialized regions of German Europe. Lutheran Ducal Prussia – roughly as large as Brandenburg itself – lay outside the Holy Roman Empire to the east on the Baltic coast, surrounded by the lands of the Polish-Lithuanian Commonwealth. It was a place of windswept beaches and inlets, cereal-bearing plains, placid lakes, marshes and sombre forests. It was not unusual in Early Modern Europe for geographically scattered territories to fall under the authority of a single sovereign, but the distances involved in this case were unusually great. Over 700 kilometres of roads and tracks – many of which were virtually impassable in wet weather – lay between Berlin and Königsberg.

It was clear that Brandenburg's claims would not go unchallenged. An influential party within the Polish diet was opposed to the Brandenburg succession, and there were at least seven prominent rival claimants to the Jülich-Kleve inheritance, of which the strongest on paper (after Brandenburg) was the Duke of Pfalz-Neuburg in western Germany. Both Ducal Prussia and Jülich-Kleve lay, moreover, in areas of heightened international tension. Jülich-Kleve fell within the orbit of the Dutch struggle for independence from Spain that had been raging intermittently since the 1560s; Ducal Prussia lay in the conflict zone between expansionist Sweden and the Polish-Lithuanian Commonwealth. The Electorate's military establishment was based on an archaic system of feudal levies that had been in steep decline for over a century by 1600. There was no standing army, beyond a few companies of life-guards and some insignificant fortress garrisons. Even supposing Brandenburg were able to acquire them in the first place, keeping the new territories would require the commitment of considerable resources.

But where would these resources come from? Any attempt to expand the Elector's fiscal base in order to finance the acquisition of new territories was sure to meet entrenched domestic opposition. Like many European princes, the Electors of Brandenburg shared power with an array of regional elites organized in representative bodies called Estates. The Estates approved (or not) taxes levied by the Elector and (from 1549) administered their collection. In return they possessed far-reaching powers and privileges. The Elector was forbidden, for example, to enter into alliances without first seeking the approval of the Estates.[14] In a declaration published in 1540 and reiterated on various occasions until 1653, the Elector even promised that he would not 'decide or undertake any important things upon which the flourishing or decline of the lands may depend, without the foreknowledge and consultation of all our estates'.[15] His hands were therefore tied. The provincial nobilities owned the lion's share of the landed wealth in the Electorate; they were also the Elector's most important creditors. But their outlook was vehemently parochial; they had no interest in helping the Elector to acquire far-flung territories of which they knew nothing and they were opposed to any action that might undermine the security of the Mark.

Elector Joachim Frederick recognized the scale of the problem. On 13 December 1604, he announced the establishment of a Privy Council (*Geheimer Rat*), a body consisting of nine councillors whose task was to oversee 'the high and weighty matters that press upon Us', especially in connection with the claims to Prussia and Jülich.[16] The Privy Council was supposed to function collegially, so that issues could be weighed up from a range of angles with a greater consistency of approach. It never became the core of a state bureaucracy – the schedule of regular meetings envisaged in the original order was never observed and its function remained primarily consultative.[17] But the breadth and diversity of its responsibilities signalled a new determination to concentrate the decision-making process at the highest level.

There was also a new westward orientation in marital policy. In February 1605, the Elector's ten-year-old grandson George William was betrothed to the eight-year-old daughter of Frederick IV, the Elector Palatine. The Palatinate, a substantial and wealthy territory on the Rhine, was the foremost German centre of Calvinism, a rigorous form of Protestantism that broke more radically with Catholicism than the Lutherans. During the second half of the sixteenth century, the Calvinist, or Reformed, faith had secured a foothold in parts of western and southern Germany. Heidelberg, capital city of the Palatinate, was the hub of a network of military and political relationships that embraced many of the German Calvinist cities and principalities, but also extended to foreign Calvinist powers, most importantly the Dutch Republic. Frederick IV possessed one of the most formidable military establishments in western Germany, and the Elector hoped that closer relations would bring him strategic support for Brandenburg's claims in the west. Sure enough, in April 1605 an alliance was formalized between Brandenburg, the Palatinate and the Dutch Republic, by which the Dutch agreed, in return for military subsidies, to maintain 5,000 men in readiness to occupy Jülich for the Elector.

This was a departure. In allying themselves with the militant Calvinist interest, the Hohenzollerns had placed themselves beyond the pale of the settlement reached at Augsburg in 1555, which had recognized the right to tolerance of the Lutherans, but not of the Calvinists. Brandenburg was now consorting with some of the Habsburg Emperor's most determined enemies. A division opened among the decision-makers in Berlin. The Elector and most of his councillors favoured a policy of caution and restraint. But a group of influential figures around the Elector's hard-drinking eldest son, John Sigismund (r. 1608–19), took a firmer line. One of these was the Calvinist Privy Councillor Ottheinrich Bylandt zu Rheydt, himself a native of Jülich. Another was John Sigismund's wife, Anna of Prussia, the carrier of the Jülich-Kleve claim. Backed by his supporters – or perhaps driven by them – John Sigismund pressed for closer relations with the Palatinate; he even argued that Brandenburg should pre-empt any dispute over the succession to Jülich-Kleve by invading and occupying it in advance.[18] Not for the last time in the history of the Hohenzollern state, the political elite polarized around opposed foreign policy options.

In 1609 the mad old Duke of Jülich-Kleve finally died, activating the Brandenburg claim to his territories. The timing could hardly have been less propitious. The regional conflict between Habsburg Spain and the Dutch Republic was still simmering, and the inheritance lay in the strategically vital military corridor to the Low Countries. To make matters worse, there had been a dramatic escalation in confessional tensions across the Empire. Following a sequence of bitter religious disputes, two opposed confessional alliances emerged: the Protestant Union of 1608 led by the Calvinist Palatinate, and the Catholic League of 1609, led by Duke Maximilian of Bavaria under the protection of the Emperor. In less troubled times, the Elector of Brandenburg and the Duke of Pfalz-Neuburg would doubtless have looked to the Emperor to resolve the dispute over Jülich-Kleve. But in the partisan climate of 1609, there could be no confidence in the Emperor's neutrality. Instead, the Elector decided to circumvent the machinery of imperial arbitration and sign a separate agreement with his rival: the two princes would jointly occupy the contested territories, pending a later resolution of their claims.

Their action provoked a major crisis. Imperial troops were despatched from the Spanish Netherlands to oversee the defence of Jülich. John Sigismund joined the Protestant Union, which duly declared its support for the two claimants and mobilized an army of 5,000 men. Henri IV of France took an interest and decided to intervene on the Protestant side. Only the French king's assassination in May 1610 prevented a major war from breaking out. A composite force of Dutch, French, English and Protestant Union troops entered Jülich and besieged the Catholic garrison there. In the meanwhile, new states flocked to join the Catholic League and the Emperor, in his fury at the claimants, bestowed the entire Jülich-Kleve complex upon the Elector of Saxony, prompting fears that a joint Saxon–imperial invasion of Brandenburg might be imminent. In 1614, after further quarrels, the Jülich-Kleve legacy was divided – pending a final settlement – between the two claimants: the Duke of Pfalz-Neuburg received Jülich and Berg, while Brandenburg secured Kleve, Mark, Ravensberg and Ravenstein.

These were acquisitions of considerable importance. The Duchy of Kleve straddled the River Rhine, jutting into the territory of the Dutch Republic. In the late Middle Ages, the construction of a system of dykes had reclaimed the fertile soil of the Rhine floodplain, transforming the territory into the bread basket of the Low Countries. The County of Mark was less fertile and less populous, but here there were significant pockets of mining and metallurgical activity. The little County of Ravensberg dominated a strategically important transport route linking the Rhineland with north-eastern Germany and possessed a flourishing linen industry concentrated mainly around Bielefeld, the capital city. The tiny Lordship of Ravenstein, situated on the River Maas, was an enclave within the Dutch Republic.

At some point it must have become clear to the Elector that he had overreached himself. His meagre revenues had prevented him from playing more than a minor supporting role in the conflict over his inheritance claim.[19] Yet his territory was now more exposed than ever. There was a further complication: in 1613, John Sigismund announced his conversion to Calvinism, thereby placing his house outside the religious settlement of 1555. The momentous long-term significance of this step is discussed in chapter 5; in the short term, the Elector's conversion excited outrage among the Lutheran population without providing any tangible short-term benefits for the territory's foreign policy. In 1617, the Protestant Union, whose commitment to Brandenburg's cause had always been fragile, withdrew its earlier support for the Brandenburg claim.[20] John Sigismund responded by resigning from the Union. As one of his advisers pointed out, he had joined it only in the hope of securing his inheritance; his own territory was 'so far away that [the Union] could be of no other use to him'.[21] Brandenburg stood alone.

Perhaps a sharpening awareness of these predicaments accelerated the Elector's personal decline after 1609. The man who had displayed such vigour and enterprise as crown prince seemed used up. His drinking, which had always been enthusiastic, was now out of control. The story later recalled by Schiller that John Sigismund ruined the chance of a marriage alliance between his daughter and the son of the Duke of Pfalz-Neuburg by punching his prospective son-in-law on the ear in a fit of intoxication may well be apocryphal.[22] But similar accounts of violent and irrational drunken behaviour in the 1610s can probably be believed. John Sigismund grew obese and lethargic, and was intermittently incapable of conducting the business of government. A stroke in 1616 left his speech seriously impaired. By the summer of 1618, when the Duke of Prussia died in Königsberg, activating another Hohenzollern claim to another far-flung territory, John Sigismund seemed, according to one visitor, '*lebendigtot*', suspended between life and death.[23]

The careful work of three generations of Hohenzollern Electors had transformed the prospects of Brandenburg. For the first time, we can discern the embryonic outlines of the sprawling territorial structure with its remote eastern and western dependencies that would shape the future of what would one day be known as Prussia. But there remained a gross discrepancy between commitments and resources. How would the House of Brandenburg defend its claims against its many rivals?

How would it secure fiscal and political compliance within its new territories? These were difficult questions to answer, even in peacetime. But by 1618, despite efforts from many quarters to broker a compromise, the Holy Roman Empire was entering an era of bitter religious and dynastic war.

2

Devastation

During the Thirty Years War (1618–48) the German lands became the theatre of a European catastrophe. A confrontation between the Habsburg Emperor Ferdinand II (r. 1619–37) and Protestant forces within the Holy Roman Empire expanded to involve Denmark, Sweden, Spain, the Dutch Republic and France. Conflicts that were continental in scope played themselves out on the territories of the German states: the struggle between Spain and the breakaway Dutch Republic, a competition among the northern powers for control of the Baltic, and the traditional great-power rivalry between Bourbon France and the Habsburgs.[1] Although there were battles, sieges and military occupations elsewhere, the bulk of the fighting took place in the German lands. For unprotected, landlocked Brandenburg, the war was a disaster that exposed every weakness of the Electoral state. At crucial moments during the conflict, Brandenburg faced impossible choices. Its fate hung entirely on the will of others. The Elector was unable to guard his borders, command or defend his subjects or even secure the continued existence of his title. As armies rolled across the provinces of the Mark, the rule of law was suspended, local economies were disrupted and the continuities of work, domicile and memory were irreversibly ruptured. The lands of the Elector, Frederick the Great wrote over a century and a half later, 'were desolated during the Thirty Years' War, whose deadly imprint was so profound that its traces can still be discerned as I write'.[2]

BETWEEN THE FRONTS (1618–40)

Brandenburg entered this dangerous era utterly unprepared for the challenges it would face. Since its striking power was negligible, it had no means of bargaining for rewards or concessions from friend or foe. To the south, directly abutting the borders of the Electorate, were Lusatia and Silesia, both hereditary lands of the Habsburg Bohemian Crown (though Lusatia was under a Saxon leasehold). To the west of these two, also sharing a border with Brandenburg, was Electoral Saxony, whose policy during the early war years was to operate in close harmony with the Emperor. On Brandenburg's northern flank, its undefended borders lay open to the troops of the Protestant Baltic powers, Denmark and Sweden. Nothing stood between Brandenburg and the sea but the enfeebled Duchy of Pomerania, ruled by the ageing Boguslav XIV. Neither in the west nor in remote Ducal Prussia did the Elector of Brandenburg possess the means to defend his newly acquired territories against invasion. There was thus every reason for caution, a preference underscored by the still ingrained habit of deferring to the Emperor.

Elector George William (r. 1619–40), a timid, indecisive man ill equipped to master the extreme predicaments of his era, spent the early war years avoiding alliance commitments that would consume his meagre resources or expose his territory to reprisals. He gave moral support to the insurgency of the Protestant Bohemian Estates against the Habsburg Emperor, but when his brother-in-law the Elector Palatine marched off to Bohemia to fight for the cause, George William stayed out of the fray. During the mid-1620s, as anti-Habsburg coalition plans were hatched between the courts of Denmark, Sweden, France and England, Brandenburg manoeuvred anxiously on the margins of great-power diplomacy. There were efforts to persuade Sweden, whose king had married George William's sister in 1620, to mount a campaign against the Emperor. In 1626, another of George William's sisters was married off to the Prince of Transylvania, a Calvinist nobleman whose repeated wars on the Habsburgs – with Turkish assistance – had established him as one of the Emperor's most formidable enemies. Yet at the same time there were warm assurances of fealty to the Catholic Emperor, and Brandenburg steered clear of the anti-imperial Hague Alliance of December 1626 between England and Denmark.

None of this could protect the Electorate against pressure and military incursions from both sides. After the armies of the Catholic League under General Tilly had defeated Protestant forces at Stadlohn in 1623, the Westphalian territories of Mark and Ravensberg became quartering areas for Leaguist troops. George William understood that he would be

2. *Portrait of George William (1619–40); woodcut by Richard Brend'amour based on a contemporary portrait*

able to stay out of trouble only if his territory were in a position to defend itself against all comers. But the money was lacking for an effective policy of armed neutrality. The overwhelmingly Lutheran Estates were suspicious of his Calvinist allegiances and unwilling to finance them. In 1618–20, their sympathies were largely with the Catholic Emperor and they feared that their Calvinist Elector would drag Brandenburg into dangerous international commitments. The best policy, as they saw it, was to wait out the storm and avoid attracting hostile notice from any of the belligerents.

In 1626, as George William struggled to extract money from his Estates, the Palatine General Count Mansfeld overran the Altmark and Prignitz, with his Danish allies close behind. Mayhem broke out. Churches were smashed open and robbed, the town of Nauen was razed to the ground, villages were burned as troops attempted to extort hidden money and goods from the inhabitants. When he was taken to task for this by a senior Brandenburg minister, the Danish envoy Mitzlaff responded with breathtaking arrogance: 'Whether the Elector likes it or not, the [Danish] King will go ahead all the same. Whoever is not with him is against him.'[3] Scarcely had the Danes made themselves at home in the Mark, however, but they were pushed back by their enemies. In the late summer of 1626, after the imperial and Leaguist victory near Lutter-am-Barenberg in the Duchy of Brunswick (27 August), imperial troops occupied the Altmark, while the Danes withdrew into the Prignitz and the Uckermark to the north and north-west of Berlin. At around the same time, King Gustavus Adolphus of Sweden landed in Ducal Prussia, where he established a base of operations against Poland, completely disregarding the claims of the Elector. The Neumark, too, was overrun and plundered by Cossack mercenaries in the service of the Emperor. The scale of the threat facing Brandenburg was made clear by the fate of the dukes of neighbouring Mecklenburg. As punishment for supporting the Danes, the Emperor deposed the ducal family and bestowed Mecklenburg as booty upon his powerful commander, the military entrepreneur Count Wallenstein.

The time seemed ripe for a shift towards closer collaboration with the Habsburg camp. 'If this business continues,' George William told a confidant in a moment of desperation, 'I shall become mad, for I am much grieved. [...] I shall have to join the Emperor, I have no alternative; I have only one son; if the Emperor remains, then I suppose I and my son will be able to remain Elector.'[4] On 22 May 1626, despite protests from his councillors and the Estates, who would have preferred a rigorous policy of neutrality, the Elector signed a treaty with the Emperor. Under the terms of this agreement, the entire Electorate was opened to imperial troops. Hard times followed, because the imperial supreme commander, Count Wallenstein, was in the habit of extracting provisions, lodgings and payment for his troops from the population of the occupied area.

Brandenburg thus gained no relief from its alliance with the Emperor. Indeed, as the imperial forces rolled back their opponents and approached the zenith of their power in the late 1620s, Emperor Ferdinand II seemed to disregard George William entirely. In the Edict of Restitution of 1629, the Emperor announced that he intended to 'reclaim', by force if necessary, 'all the archbishoprics, bishoprics, prelatecies, monasteries, hospitals and endowments' which the Catholics had possessed in the year 1552 – a programme with profoundly damaging implications for Brandenburg, where numerous ecclesiastical establishments had been placed under Protestant administration. The Edict confirmed the settlement of 1555, in that it also excluded Calvinists from the religious peace in the Empire; only the Catholic and Lutheran faiths enjoyed official standing – 'all other doctrines and sects are forbidden and cannot be tolerated.'[5]

Sweden's dramatic entry into the German war in 1630 brought relief for the Protestant states, but also raised the political pressure on Brandenburg.[6] In 1620, George William's sister Maria Eleonora had been married off to King Gustavus Adolphus of Sweden, a larger-than-life figure whose appetite for war and conquest was twinned with a missionary zeal for the Protestant cause in Europe. As his involvement in the German conflict deepened, the Swedish king, who had no other German allies, resolved to secure an alliance with his brother-in-law George William. The Elector was reluctant, and it is easy to see why. Gustavus Adolphus had spent the past decade and a half waging a war of conquest in the eastern Baltic. A series of campaigns against Russia had left Sweden in possession of a continuous swathe of territory stretching from Finland to Estonia. In 1621, Gustavus Adolphus had renewed his war against Poland, occupying Ducal Prussia and conquering Livonia (present-day Latvia and Estonia). The Swedish king had even pushed the elderly Duke of Mecklenburg into an agreement that the duchy would pass to Sweden when the duke died, a deal that directly undercut Brandenburg's longstanding inheritance treaty with its northern neighbour.

All of this suggested that the Swedes would be no less dangerous as friends than as enemies. George William returned to the idea of neutrality. He planned to work with Saxony in forming a Protestant bloc that would oppose the implementation of the Edict of Restitution while at the same time providing a buffer between the Emperor and his enemies in the north, a policy that bore fruit in the Convention of Leipzig of February 1631. But this manoeuvring did little to repel the threat facing Brandenburg from north and south. Furious warnings and threats issued from Vienna. In the meanwhile, there were clashes between Swedish and imperial troops across the Neumark, in the course of which the Swedes chased the imperials out of the province and occupied the fortified cities of Frankfurt/Oder, Landsberg and Küstrin.

Emboldened by the success of his troops in the field, the King of Sweden demanded an outright alliance with Brandenburg. George William's protests that he wished to remain neutral fell on deaf ears. As Gustavus Adolphus explained to a Brandenburg envoy:

I don't want to know or hear anything about neutrality. [The Elector] has to be friend or foe. When I come to his borders, he must declare himself cold or warm. This is a fight between God and the devil. If My Cousin wants to side with God, then he has to join me; if he prefers to side with the devil, then indeed he must fight me; there is no third way.[7]

While George William prevaricated, the Swedish king drew close to Berlin with his troops behind him. Panicking, the Elector sent the women of his family out to parley with the invader at Köpenick, a few kilometres to the south-east of the capital. It was eventually agreed that the king should come into the city with 1,000 men to continue negotiations as the guest of the Elector. Over the following days of wining and dining, the Swedes talked beguilingly of ceding parts of Pomerania to Branden-burg, hinted at a marriage between the king's daughter and the Elector's son, and pressed for an alliance. George William decided to throw in his lot with the Swedes.

The reason for this policy reversal lay partly in the intimidating demeanour of the Swedish troops, who at one point drew up before the walls of Berlin with their guns trained on the royal palace in order to concentrate the mind of the beleaguered Elector. But an important predisposing factor was the fall, on 20 May 1631, of the Protestant city of Magdeburg to Tilly's imperial troops. The taking of Magdeburg was followed not only by the sacking and plundering that usually attended such events, but also by a massacre of the town's inhabitants that would become a fixture in German literary memory. In a passage of classically measured rhetoric, Frederick II later described the scene:

Everything that the unfettered license of the soldier can devise when nothing restrains his fury; all that the most ferocious cruelty inspires in men when a blind rage takes possession of their senses, was committed by the Imperials in this unhappy city: the troops ran in packs, weapons in hand, through the streets, and massacred indiscriminately the elderly, the women and the children, those who defended themselves and those who made no move to resist them [. . .] one saw nothing but corpses still flexing, piled or stretched out naked; the cries of those whose throats were being cut mingled with the furious shouts of their assassins . . .[8]

For contemporaries too, the annihilation of Magdeburg, a community of some 20,000 citizens and one of the capitals of German Protestantism, was an existential shock. Pamphlets, newspapers and broadsheets circulated across Europe, with verbal renderings of the various atrocities committed.[9] Nothing could more have damaged the prestige of the Habsburg Emperor in the German Protestant territories than the news of this wanton extermination of his Protestant subjects. The impact was especially pronounced for the Elector of Brandenburg, whose uncle, Margrave Christian William, was the episcopal administrator of Magdeburg. In June 1631, George William reluctantly signed a pact with Sweden, under which he agreed to open the fortresses of Spandau (just north of Berlin) and Küstrin (in the Neumark) to the Swedish troops, and to pay the Swedes a monthly contribution of 30,000 thalers.[10]

The pact with Sweden proved as shortlived as the earlier alliance with the Emperor. In 1631–2 the balance of power was tilting back in favour of the Protestant forces, as the Swedes and their Saxon allies swept deep into the south and west of Germany, inflicting heavy defeats on the imperial side. But the momentum of their onslaught slowed after Gustavus Adolphus's death in a cavalry mêlée at the Battle of Lützen on 6 November 1632. By the end of 1634, after a serious defeat at Nördlingen, Sweden's ascendancy was broken. Exhausted by the war and desperate to drive a wedge between Sweden and the German Protestant princes, Emperor Ferdinand II seized the moment to offer moderate peace terms. This move worked: the Lutheran Elector of Saxony, who had joined forces with Sweden in September 1631, now came running back to the Emperor. The Elector of Brandenburg faced a more difficult choice. The draft articles of the Peace of Prague offered an amnesty and withdrew the more extreme demands of the earlier Edict of Restitution, but they still made no reference to the toleration of Calvinism. The Swedes, for their part, were still pestering Brandenburg for a treaty; this time they promised that Pomerania would be transferred in its entirety to Brandenburg after the cessation of hostilities in the Empire.

After some agonized prevarication, George William elected to seek his fortune at the Emperor's side. In May 1635, Brandenburg, along with Saxony, Bavaria and many other German territories, signed up to the Peace of Prague. In return, the Emperor promised to see to it that Brandenburg's claim to the Duchy of Pomerania would be honoured. A detachment of imperial regiments was sent to assist in protecting the Mark and George William was honoured – somewhat incongruously, given his utter lack of military aptitude – with the title of *Generalissimus* in the imperial army. The Elector, for his part, undertook to raise 25,000 troops in support of the imperial war effort. Unfortunately for Brandenburg, this mending of fences with the Habsburg Emperor coincided with another shift in the balance of power in northern Germany. After their victory over the Saxon army at Wittstock on 4 October 1636 the Swedes were once again 'lords in the Mark'.[11]

George William spent the last four years of his reign trying to drive the Swedes out of Brandenburg and to take control of Pomerania, whose duke died in March 1637. His attempts to raise a Brandenburg army against Sweden produced a small and poorly equipped force and the Electorate was ravaged by both the Swedes and the imperials, as well as by the less disciplined units of its own forces. After a Swedish invasion of the Mark, the Elector was forced to flee – not for the last time in the history of the Brandenburg Hohenzollerns – to the relative safety of Ducal Prussia, where he died in 1640.

POLITICS

Frederick the Great later described Elector George William as 'incapable of governing', and one history of Prussia noted unkindly that this Elector's worst defect was not so much 'indecision of mind' as 'the absence of a mind to make up'. Two such Electors, it added, and Brandenburg would have 'ceased to provide anything but parochial history'. Judgements of this kind abound in the secondary literature.[12] George William certainly cut an unheroic figure, and he was conscious of the fact. He had been seriously injured as a young man in a hunting accident. A deep wound on his thigh became chronically inflamed, confining him to a sedan chair and depressing his vitality. At a time when the destiny of Germany seemed to rest in the hands of physically imposing warlords, the spectacle of the Elector fleeing hither and thither in his sedan chair to avoid the various armed forces passing without leave across his territory hardly inspired confidence. 'It pains me greatly,' he wrote in July 1626, 'that my lands have been wasted in this way and that I have been so disregarded and mocked. The whole world must take me for a cowardly weakling . . .'[13]

Yet the hesitation and wavering of these years had less to do with the personal characteristics of the ruler than with the intrinsic difficulty of the choices that confronted him. There was something irreducible, something structural in his predicament. This is worth emphasizing, because it draws our attention to one of the continuities of Brandenburg (later Prussian) history. Again and again, the decision-makers in Berlin would find themselves stranded between the fronts, forced to oscillate between options. And on each of these occasions the monarch would be vulnerable to the charge that he had hesitated, prevaricated, failed to decide. This was not a consequence of 'geography' in any simplistic sense, but rather of Brandenburg's place on the mental map of European power politics. If we visualize the main lines of conflict between the continental power blocs of the early seventeenth century – Sweden-Denmark, Poland-Lithuania, Austria-Spain, and France – then it is clear that Brandenburg, with its virtually undefended appanages to the west and the east, was in the zone where these lines intersected. Sweden's power would later decline, followed by that of Poland, but the rise of Russia to great-power status would pose the same problem anew, and successive governments in Berlin would have to choose between alliance, armed neutrality and independent action.

As Brandenburg's military and diplomatic predicament deepened, competing factions emerged in Berlin with opposed foreign-political objectives. Should Brandenburg abide by its traditional allegiance to the Holy Roman Emperor and seek safety at the side of the Habsburgs? This was the view espoused by Count Adam Schwarzenberg, a Catholic native of the County of Mark who had supported the Brandenburg claim to Jülich-Berg. From the mid-1620s onwards, Schwarzenberg was the leader of a Habsburg faction in Berlin. By contrast, two of the most powerful privy councillors, Levin von Knesebeck and Samuel von Winterfeld, were strong supporters of the Protestant cause. The two camps fought bitterly for control of Brandenburg's policy. In 1626, as the Elector was forced into closer collaboration with the Habsburg camp, Schwarzenberg succeeded in having Winterfeld tried for treason and driven out of the country, despite protests from the Estates. In the autumn of 1630, on the other hand, when Sweden was in the ascendant, a pro-Swedish faction emerged, led by the Calvinist Chancellor Sigismund von Götzen, and Schwarzenberg was forced to retire to Kleve, only to return to Berlin after the initiative passed back to the imperial side in 1634 and 1635.

The women at court also had strong views on foreign policy. The Elector's young wife was the sister of the Calvinist ruler Frederick V, whose Palatine homeland had been overrun and devastated by Spanish and Catholic League troops. She naturally took an anti-imperial view, as did her mother, who had joined her in exile from Heidelberg, and the Elector's aunt, who had married the brother of Frederick V. The Elector's Lutheran mother, Anna of Prussia, was another outspoken opponent of the Habsburgs. It was she who had engineered the marriage of her daughter Maria Eleonora to the Lutheran King of Sweden in 1620, disregarding the objections of her son, Elector George William.[14] Her intention was to bolster Brandenburg's position in Ducal Prussia, but it was a highly provocative move at the time, since Sweden was at war with Poland, whose king was still formally the sovereign of Ducal Prussia. As these initiatives suggest, dynastic politics still functioned in a way that gave an important voice to consorts and female relatives of the monarch. The women in dynastic families were not just living securities for inheritance claims; they also maintained relationships with foreign courts that could be of great importance and they did not necessarily see themselves as bound by the monarch's policy.

Beyond the narrow circle of the Elector's court were the holders of power in the land, the provincial Estates, representatives of the Lutheran nobilities. These were deeply sceptical of foreign political adventures of any kind, particularly when they suspected that these were motivated by an attachment to the Calvinist interest. As early as 1623, a delegation of Estates representatives warned the Elector against the enthusiasms of 'hot-headed councillors' and reminded him that their military obligations extended only to 'what was absolutely necessary for the preservation of the land in the case of an emergency'. Even after repeated incursions by Protestant and imperial troops, the Estates remained impassive in the face of entreaties from the sovereign.[15] As they saw it, their function was to forestall unwarranted adventures and to preserve the fabric of provincial privilege against incursions from the centre.[16]

Such passive resistance was difficult to overcome in peacetime. After 1618, the problem was compounded by the fact that the war, in its early phases, deepened the Elector's dependence on the corporate local structures of his territory. George William had no administration of his own with which to collect military contributions, grain or other provisions – all this had to be done by agents of the Estates. The provincial organs of tax collection remained under Estate control. With their local knowledge and authority, the Estates also played an indispensable role in coordinating the billeting and through-marches of troops.[17] On occasion they even negotiated independently with invading commanders over the payment of contributions.[18]

Nevertheless, as the war dragged on, the fiscal privileges of the provincial nobilities began to look fragile.[19] Foreign princes and generals had no compunction in extorting contributions from the provinces of Brandenburg; why should the Elector not take his share? This would involve rolling back the ancient 'liberties' of the Estates. For this task, the Elector turned to Schwarzenberg, a Catholic and a foreigner with no ties to the provincial nobility. Schwarzenberg lost no time in imposing a new tax without any recourse to the usual provincial organs. He curtailed the power of the Estates to oversee state expenditures and suspended the Privy Council, transferring its responsibilities to the Council of War, whose members were chosen for their complete independence from the Estates. In short, Schwarzenberg installed a fiscal autocracy that broke decisively with the corporate traditions of the Mark.[20] During the last two years of George William's reign, Schwarzenberg virtually ran the war against Sweden, pulling the tattered remains of the Brandenburg regiments together and mounting a desperate guerrilla campaign against Swedish troop units. Requests for tax exemptions from impoverished, war-damaged towns were unceremoniously rejected and those who entered into negotiations with the invaders – over billets, for example – were branded as traitors.[21]

Schwarzenberg was a controversial figure among his contemporaries. The Estates had initially supported his cautious, pro-imperial foreign policy, but they later came to loathe him for his assault on their corporate liberties. His prosecutions and intrigues earned him the hatred of his opponents in the Privy Council. His Catholic faith was a further spur to their rage. In 1638–9, when Schwarzenberg's power was in its zenith, flysheets circulated in Berlin decrying the 'Hispanic servitude' of his rule.[22] In retrospect, however, it is clear that this powerful minister set a number of important precedents. What survived his military dictatorship was the notion that the state, in times of need, might be justified in sweeping aside the cumbersome machinery of Estate privilege and corporate fiscal co-regency. Seen from this perspective, the Schwarzenberg years were a first indecisive experiment in 'absolutist' rule.

WHOLESALE RUIN

For the people of Brandenburg, the war meant lawlessness, misery, poverty, deprivation, uncertainty, forced migration and death. The Elector's decision not to risk a pro-Protestant commitment after 1618 initially kept Brandenburg out of trouble. The first major incursions came in 1626, with the Danish campaign in northern Germany. During the fifteen years that followed, Danish, Swedish, Palatine, imperial and Leaguist troops overran the provinces of Brandenburg in rapid succession.

The towns in the path of advancing armies faced a choice between surrendering and admitting the enemy, defending the walls and suffering the consequences if the enemy broke through, or abandoning them altogether. The town of Plaue in the Havelland district of western Brandenburg, for example, successfully defended itself against attack by a small imperial force on 10 April 1627, but was abandoned by its population on the following day, when the enemy returned in greater numbers to renew the assault. No sooner had the imperials established themselves in the town, but it was attacked, captured and plundered by advancing Danish troops. In the city of Brandenburg, the mayor and corporation of the Old City on the right bank of the river Havel agreed to open their walls to the imperials, but the councillors of the New City on the other bank opted to seal themselves off by burning the bridges between the two precincts, barring their gates and firing on the invaders as they approached. A fierce battle followed, the defences of the New City were breached by imperial artillery, and the troops stormed through the city plundering in all quarters.[23]

The hardest-hit provinces tended to be those, like the Havelland or the Prignitz, where river passes commanding the main military transit routes repeatedly changed hands throughout the war. During the summer of 1627, Danish forces played a game of cat-and-mouse with the imperial strongholds in the Havelland, plundering and laying waste to a string of quaintly named villages: Möthlow, Retzow, Selbelang, Gross Behnitz, Stölln, Wassersuppe.[24] Most commanders regarded their armies as personal property and were thus reluctant to commit men to battle unless it was absolutely necessary. Pitched battles were thus relatively rare and armies spent most of the war years engaged in marches, manoeuvres and occupations. It was an arrangement that spared the troops, but weighed heavily on host populations.[25]

War brought a drastic rise in taxation and other obligatory payments. First there was the regular 'contribution', a combined land and poll tax levied by the Brandenburg government upon its own population to support the Elector's army. Then there were the numerous legal and illegal levies raised by foreign and home troops. These were sometimes agreed between the occupying commander and government officials or the mayors or councillors of cities and towns.[26] But there were also countless episodes of outright extortion. In the winter of 1629, for example, officers commanding troops quartered in the New City of Brandenburg demanded that the burghers pay subsistence costs for the next nine months in advance. When the latter refused, punishment billets were quartered on the locals. 'And whatever they didn't quaff or squander themselves, they smashed in two; they poured away the beer, stove in the barrels, smashed windows, doors and ovens and destroyed everything.'[27] In Strausberg, just north of Berlin, the troops of Count Mansfeld required two pounds of bread, two pounds of meat and two quarts of beer per man per day; many soldiers refused to content them-selves with their allotted ration and 'scoffed and quaffed as much as they could get'. The result was a steep decline in nutritional standards among the inhabitants, a dramatic rise in mortality rates, a pronounced fall in fertility among women of childbearing age, and even the occasional incident of cannibalism.[28] Many simply fled the town, leaving their household goods behind.[29] In the tense intimacy of protracted billets, there were endless opportunities, as many of the eyewitness accounts confirm, for one-off acts of extortion and theft.

All this meant that the people in many parts of Brandenburg were slowly crushed under successive layers of extortion. A report compiled in 1634 gives us some sense of what this meant for the district of Oberbarnim to the north of Berlin, whose population numbered some 13,000 in 1618, but had fallen to fewer than 9,000 by 1631. The inhabitants of Oberbarnim paid 185,000 thalers to imperial com-manders in 1627–30, 26,000 thalers in contributions to the Swedish-Brandenburg allied forces in 1631–4, a further 50,000 thalers in provisioning costs to the Swedes in 1631–4, 30,000 thalers in pro-visioning costs to the Saxon cavalry regiments, 54,000 thalers to various Brandenburg commanders, plus sundry other taxes and one-off levies, not counting many other informal extortions, seizures and confiscations. This at a time when a horse cost 20 thalers and a bushel of corn less than one thaler, when a third of the peasant-owned land had been abandoned or lay uncultivated, when the disruptions of war had ruined many branches of skilled manufacture, when the ripening grain around the town was regularly trampled into the ground by passing cavalrymen.[30]

Atrocity stories – narratives of extreme violence and cruelty by armed men against civilians – loom so large in the literary depictions of the Thirty Years War that some historians have been tempted to dismiss them as the accoutrements of a 'myth of all-destructive fury' or a 'fable of wholesale ruin and misery'.[31] There is no doubt that atrocity stories became a genre in their own right in contemporary reporting of this war; a good example is Philip Vincent's book *The Lamentations of Germany*, which listed the horrors suffered by the innocent, featuring graphic plates entitled: 'Croats eat Children', 'Noses and eares cut of to make hatbandes', and so on.[32] The sensationalist character of many atrocity stories should not obscure the fact that they were rooted, at least indirectly, in the lived experience of real people.[33]

Official reports from the Havelland record numerous beatings, house-burnings, rapes and wanton destruction of property. People living on the outskirts of Plaue, just a few kilometres to the east of Brandenburg city, described a through-march by imperial troops on their way to Saxony on New Year's Day 1639 during which 'many old people were tortured to death, shot dead, various women and girls raped to death, children hanged, sometimes even burnt, or stripped naked, so that they perished in the extreme cold.'[34]

In one of the most evocative memoirs that survives from Brandenburg, Peter Thiele, customs officer and town clerk at Beelitz near Potsdam, described the conduct of the imperial army that passed through his town in 1637. In order to force a certain Jürgen Weber, a baker in the town, to reveal where he had concealed his money, the imperials 'stabbed a piece of wood half a finger long into his [penis], if you will excuse me'.[35] Thiele described the 'Swedish draught', said to have been invented by the Swedes, but widely reported of all armies and a fixture in later literary representations of the war:

The robbers and murderers took a piece of wood and stuck it down the poor wretches' throats, stirred it and poured in water, adding sand or even human

3. Atrocities against women in the German lands during the
Thirty Years War, woodcut from Philip Vincent's The
Lamentations of Germany *(London, 1638)*

faeces, and pitifully tortured the people for money, as transpired with a citizen
of Beelitz called David Örttel, who died of it soon after.[36]

Another man, by the name of Krüger Möller was caught by imperial
soldiers, bound hand and foot and roasted over a fire until he revealed

the whereabouts of his money. But no sooner had his tormentors taken the money and gone, than another raiding party of imperials arrived in the town. Hearing that their colleagues had already roasted 100 thalers out of Möller, they carried him back to the fire and held him with his face in the flames, roasting him 'for so long that he died of it and his skin even came off like that of a slaughtered goose'. The cattle merchant Jürgen Möller was likewise 'roasted to death' for his money.[37]

In 1638, the imperial and Saxon armies passed through the little town of Lenzen in the Prignitz to the north-west of Berlin, where they tore all the wood and equipment from the houses before putting them to the torch. Whatever householders rescued from the flames, the soldiers took from them by force. Hardly had the imperials departed, but the Swedes attacked and plundered the town, treating the 'citizens, women and children so gruesomely that such things were never told of the Turks'. An official report compiled by the Lenzen authorities in January 1640 sketched a grim picture: 'They tied our honest burgher Hans Betke to a wooden pole and roasted him at the fire from seven in the morning until four in the afternoon, so that he gave up the spirit amidst much shrieking and pains.' The Swedes cut the calves of an elderly man to stop him from walking, scalded a matron to death with boiling water, hanged children naked in the cold and forced people into the freezing water. About fifty people, 'old and young, big and small, were martyred in this way'.[38]

The men raised by the Elector himself were not much better than the invaders. They too were ill clothed, underfed and demoralized. Officers brutalized their men with a regime of draconian punishments. The soldiers of Colonel von Rochow's regiment were 'beaten and stabbed on trivial pretexts, made to run the gauntlet, branded', and in some cases had their noses and ears cut off.[39] Unsurprisingly, perhaps, the troops were equally merciless in their dealings with local civilians, prompting bitter protests against their 'frequent extortions, plundering, murder and robbery'. So frequent were these complaints that Count Schwarzenberg convened a special meeting with the commanders in 1640 and dressed them down for vexing the civilian population with acts of insolence and violence.[40] But the effect of his admonitions soon wore off: a report filed two years later from the district of Teltow near Berlin stated that the troops of the Brandenburg commander von Goldacker had been plundering the area, threshing the corn they found and treating the local people 'in a manner as inhumane as, indeed worse than, the enemy could have done'.[41]

It is impossible to establish with any precision how frequently atrocities took place. The regularity with which such accounts crop up across a wide range of contemporary sources, from individual ego-narratives to local government reports, petitions and literary representations certainly suggests that they were widespread. What is beyond doubt is their significance in contemporary perception.[42] Atrocities defined the meaning of this war. They captured something about it that left a profound impression: the total suspension of order, the utter vulnerability of men, women and children in the face of a violence that raged unmastered, out of control.

Perhaps the most eloquent testimony to the harshness of the tribulations visited upon the people of Brandenburg between 1618 and 1648 is simply the demographic record. Diseases such as typhus, bubonic plague, dysentery and smallpox raged unchecked through civilian populations whose physical resistance had often been undermined by years of high prices and poor nutrition.[43] Across the Mark Brandenburg as a whole, about one half of the population died. The figures vary from district to district; those areas that were protected from military occupation or through-marches by water or swampland tended to be less seriously affected. In the marshy floodplains of the river Oder, known as the Oderbruch, for example, a survey conducted in 1652 found that only 15 per cent of the farms in operation at the beginning of the war were still deserted. In the Havelland, by contrast, which saw nearly fifteen years of virtually uninterrupted disruption, the figure was 52 per cent. In the Barnim district, where the population was heavily burdened with contributions and billets, 58.4 per cent of the farms were still deserted in 1652. On the lands of the district of Löcknitz in the Uckermark, on the northern margins of Brandenburg, the figure was 85 per cent! In the Altmark, to the west of Berlin, the mortality rate rose from the west to the east. Between 50 and 60 per cent are reckoned to have perished in the areas bordering on the river Elbe in the east, which were important military transit zones; the death rate sank to 25–30 per cent in the middle and 15–20 per cent in the west.

Some of the most important towns were very hard hit: Brandenburg and Frankfurt/Oder, both in key transit areas, lost over two-thirds of their populations. Potsdam and Spandau, satellite towns of Berlin-Cölln, both lost over 40 per cent. In the Prignitz, another transit zone, only ten of the forty noble families who had been running the major estates in the province were still in residence in 1641, and there were some towns – Wittenberge, Putlitz, Meyenburg, Freyenstein – where no one could be found at all.[44]

We can really only guess at the impact of these disasters on popular culture. Many of the families that repopulated the most devastated districts after the war were immigrants from outside Brandenburg: Dutch, East Frisians, Holsteiners. In some places the shock was sufficient to sever the thread of collective memory. It has been observed of Germany as a whole that the 'great war' of 1618–48 obliterated the folk memory of earlier conflicts, so that medieval, ancient or prehistoric walls and earthworks lost their earlier names and came to be known as 'Swedish ramparts'. In some areas, it seems that the war broke the chain of personal recollection that was essential to the authority and continuity of village-based customary law – no one was left of an age to remember how things were 'before the Swedes came'.[45] Perhaps this is one of the reasons for the paucity of folk traditions in the Mark Brandenburg. In the 1840s, when the craze for collecting and publishing myths and other folklore was at its height, enthusiasts inspired by the brothers Grimm found lean pickings in the Mark.[46]

The all-destructive fury of the Thirty Years War was mythical not in the sense that it bore no relation to reality, but in the sense that it established itself within collective memories and became a tool for thinking about the world. It was the fury of religious civil war – not only in his native England, but also on the continent – that moved Thomas Hobbes to celebrate the Leviathan state, with its monopoly of legitimate force, as the redemption of society. Surely it was better, he proposed, to concede authority to the monarchical state in return for the security of persons and property than to see order and justice drowned in civil strife.

One of the most brilliant German readers of Hobbes was Samuel Pufendorf, a jurist from Saxony who likewise grounded his arguments for the necessity of the state in a dystopian vision of ambient violence and disorder. The law of nature alone did not suffice to preserve the social life of man, Pufendorf argued in his *Elements of Universal Jurisprudence*. Unless 'sovereignties' were established men would seek their welfare by force alone; 'all places would reverberate with wars between those who are inflicting and those who are repelling injuries.'[47] Hence the supreme importance of states, whose chief purpose was 'that men, by means of mutual cooperation and assistance, be safe against the harms and injuries they can and commonly do inflict on one another'.[48] The trauma of the Thirty Years War reverberates in these sentences.

The argument that the state's legitimacy derived from the need to forestall disorder through the concentration of authority was widely employed in early modern Europe, but it had a special resonance in Brandenburg. Here was an eloquent philosophical answer to the resistance that George William had encountered from the provincial Estates. Since it was impossible in peace or war to conduct the affairs of a state without incurring expenses, Pufendorf wrote in 1672, the sovereign had the right to 'force individual citizens to contribute so much of their own goods as the assumption of those expenses is deemed to require'.[49]

Pufendorf thus distilled from the memory of civil war a powerful rationale for the extension of state authority. Against the 'libertas' of the Estates, Pufendorf asserted the 'necessitas' of the state. Late in his life, when he was employed as historiographer at the Berlin court, Pufendorf wove these convictions into a chronicle of Brandenburg's recent history.[50] At the centre of his story was the emergence of the monarchical executive: 'the measure and focal point of all his reflections was the state, upon which all initiatives converge like lines towards a central point.'[51] Unlike the crude chronicles of Brandenburg that had begun to appear in the late sixteenth century, Pufendorf's history was driven by a theory of historical change that focused on the creative, transformative power of the state. In this way, he engineered a narrative of great power and elegance that has – for better or for worse – shaped our understanding of Prussian history ever since.

3

An Extraordinary Light in Germany

RECOVERY

Viewed against the background of the misery and hopelessness of 1640, Brandenburg's resurgence in the second half of the seventeenth century appears remarkable. By the 1680s, Brandenburg possessed an army with an international reputation whose numbers fluctuated between 20,000 and 30,000.[1] It had acquired a small Baltic fleet and even a modest colony on the west coast of Africa. A land bridge across Eastern Pomerania linked the Electorate to the Baltic coast. Brandenburg was a substantial regional power on a par with Bavaria and Saxony, a sought-after ally and a significant element in major peace settlements.

The man who presided over this transformation was Frederick William, known as the 'Great Elector' (r. 1640–88). Frederick William is the first Brandenburg Elector of whom numerous portraits survive, most of them commissioned by the sitter himself. They document the changing appearance of a man who spent forty-eight years – longer than any other member of his dynasty – in sovereign office. Depictions from the early years of the reign show a commanding, upright figure with a long face framed by flowing dark hair; in the later images, the body has swollen, the face is bloated and the hair has been replaced by cascades of artificial curls. And yet one thing is common to all the portraits painted from life: intelligent, dark eyes that fix the viewer in a sharp stare.[2]

When he succeeded his father at the age of twenty, Frederick William had virtually no training or experience in the art of government. He had spent most of his childhood cloistered away in the fortress of Küstrin enclosed by sombre forests, where he was safe from enemy troops. Lessons in modern languages and technical skills such as drawing, geometry and the construction of fortifications were interspersed with the

4. Frederick William the Great Elector as Scipio, *painted c. 1660, attrib. to*
Albert van der Eeckhout

regular hunting of stag, boar and wildfowl. Unlike his father and grandfather, Frederick William was taught Polish from the age of seven to
assist him in conducting relations with the Polish king, feudal overlord
of Ducal Prussia. At the age of fourteen, as the military crisis deepened
and a wave of epidemics spread across the Mark, he was sent to the

relative safety of the Dutch Republic, where he would spend the next four years of his life.

The impact on the prince of these teenage years in the Republic is difficult to ascertain precisely, since he did not keep a diary or write personal memoirs of any kind. His correspondence with his parents confined itself to the exchange of compliments in an extremely distanced and formal diction.[3] Yet it is clear that the prince's Dutch education did reinforce his sense of allegiance to the Calvinist cause. Frederick William was the first Brandenburg Elector to be born of two Calvinist parents, and the composite name Frederick William, a novelty in the history of the House of Hohenzollern, was devised precisely in order to symbolize the bond between Berlin (William was his father's second name) and the Calvinist Palatinate of his uncle, Frederick V. Only with this generation of the Hohenzollern family did the reorientation launched by the conversion of his grandfather John Sigismund in 1613 come fully into effect. Frederick William consolidated the bond in 1646 by marrying the Dutch Calvinist Louise Henriette, nineteen-year-old daughter of Stadtholder Frederick Henry of Orange.

Frederick Williams's long sojourn in the Dutch Republic was also influential in other ways. The prince received instruction from professors in law, history and politics at the University of Leiden, a renowned centre of the then fashionable neo-stoical state theory. The prince's lessons emphasized the majesty of the law, the venerability of the state as the guarantor of order and the centrality of duty and obligation to the office of sovereign. A particular concern of the neo-stoics was the need to subordinate the military to the authority and discipline of the state.[4] But it was outside the classroom, in the streets, docks, markets and parade-squares of the Dutch towns that Frederick William learned his most important lessons. In the early seventeenth century, the Republic was at the height of its power and prosperity. Over more than sixty years, this tiny Calvinist country had fought successfully to assert its independence against the military might of Catholic Spain and establish itself as the foremost European headquarters of global trade and colonization. In the process, it had developed a robust fiscal regime and a distinctive military culture with recognizably modern features: the regular and systematic drilling of troops in battleground manoeuvres, a high level of functional differentiation and a disciplined professional officer corps. Frederick William had ample opportunity to observe the military prowess of the Republic at close hand – he visited his host and relative, Viceroy Prince Frederick Henry of Orange, in the Dutch encampment at Breda in 1637, where the Dutch recaptured a stronghold that had been lost to the Spaniards twelve years before.

Throughout his reign Frederick William strove to remodel his own patrimony in the image of what he had observed in the Netherlands. The training regime adopted by his army in 1654 was based on the drill-book of Prince Maurice of Orange.[5] Frederick William remained convinced throughout his reign that 'navigation and trade are the principal pillars of a state, through which subjects, by sea and by manufactures on land, earn their food and keep.'[6] He became obsessed with the idea that the link to the Baltic would enliven and commercialize Brandenburg, bringing the wealth and power that were so conspicuously on display in Amsterdam. In the 1650s and 1660s, he even negotiated international commercial treaties to secure privileged terms of trade for a merchant marine he did not yet possess. In the later 1670s, with the assistance of a Dutch merchant by the name of Benjamin Raule, he acquired a small fleet of ships and became involved in a string of privateering and colonial schemes. In 1680, Raule secured for Brandenburg a share in the west African trade in gold, ivory and slaves by establishing the small colonial fort of Friedrichsburg on the coast of modern-day Ghana.[7]

It could be said that Frederick William reinvented the Electoral office. Whereas John Sigismund and George William had addressed themselves only sporadically to the business of government, Frederick William worked 'harder than a secretary'. Contemporaries recognized this as something new and noteworthy. His ministers marvelled at his memory for detail, his sobriety and his ability to sit for an entire day in council dealing with affairs of state.[8] Even the imperial ambassador Lisola, no uncritical observer, was struck by the Elector's conscientiousness: 'I admire this Elector, who takes delight in long and exceedingly detailed reports and who expressly demands these of his ministers; he reads everything, he resolves and orders everything [. . .] and neglects nothing.'[9] 'I shall manage my responsibility as prince,' Frederick William declared, 'in the knowledge that it is the affair of the people and not mine personally.'[10] The words were those of the Roman Emperor Hadrian, but in the mouth of the Elector they signalled a new understanding of the sovereign's role. It was more than a prestigious title or a bundle of rights and revenues; it was a vocation that should rightly consume the personality of the ruler. The early histories of the reign established an image of this Elector as the model of an absolute and unstinting dedication to office. His example became a potent icon within the Hohenzollern tradition, a standard that the Elector's reigning descendants would either emulate or be measured against.

EXPANSION

In December 1640, when Frederick William acceded to the throne, Brandenburg was still under foreign occupation. A two-year truce was agreed with the Swedes in July 1641, but the looting, burning and general misbehaviour continued.[11] In a letter of spring 1641, the Elector's viceroy, Margrave Ernest, who carried the responsibility for administering the ruined Mark, offered a grim synopsis:

The country is in such a miserable and impoverished condition that mere words can scarcely convey the sympathy one feels with the innocent inhabitants. In general, We think that the cart has been driven so deep into the muck, as they say, that it cannot be extricated without the special help of the Almighty.[12]

The strain of overseeing the anarchy unfolding in Brandenburg ultimately proved too much for the margrave, who succumbed to panic attacks, sleeplessness and paranoid delusions. By the autumn of 1642, he had taken to pacing about in his palace muttering to himself, shrieking and throwing himself to the floor. His death on 26 September was ascribed to 'melancholy'.[13]

Only in March 1643 did Frederick William return from the relative safety of Königsberg to the ruined city of Berlin, a city he scarcely recognized. Here he found a population depleted and malnourished, and buildings destroyed by fire or in a parlous state of repair.[14] The predicament that had bedevilled his father's reign remained unsolved: Brandenburg had no military force with which to establish its independence. The small army created by Schwarzenberg was already falling apart and there was no money to pay for a replacement. Johann Friedrich von Leuchtmar, a privy councillor and the Elector's former tutor, summarized Brandenburg's predicament in a report of 1644: Poland, he predicted, would seize Prussia as soon as it was strong enough; Pomerania was under Swedish occupation and likely to remain so; Kleve in the west was under the control of the Dutch Republic. Brandenburg stood 'on the edge of the abyss'.[15]

In order to restore the independence of his territory and press home his claims, the Elector needed a flexible, disciplined fighting force. The creation of such an instrument became one of the consuming preoccupations of his reign. The Brandenburg campaign army grew dramatically, if somewhat unsteadily, from 3,000 men in 1641–2, to 8,000 in 1643–6, to 25,000 during the Northern War of 1655–60, to 38,000 during the Dutch wars of the 1670s. During the final decade of the Elector's reign, its size fluctuated between 20,000 and 30,000.[16] Improvements in tactical training and armaments modelled on French, Dutch, Swedish and imperial best practice placed the Brandenburg army close to the cutting edge of European military innovation. Pikes and pikemen were phased out and the cumbersome matchlock guns carried by the infantry were replaced by lighter, faster-firing flintlocks. Artillery calibres were standardized to allow for the more flexible and efficient use of field guns, in the style pioneered by the Swedes. The foundation of a cadet school for officer recruits introduced an element of standardized professional formation. Better conditions of employment – including provision for maimed or retired officers – improved the stability of the command structure. These changes in turn improved the cohesion and morale of the non-commissioned ranks, who distinguished themselves in the 1680s by their excellent discipline and low rates of desertion.[17]

The improvised forces assembled for specific campaigns during the early years of the reign gradually evolved into what one could call a standing army. In April 1655, a General War Commissioner (*Generalkriegskommissar*) was appointed to oversee the handling of financial and other resources for the army, on the model of the military administration recently introduced in France under Le Tellier and Louvois. This innovation was initially conceived as a temporary wartime measure and only later established as a permanent feature of the territorial administration. After 1679, under the direction of the Pomeranian nobleman Joachim von Grumbkow, the General War Commissariat extended its reach throughout the Hohenzollern territories, gradually usurping the function of the Estate officials who had traditionally overseen military taxation and discipline at a local level. The General War Commissariat and the Office for the Domains were still relatively small institutions in 1688 when the Elector died, but under his successors they would play a crucial role in toughening the sinews of central authority in the Brandenburg-Prussian state. This synergy between war-making and the development of state-like central organs was something new; it became possible only when the war-making apparatus was separated from its traditional provincial-aristocratic foundations.

The acquisition of such a formidable military instrument was important, because the decades that followed the end of the Thirty Years War were a period of intense conflict in northern Europe. Two foreign titans overshadowed Brandenburg foreign policy during the Elector's reign. The first was King Charles X of Sweden, a restless, obsessive figure with expansionist dreams who seemed bent on trumping the record of his illustrious predecessor Gustavus Adolphus. It was Charles X's invasion of Poland that started the Northern War of 1655–60. His plan was to subdue the Danes and the Poles, occupy Ducal Prussia and then march south at the head of a vast army to sack Rome in the manner of the ancient Goths. Instead, the Swedes became bogged down in a bitter five-year struggle for control of the Baltic littoral.

After the death of Charles X in 1660 and the ebbing of Swedish power, it was Louis XIV of France who dominated Brandenburg's political horizons. Having assumed sole regency after the death of Cardinal Mazarin in 1661, Louis expanded his combined wartime armed forces from 70,000 to 320,000 men (by 1693) and launched a sequence of assaults to secure hegemony in western Europe; there were campaigns against the Spanish Netherlands in 1667–8, the United Provinces in 1672–8 and the Palatinate in 1688.

In this dangerous environment, the Elector's growing army proved an indispensable asset. In the summer of 1656, Frederick William's 8,500 troops joined forces with Charles X to defeat a massive Polish-Tartar army in the battle of Warsaw (28–30 July).[18] In 1658, he changed sides and campaigned as an ally of Poland and Austria against the Swedes. It was a sign of Frederick William's growing weight in regional politics that he was appointed commander of the Brandenburg-Polish-imperial allied army raised to fight the Swedes in 1658–9. A chain of successful military assaults followed, first in Schleswig-Holstein and Jutland and later in Pomerania.

The most dramatic military exploit of the reign was Frederick William's single-handed victory over the Swedes at Fehrbellin in 1675. In the winter of 1674–5, the Elector was campaigning with an Austrian army in the Rhineland as part of the coalition that had formed to contain Louis XIV during the Dutch wars. In the hope of securing French subsidies, the Swedes, allies of the French, invaded Brandenburg with an army of 14,000 men under the command of General Karl Gustav Wrangel. It was a scenario that awakened memories of the Thirty Years War: the Swedes unleashed the usual ravages on the hapless population of the Uckermark, to the north-east of Berlin. Frederick William reacted to news of the invasion with undisguised rage. 'I can be brought to no other resolution,' the Elector told Otto von Schwerin on 10 February, 'than to avenge myself on the Swedes.' In a series of furious despatches, the Elector, who was bedridden with gout, urged his subjects, 'both noble and non-noble', to 'cut down all Swedes, wherever they can lay their hands upon them and to break their necks [...] and to give no quarter'.[19]

Frederick William joined his army in Franconia at the end of May. Covering over one hundred kilometres per week, his forces reached Magdeburg on 22 June, just over ninety kilometres from the Swedish headquarters in the city of Havelberg. From here, the Brandenburg command could establish through local informants that the Swedes were strung out behind the river Havel, with concentrations in the fortified cities of Havelberg, Rathenow and Brandenburg. Since the Swedes had failed to register the arrival of the Brandenburg army, the Elector and his commander Georg Derfflinger had the advantage of surprise, and they resolved to attack the Swedish strongpoint at Rathenow with only 7,000 cavalry; a further 1,000 musketeers were loaded on to carts so that they could keep pace with the advance. Heavy rain and muddy conditions impeded their progress but also concealed them from the unsuspecting Swedish regiment at Rathenow. In the early morning of 25 June, the Brandenburgers attacked and destroyed the Swedish force with only minimal casualties on their own side.

The collapse of the Swedish line at Rathenow set the scene for the Battle of Fehrbellin, the most celebrated military engagement of the Elector's reign. In order to restore cohesion to their position, the Swedish regiment in Brandenburg City pulled back deep into the countryside with the intention of sweeping to the north-west to join up with the main force at Havelberg. This proved more difficult than they had expected, because the heavy spring and summer rains had transformed the marshes of the area into a treacherous waterland broken only by islands of sodden grass or sand and criss-crossed by narrow causeways. Guided by locals, advance parties of the Electoral army blocked the main exits from the area, and forced the Swedes to fall back on the little town of Fehrbellin on the river Rhin. Here their commander, General Wrangel, deployed his 11,000 men in defensive fashion, setting the 7,000 Swedish infantry in the centre and his cavalry on the wings.

Against 11,000 Swedes the Elector could muster only around 6,000 men (a substantial part of his army, including most of his infantry, had not yet arrived in the area). The Swedes disposed of about three times as many field guns as the Brandenburgers. But this numerical disadvantage was offset by a tactical opportunity. Wrangel had neglected to occupy a low sandhill that overlooked his right flank. The Elector lost no time in positioning his thirteen field guns there and opening fire on the Swedish lines. Seeing his error, Wrangel ordered the cavalry on his right wing, supported by infantry, to take the hill. For the next few hours the battle was dominated by the ebb and surge of cavalry charge and counter-charge as the Swedes attempted to seize the enemy guns and were thrown back by the Brandenburg horse. A metaphorical fog of war shrouds all such encounters; it was thickened on this occasion by a literal summer mist of the kind that often gathers in the marshes of the Havelland. Both sides found it difficult to coordinate their forces, but it was the Swedish cavalry that gave way first, fleeing from the field and leaving their infantry – the Dalwig Guards – exposed to the sabres of the Brandenburg horse. Of 1,200 Guards, twenty managed to escape and about seventy were taken prisoner; the rest were killed.[20] On the following day, the town of Fehrbellin itself was seized from a small Swedish occupation force. There was now a great fleeing of Swedes across the Mark Brandenburg. Considerable numbers of them, more perhaps than fell on the field of battle, were hacked to death in opportunist attacks by peasants as they made their way northwards. A contemporary report noted that peasants in the area around the town of Wittstock, not far from the border with Pomerania, had slain 300 Swedes, including a number of officers: 'although several of the latter offered 2000 thalers for their lives, they were decapitated by the vengeful peasants.'[21] Memories of the 'Swedish terror' still vivid in the older generation played a role here. By 2 July, every last Swede who had not been captured or killed had left the territory of the Electorate.

Victories of the kind achieved at Warsaw and Fehrbellin were of enormous symbolic importance to the Elector and his entourage. In an era that glorified successful warlords, the victories of Brandenburg's army magnified the prestige and reputation of its founder. At Warsaw, Frederick William had stood in the thick of the fighting, repeatedly exposing himself to enemy fire. He wrote an account of the event and had it published in The Hague. His notes on the battle formed the basis for the relevant passages in Samuel Pufendorf's history of the reign – a comprehensive and sophisticated work that marked a new departure in Brandenburg historiography.[22] All this bore witness to a heightened historical self-consciousness, a sense that Brandenburg had begun to make – and to narrate – its own history. In his 'royal memoirs', a text intended for the eyes of his successor, Louis XIV observed that kings owe an account of their actions 'to all ages'.[23] The Great Elector never unfolded a cult of historicized self-memorialization to rival that of his French contemporary, but he too began consciously to perceive himself and his achievements through the eyes of an imagined posterity.

At Warsaw in 1656 the Brandenburgers had shown their mettle as coalition partners; at Fehrbellin nineteen years later the Elector's army, though outnumbered and forced to advance at lightning speed, prevailed without aid over an enemy with an intimidating European reputation. Here too the Elector, now a stout man of fifty-five, stayed at the centre of the action. He joined his riders in assaults on the Swedish lines until he was encircled by enemy troops and had to be cut free by nine of his own dragoons. It was after the victory at Fehrbellin that the soubriquet 'the Great Elector' first appeared in print. There was nothing particularly remarkable in that, since broadsheets extolling the greatness of rulers were commonplace in seventeenth-century Europe. But unlike so many other early-modern 'greats' (including the abortive 'Louis the Great', propagated by the sycophantic pamphleteers of the sun-king; 'Leopold the Great' of Austria; and 'Maximilian the Great', usage of which is now confined to die-hard Bavarian monarchist circles) this one survived, making Elector Frederick William the only non-royal early-modern European sovereign who is still widely accorded this epithet.

With Fehrbellin, moreover, a bond was forged between history and legend. The battle became a fixture in memory. The dramatist Heinrich von Kleist chose it as the setting for his play *Der Prinz von Homburg*, a fanciful variation on the historical record, in which an impulsive military commander faces a death sentence for having led a victorious charge against the Swedes despite orders to hold back, but is pardoned by the Elector once he has accepted his culpability. To the Brandenburgers and Prussians of posterity, Frederick William's predecessors would remain shadowy, antique figures imprisoned within a remote past. By contrast, the 'Great Elector' would be elevated to the status of a three-dimensional founding father, a transcendent personality who both symbolized and bestowed meaning upon the history of a state.

ALLIANCES

'Alliances are certainly good,' Frederick William wrote in 1667, 'but a force of one's own, that one can confidently rely on, is better. A ruler is not treated with respect unless he has his own troops and resources. It is these, thank God, that have made me important since I have had them.'[24] There was much truth in these reflections, composed for the edification of the Elector's son and successor. By the end of the Second Northern War, Frederick William was a man to be reckoned with. He was an attractive alliance partner who could command substantial subsidies. He also participated as a principal in major regional peace treaties – a distinction that had been denied to his predecessors.

But the army was just one factor in Brandenburg's recovery and expansion after 1640. Even before he possessed an armed force capable of tipping the scales in regional conflicts, Frederick William was able to secure major territorial gains simply by playing the international system. It was only thanks to French backing that Brandenburg emerged in such a strong position from the Peace of Westphalia in 1648. The French, who were looking for a German client state to support their designs against Austria, helped Frederick William thrash out a compromise agreement with Sweden (a French ally), under which Brandenburg received the eastern portion of Pomerania (excluding the river Oder). Then France and Sweden joined forces in pressing the Emperor to compensate Brandenburg for the still Swedish portion of Pomerania by granting it lands from the former bishoprics of Halberstadt, Minden and Magdeburg. These were by far the most significant acquisitions of Frederick William's long reign. After 1648, a swathe of Hohenzollern territory swept in a broad curve from the western borders of the Altmark up to the eastern end of the Pomeranian coastline – the gap between the central agglomeration of territories and Ducal Prussia narrowed to less than 120 kilometres. For the first time in its history, Brandenburg was bigger than neighbouring Saxony. It was now the second largest German territory after the Habsburg monarchy. And all this was achieved without discharging a single musket, at a time when Brandenburg's tiny armed force still counted for little.

The same point can be made in connection with the acquisition of full sovereignty over Ducal Prussia in 1657. To be sure: the Elector's army expanded to 25,000 men in the course of the Northern War of 1655–60. By fighting first on the Swedish and then on the Polish-imperial side, the Elector was able to prevent the powers engaged in the conflict from shutting him out of his exposed eastern duchy. After the victory at Warsaw in 1656, Charles X abandoned his plan to occupy Ducal Prussia as a Swedish fief and agreed to concede full sovereignty to Brandenburg. But once the Swedes had been driven back into Denmark, this promise became meaningless – Ducal Prussia was no longer theirs to give. The trick now was to get the Poles to follow suit and grant full sovereignty in their turn. Here again, the Elector was the beneficiary of international developments beyond his control. A crisis in relations between the Polish Crown and the Russian Tsar meant that the lands of the Commonwealth were exposed to Russian assaults. The King of Poland, John Casimir, was thus eager to separate Brandenburg from Sweden and to neutralize it as a military threat.

By a further coincidence, Emperor Ferdinand III died in April 1657, meaning that Frederick William could trade his Electoral vote for concessions over Ducal Prussia. The Habsburgs duly pressed the Polish king to grant the Elector's demand for sovereignty over Ducal Prussia, urgings that carried considerable weight, since the Poles were counting on Austrian assistance in the event of a renewed Swedish or Russian attack. In a secret treaty signed at Wehlau on 1 September 1657, the Poles agreed to cede Ducal Prussia to the Elector 'with absolute power and without the previous impositions'. The Elector promised in turn to help John Casimir against Sweden.[25] Nothing could better illustrate the intricacy and geographical scope of the mechanisms that shaped Brandenburg's opportunities. The fact that Frederick William had by now assembled sufficient troops under his command to be a useful ally was an important enabling factor in this outcome, but it was the international system rather than the Elector's own efforts that settled the question of sovereignty in his favour.

Conversely, the unilateral application of military force – even when it was successful in military terms – was of little avail in cases where Brandenburg's objectives were *not* underwritten by the broader dynamics of the international system. In 1658–9, Frederick William commanded an extremely successful joint Austrian-Polish-Brandenburg campaign against the Swedes. There was a long chain of successful military assaults, first in Schleswig-Holstein and Jutland and later in Pomerania. By the time the campaign of 1659 was over, Brandenburg troops controlled virtually all of Swedish Pomerania, excluding only the coastal cities of Stralsund and Stettin. But these successes did not suffice to secure the Elector a permanent foothold in the disputed portion of his Pomeranian inheritance. France intervened in support of Sweden, and the Peace of Oliva (3 May 1660) largely confirmed the concessions agreed at Wehlau three years before. Brandenburg thus gained nothing from the Elector's involvement in the alliance against Sweden, apart from broader international recognition of his sovereign status in Prussia. Here was a further lesson, if any were needed, in the primacy of the system over the forces at the disposal of one of its lesser members.

Exactly the same thing happened after the victory over Sweden at Fehrbellin in 1675. In the course of an exhausting four-year campaign, the Elector succeeded in driving every last Swede out of Western Pomerania. But even this was not enough to place him in possession of his claim, for Louis XIV had no intention of leaving his Swedish ally at Brandenburg's mercy. France, whose powers were waxing as the Dutch Wars came to an end, insisted that the conquered Pomeranian territories should be restored in their entirety to Sweden. Vienna agreed: the Habsburg Emperor had no desire to see 'the rise of a new king of the Vandals on the Baltic'; he preferred a weak Sweden to a strong Brandenburg.[26] In June 1679, after much impotent raging, the Elector finally renounced the claim he had fought so hard for and authorized his envoy to sign the Peace of St Germain with France.

This dispiriting conclusion to a long struggle was yet another reminder that Brandenburg was still, for all its efforts and accomplishments, a small player in a world where the big players decided the important outcomes. Frederick William had been able with some success to exploit the shifting balance of power in a regional conflict between Poland and Sweden, but he was out of his depth in a struggle in which great-power interests were more directly engaged.

Playing the system effectively meant being on the right side at the right moment, and this in turn implied a readiness to switch allegiances when an existing commitment became burdensome or inopportune. Throughout the late 1660s and early 1670s, the Elector oscillated franti-cally between France and Austria. In January 1670, a three-year train of negotiations and agreements culminated in a ten-year treaty with France. In the summer of 1672, however, when the French attacked the Dutch Republic, invading and plundering Kleve in the process, the Elector turned instead to Emperor Leopold in Vienna. A treaty was signed in late June 1672, by which it was agreed that Brandenburg and the Emperor would conduct a joint campaign to safeguard the western borders of the Holy Roman Empire against French aggression. In the summer of 1673, however, the Elector was once again in alliance dis-cussions with France; by the autumn of the same year he was already gravitating back towards a new anti-French coalition centred on a triple alliance between Emperor Leopold, the Dutch and the Spaniards. The same pattern of rapid alternation can be observed during the last years of Frederick William's reign. There was a succession of alliances with France (October 1679, January 1682, January 1684), yet at the same time a Brandenburg contingent was sent to assist in the relief of the Turkish siege of Vienna in 1683. In August 1685, moreover, Frederick William signed a treaty with the Dutch Republic whose terms were largely directed against France (while at the same time assuring the French of his loyalty and pressing them to keep up with their subsidy payments).

'[It is] in the nature of alliances,' the Austrian military strategist Count Montecuccoli sagely observed, 'that they are dissolved at the slightest inconvenience.'[27] But even in an era that saw alliances as short-term fixes, the 'feverish inconstancy' (*Wechselfieber*) of the Elector seemed remarkable. There was method in the madness, however. In order to pay for his growing army, Frederick William needed foreign subsidies. Frequent alliance-switching forced would-be partners into a bidding war and thereby pushed up the going price for an alliance. The rapid alternation of alliances also reflected the complexity of Brandenburg's security needs. The integrity of the western territories depended on good relations with France and the United Provinces. The integrity of Ducal Prussia depended on good relations with Poland. The safety of Brandenburg's entire Baltic littoral depended on holding the Swedes at bay. The maintenance of the Elector's status and the pursuit of his inheritance claims within the Empire depended upon good (or at least functional) relations with the Emperor. All these threads crossed at various points to form a neural net generating unpredictable and rapidly shifting outcomes.

Although this problem was particularly acute in the reign of the Great Elector, it did not go away after his death. Again and again, Prussian sovereigns and statesmen would face agonizing choices between conflicting alliance commitments. It was a predicament that placed considerable strain on the decision-making networks close to the throne. During the winter of 1655–6, for example, as the Elector pondered which side to back in the opening phase of the Northern War, 'Swedish' and 'Polish' factions formed among the ministers and advisers and even the Elector's own family. The resulting mood of uncertainty and indecision prompted one of the Elector's most powerful councillors to the observation that the Elector and his advisers 'want what they didn't want and do what they didn't think they would do'[28] – a charge that had also been laid at the feet of George William and would be made against various later Brandenburg sovereigns. The periodic disintegration of the policy-making establishment into factions supporting rival options would remain one of the structural constants of Prussian politics.

In switching thus from partner to partner, the Elector followed the advice of the Pomeranian Calvinist Privy Councillor Paul von Fuchs, who urged the Elector not to commit himself permanently to any one partner but always to follow a 'pendulum policy' (*Schaukelpolitik*).[29] Here was an important break with the previous reign: George William, too, had alternated between Vienna and Stockholm, but only under duress. By contrast, the word *Schaukelpolitik* implied a conscious policy of oscillation. And this in turn implied an attenuation of the Elector's sense of obligation to the Emperor. Successive efforts to mount a joint Brandenburg-Habsburg response to the threat from France in the 1670s had revealed that the two powers had widely divergent geopolitical interests (this problem was to dog Austro-Prussian relations well into the nineteenth century). And the Austrian Habsburg court showed on more than one occasion that it was happy to see the Elector thwarted in his ambition. Frederick William boiled with resentment at these slights: 'You know how the Emperor and the Empire have treated us,' he told the chief minister of his Privy Council, Otto von Schwerin, in August 1679, when Vienna supported the return of Western Pomerania to Sweden. 'And since they were the first to leave us defenceless before our enemies, we need no longer consider their interests unless they agree with ours.'[30]

Yet it is also striking how reluctant the Elector was to burn his bridges with Vienna. He remained a loyal prince of the Empire, supporting the Habsburg candidates in successive imperial elections and participating actively and constructively in imperial politics.[31] The Hohenzollern eagle shown on the ensigns of seventeenth-century Brandenburg always wore a shield proudly adorned with the golden sceptre of the Imperial Hereditary Chamberlain, a mark of the Elector's prominent ceremonial standing within the Empire. Frederick William saw the Empire as indispensable to the future well-being of his lands. The interests of the Empire were not, of course, identical with those of the Habsburg Emperor, and the Elector was perfectly aware that it might at times be necessary to defend the institutions of the former against the latter. But the Emperor remained a fixed star in the Brandenburg firmament. It was essential, the Elector warned his successor in the 'Fatherly Instruction' of 1667, 'that You bear in mind the respect that You must have for the Emperor and the Empire'.[32] This curious combination of a rebellious resentment of the Emperor with an ingrained respect for the ancient institutions of the Empire (or at the very least a reluctance to do away with them) was another feature of Prussian foreign policy that would endure into the late eighteenth century.

SOVEREIGNTY

On 18 October 1663, a colourful assembly of Estates representatives gathered before Königsberg castle. They were there to swear an oath of fealty to the Elector of Brandenburg. The occasion was a solemn one. The Elector stood on a raised platform draped in scarlet cloth. Near him were four senior officials of the ducal administration, each bearing one of the insignia of his office: the ducal crown, a sword, a sceptre and a field marshal's baton. After the ceremony, the gates of the castle courtyard were opened for the traditional display of sovereign largesse. As the people of the city crowded in to join the celebrations, chamberlains tossed gold and silver commemorative medals into the crowd. Wine – red and white from two different spouts – splashed all day from a fountain fashioned in the likeness of the Hohenzollern eagle. In the reception rooms of the palace, the Estates were entertained at twenty large tables.[33]

The choreography of this occasion invoked a tradition of great antiquity. The oath of fealty had been an accoutrement of sovereignty in western Europe since the twelfth century. It was a legal act by which the constitutional relationship between sovereign and subject was 'actualised, renewed and perpetuated'.[34] In time-honoured fashion, the Estates representatives swore that they would never 'under any circumstances imaginable to man' break their bond with the new sovereign, all the while kneeling before the Elector with the left hand laid across the chest and the right hand raised above the head with the thumb and two fingers extended. It was said that the thumb signified God the Father, the index finger God the Son and the middle finger the Holy Spirit; 'of the other two fingers, folded down into the hand, the fourth signifies the precious soul, which is hidden among mankind, while the fifth signifies the body, which is a smaller thing than the soul'.[35] A specific act of political subordination was thus merged into the permanence of man's submission before God.

These invocations of timelessness and tradition belied the fragility of Hohenzollern authority in Ducal Prussia. In 1663, when the oath was sworn in Königsberg, the Elector's legal sovereignty in the Duchy of Prussia was of recent vintage. It had been formally confirmed at the Peace of Oliva only three years before and had since been vigorously contested by the inhabitants. In the city of Königsberg, a popular movement emerged to resist the efforts of the Electoral administration to impose its authority. Only after a leading city politician had been arrested and Electoral cannon trained on the heart of the city could peace be restored, making way for the settlement that was solemnized in the palace courtyard on 18 October 1663. And yet, within a decade, the Electoral authorities once again faced open resistance and were forced to invest the city with troops. Not only in Ducal Prussia, but also in Kleve and even in Brandenburg itself, the decades that followed the Thirty Years War were marked by strife between the Electoral authorities and the guardians of local privilege.

There was nothing inevitable about the conflict between monarchs and estates. The relationship between the sovereign and the nobilities was essentially one of interdependence. The nobilities administered the localities and collected the taxes. They lent money to the sovereign – in 1631, for example, George William owed the Brandenburg nobleman Johann von Arnim 50,000 thalers, for which he pawned two domains to him as security.[36] Noble wealth provided the collateral for crown loans and in times of war noblemen were expected to provide the prince with horses and armed men to defend the territory. During the seventeenth century, however, the relationship between the two came under increasing pressure. It seemed that conflicts between the sovereign and the Estates had become the norm rather than the exception.[37]

The issue was essentially one of perspective. Again and again, Frederick William had to make the case that the Estates and the regions they represented should see themselves as parts of a single whole and thus as bound to collaborate in the maintenance and defence of all the sovereign's lands and the pursuit of his legitimate territorial claims.[38] But this way of seeing things was completely alien to the Estates, who viewed the respective territories as discrete constitutional parcels, bound vertically to the person of the Elector, but not horizontally to each other. For the Estates of the Mark Brandenburg, Kleve and Ducal Prussia were 'foreign provinces' with no claim on Brandenberg's resources.[39] Frederick William's wars for Pomerania, by the same token, were merely private princely 'feuds', for which he had – in their view – no right to sequester the wealth of his hard-working subjects.

The Estates expected from the Elector the continuation and solemn observance of their 'especial and particular privileges, freedoms, treaties, princely exemptions, marital agreements, territorial contracts, ancient traditions, law and justice'.[40] They inhabited a mental world of mixed and overlapping sovereignties. The Estates of Kleve maintained a diplomatic representative in The Hague until 1660 and looked to the Dutch Republic, the imperial diet and on occasions even to Vienna, for support against illicit interventions from Berlin.[41] They frequently conferred with the Estates of Mark, Jülich and Berg on how best to respond to (and resist) the Elector's demands.[42] The Estates of Ducal Prussia, for their part, tended to see neighbouring Poland as the guarantor of their ancient privileges. As one senior Electoral official irritably remarked, the leaders of the Prussian Estates were 'true neighbours of the Poles' and 'indifferent to the defence of [their own] country'.[43]

It was not long before the widening scope of the Elector's ambitions put him on a collision course with the Estates. The introduction of foreigners, mostly of Calvinist confession, into the most powerful administrative offices of the territories was an affront to the largely Lutheran nobility. It contravened the cherished *Indigenat*, a longstanding constitutional tradition in all the provinces, according to which only 'natives' could serve in the administration. Another sensitive question was the standing army. The Estates objected to it not just because it was expensive, but also because it displaced the old system of provincial militias, which had been under Estates control. This was of particular importance in Ducal Prussia, where the militia system was a cherished symbol of the duchy's ancient liberties. In 1655, when the Electoral administration put forward a proposal for the abolition of the militias and their replacement by a permanent force answering directly to Berlin, the Estates responded with bitter protests, declaring that if the traditional means did not suffice for an effective defence, the sovereign should order days of 'general atonement and prayer' and 'seek refuge in God'.[44] There are interesting parallels here with those outspoken 'Country Whigs' who opposed the expansion of the standing army in England, pleading for the retention of local militias under gentry control and arguing that a country's foreign policy should be determined by its armed forces, not the other way around.[45] In England, as in Ducal Prussia, the 'country ideology' of the rural elites encompassed a potent blend of provincial patriotism, the defence of 'liberty' and resistance to the expansion of state power.[46] Many Prussian noblemen would have agreed enthusiastically with the view expressed in an English anti-army pamphlet of 1675 that 'the power of *Peerage* and a *Standing Army* are like two Buckets, the proportion that one goes down, the other exactly goes up . . .'[47]

The most contentious issue of all was taxation. The Estates insisted that monetary and other levies could not legally be raised without prior agreement with their representatives. Yet the increasingly deep involvement of Brandenburg in regional power politics after 1643 meant that the administration's financial needs could not be satisfied using the traditional fiscal mechanisms.[48] During the years 1655–88 the Great Elector's military expenditures totalled some 54 million thalers. Some of this was covered by foreign subsidies under a succession of alliance compacts. Some derived from the exploitation of the Elector's own domains, or other sovereign revenues, such as the postal services, coinage and customs. But these sources together accounted for no more than 10 million thalers. The remainder had to be raised in the form of taxes from the population of the Elector's territories.[49]

In Kleve, Ducal Prussia and even in Brandenburg, the heartland of the Hohenzollern patrimony, the Estates resisted the Elector's efforts to secure new revenues for the army. In 1649, the Brandenburg Estates refused to approve funds for a campaign against the Swedes in Pomerania, despite the Elector's earnest reminder that all his territories were now 'limbs of one head' (*membra unius capitis*) and that Pomerania ought thus to be supported as if it were 'part of the Electorate'.[50] In Kleve, where the wealthy urban patriciate still regarded the Elector as a foreign interloper, the Estates revived the traditional 'alliance' with Mark, Jülich and Berg; leading spokesmen even drew parallels with the contemporary upheavals in England and threatened to treat the Elector as the parliamentary party were treating King Charles. Frederick William's threats to apply 'military executive actions' were largely futile, since the Estates were supported by the Dutch garrisons still occupying the duchy.[51] In Ducal Prussia, too, the Elector encountered determined resistance. Here the Estates had traditionally ruled the roost, meeting regularly in full session and keeping a tight grip on central and local government, the militia and the territorial finances. The traditional Prussian right of appeal to the Polish Crown meant that they could not easily be bullied into cooperating.[52]

It was the outbreak of the Northern War of 1655–60 that brought the confrontation over revenues to a head. First, coercion and force were used to break resistance. Annual levies were raised unilaterally and extracted by military 'executive action' – especially in Kleve, where the annual contribution rose more sharply during the war years than anywhere else in the Elector's lands. Leading Estates activists were intimidated or arrested.[53] Protests were ignored. In the struggle over revenues, the Elector benefited from changes in the broader legal environment that helped to undermine the pretensions of the provincial elites. In 1654, under pressure from the German Electors, most of whom were locked in conflicts of one kind or another with their Estates, the Emperor decreed that the subjects of sovereigns within the Holy Roman Empire were 'obliged obediently to give the necessary assistance to their Princes [. . .] for the support and occupation of fortified places and garrisons'. While it is perhaps an exaggeration to describe this document as the 'Magna Carta of absolutism', the decree of 1654 was an important point of departure. It signalled the advent across the Holy Roman Empire of a political climate unfavourable to the assertion of corporate rights.[54]

Of all the conflicts over Estates' rights, the one in Ducal Prussia was the most bitter. Here too, the outbreak of the Northern War was the catalyst for confrontation. The Elector summoned the Prussian Diet in April 1655 but even in August, when the threat posed by Sweden was evident, the Estates refused to promise more than 70,000 thalers – a small sum if one bears in mind that poorer and less populous Brandenburg was at this time providing an annual military contribution of 360,000 thalers.[55] The situation changed dramatically in the winter of 1655 when Frederick William and his army arrived in Königsberg. Forced payments soon became the rule and the annual military contribution rose sharply to an average of 600,000 thalers over the years 1655–9. A string of administrative reforms was put in place that allowed the Elector to circumvent the Estates. The most important were the foundation of the War Commissariat, with extensive fiscal and confiscatory powers, and the installation of an Electoral viceroy, Prince Boguslav Radziwill, whose task was to oversee the powerful and independent Supreme Councillors (Oberräte), who had traditionally ruled Prussia on behalf of the Estates.

With the issue of his full sovereignty resolved by the Treaty of Wehlau (1657) and the Peace of Oliva (1660), the Elector was determined to achieve a lasting settlement with the Prussian Estates. But the Estates contested the validity of the treaties, arguing that changes to the constitutional machinery of the province could only be made on the basis of trilateral negotiations between the Elector, the Ducal Prussian Estates and the Polish Crown.[56] During the year-long Great Diet convened in Königsberg in May 1661, the Estates unfolded a far-reaching programme of demands including a permanent right of appeal to the Polish Crown, the removal of all Electoral troops except for a few coastal garrisons, the exclusion of non-Prussians from official posts, regular diets, and automatic Polish mediation in all disputes between the Estates and the Elector. It proved extremely difficult to reach an agreement over these issues, the more so as the mood among the citizenry of Königsberg grew steadily more restless and intransigent. In order to insulate the

5. A view of the city of Königsberg (c. 1690)

negotiations from the turbulence in the ducal capital, the Elector's minister, Otto von Schwerin, ordered that the diet be moved southwards to the more tranquil setting of Bartenstein in October 1661. Only after March 1662, when a mission to Warsaw failed to secure concrete assistance from Poland, did the corporate nobility begin to back down.

In the meanwhile, the mood of the city had grown more radical, following a pattern that can also be observed in other parts of Europe. There were daily protest meetings. One of the foremost activists for urban corporate rights was Hieronymus Roth, a merchant and president of the court of aldermen of Kneiphof, one of the three 'cities' of old Königsberg. Hoping to persuade Roth to adopt a more moderate position, Otto von Schwerin invited him to a private meeting at the ducal castle in Königsberg on 26 May 1661. But the encounter went horribly wrong. According to a report by Schwerin, Roth adopted a seditious and confrontational tone, declaring among other things that 'every prince, be he ever so pious, bears a tyrant in his breast' – words that would later be cited in the alderman's indictment. Roth for his part recalled that he had defended the ancient liberties of Königsberg in a polite and reasonable way – it was Schwerin who had flown into a rage and threatened him with raised arm.[57]

Despite a sustained campaign of harassment, Roth continued to agitate against the Electoral administration, protected by a city government that refused to arrest him or limit his activities. He travelled to Warsaw, where he met with the King of Poland, presumably in order to discuss the possibility of Polish support for the Estates. In the last week of October 1661, the Elector ran out of patience and entered Königsberg with 2,000 troops. Roth was arrested, tried, summarily convicted by an Electoral Commission and imprisoned in the fortress of Peitz, far away in Cottbus, a Hohenzollern enclave in Electoral Saxony. The prison regime was not particularly arduous in the early years – Roth was served six-course lunches, had comfortably appointed rooms and was allowed to take walks along the upper walls of the fortress.

New restrictions were imposed in 1668, however, when it was discovered that he had been carrying on a secret correspondence with his stepson in Königsberg, in which he railed against the 'arrogant Calvinists' who now governed his city on behalf of the Elector. The go-between who had conveyed his letters, a Königsberg-born soldier serving on the fortress garrison, was also punished. Frederick William had initially declared that he would release Roth if the latter would acknowledge his 'guilt', show true remorse and beg for mercy. But Roth stuck to his guns, objecting that he had acted not from any ill will but out of duty to his 'Fatherland'. After the scandal of the intercepted letters, the Elector resolved that the turbulent alderman should never be released. Only some years later, at the age of seventy, did Roth write to Frederick William begging for his liberation and commending himself as the Elector's 'loyal and obedient subject'.[58] But there was no pardon and the alderman died in his fortress in the summer of 1678, after seventeen years in confinement.

The imprisonment of Hieronymus Roth cleared the way for an interim settlement with the Prussian Estates. There were further clashes over taxation in the early 1670s, during which troops were called in to enforce payment. In January 1672 there was even a political execution in Ducal Prussia – the only one of the Elector's reign.[59] But the Prussians did eventually come to accept the Elector's sovereignty and the fiscal regime that came with it. By the 1680s, the political rule of the Prussian Estates had come to an end, leaving nothing but nostalgic dreams of the 'still unforgotten blissfulness, liberty and peaceful tranquillity' they had enjoyed under the mild overlordship of the kings of Poland.[60]

COURT AND COUNTRY

The Electoral administration gradually extended its independence from the provincial elites. Since the Elector owned nearly one-third of Brandenburg and about half of Ducal Prussia, he could greatly expand his revenue base simply by improving the administration of the crown domains. During the Second Northern War, the management of these properties was streamlined under the oversight of the new Office for the Domains (*Amtskammer*). A further important step was the excise tax, an indirect duty on goods and services introduced piecemeal in the towns of Brandenburg during the late 1660s and later extended to Pomerania, Magdeburg, Halberstadt and Ducal Prussia. After local disputes over the mode of its collection, the excise was placed under the control of centrally directed tax commissioners (*Steuerräte*), who soon began to accumulate other administrative functions. The excise was an important tactical asset because it divided the different corporate elements within the Estates against each other and thus weakened them *vis-à-vis* the central administration. Since the excise applied only to the towns, it placed rural enterprises at a competitive advantage over their urban rivals and enabled the Elector to milk the commercial wealth of the regions without alienating the powerful landed families.

Frederick William also reinforced his authority by appointing Calvinists to key administrative offices. This was not just a matter of religious preference – it was a policy consciously directed against the pretensions of the Lutheran Estates. Several of Frederick William's most senior officials were foreign Calvinist princes. The long-serving viceroy of Kleve, John Moritz von Nassau-Siegen, fell into this category, as did Count (later Prince) George Frederick von Waldeck, the flamboyant ruler of a minor Westphalian principality who had served in the Dutch army and became the most influential minister of the first half of the reign. Another was John George II of Anhalt, commander of the 1672 campaign and sometime viceroy of Brandenburg. The Polish-Lithuanian Prince Boguslav Radziwill, appointed as viceroy in Ducal Prussia during the Second Northern War, was another imperial Calvinist grandee. The Brandenburg minister Otto von Schwerin, leading office-holder at the Berlin court after 1658, was a Pomeranian nobleman who had converted to Calvinism and whose activities on the Elector's behalf included the buying up of noble estates and their incorporation into the crown domains. In all, some two-thirds of senior office-holders appointed during the Great Elector's reign were of the Reformed faith.[61]

The use of foreign officials was another important development; in Brandenburg, scarcely any of the leading ministers appointed after 1660 was actually a native of the Electorate. The employment of gifted commoners (mainly lawyers) in the upper echelons of the civilian and military administrations widened the gap between government organs and the provincial elites. By the end of the seventeenth century, the Junker nobility of the Brandenburg hinterland had become a marginal presence within the nascent Hohenzollern bureaucracy, a trend accelerated by the deteriorating financial condition of an elite that was slow to recover from the disruptions of the Thirty Years War. Of all the appointments made to senior court, diplomatic and military posts between the accession of Elector Frederick William in 1640 and that of his grandson Frederick the Great one hundred years later, only 10 per cent went to members of the Brandenburg noble landowning class.[62] What emerged as they retreated was a new office-holding type, less bound to the provincial nobilities than to the monarch and his administration.

This was not a struggle for the unconditional surrender of one party to the other. The central authority did not seek direct dominance over the provincial elites as such, but control over particular mechanisms within the traditional power-holding structures.[63] The Elector never set out to abolish the Estates or to subject them entirely to his authority. The objectives of his administration were always limited and pragmatic. The most senior officials often urged the government to be flexible and indulgent in its dealings with the Estates.[64] Prince Moritz von Nassau Siegen, viceroy in Kleve, was by temperament a conciliatory figure who spent much of his time in office mediating between the sovereign and the local elites.[65] Frederick William's chief agents in Ducal Prussia, Prince Radziwill and Otto von Schwerin, were both moderate figures with considerable sympathy for the Estates' cause. A close examination of the protocols of the Privy Council reveals a veritable flood of individual complaints and requests from particular Estates, most of which were approved on the spot by the sovereign.[66]

The Estates, or at least the corporate nobilities, soon found ways of reconciling their interests with the Elector's pretensions. They acted tactically, breaking with their corporate colleagues when it furthered their interests. Their opposition to the standing army was muted by the realization that military service in a command role offered an attractive and honourable road to status and a regular income.[67] They did not contest in principle the Elector's right to formulate foreign policy in consultation with his councillors. What they envisaged was a complementary relationship between the organs of central authority and the provincial grandees. As the Kleve Estates explained in a memorandum of 1684, the Elector could not be expected to know what was going on in all of his lands and was thus dependent upon his officials. But these, being human, were prey to the usual weaknesses and temptations. The role of the Estates was thus to provide a corrective and balance to the organs of provincial governance.[68] Things had come a long way since the confrontational exchanges of the 1640s.

Force and coercion played a role in securing the acquiescence of local elites, but protracted negotiations, mediation and the convergence of interests, though less spectacular, were far more important.[69] The Brandenburg administration pursued a flexible two-track approach, with the Elector pushing hard at intervals for key concessions and his officials working to restore consensus in between. Towns too, could benefit from this pragmatic approach. In return for rendering a formal declaration of fealty to the Elector in 1665, the little Westphalian city of Soest in the County of Mark was allowed to retain its ancient 'constitution', incorporating a unique system of self-government and municipal justice run by elected functionaries recruited from the corporate elites[70]

If we survey the situation at the end of the century from the vantage point of the rural localities, then it is clear that the nobility had conserved much of its jurisdictional autonomy and socio-economic power and remained the dominant force in the land. They retained the right to assemble at their own behest in order to deliberate on issues affecting the welfare of their regions. They controlled the collection and allocation of taxes in the countryside. More importantly, Estate bodies at district level (*Kreisstände*) retained the right to elect the district governor (*Landrat*), ensuring that this crucial figure in the administration remained – into the late eighteenth century – an intermediary who answered not only to the sovereign, but also to local corporate interests.[71]

If, however, we focus instead on the political power structures of the Hohenzollern territories, it becomes plain that the relationship between the central administration and the provincial estates had been irreversibly transformed. Plenary assemblies of the corporate representatives of the provincial nobilities became increasingly rare – the last such meeting of the Altmark and Mittelmark nobilities took place in 1683. Thereafter the business of the Estates and their dealings with government were managed through small deputations of permanent delegates known as 'lesser committees' (*engere Ausschüsse*). The corporate nobility had retreated from the high ground of the state, focusing its collective attention on the locality and relinquishing its territorial political ambitions. Court and country had grown apart.

LEGACY

At the close of the seventeenth century, Brandenburg-Prussia was the largest German principality after Austria. Its long scatter of territories stretched like an uneven line of stepping-stones from the Rhineland to the eastern Baltic. Much of what had been promised in the marriage and inheritance contracts of the sixteenth century had now been made real. As the Elector told a tearful bedside gathering on 7 May three days before his death, his reign had been, by God's grace, a long and happy one, though difficult and 'full of war and trouble'. 'Everyone knows the sad disorder the country was in when I began my reign; through God's help I have improved it, am respected by my friends and feared by my enemies.'[72] His celebrated great-grandson, Frederick the Great, would later declare that the history of Prussia's ascent began with the reign of the Great Elector, for it was he who had established 'the solid foundations' of its later greatness. Echoes of this argument resound in the great nineteenth-century narratives of the Prussian school.

It is clear that the military and foreign-political exploits of this reign did define, in formal terms, a new point of departure for Brandenburg. From 1660, Frederick William was the sovereign ruler of Ducal Prussia, a territory outside the Holy Roman Empire. He had superseded his ancestral political condition. He was no longer merely an imperial potentate, but a European prince. It is a mark of his attachment to this new status that he sought from the court of Louis XIV the official denomination 'Mon Frère' traditionally accorded only to sovereign princes.[73] During the reign of his successor Elector Frederick III, the Ducal Prussian sovereignty would be used to acquire the title of king for the House of Hohenzollern. In due course, even the ancient and venerable name of Brandenburg would be overshadowed by 'Kingdom of Prussia', the name increasingly used in the eighteenth century for the totality of the northern Hohenzollern lands.

The Elector himself was alert to the import of the changes that had been wrought during his reign. In 1667, he composed a 'Fatherly Instruction' for his heir. The document began, in the manner of the traditional princely testament, with exhortations to lead a pious and God-fearing life, but it soon broadened into a political tract of a type without precedent in the history of the Hohenzollern dynasty. Sharp contrasts were drawn between past and present: the Elector reminded his son of how the acquisition of sovereignty over Ducal Prussia had annulled the 'intolerable condition' of vassalage to the Crown of Poland that had oppressed his forebears. 'All this cannot be described; the Archive and the accounts will bear witness to it.'[74] The future Elector was also urged to develop an historical perspective on the problems that beset him in the present. Industrious consultation of the archive would reveal not only how important it was to maintain good relations with France, but also how these should be balanced with 'the respect that You, as an Elector, must have for the Reich and Emperor'. There was also a strong sense of the new order established by the Peace of Westphalia and the importance of defending it if necessary against any power or powers that should set out to overturn it.[75] In short, this was a document acutely sensitive to its own location in history and charged with an awareness of the tension between historical continuity and the forces of change.

Closely linked to the Elector's alertness to historical contingency was an acute sensitivity to the vulnerability of his achievement: what had been made could always be unmade. The Swedes would always be waiting for the next chance 'by cunning or by force' to wrest control of the Baltic coast from Brandenburg. The Poles, together with the Prussians themselves, would take the first opportunity to return Ducal Prussia to its 'prior condition'.[76] It followed that the task of his successors would not be to extend further the territories of the House of Brandenburg, but to safeguard what was already rightfully theirs:

Be sure at all times that you live as far as possible in mutual trust, friendship and correspondence with all the Electors, princes and Estates of the Empire, and that you give them no cause for ill-will, and keep the good peace. And because

God had blessed our House with many lands, you should look only to their conservation, and be sure that you do not awaken great envy and enmity through the quest for further lands or jeopardize thereby what you already possess.[77]

It is worth emphasizing this note of edginess. It articulates one of the abiding themes of Brandenburg-Prussian foreign policy. Underlying Berlin's view of the world there was always a sharp undertone of vulnerability. The restless activism that would become a hallmark of Prussian foreign policy began with the remembered trauma of the Thirty Years War. We hear it resounding in the doleful phrases of the 'Fatherly Instruction': 'For one thing is quite certain, if You simply sit still, in the belief that the fire is still far from Your borders: then Your lands will become the theatre on which the tragedy is played out.'[78] We hear it again in Frederick William's words of 1671 to the chief minister Otto von Schwerin: 'I have experienced neutrality before; even under the most favourable conditions, you are treated badly. I have vowed never to be neutral again until I die.'[79] It is one of the central problems of Brandenburg-Prussian history that this sense of vulnerability proved so inescapable.

4

Majesty

CORONATION

On 18 January 1701, Elector Frederick III of Brandenburg was crowned 'King in Prussia' in the city of Königsberg. The splendour of the event was unprecedented in the history of the House of Hohenzollern. According to one contemporary report, 30,000 horses were required to relay the Electoral family, their retainers and their luggage, all packed into 1,800 carriages, eastwards along the road from Berlin to the place of coronation. On their way, they passed villages hung with decorations, their main thoroughfares lined with burning torches, or even draped with fine cloth. The celebrations began on 15 January in Königsberg, when heralds wearing blue velvet livery emblazoned with the new royal coat of arms passed through the city, proclaiming the Duchy of Prussia a sovereign kingdom.

The coronation itself began on the morning of 18 January in the audience chamber of the Elector, where a throne had been erected specially for the occasion. Dressed in a scarlet and gold coat glittering with diamond buttons and a crimson mantle with an ermine lining and attended by a small gathering of male family members, courtiers and senior local officials, the Elector placed the crown on his own head, took his sceptre in hand and received the homage of those present. He then passed into the chambers of his wife, whom he crowned as his queen in the presence of their household. After representatives of the Estates had rendered homage, the royal couple processed to the castle church in order to be anointed. Here they were greeted at the entrance by two bishops, one Lutheran and one Reformed (Calvinist), both of whom had been appointed to their offices specifically for this purpose, in deference to the bi-confessional character of the Brandenburg-Prussian state. After some hymns and a sermon, a royal fanfare of drums and trumpets announced the high point of the service: the king rose from his throne and knelt at the altar while the Calvinist Bishop Ursinus wet two fingers of his right hand in the oil and anointed the forehead and the right and left wrists (above the pulse) of the king. The same ritual was then performed upon the queen. To the accompaniment of a musical acclamation, the clergymen involved in the service gathered before the throne and rendered homage. After further hymns and prayers, a senior court official stood up to announce a general pardon for all offenders, excluding blasphemers, murderers, debtors and those guilty of *lèse-majesté*.[1]

In terms of the proportion of territorial wealth consumed, the coronation of 1701 must surely be the most expensive single event in the history of Brandenburg-Prussia. Even by the standards of an age that revelled in courtly ceremonial as an expression of power, the Prussian coronation was unusually splendid. The government levied a special crown tax to cover its expenditures, but this brought in a total of only 500,000 thalers – three-fifths of this amount were paid out for the queen's crown alone, and the royal crown, fashioned of precious metal and studded over its entire surface with diamonds, accounted for the rest and more besides. Reconstructing the total cost of the festivities is difficult, since no integrated account survives, but it has been estimated that around 6 million thalers were spent in all for the ceremony and attendant festivities, about twice the annual revenues of the Hohenzollern administration.

The coronation was singular in another sense too. It was entirely custom-made: an invention designed to serve the purposes of a specific historical moment. The designer was Frederick I himself, who was responsible for every detail, not only of the new royal insignia, the secular rituals and the liturgy in the castle church, but also for the style and colour of the garments worn by the chief participants. There was a staff of experts to advise on monarchical ceremonial. Foremost among these was the poet Johann von Besser who served as master of ceremonies at Frederick's court from 1690 until the end of the reign and possessed a wide-ranging knowledge of English, French, German, Italian and Scandinavian courtly traditions. But the key decisions always fell to the Elector.

The ceremony that resulted was a unique and highly self-conscious amalgam of borrowings from historical European coronations, some recent, others of older vintage. Frederick designed his coronation not only with a view to its aesthetic impact, but also in order to broadcast what he regarded as the defining features of his kingly status. The form of the crown, which was not an open band, but a domed metal structure closed at the top, symbolized the all-embracing power of a monarch who encompassed in his own person both secular and spiritual sovereignty. The fact, moreover, that the king, in contrast to the prevailing European practice, crowned himself in a separate ceremony before being anointed at the hands of his clergy, pointed up the autonomous character of his office, its independence from any worldly or spiritual authority (save that of God himself). A description of the coronation by Johann Christian Lünig, a renowned contemporary expert on the courtly 'science of ceremony', explained the significance of this step.

Kings who accept their kingdom and sovereignty from the Estates usually only take up the purple mantle, the crown and sceptre and mount the throne *after* they have been anointed: [...] but His Majesty [Friedrich I], who has not received His Kingdom through the assistance of the Estates or of any other [party], had no need whatever of such a handing-over, but rather received his crown after the manner of the ancient kings from his own foundation.[2]

Given the recent history of Brandenburg and Ducal Prussia, the importance of these symbolic gestures is obvious enough. The Great Elector's struggle with the Prussian Estates and particularly the city of Königsberg was still a memory with the power to disturb – it is a telling detail that the Prussian Estates were never consulted over the coronation and were informed of the forthcoming festivity only in December 1700. Equally important was the independence of the new kingdom from any kind of Polish or imperial claim. Everyone knows, the British envoy George Stepney had reported to James Vernon, Secretary of State for the Northern Department, in 1698,

the value this Elector sets upon [...] the absolute soveraignety wherewith he possesses the Ducal Prussia, for in that respect he exceeds in Power all other Electors and Princes of the Empire, who are not so independent but derive their grandeur by investiture from the Emperor, for which reasons, the Elector affects to be distinguished by some more extraordinary title than what is common to the rest of his colleagues.[3]

6. Frederick I, King in Prussia *(Elector 1688–1701; king 1701–13), painted after his coronation, attributed to Samuel Theodor Gericke*

One of the reasons for adopting the title 'King in Prussia' – an unusual title that occasioned some amusement at the European courts – was that it freed the new crown from any Polish claims pertaining to 'royal' Prussia, which was still within the Polish Commonwealth. In negotiations with Vienna, particular care was expended to ensure that the wording of any agreement would make it clear that the Emperor was not 'creating' (*creieren*) the new royal title, but merely 'acknowledging' (*agnoszieren*) it. A much disputed passage of the final agreement between Berlin and Vienna paid lip service to the special primacy of the Emperor as the senior monarch of Christendom, but also made it clear that the Prussian Crown was an entirely independent foundation, for which the Emperor's approval was a courtesy rather than an obligation.

In 1701, as so often before, Berlin owed its good fortune to international developments. The Emperor would probably not have cooperated in the Elector's elevation had it not been for the fact that he stood in urgent need of Brandenburg's support. The epochal struggle between Habsburg and Bourbon was about to enter a new and bloody phase, as a coalition of European powers gathered to oppose French designs to place a grandson of Louis XIV on the vacant Spanish throne. Anticipating a major conflagration, the Emperor saw that he would have to make concessions in order to win Frederick's support. Wooed with attractive offers from both sides, the Elector hesitated, swinging from one option to the other, but eventually decided to align himself with the Emperor in return for the Crown Treaty (*Krontraktat*) of 16 November 1700. Under this agreement, Frederick undertook to supply a contingent of 8,000 men to the Emperor and made various more general assurances of support for the House of Habsburg. The Viennese court agreed, for its part, not only to recognize the foundation of the new title, but also to work towards its general acceptance, both within the Holy Roman Empire and among the European powers.

The establishment of the royal title brought a massive expansion of the courtly establishment and a great unfurling of elaborate ceremonies. Many of these had an overtly historical dimension. There were splendid festivities to mark the anniversary of the coronation, the birthday of the queen, the birthday of the king, the conferral of the Order of the Black Eagle, the unveiling of a statue of the Great Elector. In this respect Frederick's reign institutionalized the heightened historical consciousness that had been a feature of his predecessor's understanding of his office and that had been percolating through the courts of western Europe since the late sixteenth century.[4] It was Frederick who appointed Samuel Pufendorf Court Historiographer in 1691. Pufendorf's remarkable history of the Great Elector's reign was the first to make systematic use of archived government papers.

While other courts were preoccupied with the battles and sieges of the war currently waging over the Spanish succession, one contemporary English observer remarked with a note of exasperation, life in Berlin was an unceasing round of 'shows, dancing and other such like devertions'.[5] For the foreign envoys posted in Berlin, this quantum leap in courtly splendour meant that life became more expensive. In a report filed in the summer of 1703, the British envoy extraordinary (later ambassador) Lord Raby, noted that his 'equipage, which in London was thought very fine, is nothing to those that are here'. The British despatches of this period are filled with complaints at the inordinate expense involved in maintaining appearances at what had suddenly become one of Europe's most splendid courts. Apartments had to be refurnished, servants, carriages and horses kitted out to a more exacting and costly standard. 'I find I shall be no gainer by my embassy,' Raby dolefully commented in one of many veiled pleas for a more generous allowance.[6]

Perhaps the most dramatic expression of the new taste for elaborate ceremonial was the regime of mourning that followed the death of the king's second wife, Sophie Charlotte of Hanover, in February 1705. The queen had been visiting her relatives in Hanover at the time of her death. A senior court official was ordered to take two battalions of Brandenburg troops to Hanover and bear the corpse back to Berlin, where it was to lie exposed on a bed of state for six months. Strictest orders were given that the 'deepest mourning that is possible' should be observed throughout the king's dominions. All who came to court were ordered to cover themselves in long black cloaks and all apartments, coaches and equipages, including those of the foreign envoys, were to be 'put into deep mourning'.

The court was in deeper mourning than ever I saw in my life, for the women all had black head clothes and Black veils that cover'd them all over, so no face was to be seen. The men all in long black cloakes and the rooms all hung with cloath the top as well as the bottom, and but four candles in each room, so that one could hardly distinguish the king from the rest but by the height of his cloake, which was held up by a gentleman of the bedchamber.[7]

Hand in hand with the ratcheting up of courtly splendour and ceremonial went a boom in cultural investment that was unprecedented in the history of the dynasty. The last decades of the Great Elector's reign had seen a growth in representative building in the capital city, but this paled into insignificance beside the projects launched during the reign of his successor. A huge palace complex with an extensive pleasure garden was constructed in Charlottenburg under the direction of the

Swedish master builder Johann Friedrich Eosander, and there was a proliferation of representative sculpture across the city, the most notable example being the striking equestrian statue of the Great Elector designed by Andreas Schlüter. The old war-scarred town of Berlin began to disappear beneath the broad paved streets and stately buildings of a graceful residential city.

In July 1700, as his quest for the royal title approached a successful conclusion, Frederick founded a Royal Scientific Society, later renamed the Royal Prussian Academy of Sciences, and thus acquired one of the most prized contemporary attributes of dynastic distinction.[8] A medallion designed by the philosopher Leibniz to commemorate the inauguration of the society (which was officially established on 11 July, the sovereign's birthday) displayed on one side a portrait of the Elector, on the other an image of the Brandenburg eagle flying upwards towards the constellation known as the Eagle and bearing the motto: 'he strives for the stars he knows'.[9]

Was the Prussian royal title, with all the pomp and circumstance that attended it, worth the money and effort spent acquiring and living up to it? The most famous answer to this question was a scathing negative. For Frederick's grandson Frederick II the entire exercise amounted to little more than an indulgence of the Elector's vanity, as he explained in a remarkably spiteful portrait of the first Prussian king:

He was small and misshapen, his expression was proud, his physiognomy vulgar. His soul was like a mirror that throws back every object. [...] He mistook vanities for true greatness. He was more concerned with appearances than with useful things that are soundly made. [...] He only desired the crown so hotly because he needed a superficial pretext to justify his weakness for ceremony and his wasteful extravagance. [...] All in all: he was great in small things and small in great things. And it was his misfortune to find a place in history between a father and a son whose superior talents cast him in shadow.[10]

It is certainly the case that Frederick's court establishment incurred costs that were unsustainable in the longer term, and it is true that the first king took great pleasure in magnificent festivities and elaborately choreographed ceremonies. But the emphasis on personal foibles is in some respects misplaced. Frederick I was not the only European ruler to seek elevation to kingly status at this time – the Grand Duke of Tuscany had acquired the right to be addressed as 'Royal Highness' in 1691; the same right was acquired during the following years by the dukes of Savoy and Lorraine. More importantly from Berlin's perspective, a number of rival German dynasties were angling for a royal title during the 1690s. The Elector of Saxony converted to Catholicism in order to get himself elected King of Poland in 1697, and negotiations began at around the same time over the possible succession of the Electoral House of Hanover to the British royal throne. The Bavarians and the Palatine Wittelsbachs were likewise engaged with (ultimately futile) plans to capture a royal title, either by elevation or, in the latter case, by securing a claim to the 'royal throne of Armenia'. In other words, the coronation of 1701 was no isolated personal caprice, but part of a wave of regalization that was sweeping across the still largely non-regal territories of the Holy Roman Empire and the Italian states at the end of the seventeenth century. Royal title mattered because it still entailed privileged status within the international community. Since the precedence accorded to crowned heads was also observed at the great peace treaties of the era, it was a matter of potentially grave practical importance.

The recent growth of interest in the early modern European courts as political and cultural institutions has heightened our awareness of the functionality of courtly ritual. Courtly festivities had a crucial communicative and legitimating function. As the philosopher Christian Wolff observed in 1721, the 'common man', who depended upon his senses rather than his reason, was quite incapable of grasping 'what the majesty of a king is'. Yet it was possible to convey to him a sense of the power of the monarch by confronting him with 'things that catch his eye and stir his other senses'. A considerable court and court ceremonies, he concluded, were thus 'by no means superfluous or reprehensible'.[11] Courts were also densely interlinked with each other through family diplomatic and cultural ties; they were not only focal points for elite social and political life within each respective territory, but also nodes in an international courtly network. The magnificent celebrations of the coronation anniversary, for example, were observed by numerous foreign visitors, not to speak of the various dynastic relatives and envoys who could always be found at court during the season.

The international resonance of such events within the European court system was further amplified by published official or semi-official accounts, in which scrupulous attention was paid to details of precedence, dress, ceremony and the splendour of the spectacle. The same

74

applied to the elaborately ritualized observances associated with mourning. The orders issued following the death of Queen Sophie Charlotte
were not primarily intended to lend expression to the private grief
of the bereaved, but rather to send out signals about the weight and
importance of the court where the death had occurred. These signals
were directed not only to a domestic audience of subjects, but also to
other courts, which were expected to mark their acknowledgement of
the event by entering into various degrees of mourning. So implicit were
these expectations that Frederick I was furious when he discovered that
Louis XIV had decided not to put the court at Versailles into mourning
on Sophie Charlotte's account, presumably as a means of conveying his
displeasure at Berlin's pro-Austrian policy in the War of the Spanish
Succession.[12] Like the other ceremonies that punctuated life at court,
mourning was part of a system of political communication. Seen in this
context, the court was an instrument whose purpose was to document
the rank of the prince before an international 'courtly public'.[13]

Perhaps the most remarkable thing about the coronation ritual of
1701 is the fact that it did not become the foundation stone of a tradition
of sacral coronations in Prussia. Frederick's immediate successor, Frederick William, had developed during his youth a deep antipathy to the
refinement and playfulness cultivated by his mother and showed no taste
as an adult for the kinds of ritual display that were a defining feature of
his father's reign. Upon his accession, he not only dispensed entirely
with a coronation ritual of any kind, but substantially dismantled the
court establishment his father had created. Frederick II inherited his
father's dislike of dynastic ostentation and did not restore the ceremony.
As a consequence, Brandenburg-Prussia became a kingdom without
coronations. The defining ritual of the accession remained, as in earlier
times, the oath of homage in Königsberg of the Prussian estates and in
Berlin of the other estates of the Hohenzollern dominions.

It is clear none the less in retrospect that the acquisition of the kingly
title inaugurated a new phase in the history of the Brandenburg polity.
First, it is worth noting that the rituals associated with the coronation
remained dormant within the collective memory of the dynasty. The
Order of the Black Eagle, for example, founded by Frederick I on the
eve of the coronation to reward the kingdom's most distinguished friends
and servants, was gradually alienated from its courtly function, but it
enjoyed a revival in the 1840s during the reign of Frederick William IV,

when a number of the original conferral ceremonies were reconstructed from the archives and reintroduced. King William I chose upon his accession in 1861 to dispense with the homage (which many contemporaries judged to be obsolete) and instead to revive the practice of self-coronation in Königsberg.[14] It was this same monarch who scheduled the proclamation of the German Empire in 1871 in the Hall of Mirrors at Versailles to fall on 18 January, the anniversary of the first coronation. The cultural resonance of the coronation ritual within the life of the dynasty was thus more enduring than its sudden abandonment after 1713 might suggest.

The coronation of 1701 also signalled a subtle shift in the relationship between the monarch and his spouse. Of the seventeenth-century wives and mothers of the Brandenburg Electors, several had been powerful independent figures at court. The most outstanding in this respect had been Anna of Prussia, wife of John Sigismund, a spirited, iron-willed woman who responded to her husband's intermittent drunken rages by throwing plates and glasses at his head. Anna was an important player in the labile confessional politics of Brandenburg after her husband's conversion to Calvinism; she also maintained her own diplomatic network and virtually ran a separate foreign policy. This continued even after the death of her husband and the accession of her son George William in 1619. In the summer of 1620, Anna entered into separate negotiations with the King of Sweden over the latter's marriage to her daughter, Maria Eleonora, without so much as consulting her son, the head of state. In 1631, as Brandenburg's greatest wartime crisis came to a head, it was the Elector's Palatine wife Elisabeth Charlotte and her mother Louise Juliane, rather than George William himself, who managed the delicate diplomatic relationship between Brandenburg and Sweden.[15] In other words: women at court continued to pursue interests informed by their own family networks and quite distinct from those of their husbands. The same can be said of Sophie Charlotte, the intelligent Hanoverian princess who married Frederick III/I in 1684, but who spent long sojourns at her mother's court in Hanover (she was staying there when she died in 1705) and remained an advocate of Hanoverian policy.[16] She was an opponent of the coronation project, which she saw as damaging to Hanoverian interests. (She is reported to have found the coronation itself so tedious that she took pinches of snuff during the proceedings in order to provide herself with 'some pleasant distraction'.)[17]

Against this background, it is clear that the coronation set the relationship between the Elector and his spouse within a new framework. It was the Elector who crowned his wife, having first crowned himself, and thereby made her his queen. This was, of course, a mere symbolic detail without practical consequences and, since there were no further coronations in the eighteenth century, it was not re-enacted. But the ceremony none the less signalled the beginning of a process by which the dynastic identity of the wife would be partially merged into that of her husband, the crowned head of a royal household. The concomitant masculinization of the monarchy, coupled with the fact that the House of Hohenzollern now enjoyed a clear pre-eminence among the Protestant German dynasties from which spouses were recruited, narrowed the freedom of movement available to the 'first ladies' of Brandenburg-Prussia. Their eighteenth-century successors were not without personal gifts and political insight, but they would not develop the kind of autonomous weight in politics that had been such a striking feature of the previous century.

The independent, extra-imperial sovereignty secured by the Great Elector had been solemnized in the most dramatic possible way. The special prominence that Brandenburg had acquired among the lesser European powers after 1640 by virtue of its military prowess and the determination of its leadership was now reflected in its formal standing within the international order of precedence.[18] The Viennese court recognized this and soon came to regret the role it had played in facilitating the Elector of Brandenburg's elevation. The new title also had a psychologically integrating effect: the Baltic territory formerly known as Ducal Prussia was no longer a mere outlying possession of the Brandenburg heartland, but a constitutive element in a new royal-electoral amalgam that would first be known as Brandenburg-Prussia, later simply as Prussia. The words 'kingdom of Prussia' were incorporated into the official denomination of every Hohenzollern province. It may have been true, as opponents of the coronation project were quick to point out, that the sovereign of Brandenburg already possessed the fullness of royal power and thus had no need to adorn himself with new titles. But to accept this view would be to overlook the fact that things are ultimately transformed by the names we give them.

CULTURAL REVOLUTION

It is difficult to imagine two more contrasting individuals than the first and the second Prussian kings. Frederick was urbane, genial, courteous, mild mannered and gregarious. He spoke several modern languages, including French and Polish, and had done much to cultivate the arts and intellectual enquiry at his court. He was, by the judgement of the Earl of Strafford, who had spent many years (under his earlier title, Lord Raby) as ambassador in Berlin, 'good natured, affable [. . .] generous and just [. . .] magnificent and charitable'.[19] Frederick William I, by contrast, was brusque to the point of brutality, distrustful in the extreme and given to violent rages and attacks of acute melancholy. Although possessed of a quick and powerful intelligence, he barely managed to master written German (he may well have been dyslexic). He was profoundly sceptical of any sort of cultural or intellectual endeavour that was not of immediate practical (by which he mainly meant military) utility. The sometimes harsh, contemptuous tone of his speech is conveyed in the following marginalia to incoming government papers:

10 November 1731: Ivatyhoff, the Brandenburg Agent in Copenhagen, requests an increase in his allowance. [Frederick William: 'The rasckal wants an increase – I'll count it out on his back']

27 January 1733: Letter proposing that von Holtzendorff be sent to Denmark [Frederick William: 'To gallows with Hotzedorff [sic] how dare you sujest me this rogue but as he's a curr he's good enough for the gallows go tell hym that']

5 November 1735: Report from Kuhlwein [Frederick William: 'Kuhlwein is an idiott he can kis my arss']

19 November 1735: Order to Kuhlwein [Frederick William: 'You filth don't interfeer in my family or youll find there's a barrow waiting for you in Spandau fortress']20

Within days of his accession in February 1713, Frederick William laid an axe to the tree of his father's court establishment. There was, as we have seen, no follow-up to the coronation of 1701. Having scrutinized the financial accounts of the royal household, the new king embarked on a drastic cost-cutting campaign. Two-thirds of the servants employed at the court – including the *chocolatier*, a brace of castrato singers, the cellists, composers and organ-builders – were sacked without notice; the rest had to accept salary reductions of up to 75 per cent. A substantial quantity of the jewels, gold and silver plate, fine wines, furniture and coaches accumulated during his father's reign was sold off. The lions of the royal menagerie were presented as gifts to the King of Poland. Most of the sculptors engaged during Frederick's reign promptly left Berlin when they were informed of their revised conditions of employment. A sense of panic gripped the court. In a report filed on 28 February 1713, the British envoy William Breton observed that the king was 'very busye cutting off pensions and making great retrenchments in his civill list, to the great grief of many fine gentlemen'. The queen dowager's household had been especially hard hit and 'the poore maids [had] gone home to their friends with heavy hearts.'[21]

The weeks following the accession must have been particularly traumatic for Johann von Besser, who had served Frederick III/I as his master of ceremonies since 1690. Besser had helped to shape the ritual culture of the royal court and was the author of a detailed official account of the coronation. As his life's work collapsed around him, he was unceremoniously struck from the state list. A letter he sent to the new king requesting consideration for another post was tossed into the fire on receipt. Besser fled Berlin and subsequently found employment as an adviser and master of ceremonies at the still sumptuous Saxon court in Dresden.

The court established under Frederick quickly withered away. What took its place was a leaner, cheaper, rougher and more masculine social scene. 'As the late King of Prussia was scrupulous in the ceremonies of the greatest nicety, his present Majesty, on the contrary, has scarce left the least footsteps of it,' the new British envoy Charles Whitworth reported in the summer of 1716.[22] At the centre of the monarch's social life was the '*Tabakskollegium*' or 'Tobacco Ministry', a group of between eight and twelve councillors, senior officials, army officers and assorted visiting adventurers, envoys or men of letters who gathered in the evenings with the monarch for general conversation over strong drink and pipes of tobacco. The tone was informal, often crude, and non-hierarchical – one of the rules of the Tobacco Ministry was that one did not stand to honour the arrival of the king. The subjects of discussion ranged from Bible passages, newspaper reports, political gossip, hunting anecdotes to more risqué matters such as the natural aromas given off by women. Participants were expected to speak their minds, and hefty arguments sometimes broke out; indeed, these appear on occasion to have been encouraged by the monarch himself. In the autumn of 1728, for example, a theological dispute between a Friedrich August Hackemann, a visiting professor from the University of Helmstedt, and the Berlin-based popular writer David Fassmann degenerated into a mud-slinging match, to the great amusement of the other guests. According to a contemporary report by an envoy resident in Berlin, Hackemann was eventually goaded into calling Fassmann a liar, whereupon the latter

solidly responded with the flat of his hand so promptly! and in such a manner! that [Hackemann] almost tumbled onto the king; at this point he [Hackemann] asked His Majesty whether it was [...] not a most punishable thing to behave in such a way and to attack someone thus in the presence of the all-highest?

Frederick William, who clearly took pleasure in such raucousness, merely commented that a scoundrel deserves the blows he receives.[23]

Emblematic for the tone and values that prevailed in the monarch's milieu after 1713 was the fate of Jacob Paul von Gundling. Born near Nuremberg and educated at the universities of Altdorf, Halle and Helmstedt, Gundling was one of the many academically trained men who were drawn to Berlin during the expansion of intellectual life that took place in the city under Frederick I. In addition to a professorial teaching post at a new school for sons of the nobility in Berlin, Gundling occupied an honorary court post as official historiographer for the *Oberheroldsamt* (Chief Herald's Office), an institution founded in 1706 to establish the genealogical credentials of noble applicants for public office. But disaster struck in 1713, when both of these institutions were swept away in the weeks following Frederick William's accession. Gundling managed to secure a place in the new system by adapting himself to the king's views and working freelance for a few years as an adviser on economic policy, a role in which he became known as an opponent of noble fiscal and economic privilege. He was rewarded for his services with various honorary titles (including 'Commercial Councillor' and the presidency of the Academy of Sciences) and became a frequent guest at the Tobacco Ministry. Indeed Gundling remained a

7. Satirical portrait of Jacob Paul von Gundling (anon. engraving from The
Learned Fool (Der Gelehrte Narr) *by the Gundling-baiter David F. Fassmann
(Berlin, 1729)*

courtier of sorts, dependent on the royal purse, until his death in 1731.

But neither his record of service as an educator and courtier, nor his
presidency of the academy, nor his steadily growing list of scholarly
publications could save Gundling from degenerating into a figure of
ridicule at the court of Frederick William I. In February 1714, the king
demanded that he deliver a lecture before the assembled guests on the
existence (or not) of ghosts while taking regular draughts of strong drink.

After much raucous hilarity, two grenadiers escorted the inebriated commercial councillor back to his room, where he shrieked with terror at the sight of a figure draped in a white sheet emerging from a corner. Provocations of this kind soon became the norm. Gundling was confined in a chamber where the king kept a number of young bears while fireworks were rained down into the room from above; he was forced to wear outlandish courtly attire modelled loosely on French fashions, including a towering wig in an outdated style that had belonged to the previous king; he was force-fed laxatives and locked in a cell overnight; he was pressed into a pistol duel with one of his chief tormentors, the joke being that everyone but Gundling knew that the weapons contained no shot. When Gundling refused to grasp or fire his gun, his opponent discharged a spray of burning powder into his face, setting fire to his wig, to the huge hilarity of all present. He was prevented by his debts from leaving Berlin and constrained by the pleasure of the king his master to return daily to the scene of his humiliations, where his honour and reputation were martyred for the amusement of the royal court. Under these pressures, Gundling's liking for drink soon developed into fully fledged alcoholism, a weakness that, in the eyes of his detractors, merely enhanced his suitability for the role of court fool. And yet Gundling continued to generate a flow of learned publications on such subjects as the history of Tuscany, imperial and German law, and the topography of the Electorate of Brandenburg.

Gundling even had to tolerate the presence in his bedchamber of a coffin in the form of a varnished wine barrel inscribed with a mocking verse:

> Here there lies within his skin
> Half-pig, half-man, a wondrous thing
> Clever in his youth, in old age not so bright
> Full of wit at morning, full of drink at night
> Let the voice of Bacchus sing:
> This, my child, is Gundeling.
> [...]
> Reader, say, can you divine
> Whether he was man or swine?[24]

After his death in Potsdam on 11 April 1731, Gundling's corpse was publicly displayed propped up in the barrel in a room lined with candles, dressed in a wig hanging down to the thighs, brocaded breeches and

8. The Tobacco Ministry. *Attributed to Georg Lisiewski, c. 1737.*

black stockings with red stripes – all clear references to the baroque culture of the court of Frederick I. Among those who came to ogle at this macabre spectacle were commercial travellers on their way to the great fair at Leipzig. Gundling and his barrel were buried soon afterwards under the altar of the village church outside the city. The funeral address was given by the writer (and sometime Gundling-baiter) Fassmann, the local Lutheran and Reformed clergy having conscientiously refused to take part.

Gundling's 'martyrdom' was the flip-side of the raucous masculine camaraderie of the new monarchy. The masculinization that had tentatively announced itself in the ceremony of the coronation had by now transformed the social life of the court. Under Frederick William I, women, who had played such a prominent role at the court of Frederick I, were pushed to the margins of public life. A visitor from Saxony who resided in Berlin for several months during 1723 recalled that the great festivities of the courtly season were held 'according to the Jewish manner' with the women separated from the men, and observed with surprise that there were many dinners at court at which no women appeared at all.[25]

Reflecting on the regime-change that occurred in 1713, one is tempted to describe it as a cultural revolution. There were continuities in the sphere of administration and finance, to be sure, but in the sphere of representation and culture we can speak of a comprehensive reversal of values and styles. Between them, the first two Prussian kings marked out the extremes between and by which their successors would position themselves. At one end of the spectrum we find the type-A Hohenzollern monarch: expansive and expensive, ostentatious, detached from the regular work of state, focused on image; at the other end his type-B antipode: austere, thrifty, workaholic.[26] The 'baroque' style of monarchy inaugurated by Frederick I retained, as we have seen, a certain resonance within the collective memory of the dynasty, and the epochal alternation of tastes and fashions ensured that there would be periodic revivals of courtly largesse – under Frederick William II, court expenditure exploded once again to around 2 million thalers per annum, about one-eighth of the total state budget (the figure for his predecessor, Frederick the Great, had been 220,000).[27] The last decades of the nineteenth century would witness, after a period of relative austerity, a remarkable late blooming of courtly culture around the person of the last Kaiser, William II. But the type-B kingship of Frederick William I also had a vigorous afterlife in the history of the dynasty. The harsh marginal jottings of Frederick William I were imitated (with more wit) by his illustrious son Frederick II and (at greater length and with less wit) by his more distant descendant Kaiser William II. Frederick William I's habit of wearing military uniform rather than the more expensive civilian alternative was taken up by Frederick II and remained a striking feature of Hohenzollern dynastic representation until the fall of the Prussian monarchy at the end of the First World War. The historical power of the type-B model lay not merely in its association with Prussia's later ascendancy in Germany but also in its affinity with the values and preferences of an emergent Prussian public, for whom the image of a just and thrifty monarch dedicated to the service of the state came to embody a specifically Prussian vision of kingship.

ADMINISTRATION

It has often been noted that the reigns of Frederick William the Great Elector and his grandson King Frederick William I stand in a complementary relation to each other. The Great Elector's achievement was centred on the outward projection of power. Frederick William, by contrast, has been called Prussia's greatest 'inner king', in honour of his role as the founding father of the Prussian administrative state. The opposition between the two can, of course, be overstated. There was no epochal rupture in administrative practices to match the cultural revolution at court. It is probably more accurate to speak of a process of administrative consolidation spanning the century between 1650 and 1750. This process was at first most pronounced in the spheres of revenue extraction and military administration. It was the Great Elector who began simplifying and centralizing the previously haphazard arrangements in place for the collection of the Electoral revenues – i.e. those from crown land, tolls, mines (which were the property of the crown) and monopolies. A first step was taken in this direction with the creation of an Electoral administration for the collection of the royal revenues in Brandenburg in the 1650s. Yet it was not until 1683 that the central revenues office, under the energetic East Prussian nobleman Dodo von Knyphausen, succeeded in acquiring direct control over Electoral revenues from the entirety of the Hohenzollern territories. Knyphausen's work of consolidation continued after the Great Elector's death: in 1689 he oversaw the establishment of a central Brandenburg-Prussian revenue office with a stable institutional structure. As a result of this innovation, it proved possible to draw up for the year 1689–90 the first complete balance sheet of income and expenditure in the history of Brandenburg-Prussia.[28] A further important centralizing step was undertaken in 1696 with the foundation of a unified central administration for the management of the royal domains.[29]

A parallel process of concentration can be observed in those areas responsible for the maintenance of the army and the waging of warfare. A General War Commissariat (*Generalkriegskommissariat*) was established in April 1655 to organize the army and its financial and logistical support. Under a series of capable administrators it grew into one of the key agencies of the Electoral administration, controlling all the revenues (contribution tax, excise tax and foreign subsidies) destined for military expenditures and gradually undermining the tax-collecting powers of the Estates by drawing their local officials into the sphere of its authority. By the 1680s, the commissariat had begun to arrogate to itself a more general responsibility for the health of the domestic manufacturing economy, launching a programme to establish Brandenburg as self-sufficient in wool-based textiles and mediating in local conflicts between the trade guilds and new businesses. There was nothing uniquely Prussian about this merging of financial, economic and military administration; it was undertaken in emulation of Louis XIV's powerful *contrôleur-général*, Jean-Baptiste Colbert.

With the accession of Frederick William I to the throne in 1713, the process of reform acquired a new momentum. For all his dysfunctionality as a social being, Frederick William was an inspired institution-builder with an architectonic vision of administration. The roots of this passion can be traced back to the comprehensive princely training provided by his father. At the age of only nine, Frederick William was entrusted with the management of his own personal estate at Wusterhausen to the south-east of Berlin, a task he performed with prodigious energy and conscientiousness. By this means, he acquired a first-hand familiarity with the day-to-day responsibilities of managing an estate – still the fundamental operational unit of the Brandenburg-Prussian economy. He was only thirteen when he began attending meetings of the Privy Council in 1701; his induction into other departments of the administration followed soon after.

Frederick William was therefore already well versed in the inner workings of the administration when an outbreak of plague and famine in East Prussia plunged the monarchy into crisis in 1709–10. The epidemic, which was probably brought into the region by the movement of Saxon, Swedish and Russian troops during the Great Northern War of 1700–1721, killed around 250,000 people, more than a third of the East Prussian population. In a chronicle of the small city of Johannisburg, in the south of the kingdom not far from the Polish border, one contemporary recalled that the plague had spared the city in 1709, but had returned with all the more ferocity in 1710 taking 'both the preachers, both the school teachers and most of the town councillors to their graves. The city was so emptied of people that the market place was overgrown with grass and only fourteen citizens remained alive.'[30] The impact of the disease was compounded by a famine that weakened resistance and decimated communities of survivors. Thousands of farms and hundreds of villages were abandoned; in many of the worst affected areas, social and economic life came to a complete halt. Since the areas of highest mortality were in the eastern areas of East Prussia, where the crown was the main landowner, there was an instantaneous collapse in crown revenues. Neither the central nor the provincial administration proved capable of responding effectively to the disaster as it unfolded; indeed a number of the chief ministers reacted by trying to conceal from the monarch the seriousness of the crisis.

The disaster in East Prussia highlighted the inefficiency and corruption of the ministers and senior officials, many of whom were personal favourites of the king. A party – including crown prince Frederick William – formed at court to bring down the leading minister, Kolbe von Wartenberg, and his cronies. After an official enquiry revealed misappropriations and embezzlement on an epic scale, Wartenberg was forced into retirement; his close associate Wittgenstein was incarcerated in Spandau fortress, fined 70,000 thalers and subsequently banished. The episode was a formative one for Frederick William. This was the first time he had become actively involved in politics. It was also a turning point in the reign of his father, who now began to let power pass gradually into the hands of his son. Most importantly, the East Prussian débâcle left the crown prince with a burning zeal for institutional reform and a visceral hatred of corruption, wastage and inefficiency.[31]

Within a few years of his accession to the throne, Frederick William had transformed the administrative landscape of Brandenburg-Prussia. The organizational concentration that had begun under the Great Elector was now resumed and intensified. The management of all non-tax revenues across the territories of Brandenburg-Prussia was centralized; on 27 March 1713 the Chief Domains Directory (*Ober-Domänen-Direktorium*), which managed the crown lands, and the Central Revenues Office (*Hofkammer*) were merged to form a new General Finance Directory (*Generalfinanzdirektorium*). Control over the finances of the territory now rested in the hands of only two institutions, the General Finance Directory, which dealt above all with lease income from the royal domains, and the General Commissariat (*Generalkommissariat*), whose task was to collect the excise tax levied in the towns and the contribution tax paid by people in the countryside. But this state of affairs in turn generated new tensions, for the two authorities, whose responsibilities overlapped at various points, soon became bitter rivals. The General Finance Directory and its subordinate provincial offices regularly complained that the exactions of the Commissariat were preventing their leaseholders from keeping up with their rents. When the General Finance Directory, for its part, tried to raise its rental income by encouraging its leaseholders to establish small rural businesses such as breweries and manufactures, the Commissariat protested that these enterprises placed urban taxpayers at a competitive disadvantage, since they were outside the towns and therefore not liable to excise. In 1723, after much deliberation, Frederick William decided that the solution was to merge the two rivals into an omnicompetent super-ministry that bore the unwieldy title 'General Chief Directory for Finance, War and Domains', but was known simply as the General Directory (*Generaldirektorium*). Within two weeks, the merger had been extended to cover all the subordinate provincial and local offices of both bodies.[32]

At the apex of the General Directory, Frederick William installed what was known as a 'collegial' decision-making structure. Whenever an issue had to be resolved, all the ministers were required to come together at the main table in the relevant department. Along one side sat the ministers, facing them on the other were the privy councillors of the relevant department. At one end of the table there was a chair left empty for the king – a pro forma observance, since the king scarcely ever attended meetings. The collegial system delivered several advantages: it brought the decision-making process out into the open and thereby prevented (in theory) the empire-building by individual ministers that had been such a prominent feature of the previous reign; it ensured that provincial and personal interests and prejudices were balanced out against each other; it maximized the relevant information available to the decision-makers; most importantly, it encouraged officials to take a holistic view. Frederick William sought to reinforce this tendency by urging the former employees of the General Finance Directory not to be shy in learning from their colleagues of the General Commissariat, and vice versa. He even threatened to use internal examinations in order to test whether knowledge was being transferred efficiently between the officials of what had previously been rival administrations. The ultimate objective was to forge an organic, pan-territorial body of expertise out of a plurality of separate specialist knowledges.[33]

The General Directory was still in many respects quite different from a modern ministerial bureaucracy: business was not primarily organized according to spheres of activity, but, as in most executive governmental organs in Europe at this time, by a mixed system in which provincial portfolios were supplemented with responsibility for specific policy areas. Department II of the General Directory, for example, dealt with the Kurmark, Magdeburg and the provisioning and quartering of troops; Department III combined responsibility for Kleve, Mark and various other exclaves with management of the salt monopoly and the postal services. Moreover, the lines of demarcation separating distinct spheres of competence within the new organization remained unclear, so that serious internal conflicts over jurisdiction continued well into the 1730s – the institutional rivalries that had given rise to the General Directory in the first place were thus internalized rather than resolved, and they were cross-cut with new structural tensions between locality, province and central government.[34]

On the other hand, the conditions of employment and the general ethos of the General Directory do sound a familiar note from a present-day perspective. The ministers were expected to convene at seven in the morning in summer and eight in winter. They were expected to remain at their desks until the day's work was accounted for. They were required to come into the office on Saturdays in order to check the week's accounts. If they spent more than a certain number of hours at work on any particular day, a warm meal was to be provided at the expense of the administration, but served in two sittings, so that half the ministers could keep working while their colleagues ate. These were the beginnings of that world of supervision, regulation and routine that is common to all modern bureaucracies. By comparison with ministerial posts in the era of the Great Elector and Frederick I, service in the General Directory offered fewer opportunities for illicit self-enrichment: a system of concealed supervision and reporting that ran through every tier of the organization ensured – in theory at least – that irregularities were immediately notified to the king. Serious offences met with punishments ranging from dismissal to fines and restitutions, to exemplary execution at the place of work. A notorious case was that of the East Prussian War and Domains Councillor von Schlubhut, who was hanged for embezzlement before the main meeting room of the Königsberg Chamber.

*

After the disaster of 1709–10, Frederick William was especially concerned for the condition of East Prussia. His father's administration had
already succeeded in occupying some of the vacated farms with foreign
settlers and migrants from the other Hohenzollern provinces. In 1715,
Frederick William appointed a nobleman from one of the leading
families of the province, Karl Heinrich Truchsess von Waldburg, to
oversee reforms to the provincial administration. Waldburg focused
above all on the iniquities of the existing tax system, which tended to
operate to the disadvantage of the smallholding peasants. Under the
traditional arrangements in the province, every landowner paid a flat
rate of tax for every *Hufe* of land in his possession (the *Hufe* was one
of the basic contemporary units of land; the English equivalent was
'hide'). But since the tax-collecting agencies of the administration were
still largely in the hands of the corporate nobility, the authorities tended
to turn a blind eye when noble landowners understated their taxable
landholdings. The returns of peasant households, by contrast, were
subjected to the most pedantic scrutiny, so that not a single hide was
missed. Further iniquities arose from the fact that no account was taken
of the quality and yield of the land in question, so that smallholders,
who tended in general to occupy the less fertile land, were subject to
proportionally greater burdens than the major landowners. The problem, in Frederick William's eyes, was not the fact of inequality as such,
which was accepted as inherent in all social order, but the depression of
revenues that resulted from the operation of this particular system.
Underlying his concern was the presumption, which the king shared
with some of the best-known German and Austrian economic theorists
of the era, that excessive taxation reduced productivity and that the
'conservation' of his subjects was one of the foremost tasks of the
sovereign.[35] The king's concern for peasant households in particular
represented a shift from the previous generation of mercantilist theory
and practice (embodied in the career of Louis XIV's minister of finance
Jean-Baptiste Colbert), which had tended to focus on the stimulation of
commerce and manufacturing at the expense of agrarian producers.

The East Prussian reform programme began with the compilation of
a survey of landholdings. The process revealed some 35,000 hides of
previously undeclared taxable land, amounting to an area of nearly
6,000 square kilometres. In order to correct for variations in yield,
the provincial domains administration then drew up a comprehensive

classification of all holdings according to soil quality. Once these measures were in place, a new General Hide Tax, calibrated for soil quality, was imposed on the entire province. In conjunction with new, more transparent and standardized leasing arrangements for farms on crown land, Waldburg's East Prussian reforms produced a dramatic rise in agrarian productivity and crown revenues.[36]

While arrangements for the General Hide Tax were still being put in place, Frederick William launched the long and difficult process known as the 'allodification of the fiefs' (*Allodifikation der Lehen*). The term referred to removing various bits of legal red tape left over from the feudal era, when noblemen had 'held' their lands as 'vassals' of the monarch and the sale and transfer of property were encumbered by the need to acknowledge residual claims vested in the heirs and descendants of previous owners. The sale of a noble estate was henceforth final, a state of affairs that provided new incentives for investment and agricultural improvement. In return for the reclassification of their land as 'allodial' (i.e. independently owned and unbound by any feudal obligations), the nobilities were to accept a permanent tax. The measure was legally complex, because the legacy of feudal law and custom was different in every province. It was also very unpopular, because the attachment of the nobilities to their traditional tax-exempt status was far greater than their resentment of their now largely obsolete and theoretical feudal obligations. They saw 'allodification' – not without justification – as a cunning pretext for undermining their ancient fiscal privileges. In many provinces, years of negotiation were required before the new tax could be introduced; in Kleve and Mark no agreement was reached and the tax had to be extracted through 'forced execution'. Opposition was also strong in the recently acquired and still independently minded Duchy of Magdeburg; in 1718 and 1725, delegations of noblemen from this province were successful in securing judgements supporting their case from the imperial court in Vienna.[37]

These fiscal initiatives were flanked by numerous other revenue-raising measures. The marshes of the Havelland, where the Swedish army had floundered in 1675, were drained so energetically that 15,000 hectares of excellent arable and pasture were won back within ten years. Work began on the draining of the delta region around the rivers Oder, Warthe and Netze, an epic project that would be completed only during the next reign, when the Oder River Commission established by Frederick

William's successor oversaw the reclamation of some 500 square kilometres of marshland from the Oder floodplains. Reflecting the fashionable contemporary concern with population size as the chief index of
prosperity, Frederick William launched settlement programmes to
raise productivity and stimulate manufacturing in particular regions.
Protestant immigrants from Salzburg, for example, were settled on farms
in the far east of East Prussia, and Huguenot textile manufacturers
were installed in the city of Halle in the hope of mounting a challenge
to the dominance of Saxon imports in the Hohenzollern Duchy of Magdeburg.[38] A series of regulations issued in the 1720s and 1730s dismantled
many of the localized guild powers and privileges to create a more
unified labour market in the manufacturing sector.[39]

One area of particularly sustained government activity was the grain
economy. Grain was the most fundamental of all products – it accounted
for the lion's share of economic transactions and for the greater part of
what most people bought and consumed in their daily lives. The king's
policy on grain was based on two objectives. The first was to protect
Brandenburg-Prussia's grain growers and traders from foreign imports
– the main concern here was the grain produced on Polish estates, which
was of excellent quality and less expensive.[40] The means adopted to
achieve this were high tariffs and the prevention of smuggling. How
successful the authorities were in stemming the flow of illegal grain is
difficult to say. The records indicate numerous prosecutions, some of
small dealers, such as groups of Polish peasants attempting to pass as
subjects of the Mark and carrying a few bushels of contraband grain, as
well as of more sophisticated operators, like the team of Mecklenburg
smugglers who tried to sneak thirteen wagonloads of grain into the
Uckermark in 1740.[41]

In order to prevent poor harvests from driving grain prices up to the
point where they undermined the viability of the urban manufacturing
and commercial economies, Frederick William also expanded the network of grain magazines that the Great Elector had used to provision
his standing army. These magazines had been retained during the reign
of Frederick I, but they were poorly managed and far too small to cope
with the needs of the civilian economy, as the disaster of 1709–10
revealed. Starting in the early 1720s, Frederick William set about establishing a system of large dual-purpose magazines (twenty-one in all) that
would serve the needs of his army but also perform an important role

in stabilizing the domestic grain market. The provincial commissariats and chambers were instructed to hold the price of grain as steady as possible, by purchasing stocks when prices were low and selling them off in times of dearth. The new system was to prove its worth in 1734–7 and again in 1739, when the social and economic impact of a succession of poor harvests was buffered by the sale of low-priced government grain. One of the last orders issued by the king was an instruction to the General Directory dated 31 May 1740, the day of his death, stipulating that the grain magazines of Berlin, Wesel, Stettin and Minden were to be filled again before the onset of the coming winter.[42]

There were, of course, limits to Frederick William's economic achievement and blind spots in his vision. He shared the widespread contemporary mercantilist preference for regulation and control. There is a clear contrast with the more trade-oriented policies of the Great Elector, who had acquired the colony of Gross Friedrichsburg on the west coast of Africa in the hope that this would open the door to an expansion of colonial commerce. Frederick I had kept up the ailing colony for sentimental reasons, but Frederick William sold it off to the Dutch in 1721, saying he had 'always regarded this trading nonsense as a chimera'.[43] On the domestic front there was a similar disregard for the importance of exchange and infrastructure. Frederick William never seriously tackled the problem of market integration within his territories. Work on the construction of a canal between the Oder and the Elbe accelerated during his reign, a more uniform system of grain measurement was introduced, and there was some reduction – against local protests – of internal tolls. Yet numerous obstacles remained to hinder the movement of goods across the Hohenzollern lands. Even within Brandenburg, tolls continued to be levied on the inner provincial borders. Little effort was made to integrate the outlying territories to the east and west, which were treated in economic terms as if they were foreign principalities. Brandenburg-Prussia was still worlds away from constituting an integrated domestic market when the king died in 1740.[44]

Under Frederick William, the confrontation between an increasingly confident monarchy and the holders of traditional power entered its administrative phase. By contrast with his predecessors, Frederick William refused at the time of his accession to sign the traditional 'concessions' to the provincial nobilities. There were no theatrical set-tos in the diets (which in any case became much rarer in most areas during his reign). Instead the traditional privileges of the nobilities were whittled away by successive incremental measures. The time-honoured tax immunities of the landed nobility were curtailed, as we have seen; organs that had previously answered to local interests were gradually subordinated to the authority of the central administration; the freedom of noblemen to travel for leisure or study was cut back so that the provincial elites in Brandenburg-Prussia were slowly detached from the cosmopolitan networks of the Holy Roman Empire.

This was not merely a by-product of the process of centralization; the king was quite explicit about the need to diminish the standing of the nobility and clearly saw himself as furthering the historical project inaugurated by his grandfather, the Great Elector. 'As far as the nobility is concerned,' he once remarked in relation to East Prussia, 'it previously had great privileges, which the Elector Frederick William broke through his sovereignty, and I have now brought them entirely into subordination [*Gehorsahm*] through the General Hide Tax of 1715.'[45] The central administration he built up to achieve his objectives was deliberately stocked with commoners (who were generally ennobled for their services), so that there would never be any question of corporate solidarity with the noble interest.[46] Yet, oddly enough, Frederick William always succeeded in finding talented noblemen – like Truchsess von Waldburg – willing to assist him in implementing his policies, even at the cost of their corporate comrades. The motivations behind such collaboration are not always clear; some were simply won over to the monarch's administrative vision, others may have been motivated by disaffection with the corporate provincial milieu, or joined the administration because they needed the salary. The provincial nobilities were far from monolithic; factional and family rivalries were common and local interest conflicts often overrode more general concerns. Recognizing this, Frederick William avoided categorical judgements. 'You must be obliging and gracious with the entire nobility from all provinces,' he advised his successor in the Instruction of 1722, 'and give preference to the good ones over the bad and reward the loyal ones.'[47]

THE ARMY

Your Excellency will already know [...] of the Resolution the new King has taken of increasing his army to 50,000 men. [...] When the state of war [i.e. military budget] was laid before him, he writt in the margen these words, I will augment my Forces to the number of 50,000 men which ought not to allarme any person whatsoever, since my only pleasure is my Army.[48]

When Frederick William came to the throne, the Prussian army numbered 40,000 men. By 1740, when he died, it had increased in size to over 80,000, so that Brandenburg-Prussia boasted a military establishment that seemed to contemporaries quite out of proportion to its population and economic capabilities. The king justified the immense costs involved by arguing that only a well-trained and independently financed fighting force would provide him with the autonomy in international affairs that had been denied to his father and grandfather.

Yet there is also a sense in which the army was an end in itself, an intuition reinforced by the fact that Frederick William remained reluctant throughout his reign to deploy his army in support of any foreign-political objective. Frederick William was powerfully attracted to the orderliness of the military; he himself regularly wore the uniform of a Prussian lieutenant or captain from the mid-1720s onward and he could conceive of nothing more pleasing to the eye than the sight of uniformed men moving in ever changing symmetries across a parade square (indeed he flattened a number of royal pleasure gardens in order to convert them for this purpose and tried where possible to work in rooms from which drilling exercises could be viewed). One of the few indulgences in wasteful ostentation he allowed himself was the creation of a regiment of exceptionally tall soldiers (affectionately known as '*lange Kerls*' or 'tall lads') at Potsdam. Immense sums were squandered on the recruitment from all over Europe of these abnormally tall men, some of whom were partially disabled by their condition and thus physically unfit for real military service. Their likenesses were memorialized in individual full-length oil portraits commissioned by the king; executed in a primitive realist style, they show towering men with hands like dinner plates plinthed on black leather shoes the size of plough shares. The army was, of course, an instrument of policy, but it was also the human and

9. *Portrait of Grenadier James Kirkland, soldier in the Royal Guard of King Frederick William I, painted by Johann Christof Merk, c. 1714*

institutional expression of this monarch's view of the world. As an orderly, hierarchical, masculine system in which individual interests and identities were subordinated to those of the collective, the king's authority was unchallenged, and differences in rank were functional rather than corporate or decorative, it came close to actualizing his vision of an ideal society.

Frederick William's interest in military reform predated his accession to the throne. We see it in a set of guidelines that the nineteen-year-old crown prince proposed to the Council of War in 1707. The calibres of all infantry guns should be the same, he argued, so that standard-issue shot could be used for all types; all units should employ the same design of bayonet; the men in each regiment should wear identical daggers on a model to be determined by the commanding officer; even the cartridge pouches were to be furnished according to a single design, with identical straps.[49] One of his important early innovations as a military commander was the introduction within his own regiment of a new and more rigorous form of parade drill intended to heighten the manoeuvrability of unwieldy masses of troops across difficult terrain and to ensure that firepower could be delivered consistently and to the greatest effect. After 1709, when Frederick William witnessed Prussian troops in action at the Battle of Malplaquet during the War of the Spanish Succession, the new drill was gradually extended through the Brandenburg-Prussian forces as a whole.[50]

The king's chief preoccupation during the early years of the reign was simply to increase the number of troops in service as fast as possible. At first, this was accomplished largely through forced recruitments. The responsibility for raising troops was transferred from the civil authorities to the local regimental commanders. Operating virtually without restraint, the recruiting officer became a figure of fear and hatred, especially among the rural and small-town population, where he prowled in search of tall peasants and burly journeymen. Forced recruitments often involved bloodshed. In some cases, prospective recruits even died at the hands of their captors. Complaints poured in from the localities.[51] In fact so dramatic was the first phase of forced recruitments that it prompted a wave of panic. '[His Majesty] makes use of such hasty means in levying of [his troops] as if he was in some very great danger,' wrote William Breton, the British envoy, on 18 March 1713, scarcely three weeks after the new king's accession, 'that the peasants are forced into the service and tradesmen's sons taken out of their shops very frequently. If this method continues, we shall not long have any market here, and many people will save themselves out of his Dominions . . .'[52]

Faced with the mayhem generated by forced recruiting, the king changed tack and put an end to the practice inside his territories.[53] In its place he established the sophisticated conscription mechanism that would come to be known as the 'canton system'. An order of May 1714 declared that the obligation to serve in the king's army was incumbent upon all men of serving age and that anyone fleeing the country in order to avoid this duty would be punished as a deserter. Further orders assigned a specific district (canton) to each regiment, within which all the unmarried young men of serving age were enrolled (*enrolliert*) on the regimental lists. Voluntary enlistments to each regiment could then be supplemented from enrolled local conscripts. Finally, a system of furloughs was developed that allowed the enlisted men to be released back into their communities after completion of their basic training. They could then be kept on until retiring age as reservists who were obliged to complete a stint of refresher training for two to three months each year, but were otherwise free (except in time of war) to return to their peacetime professions. In order to soften further the impact of conscription on the economy, various classes of individual were exempted from service, including peasants who owned and ran their own farms, artisans and workers in various trades and industries thought to be of value to the state, government employees and various others.[54]

The cumulative result of these innovations was an entirely new military system that could provide the Brandenburg-Prussian Crown with a large and well-trained territorial force without seriously disrupting the civilian economy. This meant that at a time when most European armies still relied heavily on foreign conscripts and mercenaries, Brandenburg-Prussia could raise two-thirds of its troops from territorial subjects. This was the system that enabled the state to muster the fourth largest army in Europe, although it ranked only tenth and thirteenth in terms of territory and population respectively. It is no exaggeration to say that the power-political exploits of Frederick the Great would have been inconceivable without the military instrument fashioned by his father.

If the canton system provided the state with a greatly enhanced external striking power, it also had far-reaching social and cultural consequences. No organization did more to bring the nobility into subordination than the reorganized Brandenburg-Prussian army. Early in the reign, Frederick William had prohibited members of the provincial nobilities from entering foreign service, or indeed even from leaving his lands without prior permission, and had a list drawn up of all the sons of noble families aged between twelve and eighteen years. From this list a cohort of boys was selected for training in the cadet school recently established in Berlin (in the premises of the academy where Gundling had once worked as professor). The king persevered with this policy of elite conscription despite bitter protests and attempts at evasion by some noble families. It was not unknown for young noblemen from recalcitrant households to be rounded up and marched off to Berlin under guard. In 1738, Frederick William inaugurated an annual survey of all young noblemen who were not yet in his service; in the following year he instructed the district commissioners to inspect the noble sons of their districts, identify those who were 'good looking, healthy and possess straight limbs' and send an appropriate annual contingent for enlistment in the Berlin cadet corps.[55] By the mid-1720s there were virtually no noble families in the Hohenzollern lands without at least one son in the officer corps.[56]

We should not see this process simply as something that was unilaterally forced upon the nobility – the policy succeeded because it offered something of value, the prospect of a salary that would assure a higher standard of living than many noble households could otherwise afford, an intimate association with the majesty and authority of the throne, and the status attaching to an honourable calling with aristocratic historical connotations. Nevertheless, it cannot be denied that the establishment of the canton system represented a caesura in the relationship between the crown and the nobilities. The human potential locked within the noble landed estate was now placed even more securely within the state's reach and the nobility began its gradual transformation into a service caste. Samuel Benedikt Carsted, pastor of Atzendorf in the Duchy of Magdeburg and sometime field chaplain in the Brandenburg-Prussian army, was thus right when he observed that the canton system constituted 'the final proof that King Frederick William had acquired the most comprehensive sovereignty'.[57]

An influential view has it that the cantonal regime created a socio-military system in which the hierarchical structures of the conscript army and those of the noble landed estate merged seamlessly to become one all-powerful instrument of domination. According to this view, the regiment became a kind of armed version of the estate, in which the noble lord served as the commanding officer and his subject peasants as the troops. The result was a far-reaching militarization of Brandenburg-Prussian society, as the traditional rural structures of social domination and disciplining were permeated with military values.[58]

Reality was more complex. Examples of noble landlords who were also local commanders are very rare; they were the exception rather than the rule. Military service was not popular among peasant families, who resented the loss of labour that occurred when young men were taken away for basic training.[59] Local records from the Prignitz (to the north-east of Berlin) suggest that the evasion of military service by flight across Brandenburg's borders into neighbouring Mecklenburg was commonplace. In order to escape service, men were prepared to resort to desperate measures – even professing their willingness to marry the women in their villages upon whom they had fathered illegitimate children – and they were sometimes supported in these efforts by noble landowners. Moreover, far from bringing a mood of submission and obedience to the estate community, the active and inactive duty soldiers were often a disruptive element, prone to exploit their military exemption from local jurisdiction against the village authorities.[60]

Relations between local communities and the military were beset with tension. There were numerous complaints about the tyrannical behaviour of regimental officers: exemptions were sometimes disregarded by the officers who came to 'collect' recruits, reservists were called up during the harvest season despite regulations to the contrary, and money was extorted in bribes from peasants seeking marriage permits from their local commanders (in some areas this latter problem was so pronounced that there was an appreciable rise in the rate of illegitimate births).[61] There were also complaints from the landlords of noble estates, who naturally resented any unwarranted meddling in the affairs of the peasants who constituted their workforce.

Despite these problems, a kind of symbiosis developed between regiments and communities. Although only a fraction of the eligible male population (about one-seventh) was actually called up, nearly all the men in rural communities were listed on the regimental rolls; in this sense, the cantonal system was based upon the principle (though not the practice) of universal conscription. Exemptions came into play only once the enrolments had taken place. All reservists were required to wear their full uniforms in church and they were thus an ever-present reminder of the proximity of the military; it was not unknown for enlisted men to gather voluntarily in town and village squares in order to practise their drilling. The pride that many men felt in their military status may have been sharpened by the fact that the exemption system tended to concentrate enrolments among the less well-off, so that there was a tendency for the sons of landless rural labourers to serve while those of the prosperous peasants did not. Soldiers and reservists thus gradually came to constitute a highly visible social group within the village, not only because the uniform and a certain (affected) military bearing became crucial to their sense of importance and personal worth, but also because the conscripts tended to be drawn from among the tallest of each age group. Boys shorter than 169 cm were sometimes called up for service as porters and baggage handlers, but, for most, diminutive stature was a free ticket out of military service.[62]

Did the canton system heighten morale and cohesion within serving regiments? Frederick the Great, who knew the Prussian army as well as anyone and observed the canton system at work during three exhausting wars, believed that it did. In his *History of My Own Times*, completed in the summer of 1775, he wrote that the native Prussian cantonists serving in each company of the army 'come from the same region. Many in fact know or are related with one another. [. . .] The cantons spur on competition and bravery, and relatives and friends are not apt to abandon each other in battle.'[63]

FATHER *VS* SON

If we survey the inner history of the Hohenzollern dynasty after the Thirty Years War, two contradictory features attract our attention. The first is the remarkable consistency of political will from each generation to the next. Between 1640 and 1797, there was not a single reign in which territorial gains were not realized. As the political testaments of the Great Elector, Frederick I, Frederick William I and Frederick the Great show, these monarchs saw themselves as involved in a cumulative historical project, each new ruler accepting as his own the unfulfilled objectives of his predecessors. Hence the consistency of intention that can be observed in the pattern of Brandenburg's expansion and the long memory of this dynasty, its capacity to recall and reactivate old claims whenever the time seemed right.

Yet this apparently seamless continuity between generations belied a reality of recurrent conflict between fathers and sons. This problem arose in the 1630s towards the end of Elector George William's reign, when the crown prince, Frederick William (the future Great Elector), refused to return from the Dutch Republic, for fear that his father was planning to marry him off to an Austrian princess. He even came to believe that Count Schwarzenberg, George William's most powerful minister, was plotting his death. The crown prince did eventually rejoin his father at Königsberg in 1638, but the damage done to their relationship was never repaired and George William made no effort to involve his son in affairs of state, treating him instead as a complete stranger. In his Political Testament for his successor the Great Elector later wrote that his own government 'would not have been so difficult at the beginning', if he had not been frozen out in this way by his father.[64]

The wisdom of experience did not suffice to prevent similar tensions arising at the end of the Great Elector's reign. The Great Elector had never been very impressed by Crown Prince Frederick – his favourite was the older brother Charles Emmanuel, who died of dysentery during the French campaign of 1674–5. Whereas Charles Emmanuel was a talented and charismatic figure with a natural aptitude for the military life, Frederick was highly strung, sensitive and partially disabled by a childhood injury. 'My son is good for nothing,' the Elector told a foreign envoy in 1681, when Frederick was a married man of twenty-four.[65] The relationship was further complicated by the coldness and mutual distrust between Frederick and the Elector's second wife, Dorothea of Holstein. Frederick had been his own mother's favourite child, but, after her death, his stepmother had borne the Elector another seven children and naturally tended to favour these over the offspring of her husband's first marriage. It was under pressure from Dorothea that the Great Elector agreed to provide for his younger sons through the testamentary partition of his lands, a decision that was concealed from Frederick and that he successfully countermanded after his accession.

The last decade of the Great Elector's life was thus soured by an increasingly tense family situation. A low point was reached in 1687, when Frederick's younger brother died unexpectedly after a bout of scarlet fever. Suspicion now deepened into outright paranoia: Frederick believed that his brother had been poisoned as part of a plot to open the way to the throne for the eldest son of the second marriage, and that he himself would be the next victim. He was suffering from frequent stomach pains at this time, probably because of the many dubious powders and potions he was taking to ward off the effects of poison. As the court seethed with rumour and counter-rumour, he fled to the home of his wife's family in Hanover and refused to return to Berlin, saying that 'it was not safe for him to be there, since it plainly appeared that his brother had been poisoned.' The Great Elector was furious and announced that he would cut the crown prince out of the succession. Not until Emperor Leopold and William III of England intervened did it prove possible to reconcile the two men, only months before the father's death.[66] Needless to say, it was quite impossible under these conditions to provide the crown prince with a proper induction into the affairs of state.

Frederick III, later crowned King Frederick I, was determined not to repeat the errors of his predecessors and went to great pains to provide his heir both with the fullest possible training in government and with a quasi-independent sphere of action in which to develop his capacities. As a teenager, he was thoroughly inducted into all the main branches of government. The youthful Frederick William was a difficult, obstreperous child who drove his teachers to distraction (it was said of his long-suffering tutor, Jean Philippe Rebeur, that he would have been happier as a galley slave than as Frederick William's tutor), but he was always fastidiously respectful in his bearing towards his father. In this case, it was the crisis of 1709–10 that placed the relationship under strain, by bringing the crown prince into open opposition to the ineptitude and mismanagement of his father's ministerial favourites. Frederick, amiable to the last, avoided an irreparable break by backing down and allowing power to pass to his son. In the last few years of his reign we can speak of a co-regency of father and son. Yet this conciliatory approach did not weaken Frederick William's resolve after his accession to erase every last trace of the exuberant baroque political culture his father had created. Many of the great administrative enterprises of Frederick William's reign – from the re-establishment of East Prussia to the purging of corruption and the expansion of the magazine system – can be understood as a reply to the perceived shortcomings of his father's rule.

The cold war that seethed between Frederick William and his own teenage son, the future Frederick the Great, puts all these earlier conflicts in the shade. Never had the struggle between father and son been waged with such emotional and psychological intensity. The roots of the conflict can be traced in part to Frederick William's profoundly authoritarian temperament. Since he himself had always been scrupulously respectful in his dealings with his father, even when he was forced by circumstance to join the opposition party, he was completely unable to understand any form of insubordination from his heir. Coupled with this was a conceptual and emotional inability to detach his own person from the administrative achievements of his reign, so that any failure of deference appeared to place his historical accomplishment, and the very state itself, in jeopardy. It seemed to him that the work he had laboured so hard to complete must collapse if the successor did not share 'his belief, his thoughts, his likes and dislikes, in short, if the successor were not his mirror-image'.[67] It became clear early in Frederick's life that he would not fulfil these exacting designs. He showed little in the way of soldierly aptitude – he often fell from his horse and was frightened of shooting. His posture and comportment were languid, his hair messy, he slept late, enjoyed being alone and was often to be found reading novels in the rooms of his mother and sister. Whereas Frederick William had been frank, even brutally honest, even as a small boy, Frederick was oblique, ironic, as if he had already learned to hide his true nature from the hostile eyes of his father. 'I would like to know what is going on in this little head,' the king remarked in 1724, when Frederick was twelve years old. 'I know for sure that he does not think as I do.'[68]

Frederick William's solution was to step up the pressure on the crown prince by subjecting him to a gruelling routine of daily chores – military reviews, inspection tours, council meetings – all timetabled to the very last minute. In a letter written when Frederick was in his fourteenth year, the imperial ambassador, Count Friedrich Heinrich von Seckendorff, observed that 'the crown prince, despite his young years, looks as elderly and stiff as if he had already served on many campaigns.'[69] But as even Seckendorff could tell, these measures were unlikely to have the desired effect. Instead they merely hardened and deepened Frederick's opposition. He became an adept at resisting his father's will by a kind of sly civility. When the king asked him at a review of the Magdeburg regiments in the summer of 1725 why he was so often late in arriving, Frederick, who had slept in, replied that he needed time to pray after he had dressed. The king answered that the prince could just as well say his morning prayers while he was being dressed, to which the boy replied: 'His Majesty will surely allow that one cannot pray properly if one is not alone, and that one must set aside a time specifically for praying. In such matters one must obey God rather than men.'[70]

By the time he was sixteen (in 1728), the prince was leading a double life. He conformed outwardly to the hard regime imposed by his father and fulfilled his duties, adopting a cold, impenetrable countenance whenever he was not among intimates. In secret, he began playing the flute, composing verse and accumulating debts. Through the good offices of his Huguenot instructor Duhan, he acquired a library of works in French reflecting a secular, enlightened, philosophical literary taste that was the diametrical antipode of his father's world. Sensing that his son was drifting away from him, Frederick William became increasingly violent. He frequently slapped, cuffed and humiliated the prince in public; after one particularly savage beating he is reported to have shouted at the crown prince that he would have shot himself if his father had mistreated him thus.[71]

In the late 1720s, the deepening antipathy between father and son acquired a political dimension. In 1725–7, Frederick William and his Hanoverian wife Sophie Dorothea had been involved in negotiations over the possible double marriage of Frederick and his sister Wilhelmine to the English Princess Amalia and the Prince of Wales respectively. Fearing that this alliance would create a western bloc that could threaten Habsburg interests, the imperial court pressured Berlin to withdraw from the double marriage. An imperial faction formed in Berlin, centred on the imperial ambassador Seckendorff and the king's trusted minister General Friedrich Wilhelm von Grumbkow, who appears to have been taking hefty bribes from Vienna.

Opposing the machinations of this faction was the queen, Sophie Dorothea, who saw in the double marriage a chance to pursue the interests both of her children and of her dynasty, the Guelph House of Hanover and Great Britain. The passion, bordering on desperation, with which she pursued this project doubtless reflected years of accumulated frustration at a court where the room for political action by women had been radically curtailed.

As the web of intrigues spun by English, Austrian, Prussian and Hanoverian diplomacy thickened, the Berlin court polarized around the two factions. The king, fearing a break with Vienna, withdrew his support for his son's marriage and sided with Grumbkow and Seckendorff against his own wife, while the crown prince was drawn ever more deeply into his mother's designs and became an active supporter of the English marriage. Predictably, it was the will of the king that prevailed and the double marriage was abandoned. There were parallels here with the last years of Elector George William in the 1630s, when the crown prince (and future Great Elector) had refused to return to Berlin for fear that his father and his chief minister (Count Schwarzenberg) would marry him off to an Austrian princess.

The struggle over the 'English marriage' set the context for Frederick's attempted flight from Brandenburg-Prussia in August 1730, one of the most dramatic and memorable episodes in the history of the dynasty.

The crown prince was not motivated by political outrage or by personal disappointment at the evaporation of his marriage to Princess Amalia, whom he had never met. It was rather that the struggles and intrigues of 1729–30 brought to boiling point his frustration and resentment at the treatment his father had meted out to him over the past years. Frederick planned his escape during the spring and early summer of 1730. His chief collaborator was a twenty-six-year-old officer by the name of Hans Hermann von Katte from the Royal Gensdarmes Regiment, a clever, cultivated man who took an interest in painting and music and had become Frederick's closest friend – a contemporary memoir reports that they 'carried on' together 'like a lover with his mistress'.[72] It was Katte who helped Frederick make most of the practical preparations for departure. The flight itself was a non-starter. Frederick and Katte went about their business with a carelessness that soon aroused suspicion. The king put the prince's tutors and servants on alert and had him watched day and night. Katte had planned to use recruitment leave from his regiment in order to flee with the prince, but his permission was withdrawn at the last minute, possibly because the king had become aware of his involvement. Frederick, who was accompanying his father on a journey into southern Germany, chose at the last minute to go ahead with the plan none the less – a decision whose recklessness conveys something of the extremity of his predicament. In the small hours of the night of 4–5 August, he slipped away from his encampment near the village of Steinfurt. A servant who had seen him leave raised the alarm and he was easily captured. His father was informed on the following morning.

Frederick William ordered that his son be carted to the fortress at Küstrin, the stronghold where the Great Elector had spent his childhood during the bleakest years of the Thirty Years War. Here he was confined to a dungeon cell and forced to wear the brown habit of a convict; the guards appointed to watch over him were forbidden to answer any questions from the prisoner and the little tallow light he was given to read his Bible by was extinguished each evening at seven.[73] In the course of the investigation that followed, the prince was subjected to a detailed inquisition. Christian Otto Mylius, Auditor-General and the official entrusted with conducting the proceedings, was given a list of more than 180 questions to put to the prince. They included the following:

179: What does he consider to be a fit punishment for his action?

180: What does a person who brings dishonour upon himself and plots desertion deserve?

183: Does he consider that he still deserves to become king?

184: Does he wish his life to be spared or not?

185: Since, in saving his life, he would ipso facto lose his honour, and, in effect, be disqualified from succeeding [to the throne], would he thus stand down in order to save his life, and renounce his right to the throne in such a manner that this could be confirmed by the entire Holy Roman Empire?[74]

The haranguing, anguished, obsessive tone of these questions and the implicit references to the death penalty convey a clear sense of the king's state of mind. To a man obsessed with control, such direct insubordination seemed the greatest abomination. There is no reason to doubt that at times the execution of his son appeared to the king to be the only possible course of action. Frederick's answers to his inquisitors were entirely in character. To question 184 he replied only that he submitted himself to the king's will and mercy. To question 185 he answered that 'his life was not so dear to him, but His Royal Highness would surely not be so harsh in his treatment of him.'[75] What is remarkable here is the level of self-restraint that the prince's deft answers display, despite the terror that he must have been feeling at this time, when his future was still so uncertain.

While Frederick's fate remained undecided, the king vented his rage on the prince's friends and collaborators. Two of his closest military companions, the subalterns Spaen and Ingersleben, were thrown into gaol. Doris Ritter, the sixteen-year-old daughter of a Potsdam burgher with whom Frederick had engaged in some tentative adolescent flirtation, was whipped through the streets of Potsdam by the hangman and incarcerated in the workhouse at Spandau, where she remained until her release in 1733. But it was Hans Hermann von Katte who bore the brunt of the king's fury. His fate entered the realm of legend and came to occupy a unique place in the historical imagination of Brandenburg. The special military court convened to try the conspirators found it difficult to agree on an appropriate sentence for Katte and eventually decided by a majority of one to impose life imprisonment. Frederick

William overturned this verdict and demanded the death sentence. He set out his reasons in an order of 1 November 1730. As he saw it, Katte, in planning to desert from a royal elite regiment and assisting the heir to the throne in an act of high treason, had committed the worst possible kind of *lèse-majesté*. He thus deserved the cruellest form of execution, namely tearing of the limbs with hot irons followed by hanging. In consideration of his family, however, the king was willing to commute this sentence to simple decapitation – to be carried out on 6 November in the fortress of Küstrin, in view of the crown prince's cell.

Katte appears to have believed that the king would ultimately show mercy. He composed a letter to Frederick William acknowledging his misdeeds, promising to dedicate the rest of his life to loyal service, and begging for clemency. The letter remained unanswered. On 3 November, a detachment of guards under the command of a Major von Schack arrived to transfer the delinquent in thirty-kilometre relays to Küstrin. During this journey, von Schack recalled that Katte expressed the desire to write to his father (also serving in the king's army), 'upon whom he had brought such misery'. Permission was given and Katte was left alone to begin writing. But when Schack entered the chamber some time later, he found the prisoner pacing up and down and lamenting that 'it was so difficult and he could make no beginning for sorrow.' After some calming words from the major, Katte composed a letter that opened with the following words:

I could dissolve in tears, my father, when I think that this letter will cause you the greatest sorrow that the heart of a father can feel; that your hopes for my well-being in this world and your comfort in old age must vanish for ever, [...] that I must fall in the springtime of my years, without having borne the fruits of your efforts . . .[76]

Katte spent the night before the execution in the fortress at Küstrin, attended by preachers and friends from among his fellow officers, singing hymns and praying. His cheerful demeanour gave way at around three o'clock, when a witness reported that one could see that 'a hard struggle of the flesh and the blood was underway.' But after sleeping for two hours he awoke refreshed and strengthened. At seven o'clock on the morning of 6 November, he was led by a detachment of guards from his room to the place of execution, where a small mound of sand had been prepared. According to the garrison preacher Besser, who was entrusted with supporting Katte on his way to execution, there was a brief last-minute exchange between the condemned man and the prince, who could be seen watching the proceedings from his cell window:

At last, after much searching and looking about, he caught sight of his beloved [companion], His Royal Highness and Crown Prince, at the window of the castle, from whom he took leave with some courteous and friendly words spoken in French, with not a little sorrow. [After hearing the sentence read aloud and removing his jacket, wig and necktie] he knelt on the mound of sand and cried: 'Jesus accept my spirit!' And as he commended his soul in this manner to the hands of his Father, the redeemed head was severed from the body by a well-aimed blow from the hand and sword of the executioner Coblentz [. . .]. There was nothing further to see but some quivering caused by the fresh blood and life in the body.[77]

In executing Katte, Frederick William had also found an exquisitely potent punishment for his son. On learning of Katte's impending fate, Frederick begged the king to allow him to renounce the throne or even to substitute his life for that of the condemned man. The prince was sentenced to watch the execution from the window of his cell; his guards were ordered to hold his face to the bars so that nothing would be missed. Katte's body, with the separated head, were to be left where they fell until two o'clock in the afternoon.[78]

Katte's death was the turning point in Frederick's fortunes. His father's rage began to cool and he turned his mind to the question of his son's rehabilitation. Over the months and years that followed, the constraints on Frederick's freedom were gradually removed, and he was allowed to leave the fortress and take up residence in the town of Küstrin, where he attended meetings of the city's Wars and Domains Chamber, the local branch office, as it were, of the General Directory. For Frederick there now began a period of outward reconciliation with the hard regime of his father. He took on the subdued comportment of the sincere penitent, endured the monotony of life in the garrison town of Küstrin without complaint and conscientiously performed his administrative duties, acquiring useful knowledge in the process. Most importantly, he resigned himself to accepting the marriage proposed for him by his father with Princess Elisabeth Christina of Brunswick-Bevern, a

10. Crown Prince Frederick greets Katte through the window of his cell. *Engraving by Daniel Chodowiecki.*

cousin of the Habsburg Empress. Her choice as bride represented a clear victory for the imperial interest over the party that had favoured the English marriage.

Was this episode in Frederick's life a trauma that transformed the prince's personality? He had fainted into the arms of his guards before the moment of Katte's decapitation in Küstrin and remained in a state of extreme terror and mental anguish for some days, partly because he initially believed that his own execution was still imminent. Did the events of 1730 forge a new and artificial persona, acerbic and hard, remote from others, locked within the nautilus shell of a convoluted nature? Or did they merely deepen and confirm a tendency towards self-concealment and dissimulation that was already well developed in the adolescent prince? The question is ultimately unanswerable.

What does seem certain is that the crisis had important implications for the prince's developing conception of foreign policy. The Austrians were closely involved not only in masterminding the collapse of the English marriage, but also in managing the crisis that broke out following Frederick's attempted flight. It is an indication of how deeply imperial and Brandenburg-Prussian court politics were interwoven during the reign of Frederick William I that the first draft of the document setting out a 'policy' for disciplining and rehabilitating the errant prince was submitted to the king by the imperial envoy, Count Seckendorff. The woman Frederick was ultimately forced to marry was effectively the Austrian candidate. 'If I am forced into marriage with her,' he warned the minister Friedrich Wilhelm von Grumbkow in 1732, 'she will be rejected [*elle sera repudiée*].'[79] Frederick would hold to this resolution after his accession in 1740, consigning Elisabeth Christina of Brunswick-Bevern to a twilight existence on the margins of public life.

Austria's imperial tutelage over the Brandenburg-Prussian court was thus both a political and a personal reality for Frederick. The crisis of 1730 and its aftermath amplified the prince's distrust of the Austrians and reinforced his cultural and political attachment to France, Vienna's traditional enemy in the west. Indeed, it was Frederick William's own growing frustration with Austrian policy during the 1730s (to which we shall later return) that opened the door to a fuller reconciliation between father and son.[80]

THE LIMITS OF THE STATE

The Prussian historian Otto Hintze observed in his classic chronicle of the Hohenzollern dynasty that the reign of Frederick William I marked 'the perfection of absolutism'.[81] By this he meant that it was Frederick William who succeeded in neutralizing the power of the provincial and local elites and welding the diverse lands of the Hohenzollern patrimony into the centralized structures of a single state ruled from Berlin. As we have seen, there is something to be said for this view. Frederick William endeavoured to concentrate power in the central administration. He aimed at the subordination of the nobilities through military service, the equalization of tax burdens, the purchase of formerly noble land and the imposition of new provincial administrative bodies answerable to the officials in Berlin. He enhanced the capacity of the administration to intervene in the velleities of the grain market.

It is important, however, not to assign disproportionate significance to these developments. The 'state', such as it was, remained small. The central administration – including royal officials in the provinces –

counted in total no more than a few hundred men.[82] A governmental infrastructure had scarcely begun to emerge. Communications between the government and many local communities remained slow and unpredictable. Official documents passed to their destinations through the hands of pastors, vergers, innkeepers and school children who happened by. An investigation of 1760 in the principality of Minden revealed that it took up to ten days for official circulars and other important documents to cover the few kilometres between neighbouring districts. Government communications were often sent in the first instance to taverns, where they were opened, passed around and read out over a glass of brandy, as a result of which they arrived at their ultimate destinations 'so dirtied with grease, butter or tar that one shudders to touch them'.[83] The days when an army of trained and disciplined postal and other local officials would penetrate the provincial districts of the Hohenzollern lands were still far in the future.

It was one thing to issue an edict from Berlin and another to implement it in the localities. An instructive case is the Schools Edict of 1717, a famous decree because it has often been seen as inaugurating a regime of universal elementary education in the Hohenzollern lands. This edict was not published in Magdeburg or Halberstadt, because the government agreed to defer to existing school regulations in these territories. Nor was it fully effective in the territories where it was published. In a 'renewed edict' of 1736, Frederick William I complained that 'our salutary [earlier] edict has not been observed', and a thorough survey of the relevant local records suggests that the edicts of 1717 and 1736 may have been completely unknown in many parts of the Hohenzollern lands.[84]

Brandenburg-Prussian 'absolutism' was thus no well-oiled machine capable of translating the monarch's will into action at every tier of social organization. Nor had the instruments of local authority wielded by the local and provincial elites simply disappeared into the woodwork. A study of East Prussia, for example, has shown that local nobilities waged a 'guerrilla war' against encroachments by the central administration.[85] The provincial *Regierung* in Königsberg continued to exercise independent authority in the territory and remained under the control of the local aristocracy. Only gradually did the king come to play a significant role in appointments to key local offices, such as the district captaincies (*Amthauptleute*). Nepotism and the sale of offices – both practices that tended to consolidate the influence of local elites – remained commonplace.[86] A study of local appointments in East Prussia from the years 1713–23 showed that of those posts whose recruitment could be reconstructed from the records, only about one-fifth involved intervention by the king; the rest were recruited directly by the *Regierung*, although the proportion rose to nearly one-third in the following decade.[87]

So pervasive were the less conspicuous, *in*formal structures of elite influence in East Prussia that one scholar has written of the persistence of a 'latent form of Estates government'.[88] Indeed, there is much evidence to suggest that the power of local elites over key administrative offices actually increased in some territories during the middle decades of the eighteenth century. The Brandenburg nobility may have been largely excluded from an active role in the central administration during Frederick William's reign, but in the longer term they more than made up for this lost ground by consolidating their control over local government. They retained the power, for example, to elect the local *Landrat* or district commissioner, a post of great importance, since it was he who negotiated taxation arrangements with the central authorities and oversaw the local allocation of tax burdens. Whereas Frederick William I had often rejected the candidates presented by the district assemblies of the nobility, Frederick II conceded their right to present a list of favoured candidates, from which the king would select his preferred incumbent.[89] Efforts by Berlin officials to interfere in elections or to manipulate the behaviour of incumbents became increasingly rare.[90] The government thus conceded a measure of control in order to secure the cooperation of local mediators enjoying the trust and support of the district elites.

The concentration of provincial authority achieved through this process of negotiated power-sharing was durable precisely because it was latent, informal. The persistence of provincial corporate power and solidarity helps in turn to explain why, after a long period of relative quiescence, the provincial nobilities were in such a strong position to challenge and resist government initiatives during the upheavals of the Napoleonic era. The emergent core bureaucracy of the Hohenzollern lands did not displace or neutralize the structures of local and provincial authority. Rather, it entered into a kind of cohabitation, confronting and disciplining local institutions when the fiscal and military prerogatives of the state were at stake, but otherwise letting well enough alone. This helps to explain the curious and apparently paradoxical fact that what is sometimes called the 'rise of absolutism' in Brandenburg-Prussia was accompanied by the consolidation of the traditional nobilities.[91] In the eighteenth century, as in the era of the Great Elector, absolutism was not a zero-sum contest pitting the centre against the periphery, but rather the gradual and complementary concentration of different power structures.

5

Protestants

On Christmas Day 1613, Elector John Sigismund took communion according to the Calvinist rite in Berlin Cathedral. The candles and crucifix that usually adorned the altar for Lutheran worship had been removed. There was no kneeling or genuflection before the Eucharist and no communion wafer, just a long piece of bread that was broken and distributed among the worshippers. For the Elector, the occasion was the public culmination of a private journey. His doubts about Lutheranism dated back to his teenage years, when he came under the influence of the Rhenish Calvinists circulating at his father's court; it is thought that he embraced the Reformed faith in 1606 during a visit to Heidelberg, capital city of the Palatinate, the powerhouse of early seventeenth-century German Calvinism.

John Sigismund's conversion placed the House of Hohenzollern on a new trajectory. It reinforced the dynasty's association with the combative Calvinist interest in early seventeenth-century imperial politics. It augmented the status of the Calvinist officials who were beginning to play an influential role in the central government. Yet there is no reason to suppose that political calculations were decisive, for the conversion brought more risks than benefits. It placed the Elector in a religious camp for which no provision had been made in the Peace of Augsburg. Not until the Peace of Westphalia in 1648 would the right of the Calvinists to toleration within the confessional patchwork of the Holy Roman Empire be enshrined in a binding treaty. The conversion of the monarch also drove a deep confessional trench between dynasty and people. Inasmuch as there existed a sense of territorial 'identity' in late sixteenth-century Brandenburg, this was intimately bound up with the Lutheran church, whose clergy spanned the length and breadth of the Mark. It is no coincidence that the earliest historical chronicles of

Brandenburg were the work of Lutheran parochial clergymen. Andreas Engel, a pastor from Strausberg in the Mittelmark, opened his *Annales Marchiae Brandenburgicae* of 1598 with a long disquisition on the virtue and naturalness of love for one's fatherland.[1] After 1613, the dynasty ceased to be a beneficiary of this embryonic territorial patriotism. A ruling family that had succeeded, during the middle decades of the sixteenth century, in shepherding its subjects with great circumspection through one of the most gradual, moderate and peaceful Reformations in Europe now cut itself off in one fell swoop from the bulk of the population, and this at a moment in European history when confessional tensions could ignite revolutions and overturn thrones.

CALVINIST MONARCH –
LUTHERAN PEOPLE

Bizarrely enough, the Elector and his advisers failed to foresee the difficulties his conversion would create. John Sigismund believed that his own conversion would give the signal for a generalized – and largely voluntary – 'second Reformation' in Brandenburg. In February 1614, the Elector's Calvinist officials and advisers even drew up a proposal outlining the steps by which Brandenburg could be transformed into a Calvinist territory. The universities were to be stocked with Calvinist appointees so that they could serve as centres for the Calvinization of clergy and officialdom. Liturgical and other religious usages were to be purged from Lutheran services through a stepped process of reform. A Calvinist Church Council would oversee and coordinate all reforming measures.[2] An edict issued in the same month ordered that the clergy of the Mark Brandenburg were henceforth to preach the word of God 'pure and undefiled, [...] without any distortion and without the self-devised glosses and doctrinal formulae of certain idle, ingenious and presumptuous theologians'. The list of authoritative texts that followed omitted the Augsburg Confession and the Formula of Concord, the two foundational documents of Brandenburg Lutheranism. Pastors who found it impossible to comply with these injunctions, the edict declared, were free to leave the country. The Elector and his advisers assumed that the inherent superiority and clarity of Calvinist doctrine, when cogently and accessibly presented, would suffice to recommend it to the great majority of subjects.

They could hardly have been more mistaken. The tampering of the Calvinists with the traditional Lutheran church settlement of Brandenburg aroused resistance at every level of society. The most serious single confessional tumult took place in the residential city of Cölln (sister-city of Berlin across the river Spree) in April 1615. The Elector happened to be away in Königsberg seeing to the future handover arrangements for Ducal Prussia, and Cölln-Berlin was under the authority of his Calvinist brother, Margrave John George of Brandenburg-Jägerndorf. It was the margrave who triggered unrest when he ordered the removal of 'idolatrous' images and liturgical paraphernalia from the ornately decorated Berlin Cathedral. On 30 March 1615, the altars, baptismal font, a large wooden crucifix and numerous artworks, including a celebrated sequence of panels on the passion of Christ whose foundation drawings were the work of Lucas Cranach the Younger, were stripped from the cathedral. To add insult to injury, the Calvinist court preacher Martin Füssel used the occasion of his Palm Sunday sermon in the cathedral a few days later to thank God 'for cleansing His house of worship of the dirt of papal idolatry'.

Within hours of this address (which was given at nine o'clock in the morning), the Lutheran deacon of the nearby church of St Peter's was delivering a furious counter-volley from the pulpit, in which he charged that 'the Calvinists call our place of worship a whorehouse [. . .]; they strip our churches of pictures and now wish to tear the Lord Jesus Christ from us as well.' So stirring was the effect of his oratory that an assembly of more than one hundred Berlin burghers met on the same evening to pledge that they would 'strangle the Reformed priests and all other Calvinists'. On the following day, a Monday, a full-scale riot broke out in the city, in the course of which shots were fired and a crowd of over 700 people raged through the town centre, sacking the houses of two prominent Calvinist preachers, including Füssel, who was forced to escape by climbing over a neighbour's roof in his underwear.[3] At one point, the Elector's brother was caught up in a confrontation with the crowd and only narrowly escaped serious injury. A chain of similar (if generally less spectacular) conflicts broke out in other towns across the Mark. So serious was the sense of emergency that a number of the Calvinist councillors in Berlin considered leaving the territory. At the end of the year, as he made to retire to his estates in the county of Jägerndorf (in Silesia), Margrave John George lugubriously advised his brother the Elector to expand his bodyguard.

In addition to this pressure from the street, John Sigismund faced concerted resistance from the Estates. Dominated by the Lutheran provincial nobilities, the Estates exploited their control over taxation to extract concessions from the deeply indebted Elector. In January 1615, they informed him that the approval of further funds would be dependent upon his granting certain religious guarantees. The status of the Lutheran church establishment must be confirmed; the church patronage rights that placed the power of clerical appointment in the hands of local elites must be respected, and the Elector must promise not to use his own patronage rights to appoint teachers or clergymen who appeared suspect in the eyes of the Lutheran populace. John Sigismund responded with outraged blustering – he would rather shed the last drop of his blood, he declared, than yield to such blackmail. But he backed down. In an edict of 5 February 1615 he conceded that subjects who were attached to the doctrine of Luther and the key texts of the Lutheran tradition were entitled to remain so and must not be in any way pressed or compelled to relinquish them. 'For His Electoral Highness,' the edict continued, 'in no way arrogates to himself dominion over consciences and therefore does not wish to impose any suspect or unwelcome preachers on anyone, even in places where he enjoys the right of patronage . . .'[4] This was a serious setback. At this point, at the very latest, it must have dawned on the Elector that the 'second Reformation' might have to be postponed or even deferred indefinitely.

What exactly was at stake in these struggles? Clearly there was a power-political dimension. Even before 1613, the Electors' use of 'foreign' Calvinist officials had been controversial, not just on religious grounds but also because it contravened the '*ius indigenatus*' by which appointments to senior offices were reserved to the native-born elites. There was also, as we have seen, a widespread reluctance to accept the costs incurred by a Calvinist foreign policy. Townsfolk clearly resented Calvinist officials and clergy as intruders into an urban space whose key cultic monuments were also focal points of urban identity. But it would be wrong to reduce the Calvinist-Lutheran quarrels to a 'politics of interest', in which denunciations and complaints are seen as encoded bids for advantage.[5] For on both sides in the confrontation, powerful emotions were engaged. At the heart of the most committed forms of Calvinism was a fastidious shudder of disgust at the strands of papalism that survived within Lutheran observance.

This was in part an aesthetic issue: to the colourful extravagance of a Lutheran church interior, with its candles and images graven and painted glowing with reflected fire, the Calvinists opposed the white space of a purified church, suffused with natural light. There was also an authentic apprehension that Catholicism remained a latent force *within* Lutheranism. A particular focus of concern was the Lutheran communion rite; Elector John Sigismund objected to Luther's doctrine of the real presence in the Lord's Supper, calling it a 'false, divisive and highly controversial teaching'. In the words of the Calvinist theologian Simon Pistoris, author of a controversial tract published in Berlin in 1613, Luther 'derived his views from the darkness of papacy, and thus inherited the errors and false opinions of transubstantiation, whereby the bread is changed into the body of Christ'. As a consequence, the Lutheran faith had become 'a pillar and a prop to the papacy'.[6] In other words, the Reformation remained incomplete. If a complete break with the darkness of the Catholic past were not accomplished, then the danger of re-Catholicization loomed. The Calvinists felt implicitly that the forward progress of time itself was at stake: if the confessional accomplishments of the recent past were not consolidated and expanded, they would be reversed and expunged from history.

The Lutherans, for their part, were motivated by a powerful attachment to their festal ceremonies and the paraphernalia, visual and liturgical, of their worship. There was a rich historical irony here. It was the achievement of the sixteenth-century Hohenzollern Electors of Brandenburg to have slowed and moderated the spread of reform within Brandenburg, with the result that the territory's Lutheran Reformation was one of the most conservative in the Empire. Brandenburg Lutheranism was marked by doctrinal orthodoxy and a powerful attachment to traditional ceremony, tendencies that were reinforced by the Electoral administration throughout the last decades of the sixteenth century. A widespread fear of Calvinism and sporadic bursts of anti-Calvinist polemic towards the end of the century helped to focus Lutheran allegiances on the foundational documents of the territorial church, such as the Augsburg Confession of 1530 and the Formula of Concord of 1577, which defined its doctrinal substance. It could thus be argued that the dynasty itself had helped to create a brand of Lutheranism uniquely resistant to the Calvinist appeal.

The strength of this resistance forced the Elector and his Calvinist advisers to abandon their hopes of a Second Brandenburg Reformation. They settled instead for a 'court reformation' (*Hofreformation*), whose religious energies petered out on the fringes of the political elite.[7] Yet even within the confines of court society Calvinism did not enjoy unchallenged hegemony. John Sigismund's wife, the redoubtable Anna of Prussia, upon whose blood lines depended the claims to Ducal Prussia and the Jülich succession, remained a staunch Lutheran and continued to oppose the new order. The fact that Lutheran services were held for her in the palace chapel provided an encouragement and a focal point for popular resistance. She also maintained close contacts with neighbouring Saxony, the chief engine-house of Lutheran orthodoxy and the source of unending Lutheran polemics against the godless Calvinists in Berlin. In 1619, when John Sigismund died, she invited a prominent Saxon Lutheran controversialist, Balthasar Meisner, to Berlin to offer her spiritual consolation. Meisner, whose sermons in the palace chapel were open to the public, used the opportunity to stir up Lutheran passions against the Calvinists. The mood in Berlin became so tense that the viceroy of Brandenburg made an official complaint to Anna and insisted that he leave the country. But Meisner continued in his efforts (as he himself put it) to 'blow away the Calvinist locusts'. In a pointed symbolic gesture, Anna had the corpse of her husband laid out in the Lutheran style with a crucifix in one hand, a detail that predictably lent credibility to rumours that the Elector had repudiated Calvinism and undergone a deathbed reconversion to Lutheranism.[8] Only with Anna's death in 1625 did the Electoral family achieve a measure of confessional harmony. Born in 1620, Frederick William (the future Great Elector) became the first Hohenzollern prince to grow up within an entirely Calvinist nuclear family.

It took a long time for the emotion to drain out of the Lutheran-Calvinist confrontation. Tension levels fluctuated with the ebb and flow of confessional polemic. During the years 1614–17, the controversy over John Sigismund's conversion generated no fewer than 200 books and pamphlets circulating in Berlin, and the dissemination of Lutheran tracts condemning Calvinism remained a problem throughout the century.[9] Care had to be taken to ensure that the dynastic ceremonies were designed to accommodate the expectations of both faiths. In terms of its public ceremony and symbolism, Brandenburg-Prussia evolved into a bi-confessional state.

The new Elector's view of these matters was equivocal. On the one hand, he repeatedly assured his Lutheran subjects that he had no intention of forcing the conscience of any subject.[10] On the other hand, he appears to have cherished the hope that the two camps would set aside their differences once they developed a fuller and truer understanding of each other's positions (by which he really meant: if only the Lutherans could be brought to a fuller understanding of the Calvinist position). Frederick William hoped that a bi-confessional conference would facilitate 'friendly and peaceful discussion'. The Lutherans were sceptical. They saw discussions of this kind as opening the door to a godless syncretism. 'Spiritual war and conflict', the Lutheran clergy of Königsberg observed sullenly in a joint letter of April 1642, were preferable to 'a union of true doctrine with error and unbelief'.[11] Predictably enough, a conference of Lutheran and Calvinist theologians which did actually meet at the Electoral palace in Berlin in 1663 merely sharpened the differences between the two camps and led to a new wave of mutual denunciations.

Throughout the reign, and especially from the early 1660s, the Electoral administration sought to keep the peace by forbidding theological polemic. Under an 'edict of tolerance' issued in September 1664, Calvinist and Lutheran clergymen were ordered to abstain from mutual disparagements; all preachers were required to signal their acceptance of this order by signing and returning a pre-circulated reply. In Berlin, two preachers who refused to do so were summarily dismissed from their livings; conversely, one preacher who did comply encountered such ill-will from his parishioners that his sermons remained unattended until his death shortly thereafter. Among those who were suspended for refusing to sign was Paul Gerhardt, greatest of the Lutheran hymnists.[12] The most spectacular single incident was the arrest and incarceration of David Gigas, a Lutheran preacher at the Church of St Nikolai in Berlin. Gigas initially signed and returned the government questionnaire. Faced with a mutiny by his own parishioners, however, he reneged on his compliance and gave a rousing sermon on New Year's Day 1667, in which he warned that religious coercion provoked 'rebellions and unhappy wars'. Gigas was arrested and carted off to the fortress at Spandau.[13]

If the confessional divide remained a live issue in the Hohenzollern lands, this was in part because it became entwined with the political struggle between the central administration and the holders of provincial power. In his battle against entrenched local privilege, the sovereign found himself face to face with Lutheran elites jealous of their rights and hostile to the unfamiliar confessional culture of the central government. Under these conditions Lutheranism, sustained institutionally by the network of local church patronage, became the ideology of provincial autonomy and resistance to central power. The Elector, for his part, never gave up working to reinforce the position of the Calvinist minority in the Hohenzollern lands – the great majority of around 18,000 Protestant immigrants who entered the Hohenzollern lands from France, the Palatinate and the Swiss cantons were adherents of the Reformed faith. Their presence helped to spread the influence of the Elector's religion beyond the narrow confines of the court, but also provoked protests and complaints from the Lutheran elites. The conflict between centre and periphery that we associate with the 'age of absolutism' thus acquired a distinctive confessional flavour in Brandenburg-Prussia.

It has often been observed that the minority status of the dynasty and its Calvinist agents forced the political authorities in the Electorate to adopt a policy of tolerance in religious affairs. Tolerance was thereby 'objectively' built into the practice of government.[14] It was also imposed as a principle of governance, where this was possible, on the provincial authorities. In 1668, for example, five years after the Estates of Ducal Prussia had formally accepted his sovereignty in the territory, Frederick William at last succeeded in forcing the three cities of Königsberg to allow Calvinists to acquire property and become citizens.[15] This was tolerance in a very narrow sense, of course. It was more a matter of historical contingency and practical politics than of principle. Since it had nothing to do with the notion of minority rights in a present-day sense, it was not necessarily transferable to other minorities. Frederick William was opposed, for example, to the toleration of Catholics in the core territories of Brandenburg and Eastern Pomerania, but he accepted it in Ducal Prussia and the Hohenzollern territories of the Rhineland, where Catholics enjoyed the protection of historic treaties. The famous Edict of Potsdam (1685), by which Frederick William threw open the doors of his lands to Huguenot (Calvinist) refugees fleeing from France, struck a blow for tolerance against persecution. But the same edict also included an article forbidding Brandenburg Catholics to attend mass in the chapels of the French and imperial ambassadors' homes. In 1641, when Margrave Ernest, viceroy of Brandenburg, proposed that Frederick William might consider readmitting the Jews (expelled from the Electorate in 1571) as a means of alleviating the financial strains of the war, the latter replied that it was best to leave well enough alone – his ancestors must have had 'sure and weighty reasons for extirpating the Jews from our Electorate'.[16]

Yet there are signs that the peculiar confessional geography of his lands did gradually propel the Elector towards a more principled commitment to tolerance. He repeatedly renounced any intention of compelling the consciences of his subjects and enjoined his successor in the Political Testament of 1667 to love all his subjects equally, regardless of their religion. He supported the admission into Ducal Prussia of nonconformist Protestant sectaries fleeing from persecution in neighbouring Catholic Poland and was prepared to tolerate the private practice of their religion. He even, in later years, encouraged the immigration of Jews. There was a small Jewish community in the territories of Kleve and Mark, but the Jews were prohibited from settling in Brandenburg or Prussia. In 1671, when Emperor Leopold expelled the Jews from most of the Habsburg lands, Frederick William offered the fifty wealthiest families a domicile in Brandenburg. Over the following years, he supported them against the bitter complaints of the Estates and other local interests.

This policy was of course motivated by economic calculation, but the Elector's justification for it also reveals a striking absence of prejudice. 'It is known that cheating in trade takes place among Christians as well as Jews and with more impunity,' he told a group of delegates from the district of Havelland who had demanded that the Jews be expelled.[17] In 1669, when a Christian mob destroyed the synagogue in Halberstadt, he admonished the local Estates and ordered his officials to pay for its reconstruction.[18] It is difficult to know precisely why the Elector adopted these untypical views, but plausible to suppose that they may date back to his upbringing in the Dutch Republic, home to a flourishing and respected Jewish community. A letter he had drafted by his secretary in 1686 suggests that he may also in his own mind have connected the imperative of tolerance with the remembered strife of the Thirty Years War. 'Differences between religious communities certainly produce violent hatreds,' he wrote. 'But older and holier is the law of nature, which obliges men to support, tolerate and help one another.'[19]

THE THIRD WAY: PIETISM IN BRANDENBURG-PRUSSIA

On 21 March 1691, Philipp Jakob Spener, the Lutheran Head Chaplain to the Saxon court in Dresden, took up a senior church post in Berlin. It was a provocative appointment, to say the least: Spener was already well known as one of the leading lights in a highly controversial movement for religious reform. In 1675, he had achieved instant notoriety with the publication of a short tract called *Pious Hopes* that decried various deficiencies in contemporary Lutheran religious life. The orthodox ecclesiastical establishment, he argued, had become so absorbed in the defence of doctrinal correctness that it was neglecting the pastoral needs of ordinary Christians. The religious life of the Lutheran parish had become desiccated and stale. In a pithy and accessible German, Spener proposed various remedies. Christians might try revitalizing the spiritual life of their communities by founding groups for pious discussion – Spener called them 'colleges of piety' (*collegia pietatis*). The spiritual intensity of these intimate circles, he suggested, would transform nominal believers into reborn Christians with a powerful sense of God's agency in their lives. The idea proved enormously appealing and colleges of piety began to pop up across the parishes of the Lutheran states. The Lutheran establishment responded with alarm to what they saw as a subversive campaign to dilute the spiritual authority of the ordained pastorate.

By 1690, the Spenerite reformers – dubbed 'Pietists' by their detractors – were under attack from the orthodox authorities at the Lutheran universities. August Hermann Francke, a graduate student in theology at the University of Leipzig and a follower of Spener, caused a huge stir in 1689 when he encouraged the formation of colleges of piety under student supervision, and denounced the traditional Lutheran theological curriculum, prompting some students to burn their textbooks and lecture notes.[20] The academic authorities soon found themselves faced with a formidable student movement, and the Saxon government intervened in March 1690 to prohibit all 'conventicles' (a term widely used by contemporaries for non-official religious gatherings) and to stipulate that 'Pietist' students – it was in the course of this conflict that the term entered general usage – be excluded from admission to clerical office. Francke himself was hounded out of the university and subsequently took up a minor clerical post in Erfurt. Wherever recognizable Pietist groups emerged there were bitter – sometimes violent – conflicts with the Lutherans.[21]

Pietism was controversial because it represented a critical counter-culture within German Lutheranism. It was one of that broad palette of seventeenth-century European religious movements that challenged the authority of ecclesiastical establishments by calling for a more intense, committed and practical form of Christian observance than was usual within the formal church structures. Pietism was about living to the full Luther's 'priesthood of all believers'; Pietists cherished the *experience* of faith; they developed a refined vocabulary to describe the extreme psychic states that attended the transition from a merely nominal to a truly heartfelt belief in redemption through reconciliation with God. Perhaps because it was driven by such explosive emotions, Pietism was also dynamic and unstable. Once elements of the movement began to distance themselves from the established Lutheran churches, it proved difficult to arrest the process of disintegration. In many places, newly formed conventicles spiralled out of control, falling under the influence of radicals who ultimately severed themselves entirely from the established churches.[22] Spener himself had never intended the conventicles to function as vehicles for separatism.[23] He was a devout Lutheran who respected the institutional structures of the official church; he insisted that religious meetings take place under clerical supervision and be disbanded with good grace if they incurred the disapproval of the church authorities.[24]

The movement developed a momentum of its own. In Dresden, where Spener had occupied the position of Senior Court Chaplain since 1686, the escalating conflict with the Orthodox Lutherans – exacerbated by the reformer's stern rantings against the moral laxity of the Saxon court – soured relations with his employer, Elector John George. In March 1691, the Elector, whose own sexual morality was rather relaxed, ran out of patience and asked his privy councillors to 'have Spener quit his post without further ado, since we do not want to see nor hear this man any more'.[25] In the following year, the Lutheran theological faculty at the University of Wittenberg officially confirmed Spener's heterodoxy, identifying no fewer than 284 doctrinal 'errors' in his writings.[26]

Help was at hand. Just as Spener wore out his welcome in Dresden, Frederick III of Brandenburg offered him a senior ecclesiastical and pastoral post in Berlin. Frederick also allowed him to recruit numerous beleaguered Pietist activists to clerical and academic offices in Brandenburg-Prussia. One of these was August Hermann Francke, who, having left Leipzig, had been forced only one year later to leave his post as deacon in Erfurt. In 1692, Francke was appointed to a vicarage in Glaucha, a satellite town of Halle, and professor of Oriental languages at the new University of Halle. The theologian Joachim Justus Breithaupt, who had fallen from favour in Erfurt for defending Francke against the Orthodox, became the University's first professor of theology in 1691. A further veteran of the Leipzig quarrels, Paul Anton, was also appointed to a professorship. At the same time, Spener gathered and instructed a new generation of Pietist leaders in a college of piety that met twice weekly in Berlin.[27] This deliberate state sponsorship of the movement was at variance with the policies adopted in most other territories and it represented an important point of departure, both in the history of the Pietist movement and in the cultural history of the Brandenburg-Prussian polity.

The reason for Brandenburg's co-option of Pietism lay in the peculiar confessional predicament of the Calvinist ruling house. Repeated efforts to stifle Lutheran polemic had failed utterly and the prospect of a voluntary union of the two confessions remained as remote as ever. Spener's outspoken condemnations of inter-confessional squabbling were therefore music to the ears of the Elector and his family. The fourth of the six proposals in *Pious Hopes* was that theological polemics should be curtailed: it was 'the holy love of God' rather than disputation, Spener argued, that anchored the truth in each individual; exchanges with those whose beliefs differed from one's own should therefore be undertaken in a pastoral, not a polemical, spirit.[28] Throughout Spener's theological and pastoral writing dogmatic issues were marginalized by an overwhelming concern for the practical, experiential dimension of faith and observance. Christians were urged to practise 'spiritual priesthood' in their own lives by tending actively to the well-being of their fellows, observing, edifying and 'converting' them.[29] 'If we awaken in our Christians an ardent love, for each other in the first instance and thereafter for all mankind [. . .] then we have achieved virtually everything we desire.'[30]

Spener always remained respectful of the established Protestant churches and their liturgical and doctrinal traditions, and he was never a supporter of unionist projects.[31] Nevertheless, it was possible to see in his writings – as in the individualized, experience-oriented devotional culture of the Pietist movement as a whole – the outlines of a confessionally impartial Christianity that transcended the boundaries between Calvinist and Lutheran Protestantism. By playing down the significance of dogma and the sacraments, and by emphasizing the indivisibility of the apostolic true church, pietism promised to cement the 'inner basis' for the Prussian monarchy's claim to supreme episcopacy over the two Protestant confessions.[32]

There were also good reasons why the Elector should have chosen Halle as the place in which to furnish the Pietist movement with a provincial stronghold. Halle was one of the largest cities in the Duchy of Magdeburg. Brandenburg had acquired the inheritance rights to Magdeburg as part of the peace settlement of 1648, but the territory changed hands only in 1680. Magdeburg was a bastion of Lutheran orthodoxy, where the Lutheran Estates had traditionally ruled without hindrance from the nominal sovereign, the archbishop of Magdeburg. Until 1680, Calvinists were forbidden to own land in the duchy and possessed no civil rights. The takeover was followed by a period of tense confrontation between the government in Berlin and the local Estates. Against the wishes of the Lutherans, a Calvinist chancellor was installed to administer the duchy.

In this context, the significance of state support for the local Pietist movement becomes clear. The Pietists were to function as a kind of fifth column, whose task was to assist in the cultural integration of an ultra-Lutheran province. Throughout the 1690s, the Electoral government intervened to protect the Pietists against attacks and obstruction from the local Lutherans – municipal authorities, guildsmen and local landowners.[33] The keystone of the government's cultural policy in the region was the foundation of the University of Halle in 1691 as the leading university of the Hohenzollern lands. With Pietists and distinguished secular thinkers in key administrative and academic positions, the University of Halle would mellow the combative Lutheranism of the province. As a training institute for future pastors and church officials, it would offer a congenial alternative to the combative and anti-Calvinist theological faculties of neighbouring Saxony, where much of the Lutheran pastorate of Brandenburg had hitherto been educated.

The Pietists also became involved in the provision of social services. Spener had long believed that poverty and its concomitant evils, idleness, beggary and crime could and should be eliminated from Christian society by judicious reforms involving the forced or voluntary participation of the indigent in work programmes.[34] In this respect, as in his conciliatory confessional outlook, he found himself in tune with the aspirations and policies of the Brandenburg state. At the Elector's request, Spener submitted a memorandum recommending the suppression and policing of beggary in Berlin and the centralization of charitable provision for persons requiring temporary or permanent care. The necessary funds, he argued, could be raised through a combination of church poor-boxes, donations and state subsidies. The consequence was a general prohibition of beggary, the creation of a permanent Poor Commission and the establishment in Berlin of the Friedrich-Hospital for the Sick, the Elderly and Orphans (1702).[35]

In Halle, too, the local Pietists battled poverty and indigence. Around the charismatic figure of August Hermann Francke there was an extraordinary flowering of Christian voluntarism. In 1695, Francke opened a poor-school financed by pious donations. Such was the scale of public generosity that he was soon able to expand the school into an 'orphanage' offering accommodation and maintenance as well as free elementary tuition. The daily routine within this institution was structured around practical and useful tasks, and the 'orphans' (many of whom were in fact the children of local poor families) were regularly taken to visit the workshops of artisans, so that they might form a clear idea of their prospective professions. In the early years, Francke experimented with plans to finance the orphanage through the sale of items produced using child labour, but even after this idea had been abandoned as impracticable, skilled manual crafts remained a crucial component of the orphanage's pedagogical programme.[36] It was above all this striking combination of education, socialization through labour and charitable provision that aroused the interest and admiration of contemporaries in Brandenburg-Prussia and beyond.

With the revenues generated by the new school, Francke built the broad and graceful stone building that today still dominates the Franckeplatz in central Halle. New fee-paying schools were founded to accommodate children from specific social and occupational backgrounds, with a system of bursaries and 'free tables' to shield the less prosperous students from the impact of economic fluctuations.[37] The Pädagogium, founded in 1695, specialized in the education of children whose parents – many of whom were of noble estate – could afford the most costly education and care. One of its early alumni was Hans Hermann von Katte, the intimate of Crown Prince Frederick who would later be decapitated for his role in the prince's attempted flight from Brandenburg. The 'Latin School', founded two years later, offered instruction in the 'foundations of learning' (*fundamentis studiorum*); the curriculum included Latin, Greek, Hebrew, history, geography, geometry, music and botany, all of which were taught by specialist teachers, a significant departure from contemporary educational practice. Among its distinguished alumni was the Berlin publisher Friedrich Nicolai, one of the luminaries of the Prussian enlightenment.

The Halle Pietists understood the importance of publicity. Francke supported his establishments with oceans of printed propaganda in which evangelical sermonizing blended seamlessly with appeals to the generosity of readers. The most widely known and influential publication disseminating news of the Pietist enterprises in Halle was *Footsteps of the still living and reigning benevolent and true GOD / for the shaming of unbelief and the strengthening of faith*, published from 1701 in numerous new editions and reprintings.[38] With their exalted rhetoric and air of unshakeable self-confidence, these publications, distributed along a network of Pietist sympathizers spanning the breadth of Europe, conveyed a sense of the breathtaking ambition behind the Halle institutes. Halle Pietist publications interspersed reports on the good works and expansion of the Halle foundations with news of the flow of donations and material recycled from correspondence. They awakened a sense of immediacy and involvement among those who supported the work of the Halle foundations. Indeed, they anticipated in many respects the fund-raising development campaigns of our own day. They also created a sense of belonging that was at least partly independent of place. Lutheran networks were densely woven around specific localities; they were quickened by a sense of intimacy with a particular setting. By contrast, the Pietists created a decentred epistolary network of agents, helpers and friends that could be infinitely extended – across Central Europe into Russia and across the Atlantic to the North American colonies, where Halle Pietists made an important contribution to the evolution of new world Protestantism.[39]

Francke's intention was that the entire Halle complex should ultimately be autonomous and self-funding; it should be a 'City of God', a microcosmic emblem of the capacity of faithful labour to achieve a comprehensive transformation of society.[40] In order to achieve a degree of self-sufficiency in practice, Francke encouraged commercial operations within the orphanage. The most financially important were the publishing house and the pharmacy. In 1699, the orphanage began selling its books (printed on its own presses) at the Leipzig autumn fair. In 1702, an orphanage branch store opened in Berlin, followed by branches in Leipzig and Frankfurt/Main. Working closely with faculty staff at the University of Halle, the orphanage press secured an uninterrupted flow of saleable manuscripts, including works of religious interest and secular treatises of high quality. The house catalogue of 1717 listed 200 titles by seventy authors. Between 1717 and 1723, the orphanage printed and sold no fewer than 35,000 tracts containing sermons by Francke.

Even more lucrative was the mail order trade in pharmaceuticals (from 1702), for which the orphanage employed a sophisticated system of commissioned agents spanning central and eastern Europe. Only with the growth of this business did the commercial value of Pietism's far-flung networks become apparent. With annual profits of around 15,000 thalers in the 1720s, the *Medikamentenexpedition* was to become the most substantial single contributor to the orphanage coffers. Further income accrued from brewing, newspaper and trading operations run from within the Halle complex. By 1710, the original orphanage building had become the edifice of a large self-contained compound of commercial and pedagogical establishments stretching southwards into the vacant land away from the centre of the city.

Success on this scale would have been unthinkable without the concerted support of the government in Berlin and its servants in the province.[41] Francke was acutely aware of the movement's dependence on the

11. *The Orphanage complex in Halle. A portrait of its founder, August Hermann Francke, is borne aloft by a Prussian eagle, with the assistance of cherubs.*

patronage of its powerful friends and he was as assiduous as Spener had been in cultivating court and government contacts, a task to which he brought all the charisma and intense sincerity that had moved his student audiences at the University of Leipzig. After a meeting with Francke in 1711, Frederick granted the orphanage a privilege that placed it directly under the authority of the new Prussian Crown. Further privileges followed, securing revenues from a variety of official sources.

The accession of Frederick William I, whom Francke had cultivated as crown prince, inaugurated an era of even deeper cooperation. The new monarch was a restless, driven, unstable personality prone to bouts of extreme melancholy and mental anguish. At the age of twenty, after the death of his first son, he had passed through a 'conversion' that introduced an intensely personal dimension to his faith. There was an affinity here with Francke, whose dynamism was powered in part by a sense of the existential fragility of faith and a desire to evade the despair and fear of meaninglessness that had tormented him before his 'conversion'. In both men, inner conflicts were channelled outwards into 'constant work and limitless sacrifice', characteristics that were reflected both in the extraordinary colonizing energy of Halle Pietism and in the indefatigable zeal of the 'soldier king'.[42]

The collaboration between the monarchy and the Pietist movement steadily deepened.[43] The establishment of Halle-style educational foundations continued. Frederick William I employed Halle-trained Pietists to run the new military orphanage at Potsdam and the new Cadet School in Berlin. In 1717, when the king issued legislation for compulsory schooling in Brandenburg-Prussia, 2,000 schools were planned (not all of which were actually built) on the Halle model.[44] By the late 1720s, training for at least two semesters at the Pietist-dominated University of Halle (four semesters from 1729 onwards) had become a prerequisite for state service in Brandenburg-Prussia.[45] Pietist appointments to the University of Königsberg created a parallel power base in East Prussia; here, as in Halle, Pietist patronage networks ensured that like-minded students found their way to parishes and ecclesiastical offices.[46] After 1730, the education, not only of civil servants and clergymen but also of the greater part of the Prussian officer corps, took place in schools based on the Halle model and run by Pietists.[47]

Field chaplains were the most important propagators of Pietist values within the Prussian military.[48] In 1718, Elector Frederick William separated the administration of the military clergy from that of the orthodox-controlled civilian church and appointed a Halle graduate, Lampertus Gedike, as its director. Gedike acquired new powers over the appointment and supervision of army chaplains and used them energetically in favour of Halle candidates. Of all the army chaplains appointed to posts in Ducal Prussia between 1714 and 1736, for example, over one-half were former theology students from Halle.[49] The education of cadets, war orphans destined for army service, and the children of serving soldiers also fell increasingly into Pietist hands.

How far-reaching were the effects of this impressive record? It is difficult to isolate the impact of the Pietists within the training and pastoral structure from the effects of other changes in organization and administration of the military under Frederick William I (such as better training or the introduction of the cantonal system of recruitment). Not all Pietist field chaplains managed to make a mark in the raw world of the Prussian army. One chaplain was victimized by his officers because he had preached against dancing and powdering the hair; another was reduced to tears by the mockery and abuse of his regiment. The field

chaplains were not recruited through the canton system and they sometimes found it difficult to secure the respect of soldiers who regarded
them as 'foreigners' because they hailed from a different province.[50]
Nevertheless, there seems little doubt that the ideals and attitudes propagated by the movement did help to shape the corporate ethos of the
Prussian army. It is at least plausible that the relatively low rates of
desertion – by western European standards – among the Prussian
common soldiery during the three Silesian wars of 1740–42, 1744–5
and 1756–63 reflected the heightened discipline and morale instilled in
generations of recruits by Pietist chaplains and instructors.[51]

Among the officer corps, where the Pietist movement had a number
of influential friends, it is likely that the Pietists, with their moral rigour
and sacralized sense of vocation, helped to discredit an older image of
the officer as a swashbuckling, rakish gambler and to establish in its
place a code of officerly conduct based on sobriety, self-discipline and
serious dutifulness that came to be recognized as characteristically
'Prussian'.[52] With its at once worldly and sacralized concept of vocation,
its focus on public needs and its emphasis on self-denial, Franckean
Pietism may also have contributed to the emergence of a new 'ethics of
profession' that helped to shape the distinctive identity and corporate
ethos of the Prussian civil servant.[53]

The innovations in schooling introduced by Francke and his successors
also had a transformative impact on pedagogical practice in Prussia. The
close alliance between the Halle Pietists and the monarch contributed to
the emergence of schooling as a 'discrete object of state action'.[54] It
was the Pietists who introduced professional training and standardized
certification procedures for teachers and general-issue elementary textbooks for pupils. The orphanage schools also created a new kind of
learning environment characterized by the close psychological observation of pupils, an emphasis on self-discipline and an acute awareness of
time (Francke installed hourglasses in every classroom). The day was
sharply subdivided into periods of coordinated study in a range of
subjects and periods of free time; in this respect, the Halle regime
anticipated the polarization of work and leisure characteristic of modern
industrial society. Under these conditions, the classroom became the
sealed-off, purpose-dedicated space we associate with modern schooling.

The transformation of schooling in Prussia along these lines was, of
course, incomplete when Frederick William I died in 1740 and the

movement lost its powerful sponsor. But the Halle model remained influential; in the 1740s and 1750s, the educationalist Johann Hecker, a former teacher at the Pädagogium who had been trained at Francke's Teachers' College in Halle, founded a network of 'pauper schools' in Berlin catering to the neglected and potentially delinquent offspring of the town's numerous soldiers. In order to ensure an adequate supply of properly trained and motivated teachers, Hecker established a teachers' college on the Franckean model; he was one of several graduates of the Halle college to set up such institutes in Prussian cities. He also founded a *Realschule* in Berlin, the first to offer children of the middle and lower-middle classes tuition in a range of vocational subjects, as an alternative to the Latin-based, humanistic curriculum of the traditional secondary school. It was Hecker who popularized the practice of teaching pupils of like ability collectively, so as to maximize the efficiency of the teaching process; this was a crucial and lasting innovation.

As well as contributing to the standardization of education and public service, the Pietists directed their attention to the education of the Lithuanian and Masurian (Polish-speaking Protestant) minorities. In 1717, when the Pietist Heinrich Lysius became Inspector of Schools and Churches for East Prussia, he called for the specialized training of clergymen for missionary and teaching work among the non-German-speaking communities in the East Prussian dioceses. As a result, after some initial disagreements, Lithuanian and Polish seminars were established at the University of Königsberg.[55] The aim was to train Pietist aspirants for work in the Lithuanian and Masurian parishes. The Pietists also helped to establish the minority languages of the province as serious objects of study. Major dictionaries of the Lithuanian language were published in Königsberg in 1747 (Ruhig) and 1800 (Mielcke), both with the sponsorship of the Prussian authorities.[56]

The Pietists also provided support in the integration of the 20,000-odd Lutherans who entered Prussia as refugees from the archbishopric of Salzburg in 1731–2, most of whom were sent by Frederick William I to live as farmers in the depopulated region of Prussian Lithuania (see below). Pietists accompanied the Salzburgers on their trek through Prussia, organized fund-raising campaigns and financial support, supplied the new arrivals with devotional texts printed at the orphanage and provided their communities in the east with pastors.[57]

A further – often overlooked – area of evangelizing activity was the Pietist mission to the Jews. From 1728, there existed a Judaic Institute in the city of Halle, under the management of the Pietist theologian Johann Heinrich Callenberg, which ran a well-organized mission – the first of its kind – to the Jews of German-speaking Europe. The missionaries, who received language training in Halle at the first academic Yiddish seminar in Europe, travelled far and wide across Brandenburg-Prussia, buttonholing travelling Jews and trying without much success to persuade them that Jesus Christ was their messiah. Closely intertwined with the orphanage complex, the institute was sustained by the eschatological hope for a prophesied mass conversion of Jewry articulated in the writings of Philipp Jakob Spener. In practice, however, its missionary efforts were focused largely on the conversion and occupational retraining of impoverished itinerants known as 'beggar Jews' (*Betteljuden*) whose numbers were on the increase in early eighteenth-century Germany.[58] The mission to the Jews thus embodied a characteristically Pietist blend of social awareness and evangelizing zeal. In their missionary endeavours, as in the other spheres of their activity, the Pietists earned official approval by contributing to the tasks of religious, social and cultural integration that faced the administration of the Brandenburg-Prussian state, helping to bring about the 'domestication', as one historian has called it, of 'wild elements'.[59]

By the 1720s and 1730s, Pietism had become respectable. As often happens in such cases, it had changed in the process. It had begun as a controversial movement with a precarious foothold in the established Lutheran churches. As Pietism gathered new adherents during the 1690s and into the new century, it continued to be burdened by a reputation for excessive zeal.[60] By the 1730s, however, the moderate wing of the movement enjoyed unchallenged dominance, thanks to the groundwork laid by Spener and the tireless work of Francke and his Halle collaborators in channelling the surplus spiritual energies of Lutheran nonconformism into a range of institutional projects. A variety of radical Pietisms, some of them overtly separatist, continued to flourish in the other German states, but the Prussian variant shed its embarrassing extremist fringe and became an orthodoxy in its own right. Infused with confidence, the second generation of Pietists used their positions within key institutions to silence or remove opponents, much as the Lutheran

Orthodox had done in an earlier era. The Pietist movement became a patronage network in its own right.[61]

This position of dominance could not be sustained in the longer term. By the mid-1730s, the most influential and talented members of the founding generation of Halle theologians were dead: Francke (1727), Paul Anton (1730) and Joachim Justus Breithaupt (1732); the succeeding generation did not produce theologians of comparable quality or public profile. The movement was further weakened in the 1730s by internal controversy over a campaign launched by Frederick William I to purge 'Catholic' elements in Lutheran ceremonial. Some leading Pietists supported the initiative, but most remained respectful of Lutheran tradition and opposed the king's liturgical tampering. In this, they found themselves at one with the orthodox leadership of the Lutheran church, a fact that did much to repair the damage done by decades of feuding.[62]

The allegiance to the state that had won the movement such prominence thus threatened to sunder it. There were signs that the traditional Pietist tolerance of confessional difference was being supplanted, from within the movement itself, by a proto-enlightened enthusiasm for confessional convergence. Then there was the problem that the policy of favouring Pietists for civil service and pastoral posts encouraged ambitious candidates to employ adaptive mimicry in the service of their careers. Many succumbed to the temptation to manufacture narratives of conversion to a truer and more heartfelt faith, or even to counterfeit the grave countenance and demeanour (one source speaks of Pietist 'eye-rolling') associated with the more zealous adherents of the movement. This phenomenon – a consequence of the movement's success – was to leave the term 'Pietist' enduringly tainted with the connotation of religious imposture.[63]

After 1740, Pietism quickly declined in the theological faculties of the universities and within the clerical networks of Brandenburg Prussia. This was in part the result of a withdrawal of royal support. Frederick the Great was personally antipathetic to the 'Protestant Jesuits' who had enjoyed his father's protection, and consistently favoured enlightened candidates for posts in church administration, with the consequence that Berlin became a renowned centre of the Protestant enlightenment.[64] The University of Halle, once the bastion of the movement, became a leading centre of rationalism, and was to remain so well into the following century. There was a gradual fall in the number of persons attending the orphanage complex in Halle, and a corresponding decline in the circle of donors willing to support its activities. All this was reflected in the waning fortunes of the Pietist mission to the Jews in Halle, whose final annual report, published in 1790, opened with the observation that 'if we compare the earlier days of our institute with the present, then the two are as body and shadow . . .'[65]

How far-reaching was the impact of the Pietist movement on Prussian society and institutions? Pietists valued restraint and understatement and despised courtly luxury and wastefulness. At court and in the organs of military and civilian education they systematically extolled the virtues of modesty, austerity and self-discipline. In this way they amplified the impact of the cultural change wrought by Frederick William I after 1713, when towering wigs and richly embroidered jackets became the despised trifles of a bygone era. Through their role in the cadet schools, they helped to shape attitudes and comportment within the provincial nobilities, more and more of whose sons were passing through the cadet system by the middle decades of the eighteenth century. This may in turn account for the dislike of ostentation that came to be seen as a hallmark of the Prussian Junker caste. If the fabled modesty of the Junker was in many individual cases pure affectation and posturing, this merely testifies to the power of the persona popularized by the Pietist movement.

Pietism also helped to prepare the ground for the Prussian enlightenment.[66] The movement's optimism and its future-oriented focus bore an affinity with the enlightened idea of progress, just as its preoccupation with education as a means of shaping personality 'gave rise to that comprehensive pedagogization of human existence that was an essential characteristic of the enlightenment'.[67] The development of the natural sciences at the University of Halle reveals how closely Pietism and enlightenment, despite their many differences, were intertwined; the 'field of force' between them shaped the assumptions guiding scientific enquiry.[68] The Pietist emphasis on ethics over dogma and the commitment to tolerance in dealing with confessional difference likewise prefigured the fashions of the later eighteenth century – witness Kant's conception of morality as the highest sphere of rationally accessible truth, and his tendency to subordinate religious to moral intuitions.[69]

Some of the most influential Prussian exponents of enlightened and romantic philosophy were reared within a Pietist milieu. The cult of

introspection associated with the romantic movement had a Pietist ante-
cedent in the Pietist 'spiritual biography', of which Francke's own widely
read narrative of his conversion became an archetype. Its secular successor, the 'autobiography', emerged as an influential literary genre in
the mid to late eighteenth century.[70] The romantic philosopher Johann
Georg Hamann was educated at the Kneiphof School in Königsberg, a
stronghold of moderate Pietism, and subsequently attended the city's
university, where he came under the influence of the Pietist-inspired
philosophy professor Martin Knutzen; the introspective and ascetic quality of the Pietist outlook can be traced in his writings. Hamann even
underwent a conversion experience of sorts, brought on by a period of
close Bible-reading and penitential self-observation.[71] The influence of
Württemberg Pietism can be discerned in the writings of G. W. F. Hegel,
who came to exercise a profound influence on the development of
philosophy and political thought at the University of Berlin; Hegel's
conception of teleology as a process of self-realization was underpinned
by a Christian theology of history with recognizably Pietist features.[72]

And what of the Brandenburg-Prussian state? Moulded on to the
frieze that dominates the façade of Francke's orphanage building in
Halle are two black Prussian eagles, their wings outspread, a vivid
reminder to all who passed by of the movement's proximity to state
power. The positive contribution rendered by the Pietists to the consolidation of dynastic authority in Brandenburg-Prussia offers a striking
contrast with the political neutrality of the contemporaneous Pietist
movement in Württemburg and the subversive impact of Puritanism in
England.[73] As a fifth column within Brandenburg-Prussian Lutheranism,
the Pietists were a much more effective ideological instrument than
the Calvinist confessional prescriptions and censorship measures of the
Electors and kings could ever have been. But the Pietists did more than
merely assist the sovereign; they fed the energy from a broadly based
movement of Protestant voluntarism into the public enterprise of Brandenburg-Prussia's newly elevated dynasty. Above all, they propagated the
idea that the objectives of the state might also be those of conscientious
citizens, that service to the state could be motivated not just by obligation
or self-interest, but also by an encompassing sense of ethical responsibility. A community of solidarity emerged that extended beyond the networks of patron–client relationships. Pietism created the beginnings

of a broad-based activist constituency for the monarchical project in Brandenburg-Prussia.

PIETY AND POLICY

Does it make sense to speak of Brandenburg-Prussia's external relations in terms of a 'Protestant foreign policy'? Historians of power politics and international relations have often been sceptical about such claims. Even in the era of 'religious war', they point out, the imperatives of territorial security overrode the demands of confessional solidarity. Catholic France supported the Protestant Union against Catholic Austria; Lutheran Saxony sided with Catholic Austria against Lutheran Sweden. Confessional allegiances were only very rarely strong enough to prevail against all other considerations – the readiness of the Calvinist Palatinate under Frederick V to risk everything for the sake of the Protestant interest in 1618–20 was rare, perhaps even exceptional.

Yet it would be misleading to conclude that foreign policy was formulated on the basis of an entirely secular calculus of interest or that confession was an unimportant factor. It played an important role in structuring dynastic marital alliances, for one thing, and these in turn had important consequences for external policy, not least because they often entailed new territorial claims. It is clear, moreover, that many Protestant rulers perceived themselves as members of a Protestant community of states. This was certainly true of the Great Elector, who advised his successor in the Political Testament of 1667 to work wherever possible in concert with the other Protestant territories and to be vigilant in defending Protestant liberties against the Emperor.[74] Confessional factors featured prominently in policy debates within the executive. Arguing against an alliance with France in 1648, the privy councillor Sebastian Striepe pointed out that Cardinal Mazarin was hostile to the reformed faith and was likely to press forward with the Catholicization of France.[75] In the 1660s, as the mistreatments of French Calvinists intensified, the Elector wrote to Louis XIV to express his concern.[76] In the 1670s, Frederick William switched to the anti-French coalition in order to prevent the subjugation of the Dutch Republic, the centre of northern European Calvinism. Geopolitics and the promise of subsidies drew him back to France in the early 1680s, but his return to the Brandenburg-imperial alliance of 1686 was motivated in part by disquiet over the brutal persecution of the Calvinist Huguenots in France.[77]

One way of demonstrating confessional solidarity without risking armed conflict was to offer asylum and other forms of assistance to persecuted co-religionists in another state. The most celebrated example of this type of gesture politics was the Edict of Potsdam of 1685, by which the Elector invited persecuted French Calvinists to settle in the lands of Brandenburg-Prussia. It was Frederick William's answer to the French king's quashing of the rights granted to the Huguenots under the Edict of Nantes (1598). In all, some 20,000 French Calvinist refugees settled in the lands of the Elector. They tended to come from the poorer strata of the Reformed population – the wealthiest had generally chosen economically more attractive destinations such as England and Holland. Their resettlement was supported (by contrast with Holland and Britain) with state-subsidized assistance, cheap dwellings, tax exemptions, discounted loans and so on. Since Brandenburg, whose population had still not recovered from the mortalities of the Thirty Years War, stood in sore need of skilled and industrious immigrants, this was a self-interested but highly effective gesture. It irritated Louis XIV profoundly[78] (which, of course, was a part of its purpose) and earned the approbation of Protestants across the German lands. There was an intriguing disproportionality in this: of the 200,000-odd Huguenots who fled France in the face of persecution, only about one-tenth fetched up in the Prussian lands, yet it was the Elector, more than any other sovereign, who succeeded in capturing the moment for his reputation. Pitched in a lofty, universalizing moral register, the edict has (somewhat misleadingly) been celebrated ever since as one of the great monuments to the Prussian tradition of tolerance.

So successful was the 'politics of religious rights' inaugurated at Potsdam that it became a sort of fixture in Hohenzollern statecraft. In a proclamation of April 1704, Frederick I broadcast in similar terms his determination to assist persecuted French Calvinists in the Principality of Orange, a Protestant territorial enclave in the south of France to which the Hohenzollerns had a strong inheritance claim:[79]

Whereas the zeal that we harbour for the glory of God and for the good of His Church has made Us take to heart the sad state to which Our poor brothers in faith have seen themselves reduced by the rough persecution that providence allowed to rage in France some years ago, and has engaged Us to receive them charitably and at great cost in our States, Therefore We find Ourselves under an even greater obligation to exert the same charity towards Our own subjects, who have been forced to abandon Our Principality of Orange and all the goods that they possessed there [...] so that they might find a refuge under Our protection . . .[80]

Here was a characteristic combination of high-minded rhetoric with cool self-interest. The charitable offer in the proclamation was coupled with a claim to disputed territory. In an instruction to the councillors entrusted with receiving the refugees, moreover, the king urged that they were not to be maintained in idleness but set up as quickly as possible in an appropriate occupation, 'so that the King may profit from their establishment'.[81]

If the logic of confessional solidarity could occasionally provide a useful diplomatic instrument on the European scene, it was far more potent within the context of the Holy Roman Empire, for here the effect of confessional quarrels was amplified by the dualist structure of the imperial diet. The articles of the Peace of Westphalia stipulated that when confessional issues came up for debate at the diet, these must be discussed in separate session by two permanent caucuses of Protestant and Catholic representatives, the *corpus evangelicorum* and the *corpus catholicorum*. The purpose of this mechanism, known as the *itio in partes* or 'going into parts', was to ensure that potentially delicate confessional issues could be debated on both sides without unwelcome interference from the other party. Its practical effect, however, was to create a trans-territorial public forum for the airing of confessional grievances, particularly for the Protestants, who stood in greater need of corporate mobilization than the structurally dominant Catholics.

Frederick William I's spectacular intervention in a conflict over the fate of the Protestant minority in Salzburg demonstrated how useful this mechanism could be. In 1731, the discovery that there were nearly 20,000 persons living in the steep valleys of the Pinzgau and Pongau districts of Salzburg who called themselves Protestants unsettled the Catholic authorities and revealed the profound cultural gulf that separated the city of Salzburg from its Alpine hinterland. When missionary expeditions failed to wean the farmers from their heresy,

Archbishop Anton Firmian resolved to enforce their expulsion. This confrontation between a wealthy archiepiscopal administration and a semi-literate population of hardy Protestant hill-farmers caught the imagination of the Protestant caucus of the imperial diet. Pamphlets and broadsheets appeared arguing the farmers' cause. The Catholic authorities in Salzburg responded with vehement counter-attacks. Both sides published selected documents relating to the case and the Salzburgers became a *cause célèbre* in the German Protestant lands.

One of the first to recognize the potential in this conflict was King Frederick William I of Prussia. He desperately needed farmers for the under-exploited terrain of Prussian Lithuania on the eastern marches of Ducal Prussia – an area that had scarcely begun to recover from the famine and pestilence of 1709–10. At the same time, he was keen to establish Brandenburg-Prussia as a universal guarantor of Protestant rights, a role that implicitly challenged the Habsburg Emperor's claim to be the neutral ombudsman in confessional disputes between and within member states. Frederick William therefore offered to re-establish the Salzburg Protestants in his own lands.

The Elector's plan seemed at first unlikely to succeed. The archbishop had no intention of letting his farmers go; he intended to crush the agitation in the Alps by military means – indeed he had already appealed to the Bavarians and the Emperor for troops to carry out the task. But the constitutional machinery of the Empire came once again to the Elector's aid. Emperor Charles VI was hoping to secure the support of the Reichstag for a 'pragmatic sanction' that would confirm the succession of his daughter Maria Theresa to the Habsburg throne after his death. He needed the vote of the Elector in Berlin. The scene was set for a mutually beneficial transaction: in return for Frederick William's support for the pragmatic sanction, the Emperor agreed to pressure the Archbishop of Salzburg into allowing a mass transfer of his protestant subjects to eastern Ducal Prussia.

Between April and July 1732, twenty-six columns of Salzburger families – each containing about 800 people – left for the long march through Franconia and Saxony to Prussia, exchanging the grassy slopes of their Alpine home for the flatlands of Prussian Lithuania. The emigration in itself was a sensation. The long lines of Salzburgers trudging steadfastly northward through Protestant towns and cities in their outlandish Alpine gear had an electrifying effect on spectators. Peasants

12. King Frederick William I of Prussia greets the Protestant exiles from the archbishopric of Salzburg; *illustration from a contemporary pamphlet.*

and townsfolk brought food, clothes or gifts for the children, others threw coins from open windows. Many were reminded of the children of Israel on their way out of Egypt. There was a flood of confessional propaganda; books and prints depicted the expulsion, praised the obdurate faith of the emigrants and lauded the pious Prussian king whose country had become a promised land for the oppressed. Over 300 independent titles (not counting periodicals) were published in sixty-seven different German cities during the years 1732 and 1733 alone. Throughout the eighteenth and nineteenth centuries, the legend of the emigration was endlessly recycled in sermons, pamphlets, novels and plays.

The emigration was thus a propaganda coup of incalculable value to the Hohenzollern dynasty and the Brandenburg-Prussia state. It marked, moreover, an important point of departure, for the Salzburgers were not Calvinists (like the Huguenots and Orange refugees), but Lutherans. The claim to trans-confessional Protestant authority that the Pietists had helped to realize within Brandenburg-Prussia now reverberated across the Empire.

6

Powers in the Land

TOWNS

Just off the Mühlentorstrasse in the Old City of Brandenburg is the
shaded yard of St Gotthard's church. Like many of the medieval churches
in the Electorate of Brandenburg, St Gotthard's is a huge barn of dark-
red brick. The buttresses that support the soaring vaults of the interior
are concealed beneath a vast roof of ochre tiles whose frowning eaves
convey a sense of impregnability. At the western entrance, a graceful
baroque tower has been incongruously grafted on to the trunk of its
Romanesque predecessor. At the height of summer, spreading trees
shade the churchyard. The place has a dreamy peripheral feel, yet this
is the ancient core of the city. From here the medieval German settlement
spread out to the south along three streets, following the curve of the
river Havel.

A traveller who walks into the coolness of St Gotthard's church will
be surprised by the height and breadth of the interior. The inner walls
are lined with ornately carved memorials. These epitaphs are grandiose
things, carved tablets of stone up to two metres high and elaborately
inscribed. One of them commemorates the life and death of Thomas
Matthias, a sixteenth-century mayor of Brandenburg and descendant of
a distinguished family of clothiers, who rose to high political office
under Elector Joachim II but fell swiftly from favour when his successor
John George held him responsible for the debts accumulated during the
previous reign, and died of the plague in his home town in 1576. The
relief on the memorial depicts the children of Israel mounting the far
bank of the Red Sea as they flee from Egyptian captivity. On the left-hand
side we see a surging crowd of men and women in lavishly rendered
urban clothing, clutching their children and belongings and turning only

*13. Carved frieze from the epitaph of Mayor Thomas Matthias, 1549/1576,
St Gotthard's Church, Brandenburg*

to look back at the disaster unfolding behind them, where men in armour founder and are submerged in curled scrolls of thick grey water. Another memorial inscription, dated 1583, is surmounted by a beautifully carved relief, in which scenes from the passion of Christ take place between the columns of a two-storeyed neo-classical façade. In the upper storey Christ hangs naked, his hands bound tight to a lintel above his head, his body bending and twisting under the kicks and blows of three men with clubs and whips. This astonishingly dynamic and naturalistic sculpture commemorates Joachim Damstorff, a mayor of the city of Brandenburg, and his wife, Anna Durings; their names and dates are seen engraved in the stepped frieze at the base of the epitaph. Portraits of Damstorff and his wife, both dressed in the ornate attire of the urban oligarchy, peep out from circular niches at the bottom left and right of the sculpture, looking almost as if they were trying to catch each other's eye across the crowded scene between them.

A large epitaph, surmounted by a finely carved allegorical relief depicting Lazarus and the rich man, commemorates two generations of the Trebaw family, another mayoral lineage. These stepping stones of memory run well into the eighteenth century – a richly decorated two-metre tablet to the right of the altar commends the 'distinguished councillor and celebrated merchant and trader of the Old City of Brandenburg' Christoph Strahle, who died at the age of eighty-one in 1738. What is striking about these objects, apart from their artistic virtuosity, is the powerful sense of civic identity that they project. They are not simply memorials to individuals but expressions of the pride and corporate identity of an oligarchy. Many of the tablets commemorate several generations of the same family and provide detailed information about children and marriages. The most impressive monument in St Gotthard's is the pulpit itself, an extraordinary composite sculpture in sandstone in which scenes from the Old and New Testaments follow the spiral stairs up to the chancel, and the whole structure rests upon a large and superbly worked bearded figure in white stone whose head is bowed over an open book. This remarkable ensemble, executed by Georg Zimmermann and dated 1623, was sponsored by the Clothiers' Guild of the Old City, and we find their memorial tablet fixed to the column adjoining the pulpit. In addition to ten individual portraits of prominent clothiers – all of them formidable figures wearing the austere dark costume and white ruffs of the early seventeenth-century bourgeoisie – the tablet shows the house marks and names of a hundred individual master clothiers. It is hard to imagine a more emphatic and dignified advertisement of corporate bourgeois self-importance.

This is by no means a phenomenon unique to St Gotthard's church. We find similar seventeenth- and eighteenth-century bourgeois urban memorials in the churches of other Brandenburg towns. St Laurence's of Havelberg, for example, nestled in the historic city centre on an island in the middle of the river Havel, offers a similar array of stone memorials, though these are executed in a somewhat less exalted register. Here too, the dedications are mainly to tradesmen – merchants, lumber-dealers, brewers – as well as to prominent mayoral families. The memorial to the 'respected merchant and trader' Joachim Friedrich Pein (d. 1744) is especially noteworthy for its affecting simplicity:

Unter diesem Leichen-Stein	Beneath this burial-stone
Ruh ich Pein ohn' alle Pein	I, Payne, lie free of pain
Und erwarte mit den meinen	And wait before God to appear
Selig für Gott zu erscheinen	Saved with my near and dear

In Havelberg, as in Brandenburg, the significance of the city church as a forum for the collective self-expression of an urban congregation is heightened by the fact that both cities are cathedral seats. There is thus an implicit dichotomy between the urban church at the medieval core of the city, whose congregation is dominated by the guilds and urban officials – and the cathedral, whose chapter was traditionally recruited from members of the imperial aristocracy. This is very clearly expressed in the geography of Havelberg, where the cathedral, an

14. Havelberg Cathedral

imposing structure that resembles a fortified castle, looks down from the heights of the northern riverbank over the little island of the Old City with its shops and stalls and narrow streets. Well into the nineteenth century, the social character of the two congregations was correspondingly polarized: St Laurence remained the church of the townsfolk (as well as of enlisted men stationed in the local garrison), while the nobility patronized the socially and geographically more elevated cathedral.

The church memorials of Havelberg and Brandenburg remind us of a world that is often overlooked in general accounts of the history of the Prussian lands. This is the world of the towns, a social milieu dominated by master artisans and patrician family networks, whose identity derived from an entrenched sense of autonomy and privilege, both political and cultural, *vis-à-vis* the surrounding countryside. If towns have traditionally occupied a marginal place in the history of Brandenburg-Prussia, this is partly because the urban sector was never especially strong in this part of German Europe – of the thirty German cities with populations of 10,000 or more in 1700, only two (Berlin and Königsberg) were in Brandenburg-Prussia. In any case, it is widely believed that the towns and, more importantly, the spirit of self-administration, civic responsibility and political autonomy that they nurtured, were among the casualties of Hohenzollern absolutism. Indeed, one historian has written of the deliberate 'destruction' of the Brandenburg bourgeoisie by the centralizing monarchical state.[1] The consequence was a political culture that was strong on obedience, but weak on civil courage and civic virtue. Here again, we sense the powerful negative attraction of the 'special path'.

There is certainly something to be said for the idea that the seventeenth and eighteenth centuries were an era of urban decline, especially if by this we mean the decline of urban political autonomy. Königsberg is perhaps the most dramatic example of a city struggling unsuccessfully to retain its traditional political and economic independence in the face of an aggressive monarchical power. In 1640, when the Great Elector came to the throne, Königsberg was still a wealthy Baltic trading city with a corporate representation in the diet that placed it on a par with the provincial nobility. By 1688, Königsberg's political autonomy, its influence within the diet and much of its prosperity had been broken. Here, the struggle between the urban authorities and the Berlin administration was especially bitter. Königsberg was a special case, of course, but developments in other towns across the Prussian lands followed a broadly analogous course.

In many towns, the downgrading or removal of political privileges coincided with the introduction of the new excise, a tax on goods and services introduced in stages during the 1660s. Since it was raised directly on goods and services (i.e. at point of sale) the excise did away with the need for fiscal negotiations with urban Estate representatives. The towns thus disappeared as a corporate presence both from the provincial diets and from the 'permanent committees' of senior provincial delegates that increasingly managed negotiations between the Estates and the crown. This process of gradual disenfranchisement was reinforced by the imposition, first in Berlin in 1667, and later in all towns, of royally appointed tax commissioners, who soon began to extend the scope of their authority.[2] The pace of centralization slackened during the reign of Frederick III/I, but picked up again under his successor, Frederick William I, whose Council Regulation (*Rathäusliches Regiment*) of 1714 transferred urban budgeting authority to royal officials and curtailed the powers of urban magistrates. Further laws were issued during the reign of Frederick II, who transferred all remaining policing powers from magistrates to royal officials and imposed a system of state authorizations on all sales of urban property.[3] In the western provinces, too, the communal independence of the towns was largely abolished during the reigns of Frederick William I and Frederick II. The unique constitutions and privileges of towns such as Soest in the Westphalian county of Mark or Emden in East Friesland, were dismantled.[4]

For most towns, the late seventeenth and early eighteenth centuries were also a period of economic stagnation or decline. In much of Brandenburg and Eastern Pomerania, the poor quality of the soils and the weakness of regional trade meant that the towns were poorly endowed to start with. The impact on the towns of the excise tax is difficult to assess. Initially, some towns were keen on the new tax, since they saw it as a way of rebalancing the fiscal load in their favour (the towns had previously paid a higher rate in contribution tax than the countryside); in some cases the municipal authorities were even pressured by urban taxpayers into begging the government to introduce it. There is some fragmentary evidence suggesting that the excise had a stimulating effect on urban economies. In Berlin, for example, the early excise years saw a boom in construction that began to make good the appalling damage done during the war, a consequence of the fact that the excise redistributed the tax burden within the cities away from land and property towards commercial activities of all kinds.

The worst drawback of the excise was simply the fact that *only* the towns paid it; rural areas still paid the old contribution. This was not how things had been planned. The Great Elector had initially intended to levy the excise on town and countryside alike, but pressure from the provincial nobilities persuaded him to restrict it to the cities. What this meant was that urban manufacturers now faced competition from rural producers whose goods were duty-free as long as they were not sold within the excise towns. Many noble estate owners exploited this state of affairs by having merchandise carted direct to the major regional markets, where they could undercut urban competitors in their own region. The problem was reinforced in areas dependent upon trade by the fact that the excise undermined the regional competitiveness of manufacturers and traders trying to shift goods across the border – this complaint was often heard in Kleve, for example, where it was felt that the excise had cut the volume and profitability of the Rhine river trade, and in Geldern where the excise was seen as having depressed trading activity on the Maas.[5]

The impact of the growing Prussian army – and in particular of garrisons – on the towns of Brandenburg-Prussia was ambivalent. On the one hand, the soldiers and their wives and children stationed in garrison towns represented both consumers and a supplementary workforce. Since military service was not a full-time occupation, soldiers in garrisons augmented their meagre military wage by working for townsfolk. In a garrison town like Prenzlau in the Uckermark to the north of Berlin, or Wesel in the Rhenish Duchy of Kleve, many soldiers chose, when not on duty, to work in the workshops and manufactures of the masters in whose houses they were billeted. In this way they could earn several times their basic military wage. If they were married, their wives might seek employment in the town's textile manufactury. The presence of soldiers thus contributed to the consolidation of a textiles manufacturing sector that was partly dependent upon cheap unguilded labour. Military service may also have helped to stabilize urban social structures by providing the most vulnerable strata of the community with a small but tolerable income.[6] Since wealthier burghers who preferred not to billet a soldier could pay poorer householders to take him instead, the billeting system had a small redistributive effect.

But there was a downside. Although the highly flexible billeting system used in the garrison towns worked astonishingly well, there were also many incidents of tension between householders and billeted servicemen. The presence in the city of substantial numbers of men who were subject to the authority of the military courts generated jurisdictional disputes. Military commanders sometimes succumbed to the temptation to flaunt the municipal authorities by requisitioning supplies from civilian sources or forcing local burghers to serve in the guards. The low-wage labour provided by off-duty soldiers undercut craft apprentices in workshops where troops were not employed, sowing tension within the ranks of the city's incorporated professions.[7] In lean times, when additional work was hard to come by, the dependants of garrison soldiers might be seen begging on the streets.[8] Soldiers, with their privileged knowledge of the fortifications surrounding the city, were also involved in the smuggling of goods across the excise boundaries.[9] More ominously, one scholar has suggested that the 'militarisation of civic society led to an arbitrary and little-regulated domination of garrison cities by the army, fostering an atmosphere of passivity among the burgher population and magistracies'.[10]

This argument should not be pushed too far. Soldiers were certainly a familiar sight on the streets of garrison towns and a crucial ingredient in the social scene at all levels – from the tavern to the patrician salon. But there is little evidence that this involved the permeation of urban civil society with militarist values or patterns of comportment. The conscription system established in Prussia allowed for a wide range of exemptions freeing young men of the burgher classes from the legal obligation to serve. These included not only the sons of upper-middle-class fathers, who were expected to pursue an academic degree or a career in trade or economic management, but also the sons of master artisans in various privileged trades, who were trained to work in their father's trade. It has been estimated that across the Hohenzollern lands, some 1.7 million men benefited from such exemptions.[11]

The eighteenth-century peacetime Brandenburg-Prussian military was not, in any case, an institution capable of transforming the outlook and sensibility of its own recruits through systematic socialization and indoctrination. The military in the eighteenth-century towns was porous and loosely organized. Basic training lasted for less than a year (its duration was locally determined and varied widely from place to place), and even during this phase, soldiers were not 'de-civilianized' through isolation from the society around them. On the contrary: if they were married, they lived in barracks with their wives and other dependants – the military was not yet the exclusively masculine domain it would later become. (Indeed, marriage was encouraged for foreign recruits as a way of binding them more firmly to the Prussian service.[12]) If they were unmarried, they were expected to find lodgings with burghers. As for those soldiers who wished to remain in service after completion of their basic training, we have seen that their military duties consumed so little of their time that they were able to supplement their income through various forms of casual labour. Some soldiers picked up extra pocket money by standing guard duty in lieu of others who were off working for wages. It is clear that a symbiosis did evolve between military personnel and town populations,[13] just as large numbers of student lodgers made a distinctive contribution to the social mix and local economy of university towns. But the soldiers no more 'militarized' their garrison towns than the students 'academicized' theirs. There were, of course, disputes between town councils and military authorities (just as there were between burghers and students), but these mostly demonstrate the readiness of 'civilian' authorities to protest when they

15. Soldier's wife begging.
Engraving by Daniel
Chodowiecki, 1764.

saw local commanders overstepping the boundaries of their authority.

There is little reason to believe that the administrative penetration of the towns by a rudimentary state officialdom had the effect of suppressing the spirit of local initiative. The royal officials appointed to administrative posts in the larger towns did not function as the imperious agents of a central policy bent on disempowering the urban elites. On the contrary, many of them 'went native', socializing or even intermarrying with the town elite and siding with the town authorities in disputes with local military commanders or other central government organs. The continuation of corruption and nepotism in many city governments – a sure sign that local patronage networks were alive and kicking – suggests that the oligarchies who held a controlling interest in the affairs of the cities were not displaced by state penetration. The oligarchies, for their part, assiduously cultivated newly arriving government officials and succeeded in many cases in suborning them to local interests.[14]

There were, moreover, dynamic and innovative elements within the urban bourgeoisie well before 1800. During the last third of the eighteenth century, changes in the structure of town-based manufacture and commerce produced a new elite composed mainly of merchants, entrepreneurs and manufacturers (rather than the guildsmen who had dominated the traditional scene).[15] Members of this elite were involved in many ways – on a voluntary or honorary basis – in local urban administration. They sat on the municipal governing bodies (*Magistrats-kollegien*), on the councils of guilds and corporations, on the administrative boards of schools, churches and local charitable organizations.

This tendency was particularly pronounced in the small and middle-sized towns, because here the local administration was absolutely dependent upon the help of volunteer notables. The wool manufacturer Christian H. Böttcher, for example, sat on the town senate in Osterwieck in the province of Halberstadt; in Prenzlau (Uckermark), the merchant Johann Granze was also assistant judge in the city court. The mayors of the cities of Burg and Aschersleben were both local businessmen.[16] One could list a hundred such cases from across the Prussian lands. The governance of the Prussian towns did not, in other words, lie exclusively in the hands of salaried state servants but rather depended on formidable reserves of local voluntarism among the more enterprising and innovative elements of the bourgeoisie. What had 'declined' in the towns of the Prussian lands – and indeed across much of western Europe – were the privileges and local autonomy of the traditional corporate system sustained by the ancient customs and honour codes of the skilled crafts. What was replacing them was a new and dynamic elite whose ambition expressed itself in entrepreneurial expansion and the assumption of informal leadership in urban affairs.

The voluntary societies founded in some middle-sized towns during the last third of the eighteenth century are a further indication of growing cultural and civic vitality among the burgher classes. There was a highly active Literary Society in Halberstadt from 1778, for example, which served as a meeting place for the educated burghers of the city and whose considerable printed output reflected a blend of regionalist pride and Prussian patriotism. In Westphalian Soest, a local judge founded a Society of Patriotic Friends and Enthusiasts of Regional History whose purpose – advertised in a regional journal, *Das Westphälische Magazin* – was to collate the first comprehensive and archivally researched history of the town. In the university town of Frankfurt/Oder, a German Society founded in the 1740s concerned itself with the cultivation of language and literature; it was later joined by a Learned Society and a Masonic lodge.[17] In these cities, but also in many smaller country towns, education was becoming the crucial marker of a new social status. From around the middle of the century in particular, the educated bourgeoisie (consisting of lawyers, school teachers, pastors, judges, doctors and others) began to separate itself from the traditional craft-based elites, forming its own social networks within and between towns.[18]

It was often the leading burghers of individual towns who achieved improvements in local schooling, an area where, for all its repeated edicts, the state had in many places failed utterly. From the 1770s, a wave of new or improved schools testifies to the rising demand, even in the most modest towns, for better and broader educational provision.[19] In Neuruppin, idyllically situated on the edge of a long narrow lake to the north-west of Berlin, a group of enlightened pastors, city officials and school teachers formed in the 1770s an association whose sworn objectives were to enact a major educational reform for the town and to improve its economic standing.[20] Thanks to their efforts along with donations from the city magistrate and leading burghers, the Neuruppin teacher Philipp Julius Lieberkühn was able to develop an innovative anti-authoritarian pedagogical programme that would become a model for educational reformers across Germany. 'The teacher strives,' Lieberkühn wrote in a general outline of his educational philosophy, 'to let all the natural faculties and strengths of his pupils develop freely and have sway, because this is a fundamental law of rational education.'[21] It was a formulation that breathed the spirit not only of enlightenment, but also of bourgeois civic pride.

THE LANDED NOBILITY

The ownership and management of land was the defining collective experience of the Brandenburg-Prussian nobilities. The proportion of land in noble hands varied considerably from territory to territory, but it was high by European standards. The averages for Brandenburg and Pomerania (according to figures from around 1800) were about 60 and 62 per cent respectively, while the equivalent figure for East Prussia (where the crown was the dominant landowner) was 40 per cent. By contrast, the French nobility owned only about 20 per cent of the cultivable land in France, while the figure for the nobility of European Russia was as low as 14 per cent. On the other hand, Brandenburg-Prussia looks less anomalous if we compare it with late eighteenth-century England, where the nobility controlled about 55 per cent of the land.[22]

The landed nobility of the East-Elbian regions of Germany were and are known collectively as 'Junkers'. Deriving from 'jung Herr', the term originally meant 'young lord' and referred to those German noblemen

– often second and younger sons – who helped to conquer or settle and defend the lands taken from the Slavs during the waves of German eastward expansion and settlement in the middle ages. In return for their military services they were granted land and perpetual tax exemptions. There were substantial disparities in wealth. In East Prussia, there was a small minority of true magnate families descended from mercenary commanders who had fought in the employ of the Teutonic Order during the Thirteen Years War against Poland (1453–66). In Brandenburg, where most noble families descended from settler-landowners, the average Junker estate was quite modest by European standards.

Since it was in the interest of the colonizing sovereigns of the Middle Ages to settle as many warrior-nobles as possible in areas vulnerable to Slav reprisals, noble land concessions were often small and close together, so that a single village might be partitioned among several families. The statistically dominant group, accounting for around half of the nobility, was that of noble families whose possessions encompassed between one and several estates and villages.[23] But even within this group, there were wide disparities. A gulf separated families such as the Quitzows (later the Kleists), for example, whose lordship at Stavenow in the Prignitz encompassed 2,400 acres of demesne arable, from the general run of Junker families in the district, who had to get by with less than 500. In such a setting it was natural that the lesser noble families should concede leadership in local and provincial politics to a small circle of wealthy and often intermarried elite families. It was from this 'dress-circle' of landed families that the key mediators in negotiations with the crown tended to be drawn.

The localized political structures of the seventeenth-century Hohenzollern territories militated against a shared political identity centred on Berlin. The Junkers – especially in Brandenburg – were largely shut out of senior state offices during the later decades of the Great Elector's reign and made only slow inroads into this area during the eighteenth century. Their political ambitions focused above all on Estate-controlled offices at district and provincial level and their horizons thus tended to be rather narrow, a condition reinforced by the fact that many of the less well-off families could not afford to educate their children away from home. The regional specificities of the various Hohenzollern territories were reflected in patterns of kinship and intermarriage. In Pomerania and East Prussia there were strong kinship links with Sweden and Poland, while houses in Brandenburg frequently intermarried with families in neighbouring Saxony and Magdeburg.

The eighteenth-century Hohenzollern monarchs, for their part, never spoke of a 'Prussian' nobility but always of a plurality of provincial elites possessing distinct personalities. In his Instruction of 1722, Frederick William I declared of the Pomeranian nobles that they were 'as loyal as gold'; though they might argue a little, they would never oppose the orders of the sovereign. The same was true of the Neumark, the Uckermark and the Mittelmark. By contrast, the nobles of the Altmark were 'bad, disobedient people' and 'impertinent in their dealings with their sovereign'. Almost as bad were the Magdeburg and Halberstadt nobilities, who, he urged, should be kept away from official posts in their own or neighbouring provinces. As for the nobles of the western provinces, Kleve, the county of Mark and Lingen, these were 'stupid and opinionated'.[24]

Nearly half a century later, in his Political Testament of 1768, Frederick the Great spoke along similar lines of the territorial nobilities within his monarchy, declaring that the East Prussians were spirited and refined, but still too attached to their separatist traditions and thus of dubious loyalty to the state, while the Pomeranians were obstinate but upstanding and made excellent officers. As for the Upper Silesians, whose homeland had only recently been conquered and annexed to the Hohenzollern lands, these were lazy and uneducated and remained attached to their former Habsburg masters.[25]

It was only very gradually that a more homogeneous Prussian elite emerged. Intermarriage played a role in this process. Whereas virtually all Brandenburg families married within their own provincial elite until the end of the seventeenth century, things had changed by the 1750s and 1760s, when there were signs of an increasingly enmeshed kinship structure. Almost one-half of the marriages contracted by leading families in Brandenburg, Pomerania and East Prussia were to lineages based in another Hohenzollern territory. The most important institutional driver of homogenization was the Prussian army. The rapid expansion of the eighteenth-century officer corps forced the administration to recruit energetically among the provincial elites. New state-subsidized academies were established at the beginning of the eighteenth century in Berlin, Kolberg and Magdeburg; shortly after his accession, Frederick William I integrated these into the central Cadet Corps School in Berlin.

Although there were certainly efforts to pressure noble families into forwarding their sons for military training, many leapt at the chance created by the cadet system. It was particularly attractive to those numerous families who could not afford to educate their sons in the privately run academies frequented by the monied nobility. Promotion to the rank of captain and above brought the opportunity to earn a better income than many lesser landed estates could sustain.[26] A characteristic example of the new generation of career officer was Ernst von Barsewisch, the son of a small estate-owner in the Altmark, who was sent to the Berlin Cadet Corps School in 1750, because his father could not afford to send him to university to be trained for state service. In his memoirs, Barsewisch recalled that the cadets (of whom there were 350 when he attended the school) were taught writing, French, logic, history and geography, engineering, dancing, fencing and 'military draughtsmanship' (militärische Zeichenkunst).[27]

The shared experience of military training and, more importantly, of active military service doubtless fostered a strong sense of esprit de corps, though this was achieved at appalling cost. Some families in particular became specialist suppliers of boys for sacrifice on the field of battle – the Wedels notably, a Pomeranian family, lost seventy-two (!) of their young men during the wars of 1740–63. Fifty-three male Kleists perished in the same battles. Of the twenty-three men in the Belling family of Brandenburg, twenty were killed during the Seven Years War.

The association between noble status and officer rank was reinforced during the reign of Frederick the Great by the practice of obstructing the promotion of non-nobles. Although the king was forced to admit commoners to senior military posts during the Seven Years War when noble candidates were in short supply, many of them were later purged or marginalized. By 1806, when the officer corps numbered 7,000 men, only 695 were of non-noble descent and most of these were concentrated in the less prestigious artillery and technical arms of the service.[28]

Yet this increasingly close identity of interest with the crown could not inure the nobility against the effects of social and economic change. During the second half of the eighteenth century, the landed nobility entered a period of crisis. The wars and economic disruption of the 1740s and 1750s–60s, aggravated by government manipulation of the grain market through the magazine system and demographic overload through the natural expansion of estate-owning families placed the landowning class under increasing strain. There was a dramatic growth in the indebtedness of Junker estates, leading in many cases to bankruptcies or forced sales, often to commoners with cash in hand. The growing frequency with which estates changed hands raised questions about the cohesion of the traditional rural social fabric.[29]

This was not a matter the king took lightly. Frederick II was more socially conservative than his father had been. The nobilities were the only corporate group (in Frederick's view) capable of serving as officers in the military. From this it followed that the stability and continuity of noble property were crucial to the viability of the Frederician military state. Whereas Frederick William I had deliberately set out to dilute the social pre-eminence of the nobility, therefore, Frederick adopted a policy of conservation. The crucial objective was to prevent the transfer of noble land into non-noble ownership. There were generous tax concessions, ad hoc cash gifts to families in financial straits, and efforts – largely futile – to prevent landowners from over-mortgaging their estates.[30] When these measures failed, Frederick's instinctive response was to tighten state control of land sales, but this proved counterproductive. Transfer controls involved an aggressive curtailment of the freedom to dispose of property. The administration thus had to reconcile conflicting priorities. It wished to restore and preserve the dignity and economic stability of the noble caste, yet it sought to achieve this by curtailing the fundamental liberties of the estate-owning class.

The quest for a less interventionist and controversial method of supporting the noble interest ultimately led to the foundation of state-capitalized agricultural credit unions (*Landschaften*) for the exclusive use of the established Junker families. These institutions issued mortgages at subsidized interest rates to ailing or indebted landowning families. Separate credit unions were established for each province (Kurmark and Neumark in 1777, Magdeburg and Halberstadt in 1780, and Pomerania in 1781). Interestingly enough, the idea of using such institutions to consolidate noble landholdings seems to have come from a commoner, the wealthy Berlin merchant Büring, who presented his ideas to the king during an audience of 23 February 1767, although there were also longstanding traditions of noble corporate financial self-help in a number of provinces.

The credit unions were at first very successful, if this can be measured by the rapid increase in the value of their letters of credit, which soon became an important medium of financial speculation. Credit union loans certainly helped some ailing estates to make productivity improvements. But the legal requirement that loans be tied to 'useful improvements on the estate' was often very loosely interpreted, so that the government's subsidized credit was tapped for purposes that did little to consolidate noble landownership. The credit unions did not in any case suffice to tackle the looming problem of indebtedness across the entire rural sector, since landowners who ran out of cheap credit with the *Landschaften* simply went to other lenders. By 1807, while the combined credit unions held 54 million thalers of mortgage debt in all, a further 307 million thalers of estate-based debt were held by bourgeois lenders.[31]

As these developments suggest, the relationship between the Junkers and the sovereign house had now turned full circle. In the sixteenth century, it was the Junkers who had kept the Electors afloat; by the last third of the eighteenth century, the polarities of their interdependency had been reversed. Some historians have spoken of a 'power compromise' (*Herrschaftskompromiss*) between the crown and the Junkers whose effect was to consolidate the domination of the state and the traditional elites at the expense of other forces in society. The problem with this metaphor is firstly that it implies that at some point both 'parties' agreed on a kind of steady-state power-sharing arrangement. But the opposite was true. The relationship between the crown (and its ministers) and the various provincial nobilities was one of never-ending friction, confrontations and renegotiation. A second problem with the 'power compromise' thesis is that it overstates the stabilizing potential of collaboration between the state and the traditional elites. The truth is that, despite their best efforts, the crown and its ministers proved completely unable to arrest the processes of social and economic change that were transforming the face of rural society in the Prussian lands.

LANDLORDS AND PEASANTS

To work the soil was the destiny of most inhabitants of German Europe in the eighteenth century. Cultivated land accounted for about one-third of total land surface and about four-fifths of the population depended on agriculture for survival.[32] The power relations governing the ownership and exploitation of land were thus of overwhelming importance, not only for the generation of nutrition and wealth, but also for the political culture of the state and society more generally. The collective power of the nobility over Brandenburg-Prussian rural society was rooted only partly in its controlling share of landed wealth. There was also a crucial legal and political dimension. From the middle decades of the fifteenth century, the Junkers succeeded not only in restructuring their landholdings so that the best arable land fell to the lordship, but also in supplementing their economic advantage with political powers enabling them to exert direct authority over the peasants on their estates. They acquired, for example, the right to prevent peasants from leaving their farms without prior permission, or to bring back (if necessary by force) peasants who had absconded and taken up domicile either in a town or on another estate. They also demanded, and gradually secured, the right to impose labour services on their peasant 'subjects'.

It is still not entirely clear why these changes came about, especially as they ran counter to prevailing developments in contemporary western Europe, where the trend was towards the legal emancipation of formerly subject peasants and the commutation of compulsory labour services into money rents. It may be that because the lands east of the river Elbe were zones of comparatively recent German settlement, traditional rights among the peasantry were relatively weak. The population decline and widespread desertion of cultivable land during the long agrarian depression of the late Middle Ages certainly placed noble landlords under pressure to maximize revenues and cut cash costs. The contraction of the urban economy undermined one potential source of resistance, since it was the towns that had most energetically contested the right of landlords to retrieve peasant absconders. Another important factor was the weakness of state authority. Deeply indebted and heavily dependent upon the provincial nobilities, the Electors of fifteenth- and sixteenth-century Brandenburg had neither the power nor the inclination to resist the consolidation of noble legal and political power in the localities.

Whatever the causes, the result was the emergence of a new form of landlordship. It was not a system of 'serfdom', properly speaking, since the peasants themselves were not the property of their masters. But it did involve a measure of subjection to the personal authority of the lord. The noble estate became an integrated legal and political space. The landlord was not only the employer of his peasants and the owner of their land; he also held jurisdiction over them through the manorial court, which was empowered to issue punishments ranging from small fines for minor misdemeanours to corporal punishments, including whippings and imprisonment.

Historians have long been preoccupied with the authoritarian features of the Prussian agrarian system. The émigré German scholar Hans Rosenberg described a regime of miniature autocracies in which

Local dominance was complete, for, in the course of time, the Junker had become not only an exacting landlord, hereditary serf master, vigorous entrepreneur, assiduous estate manager, and nonprofessional trader, but also the local church patron, police chief, prosecutor, and judge. [. . .] Many of these experts in local tyranny were experienced in whipping the backs, hitting the faces and breaking the bones of 'disrespectful' and 'disobedient' peasant serfs.[33]

For the bulk of Prussian subjects the consequence of this aristocratic tyranny was 'abject poverty' and 'helpless apathy'; peasants in particular suffered 'legal and social degradation, political emasculation, moral crippling and destruction of [their] chances of self-determination'. But they were, in the words of another study, 'too down-trodden to revolt'.[34] This view is widely echoed in the literature on the German special path, where it is presumed that the Junker-dominated agrarian system, by instilling habits of deference and obedience, had deleterious and lasting effects on Prussian – and by extension German – political culture. The historiographical black legend of Junker tyranny has been remarkably tenacious, partly because it chimes with a broader cultural tradition of anti-Junker sentiment.[35]

In recent years, a rather different picture has emerged. Not all peasants in the East-Elbian lands were the subjects of lords. A substantial proportion were free tenant farmers, or non-subject employees. In East Prussia in particular, free peasants – the descendants of free settler-colonists – ran 13,000 out of 61,000 peasant farms across the province by the end of the eighteenth century. In many areas, the settlement of immigrants on crown and noble land created new concentrations of non-subject farmers.[36] Even traditional lordships in the Brandenburg heartland incorporated a substantial contingent of persons who were paid wages for their labour or operated as specialist subcontractors managing particular resources, such as dairy herds, on an entrepreneurial basis. The Junker estates, in other words, were not lazily run cereal monocultures, in which labour was free and incentives for innovation non-existent. They were complex businesses that involved substantial operating costs and high levels of investment. Waged labour of various kinds played a crucial role in sustaining the manorial economy, both at the level of the lordship itself and among the ranks of the better-off subject villagers, who themselves frequently employed labour in order to maximize the productivity of their own holdings.

There was, to be sure, an extensive regime of compulsory labour services. In eighteenth-century Brandenburg, labour services were generally limited to between two and four days a week; they were heavier in the Neumark, where peasants rendered labour service for four days a week in winter and six in summer and autumn.[37] Services also varied within individual lordships. On the estate of Stavenow in the Prignitz, for example, the inhabitants of the village of Karstädt were required to 'come to the manor at six in the morning on Mondays, Wednesdays, and Fridays with a horse team, or if horses are not needed, with another person on foot, and to stay until they are told they can come in from the fields with the cowherder'. By contrast, the smallholders of the little fishing village of Mesekow on the same estate were liable to 'serve with the hand as often as they were told'.[38]

Yet these burdens were balanced to some extent by the strong hereditary property rights enjoyed by many subject peasants. In the light of these rights, it seems plausible to describe labour services not simply as feudal impositions, but as rents. While most fullholding peasants would dearly have loved to commute their hated labour services to money rents, it does not seem that the services were so burdensome as to prevent them from making a reasonable living out of their plots, or to prevent settler-farmers from other parts of Germany from accepting subject status in return for hereditary land titles. A study of the Stavenow estate in the Prignitz suggests that, far from being condemned to 'abject poverty', the average Brandenburg village peasant may actually have been better off than his southern and western European counterparts. In any case, seigneurial labour burdens were not engraved in stone; they could be, and sometimes were, renegotiated. This happened, for example, in the years following the devastation of the Thirty Years War, which left a huge number of farms deserted. Faced with a desperate labour shortage, landlords on many estates caved in to the demands of peasants for reductions in their services. Indeed, many landlords conspired in pushing labour rents down by outbidding their neighbours for incoming settlers looking to establish themselves on farmsteads.[39]

The state authorities, moreover, intervened to protect peasants against high-handed action by landlords. Laws and edicts issued by successive sovereigns after 1648 gradually subjected the patrimonial courts of the Junker lordships to the norms of territorial law. Whereas the consultation of lawyers in patrimonial cases had been a rarity in the sixteenth and early seventeenth centuries, landlords tended after the Thirty Years War to employ legally qualified court administrators. In 1717, Frederick William I ordered under the threat of severe penalties that every court was to acquire a copy of the newly published Criminal Code (*Criminal-Ordnung*) and to operate in conformity with its guidelines in all criminal cases. Patrimonial courts were also required to render a full quarterly report of trials conducted. This trend continued under Frederick II.

From 1747–8 onwards, all patrimonial courts were obliged to employ government-certified, university-trained jurists as judges. The giving of law was thereby de-privatized and drawn back into the sphere of state authority. The result was a gradual standardization of procedures and practices across different patrimonial jurisdictions.[40] These trends were reinforced by the activity of the Berlin Chamber Court, Brandenburg's highest tribunal and court of appeal. The role of the Chamber Court in adjudicating conflicts between villagers and landlords across Brandenburg over an extended period has yet to be comprehensively analysed. But among those individual cases that have received close attention, there are many that demonstrate the court's willingness to support the complaints of villagers or stay the hand of over-zealous Junkers.[41] Moreover, access to this court became easier during the reign of Frederick II, when the reforms initiated by Justice Minister Samuel von Cocceji established faster and cheaper appellate justice.

The history of disputes between landlords and subjects suggests an impressive capacity for concerted action, as well as a strong sense, among landed and landless agrarian workers alike, of their customary entitlements and dignity. We see this in the disputes over labour services that became increasingly common towards the end of the seventeenth century, as the population began to recover from the Thirty Years War and the balance of bargaining power between rural subjects and landowners began to tilt back in the latter's favour. In the face of demands for increased labour rents, peasants showed an elephantine memory of the customary limits to their labour obligations and a rock-hard determination not to permit the imposition of new and 'illegitimate' services.

In 1656, for example, it was reported that peasants in the Prignitz were refusing to pay their taxes or perform their labour services. The ringleaders had passed notes from village to village threatening that anyone who refused to join the protest would be fined three thalers.[42] In 1683, when a dispute over labour services broke out on an estate in the district of Löcknitz in the Uckermark to the north-east of Berlin, twelve peasant communes joined in a labour strike against the lordship and even formulated a joint petition to the Elector complaining grandilo-quently of the administrator's 'great illegitimate procedures' (*'grosser unverandtwordtlicher Proceduren'*).[43] In a letter countering these com-plaints, the administrator reported to the authorities that the peasants of his lordship had refused to perform their services, stayed away from the demesne whenever they felt like it, arrived only at 10.30 in winter, and brought only tired animals and the smallest wagons to the lordship's farm. When the lordship's stewards pressed them to get on with their work, the peasants beat them or threatened to kill them, laying their scythes about their necks. Since the dispute remained unresolved, joint representations by the peasants continued over the following years, supported, it seems, by the local pastor. Attempts by the authorities to divide the resistance by offering each commune a different deal failed. Despite the appearance of troops and the infliction of corporal penalties on some of the ringleaders, the resistance 'movement' rumbled on for over a decade as the peasants thwarted the lordship's attempts to extract more value out of the subject villagers. There was little sign here of the emasculated serf whose will has been abolished by habits of deference and obedience. When an administrator on the same estate made to hurry a labourer along with his whip during the harvest of 1697, another worker nearby threatened him with his scythe, saying: 'Master, hold back, that does no good and will make you no friends, we don't let ourselves be beaten.'[44]

This was no isolated stand. In the Prignitz, to the north-west of Berlin, a regional protest movement broke out among the peasants in 1700, again triggered by demands for increased labour rents. The peasants showed an impressive ability to organize themselves. A letter of com-plaint from the local nobility observed that 'the common peasantry' had 'joined together most punishably' in order to free themselves from dues and services, and had 'duly collected money from house to house in all villages [of the Prignitz]'. To the chagrin of the noble signatories, the government, instead of simply arresting and punishing the ringleaders, had forwarded the peasants' supplications to the Berlin Chamber Court for consideration. In the meanwhile, no fewer than 130 villages drew up petitions listing their grievances. These documents focused on the efforts of the Junker landlord to reintroduce defunct and illegitimate labour services, such as the cartage of demesne produce to Berlin, without offsetting this against other obligations; there were also complaints about a hidden rise in grain rents through the introduction of larger grain unit measures and the mistreatment of some peasants who had been manacled in the lordship's newly built jail.[45]

What is striking about this and other similar protests (there were major conflicts at around the same time in the Mittelmark and parts of the Uckermark[46]) is the capacity for concerted action and the confidence in higher justice that many peasant protests demonstrate. Events of this kind were ordered by a latent collective memory of the techniques of protest – participants 'knew' how to proceed without being told. The few detailed studies we have of such upheavals also show that peasants found it easy to secure the help and guidance of persons outside their own narrower social milieu. In the protests of the Löcknitz district, the local pastor helped formulate the grievances of villagers in a language that would make sense to the higher authorities of the lordship and the appeal court. In the Prignitz uprising, a local estate administrator, an educated man, took a considerable personal risk in helping to draw up supplications and write letters for the insurgents.[47]

Even in cases where peasant protests did not achieve their immediate end and new labour services were exacted against their will, there were ways of getting around the landlord by stealth. The easiest was simply to sabotage the system by performing labour services to the minimum standard of competence and effort. In a letter of January 1670, the local administrator Friedrich Otto von der Gröben complained to the Elector that the winter services performed by the peasants of Babitz in the Zechlin district were of poor quality – the local people often sent their children to perform services, or arrived for work at ten or eleven in the morning and left again at two, so that a whole week (three days) of services scarcely amounted to one full day's work.[48] In 1728, Major von Kleist, whose family had bought the Stavenow estate in 1717, complained to his peasants that 'many disorders have been observed in the performance of manorial services, since some people bring such poor horse-teams that they can't finish the job, while others work so unconscientiously and disobediently that nothing gets done.' An announcement to this effect was read out to the subjects before the manorial court, but a number of them failed to turn up for the reading and it had little effect.[49] The evidence available suggests that this was a widespread problem in the East-Elbian lands. On estates where rental arrangements were not perceived as legitimate, open protests were merely isolated peaks of resistance in a broader landscape of non-compliance.[50]

The impact of such resistance on the landlords as an economic elite is difficult to assess with any precision. It does seem clear, however, that the readiness of peasants to protest at unilateral hikes in labour rents and to undermine their long-term effectiveness through under-performance or sabotage placed landlords under constraint. When one of the von Arnims inherited part of an estate complex at Böckenberg in the Uckermark in 1752, he found that the fields were full of thorns and 'had been reduced to the poorest condition by peasant labour services'. Von Arnim decided instead to build dwellings with his own capital and settle the land with families of waged labourers working directly for him.[51] Here was one clear example of how peasant recalcitrance depressed the value of labour services, encouraged the use of waged labour, and hastened the transition to a fully wage-based system that would gradually hollow out the 'feudal' constitution of the East-Elbian estates.

GENDER, AUTHORITY AND ESTATE SOCIETY

A very obvious and yet little-remarked feature of the image of the 'Prussian Junker' is its emphatically masculine character. One of the crystallization points for the corporate noble ideology that emerged in the Prussian lands during the late eighteenth and early nineteenth centuries was the concept of the 'integral household' (*ganzes Haus*) under the authority of a benign paterfamilias or *Hausvater*, whose authority and stewardship extended beyond his nuclear family to the peasants, half-holders, domestic servants and others who inhabited the estate. During the seventeenth and eighteenth centuries a flourishing genre of non-fiction works dedicated itself to the notion of the ideal estate, well ordered and self-sufficient, held together by bonds of mutual dependence and obligation and guided by the leadership of a patriarchal family head.[52]

Distant echoes of this ideal type can be discerned in Theodor Fontane's remarkable elegy to the old nobility, *Der Stechlin*, in which the humane virtues of an idealized social elite whose time is passing are embodied in the gruff but lovable country squire Dubslav von Stechlin. The archetype of the paterfamilias is still recognizable in the elderly Stechlin, but the broader appurtenances, male and female, of the household have faded into the background; the head of the house has been lifted out of his setting in order that he might represent the predicaments and subjectivity of his class as a whole (Fontane makes this possible by having Stechlin's wife die young before the novel's action begins). In this sense, Fontane masculinizes the world of the estate in a way that seems alien even to the patriarchal world invoked by the *Hausvaterliteratur* of the previous century. So powerful was Fontane's nostalgic evocation of the Junker caste that it became a kind of virtual memory for the literary classes of late nineteenth- and early twentieth-century Prussia. It was the world of Fontane that the historian Veit Valentin invoked when he described the Prussian Junkers as 'quiet phlegmatic men, arrogant and amiable, splendid and impossible, who rejected anything different from their ilk, were too elevated to boast, called their country seat "house" and their park "garden"'.[53]

The tendency to conceive of the Junker as an emphatically masculine type was reinforced by the association with military service, which left an indelible imprint on the visual imaginings of the Junker class that still shape our perception of who they were. The caricatures that proliferated in the satirical journals of the 1890s and 1900s focused above all on officers in uniform. In the pages of the Munich journal *Simplicissimus*, 'the Junker' is a vain, feckless young man buttoned into grotesquely tight military dress and bent on squandering his inherited wealth at the gaming tables, or a ruthless womanizer and ignoramus who thinks 'Charles Dickens' is the name of a racehorse and mistakes 'matriculation'

16. 'The Junker'. Caricature by E. Feltner from the satirical journal Simplicissimus.

for a Jewish holiday. The physical type immortalized by Erich von Stroheim in Jean Renoir's 1937 film *La Grande Illusion* is still entirely recognizable as one of the canonical modern European types: a slim narrow-waisted body held ramrod-straight, cropped hair, strict moustaches, a posed, unexpressive countenance and the glittering monocle (which can be allowed to drop at intervals for theatrical effect).[54]

The point of this brief digression is not to denounce such constructions as false (for they certainly captured important aspects of what 'the Junker class' meant to their bourgeois admirers and detractors and were, furthermore, internalized to some extent by the Junkers themselves). The point is rather that one of their effects has been to efface from view the women who made estates function in the classic era of commercial manorialism, not only by sustaining the sociability and communicative networks that made life in the Prussian provinces bearable, but by their contributions to financial and personnel management. If we return to the Kleist estate at Stavenow, we find that, during the two decades between 1738 and 1758, the entire estate was managed by Maria Elisabeth von Kleist, the widow of Colonel Andreas Joachim, who had died in 1739. Frau von Kleist pursued outstanding debts with great energy, both through her own manorial court and through suits filed with the Chamber Court in Berlin; she supervised the workings of patrimonial justice on the estate, lent a substantial sum on 5 per cent interest to a neighbour, accepted small savings deposits from various locals (including an apothecary, a fisherman, her carriage-driver, an innkeeper), invested in war bonds and an interest-bearing deposit with the local credit institute of the corporate nobility, and generally oversaw and managed the family estate as a business.[55]

Another striking case is that of Charlotte Helene von Lestwitz, who in 1788 inherited the lordship of Alt-Friedland about seventy kilometres east of Berlin on the edge of the Oder floodplain. Having acquired the estate, she adopted the name 'von Friedland', presumably in order to reinforce her identification with the locality and its people. In the early 1790s, a dispute broke out over use-rights to a lake known as the Kietzer See that lay between her estate and the neighbouring town of Alt-Quilitz. The villagers of Alt-Quilitz claimed the right to cut rushes and grass on the margins of the lake during late autumn when fodder was becoming scarce and winter stores were needed for the cattle. They also claimed the right to dye hemp and flax on the small sandy beaches that dotted the lakeshore on the Alt-Quilitz side. These claims were energetically disputed by Frau von Friedland, who claimed that rush-cutting rights for the entire lake belonged to her lordship – she even conducted a survey of her own subjects with a view to establishing the oral history, as it were, of usage rights to the Kietzer See.

In January 1793, after repeated complaints to the lordship of Alt-Quilitz had failed to provide satisfaction, Frau von Friedland filed a suit with the Berlin Chamber Court. She also authorized her subjects and administrators to arm themselves with clubs, arrest rush-cutting Quilitzer and confiscate their ill-gotten rushes. Her subjects set about this task with zeal and evident enjoyment. When the Berlin Chamber Court finally concluded its deliberations, the outcome was a compromise that aimed to save face for both parties and apportion usage rights to the lake between them. But this was not good enough for Frau von Friedland, who promptly launched an appeal against the verdict. She now shifted the burden of her argument from the scandalous rush-cutting of her neighbours to the deleterious effects of their hemp-dyeing on the fish population of the lake. Guards were posted along the shores by the Friedland lordship to prevent hemp-dyeing, but these were summarily arrested and carried off by a numerically superior force of Quilitz townsfolk. In a subsequent sortie, the hunter (*Jäger*) of the Friedland estate managed to chase off a gang of hemp-dyers by menacing them with his gun; in the confusion that followed, however, the Quilitzer succeeded in seizing and making away with the punt of a Friedland fisherman by the name of Schmah. During the two years while the appeal case ran, Frau von Friedland continued to lead her subjects in their struggle for control of the lake and its resources.

Surveying this case, one is struck not only by the remarkable solidarity between subjects and lordship and the use of ecological arguments, but also by the prominence of the energetic and quarrelsome Frau von Friedland, who was clearly something of a local titan. She was also an 'improving landlord' of a kind that was becoming fashionable in later eighteenth-century Brandenburg. She pioneered the rent-free loan of cattle from her own stud to her subjects (to keep them in manure), she introduced new plants and she restocked depleted woodland – her picturesque forests of oaks, lindens and beeches are today still one of the most attractive features of the area. She also improved schooling on the estates and trained villagers to take on positions as administrators and dairy farmers.[56]

How frequently such matriarchs make an appearance in the annals of the landowning classes and how the conditions for such rural female activism changed over time are difficult to establish. But there is nothing in the sources on the Kietzer See conflict to suggest that contemporaries perceived Frau von Friedland as a bizarre anomaly. Moreover, there are other cases sprinkled across the literature in which we find women zealously engaged as the owners and lords of their estates.[57] These examples suggest, at the very least, that the image promulgated in the prescriptive eighteenth-century literature of manners of the 'Junkerin' knitting, darning, minding the kitchen garden and tending to 'all manner of women's work'[58] did not apply to all households, and that the normative power of such wishful image-making may have been less than we suppose. There is certainly much to suggest that the roles of men and women were less polarized in the noble rural household of the *ancien régime* than they would later become in the bourgeois household of the nineteenth and twentieth centuries. The capacity of eighteenth-century female estate-owners to operate as autonomous agents was underpinned by strong female property rights under law that would be downgraded in the course of the following century.[59]

To a certain extent, these observations about the noble household can be extended to the social milieu of the peasants, villagers and servants, subject and free, who lived on the Junker estates. Here too, although there can be no doubt about the profound structural inequalities between the genders, women were in a stronger position than one might suppose: they co-managed their households (including, in many cases, the control and management of money and accumulation of savings). Women who had brought substantial dowries into a marriage might be co-owners of the household's assets. Women also featured as semi-independent village entrepreneurs, especially in the role of tavern mistress; it was not unusual for blacksmiths or other lesser village notables to lease taverns from the lordship and run them under the management of their wives, who thereby acquired a certain status and social prominence within the village. Women frequently performed agricultural labour, especially when male labour was scarce – the sexual division of labour was less rigid in rural communities than in the towns, where male-dominated guilds made it difficult for women to break into industry.[60] Marrying into the family of her husband did not sever a woman's ties with her own kinship network, so that wives locked in disputes with their husbands could often count on support from members of their own lineage. The importance of such ties was symbolized in the retention by peasant women of the paternal (rather than the marital) surname.[61]

As a factor in determining power relations, gender interacted with the many other social gradations that structured rural society. Whereas the dowried wife of a fullholding peasant was in a relatively strong position to protect her own livelihood against other claimants to income from her household, even after her husband's death or retirement, a less well-off woman who married an already retired peasant was in a far more vulnerable position, since there was no way of ensuring that the household of her husband would continue to finance her upkeep after his death. The question of a woman's retirement benefits after the death of her husband was so sensitive that it was sometimes the subject of special stipulations in the farm occupancy deeds that were signed when a woman married into a new household. In other cases, benefits were settled at the moment of retirement, when the older generation yielded management of the holding to their heirs. Where there was good will, widowed older women could count on certain customary local assumptions about what was a fitting level of provision; where good will was lacking, they might have to seek enforcement of their rights through the manorial court.[62]

The study of disputes arising over illegitimate births has also shed light on how gender roles operated and were defined within rural society. Some parts of Prussia, such as the Altmark, had a surprisingly high rate of illegitimate births. One sample count in the parish of Stapen on the lordship of the Schulenburg family revealed that for ninety-one marriages solemnized in the parish over the period 1708–1800, there were twenty-eight illegitimate births.[63] In such cases, the court authorities were mainly concerned to establish paternity and to define the mother's right to claim support from the male. Court records reveal widely divergent assumptions about male and female sexuality; whereas women were viewed as naturally passive and defensive in sexual transactions, men were seen as driven by an unequivocal will for intercourse. This meant that the burden of the investigation into illegitimate births generally rested on establishing why the woman had complied with the man's wish for sex. If it could be shown that he had won her over with a promise of marriage, her claim to child support might be strengthened. If, conversely, it could be shown that she had a reputation for promiscuity, this might weaken her position. By contrast, the sexual history of the man in question was regarded as irrelevant. In these ways, such investigations were tilted in favour of men. And yet, court proceedings were less discriminatory than one might suppose. Considerable effort was invested to establish the precise circumstances of the impregnation as securely as possible and although fathers were only rarely forced to marry, if they could be clearly identified they were generally made to share in rearing costs.[64]

In any case, gender was only one of several variables that could influence judicial outcomes. Women from high-status peasant families were far better placed than poor ones. They were more likely to receive support from the village elite, which could be decisive in determining the verdict. The men impugned were also more likely to agree to marry them.[65] Poorer women were less well placed in both these respects, but even for them there were ways of getting by as an unmarried mother. Women in this position could make ends meet by performing domestic labour, such as spinning and sewing in other peasant households. They might sometimes succeed in marrying later down the line – the stigma associated with illegitimate birth largely dissipated (even without marriage) if a father could be identified and acknowledged his responsibilities. There is even evidence to suggest that poor women bringing up children on their own, assuming they kept their good health, were in a better position to generate income than married women of the same social status who were bound to a specific household.[66]

One of the most interesting things that emerge from court proceedings of this kind is the self-policing character of village society on the East-Elbian estates. The peasants and other villagers were not helpless, cowering subjects exposed to the arbitrary blows of an alien seigneurial justice. The manorial court was for much of the time the enforcer of the village's own social and moral norms. This is particularly clear in cases where family disputes threatened to leave old or otherwise fragile people without adequate means of support; here the function of the manorial court was often to see to it that the village's own moral economy was enforced in favour of its most vulnerable members.[67] In many cases involving sexual misdemeanours, the proceedings began with a preliminary investigation by the village itself. It was the village that informed the court that there was a case to be answered. The village also oversaw the payments of alimony that followed successful paternity suits. The manorial court thus operated in partial symbiosis with the self-governing structures of the village.[68]

INDUSTRIOUS PRUSSIA

'The power of Prussia,' Frederick II noted in the Political Testament of 1752, 'is not founded on any intrinsic wealth, but uniquely on the efforts of industry' (*gewerblichen Fleiss*).[69] From the reign of the Great Elector onwards, the development of domestic industry was one of the central objectives of the Hohenzollern administrations. Successive Electors and kings sought to achieve this by encouraging immigration to expand the native workforce and by fostering the foundation and expansion of native enterprises. Some existing industries were protected with import bans and tariffs. In certain cases, where the product in question was deemed to be of strategic significance or promised to yield very substantial revenues, the government itself operated a monopoly, appointing managers, investing funds, controlling quality and collecting income.

An effort was made to ensure – in accordance with mercantilist principle – that raw materials did not leave the territory for processing elsewhere. One of Frederick's first decisions as king was to found a new administrative organ, the Fifth Department of the General Directory, whose task was to oversee 'commerce and manufacturing'. In an instruction to its founding director, the king declared that the department's objectives were to improve existing factories, to introduce new manufacturing industries and to attract as many foreigners as possible to take up places in manufacturing enterprises.

Prussian colonization agencies opened in Hamburg, Frankfurt/Main, Regensburg, Amsterdam and Geneva. Wool spinners were recruited from neighbouring Saxony to provide the wool manufacturers of the Prussian lands with much needed labour. Skilled labourers came from Lyon and Geneva to work in the Prussian silk factories, though many of these later returned to their homelands. Immigrants from the German territories of the Empire founded factories manufacturing knives and scissors. Immigrants from France (including Catholics now, in addition to the Protestants of an earlier generation) helped to build up the Prussian hat and leather industries.

Frederick's 'economic policy' took the form of one-off interventions in specific sectors that he judged to be of special importance to the state. Particular attention was paid to the Prussian silk industry, partly because silk was a product for which the raw materials could theoretically be generated within the Prussian lands (provided one found a way of protecting young mulberry tree plantations against the frosts of the winter), partly because the purchase of luxury items made of foreign silk was seen as a major drain on the state's income, and partly because silk was a prestigious commodity associated with elegance and an advanced state of civilization and technical knowledge.[70]

The techniques adopted to stimulate production employed a characteristic mix of incentives and controls. Garrison towns were ordered to plant mulberry trees within their walls. A royal order of 1742 stated that anyone proposing to establish a mulberry plantation was to be provided with the necessary land. Growers who maintained plantations of 1,000 trees or more from their own funds were to be offered a state subsidy to cover the wages of a gardener until the business started to generate a profit. Once the trees were sufficiently mature, growers would be entitled to grants of Italian silkworm eggs free of charge from the government. The government undertook, moreover, to purchase any silk produced on such plantations from their owners. The nascent silk sector was hedged about with special export subsidies, tariff protection and tax exemptions. From 1756, the importation of foreign silk was forbidden altogether for the Prussian territories east of the river Elbe. It is estimated that in all some 1.6 million thalers of government money was invested in the production of silk, most of it dispensed by a special government department with responsibility for silk manufacture alone. This determined nurturing of a favoured industry undoubtedly produced an increase in overall capacity, but there was controversy, even among contemporaries, as to whether this heavily interventionist approach was really the best way to stimulate productivity growth across the manufacturing sector.[71]

In the case of the silk industry, the state was the chief investor and the foremost entrepreneur. The same pattern could be observed across a range of other industries deemed to be of strategic or fiscal importance. There was a royal shipyard at Stettin, for example, and state monopolies in tobacco, timber, coffee and salt, managed by businessmen under the supervision of state officials. There were also a number of private–public partnerships, like that with Splitgerber and Daum, a Berlin firm specializing in war-related industries, including the purchase and resale of foreign munitions, which operated as a private enterprise but was protected by the state from competition and provided with a regular flow of government orders. A much celebrated example of state-driven entrepreneurship was the consolidation of the Upper Silesian iron ore industry. In 1753, the Malapane Hütte in Silesia became the first German ironworks to operate a modern blast furnace. The government also assisted in the expansion of the Silesian linen industry, attracting new workers and technicians through special settlement schemes offering various incentives (such as free looms for newly arriving immigrant weavers).[72] All of these enterprises were protected by a regime of protective tariffs and import bans.

Intervention, at this level of depth, involved the state, and indeed the sovereign himself, in the time-consuming micro-management of specific sectoral problems. We can see this in the government's handling of the ailing salt industry in Halle, Stassfurt and Gross Salze towards the end of Frederick's reign. The salt-works of these towns had lost their traditional markets in Electoral Saxony and repeatedly petitioned the

king for help. In 1783 Frederick entrusted one of his ministers, Friedrich
Anton von Heinitz, with the task of finding out 'whether it would be
possible to process some other product from the salt-pit, such as a
saltpetre or whatever, so that these people can help themselves to some
extent and then sell this product'.[73] Heinitz hit upon the idea of manufacturing blocks of mineral salt and selling them on to the domains administration in Silesia as saltlicks for grazing cattle. He persuaded the local
salt-miners' corporation (*Pfännerschaft*) of Gross Salze to conduct the
necessary experiments and provided them with a royal subsidy of 2,000
thalers to cover costs. The first experiment failed because the ovens in
which the mineral salt was to be extracted were of inadequate quality and
collapsed during firing. A substantially larger subsidy from ministerial
discretionary funds was required to finance the construction of higher-
quality ovens. Heinitz also requested Carl Georg Heinrich Count von
Hoym, the Minister for Silesia and a particular favourite of the king, to
purchase 8,000 hundredweight of his product in the summer of 1786.
Hoym acceded in the first instance but refused to renew the order in the
following year because the salt from the new works at Gross Salze was
of poor quality and far too expensive. Here we see a readiness to
improvise and innovate combined with an ultimately counterproductive
preference for government- (as opposed to market-) driven solutions.[74]

As his heavily interventionist and controlling approach revealed,
Frederick II was out of touch with those contemporary trends in (especially French and British) economic thought that had begun to concep-
tualize the economy as operating under its own autonomous laws and
saw individual enterprise and the deregulation of production as the key
to growth. There was growing controversy – especially after the Seven
Years War – as businessmen began to chafe under the government's
economic restrictions. During the 1760s, independent merchants and
manufacturers in the Brandenburg-Prussian cities protested against the
restrictive and discriminatory practices of the government. They found
some support from within the king's own bureaucracy. In September
1766, Erhard Ursinus, Privy Finance Secretary of the Fifth Department,
submitted a memorandum criticizing government policy and focusing
in particular on what he saw as the over-subsidization of the velvet and
silk industries, both of which produced material of inferior quality at
much higher prices than imported foreign equivalents. The network of
government monopolies, Ursinus went on to argue, created an environ-

17. Frederick the Great visits a factory. *Engraving by Adolph Menzel, 1856.*

ment hostile to the flourishing of trade.[75] Ursinus was not rewarded for his candour. After revelations that he had been accepting bribes from powerful figures in the business community, he was imprisoned in the fortress at Spandau for one year.

A more historiographically influential critique was that of Honoré-Gabriel Riquetti, Count Mirabeau, author of a widely discussed eight-volume treatise on the agricultural, economic and military organization of the Prussian monarchy. A passionate partisan of physiocratic free trade economics, Mirabeau found little to commend in the elaborate system of economic controls employed by the Prussian administration to sustain domestic productivity. There were, he declared, many 'true and useful ways' of encouraging the growth of industry, but these did not include the monopolies, import restrictions, and state subsidies that were the norm in the Kingdom of Prussia.[76] Instead of allowing manufactures to 'establish themselves of their own accord' on the basis of the capital naturally accumulated in agriculture and trade, Mirabeau argued, the king had wasted his resources on ill-advised investment schemes:

The King of Prussia recently gave six thousand écus for the establishment of a watch factory at Friedrichswalde. Such a small project was not worthy of this gift. It is easy to foresee that if this factory is not continually fed with further benefits, it will not sustain itself. Of all useless accoutrements, there is none more useless than a bad watch.[77]

The legacy of nearly half a century of Frederician rule, Mirabeau concluded, was a grim landscape of economic stagnation in which production chronically exceeded demand and the spirit of enterprise was stifled by regulation and monopoly.[78]

This was an overly negative assessment, whose ultimate purposes were polemical (Mirabeau's real target was the French *ancien régime*, which he helped to overturn in June 1789). In defence of the Frederician experiment, one could point out that a number of the state projects launched during this era established the foundations for longer-term growth. The Silesian iron industry, for example, continued to flourish after Frederick's death under the supervision of Count von Reden, Special Industrial Commissar for Silesia. Between 1780 and 1800, its workforce and output increased by 500 per cent. By the mid nineteenth century, Silesia possessed one of the most efficient metallurgical industries in continental Europe. Here was an example of successful state-induced long-term growth and development.[79] The same point can be made for the state-sponsored wool industry established in the Luckenwalde district in the Mittelmark to the south of Berlin. The state may not in the first instance have created a congenial climate for free competition and entrepreneurship, but it did successfully substitute for the absence of a local entrepreneurial elite. No merchant, however wealthy or enterprising, would have seized upon the idea of settling artisans in an area such as Luckenwalde, where there was as yet no industry to speak of. The fructifying activity of the entrepreneurs could begin only at a later point, when a settlement, together with the necessary concentration of local resources and expertise, had already been established with the encouragement of the state. In other words, state-induced development and entrepreneurship were not mutually exclusive – they could be successive stages of the process of growth. As the great nineteenth-century social and economic historian Gustav Schmoller put it: the regime of protectionism and state-induced growth 'had to fall in order that the seeds it had sown could bloom under the sun of [nineteenth-century] industrial liberalism'.[80]

In any case, mid eighteenth-century Brandenburg-Prussia was not an economic wasteland in which the state was the only innovator and the only entrepreneur. The importance of the royal administration as the manager of large-scale manufactures should not be exaggerated.[81] In the Berlin-Potsdam residential city complex, the dominant centre of economic growth in the Prussian central provinces, only one in every fifty factories (*Fabriquen*) belonged to the state or to a public corporation. To be sure, these included some of the biggest concerns, such as the Lager-haus founded by Frederick William I to supply the army, and the por-celain, gold and silver manufactures. However, a number of these enterprises were not controlled directly by the state, but leased out to wealthy businessmen. The role of the state was less prominent in the western provinces, where there were major independent centres of metallurgy (in the county of Mark), silk manufacture (in and around Krefeld) and textiles (around the city of Bielefeld). In these areas, the dominant force in economic life was a confident mercantile and manu-facturing bourgeoisie whose wealth derived not from state contracts but from regional trade, especially with the Netherlands. In this sense, the western territories were an 'object lesson in the limits of state influence on economic developments'.[82]

Even in the central provinces of the Prussian conglomerate, growth in the state sector was dramatically outstripped by the expansion of private sector enterprise. Especially after the Seven Years War, the rapid growth of privately funded and managed middle-sized manufacturing enter-prises (employing between fifty and ninety-nine workers) bore witness to the declining importance of government-steered production. Particularly striking was the growth of the cotton sector, which unlike those of wool and silk, received little governmental assistance. Although Berlin-Potsdam and Magdeburg were the only two production centres of supra-regional importance to compare with Hamburg, Leipzig or Frankfurt/ Main, there were many lesser centres of production in the middle prov-inces of the kingdom. Even in quite small towns, where the chief source of income was agriculture, there could be substantial local concen-trations of craft-based manufacturing activity. Stendal in the Altmark to the west of Berlin, for example, boasted no fewer than 109 master artisans in the textile sector. In many such locations, the second half of the eighteenth century saw considerable structural change, as individual workshops were gradually integrated into dispersed manufacturies. Even small craft towns could be important 'islands of progress' capable of laying the foundations of later industrial development.[83]

Overseeing this accelerated growth outside the state sector was a diverse entrepreneurial elite whose relationship with the government's economic agencies was more complex than the mercantilist model allows. The decades after 1763 saw the rapid consolidation of a new economic elite of manufacturers, bankers, wholesalers and subcontractors. Although they remained closely tied to the old town oligarchies, their economic activities gradually dissolved the structures of the traditional corporate social order. These were not craven 'subjects' whose highest ambition was to capture a few crumbs from the table of the state enterprises, but independent entrepreneurs with a strong sense of their individual and collective interests. They frequently sought to influence the behaviour of the government, sometimes through open protest (such as during the depression of the 1760s, when there was collective protest against government trade restrictions) but more often through personal contacts. This could occur at many levels, from petitions to the monarch himself, to letters to senior central or provincial bureaucrats, to contacts with state agents in the locality, such as tax commissioners and factory inspectors (*Gewerksassessoren*). The investigation into the alleged corruption of Privy Councillor Ursinus of the Fifth Department threw up abundant evidence of private and official contacts with the most respected merchants and manufacturers of Berlin – Wegely, Lange, Schmitz, Schütze, van Asten, Ephraim, Schickler. Such contacts between businessmen and officials were commonplace. We find evidence of them, for example, in the correspondence of Privy Finance Councillor Johann Rudolf Fäsch, Director of the Fifth Department after the departure of Marschall. In Frankfurt/Oder, local officials and businessmen even held regular conferences at which they debated the government's measures to stimulate trade. In 1779, for example, a posse of cotton entrepreneurs – de Titre, Oehmigke, Ermeler, Sieburg, Wulff, Jüterbock and Simon – marched down to the Fifth Department to deliver a stiff protest against recent government measures.[84]

The state, for its part, was more open to influence from this sphere than Frederick's famed contempt for merchants might suggest. The king counted at least a dozen renowned entrepreneurs and manufacturers among his closest personal advisers. The textile entrepreneur Johann Ernst Gotzkowsky, for example, and the Magdeburg merchant

Christoph Gossler were sometimes asked for formal reports on matters of state policy, as were the powerful Krefeld silk manufacturers Johann and Friedrich von der Leyen, who were awarded the title 'Royal Commercial Councillor' (*königlicher Kommerzienrat*) in 1755 for their services to the king.

If the monarch himself and the officials of the central bureaucracy were open to influences from the business community, the same applied to an even greater degree to the local agents of the state in the towns. Many tax commissioners saw themselves less as the executor of the state's will in the locality than as conduits for information and influence from the periphery to the centre. They were easily pressed into the service of local entrepreneurs – in 1768, for example, we find Tax Commissioner Canitz of Calbe on the river Saale demanding that trade restrictions with Saxony be lifted so that local wool manufacturers can sell their wares at the Leipzig trade fair. The candour (even brusqueness) of the reports filed by some provincial officials suggests that they saw their input, based on familiarity with local conditions, as a crucial corrective to the misconceptions of the central bureaucracy.[85]

7

Struggle for Mastery

On 16 December 1740, Frederick II of Prussia led an army of 27,000 men out of Brandenburg across the lightly defended frontier of Habsburg Silesia. Despite the wintry conditions, the Prussians swept through the province meeting only light resistance from Austrian forces. By the end of January, only six weeks later, virtually all of Silesia, including the capital Breslau, was in Frederick's hands. The invasion was the most important single political action of Frederick's life. It was a decision taken by the king alone, against the advice of his most senior diplomatic and military advisers.[1] The acquisition of Silesia changed permanently the political balance within the Holy Roman Empire and thrust Prussia into a dangerous new world of great-power politics. Frederick was fully aware of the shock effect his assault would have on international opinion, but he could hardly have foreseen the European transformations that would unfold from that easy winter campaign.

'FREDERICK THE UNIQUE'

It is worth pausing to reflect on the man who single-handedly launched the Silesian wars and remained the custodian of the Hohenzollern territories for forty-six years – nearly as long as his illustrious predecessor the Great Elector. The persona of this gifted and spirited monarch enthralled contemporaries and has fascinated historians since. Getting a sense of who the king was is no simple matter, however, for Frederick was enormously loquacious (his posthumously published oeuvres run to thirty volumes), but rarely self-revealing. His writing and speech reflected a quintessentially eighteenth-century esteem for *esprit* – the style was aphoristic, light and economical, the tone always detached:

encyclopaedic, amused, ironic or even mocking. But behind the laboured gags of the satirical verses and the cool, reasoning prose of the historical memoirs and the political memoranda, the man himself remains elusive.

About the superiority of his intellect there can be no doubt. Throughout his life, Frederick devoured books: Fénelon, Descartes, Molière, Bayle, Boileau, Bossuet, Corneille, Racine, Voltaire, Locke, Wolff, Leibniz, Cicero, Caesar, Lucian, Horace, Gresset, Jean-Baptiste Rousseau, Montesquieu, Tacitus, Livy, Plutarch, Sallust, Lucretius, Cornelius Nepos and hundreds more. He was always reading new books, but he also regularly reread the texts that were most important to him. German literature was a cultural blind spot. In one of the eighteenth century's funniest effusions of literary bile, Frederick, a grumpy old man of sixty-eight, denounced the German language as a 'semi-barbarian' idiom in which it was 'physically impossible', even for an author of genius, to achieve superior aesthetic effects. German writers, the king wrote, 'take pleasure in a diffuse style, they pile parenthesis upon parenthesis, and often you don't find until you reach the end of the page the verb on which the meaning of the entire sentence depends'.[2]

So visceral was Frederick's need for the company and stimulation of books that he had a mobile 'field library' fitted up for use during campaigns. Writing (always in French) was also important, not just as a means of communicating his thoughts to others, but also as a psychological refuge. It was always his aspiration to combine the daring and resilience of the man of action with the critical detachment of the *philosophe*. His coupling of the two species, encapsulated in the youthful self-description 'roi philosophe', meant that neither of his roles had an absolute claim over him: he passed as a philosopher among kings and a king among philosophers. His letters from the battlefield at the lowest points in his military fortunes pretend to the true stoic's fatalism and immunity from care. The essays on practical and theoretical matters, conversely, breathe the confidence and authority of one who wields real power.

Frederick was also an accomplished musician. His preference for the flute was entirely in character, for this instrument more than any other was associated with the cultural prestige of France. The transverse flutes that Frederick played were a recent invention of the French instrument makers who had transformed the old cylindrical, six-holed flute into the subtle and chromatically versatile conically bored instrument of the baroque era. The most renowned players of the early eighteenth century

18. Johann Gottlieb Glume,
Frederick the Great before
the Seven Years War

were all French. French composers – Philidor, de la Barre, Dornel, Monteclaire – also dominated the flute repertoire. This instrument thus carried a strong note of that cultural superiority that Frederick and many of his German contemporaries associated with France. The king took his flute-playing seriously. His tutor, the virtuoso flautist and composer Quantz, was paid a salary of 2,000 thalers a year, which placed him on a par with some of the most senior civil servants in the kingdom – by contrast, Carl Philipp Emmanuel Bach, a composer of infinitely greater historical significance who worked for Frederick as a keyboard player, was paid only a fraction of this sum.[3] Frederick practised and performed on the flute incessantly, with a perfectionism verging on the obsessive. Even during campaigns, his tuneful warbling could be heard at evening across the Prussian encampments. He was also a gifted composer, though his works were competent and graceful rather than brilliant.

The relationship between Frederick's political writing and his practice as ruler was remarkably straightforward. At the centre of his thinking was the maintenance and extension of the state's power. Notwithstanding its rather misleading title, Frederick's famous early essay *The Anti-Machiavel* set out quite clearly his position on the permissibility of the pre-emptive strike and the 'war of interest', in which rights are in dispute, the prince's cause is just and he is obliged to resort to force in order to prosecute the interests of his people.[4] A clearer blueprint for the seizure of Silesia in 1740 and the Saxon invasion of 1756 could hardly be asked for. He was even more outspoken in the two Political Testaments (1752 and 1768) he penned for the private edification of his successor. The Second Testament spoke with remarkable *sang froid* about how 'useful' it would be for Prussia to absorb Saxony and Polish Prussia (the territory dividing East Prussia from Brandenburg and Eastern Pomerania), thus 'rounding out' its borders and rendering the eastern extremity of the kingdom defensible. There was no reference to the liberation of co-religionists or the defence of ancient right, just uninhibited fantasizing about the state's expansion.[5] It is here that Frederick comes closest to the 'foreign-political nihilism' of which one historian has accused him.[6]

Frederick was also a formidable and highly original historian. Taken as a whole, the *History of the House of Brandenburg* (completed in February 1748), the *History of My Own Times* (completed in a first draft in 1746), the *History of the Seven Years War* (completed in 1764) and his memoir on events during the decade between the Peace of Hubertusburg and the first Polish partition (completed in 1775) amount to the first comprehensive historical reflection on the evolution of the Prussian lands, despite a tendency to superficial judgements.[7] So attractive and cogent are Frederick's historical notes and memoirs that they have shaped perceptions of his reign – and those of his predecessors – ever since. In Frederick II, the sharp awareness of historical change that one senses in the political testaments of the Great Elector and Frederick William I is raised to the level of self-consciousness. Perhaps this was because the absence of a divine providence from Frederick's universe made it impossible for him to embed himself and his work within a timeless order of truth and prophecy. Whereas his father Frederick William I closed his Political Testament of February 1722 with the pious wish that his son and his successors might prosper until the 'end of the world' with 'the help of God through Jesus Christ', the opening passage of Frederick's Testament of 1752 confronted the contingent and fleeting character of all historical achievement: 'I know that the moment of death destroys men and their projects and that everything in the cosmos is subject to the laws of change.'[8]

Throughout his life, Frederick displayed a remarkable disregard for the conventional pieties of his era. He was vehemently irreligious: in the Political Testament of 1768, he described Christianity as 'an old metaphysical fiction, stuffed with miracles, contradictions and absurdities, which was spawned in the fevered imaginations of the Orientals and then spread to our Europe, where some fanatics espoused it, some intriguers pretended to be convinced by it and some imbeciles actually believed it.'[9] He was also unusually relaxed on questions of sexual morality. Voltaire's memoirs recall the case of a man who was sentenced to death for engaging in sexual intercourse with a she-donkey. The sentence was personally annulled by Frederick on the grounds that 'in his lands one enjoyed freedom of both conscience and penis'.[10] Whether or not this story is true (and Voltaire is not always to be trusted on such matters), it conveys an authentic sense of the libertinism that prevailed in Frederick's milieu. Jules Offray de la Mettrie was a sometime star of Frederick's court and author of the materialist treatise *Man as Machine* (*l'Homme Machine*) in which he expounded the view that man is merely a digestive tract with a sphincter at both ends. Mettrie found time during his sojourn in Berlin to write two essays on scurrilous themes: *The Art of Orgasm* (*l'Art de jouir*) and *The Little Man with a Big Prick* (*Le Petit Homme à grande queue*). Baculard d'Arnaud, another of Frederick's French guests, was the author of a study on *The Art of Fucking* (*l'Art de foutre*); Frederick himself is believed to have written a verse (now sadly lost) exploring the pleasures of the orgasm.

Was Frederick homosexual? A contemporary *mémoire secrète* published pseudonymously in London alleged that the Prussian king presided over a court of catamites, enjoying sex with courtiers, stable hands and passing boys at regular intervals during the day. The thankless Voltaire – who had himself once professed his love for Frederick in openly erotic terms – later alleged in his memoirs that the king was in the habit after his *lever* of enjoying a quarter-hour of 'schoolboy amusements' with a chosen lackey or 'young cadet', though he added bitchily that 'things didn't go all the way' because Frederick had never recovered from his father's ill-treatment and was 'unable to play the leading role'.[11] German memoirists responded with dutiful counterblasts stressing the young Frederick's vigorous heterosexuality. It is difficult to say which of these views comes closer to the truth. Voltaire was writing after his estrangement from the king with an eye to the lubricious tastes of the Paris reading public. The tales of early 'mistresses' all come from the world of court rumour, gossip and hearsay. Frederick certainly confided to Grumbkow, one of the most influential ministers at his father's court, that he felt too little attracted to the female sex to be able to imagine marriage.[12] It is impossible – and unnecessary – to reconstruct the king's sexual history; he may well have abstained from sexual acts with anyone of either sex after his accession to the throne, and possibly even before.[13] But if he did not do it, he certainly talked about it; the conversation of the inner court circle around him was peppered with homoerotic banter. Frederick's satirical poem *Le Palladion* (1749), which was read out to great amusement at the king's *petits soupers*, offered reflections on the pleasures of 'sex from the left' and painted a lurid scene in which Darget, one of the Potsdam favourites, was sodomized by a band of lecherous Jesuits.[14]

This was men-only, locker-room stuff and indeed one of the enduring features of Frederick's narrower social milieu was its pungently masculine tone. In this sense, the Frederician court was an elaboration of the Tobacco College he had contemplated with such disgust during his father's reign. The masculinization that had transformed court life after 1713 was not reversed, indeed in some respects it was reinforced. Only during the Rheinsberg years, when Frederick was still crown prince, were women integrated into the social life of his court. Clearly there was not much room within this constellation for a functioning heterosexual marriage. Whether the union between Frederick and his wife, Elisabeth of Brunswick-Bevern, was ever consummated is unclear. What is certain is that from the time of his accession to the throne, Frederick severed social relations with his wife, consigning her to a twilight zone in which she retained her formal rights and attributes as consort and occupied a modest residence of her own (on a very tight budget), but was not encouraged to seek contact with the king.

This was an unusual course of action: Frederick took none of the more obvious contemporary options – he did not divorce her, nor did he banish her from the country or replace her with mistresses. Instead he condemned her to a kind of suspended animation, in which she was scarcely more than a 'representative automaton'.[15] From 1745, she was *persona non grata* at Sans Souci; other women were invited to the king's elegant summer refuge (mostly to Sunday lunch), but not his wife. During the twenty-two years from 1741 to 1762, Frederick was only twice present to celebrate her birthday. Although she continued to preside over what remained of the Berlin court, the horizons of her life gradually narrowed to the perimeter of her suburban residence at Schönhausen. In a letter written in 1747, when she was thirty-one years old, she talked of 'peacefully waiting for death, when God will be pleased to take me from this world in which I have nothing more to do [...].'[16] Frederick's correspondence with her was conducted for the most part in a tone of icy formality and there were occasions on which he treated her with a remarkable lack of feeling. Best known of these is the unforgettable greeting 'Madame has grown fatter', with which he saluted his wife, after years of separation, on his return from the wars in 1763.[17]

Whether all this gets us any further in the quest for the 'real Frederick' is a moot question. Frederick's persona was fashioned around a rejection of authenticity as a virtue in its own right. To the injunction of his brutish father: 'be an honest fellow, just be honest', the teen-age Frederick had responded with a sly, foppish civility, striking the pose of the wry, dissembling, morally agnostic outsider. In a letter of 1734 to his former tutor, the Huguenot Duhan de Jandun, he compared himself to a mirror that, being obliged to reflect its surroundings, 'does not dare to be what nature made it'.[18] A tendency to efface himself as a subject, as an individual, runs like a red thread through his writings. It can be found in the affected stoicism of his wartime correspondence, in the sarcasm and pastiche with which he kept even close associates at a distance, and in his inclination, when reflecting on matters of political principle, to merge the person of the king into the abstract structure of the state. Even Frederick's lust for work, which was immense and never-ending, could be construed as a flight from the introversion that idleness brings. The protective screen Frederick threw up against the cruel regime imposed by his father was never dismantled. Frederick remained the self-styled misanthrope, lamenting the turpitude of humanity and despairing of happiness in this life. In the meanwhile he continued, with astonishing energy, to consolidate his cultural capital. He endlessly practised and played his flute until his teeth fell out, leaving his embouchure in ruins. He read and reread the Roman classics (in French) and honed his French prose-writing skills, devouring the latest works of philosophy and recruiting new conversation partners to fill the places vacated by friends who had died or betrayed him by taking wives.

THREE SILESIAN WARS

Why did Frederick invade Silesia and why did he do so in 1740? A banal answer to this question would be: because he could. The international setting was highly favourable. In Russia, the death of the Tsarina Anna in October 1740 had paralysed the political executive, as court factions struggled to dominate the regency of the infant successor Ivan VI. Britain, though a friend of Austria, had been at war with Spain since 1739 and was thus unlikely to intervene. Frederick also calculated (correctly) that the French would be generally supportive. He possessed the means to carry it off. His father had left to him an army of some 80,000 men, rigorously trained and well supported and equipped, but untested in battle. Frederick had also inherited a substantial war chest of 8 million thalers in gold, bagged in hessian sacks and piled in the cellars of the royal palace in Berlin. By contrast, the Habsburg monarchy, having suffered a sequence of disastrous setbacks in the War of the Polish Succession (1733–8) and the Turkish war (1737–9), was close to exhaustion.

The new Habsburg monarch, Maria Theresa, was a woman. This was problematic, because the laws governing inheritance within the House of Habsburg did not provide for female succession. Foreseeing this difficulty, Emperor Charles VI, the father of three daughters, had invested much effort and money in securing domestic and international approval for the 'Pragmatic Sanction', a technical device that would allow the dynasty to bend the rules. By the time of his death, most of the key states (including Prussia) had signalled their acceptance of the Pragmatic Sanction. But it was doubtful that these undertakings would actually be honoured. Two German dynasties in particular, the Saxon and the Bavarian, had married their eldest sons to nieces of the Emperor in 1719 and 1722 respectively; they later argued that these compacts entitled them, in the absence of a male Habsburg heir, to parts of the monarchy's hereditary lands. During the early 1720s, the Saxons and the Bavarians signed various treaties by which they promised to work together in making good these dubious claims. The Elector of Bavaria even went so far as to forge a sixteenth-century Austro-Bavarian marriage treaty that supposedly awarded most of the Austrian hereditary lands to Bavaria in the absence of a direct male line of succession. There were thus clear indications even before 1740 that trouble would break out when the Emperor died.

Prussia was among those German states that had ratified the Pragmatic Sanction, partly in order to expedite negotiations over the transfer of the Salzburg Protestants to the eastern borderlands of the Kingdom of Prussia in 1731–2. But relations between Prussia and the House of Austria had been deteriorating for some time. The Habsburgs had long regretted their support for Prussia's acquisition of a royal crown in 1701, and from around 1705, when Emperor Joseph I came to the throne, they pursued a policy of containment that aimed at preventing any further consolidation of the Hohenzollern dynasty in Germany. Prussia and Austria fought on the same side, broadly speaking, during the War of the Spanish Succession, but the reports of the British envoys in Berlin reveal frequent tensions and resentments over issues ranging from the acknowledgement of titles to the deployment of coalition troops and delays in the payment of subsidies.[19] Although Frederick William I (who acceded in 1713) was something of an imperial patriot who had no wish to contest the Emperor's primacy, there was periodic friction over Protestant rights within the Empire and fury in Berlin over the Emperor's willingness to have the complaints of the Estates of the Hohenzollern lands aired before the Imperial Aulic Council in Vienna, as if the King in Prussia were just a minor imperial potentate, a 'Prince of Zipfel-Zerbst', as Frederick William himself put it.

The breaking point for Frederick William I was the Emperor's failure in 1738 to support the still outstanding Brandenburg claim to the Rhenish Duchy of Berg. Frederick William's foreign policy was almost exclusively focused on securing the Berg title, and the Emperor had promised, as a quid pro quo for Berlin's approval of the Pragmatic Sanction, to support Brandenburg against the other claimants in the region. In 1738, however, Austria broke this commitment and supported a rival claim. This came as a bitter blow to Frederick William, who is said to have pointed to his son, saying: 'There is the man who will avenge me!'[20] A shared rage over Austrian 'betrayal' did much to bridge the divide between father and son during the last years of the reign, and a secret treaty of April 1739, by which France acknowledged Brandenburg's 'ownership' of the Duchy of Berg, foreshadowed the orientation away from Austria and towards France that would be a feature of his son's early reign. In his 'last address' to his son, delivered when the old king was dying on 28 May 1740, Frederick William warned the crown prince that the House of Austria should not be trusted and would always strive to diminish the standing of Brandenburg-Prussia: 'Vienna will never forsake this invariable maxim.'[21]

Why Silesia? There was an outstanding Hohenzollern territorial claim to various parts of the province, based on the Habsburgs' earlier appropriation of the Hohenzollern fief of Jägerndorf (1621), and the Silesian Piast territories of Liegnitz, Brieg and Wohlau (1675), to which the Hohenzollerns claimed the right of succession. Frederick himself made light of these moth-eaten titles and historians have generally followed him in this, seeing the legal briefs drawn up in support of the Silesian claim as a mere fig-leaf for an act of naked aggression. Whether they should be dismissed altogether is questionable, given the elephantine memory of the Hohenzollern dynasty – and indeed of early-modern European dynasties in general – for unfulfilled inheritance claims.[22] But a more pressing reason for the choice of Silesia was simply that this was the only Habsburg province that shared a frontier with Brandenburg. It happened also to be very lightly defended – there were only 8,000 Austrian troops stationed in the province in 1740. It was a long, thumb-shaped territory that extended to the north-west from the borders of Habsburg Bohemia to the southern margin of the Neumark. Through its length ran the river Oder, whose stream rises in the mountains of Upper Silesia and meanders to the north-west, bisecting Brandenburg and entering the sea at Stettin in Pomerania. Silesia yielded more income in tax to Vienna than any other of the hereditary Austrian lands. It was one of the most densely industrialized areas of early modern German Europe, with a substantial textiles sector specializing in linen manufacture, and its annexation would bring to the Prussian lands an element of productive intensity that they had hitherto lacked.

Yet there is little evidence to suggest that economic factors weighed heavily in Frederick's calculations – the habit of assessing the value of territories in terms of their productive potential had not yet established itself. Strategic considerations were more important. Of these the foremost was probably the apprehension that the Saxons, who also had claims to make against the Austrians, would themselves attempt to take the province, or part of it, if the King of Prussia did not act first. Like Britain and Hanover, Saxony and Poland were at this time in personal union, Elector Frederick Augustus II of Saxony doubling as King

Augustus III of Poland. The lands of the Saxon dynasty thus lay on either side of Silesia and it seemed highly likely that the Saxons would attempt to close the gap in some way. Sure enough, when Charles VI died, the Saxons offered Maria Theresa their support in return for the cession of a land corridor across Silesia between Saxony and Poland. Had this project been realized, the Saxon monarchy would have controlled a vast swathe of contiguous territory completely enclosing Brandenburg to the south and the east. It might well have eclipsed Prussia permanently, with long-term consequences that are difficult to imagine.

Frederick's behaviour around the time of the attack on Silesia suggests a spontaneity verging on recklessness. He acted with breathtaking speed. He appears to have reached his decision to invade within a few days – perhaps in one day – of receiving the news of Charles VI's unexpected death.[23] His contemporary utterances convey a tone of youthful machismo and a thirst for renown. 'Depart for your appointment with glory!', he called to officers of the Berlin regiment about to leave for Silesia. References to his 'rendez-vous with fame' and his desire to 'see his name in the gazettes' recur frequently in the correspondence.[24] To this we should add the personal animus that Frederick had harboured against the House of Habsburg since their involvement in the crisis precipitated by his attempted flight in the summer of 1730. Frederick had experienced in the most intimate way the meaning of Brandenburg-Prussia's subordinate position within the Empire, and though he bore his tribulations with an outward show of equanimity, a smouldering resentment of his lot made itself felt in his refusal to be reconciled to the marriage arranged for him – with Austrian approval – to Elisabeth of Brunswick-Bevern. The emphasis on emotional motivation may run against the grain of Frederick's later historical chronicles, in which he presents himself as the hyper-rational executor of a bloodless *raison d'état*, but it is fully in accordance with his more fundamental beliefs about the motive forces behind historical change: 'It is the lot of human affairs to be guided by the passions of men,' he wrote in his *History of the House of Brandenburg*, 'and reasons which were originally childish can ultimately lead to great upheavals.'[25]

Whatever the relative weight of the motives behind it, the invasion of Silesia committed Frederick to a long, hard struggle over the newly won province. The Austrians counter-attacked in the spring of 1741, but the momentum of their campaign was broken on 10 April by a Prussian victory at Mollwitz to the south-east of Breslau, which gave the signal for a general war of partition, known as the War of the Austrian Succession. By the end of May, France and Spain had pledged in the Treaty of Nymphenburg to support the Bavarian Elector Charles Albert's candidacy for the imperial throne and his dubious claim to most of the Habsburg hereditary lands (France and Spain were to be awarded Belgium and Lombardy for their pains). The League of Nymphenburg eventually included not only France, Spain and Bavaria, but also Saxony, Savoy-Piedmont and Prussia. Had the plans hatched by this coalition been realized, Maria Theresa would ultimately have been left with only Hungary and Inner Austria. Hyena-like, the states of western Europe gathered for the kill, each warily watching the others.

Although the emergence of the Nymphenburg coalition served Frederick's interests in 1741, his commitment to it was half-hearted. He did not wish to see Austria dismembered and he certainly had no desire to see Saxony or Bavaria aggrandized at Austria's expense. After the spring campaign, his money was running out fast and he had no intention of being dragged into further adventures by a coalition whose objectives he did not share. In the summer of 1742, Frederick abandoned his coalition partners and signed a separate peace with Austria. Under the terms of the Treaty of Breslau and a supplementary agreement signed in Berlin, Brandenburg-Prussia agreed to abstain from further campaigning in return for formally acknowledged possession of Silesia.

During the following twenty-four months, Frederick stayed outside the fight, monitoring its progress and making various military improvements. In August 1744, when the balance tipped back in Austria's favour and a renewed counter-offensive against Silesia seemed likely, he re-entered the fray, scoring two further impressive victories at Hohenfriedberg (June 1745) and Soor (September 1745). In December 1745, following a further Prussian victory at Kesseldorf, Frederick once again left the Nymphenburg allies in the lurch to sign a separate peace with Austria. Under the terms of the Peace of Dresden, he agreed to withdraw once again from the war in return for a renewed ratification of his possession of Silesia. Having won two Silesian wars (1740–42 and 1744–5), Prussia would remain a non-combatant throughout the remainder of the War of the Austrian Succession. The Peace of Aix-la-Chapelle, signed in October 1748, formally ended the war and reconfirmed Prussian ownership of Silesia with an international guarantee signed by Britain and France.

Frederick had pulled off an extraordinary coup. For the first time, a lesser German principality had successfully challenged Habsburg primacy within the Empire to place itself on an equal footing with Vienna. In this, the army created by Frederick's father played a crucial role. The Prussian victories of the first two Silesian wars were due above all to the discipline and striking power of Frederick William's infantry. At the battle of Mollwitz (10 April 1741) in southern Silesia, for example, the Prussians initially lost control of the field after an Austrian cavalry charge against the Prussian right-flank cavalry. So great was the panic and confusion among the Prussian horsemen that Frederick was prevailed upon by his experienced commander General Kurt Christoph von Schwerin to flee the field – an incident that would often be retold and embellished by his enemies. But in the meanwhile, the infantry, packed in their lines between the two Prussian flanks, unaware that the king had left the field, moved forward in perfect order, 'like moving walls', according to an Austrian observer, using their coordinated weapon drill to concentrate firepower against the Austrian infantry lines and sweeping all before them. By evening, it was clear that the Prussians, despite heavy casualties, controlled the field.

This was hardly a triumph of resolute leadership, but it demonstrated the potency of the weapon fashioned by Frederick William I. The battle of Chotusitz on the Bohemian-Moravian border (17 May 1742) exhibited some analogous features: on this occasion the Prussian cavalry was worsted by the Austrian horse early on in the action; it was the infantry, deploying with rigour and flexibility on uneven terrain, that broke the Austrian lines with tightly focused enfilade fire. Frederick's rather inept dispositions on the eve of the battle gave as yet little hint of the strategic talent for which he would later be celebrated. At Hohenfriedberg, perhaps the most decisive of the battles fought during the Second Silesian War, Frederick was more securely in control of events and showed an impressive ability to tailor his plans to changing conditions on the field. Here too, the decisive strokes were delivered by the infantry, advancing three ranks deep towards the Austrian and Saxon lines, shoulder to shoulder with sword bayonets fixed, at the regulation speed of ninety paces a minute, slowing to seventy as they closed with the enemy – relentless, unstoppable.[26]

Frederick had opened hostilities in December 1740 with a spontaneous and unprovoked attack, and historians of the later twentieth century viewing these events through the lenses of two world wars have sometimes seen Frederick's invasion as an unexampled act of criminal aggression.[27] Yet there was nothing exceptional in the context of contemporary power politics about an attack of this kind on another's territory – one need point only to the long history of French aggressions in Belgium and the western German lands, or the seizure of the island of Gibraltar by an Anglo-Dutch raiding force in 1704 during the War of the Spanish Succession, or, closer to home, to the bold partition plans of Saxony and Bavaria. One impressive feature of Frederick's war planning was his capacity to stay focused on a specific, circumscribed objective (in this case the acquisition of Silesia) and not to be seduced by allies or good fortune into gambling for higher stakes. This helps to explain why Prussia spent fewer years at war during Frederick's reign than any major European power.[28]

What amazed contemporaries about Frederick's Silesian adventure was the combination of its speed and success with the apparent mismatch between the two opponents – Prussia, a third-rank player in the European system, and Austria, the leading dynasty of the Holy Roman Empire and an established member of the great-power club. Prussia's achievement seemed all the more striking for the fact that it contrasted so sharply with the contemporary fortunes of Bavaria and Saxony. The Bavarians suffered a chain of defeats, in the course of which the Elector Charles Albert was forced to seek refuge outside his country. The Saxons fared little better; having found that there was nothing to gain through their collaboration with the League of Nymphenburg, they changed sides to fight with the Austrians in 1743, in time to stand against Prussia on the losing side at Hohenfriedberg. This unimpressive record cast the Prussian success in sharp relief. In 1740, Prussia had been just one – and certainly not the wealthiest – of a group of German territorial states with the potential to transcend their status within the Holy Roman Empire. But by 1748, Prussia had pulled ahead, eclipsing its closest German rivals.

It was by no means clear, however, that Frederick would succeed in holding on to his booty. The taking of Silesia had created a new and potentially very dangerous situation. The Austrians absolutely refused to be reconciled to the loss of the monarchy's richest province, and declined to sign the Peace of Aix-la-Chapelle in 1748, because it for-malized Prussian possession of the stolen province. The creation of an anti-Prussian coalition capable of prising Silesia out of Frederick's hands and thrusting Prussia back into the ranks of the lesser German territories now became the leitmotif of Habsburg policy. Russia could already be counted on: alarmed at Prussia's unexpected military success, Tsaritsa Elisabeth and her chief minister, Chancellor Alexis P. Bestuzhev-Riumin, came to see Brandenburg-Prussia as a rival for influence in the eastern Baltic and a potential block to Russian westward expansion. In 1746, the Russians signed an alliance with Vienna; one of its secret clauses foresaw the partition of the Hohenzollern monarchy.[29]

So powerful was the Habsburg fixation with Silesia that it brought about a fundamental reorientation of Austrian foreign policy. In the spring of 1749, Maria Theresa convened a meeting of the Privy Confer-ence (*Geheime Konferenz*) whose purpose was to sort out the implica-tions of the Silesian disaster. Present at the meeting was a brilliant young minister, the 37-year-old Count Wenzel Anton von Kaunitz. Kaunitz argued for a fundamental policy rethink. Austria's traditional dynastic ally was Britain and her traditional foe was France. But a detached look at the history of the British alliance, Kaunitz argued, showed that it had yielded little of real use to the Habsburg monarchy. Only the year before, the British had played an ignominious role in the negotiations at Aix-la-Chapelle, pressing the Austrians to accept its loss as irreversible and hurrying to guarantee Prussian possession of Silesia. The root of the problem, Kaunitz argued, lay in the fact that the geopolitical interests of a maritime power such as Britain and those of a continental power such as Austria were objectively too divergent to sustain an alliance. The interests of the monarchy thus demanded that Vienna abandon her unreliable British ally and sue instead for the friendship of France.

This was a radical stance in the Austrian setting, not only because it involved a transformation of the traditional alliance structure, but also because it was grounded in a new kind of reasoning framed not in terms of dynastic authority and tradition, but of the 'natural interests' of a state, as defined by its geopolitical position and the immediate security needs of its territory.[30] Kaunitz was the only participant at the Privy Conference debate of 1749 to take this position; the others, all of whom were older than he, shrank from his extreme conclusions. Yet it was Kaunitz's view that Maria Theresa chose to adopt, and he was duly sent off to work towards a French alliance as ambassador to the court at Versailles. In 1753 he was appointed state chancellor with responsibility for the Habsburg monarchy's foreign policy. The Silesian shock thus dislodged Habsburg foreign policy from the web of assumptions in which it had traditionally been embedded.

The Seven Years War (1756–63) that followed happened because these Austrian and Russian calculations became entangled with the escalating global conflict between Britain and France. During 1755, there were skirmishes between British and French troops in the remote watery plains of the Ohio river valley. As London and Paris drifted back into open war, King George II of Britain looked to prevent Prussia, an ally of France, from falling upon Hanover, the king's German homeland. Just as the French had used the Swedes to menace the Brandenburgers in Pomerania in the early 1670s, the British now offered to finance Russian troop and naval deployments along the borders of East Prussia. The details were set out in the Convention of St Petersburg, which was agreed (though not yet ratified) in September 1755.

Frederick II was deeply alarmed at this threat on his eastern frontier – he was well aware of Russian designs on East Prussia and always tended to overestimate Russian power. Desperate to alleviate the pressure on his eastern frontier, he entered into a curiously open-ended agreement with Britain, the Convention of Westminster of 16 January 1756. The British agreed to withdraw their offer of subsidies from the Russians and the two states decided to undertake joint defensive action in Germany in the event that France should attack Hanover. This was a hasty and ill-judged move on Frederick's part. He did not take the trouble to consult his French allies, although he ought to have guessed that this unforeseen pact with France's traditional enemy would infuriate the court at Versailles and drive the French into the arms of the Habsburgs. Frederick's panic reflex of January 1756 exposed the weakness of a decision-making system that depended exclusively on the moods and perceptions of one man.

Prussia's position now unravelled with perilous speed. The news of the Convention of Westminster sparked fury at the French court, and Louis XV responded by accepting the Austrian offer of a defensive alliance (the First Treaty of Versailles, 1 May 1756), under which each of the two parties was obliged to provide 24,000 troops to the other in the event of its coming under attack. The withdrawal of the British subsidy offer also enraged Elisabeth of Russia, who agreed in April 1756 to join in an anti-Prussian coalition. Over the next few months, it was the Russians who were the driving force towards war; while Maria Theresa took care to confine her preparations to relatively inconspicuous measures, the Russians made no effort to conceal their military build-up. Frederick now found himself encircled by a coalition of three powerful enemies whose joint offensive, he believed, would be launched in the spring of 1757. When the king demanded categorical assurances from Maria Theresa to the effect that she was not combining against him and had no intention of starting an offensive, her answers were ominously equivocal. Frederick now resolved to strike first, rather than waiting for his enemies to take the initiative. On 29 August 1756, Prussian troops invaded the Electorate of Saxony.

Here was another totally unexpected and profoundly shocking Prussian initiative, and the king was alone in deciding upon it. To a certain extent, the invasion was based upon a misapprehension of Saxon policy. Frederick believed (wrongly) that Saxony had joined the coalition against him and had his officers search the Saxon state papers (in vain) for documentary proof. But his action also served broader strategic objectives. In his *Anti-Machiavel*, published shortly after his accession to the throne, Frederick had delineated three types of ethically permiss-ible war: the defensive war, the war to pursue just rights, and the 'war of precaution', in which a prince discovers that his enemies are preparing military action and decides to launch a pre-emptive strike so as not to forgo the advantages of opening hostilities on his own terms.[31] The invasion of Saxony clearly fell into the third category. It allowed Fred-erick to start the war before his opponents had amassed the full strength of their forces. It provided him with control of a strategically sensitive area that would otherwise almost certainly have been used as a forward base – only eighty kilometres from Berlin – for enemy offensives. Saxony was also of considerable economic value; it was ruthlessly milked during the war, supplying more than one-third of Prussia's entire military expenditure, though it is difficult to establish how heavily the issue of finance and resources weighed in Frederick's calculations.

The invasion of Saxony might have been defensible in purely strategic terms, but its political impact was nothing short of disastrous. The anti-Prussian coalition acquired the momentum of self-righteous out-rage. Russia had already put an offensive construction upon the alliance, but the French had not. They may well have remained neutral if Frederick had bided his time and become the victim of an unprovoked attack by either the Austrians or the Russians. Instead, France and Austria now contracted a Second Treaty of Versailles (1 May 1757) with an openly offensive character, in which France promised to supply 129,000 troops and 12 million livres each year until the recovery of Silesia had been accomplished (France was to be rewarded with control of Austrian Belgium). The Russians joined the offensive alliance with a further 80,000 troops (they planned to annex Polish Courland to Russia and compensate a Russian-controlled Poland with East Prussia); the territories of the Holy Roman Empire put forward an imperial army of 40,000 men; even the Swedes joined in, in the hope of grabbing back some or all of Pomerania.

This was not, in other words, just a war to decide the fate of Silesia. It was a war of partition, a war to decide the future of Prussia. Had the allies succeeded in their objectives, the Kingdom of Prussia would have ceased to exist. Shorn of Silesia, Pomerania and East Prussia, along with the lesser territories claimed by various members of the imperial contingent, the Hohenzollern composite state would have returned to its primordial condition: that of a landlocked north German electorate. This would have been in precise accordance with the plans of the key Austrian policy-makers, whose objective was, as Kaunitz crisply put it, 'la réduction de la Maison de Brandebourg à son état primitif de petite puissance très secondaire'.[32]

That Frederick should have prevailed against such a massive preponderance of forces appeared miraculous to contemporaries and still seems remarkable to us. How can it be explained? Clearly the Prussians enjoyed certain geographical advantages. Frederick's control of Saxony gave him a compact territorial base (excluding East Prussia and the Westphalian principalities, of course) from which to launch operations. He was sheltered on the southern fringes of Silesia by the Sudeten mountains of northern Bohemia. His western flank was covered by the British-financed Army of Observation in Hanover; this sufficed to keep the French at bay for a time in that sector. For the four years 1758–61, Prussia received a hefty annual subsidy of £670,000 (roughly 3,350,000 thalers) from the British government, a sufficient sum to cover about one-fifth of Prussian war expenditures. Frederick (who decided early on not to defend either East Prussia or the Westphalian territories) also enjoyed the advantage of internal defensive lines, while his enemies were operating (with the exception of Austria) at a great distance from home. Dispersed around the periphery of the main theatre of operations, the allies found it difficult to coordinate their movements effectively.

There was also, as in virtually all instances of coalition warfare, a problem of motivation and trust: Maria Theresa's obsession with the destruction of the Prussian 'monster' was not shared by most of the other partners, who had more limited objectives. France's concerns were focused primarily on the Atlantic conflict and French interest in the struggle with Prussia dwindled fast after the devastating Prussian victory at Rossbach (5 November 1757). Under a renegotiated Third Treaty of Versailles, signed in March 1759, the French cut their military and financial commitments to the coalition. As for the Swedes and the assorted German territories represented in the imperial army, they were in it for easy pickings and had little inclination to persevere with an exhausting war of attrition. The strongest link in the coalition was the Austro-Russian alliance, but here too there were problems. Neither wished to see the other benefit disproportionately from the conflict and, on at least one crucial occasion, this distrust translated into Austrian reluctance to commit forces to the consolidation of a Russian victory.

But this should not be taken to imply that Prussia's ultimate success was in any sense a foregone conclusion. The Third Silesian War dragged on for seven years precisely because the issue proved so difficult to resolve militarily. There was no uninterrupted string of Prussian victories. This was a bitter struggle, in which success, for Prussia, meant surviving to fight another day. Many of the Prussian victories were narrowly won, costly in casualties and insufficiently decisive to shift the balance of forces engaged in the conflict definitively in Prussia's favour. At the battle of Lobositz (1 October 1756), for example, the Prussians managed to gain tactical control of the battlefield, at heavy cost in men, but left the main body of the Austrian army unbroken. Much the same can be said of the battle of Liegnitz (15 August 1760) against the Austrians in Silesia; here Frederick accurately assessed enemy positions and moved quickly to strike at one of the two separated Austrian armies and disable it before the other could respond effectively. This initiative was successful, but left the Austrian forces in the area largely intact.

There were a number of battles in which Frederick's intelligence and originality as a field commander were brilliantly in evidence. The single most impressive victory was at the battle of Rossbach (5 November 1757) against the French. Here 20,000 Prussians found themselves outnumbered two to one by a combined French-imperial force. As the French-imperials wheeled around the Prussian position, hoping to outflank them on their left, Frederick redeployed with impressive speed, despatching cavalry to sweep away the regiments of horse at the front of the allied advance and repositioning his infantry in a lethal scissors formation from which they could subject the French and imperial columns to heavy fire and attack. Prussian losses totalled 500 men to the enemy's 10,000.

One of the central traits of Frederick's battle-craft was a preference for oblique over frontal orders of attack. Rather than approach in parallel frontal array, Frederick tried where possible to twist his attacking lines so that one end, often reinforced by cavalry, cut into the enemy position before the other. The idea was to roll the enemy up along his own lines rather than assault him head on. It was a mode of manoeuvre that required especially skilled and steady infantry work, particularly where the terrain was uneven. In a number of battles, Prussian attacks from the flank using complex infantry deployments worked with devastating effect. At Prague (6 May 1757), for example, where Prussian and Austrian numbers were roughly matched, Frederick managed to wheel the Prussians around on to the right flank of the Austrians. When the latter redeployed in haste to meet his advance, local Prussian commanders recognized and exploited a gap in the 'hinge' between the old and the new positions and drove a salient through it, irreparably shattering the Austrian force. The classic example of the oblique marching order in action was the battle of Leuthen (5 December 1757), where the Prussians were outnumbered by the Austrians nearly two to one; here a Prussian feint attack gave the impression of a frontal approach while the mass of the Prussian infantry swept around to the south to scoop up the Austrian left wing. In this extraordinary set piece, the 'moving walls' of the Prussian infantry were flanked by coordinated artillery fire as the Prussian guns moved from firing position to firing position along the line of attack.

However, the very same tactics could also fail if they found the enemy prepared, were not supported by sufficient troop numbers or were based on a faulty understanding of the situation in the field. At Kolin (18 June 1757), for example, Frederick tried as usual to wheel around the

19. Battle of Kunersdorf, 12 August 1759. Contemporary engraving.

Austrian right flank and roll the enemy up from the wing, but found that the Austrians, in anticipation of this, had extended their lines across his route of approach, committing him to a disastrous uphill frontal assault against heavily defended and numerically superior positions – here it was the Austrians who won the field, at a cost of 8,000 men to Prussia's 14,000.[33]

In the battle of Zorndorf (25 August 1758) against the Russians, Frederick completely misread the Russian deployment and, wheeling around from the north to roll up the Russian left wing, found that the enemy was in fact facing him head-on; the fighting was savage and losses were very high – 13,000 Prussian and 18,000 Russian casualties. It is still unclear whether we should regard Zorndorf as a Prussian victory, a defeat or simply a brutal stalemate. Frederick's next major encounter with the Russians exhibited some similar features. The battle of Kunersdorf (12 August 1759) opened promisingly with accurate Prussian artillery and infantry fire on the Russian right flank, but soon became a disaster as the Russians turned to construct a solid local front against the Prussian advance and the Prussian infantry got themselves jammed into a narrow depression where they were exposed to the Russian guns. Here again, Frederick showed a flawed awareness of how the battle was unfolding; the unevenness of the terrain made cavalry reconnaissance difficult and he seems to have failed to take adequate account of the poor quality of his intelligence. The cost was hair-raising: 19,000 Prussian casualties of which 6,000 were dead on the field.

Frederick was not, then, infallible as a military commander. Of the sixteen battles he fought during the Seven Years War, he won only eight (even if we give him the benefit of the doubt and count Zorndorf as a victory).[34] Yet it is clear that in most respects he had the edge over his opponents. His isolation was also a kind of advantage – he had no allies to consult. By comparison with Russia, France and Austria, the Prussian military decision-making process was fantastically simple, since the commander-in-chief in the field was also the sovereign and (effectively) the foreign minister. There was no need for the kind of elaborate discussion that slowed the reflexes of the Habsburg monarchy. This advantage was reinforced by the king's personal indefatigability, talent and daring, and by his readiness to recognize where mistakes had been made (including by himself). If one contemplates the course of the Third Silesian War as a whole, it is surprising how often Frederick succeeded in throwing his enemies on to the tactical defensive, how often it was he who defined the terms on which battle would be joined. This was partly due to the by now widely acknowledged superiority of Prussian drill training, which allowed the walls of blue uniforms to turn at will as if on invisible pivots, and to redeploy at twice the speed of most European armies at this time.[35] With these assets Frederick combined the ability to keep a cool head at times of crisis. Nowhere was this more evident than after the catastrophe at Hochkirch (1758), where the king, drenched in the blood of his horse, which had been hit under him by a musket ball, commanded and oversaw a calm and effective withdrawal under fire from the killing ground to a safe defensive position, and thereby prevented the Austrians from driving home their advantage.

Frederick's ability to keep recovering from defeats and inflicting new and painful blows on his enemies was not enough to win the war on its own, but it sufficed to keep Prussia above water for as long as it took for the allied coalition to fall apart. Once it became clear that Tsaritsa Elisabeth was terminally ill, Russia's days in the coalition were numbered. Elisabeth's death in 1762 led to the succession of Grand Duke Peter, an ardent admirer of Frederick, who lost no time in negotiating an alliance with him. Peter did not survive for long – he was thrust from

*20. Portrait of Frederick the Great by Johann Heinrich Christoph Franke
(copy)*

the throne by his wife, Catherine II, and murdered shortly afterwards
by one of her lovers. Catherine withdrew the offer of an alliance, but
there was no resumption of the Austro-Russian compact. The Swedes,
who had little hope of securing their objectives in Pomerania without

great-power support, soon defected. After a string of shattering defeats in India and Canada, the French, too, lost interest in pursuing further a war whose objectives now seemed strangely irrelevant. The peace they signed with Britain at the Treaty of Paris (3 February 1763) left the Austrians high and dry. Their treasury was exhausted. At the Peace of Hubertusburg (15 February 1763), after seven years of bitter struggle and prodigious sacrifice in money and lives, Maria Theresa confirmed the *status quo ante bellum*. In return, Frederick promised that in the next imperial election, he would vote for her son, the future Joseph II.

There is a tendency, when we reflect on the European wars of the mid eighteenth century, to visualize them as diagrams with rectangles and sweeping arrows, or as compact arrays of brightly painted soldiers on the green baize of the war-gamer's table. When we focus on 'moving walls', 'oblique marching orders' and the 'rolling up' of enemy flanks it is easy to lose sight of the terror and confusion that reigned on most battlefields as soon as the serious fighting began. For the troops on an exposed front or flank, coming under fire meant maintaining formation and discipline while projectiles ranging from musket balls to canister shot and cannon balls scythed through closely packed rows of standing men. Opportunities to display individual dash and daring were limited – it was more a matter of mastering an overwhelming instinct to flee and take cover. Officers stood in especially exposed positions and were expected to display absolute calm before their men and each other. It was a question not just of personal bravado, but of the collective ethos of an emergent military-noble caste.

Ernst von Barsewisch, the son of a modest Junker landowner in the Altmark, had been educated at the Berlin Cadet School and later served as a Prussian officer in many of the battles of the Seven Years War. His memoirs, based on diary entries sketched while on campaign, capture the mixture of samurai fatalism and schoolboy camaraderie that could sometimes be observed among officers in action. At the battle of Hoch-kirch, Barsewisch happened to be positioned near the king on a section of the Prussian wing that came under Austrian attack. There was a thick hail of musket balls, most of which were aimed at the chests and faces of the standing men. Just next to the king, a Major von Haugwitz was shot through the arm and shortly afterwards another ball buried itself in the neck of the king's horse. Not far from where Barsewisch was standing, Field Marshal von Keith (a favourite of the king's) was torn from his horse by a shell and died on the spot. The next commander to fall was Prince William of Brunswick, brigadier of Barsewisch's regiment, who was drilled through by a musket ball and fell dead to the ground. His terrified horse, an immaculate white stallion, galloped riderless back and forth between the lines for nearly half an hour. To help master their nerves, Barsewisch and the young noblemen around him engaged in light-hearted banter:

Early in the action I had had the honour that a musket ball had drilled through the peak of my hat at the front just above my head; not long afterwards, a second ball shot through the large upturned rim on the left side of the hat, so that it fell from my head. I said to the von Hertzbergs, who were standing not far from me: 'Gentlemen, should I put this hat back on my head, if the Imperials want it so badly?' 'Yes, do,' they said – 'the hat does you honour.' The eldest von Hertzberg took his snuff box in his hand and said: 'Gentlemen, take a pinch of courage!' I stepped up to him, took a pinch and said: 'Yes, courage is what we need.' Von Unruh followed me and the brother of von Hertzberg, the youngest, took the last pinch. Just as the eldest von Hertzberg had taken his pinch of snuff from the box and was raising it to his nose, a musket ball came and flew straight into the top of his forehead. I was standing right beside him, I looked at him – he cried out 'Lord Jesus' – turned around and fell dead to the ground.[36]

It was through this collective sacrifice of its young men – note the presence of three von Hertzberg brothers on one section of the Prussian line! – that the Junker nobility earned its special place within the Frederician state.

The great majority of first-person battle narratives stem from officers, mostly of noble birth, but this should not be allowed to overshadow the phenomenal sacrifice of humbler men in the field. For every officer killed at the battle of Lobositz, more than eighty private soldiers were slain. In a letter to his family, the cavalryman Nikolaus Binn from Erxleben near Osterburg in the Altmark reported twelve deaths among the men from his home district, including an Andreas Garlip and a Nicolaus Garlip who must have been brothers or cousins, and added reassuringly: 'all those who are not named as dead are in good health.'[37] On 6 October, five days after the battle, Franz Reiss, a soldier of the Hülsen Regiment, described his arrival at the battlefield. As soon as he and his fellows had formed up in line, he wrote, they had come under heavy Austrian cannon fire:

So the battle began at six o'clock in the morning and dragged on amidst thundering and firing until four in the afternoon, and all the while I stood in such danger that I cannot thank God enough for [preserving] my health. In the very first cannon shots our Krumpholtz took a cannon ball through his head and the half of it was blown away, he was standing just beside me, and the brains and skull of Krumpholtz sprayed into my face and the gun was blown to pieces from my shoulder, but I, praise God, was uninjured. Now, dear wife, I cannot possibly describe what happened, for the shooting on both sides was so great, that no-one could hear a word of what anyone was saying, and we didn't see and hear just a thousand bullets, but many thousands. But as we got into the afternoon, the enemy took flight and God gave us the victory. And as we came forward into the field, we saw men lying, not just one, but 3 or 4 lying on top of each other, some dead with their heads gone, others short of both legs, or their arms missing, in short, it was an amazing sight. Now, dear child, just think how we must have felt, we who had been led meekly to the slaughterhouse without the faintest inkling of what was to come.[38]

In the aftermath of an action the battlefield descended into chaos. To remain wounded on the field could be a miserable fate. In the nights that followed the battles of Zorndorf and Kunersdorf, the battlefield echoed with the shrieks of the Prussian wounded being killed by Cossack light troops of the Russian army. Even if they escaped deliberate brutality, wounded soldiers needed determination and good luck to survive. The Prussian army had a relatively large and well-organized surgical support service by the standards of the day, but in the disorder following an action (especially a lost one), the chances of finding one's way in time to proper care might be very slim. The quality of treatment varied enormously from surgeon to surgeon and the facilities for handling infected wounds were very rudimentary.

After Leuthen, where a musket ball bored through his neck and lodged itself between his shoulder blades, Ernst von Barsewisch had the good fortune to run into a captured Austrian soldier who happened to be a Belgian graduate of the surgical school at the University of Lyon. Sadly, the Belgian no longer had his fine surgical tools to work with – his Prussian captor had snatched them as booty. Using the 'very bad and blunt knife' of a shoemaker, however, he was able to hack the ball out of Barsewisch's back with 'ten or twelve cuts'. Less fortunate was Barsewisch's comrade Baron Gans Edler von Puttlitz, whose foot had been shattered by canister shot and had grown infected while he lay out in the cold untended for two nights and a day. The captured surgeon told him that an amputation of the leg below the knee was his only hope, but Puttlitz was too confused or too terrified to consent. The infection gradually spread and he died a few days later. Shortly before he died, he told Barsewisch that he was his parents' only child and begged him to be sure that they were informed of the place of his burial. 'This death affected me greatly,' wrote Barsewisch, 'because this was a young person of about seventeen years, and from his wound he had watched his death draw nearer, creeping slowly, hour by hour.'[39]

The Seven Years War, unlike the Thirty Years War of the previous century, was a 'cabinet war' fought by relatively disciplined bodies of troops equipped and supplied by their own governments through relatively sophisticated logistical organizations. It was thus not marked by the kind of pervasive anarchy and violence that had traumatized the populations of the German territories in the 1630s and 1640s. But this did not mean that the civilians in occupied areas or theatres of combat were not subject to arbitrary exactions, reprisals and even atrocities. Following their invasion of Pomerania, for example, the Swedes demanded from the neighbouring Uckermark in northern Brandenburg contributions totalling 200,000 thalers, double the amount of contribution raised annually by the king from that province.[40] The Hohenzollern provinces of Westphalia were under French and Austrian occupation for much of the war; here the military authorities imposed an intricate system of contributions and extortions, often supported by the kidnapping of local notables as hostages.[41] French soldiers from the defeat at Rossbach committed numerous excesses as they passed through Thuringia and Hessen. 'If one wished to relate all of these disorders, one would never get to the end of it,' one French general reported. 'Over a forty-league compass, the ground was swarming with our soldiers: they pillaged, killed, raped, sacked, and committed every possible horror . . .'[42]

Particularly problematic were the 'light troops' used by most armies at this time. These units were recruited on a voluntary basis, operated semi-autonomously from the regular army, were not provided with the standard logistical support, and were expected to support themselves entirely through exactions and the acquisition of booty. The best-known examples of such troops were the Russian Cossacks and the exotically clothed Austrian 'Panduren', but the French too retained the services of such units. During the first phase of the Russian occupation of East Prussia, some 12,000 light troops made up of Cossacks and Kalmucks rampaged through the country with fire and sword: in the words of one contemporary, they 'murdered or mangled unarmed and defenceless people, they hanged them from trees or cut off their noses or ears; others were hacked in pieces in the most cruel and disgusting manner . . .'[43] During 1761, the Fischer Free Corps, a light unit in French service, broke into East Frisia – a small territory in the north-west of Germany that had fallen to Prussia in 1744 – and terrorized the civilian population with a week of rape, murder and other atrocities. The peasants, drawing on a local tradition of collective protest and resistance, responded with an uprising that reminded some contemporaries of the Peasants' War of 1525. Only through the deployment of French regular army units stationed nearby could peace be restored in the area.[44]

Conflict at this level of intensity was the exception, not the rule, but in all provinces touched by the war, there were substantially raised mortalities, mainly through the so-called 'camp epidemics' that spread from overcrowded troop hospitals. In Kleve and Mark, the mortality for the war years amounted to 15 per cent of the population. In the city of Emmerich, situated on the bank of the Rhine in Kleve, 10 per cent of the townsfolk died during 1758 alone, mainly of diseases contracted from French soldiers fleeing out of north-west Germany. The demographic losses for nearly all of the Prussian lands were breathtaking: 45,000 in Silesia, 70,000 in Pomerania, 114,000 in the Neumark and the Kurmark combined, 90,000 in East Prussia. In all it seems that the war took the lives of about 400,000 Prussians, amounting to roughly 10 per cent of the population.

THE LEGACY OF HUBERTUSBURG

The diplomatic reorientation of 1756, in which the Austrians and the French overcame their ancestral antipathies to form a coalition, was so out of tune with the traditional pattern of inter-dynastic partnerships that it came to be known as the 'diplomatic revolution'.[45] And yet, as we have seen, the events of that year were in large part the working out of a process of change that had been set in train in December 1740.

The Prussian invasion of Silesia was the real revolution. Without this powerful stimulus, the Austrians would not have abandoned their British allies to embrace their French enemies. From here unfolded a sequence of shocks and realignments that runs like a long fuse through the history of modern Europe.

In France, the alliance with Austria, and especially the abject defeat at Rossbach, played disastrously with the home public, raising doubts about the competence of the Bourbon regime that would persevere until the revolutionary crisis of the 1780s. 'More than ever before,' the French Foreign Minister Cardinal de Bernis observed in the spring of 1758, 'our nation is outraged against the war. Our enemy, the king of Prussia, is loved to the point of distraction . . . but the court of Vienna is hated because it is seen as the bloodsucker of the state.'[46] In the eyes of critical French contemporaries, the treaties with Austria of 1756 and 1757 were 'the disgrace of Louis XV', 'monstrous in principle and disastrous for France in practice'. The defeats of this war, the Comte de Ségur recalled, 'both wounded and aroused French national pride. From one end of the kingdom to the other, to oppose the Court became a point of honour.' The first partition of Poland in 1772, in which Prussia, Austria and Russia joined in despoiling one of France's traditional clients, deepened such apprehensions by demonstrating that the new alliance system operated to the benefit of Austria and the detriment of France.[47] To make matters worse, the French monarchy chose to cement the Austrian alliance by marrying the future Louis XVI to the Habsburg princess Marie Antoinette in 1771. She later came to personify the political malaise of Bourbon absolutism in its terminal phase.[48] In short, we can follow at least one strand of the crisis that culminated in the fall of the French monarchy back to the consequences of Frederick's invasion of Silesia.

For Russia, too, the end of the Seven Years War inaugurated a new era. Russia did not achieve the territorial objective Elisabeth had set herself, but it emerged from the conflict with its reputation substantially enhanced. This was the first time Russia had played a sustained role in a major European conflict. Its place among the European great powers was confirmed in 1772, when Russia joined Austria and Prussia in the synchronized annexation of territories on the periphery of the Polish-Lithuanian Commonwealth, and again in 1779, when Russia acted as guarantor of the Treaty of Teschen, signed between Prussia and Austria. The long journey towards full membership of the European concert of powers that had begun with the reign of Peter the Great was now complete.[49]

Russia's combination of expansionism, power and invulnerability eclipsed the threat once posed by the Swedes and the Turks. Russia would henceforth play a crucial role in the power struggle within German Europe – in 1812–13, 1848–50, 1866, 1870–71, 1914–17, 1939–45, 1945–89 and 1990, Russian interventions determined or helped to determine power-political outcomes in Germany. From this moment onwards, the history of Prussia and the history of Russia would remain intertwined. Frederick was no clairvoyant, but he could sense Russia's arrival and was intuitively aware of its irreversibility. After the slaughter at Zorndorf and Kunersdorf, he could never contemplate the spectacle of Russian power without a frisson of dread. The Empire of Catherine II, he told his brother Prince Henry in 1769, was 'a terrible power, which will make all Europe tremble'.[50]

In Austria, the protracted struggle with Prussia prompted, as we have seen, a radical rethinking of external policy. Kaunitz, the mastermind behind the realignment of 1748–56, remained in office until 1792, although his authority declined after the death of Joseph II in 1790. The Prussian challenge also had profound domestic implications. The raft of initiatives launched in 1749–56 and known as the First Theresian Reform focused exclusively on tightening the administration of the Habsburg monarchy in ways that would enable it to strike back effectively at Prussia. The central executive was substantially recast so as to centralize and simplify the most important administrative organs. A new tax regime was introduced, indirectly inspired by the new Prussian administration in Silesia, which was closely watched by the Austrians. The architect of these changes was Count Friedrich Wilhelm von Haugwitz, a convert to Catholicism who had fled his native Silesia when the Prussians invaded. No one was more determined to learn from the example set by Frederick II than Maria Theresa's eldest son and successor, Joseph II. It was partly from contemplating Frederick's achievement that Joseph derived his passionately held view that the Habsburg monarchy must become more like a unitary state if it were to master the challenges it faced in a competitive European environment. His attempts to bring this about in the 1780s would bring the Habsburg monarchy close to internal collapse.[51]

Prussia too bore the marks of the three wars it had fought for Silesia.

The Prussian lands had been extensively devastated and the tasks of reconstruction consumed the lion's share of domestic investment during the last two decades of Frederick's reign. The population of deserted areas and the draining of marshes for new arable land and pasture remained a high priority. In largely agrarian Polish-speaking Masuria, for example, colonists were lured in from Württemberg, the Palatinate and Hessen-Nassau to live and work in a host of new settlements: Lipniak (1779), Czayken (1781), Powalczyn (1782), Wessolowen (1783), Ittowken (1785) and Schodmak (1786). These settlements advanced in parallel with the construction of an extensive canal network designed to drain the waterlands of southern Masuria, hitherto one of the most isolated and underdeveloped regions of the kingdom. The excess water was drawn away into the rivers Omulef and Waldpusch and new villages sprang up on what had once been a vast impassable marsh.[52]

It was above all in the aftermath of 1763 that Frederick began to show an expanded sense of the state's social obligations – especially to those who had risked life and limb in the service of his armies. 'A soldier who sacrifices for the general good his limbs, his health, his strength and his life,' Frederick declared in 1768, 'has a right to claim benefits from those for whom he risked everything.' An institute was established in Berlin to house and care for 600 war invalids and a fund was set up in the war chest from which payments were made to poverty-stricken soldiers who had returned to their rural homes. Low-wage jobs with the excise, customs and the tobacco monopoly and other minor government-paid posts were reserved for soldiers who had fallen on hard times.[53] Perhaps the most dramatic expression of the king's heightened willingness to use the apparatus of the state for the purposes of social provision in the broadest sense was the intensified use of the grain excise and magazine system to counter the effects of food shortages, price rises and famines. In 1766, for example, Frederick suspended the excise on grains in order to ease the flow of cheap imports into Prussia; three years later the excise was reintroduced, but only for wheat, so that the burden of the bread tax fell exclusively on the better-off consumers who chose to purchase white bread. The high point of Prussia's post-war food policy came in the winters of 1771 and 1772, when the administration kept a Europe-wide famine at bay through the controlled release of large amounts of grain from the magazine stocks. The needs of the civilian population were allowed to override the military imperatives for which the magazine system had originally been fashioned. We can thus speak of these massive subsidies in kind as an exercise in social welfare policy.[54]

The war also slowed the pace of administrative integration. In the early years of his reign, Frederick had furthered this process through the creation of new administrative organs such as the Fifth Department, responsible for industrial policy throughout the territories, or the Sixth Department for Military Affairs, another authority with all-Prussian responsibility.[55] Yet the momentum of integration was not maintained after 1763, mainly because the experience of war had taught Frederick that he would never be able to defend his peripheral possessions against attack – it was characteristic that he should allow this geostrategic consideration to determine his economic priorities in peacetime. East Prussia was thus never fully integrated into the grain magazine system, and after the Seven Years War grain transfers from East Prussia to the core provinces were gradually scaled down to make way for cheaper Polish imports.[56] The effort to integrate the western provinces into the fiscal structure of the core provinces also flagged from 1766, when the project of a unitary excise regime was abandoned and the grip of Berlin on the local administrations loosened tangibly thereafter.[57] It is worth emphasizing these retardatory effects, since it is often assumed that war was the crucial driver of state-building in the Prussian lands.

Frederick had greatly increased the international standing of his kingdom through the acquisition of Silesia, yet it would be wrong to presume that this imbued him with confidence and a sense of strength. Indeed, quite the opposite was the case. Frederick remained acutely aware of the fragility of his achievement. In the Political Testament of 1768, he observed that the European continental 'system' comprised only 'four great powers, which overshadow all the others'; Prussia was not among them.[58] In 1776, after a spell of serious illness, the king became preoccupied with the idea that the state he had worked so hard to consolidate would disintegrate after his death.[59] Frederick recognized that there was a fundamental mismatch between Prussia's international reputation and its meagre domestic resources.[60] There was thus, in his eyes, no excuse for complacency. Prussia stood in desperate need of measures to compensate for its power-political weakness. The years after 1763 thus witnessed, as we have seen, a programme of intensified domestic reconstruction. In the diplomatic sphere, Frederick's first priority was to neutralize the threat from Catherine the Great's expanding Russia. In keeping with his own doctrine that a prince should always ally himself with the power best placed to strike at him, Frederick focused his efforts on securing a non-aggression pact with Russia. The high point of this diplomacy was the Prussian-Russian alliance of 1764, which cancelled at one stroke the threat from Russia and the danger of an Austrian revanche.[61]

Since alliances are flimsy things whose duration depends upon the good will of individuals – the treaty of 1764, for example, collapsed in 1781 with the fall from power of the Russian Foreign Minister Nikita Panin – Frederick's ultimate security was still the deterrent effect of his army. Prussia remained heavily armed after the Peace of Hubertusburg. In 1786, it was the thirteenth largest European state in population and the tenth largest in area, yet boasted the third largest army. With a population of 5.8 million, Prussia sustained an army of 195,000. In other words, there was a soldier for every twenty-nine subjects. The size of the army, expressed as a percentage of the total population, was thus 3.38 per cent, a figure that compares with the highly militarized states of the Soviet bloc during the Cold War (the figure for the German Democratic Republic in 1980, for example, was 3.9 per cent). It was the size of this army that moved Georg Heinrich Berenhorst, an adjutant to Frederick II during the Seven Years War, to make the memorable observation that 'the Prussian monarchy is not a country which has an army, but an army which has a country, in which – as it were – it is just stationed.'[62]

Yet the percentage figure is somewhat misleading, since only 81,000 of these soldiers were native-born Prussians. Expressed as a percentage of total population this yields a figure of only 1.42 per cent, which is comparable with the western European states of the late twentieth century (the figure for the German Federal Republic in 1980, for example, was 1.3 per cent). Prussia was thus a highly militarized *state* (i.e. one in which the military consumed the lion's share of resources), but not necessarily a highly militarized society. There was no universal conscription. Peacetime training was still short and perfunctory by present-day standards, the social structure of the army still porous. The hiving off of the military into barracks, where troops could be concentrated and indoctrinated over years of training, was still in the distant future.

And what of the Holy Roman Empire of the German Nation?

Observing the progress of the Seven Years War, the Danish minister Johann Hartwig Count Bernstorff noted that the issue at stake in this great conflict was not simply the ownership of a province here or there, but the question of whether the Holy Roman Empire should have one head, or two.[63] We have seen that the relationship between Brandenburg and Austria had always been troubled by intermittent tension. As Brandenburg began to operate with a degree of autonomy within imperial politics, the potential for conflict grew. Yet for a long line of successive Electors, the pre-eminence of the Emperor and, by extension, of the House of Habsburg, was beyond question. With the invasion of 1740, all this changed. The annexation of Silesia provided Prussia not only with money, produce and subjects, but also with a broad corridor of land extending from the Brandenburg heartland straight to the margins of Habsburg Bohemia, Moravia and the Austrian hereditary lands. It was a dagger poised over the heart of the Habsburg monarchy. (This would prove decisive in the Austro-Prussian War of 1866, when two of the four Prussian army groups entered Bohemia from assembly points in Silesia to crush the Austrian army at Königgrätz.) 'Never will Austria get over the pain of Silesia's loss,' Frederick wrote in his Political Testament of 1752. 'Never will it forget that it must now share its authority in Germany with us.'[64]

For the first time, the political life of the Empire began to orient itself around a bipolar balance of power. The era of Austro-Prussian 'dualism' had begun. Henceforth, Prussian foreign policy would focus first and foremost on safeguarding its place in the new order and containing Vienna's efforts to redress the balance in its own favour. The most prominent example of such power-political sparring was the conflict that broke out over the Bavarian succession in 1778. In December 1777, the Bavarian Elector Maximilian III Joseph died, leaving no direct heirs. His successor, Charles Theodore, agreed with Vienna to exchange his prospective Bavarian inheritance for the Austrian Netherlands (Belgium), and a small contingent of Austrian troops entered Bavaria in mid-January 1778. Prussia's first response was to demand territorial compensation – in the form of inheritance rights to the Franconian duchies of Ansbach and Bayreuth – for Austria's acquisition of Bavaria. But Kaunitz was having none of it and refused to heed Berlin's threats of armed intervention.

In the summer of 1778, Frederick decided to take action and entered

Bohemia, aged sixty-six, at the head of a Prussian army. He now claimed to be acting on behalf of a rival heir to Bavaria, Duke Charles of Zweibrücken. In northern Bohemia Frederick found his progress blocked by a large and well-managed Austrian force. There followed long months of manoeuvring without a serious engagement, in increasingly cold and wet conditions. Frederick was eventually forced to winter his troops in the Sudeten mountains. In withering cold, Austrian and Prussian foraging parties skirmished over patches of frozen potatoes. Although the 'Potato War' produced no decisive engagement, Maria Theresa was keen to bring it to a swift end, even if this meant making concessions. Under the terms of the Treaty of Teschen (13 May 1779), negotiated through Russian and French mediation, she agreed not only to relinquish all of Bavaria, but also to accept Prussia's eventual succession to the duchies of Ansbach and Bayreuth. The episode revealed the extent of Austrian unwillingness to stand alone against Frederick, a symptom of the enduring trauma inflicted by the Silesian wars and a mark of the respect in which his armed forces were now held. Equally significant was the response of the other German states. Many of these sided with Prussia, seeing Frederick as the defender of the Empire's integrity against a predatory power play by the House of Habsburg. In 1785, when Joseph made a second attempt to trade the Austrian Netherlands for Bavaria, Frederick emerged once again as the defender of the Empire against the designs of the Emperor. In the summer of that year, he joined with Saxony and Hanover and a handful of lesser territories in a League of Princes (*Fürstenbund*) whose objective was to defend the Empire against the designs of the Emperor. Within eighteen months, the league counted eighteen members, including the Catholic archbishop of Mainz, vice-chancellor of the Holy Roman Empire and traditionally a Vienna loyalist.[65]

The poacher had become the gamekeeper. It was a role that Frederick learned to play with great panache. Nowhere is this more evident than in his exploitation of the complex confessional machinery of the Empire. The balance between the Catholic and Protestant camps within the Empire remained a live issue in the mid and later eighteenth century. In the reigns of the Great Elector, Frederick III/I and Frederick William I, Prussia had gradually emerged as a champion of the Protestant cause within the Empire. Although his personal interest in confessional squabbles was minimal, Frederick II was an astute executor of this tradition, successfully intervening, for example, in support of the Protestant Estates in territories whose ruling houses had converted to Catholicism (there were thirty-one such conversions between 1648 and 1769). In Hessen-Kassel (1749), Württemberg (1752), Baden-Baden (1765) and Baden-Durlach (1765), Frederick became a co-signatory and guarantor of contracts securing the rights of Protestant Estates against Catholic-convert monarchs. In such cases, he acted, with the enthusiastic support of the Protestant caucus of the imperial diet, as the supposed champion and enforcer of the rights enshrined in the Peace of Westphalia.

What better way for a Protestant power like Prussia to use the structures of the Empire to its own advantage than to define itself as the protector of all Protestants in the German territories? Such a posture vindicated the Protestant view of the Empire, namely that it was not a form of Christian universal monarchy, but rather a power-sharing arrangement between two separate confessional parties who were obliged to practise solidarity and self-help. At the same time, it undermined the standing of the Habsburg Emperor, who was in theory supposed to be the guarantor of the rights of all imperial subjects adhering to a tolerated confession. The Catholic Emperor in Vienna now faced a Protestant anti-emperor in Berlin.[66]

The Seven Years War marked a high point in the confessional polarization of the Empire. By allying with France and continuing to discriminate against her Protestant subjects, Maria Theresa swelled the sails of Frederick's pretensions. So did her husband, Emperor Francis Stephen I, who unwittingly played the Prussians' game, repeatedly urging the Catholic princes to take united action against the *'ligue protestante'* and thereby further accelerating the bifurcation of the Empire into two confessional warring parties. Enormous use was made on both sides of printed propaganda with a confessional bent. Prussian wartime propaganda consistently played up the confessional element in the conflict, arguing that the Habsburg court, in allying with Catholic France, was attempting to inflict a new war of religion on the Holy Roman Empire. In the face of this threat, Prussia represented the only hope for the integrity of the constitutional order established in 1648, indeed its interests were identical with those of 'Germany' itself. Prussian propaganda thus played on the traditional strengths of Hohenzollern confessional policy, pushing Prussia's claim to represent a larger 'Protestant interest'.

What was perhaps less familiar was the tendency to equate this community of interest with the German fatherland *tout court*, an argument that anticipated in some points the idea of a Prussian- and Protestant-dominated 'lesser Germany' that would come to the fore during the dualist struggles of the nineteenth century.[67] These efforts yielded results. A French envoy observed at the end of the Seven Years War that the Peace of Hubertusburg found the Prussians in a stronger position at the imperial diet than ever before, because the Prussians had succeeded in placing themselves at the head of a largely Protestant anti-imperial (for which read anti-Austrian) party in the diet.[68]

PATRIOTS

On 11 December 1757, Karl Wilhelm Ramler attended a service of thanksgiving in the Cathedral of Berlin for the recent Prussian victory at Rossbach. Returning to his apartments, he dashed off a letter to the poet Johann Wilhelm Gleim:

My dearest friend, [. . .] I have just come out from hearing the victory sermon of our incomparable [Court Chaplain] Sack. Almost all eyes were weeping for love, for gratitude. [. . .] If you would like to read some of our victory sermons, I can send them to you. The one on the victory at Prague and the one he gave today are without doubt the best that Mr Sack has held. Our young men have not stopped firing off victory shots and there is shooting all around me as I write these lines. Our merchants have produced every sort of silk ribbon in honour of both victories and we have festooned our vests, hats and swords with them.[69]

The upsurge of patriotic sentiment in the Prussian lands during the Seven Years War is one of the most remarkable features of the conflict. Today it seems natural to assume that wars will reinforce patriotic allegiances, but this had not always been the case in Prussia. The devastating conflicts of the Thirty Years War had rather the opposite effect. In the 1630s, the Elector's subjects did not for the most part identify with him or the territorial composite over which he reigned. Indeed, many felt stronger ties of sympathy with Brandenburg's Lutheran Swedish enemies than with the Calvinist Elector in Berlin. The Brandenburg army of the later 1630s was hated and feared almost as vividly as the occupying forces of the enemy. Even after the notable victory of the

Great Elector against the Swedes at Fehrbellin in 1675, there was little sign of popular enthusiasm for Brandenburg's cause, or of popular identification with the struggles of its head of state. The exalted sense of history in the making that attended the events at Fehrbellin remained confined for the most part to a tiny court-centred elite. Nor was there much popular interest in Prussia's contribution to the Wars of the Spanish Succession (1701–14); these were complex coalition campaigns fought for arcane political objectives in which Prussian troops served far from home.

By contrast, the defeats and victories of the Prussian armies in the Seven Years War generated a widespread sense of solidarity with the objectives and person of the monarch. Johann Wilhelm Archenholtz, an officer who had served in the Prussian army for the greater part of the war and later wrote an epic narrative of its course, recalled the wave of enthusiasm that had animated his fellow Prussians during the darkest years of the conflict. Prussian subjects, he wrote, 'looked upon the king's ruin as their own' and 'took part in the fame of his great deeds'. The Estates of Pomerania had come together of their own accord to raise 5,000 men for the king's service; their example was emulated in Brandenburg, Magdeburg and Halberstadt. 'This war,' Archenholtz concluded, 'generated a love of fatherland that had until then been unknown in the German lands.'[70]

The churches played a crucial role in stirring public enthusiasm for the wartime exploits of the monarch, encouraging the faithful to see Frederick as the instrument of a divine providence. After the – in fact rather marginal – Prussian victory at the battle of Prague in 1757, Court Chaplain Sack delivered a thundering sermon from the pulpit of Berlin Cathedral:

The king has won a victory and lives! Give honour to our God! [. . .] For what would all our victories and conquests be worth, if we had already lost our father? But the providence that protects us was once again his guard and an angel of God shielded him in the hour of greatest danger from all the darts fired down on him by death.[71]

Another preacher celebrating the victory declared that God himself had chosen to distinguish Prussia above all lands and had chosen the Prussians as 'his particular people', 'so that we may walk before him in the light as his chosen people'.[72] The impact of such performances reverberated far beyond the congregations who heard them. Sack's sermons in particular appeared in various printed editions and were widely reread at private gatherings across the central provinces of the Prussian lands.[73]

These efforts to mobilize the population from the pulpit were supplemented by agitation from Prussian literary patriots. There was a striking contrast here: in 1742, Prussia's acquisition of most of Silesia in the Peace of Breslau was greeted by the publication of a small number of Prussian panegyrical texts. Composed in Latin and published in expensive folio or quarto editions, these were clearly intended for a circumscribed and highly educated audience. By the 1750s, however, propagandist scribes and freelance patriots were churning out large numbers of texts in cheap, German-language octavo editions.[74] One highly influential example was the tract *On Death for the Fatherland*, published in 1761 at the nadir of Prussia's military fortunes by Thomas Abbt, a professor of philosophy at the University of Frankfurt/Oder. Abbt's lively and accessible essay argued that the classical values of patriotism, conventionally associated with the ancient republics, were actually better suited to monarchical states, where the monarch personified the abstract power of the state and provided a focus for the loyalty and sacrifice of his subjects. In a 'well-established' monarchy, Abbt suggested, the attachment of the subject to the homeland was reinforced by a love for the person of the monarch, a love so intense that it abolished fear and sanctified death in battle.

[When I behold the king surrounded by his brave soldiers, living and dead,] I am overcome with the thought that it is noble to die fighting for one's fatherland. Now this new beauty that I am reaching for comes more sharply into focus: it delights me; I hasten to take possession of it, tear myself away from anything that could hold me back in an effeminate tranquillity; I do not hear the call of my relatives, but only that of the fatherland, not the din of the fearful weapons, but only the thanks that the fatherland sends me. I join the others who form a wall around the defenceless [king]. Perhaps I will be torn down, satisfied that I have given another the chance to take my place. I follow the principle that the part must, when necessary, be lost in order to preserve the whole.[75]

Death in battle was also an important theme for Christian Ewald von Kleist, a poet, dramatist and melancholic who also served as an officer in the Prussian army. In 1757 he composed a poem in the form of an inscription for the grave of Major von Blumenthal, a friend who was killed during a skirmish with Austrian troops near the town of Ostritz in Upper Lusatia. His verses for the fallen major acquired a certain poignancy in retrospect, because they seemed to foretell Kleist's own death only eighteen months later as a result of a wound received at the battle of Kunersdorf:

> Death for the fatherland is worthy
> Of eternal veneration!
> And how gladly will I die
> This noble death –
> When my fate summons me.[76]

Kleist subsequently became an early prototype of the fallen patriot poet – his poetry and his death merged to become part of the same oeuvre. The verses bestowed unique meaning upon the death by transforming it into a voluntary and conscious act, while the death wove a glimmering halo of sacrifice around the writings and the narrative of his life.

Among the most vociferous of the patriot publicists was the Halberstadt poet and dramatist Johann Wilhelm Ludwig Gleim. Gleim followed the campaigns of the Prussian armies with passionate interest, relying on reports sent to him from the field by his old friend Kleist. Before the outbreak of war, Gleim was best known as the author of esoteric, classically inspired poems on the themes of love, wine and the pleasures of sociability, but after 1756 he became a military balladeer and cheerleader for the Prussian troops in the field. His *Prussian War Songs in the Campaigns of 1756 and 1757 by a Grenadier*, published in 1758 with a supportive foreword by the dramatist Gotthold Ephraim Lessing, represented an innovative attempt to achieve immediacy and emotional impact by adapting the idiom and tone of the marching song. Gleim evoked the movement and confusion of battle; his imaginary protagonist, the Prussian grenadier, provided him with a hinge on which to swivel the perspective of the battle narrative – the grenadier looks to his commander, then to the flag, then to the king, then to his fellow soldiers, then to the enemy. The result was a succession of scenes delivered with a disorienting immediacy, as if through a hand-held camera. This technique seems hackneyed to us, but to contemporaries it was fresh and arresting. It took the reader into the theatre of battle in a way that was new for the Prussian reading public.

The impact of this kind of patriotic literary production was broader than one might imagine. Abbt's *On Death for the Fatherland* quickly sold out in its first edition and appears to have had a powerful mobilizing effect upon readers. Johann Georg Scheffner, a former volunteer who served in the years 1761–3, later recalled that as young men he and his friends in his native city of Königsberg had walked with copies of Abbt's tract in their pockets to the recruitment offices of the Prussian army.[77] In a novel published over a decade after the war, the Berlin publicist Friedrich Nicolai described the wife of a pastor – the main protagonist – who had fallen under the spell of Abbt's rhetoric and demanded that her husband preach the gospel of patriotic sacrifice from his pulpit.[78] Gleim's 'Grenadier Songs' sold out in individual editions and were subsequently reprinted as an anthology.

For the first time, there was widespread interest in the contours of specific battles, not only among academically trained literati, but also within the artisan classes of the towns. The Berlin master baker Johann Friedrich Heyde is a case in point: his diary interspersed notes on the price of rye and other grains (a matter of existential interest for a master baker) with often detailed descriptions of the movements of the Prussian army and of its deployments in key battles. Heyde's involvement in these often distant events is testimony not only to the expansion of patriotic commitments, but also to the rapid popularization of military knowledge. For Heyde there was also a personal dimension; like many Prussian subjects, he had sons serving in the field. The symbiotic relationship between the Prussian garrisons and the towns in which they were stationed and the deep roots that the canton system had put down within the villages ensured a wider and deeper form of sympathetic engagement with the Prussian military enterprise than had ever been witnessed in the Hohenzollern lands before.[79]

In the western provinces, too, there were expressions of sentimental attachment to Prussia, or at least to its ruling dynasty. In Kleve and Mark, for example, there were many who provoked the Austrian occupation authorities by demonstratively wearing black to mark the death of Frederick's brother, August William, heir to the Prussian throne, in 1758. In 1761 there were newspaper reports of a 'patriotic soirée' on the occasion of the king's name day, but the Austrians never succeeded in finding out where it had been held. These manifestations of solidarity with the dynasty were confined to an elite consisting of officials, academics and Protestant clergy, but patriotic images and messages were also transmitted through more popular media. The most striking example must be the famous tobacco tins manufactured for the mass market in Iserlohn (Kleve) during the war. These enamelled containers, decorated with images depicting the victories of the Prussian and allied armies or idealized portraits of the Hohenzollern king and his generals, were enormously popular, not only in the Hohenzollern territories, but across north-western Germany and the Protestant Netherlands. In silk-producing Krefeld, the manufactures churned out silken 'long-live-the-king sashes' (*Vivatbänder*) bearing patriotic slogans and emblems.[80] Patriotism was good business.

Prussian patriotism was a complex, polyvalent phenomenon that expressed much more than a straightforward love for homeland. It reflected a contemporary esteem for extreme affective states – this was, after all, an age of the sentimental, in which a capacity for empathetic emotional response was regarded as a mark of superior character. Tied in with the patriot wave was also the idea that love of fatherland might form the basis for a new kind of political community. As Thomas Abbt argued in his tract on death for the fatherland, patriotism was a force that could overcome the boundaries between the different estates of society. 'Seen from this perspective, the difference between peasant, burgher, soldier and nobleman disappears. For every burgher is a soldier, every soldier a burgher and every nobleman a burgher and a soldier . . .'[81] In this sense, patriotism expressed a yearning for that 'universal society of burghers' that would become the political ideal of generations of nineteenth-century liberals. There was also much enthusiasm for the idea that the bond honoured by the patriot was founded not on compulsion or obligation, but on an entirely voluntary allegiance. As she read Abbt's lines, the pastor's wife in Nicolai's novel experienced 'rapture at the thought that even the subject of a monarchy was not a mere machine, but rather had his own particular value as a person, that love for the fatherland of a nation could vouchsafe a great and new way of thinking . . .'[82]

In other words, patriotism resonated because it bundled together various contemporary preoccupations. Not all the ingredients in the mix were positive or emancipatory. The flip-side of a heightened allegiance to the beleaguered Prussian polity was an intensified derision or even hatred for its foes. The Russians in particular (and especially the Cossacks) figured in most patriotic narratives as bestial, cruel, brutal, blood-thirsty, wretched and so on. Such stylizations drew to some extent on the actual behaviour of Cossack light troops, but they were also rooted in an older set of stereotypes about 'Asiatic' and 'barbarian' Russia that would resonate in Prussian and German culture over the next two centuries. The French were mocked as cowards and braggadocios who talked big but turned tail when the going got tough. Even the German territories fighting in alliance with Austria came in for a drubbing. Gleim's victory hymn after Rossbach includes a long list of strophes lampooning the German contingents; they feature (among others) a Palatine trooper who stands wailing on the field because he has burned his finger; a soldier from Trier who falls while fleeing and mistakes his bleeding nose for a war-wound; a Franconian who squeals 'like a cat in a trap'; a soldier from Bruchsal who tries to evade capture by donning a woman's bonnet; a Paderborner who dies of sheer fright when he sees the Prussians, and many more.[83]

Perhaps the most striking feature of the patriot wave of the 1750s was its fixation on Frederick II. For Abbt, it was above all the flesh-and-blood person of the monarch – rather than the political order that he represented, or the character of the homeland – that commanded the love of the patriot.[84] Throughout the war years there was a flood of poems, engravings, biographies, pamphlets and books celebrating the achievements of the Prussian king, 'Frederick the Great', or in another widely used contemporary epithet, 'Frederick the Unique'. The victories of the Prussian armies were universally celebrated – reasonably enough – as victories of the king. The king's birthdays – formerly rather down-beat events – served as occasions for demonstrative celebrations involving the firing of rifles and the wearing of various royalist memorabilia. In many representations, the king appeared as a towering, almost super-natural figure, as in this dreamlike, almost cinematic passage from Gleim's *Ode to the Muse of War*, written after the slaughter at Zorndorf:

> From a stream of black murderer's blood
> I trod with timid foot upon a hill
> Of corpses, saw about me far and wide
> That none was left to kill, stood up
> And peered, and searched with craning neck
> Through pitch-black clouds of battle-smoke

For the Anointed One, fixed upon him
And the envoy of God, his guard,
My eyes and thoughts . . .

The reference to Frederick as 'the Anointed' (*der Gesalbte*) is noteworthy – Frederick I had been anointed as part of his coronation ceremony, but as there were no further coronations, this ritual was not
performed upon his successors. Here we discern muted echoes of the
exalted conception of monarchy inaugurated by the first king.[85] Frederick was frequently apostrophized, moreover, with the familiar form
'*du*', a usage that suggested a utopian intimacy with the person of the
monarch while awakening associations with the language of prayer and
liturgy. In a verse composed for the occasion of Frederick's return from
the Seven Years War, the celebrated poet Anna Louise Karsch blended
panegyric with the private intensity of prayer, invoking the intimate
mode of address no fewer than twenty-five times over forty-four lines.[86]
In other contexts, the king could appear pitiable, suffering, self-
sacrificial, masked in perspiration and dust, trembling for his men,
drenched in tears for the slain, a man of pains in need of comfort and
protection. It was one of the central themes of Abbt's tract that the
subject's love for the king arises not from the fear of his power, but
from the desire to shield him against the overwhelming might of his
enemies.

There was a sharp irony here, for the king, though sensitive to public
opinion in a general way and aware of the need to impress (especially
when it came to foreign potentates and envoys) appears to have found
this adulation deeply distasteful. He refused, for example, to play any
part in the celebrations organized by the city of Berlin to mark his return
to the capital at the end of the Seven Years War. On 30 March 1763, a
delegation of worthies gathered at the Frankfurt Gate and honour guards
of mounted burghers and liveried torchbearers formed up to accompany
the royal carriage as it re-entered the city and made its way to the palace.
Appalled by the prospect of this welcome, Frederick delayed his arrival
until dusk, slipped away from his hosts and drove unaccompanied to
the palace by an alternative route.[87]

This epic display of diffidence set the tone for the rest of his reign.
Frederick had spent much of his year away from the Berlin court since
the late 1740s, but after 1763 he withdrew almost entirely from the

capital and retreated to the residential complex in Potsdam, spending his winters in the Potsdam city palace and the summers in Sans Souci.[88] The king was content to project the majesty of the state with representative buildings, such as the Neues Palais (which was built at great expense after the Seven Years War but reserved solely for official purposes), but hostile to efforts to focus adulation on his own person.[89] Frederick refused, for example, to sit for official portraits after his accession to the throne. When the renowned engraver Daniel Chodowiecki produced an elaborate image showing the king returning in triumph from the Seven Years War, Frederick rejected it as excessively theatrical.

With the exception of coins such as the Friedrich-d'or and various medallions displaying the king crowned in the laurels of victory,[90] the only image of himself that Frederick deliberately propagated was a likeness of 1764 by the painter Johann Heinrich Christoph Franke (see p. 205). In this painting, the king appears as an old man with sunken lips, sagging face and bent back. He is presented in casual pose, as if captured unawares, raising his trademark three-cornered hat and turning to glance at the viewer as he passes a stone plinth behind him. It is not known whether Franke's painting was commissioned or not, but it was not in any case painted from life. Frederick took to it, sending engraved versions as a mark of his good will to favoured subjects. What precisely he liked about the picture is not known. The modesty of the pose and the sketchiness of the execution may have appealed to him. He may also have seen in the tired old man depicted by Franke a faithful reflection of his own self-image.[91]

The concentration of interest in Frederick's person proved the most lasting legacy of the patriot wave in Prussia. After 1786, when the king died, the Frederician cult roared back into life with a redoubled intensity. There was a massive proliferation of objects commemorating the dead king, from sculpted mugs, tobacco tins, ribbons, sashes and calendars to ornamental chains, newspapers and books.[92] There was a wave of new publications celebrating Frederick. Of these, the most famous and successful was a two-volume compendium edited by Friedrich Nicolai, the most important publisher of the Berlin enlightenment. Nicolai was one of the great majority of Prussian subjects alive in the late 1780s to whom Frederick seemed always to have been on the throne. As Nicolai himself observed, his recollections of the king's life and achievements were intertwined with memories of 'the happy years of my youth and

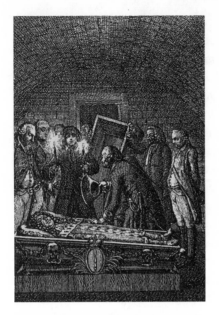

21. *Frederick the Great opens the sarcophagus of the Great Elector in 1750, saying: 'Messieurs, this man accomplished so much!' Engraving of 1789 by Daniel Chodowiecki. By the reign of Frederick the Great, Prussian kingship was marked by an intense awareness of historical legacy.*

the flowering of my manhood'. He had been an 'eyewitness' to the 'indescribable enthusiasm' that had taken hold of his fellow subjects during the Seven Years War, and the extraordinary efforts the king had invested in the reconstruction of war-torn Prussia after 1763. The anecdote collection (which took Nicolai four years to complete) was thus a project that connected the passions of a private identity with the public work of patriotic memory. To contemplate the king, Nicolai declared, was 'to study the true character of one's fatherland'.[93]

Nicolai's was only one – though perhaps the most authoritative – of many such volumes of anecdotes. Anecdote became the most important vehicle for the remembrance and mythologization of the dead king. In these apparently random tatters of memory, the king appeared falling from his horse, responding to impertinence with an indulgent witticism, forgetting someone's name, prevailing over adversity through sheer nerve.[94] He is sometimes the hero, but the majority of anecdotes accentuate his physical presence, his mortality, his modesty, the ordinary trappings of an extraordinary individual. We are presented with a king who commands our respect precisely because he refuses to adopt royal airs.

Being compact and memorable, anecdotes circulated as swiftly in oral as in literary culture, much as jokes do today. Like today's celebrity magazines they catered to an appetite for intimate glimpses of the revered personality. Charged with the humanity of the king, they appeared innocent of politics. Their apparently random quality concealed the artificiality of the image being offered up for consumption. Anecdotes could also take pictorial form. The supplier of the most sophisticated visual anecdotes was the Berlin engraver Daniel Chodowiecki, who provided illustrations for some anecdotal collections, but whose images also circulated independently. Many of these depict poignant unguarded moments in the life of the king, creating an energetic tension between the modesty of his person and the singularity of his status. Like verbal anecdotes, Chodowiecki's images were concise enough to be memorable in their entirety, concentrated enough to reproduce themselves in the mind of the observer. Adolph Menzel's remarkable mid nineteenth-century series of history paintings, which fixed the image of the king for generations of modern Prussians, also preserved the kaleidoscopic quality of the anecdotal tradition, as did the cinematic narratives of his life produced by the film studios of the Weimar Republic and the Third Reich.

Not everyone was inundated by the patriot wave. There was much less enthusiasm for the Prussian cause in the Catholic than in the Protestant areas of the western provinces during the Seven Years War.[95] It is probably safe to assume that Prussian patriotism was a phenomenon above all of the Protestant core areas (including East Prussia), much as it was in late eighteenth-century Great Britain.[96] Here we can speak of a process by which literate Prussian subjects 'discovered' themselves as members of a common polity. Prussianness acquired the 'critical mass' it required to sustain a stable collective identity.[97] By the last decades of the century, the composite term 'Brandenburg-Prussia' was scarcely heard. Frederick was no longer (as of 1772) King *in*, but King *of* Prussia.[98] Contemporaries spoke of 'the Prussian lands' or simply 'Prussia' (although the latter was officially adopted only in 1807 as the collective term for the Hohenzollern territories).

We can thus speak of a thickening of collective allegiances in late eighteenth-century Prussia. It was the visible face of a sedimentary formation whose deeper layers recalled earlier phases of mobilization – the confessional solidarities of the early-modern era, the service ethic, at once dutiful and egalitarian, of Pietism, the remembered trauma of warfare and invasion. And yet there was something fragile about the perfervid patriotism of the Prussians. While British, French and

American patriots died – in theory at least – for their country or for the nation, Prussian patriotic discourses focused above all on the person of Frederick the Great. When Thomas Abbt talked about death for the fatherland, it is difficult to escape the impression that he really meant death for the king. The highly textured stereotypes of national self-identification that we see emerging in the literary and print culture of late eighteenth-century Britain had no counterpart in Prussia. Prussian patriotism was intense, but also rather narrowly focused. With the death of 'Frederick the Unique', Prussian patriotism acquired a flavour of retrospection and nostalgia that it would never quite shake off.

PRUSSIAN POLAND

During the last third of the eighteenth century, the Polish-Lithuanian Commonwealth, a country larger than France, disappeared from the political map of Europe. In the first partition of 1772, Prussia, Austria and Russia joined in slicing off and annexing large pieces of Polish territory on the western, southern and eastern peripheries of the Commonwealth. The second partition of Poland, formalized in the Treaty of St Petersburg in January 1793, saw Prussia and Russia carry off further spoils, leaving to the Poles a grotesquely depleted rump of land stretching from northern Galicia to a narrow stretch of Baltic coast. In the third partition two years later, all three powers joined in gobbling up what remained of the once-mighty Commonwealth.

The roots of this unprecedented erasure of a great and ancient polity lay partly in the deteriorating condition of the Commonwealth. The Polish monarchy was elective, a fact that opened the system to chronic international manipulation as rival powers fought to establish their clients on the throne. The vagaries of the Polish constitution paralysed the system and obstructed efforts to reform and strengthen the state. Particularly problematic were the '*liberum veto*', according to which each individual member of the Polish diet, or Sejm, had the right to obstruct the will of the majority, and the right to form 'confederations' – armed associations of nobles who convened their own diets – to support or oppose the crown. Recourse to this form of 'legalized civil war' was especially common in the eighteenth century, when major confederations formed in 1704, 1715, 1733, 1767, 1768 and 1792, more frequently, indeed, than the diets of the Commonwealth itself.[99]

Poland's inner turmoil was exacerbated by the interventions of its neighbours, and of Russia and Prussia in particular. The policy-makers in St Petersburg viewed Poland as a Russian protectorate and westward salient from which to project Russian influence into Central Europe. Prussia had longstanding designs on the Polish territory between East Prussia and Brandenburg. Neither state had any interest in allowing the Commonwealth to reform itself to the point where it might regain the autonomy and influence it had once enjoyed in European affairs. In 1764, Prussia and Russia collaborated in excluding the Saxon Wettin candidate from the Polish education and installing the Russian client Stanisław-August Poniatowski on the Warsaw throne. When Poniatowski emerged, to everyone's surprise, as a Polish reformer and patriot, Prussia and Russia intervened to thwart his plans. His efforts to establish a unified Polish customs zone met with reprisals from the Prussians. In the meanwhile, the Russians intervened with armed force, extending their patronage networks and supporting the opponents of reform. By 1767, the commonwealth had polarized into two armed camps.

It was against this background of deepening anarchy in Poland that Frederick II produced a first Polish partition proposal in September 1768. The acquisition of a chunk of Poland was one of Frederick's long-cherished dreams – he had mused on this theme in the Political Testament of 1752 – where he famously described Poland as an 'artichoke, ready to be consumed leaf by leaf' – and he periodically returned to it in later years.[100] Of particular interest to him was the area known as 'Royal Prussia', which had been subject to the authority of the Polish Crown since 1454. Royal Prussia was the western half of the ancient principality of Prussia, whose name the Brandenburg Electors and kings had adopted for themselves after 1701. A small part of Royal Prussia was already under Prussian administration, thanks to a complex system of leases that dated back to the beginning of the eighteenth century.[101] Yet it would be overstating the case to call Frederick the sole or chief architect of the partition.[102] It was the Austrians who took a small first bite from the Polish pie, by invading and occupying first Spisz, an archipelago of Polish enclaves in northern Hungary, and then the adjoining territories of Nowy Targ and Nowy Sącz in 1769–70. And it was

Russia whose increasingly aggressive involvement in Polish affairs had done most to undermine the autonomy and peace of the Commonwealth. This in turn provoked legitimate concern over the westward extension of Russian power and fed fears that Poland's disorder might eventually draw the three regional powers into a major conflict.[103]

As turmoil spread across the kingdom of Poland in 1771, Russia and Prussia agreed a partition in principle; Austria joined in the following year. The Convention of Partition of 5 August 1772 justified this act of cold-blooded predation with an almost comically cynical preamble:

In the Name of the Most Holy Trinity! The spirit of faction, the troubles of intestine war which had shaken the Kingdom of Poland for so many years, and the Anarchy that acquires new strength with each passing day [...] give just grounds for expecting with apprehension the total decomposition of the state ... [104]

The smallest share went to Prussia, which acquired 5 per cent of the Commonwealth's territory (the Russians took 12.7 per cent and the Austrians 11.8 per cent). In addition to Royal Prussia itself, the Prussians annexed two adjacent territories, namely the Netze district, a long river valley adjoining the southern border of West Prussia, and the bishopric of Ermland to the east. This regional agglomerate covered the territory that still divided East Prussia from the core provinces of the Hohenzollern monarchy; its acquisition was thus of immense strategic value. The area was also of considerable economic importance to the region, since whoever controlled it could exert a stranglehold on the Polish trade routes via Danzig and Thorn (both of which remained Polish) into the Baltic.

The legal justification for the invasion of Silesia had been slender enough; in the case of Royal Prussia there was no question of any authentic rationale for the annexation beyond the security interests of the Prussian state. The Prussians advanced various fanciful claims along the lines that Brandenburg's inheritance rights to the annexed territories had been usurped in times of yore by the Teutonic Knights and the Polish Commonwealth, and that they were thus merely reclaiming a long-lost heritage.[105] These claims were solemnly reiterated in various official documents, but it is hard to believe that anyone within the Prussian administration took them seriously. It is also worth noting that Frederick made no use – even in internal communications – of ethnic arguments in staking his claim for Royal Prussia. This may appear surprising in retrospect, given that the annexed territories included substantial areas of predominantly German (i.e. German-speaking Protestant) settlement. Germanophone Protestants accounted for about three-quarters of the urban population of Royal Prussia and the Netze district combined, and for about 54 per cent of the population as a whole. In the later nineteenth and twentieth centuries, German nationalist historians cited this German ethnic presence in Royal Prussia as grounds for its rightful annexation.[106] Yet this is a profoundly anachronistic view. The notion that Brandenburg-Prussia had a 'national' mission to unite the German nation under German rule was utterly alien to the Francophone Frederick the Great, who was famously dismissive of contemporary German culture and believed in the primacy of the state, not that of the nation.

Far more important in reinforcing the self-righteousness of the usurpers was a generalized (and characteristically enlightened) assumption that their rule would establish a fairer and more prosperous and efficient administration than had hitherto been known in the region. Prussian views of Polish governance were in general extremely negative – the proverbial expression '*polnische Wirtschaft*' ('Polish management') was used – and still is in some quarters – to describe a chaotic or disordered state of affairs. The Polish nobility (*szlachta*) was widely viewed as wasteful, lazy and negligent in its custodianship of the land. The Polish towns were denounced for their dilapidated condition. The Polish peasantry was held to be languishing in the deepest servitude and misery under the yoke of the imperious *szlachta*. Prussian rule would thus mean the abolition of personal serfdom and liberation from 'Polish slavery'.[107] These were all, needless to say, tendentious and self-interested justifications. The notion that a record of negligent custodianship might attenuate ownership rights, and that acts of usurpation and annexation might be legitimated through an enlightened appeal to the idea of 'improvement' was already a commonplace in the imperialist political cultures of Britain and France, and it served the Prussians well in their new Polish lands.

Frederick renamed his new province 'West Prussia' and throughout the last fourteen years of his reign he intervened more intensively in its domestic affairs than in those of any other province of his kingdom. It was a reflection of his low regard for the native Polish administration

Spisz, Nowy Targ
and Nowy Sącz
occupied by Austria
1768-69

The First Partition of Poland, 1772

|||||| Territories lost to Prussia

Territories lost to Austria

Territories to Russia

The Kingdom of Prussia

–·–·–·– Boundary of Poland

Sebesh

Polotsk

Smolensk

Minsk

Gomel

Chernigov

RUSSIA

Kiev

N
W — E
S

0   50   100   150   200 Miles
0   100   200   300 Kms

that he adopted a relatively centralized approach, sweeping aside the traditional organs of local governance and imposing an alien cohort of officials drawn mainly from the Berlin and East Prussian bureaucracies. Of all the district commissioners appointed to posts in West Prussia following the annexation, only one hailed from the province; most of the rest were East Prussians. There were clear contrasts here with the handling of Silesia thirty years earlier.

In Silesia, too, there was a major administrative restructuring, but an effort was made wherever possible to preserve continuity at the level of the local elites; the reformed judiciary in particular was staffed almost entirely by native-born Silesians.[108] The office of the Silesian provincial minister also ensured Silesia a distinctive place within Berlin's quasi-federal governmental system. The provincial minister, a kind of viceroy with wide-ranging powers who reported only to the king himself, was in a position to resolve key conflicts of interest in a way that was sensitive to the special conditions of the province. By contrast, there was no authoritative centre in West Prussia that was capable of ensuring even a minimal degree of self-administration. The most senior West Prussian official after 1772 was the Chamber President Johann Friedrich Domhardt, but he had no control over the fiscal administration in the province, and the judiciary and military both reported directly to Berlin.[109]

The Catholic church was handled with particular caution. During the preliminary negotiations for the first partition, Frederick had expressed concern that the news of an impending Prussian annexation of exclusively Catholic areas such as the bishopric of Ermland on the eastern periphery of Royal Prussia would provoke public outrage. After 1772, as in Silesia thirty years before, the Prussians went to great pains to preserve the appearance of Catholic institutional continuity in the annexed areas. There was thus no outright expropriation of episcopal properties. Instead ecclesiastical properties were placed under the control of the chamber administrations in East and West Prussia. They thus remained church property in a formal sense; thanks to heavy taxation and other costs, however, only about 38 per cent of the church's gross domain income actually made its way back into the coffers of the clergy.[110] The West Prussian clergy was even worse off; it seems that the state paid only about one-fifth of ecclesiastical estate income back to the church. One might therefore speak of a process of secularization

by stealth. Here again, there were contrasts with the rather more generous arrangements made for the Silesian clergy after 1740.

The mainly Polish nobility of West Prussia did not, by and large, offer
any resistance to the Prussian annexation. In some areas, such as the
Netze district, local landed families boycotted the homage ceremonies
to the new monarch, but there were virtually no acts of outright opposition.[111] Yet this did not suffice to endear the Polish nobles to Frederick,
who spoke of them with contempt in numerous internal government
documents. They were taxed at a higher rate in contribution than their
Protestant (German) counterparts; they were forbidden to meet in
county diets; they were not permitted to form a provincial credit
society.[112] The policies adopted by the king in his other lands to consolidate noble land ownership were inverted in the new province: Frederick
actively encouraged Polish noblemen to sell up their lands and urged the
provincial administration to find Protestant buyers, whether or not these
were of noble stock. As a result, the proportion of noble land in bourgeois hands in West Prussia rose at almost twice the average rate across
the Hohenzollern lands.[113] The reason for these measures, Frederick
declared, was that the Polish magnates were sucking wealth out of the
country by drawing income from their West Prussian estates and spending it in Warsaw. In June 1777 he issued an ultimatum demanding that
landowners with properties on both sides of the Polish border take up
sole residence within West Prussia or lose their West Prussian estates.

The impact of these policies is difficult to establish with any precision.
There was often more bark than bite in Frederick's orders; little seems
to have been done, for example, to implement the ultimatum of 1777.
The king's anti-nobiliary policies were in any case directed mainly at the
small elite of true magnate nobles, such as the Czapskis, Potockis,
Skorzowskis, Prebendows and Dabskis, who remained attached to the
Warsaw court and social scene; Frederick was far less hostile to the
minor Polish nobility in West Prussia and actually took steps to conserve
it.[114]

West Prussia became a focus of energetic administrative intervention:
money was set aside for the improvement of the towns, especially Bromberg and Kulm; marshes were drained; forests were cut back to open up
new arable and pasture land; a new canal was built linking the river
Netze with the Brahe, thereby permitting ships to transfer from the Oder
to the Vistula. Frederick threw himself into countless matters of detail,

ordering, for example, that fruit trees be planted, schools founded, potatoes introduced, dikes built and cheap seed grain made available to the peasantry.[115] The impact of the new regime on the peasants who made up the bulk of the population in the annexed areas was mixed. The talk of 'liberating' them from their former 'Polish servitude' was largely propaganda, since peasants in Polish Royal Prussia had already enjoyed extensive freedom of movement. On the other hand, the installation of independent judicial organs within the domains administration did provide peasants with enhanced legal protection against the caprice of landlords.[116] As the rigorous fiscal regime of the Brandenburg-Prussian state was imposed, taxes naturally went up for everyone, just as they had in Silesia, though they were now more transparent and more evenly distributed. By the mid-1770s, the new province was contributing 10 per cent of Brandenburg-Prussian state revenues, a share that was fully proportional to its size and population. The major capital investments made in the province could thus largely be funded without recourse to external income.

The impact of the annexation on the regional economy is difficult to assess in the absence of precise statistics. Population growth in the urban sector was very slow; this may suggest that heavy taxation drew money away from local investment. The effort to maintain a substantial war chest ensured that much local wealth was taken permanently out of circulation. The introduction of tariffs on the Polish border inevitably caused serious disruption, since they blocked the north–south trade routes that had traditionally been the bread and butter of the towns. On the other hand, the agrarian sector benefited from the boom conditions driven by the opening up of the real estate markets and Britain's enormous appetite for imported grain, a state of affairs reflected in the rapidly rising cash value of landed estates.

The success of the royal administration in winning the trust and loyalty of its new subjects varied from region to region. The ethnically German Protestants who formed the majority in the towns were quickly assimilated into the new system, despite some early cries of protest. Feelings among the Catholics were less favourable, despite Frederick's repeated promises that he would respect the liberty of all Catholics to worship in the accustomed fashion. Among the Polish nobility there was, with good reason, a general feeling of distrust towards the new masters. 'After the sovereign became Prussian,' one observer of conditions in the

Netze district noted in 1793, 'the Polish nobility was no longer what it had been; an element of bitterness entered its character and a distrust of Germans that will long endure.'[117] Yet much depended upon one's precise location within the social structure of the province: the new Cadet School at Kulm, for example, was popular with families of the lesser Polish nobility and after the turn of the century, we encounter many double-barrelled surnames in which the original Polish names have been paired with adopted German equivalents – Rosenberg-Gruszczyński, Hoike-Truszczyński and so on.[118] Among the Kashubian peasants and landlords who farmed the poor sandy soils in the north of the province, there is even some indirect evidence – in the form of Polish-language anecdote collections – for participation in the fashionable cult of Frederick the Great.

Perhaps the people most completely won over to the promises and propaganda of the new regime were the Prussian administrators themselves. Again and again in the documents relating to the administration of West Prussia, we find references to the need to set local institutional and economic life on a 'Prussian footing'.[119] The term 'Prussian' occurs as an antonym to the allegedly Polish vices of servitude, disorder, lassitude. The idea that Prussianness stood for certain abstract virtues acquired a sharper focus in this protracted encounter with subjects from outside the ambit of the Holy Roman Empire. It has often been observed that the experience of colonial government in India and elsewhere gave rise to a ritualized enactment of Britishness that found full articulation only as part of a discourse of moral and cultural superiority. In the same way, an overwhelmingly negative perception of native Polish traditions blended with the sanguine ameliorism of the enlightenment to heighten confidence in the distinctive merits of the 'Prussian way'.

THE KING AND THE STATE

What kind of state did Frederick II bequeath to his successors? 'The state' was one of the central themes in Frederick's political writings. His father, Frederick William I, tended, as we saw in chapter 5, to legitimate his policies in terms of the need to consolidate his own 'sovereignty'. By contrast, Frederick insisted upon the primacy of the state as an abstract structure quite separate from his own person. 'I have held it to be my duty,' he wrote in the Political Testament of 1752, 'to work for the good of the state and to do this in all domains.'[120] 'I have devoted my life to the state,' he told his brother Henry in February 1776. The state represented, in a subjective sense, a vicarious form of immortality: whereas the death of the king would extinguish his consciousness, rendering his hopes for the future meaningless, the state would endure. 'I am thinking only of the state,' Frederick wrote, 'for I know only too well that everything – even if the sky should crash in upon the earth – will be a matter of absolute indifference to me from the moment of my death.'[121] Taken to its logical conclusion, the primacy of the state implied a relativization, a demotion, of the ruler's status. Nowhere is this more pointedly expressed than in the Political Testament of 1752, where Frederick observed that 'the ruler is the first servant of the state. He is paid well so that he can maintain the dignity of his office. But he is required in return to work effectively for the well-being of the state.'[122]

This idea was not new – the idea of the sovereign as the '*premier domestique*' of the state can be found in the writings of Fénelon, Bossuet and Bayle.[123] Samuel Pufendorf, biographer of the Great Elector and the most influential German student of Hobbes, defined the sovereign in functional terms as the guarantor of the state's collective interest. The same line of argument runs through the works of the sometime professor of philosophy at Halle Christian Wolff, whose works Frederick read with admiration as crown prince. Wolff celebrated the ascendancy of an abstract legal and bureaucratic state with wide-ranging responsibilities for health, education, labour protection and security.[124] But no Prussian dynast had ever made this concept so central to his understanding of the sovereign office. It explains (or at least rationalizes) his distaste for the Frederician personality cult and his renunciation of the conventional trappings of dynastic kingship. His insistence on wearing a worn blue officer's coat, stained at the front with long streaks of Spanish snuff, signified the self-subordination of the monarch to the political and social order he represented.

So completely did Frederick personify the idea of the state, that prominent officials came to see serving the monarch and serving the state as one and the same thing. In his inaugural address to the new chamber in Glogau (Silesia), the Provincial President Ludwig Wilhelm Count von Münchow declared that the highest aim of the Prussian administration must be 'to serve the best interest of the King and the country without any ulterior motive'; 'no day – indeed, if possible, not even an hour – should pass without our having rendered some service to the king.'[125] The king was thus more than an employer; he was a model whose values and way of life were internalized by senior civil servants. We get a sense of what this could mean for an individual official from the service diary of Friedrich Anton von Heinitz, head of the Mines and Foundries Department of the General Directory. Heinitz was not a Prussian but a Saxon who had entered Frederick's service in 1776 at the age of fifty-two. In a diary entry dated 2 June 1782, Heinitz noted that one should view hard work in the public cause as an act of divine worship. 'You have as your example the King; who can match him? He is industrious, places obligation before recreation, sees first to his business [. . .]. There is no other monarch like him, none so abstemious, so consistent, none who is so adept at dividing his time . . .'[126]

Frederick also projected the abstract authority of the state through architecture. Nowhere is this idea more eloquently realized than in the ensemble of public buildings that bordered the Forum Fridericianum (now the Bebelplatz) at the beginning of Unter den Linden in the centre of Berlin. One of Frederick's first acts as king was to order the court architect Georg Wenceslaus von Knobelsdorff to build an opera house on the eastern side of the square. The resulting theatre was one of the largest in Europe, capable of seating 2,000 people. Flanking the opera house on the southern side was St Hedwig's Cathedral, built in honour of the king's Catholic subjects – a remarkable monument to inter-confessional tolerance in the heart of a Lutheran city. To drive the message home, the portico of the church was modelled on the syncretic Pantheon of ancient Rome. In the 1770s, a new and capacious royal library was erected on the western side.

There were, to be sure, elements of traditional monarchical self-representation in these projects. But the Forum was also a highly conscious articulation of the cultural purposes of the state.[127] Plans and elevations of the new buildings and of the square as a whole were widely circulated; they were the subject of sometimes controversial discussion in the Berlin journals and salons. Both the opera and the library remained open to the general public after their completion.[128] Perhaps the most remarkable feature of the whole ensemble was the absence of a royal palace. Frederick had originally intended to include one, but he lost interest in the idea after the Second Silesian War. The opera house was thus the first building of its kind north of the Alps not to be physically joined to a royal palace. The royal library was likewise a freestanding structure, highly unusual for the period. The Forum was, in other words, a *Residenzplatz* without a *Residenz* (palace); the contrast with virtually every European square of this kind was not lost on visitors.[129] In architecture, as in the person of the king, the representation of the Prussian state was uncoupled from that of the Prussian dynasty.

If the state were to wean itself from the need for constant dictatorial interventions by the sovereign, it needed to have a coherent fabric of law; here too Frederick practised what he preached, rationalizing the court system and setting the leading jurists of the day to the work of constructing a general law code for the Prussian lands. Though unfinished at his death, the Prussian General Code of Law (1794) would later serve as a kind of constitution for the kingdom of Prussia.[130] In his work towards the post-war reconstruction of Prussia, Frederick was a conscientious servant of the general interest – villages devastated during the wars were rebuilt in accordance with the principle later set out in the General Code that the state is obliged to 'compensate' those who have been 'forced to sacrifice their special rights and advantages to the welfare of the generality'.[131] By the same token, as we have seen, Frederick accepted that the state had an obligation to war-orphans and invalids, and institutional care for these groups was expanded during his reign.

The doctrine of the primacy of the state also framed Frederick's attitude to the international context. It implied, firstly, a fairly cavalier attitude to treaties and other such obligations, since these could at any time be cast aside if they no longer served the state's interest. Frederick applied this idea in practice when he abandoned the Nymphenburg coalition in 1742 and 1745, leaving his allies in the lurch while he settled a separate peace with the Austrians. It can also be seen at work in the invasion of Silesia, which tore holes in the international legal order of the Holy Roman Empire. Yet this was of no concern to Frederick, who, unlike his father, regarded the Empire with contempt. Its mode of governance, he observed in the Political Testament of 1752, was 'bizarre and outdated'.[132] From Frederick's standpoint (and that of Pufendorf and many eighteenth-century German critics of the Reich), the Holy Roman Empire, with its overlapping jurisdictions and its multiple, interpenetrating layers of sovereignty, represented the antithesis of the state principle. There were still angry memories of 1718 and 1725, when delegations of noblemen from the province of Magdeburg had succeeded in winning an appeal against a new Prussian tax before the imperial court in Vienna. One of the important steps by which Frederick consolidated the constitutional autonomy of his kingdom was the agreement of 1746, by which the Habsburg Emperor formally renounced imperial jurisdiction over the territories of Prussia. Frederick could now instruct Samuel von Cocceji, a brilliant jurist who had already served under his father, to draw up a general law code based 'solely upon reason and the legal practices in the [Prussian] territories'. This was an important moment, because it signalled the beginning of the end for the old imperial system. The struggle between Prussia and Austria represented in this sense a conflict between the 'state principle', based on the primacy of the state over all domestic and supra-territorial authorities, and the 'imperial principle' of diffused authority and mixed sovereignty that had been a defining feature of the Holy Roman Empire since the Middle Ages.

For all the sincerity of Frederick's commitment to the abstract authority of the state, however, there were some glaring discrepancies between theory and practice. Although Frederick acknowledged in principle the inviolability of the published laws and rules of procedure, he was prepared, when he deemed it necessary, to override the kingdom's judicial authorities. The most famous example of such unilateral intervention was the 'Miller Arnold Affair' of 1779–80. A miller by the name of Christian Arnold had refused to pay lease-rent to his landlord, Count Schmettau, because the local district commissioner, Baron von Gersdorff, had excavated a system of carp-ponds that had cut off the stream to his mill-wheel and thus deprived him of his livelihood. Having been condemned to eviction by the local court, Arnold and his wife sought the help of the king himself. Despite an irritable cabinet order from the king to the effect that the judgement against Arnold was to be suspended, the Justice Department in Küstrin confirmed the original verdict. Furious at what he saw as the manipulations of a provincial oligarchy, Frederick ordered that the case be transferred to the Chamber Court in Berlin. When the Chamber Court in its turn confirmed the verdict against Arnold, Frederick ordered that the three judges responsible be arrested and detained for one year in a fortress. The commissioner's carp-ponds were to be demolished, the water-course to

Arnold's mill-race restored, and all his costs and losses made good. The case scandalized the senior administration, but it was also a public sensation. In a cabinet order published in newspapers and gazettes across the kingdom, the king justified his actions, stating that his intention was to ensure that 'every man, be he of high or low estate, rich or poor' should receive 'prompt justice' at the hands of an 'impartial law'. In short: a gross breach in legal procedure was justified in terms of a higher ethical principle.[133]

Frederick's concept of the state was also less inclusive in a territorial sense than his father's had been. He was much less concerned with the integration of the outlying territories. Many of the mercantilist economic regulations applied to the Brandenburg heartland were not extended to the western provinces, whose goods were treated for taxation purposes like foreign merchandise. The government's efforts to integrate East Prussia into the grain economy of the entire kingdom through the magazine system slackened during Frederick's reign. The canton system was not extended throughout the western provinces. The three regiments of the city of Wesel, he noted in 1768, have no cantons, 'because the population of these provinces is not suitable for military service; it is limp and soft, and when the man of Kleve is transferred far from his home, he suffers from homesickness, like the Swiss'.[134] Little attempt was made to integrate the small outlying principality of Neuenburg-Neuchâtel, a French-speaking canton of Switzerland acquired in personal union by Frederick I in 1707. The Prussian governor was absent during long periods of the reign of Frederick the Great, so that the influence of Berlin was scarcely felt.[135]

Frederick assigned clear priority to the central provinces of the kingdom. In a revealing passage of the Political Testament of 1768, he even declared that only Brandenburg, Magdeburg, Halberstadt and Silesia 'constituted the actual body of the state'. This was in part a matter of military logic. What distinguished the central lands was the fact that they could 'defend themselves, as long as the whole of Europe [did] not unite against their sovereign'.[136] East Prussia and the western possessions, by contrast, would have to be given up as soon as hostilities began. Perhaps this helps to explain why Frederick discontinued the momentous East Prussian reconstruction programme his father had launched.[137] The conduct of his subjects under foreign occupation during the Seven Years War also seems to have given him pause. He was particularly resentful of the fact that the Estates of East Prussia had sworn an oath of fealty to his nemesis Tsaritsa Elisabeth in 1758. After 1763, Frederick, the indefatigable chief inspector of his realm, never made a single visit to East Prussia. He simply ordered the East Prussian chamber presidents to report to him in Potsdam or to attend him at his headquarters during the annual manoeuvres in West Prussia.[138] This reflected a significant demotion in the importance of this province, which had been something of a fetish to Frederick William I and his grandfather the Great Elector.

If we read them literally, Frederick's comments on the state sometimes seem to imply that the functions of the sovereign have been partly absorbed into the impersonal collective structures of an administration working in accordance with transparent rules and regulations. Yet the reality could hardly have been more different, for the governance of Prussia during Frederick's reign was an intensely personal affair; indeed, in some respects the political process was even more concentrated on the person of the king than it had been under his father, Frederick William I. His father had created a collegial system of ministerial government in which the monarch often took his cue from the recommendations of a powerful council of ministers. But this system fell into disuse after Frederick's accession to the throne. His personal contacts with ministers became ever more rare after 1763, as their functions were duplicated and partly displaced through the king's growing reliance on cabinet secretaries attached directly to his own person.

The political process thus came to centre more and more around the small team of secretaries who controlled access to the king, oversaw his correspondence, kept him up to date on developments and advised him on policy issues. Whereas the secretaries travelled around with the monarch, the ministers generally remained in Berlin. While the ministers tended to be aristocratic grandees such as Karl Abraham Freiherr von Zedlitz (the minister charged with educational affairs), the secretaries were mostly commoners. A characteristic example was the reclusive but enormously influential August Friedrich Eichel, the son of a Prussian army sergeant who usually began work at four o'clock in the morning. Under Frederick William I, responsibility and influence had been tied to the function of the individual within the administrative system; under Frederick, by contrast, proximity to the sovereign was the decisive determinant of power and influence.

Paradoxically, this concentration of power and responsibility in the king reversed the centralizing impetus of the reforms introduced by Frederick William I. By communing directly with the chamber officials in the provinces, Frederick undermined the authority of the General Directory, whose purpose was to act as the supervisory authority overseeing the various provincial officialdoms. On many occasions, Frederick even issued orders to the provincial chambers without informing the central administration, thus enhancing the authority of the provincial administrators, shifting power away from the centre and loosening the sinews of the territorial state structure.[139]

Frederick saw no reason to doubt the efficacy of this highly personalized system. As he pointed out in the Political Testament of 1752, it was necessary 'in a state like this one that the prince conducts his affairs himself, because if he is clever he merely pursues the interest of the state, whereas a minister always follows ulterior motives that touch upon his own interests . . .'[140] In other words, the interests of the state and those of the monarch were quite simply identical in a way that did not apply to any other living person. The hitch with this arrangement lay in the conditional clause 'if he is clever'. The Frederician system worked well with the indefatigable, far-sighted Frederick at the helm, applying his quick and capacious intellect, not to mention his courage and decisiveness, to the problems that came to his desk. But what if the king were not a genius-statesman? What if he found it difficult to resolve dilemmas? What if he were hesitant and risk-averse? What, in short, if he were an ordinary man? With a monarch like that in the driving seat, how would this system function under pressure? Frederick, we should remember, was the last of a freakish run of abnormally gifted Hohenzollern rulers. Their like would not be seen again in the history of the Hohenzollern dynasty. Without the discipline and focus of a powerful figure at the centre, there was the danger that the Frederician system might splinter into warring factions, as ministers and cabinet secretaries competed for control of their overlapping jurisdictions.

8

Dare to Know!

CONVERSATION

The Prussian enlightenment was about conversation. It was about a critical, respectful, open-ended dialogue between free and autonomous subjects. Conversation was important because it permitted the sharpening and refinement of judgement. In a famous essay on the nature of enlightenment, the Königsberg philosopher Immanuel Kant declared that

Enlightenment refers to man's departure from his self-imposed tutelage. Tutelage means the inability to make use of one's own reason without the guidance of another. This tutelage is self-imposed if its cause lies not in intellectual insufficiency, but in a lack of will and courage [. . .]. Dare to know! [*Sapere aude!*] Have the courage to use your own reason! This is the motto of the Enlightenment.[1]

Read in isolation, this passage makes enlightenment seem a solitary business, encapsulated in the struggle of an individual consciousness to make sense of the world. But at a later point in the same essay, Kant observes that this process of self-liberation through reason has an unstoppable social dynamic.

It is possible that a public may enlighten itself; indeed if its freedom is not constrained this is virtually inevitable. For there will always be a few individuals who are capable of thinking for themselves despite the established authorities that claim to exercise this right in their name, and who, as soon as they have cast off the yoke of tutelage, will spread about them the spirit of a reasoned appreciation of one's own worth and the duty of every person to think for himself.[2]

In the percolation through society of this spirit of critical, confident independence, conversation played an indispensable role. It flourished in the clubs and societies that proliferated in the Prussian lands – and more broadly in the German states – during the second half of the eighteenth century. The statutes of the 'German societies', a supraterritorial enterprise whose network included a society founded in Königsberg in 1741, explicitly defined the formal conditions for fruitful conversation among the members. During the discussion that followed readings or lectures, members were to avoid arbitrary or ill-considered comments. Critiques should engage in a structured way with the style, method and content of the lecture. They should employ, in Kant's phrase, 'the cautious language of reason'. Digressions and interruptions were strictly prohibited. All members were ultimately guaranteed the right to have their say, but they must wait their turn and make their comments as concise as possible. Satirical or mocking remarks and suggestive wordplay were unacceptable.[3]

We find the same preoccupation with civility among the Freemasons, whose movement had grown to encompass between 250 and 300 German lodges with 15–18,000 members by the end of the eighteenth century. Here too, there were injunctions to avoid immoderate speech, frivolous or vulgar commentary and the discussion of topics (such as religion) that would stir divisive passions among the brothers.[4] This may all sound stiflingly prim from a present-day perspective, but the purpose of such rules and norms was serious enough. They were designed to ensure that what mattered in discussion was not the individual but the issue, that the passions of personal relationships and local politics were left behind when members joined the meeting. The art of polite public debate had still to be learned; these statutes were the blueprints of a new communicative technology.

Civility was important, too, because it helped to iron out the asymmetries of status that otherwise threatened to cramp discussion. Freemasonry was not, as one historian of the movement has claimed, an 'organisation of the emergent German middle classes'.[5] It attracted a mixed elite constituency that included members of the nobility and educated or propertied commoners in almost equal measure. Although some German lodges began life by opening their doors exclusively to one or the other of these two groups, most of these soon merged. In such mixed society, the observance of transparent and egalitarian rules of engagement was essential if status differences were not to cripple debate from the outset.

The conversation that powered the Prussian enlightenment also took place in print. One of the distinctive features of the periodical literature of this era was its discursive, dialogical character. Many of the articles printed in the *Berlin Monthly* (*Berlinische Monatsschrift*), for example, the most distinguished press organ of the German late enlightenment, were in fact letters to the editor from members of the public. Readers were also treated to extensive reviews of recent publications, and sometimes also to lengthy replies by authors with a bone to pick with their reviewers. Occasionally the journal would call for views on a specific question – this was the case, for example, with the famous discussion on the theme 'What is enlightenment?' that began with a query posted by the theologian Johann Friedrich Zöllner in the pages of the *Berlin Monthly* in December 1783.[6] There was no permanent staff of journalists, nor were most of the articles in each issue directly commissioned by the journal. As the editors, Gedike and Biester, made clear in the foreword to the first edition, they depended upon interested members of the public to 'enrich' the journal with unsolicited contributions.[7] The *Berlin Monthly* was thus above all a forum in print that operated along similar lines to the associational networks of the towns and cities. It was not conceived as fodder for an essentially passive constituency of cultural consumers. It aimed to provide the public with the means of reflecting upon itself and its foremost preoccupations.

The resonance of the *Berlin Monthly* and other journals like it was greatly enhanced by the proliferation across northern Germany of reading societies.[8] The purpose of these groups was to pool money for the purchase of subscriptions and books in a society where public libraries were as yet unknown. Some were relatively informal gatherings with no permanent home that met in the house of one of the better-off members. Others were reading circles specializing in the dissemination of specific journals. In some towns, local book dealers ran a library service that allowed readers to gain temporary access to new publications without paying the full purchase price. Associations of this kind multiplied at a remarkable rate during the last decades of the eighteenth century. Whereas there were only about fifty of them in the German states in 1780, the number increased to around 200 during the next ten years. They tended increasingly to meet in premises rented or bought for their own use that provided a congenial setting for discussion and debate. Statutes ensured that every member joined the meeting on equal terms and that the imperatives of politeness and reciprocal respect were observed. Parlour games and gambling were prohibited. In all, the German reading societies encompassed a membership of between fifteen and twenty thousand.

Bookshops were another important venue for enlightened sociability. The main room of Johann Jakob Kanter's bookshop in Königsberg, founded in 1764, was a large, attractive, bright space that served as the city's 'intellectual stock exchange'. It was a *café littéraire* in which men and women, young and old, professors and students could leaf through catalogues, read newspapers and buy, order or borrow books. (Since Kant owned only 450 books when he died in 1804, it is likely that, like other intellectuals in the city, he borrowed many of his books from Kanter.) Here, too, patrons were expected to cultivate a respectful and civil tone in their dealings with each other. Kanter not only sold books, he also produced a compendious catalogue of publications (which ran to 488 pages in 1771), a bi-weekly newspaper and various political tracts – including a blistering essay attacking Frederick the Great by the young Königsberg philosopher Johann Georg Hamann.[9]

Beyond the reading societies, lodges and patriotic associations was a network of other gatherings: literary and philosophical associations and learned groups specializing in natural science, medicine or languages. There were also more informal circles, such as the group of writers and aspirant poets around the Berlin Cadet School master Karl Wilhelm Ramler, whose close associates included the publisher Friedrich Nicolai, the dramatist Gotthold Ephraim Lessing, the patriot poet Johann Wilhelm Ludwig Gleim, the biblical scholar Moses Mendelssohn, the jurist Johann Georg Sulzer and many other prominent figures in the Berlin enlightenment. Ramler belonged to at least one of the many Masonic lodges in Berlin and was a member of several clubs; he was also a poet in his own right – albeit of third-rate verse. What contemporaries cherished in him was above all his gift for friendship and his lively, courteous sociability. After his death in April 1798, an obituary recalled that Ramler, who remained unmarried until his death, had lived 'only for his art and his friends, whom he loved dearly without making a show of it. He had many [friends] in all walks of life, especially among scholars and businessmen.'[10]

Another analogous figure was the patriot activist Johann Wilhelm Ludwig Gleim. He too was unmarried, entertained literary aspirations and used his financially secure position as an ecclesiastical official in the city of Halberstadt to support a circle of aspiring young writers and poets in the city. Like Ramler, Gleim maintained an extensive correspondence with many of the luminaries of contemporary Prussian letters. The sociable conversation that drove the enlightenment in Prussia was not sustained by statutes and subscriptions alone; it owed much of its intensity and inclusiveness to men like Ramler and Gleim, for whom the unselfish cultivation of a wide circle of friends was a life's work. Writers, poets, editors, club, society and lodge members, readers and subscribers, these were the 'practitioners of civil society' whose engagement with the great questions of the day, literary, scientific and political, helped to create a lively and diverse public sphere in the Prussian lands.[11]

It would be a mistake to think of this emergent public sphere either as a supine, passive mass of apolitical burghers, or as a seething force of opposition and latent rebellion. One of the most striking things about the social networks that sustained the Prussian enlightenment was their proximity to, and indeed partial identity with, the state. This was in part a matter of the intellectual tradition out of which the Prussian enlightenment grew. The links with cameralism, the 'science' of state administration established at the Prussian universities during the reign of Frederick III/I, and further consolidated under Frederick William I, were only gradually severed. Then there was the social location of the Prussian intelligentsia. Whereas men of independent means or free-lance writers played an important role in contemporary French letters, the dominant group within the Prussian enlightenment was that of the civil servants. A study of the *Berlin Monthly* has shown that of all contributors to the journal over the thirteen years of its existence (1783–96), 15 per cent were noblemen, 27 per cent were professors and school teachers, 20 per cent were senior officials, 17 per cent were clergy, and 3.3 per cent were army officers. In other words, more than half of the contributors were in paid state employment.[12]

A striking example of the convergence between the state and elements of civil society was the Berlin Wednesday Club, a 'private society of friends of learning' that met regularly during the years 1783 to 1797 (virtually the same years as the *Berlin Monthly* was in existence). The members of this group, which numbered first twelve and later twenty-four participants, included senior officials such as the minister of state Johann Friedrich Graf von Struensee and the legal officials Karl Gottlieb

Svarez and Ernst Klein; among other members were Johann Biester, who was both editor of the *Berlin Monthly* and secretary of the Wednesday Club, and the publisher and sometime patriot activist Friedrich Nicolai. Nicolai's old friend Moses Mendelssohn, the by now renowned Jewish scholar and philosopher, was an honorary member. Meetings were held in the home of one of the group. Although discussions sometimes focused on scientific topics of general interest, most meetings were concerned with contemporary political issues. Debates were often heated, but an effort was made to observe the forms of civilized discussion, namely mutual respect and reciprocity, impartiality, and a commitment to eschewing opinion and vacuous generalizations in favour of rigorous fact-based interpretation. Preparation for a meeting began with the pre-circulation of a treatise on some matter of government administration, finance or legislation. This served as the basis for debate. Comments could also be submitted in writing. Essays that had been debated by the society sometimes later appeared in the *Berlin Monthly*.

It is difficult to imagine a better illustration of the fundamentally conversational character of enlightened literary culture. The Wednesday Club could hardly be described as an institution of the 'public sphere', since its meetings were shrouded in the strictest secrecy – an essential measure, given that several of the group were serving ministers. Yet it does demonstrate the kinds of synergy that were becoming possible between the informal networks of civil society and the state during the last years of Frederick II's reign.

It was easy for progressive scholars, writers and thinkers to see the state as a partner in the enlightened project, because the sovereign himself was a renowned champion of its values. Immanuel Kant's suggestion that the phrases 'age of enlightenment' and 'age of Frederick' were synonymous was no pious platitude.[13] Of all the monarchs of eighteenth-century Europe, Frederick came closest to personifying the values and outlook of enlightenment. He joined a Masonic lodge in 1738, while he was still crown prince. He was, as we have seen, a sceptic in religious questions and an exponent of religious tolerance. When asked in June 1740 whether a Catholic subject should be permitted to enjoy civic rights in the city of Frankfurt an der Oder, he replied that 'all religions are just as good as each other, as long as the people who practise them are honest, and even if Turks and heathens came and wanted to populate this country, then we would build mosques and temples for them.'[14] He gathered about him some of the leading figures of the French enlightenment. Voltaire in particular, with whom Frederick sustained a long if intermittently fractious conversation, was for many years the foremost literary star of the enlightenment and his close association with the Prussian king was famous throughout the continent. Frederick's own writings were composed in imitation of the sparkling but cool and detached tone of the contemporary French masters.

Then there were those early sovereign acts by which Frederick revealed his readiness to translate ideas and convictions into practice. On his accession to the throne, he ordered that the journal *Die Berlinischen Nachrichten* was no longer to be subject to censorship, and that the rationalist philosopher Christian Wolff, who had been driven away from the University of Halle by the Pietists in the 1720s, should be recalled forthwith.[15] Even more striking was his decision, against the advice of the leading Prussian jurist of the era, Samuel von Cocceji, to suspend the use of judicial torture in his lands. Torture was still widely used by the European judicial systems to secure confessions from suspects. In 1745, Zedler's *Universallexikon*, one of the canonical encyclopaedias of the German enlightenment, defended the use of torture as an investigative tool, and the practice was retained in the *Theresiana*, the great codex of Austrian law published in 1768.[16]

But on 3 June 1740, only three days after his father's death, Frederick ordered that torture was no longer to be used, except in a small range of extreme cases involving crimes against king or country, or instances of multiple murder where robust interrogation was required to secure the identity of unknown accomplices. In a further order of 1754, Frederick extended this ban into a blanket prohibition, on the grounds that torture was not only 'cruel' (*grausam*) but also unreliable as a means of getting at the truth, since there was always the danger that suspects would implicate themselves in order to avoid further torture.[17] This radical measure left many judges and legal officials complaining that there now existed no means of extracting a confession – the queen of proofs under all the *ancien régime* legal systems – from recalcitrant offenders. A new evidential doctrine had to be improvised to cover cases where there was a plenitude of evidence, but no confession.

Frederick also reduced the number of crimes punishable by death and made a small but significant change to the arrangements for execution by the wheel. This gruesome practice involved breaking the body of the offender on the scaffold with blows from a cartwheel and expressed a characteristically early-modern understanding of public executions as a quasi-religious ritual centred on the scourging of the malefactor in preparation for his or her departure into the afterlife. Frederick ordered that in future executions of this kind, the offender was to be strangled by the executioner out of view of the crowd *before* the application of the wheel. His intention was to preserve the deterrent effect of the punishment while doing away with the infliction of unnecessary pain.[18] Here, as in the case of torture, a rational assessment of the utility of the practice was coupled with an enlightened distaste for acts of cruelty (for, if you strip the religious dimension from the torments meted out to the offender, nothing remains but cruelty). These achievements should not be downplayed – in 1766, it was still possible in France for a youth found guilty of blasphemy and the desecration of a wayside shrine to have his right arm hacked off and his tongue torn out before being burned at the stake.[19]

Frederick even granted refuge in Berlin to the radical Spinozist Johann Christian Edelmann. Edelmann was the author of various tracts arguing, among other things, that only a deism purged of all idolatry could redeem and unite humanity, that there was no need for the institution or sacrament of marriage, that sexual freedom was legitimate, and that Christ was a man like any other. Edelmann had been driven out of some of the most tolerant states of the German lands by hostile Lutheran and Calvinist establishments. During a brief visit by Edelmann to Berlin in 1747, the local Calvinist and Lutheran clergy attacked him as a dangerous and offensive sectary. He even attracted the hostile notice of Frederick for his principled opposition to royal absolutism and his dismissive (printed) remarks about Voltaire's eulogy celebrating the king's accession. Yet he was permitted to make his home in Berlin – even as his works were being furiously condemned across the length and breadth of the German lands – on the condition that he ceased to publish. In May 1750, as Edelmann whiled away his time in Berlin (under a false name to protect him against reprisals by Christian fanatics), there was a massive burning of his books in the city of Frankfurt/Main under the auspices of the Imperial Book Commission. With the entire magistracy and municipal government in attendance and seventy guards to hold back the crowds, nearly 1,000 copies of Edelmann's books were tossed on to a tower of flaming birch wood. The contrast in tone and policy with Berlin could hardly have been more conspicuous. Frederick had no objections to Edelmann's religious scepticism, his deism or his moral libertinism. The Prussian capital, he observed in a characteristically back-handed quip, already contained a great many fools and could surely accommodate one more.[20]

Frederick was thus – unlike his French counterpart Louis XVI – a plausible partner in the project of enlightenment in the Prussian lands. Indeed for many within the literary and political elite, the monarch's legitimate *personal* claim to enlightenment bestowed a unique meaning upon the relationship between civil society and the state in Prussia. We saw in chapter 7 how the personal reputation of the king suffused political discourses in Prussia during and after the Seven Years War. At that time, patriot publicists argued that love of the king could transform mere subjects into active participants in the public life of the fatherland.

In his landmark essay of 1784, Immanuel Kant argued that the convergence of authority and enlightenment in the same sovereign person utterly transformed the relationship between political and civil liberties, for, where the monarch was enlightened, his power constituted an asset, rather than a threat to the interests vested in civil society. The result, Kant argued, was a paradox: under a truly enlightened sovereign, moderate constraints on the degree of political liberty might actually 'create a space in which the people may expand to the fullness of its powers'. The famous formula Kant placed in the mouth of Frederick: 'Argue as much as you will about whatever you choose; but obey!' was not presented as the slogan of a despot. Rather it encapsulated the self-transforming potential within an enlightened monarchy. In such a polity, public argument and public criticism – a conversation, in short, between civil society and the state – ensured that the values and objectives of the state itself would ultimately merge harmoniously with those of the people, so that the duty to obey ceased to be a burden upon the subject.

For once the [. . .] inclination and commitment to *free thinking* has germinated and taken root, this gradually exerts its influence upon the outlook of the people (steadily reinforcing its *freedom of action*) and ultimately upon the principles of the *government* itself . . .[21]

This vision of a virtuous political convection, in which the ideas of enlightened luminaries first leavened the dough of civil society before communicating themselves to the organs of government, was not entirely detached from reality. Government in Prussia was in general far more consultative than we are inclined to think. Virtually all major legislative initiatives were the result of extensive negotiations or discussion with local interests. Sometimes this was conducted through the medium of the Estates, as in the protracted consultations over restrictions on the sale of noble landed property, sometimes through local town or district officials who were themselves in consultation with a wide range of locals, and sometimes through informal networks of experts, such as jurists, for example, or businessmen. None of this was especially 'enlightened'; it was an essential, though underemphasized, part of the gathering of opinions and information that made government possible. What changed in the later eighteenth century was the emergence of a network of enlightened activists who claimed to be trustees of the public interest, as well as partners and critics of the sovereign power.[22] It was a claim that the government came largely to accept. In 1784, when Frederick II embarked on a thoroughgoing legal reform that would culminate in a new and comprehensive law code for the Prussian lands, he chose to submit early drafts of the new code to the judgement of public opinion. Initially this denoted a fairly narrow circle of leading jurists and constitutional lawyers, as well as various 'men of practical wisdom'. But the net was later greatly widened through the institution of a public essay competition, a technique that the government borrowed from the older generation of patriotic-beneficial voluntary societies.[23] This remarkable step revealed a surprising confidence in the virtue of intellectual competition and demonstrated the king's tacit acknowledgement that public opinion was now, as one of his senior officials later put it, 'a mighty tribunal' judging each act of government.[24]

There may not have been freedom of the press in Prussia – in the sense of a generalized legal right to the public expression of opinions – but censorship was sufficiently mild to permit lively and robust political debate, both in print and in speech. The Scottish travel writer John Moore, who visited Berlin in 1775, later recorded his impressions of Prussia's capital city:

Nothing surprised me more, when I first came to Berlin, than the freedom with which many people speak of the measures of government, and the conduct of the King. I have heard political topics, and others which I should have thought still more ticklish, discussed here with as little ceremony as at a London coffee-house. The same freedom appears in the booksellers' shops, where literary productions of all kinds are sold openly. The pamphlet lately published on the division of Poland, wherein the King is very roughly treated, is to be had without difficulty, as well as other performances, which attack some of the most conspicuous characters with all the bitterness of satire.[25]

PRUSSIA'S JEWISH ENLIGHTENMENT

In the 1770s, the Jewish community of Berlin was the wealthiest and most acculturated of the German states. At its core was an elite of military contractors, bankers, merchants and manufacturers. The houses of the wealthiest families were located in the most fashionable areas of the city – Berlin was the only court city in the German lands where Jewish residents were not confined to a ghetto. In 1762, the banker Daniel Itzig bought a small palace in the Burgstrasse, right on the bank of the river Spree, and converted it into an elegant two-winged residence. Here he assembled a superb collection of art treasures, including Rubens's *Ganymede*, works by Terborch, Watteau, Joseph Roos and Antoine Pesne, and a 'large view with many figures by Canaletto'.[26] Nearby, on the corner of Poststrasse and Mühlendamm, was the three-storeyed palace of the court jeweller and mintmaster, Veitel Heine Ephraim. Designed by the master builder Friedrich Wilhelm Diterichs and decorated in the rococo style with columns, pilasters and elegant balconies with gilded railings, the Ephraimpalais is still a landmark in today's Berlin.

Itzig and Ephraim, like most other members of the Jewish financial elite, were men who had made their fortunes through collaboration with the Prussian state. Both were members of the business partnership entrusted by Frederick II with managing Prussia's coin supply during the Seven Years War. When war broke out in 1756, the king resolved to fund his campaigns with a coin inflation. Prussia had no native silver to speak of and thus had to import all its coin bullion – a business that had traditionally been in the hands of Jewish agents. By reducing the proportion of silver in the Prussian coinage, he would be able to extract a 'mint charge' in the form of the unused silver. Frederick had always made more intensive use of Jewish financial managers than his predecessors and he obliged a consortium of Jewish bankers and bullion merchants – including Ephraim and Itzig – to accept responsibility for minting the debased coins. The profits generated by this enterprise – amounting to about 29 million thalers – made a significant contribution to the king's war costs.[27] By the end of the hostilities, the Jewish mint managers – together with an array of other Jewish businessmen specializing in the supply of war provisions – were among the wealthiest men in Prussia.

These were the most prominent members of the Jewish minority in Prussia, but they were hardly typical. Jewish life in Prussia was a study in contrasts. While a small minority enjoyed great wealth and legal privilege, the majority were weighed down by onerous restrictions. In 1730, Frederick William I issued a General Jewry Regulation that restricted Jewish trade, forbade Jews to practise in guild-controlled artisan crafts or to peddle wares in the cities, and prohibited them from purchasing houses. The trend towards ever-tighter state regulation continued during the reign of Frederick II. The elaborate Revised General Code of 1750 divided the Jews of Prussia into six discrete classes. At the top was a tiny minority of 'generally privileged' Jews who could purchase houses and land and operate commercially on the same footing as their Christian fellows. In special cases, members of this class might even be granted hereditary citizenship rights. The 'privileged protected Jews' of the next class, however, could not choose their place of residence and could pass their status only to one of their children. The third class of 'unprivileged protected Jews' comprised practitioners of specific professions – opticians, engravers, painters, physicians – deemed useful enough to justify conditional residence permits. Class four encompassed community employees, such as rabbis, cantors and kosher slaughterers, and entailed no hereditary rights. The fifth class comprised 'tolerated Jews' enjoying the patronage of a Jew in the upper three classes, as well as the non-inheriting children of Jews of the second and third classes. Class six, the least of them all, covered the private employees of Jewish businesses and households; residence permits in this class were dependent upon contracts of employment.

Confronted with the Jews, the king's famed enlightenment narrowed to a purely instrumental rationale. Frederick was determined to use them as revenue-generators and was prepared for that purpose to grant extremely wide-ranging freedoms to the most useful of his Jewish subjects. Indeed he pressed Jews into those sectors of the economy where entrepreneurial ventures were most sorely needed – the bullion trade, iron foundries, cross-border commercial operations in peripheral regions and various branches of manufacture. He also raised special taxes and levies on Jewish subjects and required them to purchase surplus figurines from the Royal Porcelain Manufactures – these items, reluctantly accepted in the 1770s, became the cherished heirlooms of later generations.

Underlying the superficially utilitarian measures of the state were social tensions and a lively vein of prejudice. Part of the pressure for state regulation came from the Christian corporate oligarchies of the Prussian towns, who pelted the central and provincial administrations with endless complaints and petitions against the commercial activities of the Jews.[28] Jews in Prussia, as in all the German lands, were caught in the crossfire between the state and the local communities. In seeking to settle new Jewish residents or to protect their enterprises, the state ran into concerted resistance from town guildsmen and shopkeepers who feared Jewish competition and were hostile to the economic innovations pioneered by the newcomers. Here, as in other spheres of action, the authorities had to tread a careful line between grassroots opinion and the larger interests of the state.

This is not to suggest that the king himself was free of prejudice. On the contrary, Frederick was almost as hostile to the Jews as his father – who described them as 'locusts' – had been.[29] In his Political Testament of 1752, he denounced them as the most dangerous of all sects, declaring that they harmed Christian trade, and arguing somewhat hypocritically that the state should make no use of their services. These views were reiterated in the Testament of 1768, despite the close and productive collaboration of the war years.[30] Jewry regulations consequently carried a discriminatory symbolic charge. Jews were subject to a 'body tax' otherwise levied on cattle; they were constrained to enter and leave the capital city by one of two gates. Unlike any other minority group in Prussia, they could be punished on the basis of collective liability. A cabinet order of 1747 stated that the elders of each Jewish community were co-responsible for any robbery involving a member; the same applied to losses incurred through bankruptcies and penalties imposed for receiving or concealing stolen goods.[31]

Although the wealthy Jewish entrepreneurs have tended to dominate the historical record, the great majority of Jews in the Prussian lands were very modest individuals. Large-scale commerce of the sort practised by Ephraim and Itzig was the domain of a tiny elite. The small Jewish trader or *Hausierer* working from door to door was a far more frequent and familiar figure. Those Jews who did not possess letters of protection allowing them to trade in an open shop or stall were restricted to itinerant dealing in second-hand goods. The proportion of Prussian Jewry in this position rose steadily as the successive trade restrictions of the early and mid eighteenth century pushed many formerly prosperous merchants into marginal sectors of the economy.[32] Their ranks were continuously swollen by the illegal immigration of Jews from Poland, many of whom were poor and obliged to live from very marginal forms of itinerant employment. Attempts to close the eastern borders to these economic refugees failed to have any appreciable effect. Repeated ordinances against 'beggar Jews', issued in 1780, 1785, 1788 and 1791, indicate that this migration, doubtless aggravated by the partitions of Poland, remained unchecked at the end of the century.[33] The Pietist missionary agents who worked from the Institutum Judaicum in Halle from the 1730s onwards often encountered gaggles of 'poor travelling Jews' who were unable to pay the gate tax and gathered before the walls, trading in small portable items such as prayer books or calendars.[34]

By the middle decades of the eighteenth century, a process of cultural change was under way among the Prussian Jews that would ultimately transform Judaism. The Jewish enlightenment or Haskalah (from the Hebrew *le-haskil*, 'enlighten, clarify with the aid of the intellect') first took hold in Berlin. One of its earliest and most emblematic exponents was the philosopher Moses Mendelssohn, who lived and worked in the city from 1743 until his death in 1786. Mendelssohn hailed from a humble family in the Saxon city of Dessau. His father struggled to support the family as a *Schulklopfer*, a synagogue door knocker, whose task was to instruct young children in the Torah and run from house to house rousing the congregation to prayer in the mornings. At the age of six, Moses began studying with rabbi David Fränkel, a distinguished scholar of the Talmud and its commentaries. When Fränkel moved to Berlin to accept the post of chief rabbi in 1743, his fifteen-year-old student followed. The penniless Mendelssohn would have been turned back at the Rosenthal Gate, had his mentor not found him a place in the household of one of Berlin's 'protected Jews'.

It was the beginning of a brilliant career. A train of publications soon established Mendelssohn's reputation as a commentator on themes drawn from Plato, Spinoza, Locke, Leibniz, Shaftesbury, Pope and Wolff. Mendelssohn wrote in an elegant lively German, but he also kept up a stream of publications in Hebrew. He launched the first-ever Hebrew periodical, *Kohelet Musar* (*The Moralist*), in 1755. Modelled on the 'moral weeklies' of early eighteenth-century England, *Kohelet Musar* aimed to disseminate enlightened ideas within the educated stratum of Jewry. In 1784, Mendelssohn joined the debate on the meaning of 'enlightenment' in the pages of the *Berlin Monthly*. Here he argued that enlightenment denoted not a state of affairs, but a process of maturation in which individuals learned gradually to apply their 'reason' to the problems before them.

This was an utterly new and distinctive voice. Here was a Jewish scholar who, while continuing to avow his attachment to Jewish tradition, reached out to a mixed audience of Jews and Christians, speaking of reason, sentiment and beauty in a captivating, undogmatic idiom. In using Hebrew for *Kohelet Musar*, Mendelssohn brought the sacred language of the synagogue out into the open air of an enlightened public sphere. For some of his Jewish readers, there was an almost giddy sense of displacement and liberation. Young Jews from across the Prussian lands and beyond came to gather at his home, where there were lively debates on matters of enlightenment. It was here that a specifically Jewish enlightenment began to take shape. The luminaries of the early Berlin Haskalah – Naphtali Herz Wessely, Herz Homberg, Solomon Maimon, Isaac Euchel and others – were all formed in this exciting milieu. In 1778, the Mendelssohn disciple David Friedländer, son of a Königsberg banker, joined with Isaac Daniel Itzig (son of Daniel) to found a Jewish Free School in Berlin – Mendelssohn had a hand in designing the curriculum. By the early 1780s, Mendelssohn had established a genuinely Prussian literary network; a list of the 515 subscribers to his German translation of the Pentateuch (1781–3) includes names from across the kingdom, with major concentrations in Breslau, Königsberg and Berlin.[35]

For enlightened Christian readers too, Mendelssohn was an object of fascination, a modern Jewish sage, a 'German Socrates', a man who symbolized the ferment and potential of enlightenment. More than any other individual, he exemplified the type of the wise Jew that proliferated

22. Moses Mendelssohn examined at Potsdam's Berlin Gate. *Engraving by Johann Michael Siegfried Löwe, after Daniel Chodowiecki,* Physiognomischer Almanach *(Berlin, 1792).*

in German fiction and drama during the second half of the eighteenth century.[36] The eminent dramatist Gotthold Ephraim Lessing, a close friend and collaborator, erected a literary monument to his friend in *Nathan the Wise* (1779), a play whose hero was a benign and virtuous Jewish merchant. Mendelssohn became a cultural icon, a talisman to conjure against the darkness of intolerance and prejudice. His house was a popular stopping-place for visitors to Berlin with literary pretensions.[37]

There are many contemporary portraits of Mendelssohn, but one of the most memorable, an engraving based on a drawing by Daniel Chodowiecki, shows him presenting his papers for inspection at the Berlin Gate to the city of Potsdam in 1771. Mendelssohn stands in the centre of the scene, a short, stooped figure in modest dark dress flanked by two towering Prussian guards, one of whom raises his hat in acknowledgement. The engraving referred to a contemporary anecdote in which Mendelssohn was asked to produce a letter of commendation from the king and was quizzed on its content. The emotional tone of this image remains difficult to read – is the wry expression on Mendelssohn's lean, upturned face intended to imply an ironic gloss on this routine encounter between a Prussian officer and Prussia's most famous Jew?

The Haskalah that flowed out from Mendelssohn and his circle was no bolt out of the blue. Its roots lay in a broad process of social change. The early Jewish enlighteners were deeply indebted to a parental generation that had begun to take an interest in modern languages, philosophy and the sciences. The pressure of Prussia's interventionist state had (unwittingly) undermined the authority of the traditional rabbinate, hollowing out the space for an intellectual counter-elite. Even more important was the acculturated milieu of the great Berlin families. The patronage of the commercial elite provided the *maskilim* (exponents of Haskalah), a number of whom were impoverished itinerant scholars from far afield, with work as household tutors and opportunities to test new theories on their young charges. Mendelssohn could never have pursued his career as a thinker and writer without the financial stability provided by his relationship with the wealthy silk manufacturer Isaac Bernhard, for whom he worked first as a private tutor, later as a bookkeeper and ultimately as a business partner. The homes of the wealthy bankers – especially Daniel Itzig – were meeting places and watering-holes for the young generation of scholars – it was here that Mendelssohn received his first instruction in philosophy shortly after his arrival in the city.

But the Haskalah was also part of a distinctive moment in the history of German and Jewish-German sociability. In the mid-1750s, Moses Mendelssohn wrote to the dramatist Gotthold Ephraim Lessing to report on his deepening friendship with the Berlin publisher Friedrich Nicolai:

I visit Herr Nicolai often in his garden. (I truly love him, my dearest friend! And I believe that our own friendship can only gain by this because I cherish in him your true friend as well.) We read poetry, Herr Nicolai recites his own compositions too, and I sit on my bench, a critical judge, complimenting, laughing, approving, finding fault, until evening comes.[38]

Mendelssohn's conversation with Nicolai was a spontaneous, unstructured affair, yet it carried real symbolic weight. Here were a Jew and a Christian in a garden, meeting on equal terms, delighting in each other's company and oblivious to the passing hours – for how long had such an encounter been conceivable? In the later 1750s, Mendelssohn frequented the 'Learned Coffeehouse', a society dedicated to the dissemination of enlightenment, in which members – there were about one hundred in all – presented and discussed papers on topical themes.

This interstitial sphere of enlightened trans-confessional conviviality steadily expanded in the later decades of the eighteenth century. It reached its high point in the literary salons frequented by the Berlin cultural elite during the later 1780s and 1790s. These were loosely organized gatherings in which persons of every social station and religious creed came together for conversation and the exchange of ideas. Men and women, Jews and Christians, noblemen and commoners, professors, poets, scientists and merchants mingled in private houses to discuss art, politics, literature and the sciences, but also to cultivate friendships and love affairs. Jewish women were central to the creation of this new milieu because, as members of a socially marginal group, they were in a sense equidistant from all social strata within the mainstream society – their houses provided an ideal space for the suspension of conventional boundaries. Women from the wealthier Jewish families also disposed of the considerable means required to cater to the hungry and thirsty intellectuals of Berlin – a few *salonnières* were driven to the brink of bankruptcy by the expense of keeping open house.

The two most celebrated Berlin hostesses were Henriette Herz, daughter of the first Jewish physician to practise in Berlin, and Rahel Levin, whose father was a wealthy jewel merchant. Both women were products of the assimilated Berlin elite – they had no qualms about appearing bare-headed in public and Rahel was notorious for breaking the Sabbath with Saturday-morning rides in an open carriage. Henriette's salon, which flourished in the 1790s, was for a time the epicentre of literary and scientific culture in Berlin – its guests included the celebrated theologian Friedrich Schleiermacher, Alexander and Wilhelm von Humboldt, and the dramatist Heinrich von Kleist. Rahel Levin was at first a regular attendant at Henriette's salon, but she later formed her own literary circle. The Levin salon brought literary and academic stars into contact with members of the old Prussian elites. Rahel maintained numerous friendships among noblewomen she had met during her sojourns at the spas of Bohemia. Scions of the old Junker families – Schlabrendorffs, Finckensteins and even members of the royal family – shared sofas and tables with scientists, writers, critics and literary hopefuls. Friedrich Schlegel, Jean Paul and Johann Gottlob Fichte were among the intellectual celebrities who passed through the Levin salon. Regular attendants, whatever their social status, were expected to address each other with the familiar *du*.[39]

On whose terms did this exuberant rapprochement take place? In the minds of most educated Christian contemporaries, there was still the strong presumption that acculturation must ultimately culminate in conversion. The Zürich theologian Johann Caspar Lavater, who socialized with the enlightened elite and was a frequent visitor to Mendelssohn's home in 1763–4, surprised his former host in 1769 with an open letter in which he demanded that Mendelssohn either convert to Christianity or justify his continued attachment to the Jewish faith. Lavater's impertinent challenge and Mendelssohn's gentle rejection were a literary sensation. The episode was a signal reminder of the limits of tolerance, even within the republic of letters.

The enlightened Prussian civil servant Christian Wilhelm Dohm was another case in point. Dohm was a close friend of Mendelssohn and a frequent guest in the house of Marcus Herz (husband of Henriette). He was also one of the first great champions of Jewish legal emancipation. In 1781 he published a landmark essay entitled *On the Civic Improvement of the Jews*, which attacked Christian prejudice and called for the removal of traditional legal disabilities. The Jews, he wrote, 'have been endowed with the same capacity to become happier, better persons, more useful members of society'; it was only oppression, 'so unworthy of our age', that corrupted them. It was thus congruent with 'humaneness, justice and enlightened policy to banish this oppression and improve the condition of the Jews'.[40] But even Dohm assumed that the process of emancipation must lead to a far-reaching dilution of Jewish identity, if not to conversion. Once the pressure of legal discrimination were removed, he argued, it would be possible to woo the Jews away from the 'sophistic sayings of [their] rabbis' and divest them of their 'clannish religious opinions', inspiring them instead with patriotism and love for the state.[41]

But what if the Jews failed to honour their part of this one-sided bargain? What if, despite acculturating outwardly to the forms of the Christian mainstream, they remained in some sense Jewish and different? Scepticism on this point continued to dog the enterprise of Jewish societal assimilation. In 1803, the Berlin lawyer Karl Wilhelm Grattenauer published a mordant pamphlet in which he mounted a direct attack on the Jews of the salon-going elite. Entitled *Against the Jews*, this text focused its venom specifically on the young Jewish women who

read many books, speak many languages, play many instruments, sketch in a variety of styles, paint in all colours, dance in all fashions, embroider in all patterns and possess every single thing that could give them a claim to charm, except the art of uniting all the particulars into a beautiful femininity.[42]

This was a missile aimed right at the heart of that social milieu that had done more than any other to open channels of communication between the Jewish and the Christian elites. *Against the Jews* was widely read and discussed in Berlin and across Prussia – the conservative publicist Friedrich Gentz recalled reading it, despite initial misgivings, 'with exceptional pleasure'.[43]

One of the sourest fruits of this new critique of Jewish acculturation was the satirical farce *The Company We Keep* (*Unser Verkehr*) by the Breslau doctor Karl Borromäus Sessa. Written in 1813, Sessa's play failed to arouse much interest in Breslau, but it was an instant hit in Berlin, where it opened at the Opera House on 2 September 1815. Audiences were invited to laugh at a grotesque gallery of Jewish stereotypes. Abraham, representing the older generation of *shtetl*-Jews, is a dealer in second-hand goods who expresses himself in a hilariously contorted Yiddish jargon. But his son Jacob aims for higher things; he wants to dance, speak French, teach himself aesthetics and write theatre reviews. Yet he finds it hard to shake off the Yiddishness of his speech: 'I vant to trow away de Jew in me; I'm enlightened, no? Don't have nothin' Jewish in me.' The most assimilated character of all is the affected and well-spoken Lydia, an unmistakeable caricature of the sharp-witted *salonnières* of the Herz-Levin era, who fails despite her best efforts to conceal her essential Jewishness.[44] There was nothing gentle or affectionate about Sessa's parody. It was an outright attack on the idea that acculturation would or should suffice to close the social and political gap between Jews and their Christian fellow-Prussians.

In the meanwhile, the Haskalah and intensified contact with the Christian social environment had begun to generate profound cultural changes within Prussian Jewry. We can discern a clear break between the first generation of enlighteners, personified in the figure of Mendelssohn, who wrote eloquently in Hebrew and remained deeply rooted in Jewish tradition, and the later more radical reformers of the revolutionary era who wrote in German and ultimately sought to break the mould of traditional observance altogether. The journey away from Jewish tradition towards the periphery of the community and its world of observance led to a variety of destinations: some sought to resculpt Judaism along the lines of natural religion; others hoped – like Mendelssohn's quixotic disciple David Friedländer – to merge a rationalized Judaic faith with a Christianity purged of Trinitarian elements; and for a number, including many of the well-born young Jewish women of the salons and four of Moses Mendelssohn's six children, the road ended in the most radical assimilation of all – conversion to Christianity.[45]

The Berlin Haskalah did not lead to the dissolution of traditional Judaism – the pragmatic, flexible communal culture of western Ashkenaz was far too resilient for that – but it did produce a lasting transformation. It made possible, firstly, the emergence of a secular Jewish intelligentsia that could thrive alongside the old elite of the rabbis and Talmud scholars. In so doing, it created the foundations for a critical Jewish public sphere capable of engaging in an open-ended way with its own traditions. Religion was privatized, relegated to the synagogue, while everyday life was – though only gradually – freed from the trappings of religious authority. This was at first a phenomenon of the urban elites and their social satellites, but the shock-waves generated by Haskalah gradually penetrated the fabric of traditional Judaism, broadening the intellectual horizons of the rabbinate and encouraging the faithful to seek a secular education (especially in medicine) at the German universities. It fed into the Reform movement that modernized nineteenth-century synagogue liturgy and religious observance. But it also stimulated far-reaching change within the world of traditional rabbinical Judaism. It was due in large part to the invigorating challenge posed by Mendelssohn and his successors that the Judaisms of the nineteenth century – Reform, Conservative, Orthodox – succeeded in capturing and feeding the spiritual and intellectual commitments of new generations.

COUNTER-ENLIGHTENMENT?

'Everything has collapsed into smallness,' Count Mirabeau wrote, reflecting on the death of Frederick the Great in 1786, 'just as once everything had expanded into greatness.'[46] Certainly the transition from Frederick II to his successor and nephew,[47] Frederick William II, was attended by the usual Hohenzollern family contrasts. The uncle was misanthropic, aloof and utterly uninterested in women. The nephew was genial, gregarious and recklessly heterosexual. His first marriage, with Elisabeth of Brunswick-Wolfenbüttel, was dissolved after infidelities on both sides; the second marriage, with Frederike Luise of Hessen-Darmstadt, bore seven children; a further seven offspring were born of his life-long relationship with his mistress Wilhelmine Encke (later raised to the peerage as Princess Liegnitz) and two further (bigamous) marriages 'under the left hand'. The uncle had remained loyal to the values of the high enlightenment, espousing a rigorously sceptical rationalism that seemed old-fashioned by the 1780s. The nephew was a man of his era who took an interest in spiritism, clairvoyance, astrology and other pursuits that would have disgusted his predecessor. The uncle had demonstrated his personal attachment to the ideals of the Enlightenment by joining the Freemasons when he was still crown prince. The nephew, by contrast, joined the Rosicrucians, an esoteric and secretive offshoot of Freemasonry dedicated to mystical and occult pursuits. Frederick the Great had managed, through rigorous economies in all domains of state activity, to leave behind a treasury of 51 million thalers; this staggering sum was squandered by his successor in only eleven years.[48] And there were important differences in management styles. Whereas the uncle had constantly controlled and monitored the central executive, imposing his will on secretaries and ministers alike, the nephew was an impulsive, uncertain figure who was easily steered by his advisers.

In a sense, Prussia had returned to the European dynastic norm. Frederick William was not an especially stupid man, and he was certainly a person of deep and wide-ranging cultural interests – his importance as a patron of the arts and architecture is beyond dispute.[49] But he was incapable of providing the Prussian governmental system with a strong commanding centre. One consequence of this weakening of the sovereign's grip on policy was the re-emergence of the 'antechamber of power', that space within which advisers, ministers and would-be friends of the king competed for influence on the monarch. Among Frederick William's advisers there was one in particular whose influence over domestic affairs was unrivalled. Johann Christoph Wöllner was an intelligent and ambitious commoner who had worked his way up from humble origins to become a pastor and later, through a highly advantageous marriage to the daughter of his patron, the master of a landed estate. Wöllner held an exalted position within the inner circle of the Rosicrucian order in Berlin and established contact with Frederick

William while he was still crown prince. Frederick the Great was unimpressed by this connection, describing the crown prince's upwardly mobile companion as a 'scheming, swindling parson'. But with the accession of Frederick William II to the throne, Wöllner's day had come. In 1788, he was appointed minister of culture in place of the Baron von Zedlitz, one of the most distinguished and progressive figures in the Frederician administration. In this post, Wöllner dedicated himself to an authoritarian cultural policy whose objective was to curb the supposedly corrosive effects of scepticism on the moral fabric of school, church and university. The centrepiece of Wöllner's campaign to restabilize the ideological substance of public life in the kingdom was the famed Edict on Religion of 9 August 1788, a law designed to arrest and reverse the corrosive effect of rationalist speculation on the integrity of Christian doctrine.

It was no accident that Wöllner's strictures were directed specifically at religious speculation, for it was in the sphere of religion (and especially Protestant religion) that debate over the implications of philosophical rationalism had done most to unsettle conventional certainties. The impact of enlightenment on the Prussian clergy in particular had been reinforced by Frederick II's practice of favouring rationalist candidates for appointments to clerical office. The preamble to the edict stated baldly that 'enlightenment' – the word was printed in bold letters on a line of its own – had gone too far. The integrity and coherence of the Christian church was in danger. Faith was being sacrificed on the altar of fashion.

The edict introduced new censorship mechanisms to impose doctrinal conformity on all texts used for school and university study. The disciplinary powers of the Lutheran and Calvinist consistories – the most senior confessional administrative organs – were reinforced. Monitoring procedures were introduced to ensure that candidates appointed to clerical posts actually subscribed to the articles of faith of their respective confessions. Further measures followed. A censorship edict was published in December 1788 in an effort to stem the flow of pamphlets and articles criticizing the new measures. A Royal Examining Commission was established to flush out the rationalists in church and teaching offices. Among those subjected to investigation was pastor Johannes Heinrich Schulz of Gelsdorf, who was notorious for preaching that Jesus was a man like any other, that he was never resurrected, that the doctrine of a general resurrection was nonsense and that hell did not exist.[50] Another who came to the attention of the authorities was Immanuel Kant himself: in the autumn of 1794, he received a stiff warning in the form of a royal order stating that the essay collection published as *Religion within the Bounds of Reason Alone* 'abused [. . .] philosophy for the purpose of distorting and disparaging several principal and fundamental doctrines of Holy Scripture'.[51]

Wöllner's edict has often been seen as a reactionary backlash against the Prussian enlightenment.[52] This is certainly how some of its contemporary critics saw it. Yet in many respects, Wöllner's religious policy was deeply rooted in the traditions of the Prussian enlightenment. Wöllner had himself been a Freemason before he joined the Rosicrucians (who were in any case an outgrowth of the Masonic movement), had been educated at the rationalist University of Halle and was the author of various enlightened tracts urging agricultural improvement, land reform and the abolition of serfdom.[53] The central purpose of the edict was not – as some of its more polemical contemporary critics claimed – to impose a new religious 'orthodoxy', but rather to consolidate the existing confessional structures and thereby safeguard the pluralist compromise struck at the Peace of Westphalia in 1648. In this sense it accorded with Prussia's tradition of multi-confessional religious co-existence. Thus the edict forbade not only the public propagation of heterodox rationalist views, but also proselytizing by Catholics among members of the two Protestant faiths. It even extended the state's guardianship (in article 2) to the various 'sects previously publicly tolerated in our states', including the Jews, the Herrnhut brethren, the Mennonites and the Bohemian brethren.[54]

The edict was also notable for its essentially instrumental view of religion. Underpinning it was the – characteristically enlightened – belief that religion had an important role to play in securing public order. What mattered was not the existence of theological speculation as such, but the fact that the 'poor masses of the population' were being led away from their accustomed faith in scriptural, clerical and – by extension – sovereign authority.[55] The need for stabilizing measures seemed all the more urgent for the fact that the absorption of large tracts of Polish territory (see chapter 10 below) had greatly increased the number of Prussia's Catholic subjects and raised questions about the confessional balance of power within the kingdom. For these and other reasons, many of the most prominent enlightened theologians were happy to support the edict as a policy for the maintenance of religious peace.[56]

It thus makes little sense to see the controversy that broke out over the edict as a conflict between 'enlightenment' and a political 'reaction' bent on turning the clock back. The real struggle was between different visions of enlightenment. On the one hand, there were those enlightened defenders of the edict who saw in it a rational exercise of the state's authority in the interests of religious peace and the liberty of individuals to be 'left undisturbed in their chosen public confession'.[57] On the other, there were those radical critics who argued that the edict oppressed individual consciences; one of these, the Kantian law professor Gottfried Hufeland, even argued that public institutions should reflect the rational convictions of the individuals composing them, even though this implied that 'there must be as many churches as there are personal convictions'.[58] From one perspective, the confessional identities bequeathed by history to the present were parcels of religious liberty to be safeguarded against the anarchic individualism of the radical critics; from the other, they were a stifling legacy of the past whose continued existence was a burden upon individual consciences. The real issue turned on the locus of rational action. Should this reside in the state, as Pufendorf had proposed, or should it be vested in the unfolding reasoned enquiry of individuals, as the more radical disciples of Kant appeared to be suggesting? Was the state better placed to uphold a rational public order grounded in the principles of natural law, or should this be left to the increasingly dynamic political forces within an emergent civil society?

The public furore provoked by the edict and its flanking measures revealed the extent to which enlightened critical debate had already politicized the Prussian public. There was a new sharpness in the tone of printed comment that prompted the king to observe with alarm in September 1788 that 'freedom of the press' (*Presse-Freyheit*) had mutated into 'impudence of the press' (*Presse-Frechheit*).[59] There were also institutional frictions between the makeshift organs established by Wöllner to police the edict through censorship and the existing bodies of ecclesiastical self-governance, many of which were dominated by theological liberals. The disciplinary proceedings against the flagrantly heterodox pastor Schulz collapsed when the senior judicial and consistorial officials appointed to investigate him came to the conclusion that since he was a Christian (though not a Lutheran as such), he should be permitted to remain in office.[60] As this and many other cases revealed, there was now a network of officials at the apex of the administrative system who had passed through the crucible of the Berlin enlightenment and were prepared to defend their understanding of an enlightened political order against the authoritarian prescriptions of Wöllner and Frederick William II.[61] It was surely no coincidence that Johann Friedrich Zöllner, the consistorial official who had passed the tract for publication, Johann Georg Gebhard, the tract's Calvinist author, and Ernst Ferdinand Klein, the judge entrusted with finding a verdict for the Supreme Court, were all sometime members of Berlin's Wednesday Club.

In the face of such resistance, Wöllner's efforts to silence debate and purge the administrative structures of rationalist critics were bound to enjoy at best a limited success. In the spring of 1794, Hermann Daniel Hermes and Gottlob Friedrich Hillmer, members of the Royal Examining Commission, travelled to Halle to conduct an inspection of the city's university and high school. The University of Halle had once been the headquarters of Pietism, but it was now a bastion of radical theology whose governing body had formally protested the recent censorship measures. When Hermes and Hillmer reached the city on the evening of 29 May and made their way to their quarters in the Golden Lion Hotel, they were besieged by a crowd of masked students who stood before their windows until the small hours of the morning chanting rationalist slogans. On the following night an even larger and louder crowd of students gathered to hear one of their number deliver a speech seething, in the ears of an unsympathetic onlooker, with 'blasphemies and irreligious expressions', before bombarding the windows of the examiners' rooms with tiles, bricks and cobblestones.

To make matters worse, the academic authorities of the university refused to implement Wöllner's policy within the faculties – partly because they were hostile to the spirit of the edict, and partly because they saw the imposition of such measures from above as incompatible with academic freedom and the autonomy of their institution. 'What is our power?' Hermes exclaimed in despair during a difficult meeting with senior university officials. 'We have not yet succeeded in dislodging one single neological preacher. Everybody is against us.'[62]

By 1795, with the failure to implement the new measures in Prussia's most important university, it was clear that the Wöllner authoritarian project had run out of steam. There was, to be sure, a generalized tightening of censorship, especially as the unfolding of the French Revolution revealed the scale of the threat posed to traditional authority by political radicalism. One prominent contemporary witness to these developments was the publisher and patriot Friedrich Nicolai, who moved his own journal, the *Allgemeine Deutsche Bibliothek*, to Altona (a town adjoining Hamburg but under Danish rule) in 1792 to avoid the scrutiny of the Prussian censors. In a letter to Frederick William II of 1794, Nicolai protested against the recent measures, observing that the number of independent printing presses operating in Berlin had fallen from 181 to sixty-one as a consequence of the regime imposed after 1788, and suggesting slyly that this was damaging to royal tax revenues.[63] Whether this contraction was exclusively the result of censorship (as opposed to market forces) is doubtful. Yet there clearly was a heightened impatience with government censorship among members of the Prussian intelligentsia. This was partly a function of real constraints, but it also expressed the expansion of expectations that had occurred during the intellectual and political ferment of the 1780s. 'Freedom of speech' was defined in far more radical terms by the mid-1790s in Prussia than it had been in the previous decade, and the warm glow in which the charisma of 'Frederick the Unique' had bathed the wheels of the state machine gradually faded after 1786.

Despite this souring of the public mood, it is important not to overstate the oppressiveness of the post-Frederician administration. A recent study of the Berlin press during the French Revolution has shown that Prussian subjects had access to extremely detailed and reliable press coverage of contemporaneous events in France, not only during the liberal revolution of 1789–92, but also during the Jacobin Terror and thereafter. Reports in the Berlin press incorporated sophisticated political commentaries, which were by no means always hostile to the cause of the revolutionaries. The *Haudesche und Spenersche Zeitung* in particular was remarkable for the sympathy with which the positions and policies of the various parties (including even Robespierre and the Jacobins) were set out and explained. At no time did the Prussian government seriously attempt to prevent the dissemination of information about the French events, even at the time of the trial and execution of the king in 1792–3, or to ensure that the regicides and their allies were cast in an especially hostile light. Nor did the authorities prevent the widespread use of such contemporary reportage for educational purposes, not only in the *Gymnasien* (grammar schools) but also in village and elementary schools. Nowhere in the German states, with the possible exception of Hamburg, do we find press coverage of comparable quality and candour. Despite the pervasive fear of revolution and all the vexations of censorship, Axel Schumann writes,

the fact remains that between 1789 and 1806, four journals appeared under Prussian censorship in the capital and residential city of Berlin, in which the French Revolution was celebrated as a historic necessity and as the victory of reason over aristocratic arrogance and monarchical mismanagement.[64]

TWO-HEADED STATE

In the summer of 1796, crowds of Berliners swarmed to see the latest theatrical sensation orchestrated by the famous Swabian illusionist Karl Enslen. The show opened with a trio of beautifully fashioned automatons: a Spaniard with a flute, a woman playing the glass-organ and a trumpeter who could also speak. There followed an 'aerial hunt' involving floating animal figures filled with gas, and an android gymnast whose movements were so life-like that one would have taken him for a man, were it not for the muted creaking of the neck-joint. Towards the end of the performance, the lights were extinguished and a loud clap of thunder announced a series of ghostly apparitions culminating in a spectacular *trompe-l'oeil*.

Then there is seen far off in the distance a bright star; the star widens; and out of it there comes the very exact likeness of Frederick the second, in his usual clothing and posture [. . .]. The image grows bigger and bigger, comes nearer and nearer, until it seems to stand as large as life just before the orchestra. The effect of this apparition on the floor and in the boxes was remarkable. The clapping and jubilation was endless. When Frederick seemed about to retreat to his star many called 'Oh stay with us!' He returned into his star, but after loud cries of encore he had to come back twice.[65]

Here was a theatre of the modern type, where darkness was used to heighten the impact of illusion (a recent innovation), where tickets and seats were set at different prices for different pockets. Men and women, minor officials, craftsmen and clerks mingled in the audience, but people of noble estate were there too, and even members of the royal family – albeit only as paying customers. And here was the figure of the resurrected king summoned back to life to satisfy a crowd hungry for entertainment and prepared to pay for it. Did those royals who watched this remarkable projection feel a certain unease at the spectacle of the dead king, hailed by his people, but also at their beck and call? It is hard to think of a scene that better exemplifies the ambivalence and modernity of nostalgia.

By 1800, Berlin was – in terms of its intellectual and social life – the most vibrant city of German Europe. Its population was approaching 200,000. There was a dense network of clubs and societies, of which we know thirty-eight by name, and sixteen Masonic lodges.[66] Beyond the circles of the better-known organizations there was a further array of now-forgotten clubs catering to the lower social strata. Berlin's clubland was not just large, it was also highly textured and diverse. The Monday Club, the Wednesday Society and the Thursday Circle were small and exclusive gatherings that met the needs of intellectuals and enlightened members of the upper bourgeoisie. The city also offered a wide range of societies focused on specific interests: the Society of Naturalist Friends, for example, or the Pedagogical Society that met on the first Monday every month in a suburban council chamber at Werder, or the Economic Heating Society that discussed ways of reducing the consumption of wood, a scarce and expensive commodity at this time. The Philomatic Society, with a membership of thirty-five, catered to people with an interest in the sciences, including the Jewish Kantian philosopher Lazarus Bendavid, the sculptor Johann Gottfried Schadow and the senior official Ernst Ferdinand Klein. Then there were the Medical Club – a forerunner of the later professional organizations – and the Pharmaceutical Society, which maintained a herbarium and a small library for the use of its members. The Military Society concerned itself with the need for military reform and encompassed some 200 members – it was an early focal point for the reforming energies of those activists who would come to the fore after 1806. For those who wished to keep abreast of the latest developments in politics, science and culture, there was a wide range of reading societies and other commercial reading facilities, such as lending libraries. Newspapers and journals could also be had in the coffee houses; and the lodges often maintained considerable libraries.

As the clubs grew more numerous, their functions became ever more specialized and diverse. One popular new form of organized social activity in Berlin was the amateur theatrical society. Theatrical societies proliferated quickly in the 1780s and 1790s, catering to a wide range of social constituencies. While the Urania (founded in 1792) catered to members of the enlightened social elite, the Polyhymnia (founded in 1800) included plumbers, instrument makers, cobblers and brush makers. The theatrical clubs admitted both men and women, although the selection of works for performance was generally reserved to the men alone. It was only a matter of time before clubs sprang up combining private venues for members and their guests with a range of leisure activities and entertainments. The 'Resources' (*Ressourcen*), as they were called, were clubs that rented premises in which a wide range of services was on offer, from meals to billiards, reading rooms, concerts, balls, theatrical performances, or even, in one case, fireworks. These were large enterprises, often encompassing a membership of more than 200, and reflecting in their clientele and tone the social diversity of the capital city.

This densely textured and swiftly changing topography of voluntary organizations tells us something of the forces at work in Prussian society by the end of the eighteenth century. Berlin was a centre of royal and governmental authority, but it was also a theatre of autonomous social action where citizens could deliberate on the high matters of state, acquire scientific and other esoteric knowledge, enjoy the pleasures of a sociability that was neither private nor entirely public, consume culture and take pleasure in congenial surroundings. None of this was in any sense rebellious or revolutionary, yet it did reflect a seismic shift in the balance of power within society. Christians and Jews, men and women, nobles, burghers and artisans rubbed shoulders in this sociable urbane milieu. It was a world that had made itself out of the talents, communicative energies and ready cash of the city's population. It was courteous rather than courtly. Controlling it, censoring it, even overseeing it, were tasks beyond the resources of Berlin's modest police and censorship organs. Its very existence posed a subtle challenge to the structures and habits of traditional authority.

Within the ranks of the administration, too, there were signs of a paradigm shift. A new generation of civil servants began to orient

*23. Baron Karl vom und
zum Stein*

Prussian administrative practice towards new objectives. In 1780, a young nobleman from the city of Nassau on the river Lahn joined the Prussian civil service. Reichsfreiherr Karl vom und zum Stein hailed from an ancient imperial family and was, like so many Germans of his generation, an admirer of Frederick II. As an official within the War and Domains Chamber, Stein was made responsible for improving the efficiency and productivity of the mining sector in the Westphalian territories. The lucrative mines of the county of Mark were at this time largely under the control of the *Gewerke*, corporate, trade union-like bodies that managed the local labour market. On Stein's initiative, the powers of these unions were cut back to make way for a new unified system of wage regulations and an expanded regime of state inspection. Yet at the same time, Stein, who approved of corporate organizations as long as they did not get in the way of efficiency, achieved reconciliation with the mining unions by conceding them a greater measure of self-government, including the appointment by election of their own officers.[67]

Stein's originality and brilliance were quickly recognized and by 1788 he held two senior posts within the chamber administration in Kleve and the county of Mark. He purged outmoded regulations and privileges from the fiscal system; he also suspended guild controls in the country-side, in order to stimulate rural manufacture and eliminate smuggling. The panoply of internal tolls collected by private individuals and corporations was swept away and replaced by a state-administered border tariff set at a moderate level.[68] As provincial president of Minden-Ravensberg from 1796, Stein again targeted the traditional levies and privileges that muted the vitality of the local economy. He even attempted (without success) to get to grips with the problem of servile peasant status in the Westphalian lands (and particularly in Minden-Ravensberg, where many peasants were still personally unfree). As a member of the old imperial corporate nobility, Stein was reluctant to ride roughshod over local tradition and opted for a policy of negotiation with the provincial Estates. The aim was to introduce a compensation package that would reconcile the landed families to the curtailment of their seigneurial rights. These latter initiatives foundered on the bitter resistance of the nobility, but they signalled the advent of a bold new style in Prussian administration.[69]

Another rising civil servant with reformist ideas was Karl August von Hardenberg, who joined the Prussian administration in 1790. Like Stein, Hardenberg was a 'foreigner' with a deep admiration of Frederick II. Born on his maternal grandfather's estate at Essenrode in 1750, Hardenberg hailed from a Hanoverian family of progressive reputation.[70] As a civil servant in his native Hanover, the young Hardenberg became known as an outspoken reformer – a memorandum he composed in 1780 called for the abolition of servile peasant tenures, deregulation of the economy and the creation of a more streamlined executive based upon thematic ministries and clear lines of command and responsibility.[71] After his transfer to Prussia, Hardenberg was entrusted, from January 1792, with the administrative integration of the newly acquired Franconian territories of Ansbach and Bayreuth.[72] This was a task of great complexity, for they were criss-crossed with enclaves, exclaves and overlapping sovereignties.

Hardenberg attacked the problem with extraordinary determination and ruthlessness. The imperial nobles were shorn of their baroque privileges and constitutional rights, in flagrant breach of imperial law. Exchange agreements and jurisdictional settlements were put in place to eliminate enclaves and establish the borders as the impermeable frontiers of a homogeneous Prussian political sovereignty. The right of subjects

24. Karl August, Prince
von Hardenberg. *Marble
bust by Christian Rauch,
1816.*

to bring suits before the imperial courts was abolished, thus preventing
the corporate nobility in the provinces from taking their grievances to
the Emperor. Where there was resistance to his orders, Hardenberg was
quick to send in troops and enforce compliance. These measures were
supported by an innovative approach to public opinion – Hardenberg
maintained contacts with several important journals in the region and
discreetly cultivated friendly writers who could be depended upon to
publish articles and editorials supporting his policy.[73]

Hardenberg had made it a condition of taking office that he would
report directly to the king. He was thus a kind of viceroy in Ansbach
and Bayreuth, with powers denied to his colleagues in the capital. This
enabled him to push through far-reaching reforms without fear of their
being sabotaged by jealous superiors. The new Franconian administration he established was structured (unlike the central government in
Berlin) along modern lines: there were four thematic ministries (justice,
interior, war and finance). Under Hardenberg's leadership, the
Franconian principalities became a hothouse of administrative reform
in the old Prussia. Among those officials who moved sideways from the
core administration to take up vacant posts in Ansbach and Bayreuth
we find many of the names that later appear at the apex of the Prussian

state: Schuckmann, Koch, Kircheisen, Humboldt, Bülow. Around Hardenberg himself there gathered an eager pack of ambitious younger bureaucrats from the region. Men of the 'Franconian clique' would come to occupy senior administrative posts, not only in Prussia, but also in Bavaria, which later took over the principalities as a result of the Napoleonic Wars.[74]

Even Prussia's time-honoured grain-management system was under growing pressure to change. The first four years of the reign of Frederick William II (r. 1786–97) saw a dramatic liberalization of the grain trade. It was a short-lived experiment – controls were gradually reimposed from 1788 onwards, to the great disappointment of liberals within the administration.[75] But a chain of subsistence riots in 1800–1805 persuaded some senior officials that productivity would rise and distribution occur more efficiently if the state abandoned its controls and allowed the grain markets to function without state interference. One influential supporter of this view was the East Prussian nobleman Friedrich Leopold Freiherr von Schroetter, Prussian State Minister for East and West Prussia and vice-president of the General Directory. Schroetter was a sometime student and family friend of Immanuel Kant and a decided exponent of the agrarian liberalism that was fashionable among the East Prussian elite at the turn of the century. On 11 July 1805, he set out his views in a memorandum to the king. If subsistence riots were possible in peacetime because of failures and inefficiencies in the state system, Schroetter argued, then what could be expected if a war were to break out, and the state barges used to transport grain were needed by the army? In place of the existing regulations, Schroetter proposed a radical deregulation of the grain economy. No one, he suggested, should be obliged to sell grain against his will or at prices imposed by the government; instead of protecting the grain supply from the traders, the state should protect the traders and uphold their right to dispose freely of their property. The General Directory rejected Schroetter's proposals in August 1805. But this was a temporary setback. In the not-so-long term, it was Schroetter's liberalism – not the protectionism of the Directory – that would win the day.[76]

We can therefore speak of a process of change diffusing inwards from various points on the Prussian periphery.[77] In the 1790s, the decade of revolution in Europe, Prussia seemed to be poised between two worlds. The expansion of critical print that had taken place during the last third of the century presented the administration with a phenomenon that it could neither repress nor fully accept. The flowering of Prussian monarchical patriotism expressed an ambition among the emergent urban intelligentsia to participate in the great matters of the state for which there was as yet no outlet in Prussia's governmental system. Debate and critical discussion within and outside the administration had raised questions about virtually every domain of the political system – from the power structures of agrarian society, to the organization and tactics of the military, to the state's management of the economy.

No single text better documents the transitional condition of Prussia at the end of the eighteenth century than the General Law Code published in 1794. With its almost 20,000 paragraphs that seem to spy into the foundations of every conceivable transaction between one Prussian and another, the General Code was the greatest civilian achievement of the Frederician enlightenment. Drawn up by a team of brilliant jurists following a long process of public debate and consultation, it was without parallel at the time of its publication; only in 1804 and 1811 did France and Austria follow with similar, if less comprehensive, codices. It was also exemplary for the clarity and elegance of its language, which articulated key axioms with such lucidity and precision that many rhetorical fragments of the Prussian code survive in the civil law of today's Germany.[78]

The fascination of the General Code lies in the curiously unresolved portrait it offers of Prussian society at the end of the eighteenth century. Peering at Prussia through its paragraphs is like using a pair of binoculars with different focal lengths. On the one hand, there are glimpses of an egalitarian socio-legal order. The very first paragraph announced that 'the General Law Code contains the rules by which the rights and obligations of the residents of the state [. . .] are to be assessed.'[79] The reader is immediately struck by the choice of the latently egalitarian term 'residents' (*Einwohner*) in place of the more traditional 'subjects' (*Untertanen*), and this impression is reinforced by §22, which declares that 'the laws of the state bind all members thereof, without regard to their Estate, rank or gender.'[80] Here, the notion of 'membership' of the state is substituted for subjecthood and the egalitarian intention is made more explicit. At §82 of the Introduction, however, we are told that 'the rights of the individual' are a function, all else being equal, of 'his birth [and] his Estate'; in a later section dealing with the 'obligations and rights of the noble Estate' the code states baldly that 'the nobility is the first Estate in the State' whose chief vocation and task is the defence thereof. Further paragraphs in the same section stipulate that members of the noble Estate are to be tried only by the highest courts in the land, that nobles enjoy privileged access (assuming adequate qualifications) to the 'places of honour in the State' and that 'only the nobility is entitled to the ownership of noble landed estates.'[81]

These discrepancies seemed less mysterious to contemporaries than they do to us. For Frederick II, who gave the order to begin this great work of codification, the primacy of the nobility was an axiom of the social order and he ordered his jurists to consider not only the 'general good' but also the specific entitlements of the Estates – this element was further strengthened after his death.[82] The ambivalence that resulted can be discerned in the paragraphs covering the rights and obligations of peasant subjects on the noble landed estates. Amazingly, the law characterizes these persons as 'free citizens of the State' (*freye Bürger des Staates*) – indeed the subject peasants are the only group to enjoy this distinction. Yet the bulk of the paragraphs on this topic reinforce the existing structures of corporate domination and inequality in the countryside. Subjects must gain the permission of the lordship before marrying (though, on the other hand, this cannot be refused without good legal reason); their children must offer domestic service; they must suffer (moderate) punishments for misdemeanours; they must render their services as required under law, and so on.[83] The corporate structures of Prussian society were seen as so fundamental to the social order that they structured the law, rather than being defined by it; indeed they were 'sources of the law', as one of the titles in the preamble to the code puts it.[84]

What is really interesting about the General Code is not that these disparate perspectives exist within it, but that neither seems reducible to the other. The code looks backwards to a world already of the past, a world where each order has its place in relation to the state, a world that seemed rooted in the Middle Ages but had in fact been invented by Frederick the Great and was already dissolving when the work of codification drew to a close. But it also anticipates a world where all citizens are 'free', the state is sovereign, and kings and governments are bound by the law; indeed some historians have seen the code as a kind of proto-constitution guaranteeing the rule of law.[85] The nineteenth-century historian Heinrich Treitschke highlighted these inner tensions when he observed that the code captured 'the Janus-headedness' of the Frederician state.[86] He borrowed the idea from Madame de Staël, who observed that 'the image of Prussia offers a double face, like that of Janus, one of which is military, the other philosophical.'[87] The metaphor of the two-faced Roman god of thresholds caught on, metastasizing wildly across the historiography of Prussia until the point (in the 1970s and 1980s), when it seemed impossible to write anything at all about Prussia without pouring a libation to Janus. It was as if the divided gaze of the two-faced god captured something fundamental about the Prussian experience, a polarity between tradition and innovation that defined the historical trajectory of the Hohenzollern state.

9
Hubris and Nemesis: 1789–1806

The years between the French Revolution of 1789 and Napoleon's defeat of Prussia in 1806 are among the most eventful and least impressive epochs in the history of the Prussian monarchy. Confronted by a bewildering profusion of threats and opportunities, Prussian foreign policy embarked on a course of febrile oscillation: the traditional dualist rivalry with Austria, the consolidation of Prussia's pre-eminence in northern Germany, and the tantalizing prospect of vast territorial annexations in Poland all competed for the attention of the policy-makers in Berlin. Sly double-diplomacy, fearful wavering and spasms of rapacity alternated in rapid succession. The ascendancy of Napoleon Bonaparte brought a new and existential threat. His inability to tolerate any limit to the expansion of French hegemony on the continent and his utter disregard of international treaties and agreements tested the Prussian executive almost to breaking point. In 1806, after numerous provocations, Prussia made the momentous error of offering battle to Napoleon without first securing the military support of a major power. The result was a catastrophe that challenged the legitimacy of the traditional monarchical order.

PRUSSIAN FOREIGN POLICY IN AN ERA OF REVOLUTION

The Prussian government looked with favourable interest on the Paris events of 1789. Far from shunning the rebels, the Prussian envoy in Paris spent the autumn and winter of 1789–90 establishing friendly contacts with the various factions. The idea – so familiar to later generations – that the Revolution hinged on a fundamental choice between obedience and rebellion, between the 'providence of God' and the 'will of man', played as yet no part in Berlin's interpretation of events.

There were essentially two reasons for this indulgent response to the French upheaval. The first was simply that, from Berlin's perspective, the Revolution represented an opportunity, not a threat. The Prussians were concerned above all with diminishing Austrian power and influence in Germany. Tensions between the two German rivals had risen steadily during the 1780s. In 1785, Frederick II had taken charge of a coalition of German princes opposed to the annexation of Bavaria by the Habsburg Emperor Joseph II. In 1788, the Emperor had gone to war against the Turks, prompting fears that massive Habsburg acquisitions in the Balkans would give Austria the upper hand over her Prussian rival. But in the summer and autumn of 1789, as Austrian forces pushed back the armies of Sultan Selim III, a chain of revolts broke out across the peripheral territories of the Habsburg crown – Belgium, Tyrol, Galicia, Lombardy and Hungary. Frederick William II, a vain and impulsive man who was determined to live up to the reputation of his illustrious uncle, did his best to exploit the discomfort of the Austrians. The Belgians were encouraged to secede from Habsburg rule and the Hungarian dissidents were urged to rise up against Vienna – there was even talk of an independent Hungarian monarchy to be ruled by a Prussian prince.[1]

Seen against this background, the revolution in France was welcome news, for there was good reason to hope that a new, 'revolutionary' French administration would put an end to the Franco-Austrian alliance. As the Prussians well knew, the alliance – along with its dynastic personification, Queen Marie Antoinette – was deeply unpopular with the Austrophobe patriots of the revolutionary movement. Berlin therefore courted the various revolutionary parties in the hope of building an anti-Habsburg 'party' in Paris. The aim was to reverse the diplomatic realignment of 1756, isolate Austria, and put an end to the expansionist plans of Joseph II. When a fully fledged revolution broke out in the prince-bishopric of Liège, a strip of territory right in the middle of Belgium, the Prussians supported the rebels there too, in the hope that the upheaval would spread to the adjacent Austrian-controlled areas.

There was also an ideological dimension to this tentative support for revolutionary upheaval. In 1789, a number of the leading Prussian policy-makers, including the minister responsible for foreign affairs,

Count Hertzberg – were personally sympathetic to the aspirations of the revolutionaries. Hertzberg was a man of the enlightenment who deplored the incompetent despotism of the Bourbons in France. He saw Prussian support for the insurrection in Liège as entirely in keeping with the kingdom's 'liberal principles'. The envoy entrusted with handling Prussia's affairs in the prince-bishopric, Christian Wilhelm von Dohm, was an enlightened official and intellectual (not to mention author of the famous tract supporting the emancipation of the Jews); he was a critic of the episcopal regime in Liège and favoured a progressive, constitutional solution to the dispute between the prince-bishop and the insurrectionists of the Third Estate.[2]

It was above all the threat of a Prussian-backed revolution in Hungary that persuaded Joseph's successor, Leopold II, to seek an understanding with Prussia.[3] Leopold, a wise and temperate figure, saw at once the folly of pursuing new conquests in the Ottoman Balkans while his hereditary possessions disintegrated behind his back. In March 1790, he despatched a friendly letter to Berlin, opening the door for the negotiations that culminated in the Convention of Reichenbach of 27 July 1790. The two German powers agreed – after tense discussions – to pull back from the brink of war and put their differences behind them. The Austrians undertook to end their costly Turkish war on moderate terms (i.e. without annexations) and the Prussians promised to stop fomenting rebellions within the Habsburg monarchy.

The Convention looked innocuous, but it was more significant than it seemed.[4] The era of bitter Prusso-Austrian antagonism that had structured the political affairs of the Holy Roman Empire since the invasion of Silesia in 1740 was now over, at least for a time, and the two German powers could pursue their interests in concert, rather than at each other's expense. Following an oscillatory pattern that recalled the days of the Great Elector, Frederick William II abandoned his secret efforts to secure an alliance with Paris and switched to a policy of war against revolutionary France. Foreign Minister Hertzberg and his liberal views fell into disfavour; he was later dismissed. An important role in the new diplomacy went to Frederick William's trusted adviser and confidant, Johann Rudolf von Bischoffwerder, an exponent of war against the revolution, who was despatched to Vienna in February and June–July 1791. The resulting Vienna Convention of 25 July 1791 laid the foundations for an Austro-Prussian alliance.

The first fruit of the Austro-Prussian rapprochement was a remarkable piece of gesture politics. The Declaration of Pillnitz, issued jointly by the Austrian Emperor and the Prussian king on 27 August 1791, was not a plan of action as such, but rather a statement of principled opposition to the Revolution. It opened by stating that the sovereigns of Prussia and Austria took the fate of their 'brother' the King of France to be 'an object of common interest to all the sovereigns of Europe', and demanded that the French king be placed as soon as possible 'in a position to affirm, in the most perfect liberty, the basis of a monarchical government'. It closed with the promise that Austria and Prussia would 'act promptly' with 'the necessary forces' to obtain 'the proposed and common goal'.[5] For all the fuzziness of its formulations, this was an unequivocal statement of monarchical counter-revolutionary solidarity. Yet the additional secret articles attached to the Declaration revealed that the dark waters of power politics were still running in their accustomed courses. Article 2 stated that the contracting parties reserved for themselves the power to 'exchange for their benefit several of their present and future acquisitions', always in mutual consultation, and article 6 promised that the Emperor would 'employ willingly his good offices towards the Court of Petersburg and the Court of Poland in order to obtain the cities of Thorn and Danzig [for Prussia] . . .'[6]

The Declaration fanned the flames of political extremism in the French Assembly, strengthening the hand of the Brissotin faction, who favoured war as a means of restoring French fortunes and furthering the Revolution. During late 1791 and early 1792, the pressure for war accumulated in Paris.[7] In the meanwhile, the Prussians and Austrians defined and agreed their objectives. The plan – under the terms of an alliance concluded on 7 February 1792 – was to launch a chain of enforced territorial transfers on the western periphery of the Holy Roman Empire. The allies would first conquer Alsace, handing one part of it to Austria and the other to the Elector Palatine, who would in turn be forced to yield Jülich and Berg to Prussia.

Whether and from what precise moment the allies seriously intended an invasion of France is unclear, but a military conflict became inevitable on 20 April 1792, when the French government formally declared war on the Austrian Emperor. As they prepared for an invasion, the Prussians and the Austrians assumed the mantle of ideological counter-revolution. On 25 July, the Prussian commander and joint commander of the allied forces, Charles William Ferdinand Duke of Brunswick-Lüneburg, issued the declaration that came to be known as the Brunswick Manifesto. This inflammatory document, based on a draft composed by vengeful French émigrés, claimed (somewhat mendaciously) that the two allied courts 'had no intention of enriching themselves by conquest', promised that all those who submitted to the authority of the French king would be protected, and threatened captured revolutionary guards with draconian punishments. The declaration closed with a note of menace that further radicalized the mood in Paris:

Their said Majesties declare, on their word of honour as emperor and king, that if the Chateau of the Tuileries [where the captive king and his family were housed] is entered by force or attacked, if the least violence be offered to their Majesties the king, queen and royal family, and if their safety and their liberty be not immediately assured, they will inflict an ever memorable vengeance by delivering over the city of Paris to military execution and complete destruction, and the rebels guilty of the said outrages to the punishment that they merit.[8]

Accompanying the Austro-Prussian force as it lumbered into France in the late summer of 1792 was a small army of émigrés led by Louis XVI's brother, the Count of Artois. These proved to be more trouble than they were worth: they were deeply unpopular with the French population and ineffective as a fighting force. Their chief function was to reinforce the counter-revolutionary credentials of the invaders. French peasants and townsfolk from whom food and livestock were requisitioned received promissory notes in the name of Louis XVI together with haughty assurances that the restored king would 'pay them back' once the war was over.

In the event, the allied campaign was a fiasco. Prussians and Austrians had never found it easy to coordinate forces on the western periphery of the Empire; the French campaign of 1792 was no exception. Confusion and conflicting priorities dogged the planning of the invasion from the start and the allied advance was stopped in its tracks at the battle of Valmy on 20 September. Here the invading troops found themselves confronted by an impregnably positioned enemy deployed in a broad arc on raised ground. Both sides let fly with their artillery, but it was the French who had the better of it, scoring hit after hit in the allied ranks, until some 1,200 soldiers had been cut down by cannon balls without their units having been able to make any headway at all against the enemy positions. It was the first time that the army of the Revolution had stood to face its enemies. Discouraged by this unexpected display of resolve, the allied forces withdrew from their exposed positions, leaving the French in control of the field.

The Prussians remained formal members of the coalition after Valmy and even fought with some success against the French in Alsace and the Saar. But they never committed more than a small fraction of their resources to these campaigns, because their attention was focused elsewhere. What distracted the men in Berlin were the prospects opening up in Poland. The pattern of internal turmoil and external interference and obstruction that had produced the first partition continued throughout the 1780s. In 1788–91, while the Russians were bogged down in a costly war with the Ottoman Empire, King Stanisław August and a party of Polish reformers had taken the opportunity to press ahead with changes to the political system. The new Polish constitution of 3 May 1791 created, for the first time, a hereditary monarchy and the outlines of a functioning central government. 'Our country is saved,' its authors announced. 'Our freedoms are assured; we are a free and independent nation; we have shaken off the bonds of slavery and misrule.'[9]

Neither the Prussians nor the Russians welcomed these developments. The creation of an independent Poland ran against the grain of nearly a century of Russian foreign policy. Frederick William II officially congratulated the Poles on their new constitution, but behind the scenes there was alarm at the prospect of a Polish revival. 'I foresee that sooner or later Poland will take West Prussia from us . . .' Hertzberg told a senior Prussian diplomat. 'How can we defend our state against a numerous and well-ruled nation?'[10] On 18 May 1792, Catherine II sent 100,000 Russian troops into the kingdom. Having played with the idea of supporting the Polish opposition to the invasion (in the hope of preventing or limiting Russian annexations), the Prussians decided instead to accept a partition offer from St Petersburg. Under the terms of the Treaty of St Petersburg of 23 January 1793, the Prussians received the commercially important cities of Danzig and Thorn and a substantial triangle of territory that plugged the cleft between Silesia and East Prussia and also happened to encompass the wealthiest areas of the Polish commonwealth. The Russians helped themselves to a gigantic terrain comprising almost one half of Poland's entire remaining surface area. The agreement was manifestly unequal (in the sense that Russia's

The Second Partition of Poland, 1793

Baltic
Sea

Riga

Dvina

Memel

Königsberg

Vilna

EASTERN POMERANIA

Danzig

WEST
PRUSSIA

EAST
PRUSSIA

Minsk

Bromberg

Thorn

KINGDOM OF
POLAND

Posen

Vistula

Warsaw

Bug

Brest-
Litovsk

Breslau

Oder

SILESIA

Krakow

Lvov

Sambor

HABSBURG MONARCHY

N
W E
S

0   50   100   150   200 Miles

0   100   200   300 Kms

The Third Partition of Poland, 1795

Sebesh

Polotsk

Baltic Sea

Riga

Dvina

Dvina

Sebesh

Polotsk

Memel

Danzig

Königsberg

Vilna

Minsk

Bromberg

Vistula

Posen

Bug

Breslau

Warsaw

Brest-Litovsk

Oder

Gomel

Krakow

Lvov

Chernigov

Kiev

R U S S I A

------ Boundary of Poland 1793

Territories lost to Prussia

Territories lost to Russia

The Kingdom of Prussia

-·----·- Boundary of Poland 1772

portion was four times the size of Prussia's) but it gave the Prussians more than they had traditionally aspired to and it freed Berlin from any obligation to compensate Austria in the west.[11]

In March 1794, the uprising launched against the partition powers by the Polish patriot Tadeusz Kosciuszko set the stage for a further and final partition. Although the revolt was directed primarily against Russia, it was the Prussians who first tried to take advantage of it. They hoped, by suppressing the uprising, to stake a claim for further Polish territory on an equal footing with Russia. But with substantial troop deployments still in the west, the Prussians were already seriously over-stretched; after some early successes against the revolt they were forced to pull back and call for Russian help. Seeing their chance, the Austrians, too, joined the fray. After a desperate campaign of mass recruitment, Kosciuszko held off the armies of Russia, Prussia and Austria for nearly eight months, but on 10 October 1794, a Russian victory at Maciejowice to the south-east of Warsaw brought the uprising to an end. The way was now open to the third and last partition of Poland. After bitter quarrels among the three powers, a tripartite division was agreed on 24 October 1795, by which Prussia gained a further tranche of territory encompassing about 55,000 square kilometres of land in central Poland, including the ancient capital of Warsaw, and some 1,000,000 inhabitants. Poland was no more.

THE PERILS OF NEUTRALITY

Something extraordinary had happened: in the course of the second and third Polish partitions, Frederick William II, perhaps the least impressive figure to have mounted the Prussian throne over the last century and a half, secured more territory for his kingdom than any other sovereign in his dynasty's history. Prussia grew in size by about one third to cover over 300,000 square kilometres; its population swelled from 5.5 to around 8.7 million. With its objectives in the east more than fulfilled, Prussia lost no time in extracting itself from the anti-French coalition in the west, and signing a separate peace with France at Basle on 5 April 1795.

Once again, the Prussians had left their allies in the lurch. The scribes and pamphleteers employed to produce Austrian propaganda dutifully thundered against this foul retreat from the common cause against

France. Historians have often taken a similar line, denouncing the separate peace and the neutrality that followed as contemptible, 'cowardly', 'suicidal' and 'pernicious'.[12] The problem with such assessments is that they are founded on the anachronistic presumption that late-eighteenth-century Prussia had a German 'national' mission that it failed in 1795 to fulfil. But if we focus our attention firmly on the Prussian state and its interests, then the separate peace appears the best option. Prussia was financially exhausted, its domestic administration was struggling to digest vast swathes of newly acquired Polish territory and it could ill afford to continue campaigning in the west. A 'peace party' emerged at the Berlin court with powerful economic arguments for a withdrawal from the coalition against France.[13]

The terms of the Treaty of Basle were in any case – at least on paper – highly advantageous to Prussia. Among them was an agreement by which France and Prussia undertook to uphold the neutrality of northern Germany. The neutrality zone provided Berlin with the opportunity to extend its influence over the lesser German states within the zone. Foreign Minister Haugwitz was quick to capitalize on this by persuading a string of north German territories (including Hanover) to join the Prussian neutrality system and thereby abscond from their obligations to the defence of the Holy Roman Empire.[14] Finally, the neutrality zone left Prussia's hands free in the east and ensured that French aggression would be focused on the Austrians – to this extent it was in line with the traditional dualist policy. There was more, in other words, to neutrality than simply the avoidance of war with France. With the peace signed and Prussia safe behind the north German 'demarcation line', the king could afford to look upon what had been accomplished with a certain satisfaction.

His achievement was more flimsy, however, than it looked. Prussia was now isolated. Over the past six years, it had allied itself with – and then abandoned – virtually every European power. The king's known predilection for secret diplomacy and chaotic double-dealing left him a lonely and distrusted figure on the diplomatic scene. Experience would soon show that unless Prussia could count on the assistance of a great power in defending the German demarcation line, the neutrality zone was indefensible and therefore largely meaningless. An issue of longer-term significance was the disappearance of Poland from the European map. Even if we set aside the moral outrage committed against Poland by the partitioning powers, the fact remains that independent Poland had played a crucial role as a buffer and intermediary between the three eastern powers.[15] Now that it no longer existed, Prussia shared, for the first time in its history, a long and indefensible border with Russia.[16] From now on, the fortunes of Prussia would be inseparable from those of its vast and increasingly powerful eastern neighbour.

By taking refuge in the north German neutrality zone agreed with the French at Basle in 1795, Berlin also signalled its utter indifference to the fate of the Holy Roman Empire: the demarcation line split Germany across the middle, abandoning the south to France and the tender mercies of the Austrians. Moreover, a secret agreement appended to the Treaty of Basle in 1795 stated that if France should ultimately retain the Prussian territories she had occupied in the Rhineland, the Prussians would be compensated with territorial indemnities to the east of the Rhine – an ominous foretaste of the rush for annexations that would consume Germany at the end of the decade. The Austrians, too, abandoned any pretence of accommodating the imperial sensibilities of the lesser and least states. The Austrian forces engaged in the war with France behaved more like an army of occupation than an ally in the southern German states, and Baron Johann von Thugut, the intelligent, unscrupulous minister appointed to run Austrian foreign policy in March 1793, focused his plans for Germany around a revived version of the old Bavarian exchange project. In October 1797, Vienna concluded an agreement with Napoleon Bonaparte to trade the Austrian Netherlands for Venetia and Salzburg, one of the most prominent ecclesiastical principalities of the old Empire.[17] It seemed that the fate of Poland was about to be visited upon the Holy Roman Empire. Heinrich von Gagern, chief minister of the little County of Nassau, made this connection explicit when he observed in 1797: 'The German princes have so far found themselves in the double misfortune of wishing for a rapprochement between Prussia and Austria when they think of France and of fearing one when they think of Poland.'[18]

The chief objective of French policy *vis-à-vis* Germany during these years was the 'restoration' to France of her 'natural frontiers', a wholly bogus concept invented by the Assembly and fathered upon Louis XIV. In practice, this meant the wholesale annexation of the German territories along the left bank of the river Rhine. The area was a dense patchwork of imperial principalities, encompassing territories belonging to the Hohenzollern king of Prussia, the Electorates of Cologne, Trier and Mainz, the Elector Palatine, the Duke of Pfalz-Zweibrücken, various imperial cities and numerous other lesser sovereignties. Its absorption into the French unitary state was thus bound to have a catastrophic impact on the Empire. Yet the German territories were in no position to contest France's acquisitions in the west. The larger states – Baden, Württemberg and Bavaria – had already been forced out of the war and were looking to build bridges with France. At the Peace of Campo Formio, signed in October 1797 after Bonaparte's victorious campaign against the Austrians in northern Italy, Vienna extended formal recognition to the French conquests in the German Rhineland. It was also agreed that the consequences of the French annexations for the Empire as a whole should be decided by direct bargaining between France and representatives of the imperial territories. The scene was thus set for the protracted negotiations that would culminate in the repartitioning of German Europe. These began in November 1797 in the picturesque Badenese city of Rastatt, and ended, after various stops and starts, with the Report of the Imperial Delegation (known in German by the gargantuan term *Reichsdeputationshauptschluss*) published in Regensburg on 27 April 1803.

The report announced a geopolitical revolution. All but six of the imperial cities were swept away; of the panoply of ecclesiastical principalities, from Cologne and Trier to the imperial abbeys of Corvey, Ellwangen and Guttenzell, only three remained on the map. The main winners were the greater and middle-sized principalities. The French, pursuing their time-honoured policy of creating German client states, were especially generous to Baden, Württemberg and Bavaria, whose geographical position between France and Austria made them useful allies. Baden was the biggest winner in proportional terms: it had lost 440 square kilometres through the French annexations but was compensated with over 3,237 square kilometres of land torn from the bishoprics of Speyer, Strassburg, Constance and Basle. Another winner was Prussia, which received the Bishopric of Hildesheim, Paderborn, the greater part of Münster, Erfurt and the Eichsfeld, the abbeys of Essen, Werden and Quedlinburg, the imperial city of Nordhausen, Mühlhausen and Goslar. Prussia had lost about 2,642 square kilometres of Rhenish lands with 127,000 inhabitants, but gained almost 13,000 square kilometres of territory with a population of around half a million.

The Holy Roman Empire was on its last legs. With the ecclesiastical principalities gone, the Catholic majorities in the diet were no more and the Catholicity of the Empire was a thing of the past. Its *raison d'être* as the protective incubator for the political and constitutional diversity of traditional central Europe was exhausted. The ancient association between the imperial crown and the House of Habsburg now seemed largely meaningless, even to Leopold II's successor, Francis II, who accordingly declared himself to be the hereditary Emperor of Austria in 1804 in order to secure an independent footing for his imperial title. The formal end of the Empire, announced by the imperial herald after the usual trumpet fanfare in Vienna on 6 August 1806, seemed a mere formality and provoked remarkably little contemporary comment.

There would be further territorial reorganizations before the Napoleonic Wars were over, but the basic outlines of a simplified nineteenth-century Germany were already visible. Prussia's new territories reinforced its dominance in the north. The consolidation of Baden, Württemberg and Bavaria in the south created the core of a compact block of intermediary states that would confront the hegemonial ambitions of both Austria and Prussia in the post-war era. The disappearance of the ecclesiastical states also meant that millions of German Catholics now found themselves living as diasporal communities within Protestant polities, a state of affairs with far-reaching implications for the political and religious life of modern Germany. Amid the ruins of the imperial past, a German future was taking shape.

FROM NEUTRALITY TO DEFEAT

On 14 October 1806, the 26-year-old Lieutenant Johann von Borcke was posted with an army corps of 22,000 men under the command of General Ernst Wilhelm Friedrich von Rüchel to the west of the city of Jena. It was still dark when news arrived that Napoleon's troops had engaged the main Prussian army on a plateau near the city. The noise of cannon fire could already be heard from the east. The men were cold and stiff from a night spent huddled on damp ground, but morale improved when the rising sun dispelled the fog and began to warm shoulders and limbs. 'Hardship and hunger were forgotten,' Borcke recalled. 'Schiller's *Song of the Riders* rang from a thousand throats.'

By ten o'clock, Borcke and his men were finally on the move towards Jena. As they marched eastward along the highway, they saw many walking wounded making their way back from the battlefield. 'Everything bore the stamp of dissolution and wild flight.' At about noon, however, an adjutant came galloping up to the column with a note from Prince Hohenlohe, commander of the main Prussian army fighting the French outside Jena: 'Hurry, General Rüchel, to share with me the half-won victory; I am beating the French at all points.' It was ordered that this message should be relayed down the column and a loud cheer went up from the ranks.

The approach to the battlefield took the corps through the little village of Kapellendorf; streets clogged with cannon, carriages, wounded men and dead horses slowed their progress. Emerging from the village, the corps came up on to a line of low hills, where the men had their first sight of the field of battle. To their horror, only 'weak lines and remnants' of Hohenlohe's corps could still be seen resisting French attack. Moving forward to prepare for an attack, Borcke's men found themselves in a hail of balls fired by French sharp-shooters who were so well positioned and so skilfully concealed that the shot seemed to fly in from nowhere. 'To be shot at in this way,' Borcke later recalled, 'without seeing the enemy, made a dreadful impression upon our soldiers, for they were not used to that style of fighting, lost faith in their weapons and immediately sensed the enemy's superiority.'

Flustered by the ferocity of the fire, commanders and troops alike became anxious to press ahead to a resolution. An attack was launched against French units drawn up near the village of Vierzehnheiligen. But as the Prussians advanced, the enemy artillery and rifle fire became steadily more intense. Against this, the corps had only a few regimental cannon, which soon broke down and had to be abandoned. The order 'Left shoulder forward!' was shouted down the line and the advancing Prussian columns veered to the right, twisting the angle of attack. In the process, the battalions on the left began to drift apart and the French, bringing up more and more cannon, cut larger and larger holes in the advancing columns. Borcke and his fellow officers galloped back and forth, trying to repair the broken lines. But there was little they could do to allay the confusion on the left wing, because the commander, Major von Pannwitz, was wounded and no longer on his horse, and the adjutant, Lieutenant von Jagow, had been killed. The Regimental

Colonel Oberst von Walter was the next commander to fall, followed by General Rüchel himself and several staff officers.

Without awaiting orders, the men of Borcke's corps began to fire at will in the direction of the French. Some, having expended their ammunition, ran with fixed bayonets at the enemy positions, only to be cut down by cartridge shot or 'friendly fire'. Terror and chaos took hold, reinforced by the arrival of the French cavalry, who hoed into the surging mass of Prussians, slashing with their sabres at every head or arm that came within reach. Borcke found himself drawn along irresistibly with the masses fleeing the field westwards along the road to Weimar. 'I had saved nothing,' Borcke wrote, 'but my worthless life. My mental anguish was extreme; physically I was in a state of complete exhaustion and I was being dragged along among thousands in the most horrific chaos . . .'[19]

The battle of Jena was over. The Prussians had been defeated by a better-managed force of about the same size (there were 53,000 Prussians and 54,000 French deployed). Even worse was the news from Auerstedt a few kilometres to the north, where on the same day a Prussian army numbering some 50,000 men under the command of the Duke of Brunswick was routed by a French force half that size under Marshal Davout. Over the following fortnight, the French broke up a smaller Prussian force near Halle and occupied the cities of Halberstadt and Berlin. Further victories and capitulations followed. The Prussian army had not merely been defeated; it had been ruined. In the words of one officer who was at Jena: 'The carefully assembled and apparently unshakeable military structure was suddenly shattered to its foundations.'[20] This was precisely the disaster that the Prussian neutrality pact of 1795 had been designed to avoid. How did it come about? Why did the Prussians abandon the relative security of the neutrality pact to wage war against a French Emperor at the height of his powers?

After 1797, with the accession of Frederick William III, a hesitant, cautious individual, the neutrality adopted as an expedient by his predecessor settled into a kind of system, in the sense that the Prussians clung to it, even when there was considerable pressure – as in 1799, during preparations for the second coalition against France – to join one of the warring parties. To some extent this reflected the preferences of the monarch. Unlike his father, Frederick William III had no interest in the pursuit of renown: 'Everybody knows,' he told his uncle in October 1798, 'that I abhor war and that I know of nothing greater on earth than the preservation of peace and tranquillity as the only system suited to the happiness of human kind . . .'[21] But the neutrality policy also prevailed because so many good arguments could be cited in its support. As the king himself rather casuistically pointed out, remaining neutral left open the possibility of war later and was thus the most flexible option. His wife, Luise of Mecklenburg-Strelitz, a forceful figure with many contacts among the senior ministers, warned that war on the side of the coalition powers would bring dependency on Russia. This line of argument was based on the correct insight that Prussia remained, by a considerable margin, the least of the great powers. As such, it lacked the means to ensure that its interests would be met through a partnership with either of the warring parties. The state treasury, moreover, was still deeply in deficit; without the shelter of neutrality, it would be impossible to repair the kingdom's finances in preparation for a future conflict. Lastly, neutrality was attractive because it held out the prospect of territorial aggrandizement in northern Germany. This promise was partly realized in the secret convention signed between Prussia and France on 23 May 1802, when a handsome swathe of former imperial cities and secularized ecclesiastical principalities were promised to Prussia in pre-emption of the final Report of the Imperial Deputation published in the following year. So persuasive did the benefits of neutrality seem to the Prussian ministers and cabinet secretaries entrusted with advising the king on policy that there was virtually no serious opposition to it before 1805.[22]

The fundamental problem for Prussia during the years of neutrality was simply the kingdom's exposed location between France and Russia, which threatened to make a nonsense of the neutrality zone and Prussia's supposedly dominant place within it. Here was a geopolitical predicament that had preoccupied the Hohenzollerns since the days of the Great Elector.[23] But the threat was now even more pronounced, thanks to the French annexations in Germany and the removal of the Polish buffer zone that had once separated Prussia and Russia.[24] A case in point is the brief Prussian occupation of Hanover in March–October 1801. Joined to the British Crown by personal union, Hanover was the second largest territory within the neutrality zone and an obvious target for any state wishing to apply diplomatic pressure to Britain. In the winter and spring of 1800–1801, Tsar Paul I engineered a rapprochement with France in the hope of weakening Britain's maritime supremacy in the Baltic and the North Sea and pressured Berlin into mounting an occupation of the Electorate of Hanover, in the hope that this would persuade Britain to back down. The Prussian king was hesitant, but agreed once it became clear that France would occupy Hanover if Prussia did not – an action that would have demolished the remaining shreds of credibility left in Prussia's role as guarantor of the neutrality zone. The Prussians withdrew again at the earliest opportunity, but the episode illustrates how little room for autonomous manoeuvre they enjoyed, even within the neutrality zone they had carved out at the Peace of Basle. It also soured relations between Berlin and London, where there were many who believed that the ultimate aim of the Prussians was 'to possess the [British] king's electoral dominions'.[25]

The hollowness of Berlin's claim to hegemony within the neutrality zone was further exposed by the compensation of the lesser and middling German states for territories lost to France; rather than looking to Berlin, these states negotiated directly with Paris, bypassing the Prussians altogether.[26] In July 1803, Napoleon demonstrated his complete disregard for Prussian sensibilities by ordering the French occupation of Hanover. A further blow to Prussia's prestige followed in the autumn of 1804, when French troops broke into Hamburg and kidnapped the British envoy in the city, Sir George Rumbold. The kidnapping triggered outrage in Berlin: Rumbold had been accredited to Frederick William's court and performed his duties, as it were, under the Prussian king's protection. Moreover, the action had involved a flagrant breach of the neutrality pact and of international law. Frederick William fired off a bitter protest to Napoleon and a crisis with France was averted only when Napoleon unexpectedly backed down and released Rumbold.[27]

A further breach occurred in October 1805, when French troops marched through the Hohenzollern enclaves of Ansbach and Bayreuth on their way south to the confrontation with the Austro-Russian army at Austerlitz. In the face of such provocations, the arguments for Prussian neutrality looked increasingly threadbare. It is not known whether Frederick William III pondered on the Great Elector's troubled experience of neutrality, or whether he was reminded of Leibniz's comment, made at the height of the Northern War: 'To be neutral is rather like someone who lives in the middle of a house and is smoked out from below and drenched with urine from above.'[28]

The difficulty lay in determining what was the best alternative to neutrality. Should Prussia align itself with France or with Russia and the coalition powers? Opinions were divided. Controversy mounted within the antechamber of power as ministers, cabinet secretaries and informal advisers competed for influence over the monarch. This struggle was sanctioned by the king, who was anxious not to fall under the control of any one interest and thus continued to consult state ministers, cabinet ministers, cabinet secretaries, his wife and various friends for advice on key issues. The leading figures in the struggle to control foreign policy were the recently retired foreign minister, Count Christian von Haugwitz, and Karl August von Hardenberg, formally of Ansbach-Bayreuth, who succeeded Haugwitz after the latter's retirement on grounds of ill-health in 1804.

During the Rumbold crisis, Hardenberg began pressing for a Russian alignment and an open breach with France, partly in the hope of exploiting the débâcle of Haugwitz's neutrality policy in order to advance his career. Haugwitz, recalled from his retirement to advise the monarch, counselled caution, while at the same time manoeuvring to push Hardenberg aside and regain control over foreign policy. Hardenberg fought his corner with the usual energy and ruthlessness, taking care to curry favour with the monarch, upon whom everything depended.[29] As their struggle shows, divergences of opinion were amplified by adversarial relationships within the political elite. This was possible precisely because the Prussian security predicament in 1805–6 was such that it admitted of no easy resolution. Both options, alliance with France and alliance with the coalition powers, appeared equally plausible – and equally daunting.

International developments tipped the balance of Prussian policy first one way then the other. After October 1805, following the French breach of neutrality in Ansbach and Bayreuth, interest in a Russian alliance intensified. Late in November, Haugwitz was sent to deliver a stiff ultimatum to the French. Hardly had he left, however, but events tipped the balance back towards France. Upon arriving at Napoleon's headquarters, Haugwitz learned of the shattering defeat the Emperor's armies had just inflicted on the combined Austro-Russian forces at Austerlitz (2 December 1805). Sensing that his ultimatum was no longer opportune, the Prussian emissary offered Napoleon an alliance instead. The Treaty of Schönbrunn (15 December 1805), together with various follow-up agreements imposed by France, committed Prussia not only to a comprehensive alliance with Napoleon, but also to the annexation of Hanover and the closure of the northern sea ports to British shipping. Frederick William saw that this would mean war with Britain, but viewed such an outcome as a lesser evil than destruction at the hands of France. It looked very much as if Haugwitz had won out over his younger rival; in March 1806, he succeeded in forcing Hardenberg's resignation. 'France is all-powerful and Napoleon is the man of the century,' Haugwitz wrote to the Prussian envoy Lucchesini in the summer of 1806. 'What have we to fear if united with him?'[30]

Anxious to avoid a conflict with Russia and determined to keep his options open, Frederick William continued to pursue a secret policy aimed at rapprochment with St Petersburg. This was a welcome reprieve for Hardenberg, who now became the agent of an elaborate covert diplomacy: having seemed to withdraw in high dudgeon from public life in March, he was entrusted with responsibility for the secret relationship with Russia, which in turn made a nonsense of Haugwitz's ostensible policy of collaboration with France.[31] Never had the irresolvable complexities of the two-front dilemma produced such extravagant contortions in Berlin.

A determined political opposition now emerged within the uppermost echelons of the bureaucracy. Among the most influential dissenters was the temperamental Freiherr vom Stein, a minister in Berlin. Stein had never approved of the post-1795 neutrality, seeing in it (as indeed we might expect of a Rhenish nobleman and imperial patriot) a reprehensible abandonment of Germany. During the winter of 1805–6, as Count Haugwitz committed Prussia to an alliance with Napoleon, the annexation of Hanover and war with Britain, the Anglophile Stein found himself unable to support the government's course. He came to believe that only a thoroughgoing structural reform of the supreme executive would enable the state to formulate a more effective foreign policy. In an act that radically overstepped the boundaries of his official responsibility, he composed a memorandum dated 27 April 1806 whose title alone was a manifesto: 'Presentation of the mistaken organization of the cabinet and of the necessity of forming a ministerial conference'. Stein's document was remarkable for the strength of its language: in it the men of the king's cabinet were accused of 'arrogance, dogmatism, ignorance, physical and moral enfeeblement, shallowness, brutal sensuality, treacherous betrayal, shameless lying, narrow-mindedness and mischievous gossiping'.[32] The answer to the monarchy's current predicament, Stein argued, lay not merely in the removal of these reprobates, but also in the establishment of clearer lines of responsibility. Under the current arrangements, he argued, the king's personal advisers have 'all the power, while the real ministers have all the responsibility'. It was therefore necessary to replace the arbitrary rule of cronies and favourites with a system of responsible ministerial government.

If his Majesty will not agree to the suggested change, if he persists in ruling under the influence of a Cabinet deficient in its organisation and condemned in its personnel, it is to be expected that the state will either be dissolved or lose its independence, and the love and respect of its subjects will fail it completely. [. . .] nothing will be left for the upright official but to abandon it, covered with unmerited shame, without being able to help or take part against the wickedness that will ensue.[33]

Few documents illustrate more dramatically how rebellious the atmosphere had grown within the uppermost echelons of the Prussian administration. Fortunately, perhaps, for Stein, his remarkably forthright letter was never shown to the king. Stein passed it to General Rüchel (soon to take up his ill-fated command at Jena), asking that it be forwarded to the monarch, but the old general was reluctant. In May, Stein presented it to Queen Luise, who expressed her approval of its sentiments but thought it too 'violent and passionate' for submission to her husband. The letter did its work none the less; it circulated among the dissident senior figures within the administration, helping to sharpen the focus of their opposition. By October 1806, Stein had emerged as one of the leaders of the bureaucratic opposition.

In the meanwhile, Prussia's foreign policy dilemma remained unsolved. 'Your Majesty,' Hardenberg warned in a memorandum of June 1806, 'has been placed in the singular position of being simultaneously allied with both Russia and France [. . .] This situation cannot last.'[34] In July and August feelers were put out to the other north German states with a view to establishing an inter-territorial union; the most important fruit of these efforts was an alliance with Saxony. But the negotiations with Russia advanced more slowly, partly because of the sobering effect of the still-recent disaster at Austerlitz and partly because it took time for the confusion generated by the months of secret diplomacy to clear. Little had thus been done to build a solid coalition when news reached Berlin of a further French provocation. In August 1806, intercepts revealed that Napoleon was engaged in alliance negotiations with Britain, and had unilaterally offered the return of Hanover as an inducement to London. This was an outrage too far. Nothing could better have demonstrated Napoleon's contempt for the north German neutrality zone and the place of Prussia within it.

By this point, Frederick William III was under immense pressure from elements within his own entourage to opt for war with France. On 2 September, a memorandum was passed to the king criticizing his policy thus far and pressing for war. Among the signatories were Prince Louis Ferdinand, popular military commander and a nephew of Frederick the Great, two of the king's brothers, Prince Henry and Prince William, a cousin and the Prince of Orange. Composed for the signatories by the court historiographer Johannes von Müller, the memorandum pulled few punches. In it, the king was accused of having abandoned the Holy Roman Empire and sacrificed his subjects and the credibility of his word of honour for the sake of the policy of ill-conceived self-interest pursued by the pro-French party among his ministers. Now he was further endangering the honour of his kingdom and his house by refusing to take a stand. The king saw in this document a calculated challenge to his authority and responded with rage and alarm. In a gesture evocative of an earlier era when brothers wrestled for thrones, the princes were ordered to leave the capital city and return to their regiments. As this episode reveals, the factional strife over foreign policy had begun to drift out of control. A determined 'war party' had emerged that included members of the king's family, but was centred on the two ministers Karl August von Hardenberg and Karl vom Stein. Its objective was to put an end to the fudges and compromises of the neutrality policy. But its means implied the demand for a more broadly based decision-making process that would bind the king to a collegial deliberative mechanism of some kind.[35]

Although the king resented deeply the impertinence, as he saw it, of the memorandum of 2 September, the charge of prevarication unsettled him deeply, sweeping aside his instinctive preference for caution and delay. And so it was that the Berlin decision-makers allowed themselves to be goaded into precipitate action, although the preparations for a coalition with Russia and Austria had scarcely begun to take concrete shape. On 26 September Frederick William III addressed a letter full of bitter recriminations to the French Emperor, insisting that the neutrality pact be honoured, demanding the return of various Prussian territories on the lower Rhine and closing with the words: 'May heaven grant that we can reach an understanding on a basis that leaves you in possession of your full renown, but also leaves room for the honour of other peoples, [an understanding] that will put an end to this fever of fear and expectation, in which no one can count on the future.'[36] Napoleon's reply, signed in the imperial headquarters at Gera on 12 October, reverberated with a breathtaking blend of arrogance, aggression, sarcasm and false solicitude.

Only on 7 October did I receive Your Majesty's letter. I am extraordinarily sorry that You have been made to sign such a pamphlet. I write only to assure You that I will never attribute the insults contained within it to Yourself personally, because they are contrary to Your character and merely dishonour us both. I despise and pity at once the makers of such a work. Shortly thereafter I received a note from Your minister asking me to attend a rendezvous. Well, as a gentleman, I have kept to my appointment and am now standing in the heart of Saxony. Believe me, I have such powerful forces that all of Yours will not suffice to deny me victory for long! But why shed so much blood? For what purpose? I speak to Your Majesty just as I spoke to Emperor Alexander shortly before the Battle of Austerlitz. [. . .] Sire, Your Majesty will be vanquished! You will throw away the peace of Your old age, the life of Your subjects, without being able to produce the slightest excuse in mitigation! Today You stand there with your reputation untarnished and can negotiate with me in a manner worthy of Your rank, but before a month is passed, Your situation will be a different one![37]

Thus spoke the 'man of the century', the 'world soul on horseback' to the King of Prussia in the autumn of 1806. The course was now set for the trial of arms at Jena and Auerstedt.

For Prussia, the timing could hardly have been worse. Since the army corps promised by Tsar Alexander had not yet materialized, the coalition with Russia remained largely theoretical. Prussia faced the might of the French armies alone, save for its Saxon ally. Ironically, the habit of delay that the war party so deplored in the king was now the one thing that could have saved Prussia. The Prussian and Saxon commanders had expected to give battle to Napoleon somewhere to the west of the Thuringian forest, but he advanced much faster than they had anticipated. On 10 October 1806, the Prussian vanguard made contact with

French forces and was defeated at Saalfeld. The French then pushed past the flank of the Prussian armies and formed up with their backs to Berlin and the Oder, denying the Prussians access to their supply lines and routes of withdrawal. This is one reason why the subsequent breakdown of order on the battlefield proved so irreversible.

The relative prowess of the Prussian army had declined since the end of the Seven Years War. One reason for this was the emphasis placed upon increasingly elaborate forms of parade drill. These were not a cosmetic indulgence – they were underwritten by a genuine military rationale, namely the integration of each soldier into a fighting machine answering to one will and capable of maintaining cohesion under conditions of extreme stress. While this approach certainly had strengths (among other things, it heightened the deterrent effect upon foreign visitors of the annual parade manoeuvres in Berlin), it did not show up particularly well against the flexible and fast-moving forces deployed by the French under Napoleon's command. A further problem was the Prussian army's dependence upon large numbers of foreign troops – by 1786, when Frederick died, 110,000 of the 195,000 men in Prussian service were foreigners. There were very good reasons for retaining foreign troops; their deaths in service were easier to bear and they reduced the disruption caused by military service to the domestic economy. However, their presence in such large numbers also brought problems. They tended to be less disciplined, less motivated and more inclined to desert.

To be sure, the decades between the War of the Bavarian Succession (1778–9) and the campaign of 1806 also saw important improvements.[38] Mobile light units and contingents of riflemen (*Jäger*) were expanded and the field requisition system was simplified and overhauled. None of this sufficed to make good the gap that swiftly opened up between the Prussian army and the armed forces of revolutionary and Napoleonic France. In part, this was simply a question of numbers – as soon as the French Republic began scouring the French working classes for domestic recruits under the auspices of the *levée en masse*, there was no way the Prussians would be able to keep pace. The key to Prussian policy ought therefore to have been to avoid at all costs having to fight France without the aid of allies.

From the beginning of the Revolutionary Wars, moreover, the French had integrated infantry, cavalry and artillery in permanent divisions supported by independent logistic services and capable of sustaining autonomous mixed operations. Under Napoleon, these units were grouped together into army corps with unparalleled flexibility and striking power. By contrast, the Prussian army had scarcely begun to explore the possibilities of combined-arms divisions by the time they faced the French at Jena and Auerstedt. The Prussians were also a long way behind the French in the use of sharp-shooters. Although, as we have seen, efforts had been made to expand this element of the armed forces, overall numbers remained low, the weaponry was not of the highest standard and insufficient thought was given to how the deployment of riflemen could be integrated with the deployment of large troop masses. Lieutenant Johann Borcke and his fellow infantrymen paid dearly for this gap in tactical flexibility and striking power as they stumbled on to the killing field at Jena.

Frederick William III had initially intended to open peace negotiations with Napoleon after Jena and Auerstedt, but his approaches were rebuffed. Berlin was occupied on 24 October and three days later Bonaparte entered the capital. During a brief sojourn in nearby Potsdam, he made a famous visit to the tomb of Frederick the Great, where he is said to have stood deep in thought before the coffin. According to one account, he turned to the generals who were with him and remarked: 'Gentlemen, if this man were still alive, I would not be here.' This was partly imperial kitsch and partly a genuine tribute to the extraordinary reputation Frederick enjoyed among the French, especially the patriot networks that had helped to revitalize French foreign policy and had always seen the Austrian alliance of 1756 as the greatest error of the French *ancien régime*. Napoleon had long been an admirer of the Prussian king: he had pored through Frederick's campaign narratives and had a statuette of him placed in his personal cabinet. The young Alfred de Vigny even claimed with a certain amusement to have observed Napoleon affecting Frederician poses, ostentatiously taking snuff, making flourishes with his hat 'and other similar gestures' – eloquent testimony to the continuing resonance of the cult. By the time the French Emperor stood in Berlin paying his respects to the dead Frederick, his living successor had fled to the easternmost corner of the kingdom, evoking parallels with the dark days of the 1630s and 1640s. The state treasure, too, was saved in the nick of time and transported away to the east.[39]

Napoleon was now ready to offer peace terms. He demanded that Prussia renounce all its territories to the west of the river Elbe. After some agonized wavering, Frederick William III signed an agreement to this effect at the Charlottenburg palace on 30 October, whereupon Napoleon changed his mind and insisted that he would agree to an armistice only if Prussia consented to serve as the operational base for a French attack upon Russia. Although the majority of his ministers supported this option, Frederick William sided with the minority who preferred to continue the war at Russia's side. Everything now depended upon whether the Russians would be able to put sufficient forces in the field to halt the momentum of the French advance.

During the months from late October 1806 to January 1807, French forces had steadily advanced through the Prussian lands, forcing or accepting the capitulation of key fortresses. On 7 and 8 February 1807, however, they were repulsed at Preussisch-Eylau by a Russian force with a small Prussian contingent. Sobered by this experience, Napoleon returned to the armistice offer of October 1806, under which Prussia would merely give up its West-Elbian territories. Now it was Frederick William's turn to refuse, in the hope that renewed Russian attacks would push the balance further to Prussia's advantage. These were not forthcoming. The Russians failed to capitalize on the advantage gained at Preussisch-Eylau and the French continued throughout January and February to subdue the Prussian fortresses in Silesia. In the meanwhile, Hardenberg, who was still operating the pro-Russian policy with which he had triumphed in 1806, negotiated an alliance with St Petersburg that was signed on 26 April 1807. The new alliance was short lived; after a French victory over the Russians at Friedland on 14 June 1807, Tsar Alexander asked Napoleon for an armistice.

On 25 June 1807, Emperor Napoleon and Tsar Alexander met to begin peace negotiations. The setting was unusual. A splendid raft was built on Napoleon's orders and tethered in the middle of the river Memel at Piktupönen, near the East Prussian town of Tilsit. Since the Memel was the official demarcation line of the ceasefire and the Russian and French armies were drawn up on opposite banks of the river, the raft was an ingenious solution to the need for neutral ground where the two emperors could meet on an equal footing. Frederick William of Prussia was not invited. Instead he stood miserably on the bank for several hours, surrounded by the Tsar's officers and wrapped in a Russian

*25. Napoleon and Tsar Alexander meet on board a raft on the River Memel at
Tilsit. Contemporary etching by Le Beau, after Nadet.*

overcoat. This was just one of the many ways in which Napoleon
advertised to the world the inferior status of the defeated King of Prussia.
The rafts on the Memel were adorned with garlands and wreaths bearing
the letters 'A' and 'N' – the letters FW were nowhere to be seen, although
the entire ceremony was taking place on Prussian territory. Whereas
French and Russian flags could be seen everywhere fluttering in the mild
breeze, the Prussian flag was conspicuous by its absence. Even when, on
the following day, Napoleon invited Frederick William into his presence
on the raft, the resulting conversation had the flavour of an audience
rather than a meeting between two monarchs. Frederick William was
made to wait in an antechamber while the Emperor saw to some overdue
paperwork. Napoleon refused to inform the king of his plans for Prussia
and hectored him about the many military and administrative errors he
had made during the war.

Under pressure from the Tsar, Napoleon agreed that Prussia would
continue to exist as a state. But by the terms of the Peace of Tilsit (9 July
1807), it was stripped down to the rump: Brandenburg, Pomerania
(excluding the Swedish part), Silesia and East Prussia, plus the corridor
of land acquired by Frederick the Great in the course of the first partition

of Poland. The Polish provinces acquired through the second and third partitions were taken away to form the basis for a Franco-Polish satellite state in the east; the western territories, some of which dated back to the beginning of the seventeenth century, were also swept away to be annexed to France or incorporated into a range of Napoleonic client entities. Frederick William tried sending his wife Luise to beg the Emperor for a more generous settlement – unwittingly evoking parallels with the 1630s, when the unhappy Elector George William had sent his womenfolk out of Berlin to parley with the approaching Gustavus Adolphus. Napoleon was impressed by the determination and grace of the Prussian queen, but he made no concessions.

The dream of a Prussian custodial role in northern Germany – briefly sustained by the neutrality zone – seemed to have vanished without a trace. Gone, too, was the vision of Prussia as an eastern great power, dealing on equal terms with Russia and Austria. A large indemnity was demanded, with the precise amount to be announced in due course. The French would remain in occupation until this was settled. A small but bitter detail: having signed a separate peace with the French at Posen in December 1806 and joined the Confederation of the Rhine, an association of French satellite states in Germany, the Elector of Saxony accepted a royal crown from Napoleon's hands to become King Frederick August I of Saxony. In the following year, the Saxons were rewarded with Cottbus, a former Prussian possession. It almost looked as if Saxony's fortunes might revive to the point where Dresden could once again challenge Berlin for the captaincy of northern Germany. Napoleon encouraged these hopes. In an address to the officers of the defeated Saxon army in Jena castle on the day after the battle, the Emperor announced himself as a liberator and even claimed that he had waged war on Prussia only in order to maintain Saxony's independence.[40] This was a new twist in the long history of rivalry between Prussia and Saxony, in which the alliance of 1806 had been only a momentary interruption.

All regimes are tarnished by defeat – this is one of history's few rules. There have been many worse defeats than the Prussian disasters of 1806–7, but for a political culture so centred on military prowess the defeats at Jena and Auerstedt and the surrenders that followed were definitive none the less. They signified a failure at the centre of the system. The king himself was a commanding officer (though not an especially talented one) who had been in regimental service since childhood and made it his business to be seen riding about in uniform before his advancing regiments. The adult princes of the royal family were all well-known commanders. The officer corps was the agrarian ruling class in uniform. A question mark hung over the political order of old Prussia.

10

The World the Bureaucrats Made

THE NEW MONARCHY

In December 1806, as Frederick William III and Luise of Prussia fled eastwards from the advancing French armies, they stopped overnight in the small East Prussian town of Ortelsburg. There was no food or clean water to be had. The king and his wife were forced to share the same sleeping quarters in 'one of the wretched barns that they call houses', according to the British envoy George Jackson, who was travelling with them.[1] Here, Frederick William found time to reflect at length on the meaning of the Prussian defeat. In the aftermath of the disasters at Jena and Auerstedt, numerous Prussian fortresses had collapsed under circumstances in which they should have been able to hold out. Stettin, for example, which possessed a garrison of around 5,000 men and was fully provisioned, had surrendered to a small regiment of enemy hussars numbering only 800. The fortress at Küstrin – that shrine of Prussian memory – had surrendered only days after the king himself had left it to move eastward. The collapse of Prussia, it seemed, was as much a question of political will and motivation as of technical inferiority.

The king's rage over this chain of capitulations found expression in the Declaration of Ortelsburg, a statement composed by Frederick William on 12 December 1806 and written in his own hand. It was still too early, he observed, to draw conclusions about who or what was responsible for the 'almost total dissolution' of the Prussian forces in the field, but the fortress capitulations were a scandal 'without precedent' in the history of the Prussian army. In future, he wrote, every governor or commander who surrendered his fortress 'simply for fear of bombardment' or 'for any other worthless reason, whatever it might be', would be 'shot without mercy'. Any soldier who 'threw away his weapons out of fear' would likewise face the firing squad. Prussian subjects who entered the service of the enemy and were found with a weapon in their hand would be 'shot without mercy'.[2] Much of the document reads like a cathartic explosion of anger, but tucked away at the end was a passage that announced a revolution. In future, Frederick William wrote, any fighting man who performed with distinction should be promoted into the officer corps, regardless of whether he was a private, a warrant officer or a prince.[3] Amid the chaos of defeat and flight, a process of reform and self-renewal had begun.

In the aftermath of the defeats and humiliations of 1806–7, a new leadership cadre of ministers and officials launched a salvo of government edicts that transformed the structure of the Prussian political executive, deregulated the economy, redrew the ground rules of rural society and reformulated the relationship between the state and civil society. It was the very scale of the defeat that opened the door to reform. The collapse of trust in traditional structures and procedures created opportunities for those who had long been striving to improve the system from within, and silenced their former opponents. The war also imposed fiscal burdens that were insoluble within the parameters of established practice. There was a substantial indemnity to pay (120 million francs), but the real cost of the French occupation, which lasted from August 1807 until December 1808, was estimated by one contemporary at around 216.9 million thalers – a huge sum if we consider that in 1816 total government revenues were just over 31 million thalers.[4] The resulting sense of emergency favoured those with forceful and coherent programmes of action and the ability to communicate them persuasively. In all these ways, the exogenous shock of Napoleon's victory focused and amplified forces already at work within the Prussian state.[5]

At the centre of the reform process that began in 1807 (though his role has sometimes been under-appreciated) was the King of Prussia, Frederick William III. Important as the reforming bureaucrats were, they could not have carried out their plans without the support of the monarch. It was Frederick William III who appointed Karl vom Stein as his chief adviser in October 1807, until he was forced by Napoleon to dismiss him (after allegations that Stein was plotting against the French). After appointing Alexander Count Dohna and Karl von Altenstein (an old boy from the 'Franconian clique') as joint chief ministers, the king called Hardenberg to the ministries of finance and the interior in June

1810 and granted him the new title of *Staatskanzler*, designating him as Prussia's first prime minister.

Yet Frederick William III remains a shadowy figure. J. R. Seeley, author of a three-volume nineteenth-century portrait of Stein, described the king as 'the most respectable and the most ordinary man that has reigned over Prussia'.[6] At a time when Prussia's cultural and political life was dominated by brilliant personalities – Schleiermacher, Hegel, Stein, Hardenberg, the Humboldts – the monarch was a pedantic and narrow-minded bore. His conversation was stunted and brusque. Napoleon, who often dined with him during the summer days in Tilsit, later recalled that it was difficult to get him to talk about anything but 'military headgear, buttons and leather satchels'.[7] Though he was rarely far from the centre of Prussian high politics in the crisis years before the defeat, he appears to us as a cipher, trying to blend into the background, fleeing the moment of decision and leaning on the counsels of those closest to him. As crown prince, Frederick William had been denied the chance to learn the business of government from the inside. (By contrast, he was to offer his own son, the future Frederick William IV, a key role in Prussian domestic politics – yet another example of the dialectical alternation of paternal regimes so characteristic of the Hohenzollern dynasty.) Throughout his life, the king combined a sharp, if reticent, intelligence with a profound lack of confidence in his own abilities. Far from embracing the opportunities of kingship, Frederick William saw the crown as a 'burden' to be borne, a burden he felt many others were better qualified to carry than he.

Frederick William's accession to the throne in 1797 was attended by the usual Hohenzollern contrasts. The father had pursued territorial prizes at every conceivable opportunity; the son was a man of peace who eschewed the quest for glory and reputation. The father's reign saw the last exuberant gasp of baroque monarchy, with its displays of wasteful splendour and bevies of mistresses; the son was austere in his tastes and remained faithful to his wife. Frederick William III found the City Palace in Berlin too imposing and preferred to stay in the smaller residence he had occupied as crown prince. His favourite domicile of all was a rustic little estate he bought at Paretz near Potsdam. Here he could live in tranquil domesticity and pretend he was an ordinary country squire. Frederick William drew a clear distinction, unlike his predecessors, between his private life and his public functions. He was

26. *King Frederick William and Queen Luise with the family in the palace gardens at Charlottenburg, c. 1805; engraving by Friedrich Meyer after Heinrich Anton Dähling*

painfully shy and disliked elaborate public occasions at court. He was shocked when he learned, in 1813, that his children were in the habit of referring to him in his absence as 'the king' rather than 'papa'. He enjoyed watching lightweight comedies at the theatre, partly because he relished the opportunity to be in company without being the centre of attention.

These might appear trivial observations, were it not for the fact that contemporary observers assigned them so much significance. Throughout the early years of his reign, contemporaries repeatedly drew attention to Frederick William's unassuming, bourgeois (*bürgerlich*) comportment. In 1798, shortly after the accession, the Berlin theatre-poet Karl Alexander von Herklot, acclaimed the king in verse:

> He does not care for golden crown
> Nor robes with purple dyed.
> He is a burgher on the throne.
> To be a man's his pride.[8]

The theme of the king as an ordinary (middle-class) family man runs through much of the commentary surrounding the early years of the reign. We find it in the following verse addressed to the royal couple upon their accession:

> Be not gods to us you kings
> Nor goddesses you wives of kings;
> Nay, be what you are,
> Be worthy human beings.
> Show us in noblest model
> How one reconciles small things and great:
> A cosy life at home
> And high affairs of state.[9]

Perhaps the most striking feature of monarchical discourse after 1797 was the prominence and public resonance of the Prussian queen. For the first time in the history of the dynasty, the king was perceived and celebrated not merely as a monarch, but as a husband. The baroque warlordly portraits of his father's reign, with their gleaming armour and coils of ermine gave way to restrained family scenes, in which the king was shown relaxing with his wife and children. The queen emerged – for the first time – as a celebrated public personality in her own right. In 1793, when Luise left her native Mecklenburg to be betrothed to her future husband, her arrival in Berlin caused a sensation. When she was welcomed on Unter den Linden by a little girl reciting a verse, she broke with protocol by taking the child in her arms and kissing her. 'All hearts,' the poet de la Motte-Fouqué wrote, 'flew out to her and her grace and sweetness left none untouched.'[10]

Luise was renowned not only for her charitable work, but also for her physical beauty (a superb full-length double statue of 1795–7 by Johann Gottfried Schadow, in which a teen-aged Luise stands arm-in-arm with her sister Frederike in a virtually transparent summer dress, was closed for many years to public viewing because it was deemed too overtly erotic). Luise was a figure without precedent in the history of the dynasty, a female celebrity who in the mind of the public combined virtue, modesty and sovereign grace with kindness and sex appeal, and whose early death in 1810 at the age of only thirty-four preserved her youth in the memory of posterity.[11]

As queen, Luise occupied a much more prominent and visible place

27. The princesses Luise and Frederike of Prussia. Die
Prinzessinnengruppe *by Johann Gottfried Schadow,*
1795–97.

in the life of the kingdom than her eighteenth-century predecessors. In
a notable break with tradition, she joined the king on his inaugural
journey through the Prussian lands to receive the oath of fealty from the
provincial Estates. During the endless meetings with local worthies, it
was said that the new queen impressed everyone with her warmth and
charm. She even became a fashion icon. The neckerchief she wore to
keep colds at bay was soon widely imitated by women across Prussia
and beyond. She was also an important partner to Frederick William in
his official role. From the very beginning, she was regularly consulted
on affairs of state. She cultivated the most important ministers and made
it her business to be informed of political developments at court. It is
striking that Stein thought it appropriate to approach the queen with

his radical proposal for reform during the crisis of 1806, and equally significant that she should have chosen not to pass the document to her husband, on the grounds that it would merely vex him at a time of extreme stress. Luise provided psychological support for the hesitant king. 'The only thing you need is more self-confidence,' she wrote to him in June 1806. 'Once you have that, you will be able to make decisions much more quickly.'[12]

In a sense, the prominence of the queen betokened a re-feminization of Prussian royalty after nearly a century when women had been pushed to the margins of monarchical representation. However, the reintegration of the feminine into the public life of the monarchy took place within the parameters of an increasingly polarized understanding of the two genders and their social calling. Luise's public role was not that of a female dynast with her own court, priorities and foreign policy, but that of a wife and helper. Her formidable skills and intelligence were placed at the service of her husband. This performance of subordination was crucial to the public image of the royal couple and it explains why Luise's feminine attributes – her prettiness, sweet nature, maternal kindness and wifely virtue – were such prominent features of the cult that sprang up around her. Luise rendered the increasingly withdrawn 'private sphere' of the royal family legible to its growing middle-class public. By opening new channels of emotional identification, her celebrity diminished the affective distance between the royal house and the mass of Prussian subjects.[13]

Luise was, as we have seen, supportive of the oppositional group that emerged to challenge the government's policies and procedures in 1806 and she pressed the king to recall them to office after the Peace of Tilsit. 'Where is Baron vom Stein?' she asked, after the news of Tilsit had sunk in. 'He is my last hope. A great heart, an encompassing mind, perhaps he knows remedies that are hidden to us. If only he would come!'[14] The king needed some persuading to reappoint Stein in the summer of 1807 – he had dismissed him for arrogance and insubordination only a few months earlier. Luise was also an admirer and supporter of Karl August von Hardenberg; indeed, according to one report, his name was one of the last words she uttered to her distraught husband as she lay expiring on her deathbed in 1810.[15]

Frederick William, too, accepted that the emergency created by the Prussian defeat called for a radical rethink – he had himself demonstrated

28. *Death mask of Queen
Luise, 1810*

an interest in reform long before 1806. In 1798, he had established a
Royal Commission on Financial Reform and ordered it to propose
changes to the administration of customs regulations and toll and excise
revenue across the Prussian lands, but the members of the commission
failed to harmonize their positions, and Karl August von Struensee, the
minister in charge of excise, customs and factories, was unable to provide
a coherent summary of its findings. In the following year, Frederick
William ordered his officials to draw up plans for a reform of the
Prussian prison system. In response, Grand Chancellor von Goldbeck
proposed an elaborate – and quintessentially enlightened – system of
graded rewards and punishments to encourage the self-improvement
and rehabilitation of prisoners. Goldbeck's recommendations were subsequently incorporated in a general plan for the reform of the Prussian
prisons, issued in 1804–5.[16]

The king would doubtless have achieved more, had it not been for the
resistance to reform in many quarters, including the bureaucracy itself.
In a cabinet order of October 1798, the king instructed that the Commission on Financial Reform should investigate the possibility of increasing the basic property tax paid by the nobility. Even before the

commission had met to discuss this proposal, however, a senior official leaked the order to the *Neue Zeitung* of Hamburg, where its publication triggered protests from the Prussian provincial Estates.

In the sphere of agrarian reform too, there was a strong record of monarchical initiative. Struck by 'the unbelievably large number of complaints he had received from peasants', Frederick William III was determined to do away with servile peasant tenures on the royal domains and an order to this effect was issued in 1799, but the king's efforts encountered determined resistance from within the General Directory, which argued that tampering with the status of domain peasants would awaken similar aspirations among peasants on noble estates and trigger an 'uprising of the most numerous class of the people'.[17] Only after 1803 did Frederick William override these reservations and instruct the provincial ministers to begin phasing out all remaining peasant labour services on the royal domains.[18]

BUREAUCRATS AND OFFICERS

Stein and Hardenberg, the two most influential reformers within the Prussian administration after 1806, represented two distinct German progressive traditions. Stein's familial background had imprinted him with a deep respect for corporate representative institutions. At the University of Göttingen he had imbibed a British-style aristocratic whiggery that inclined him towards the devolution of governmental responsibilities upon local institutions. His experiences as a senior Prussian official in the Westphalian coalmining sector had persuaded him that the key to effective administration lay in dialogue and collaboration with local and regional elites.[19] Hardenberg, by contrast, was a man of the German enlightenment and sometime member of the *Illuminaten*, a radical offshoot of Freemasonry. Although he respected the historical role of the nobility in the social order, Hardenberg entertained a much less exalted conception of his caste than Stein. His reforming vision was focused above all upon the concentration of power and legitimate authority in the state. The two men were also temperamentally very different. Stein was awkward, impulsive and haughty. Hardenberg was shrewd, agile, calculating and diplomatic.

Yet they had enough in common to make fruitful collaboration possible. Both were acutely aware of the power and importance of public opinion – in this sense, they both carried the stamp of the European enlightenment. Both believed passionately in the need for structural reform at the level of the supreme executive – they had coordinated their positions on this issue during the bitter factional strife of 1806. Moreover, they were not alone: during their swift rise through the Prussian administration over more than two decades, a substantial network of younger men had coalesced around them. Some were protégés or friends, some had cut their teeth as officials in the Franconian or Westphalian administrations, and some were simply likeminded colleagues who gravitated towards the reformers as crisis loomed.

The first and in some ways the most urgent task facing the reformers was the re-establishment of Prussia as a power capable of functioning autonomously on the European stage. In addressing this problem, the reformers focused on two areas: the central decision-making executive and the military. As we have seen, there was widespread agreement among senior officials that Prussia required a more streamlined ministerial structure. A particular concern was the so-called 'cabinet system', in which one or more 'foreign ministers' competed with cabinet secretaries close to the monarch and other favoured advisers for influence over the policy-making process. This, it was claimed, was the cause of the malaise that had brought Prussia to the predicament of 1806. After his appointment in October 1807, therefore, Stein went to great pains to persuade the king to dissolve his cabinet of personal advisers, and to establish (in November 1808) a central executive consisting of five functionally defined ministries, each run by a responsible minister with direct access to the king. Taken in combination, these two measures would prevent the duplication of advisory functions between secretaries and ministers, and the appointment of multiple 'foreign ministers' in tandem. They would also force the king – in theory – to channel his official consultations through one responsible official, and prevent him from playing rival ministers and advisers off against each other.

Stein, Hardenberg and their collaborators naturally argued that these measures were essential if Prussia were to be restored to a condition where it could reverse the verdict of 1807. They based this claim on the presumption that the disaster of 1806–7 had been *caused* by the adversarial tensions within the executive, that it could have been avoided with a better decision-making structure capable of steering the monarch into the required decisions. Underlying these arguments was what Carl Schmitt once called a 'cult of the decision': everything depended upon devising a system that was supple and transparent enough to deliver swift, rational and well-informed decisions in response to changing conditions. It was difficult to counter this argument in the emotionally charged environment of post-Tilsit Prussia.

Yet the case for the reformers' 'decisionism' was less compelling than it seemed. After all, the problem for Prussian foreign policy in the years 1804–6 lay not in the fact that the king had insisted on canvassing a wide range of views, but in the intrinsic difficulty of the situations Prussia had faced. It is too easy to forget that there had never been a figure like Napoleon – the efforts at 'reunion' launched by Louis XIV on the periphery of the Holy Roman Empire during the reign of the Great Elector look pale beside the scale and ambition of Bonaparte's imperial project. There were no rules for dealing with an antagonist of this type, and no precedent by which to predict how he would act next. As the rug was pulled from under the neutrality policy, it was exceptionally difficult to judge which way Prussia should jump, the more so as the international balance of power and the incoming signals from potential alliance partners were constantly shifting. The Great Elector had spent long periods of agonized wavering between options during the Northern War and the various French wars of Louis XIV, not because he was by nature indecisive or fearful, or because he lacked an adequately streamlined executive, but because the predicaments he faced demanded careful weighing up and were not susceptible to obvious solutions. Yet the judgements Frederick William III was called upon to make were finer, involved more variables, and were freighted with greater risks. There is no reason to suppose that the system advocated by the reformers, had it been implemented, say, in 1804, would have generated better outcomes than the cabinet system they so fiercely attacked – after all, the king's ill-fated decision to go to war was supported at the time by those who opposed the old system.[20]

If the reformers nevertheless pressed for executive streamlining in the sphere of foreign policy, this was in part because the concentration of the executive was guaranteed to consolidate the power of the most senior officials. In place of the jockeying for influence that had gone on within the antechamber of power before 1806, the new system promised the five ministers a stable place at the policy-making table. Under the old system, the influence of an individual adviser waxed and waned unpredictably as the king's ear turned in different directions. One day's careful work of argument and persuasion could be wiped out on the next. Under the new arrangements, however, it would be possible to work *with* the other ministers to *manage* the king, and it is interesting, though hardly surprising, to note that nearly every senior official who called for executive streamlining during the period 1805–8 envisaged that one of the key offices would fall to himself.[21]

The reformers always stressed – it would have been extremely impolitic not to – that their objective was to sharpen the focus and reach of the monarch's authority by placing him in control of a better decision-making tool. In reality they were limiting his freedom of movement by confronting him with a closed bench of advisers. They aimed to bureaucratize the monarchy, embedding it in the state's broader structures of responsibility and accountability.[22] The king saw this clearly enough, and therefore baulked when Stein proposed that in future decrees issued by the king should be valid only if they bore the signatures of the five ministers.[23]

The Prussian army was understandably the focus of intense interest after Jena and Auerstedt, but debate over military reform was nothing new. Within a few years of the death of Frederick the Great, there had been voices, civilian and military, calling for a critical re-examination of the Frederician system. The debate continued after 1800, as the more receptive military intellectuals absorbed the lessons of the revolutionary and early Napoleonic campaigns. The adjutant and military theorist Colonel Christian von Massenbach, a south German who had entered Prussian service in 1782 (at the age of twenty-four), and was close to Frederick William III, argued that the new practice of 'big war' exemplified by Napoleon's campaigns necessitated the professionalization of military planning and leadership. The fate of Prussia should not depend on whether the monarch himself was a gifted strategist. Enduring structures should be set in place to assure that all the available information was collated and weighed up before and during any campaign. Command functions should be concentrated in one decision-making organ.[24] There are clear parallels between these early sketches of a modern general staff system and the contemporaneous debate over executive reform, in which Massenbach was also an exponent of streamlining.[25]

The most important forum for debate on army reform was the Military

29. Gerhard Johann von Scharnhorst, *before 1813, by Friedrich Bury*

Society, founded in 1802, at which officers read papers to each other and discussed the implications for Prussia of the current European military situation. The dominant figure in the society was Gerhard Johann David von Scharnhorst, a man of peasant birth who had risen swiftly through the ranks in his native Hanover and entered the Prussian service in 1801 at the age of forty-six. Scharnhorst called for the introduction in Prussia of the Napoleonic divisional system, and the establishment of a territorial militia as a reserve force. Others, such as Karl Friedrich von dem Knesebeck (a born Prussian subject), drew up ambitious plans that foresaw the creation of a genuinely 'national' Prussian force.[26] As these efforts show, the Prussian military did not remain sealed off from the process of criticism and self-scrutiny that had begun to transform the relationship between the state and civil society in the 1780s and 1790s.

Little was done before 1806 to put these ideas into effect. All major reforms threaten vested interests and tentative efforts to install a vestigial general staff organization in 1803 were greeted with open hostility by office-holders within the traditional administration. There was strong resistance to innovation among the long-serving senior officers, some of whom, such as Field Marshal Möllendorf, owed their reputations to distinguished service in the Seven Years War. Möllendorf, a blimpish figure who was eighty-two when he walked calmly through the French fire at Jena, is reported to have responded to all reformist proposals with the words: 'This is altogether above my head.' But such men commanded enormous respect within the old Prussian army and it was psychologically difficult for anyone, even the king himself, who had grown up under the shadow of his famous uncle, to stand up to them. In a revealing conversation from 1810, Frederick William recalled that he had wanted a thorough reform of the military long before the war of 1806–7:

... but with my youth and inexperience, I didn't dare, and instead trusted those two veterans [Möllendorf and the Duke of Brunswick] who had grown grey under their laurels and surely understood all this better than I could [...] If I had tried as a reformer to oppose their opinions and it had gone badly, everyone would have said: 'The young gentleman has no experience!'[27]

The defeats at Jena and Auerstedt changed this situation utterly and the monarch was quick to seize the initiative. In July 1807, when the shock of Tilsit was still fresh, the king established a Military Reorganization Commission, whose task was to draw up all the necessary reforms. It was as if the Military Society of the pre-war years had been reincarnated as an organ of government. The presiding spirit was Scharnhorst, supported by a quartet of gifted disciples – August Wilhelm Neidhardt von Gneisenau, Hermann von Boyen, Karl Wilhelm Georg von Grolman and Karl von Clausewitz. Gneisenau was the son of a non-noble Saxon artillery officer who had joined the Prussian army as a member of the royal suite (a predecessor of the general staff) in 1786. Promoted to major after the battles of October 1806, Gneisenau found himself in command of the fortress of Kolberg on the Baltic coast of Pomerania, where he managed, with the help of some patriotic townsfolk, to hold out against French forces until 2 July 1807.

Boyen was the son of an East Prussian officer who had attended the lectures of Immanuel Kant at the University of Königsberg and had been a member of the Military Society since 1803. Grolman had served as an adjutant under Hohenlohe at Jena, before fleeing to East Prussia, where he joined the staff of the L'Estocq Corps, the Prussian force that fought the French alongside the Russians at Preussisch-Eylau. Like Gneisenau, Grolman had the good fortune to be associated with the continued Prussian resistance in 1807, rather than with the defeat of the previous autumn. Clausewitz, the youngest of the group (he was twenty-six in 1806), had joined the army as a twelve-year-old cadet and was selected in 1801 for admission to the Institute for Young Officers in Berlin, an elite training facility of which Scharnhorst had just been appointed director.

These men attempted to carve a new kind of military entity out of the ravaged hulk of the Prussian army. There were important structural and technical improvements. The military executive was tightened up along the lines proposed by Stein. This involved, among other things, the creation of a ministry of war, within which the rudiments of a general staff organization could begin to coalesce. Greater emphasis was placed on the deployment of flexible units of riflemen operating in an open order of battle. Scharnhorst oversaw crucial improvements to training, tactics and weaponry. Appointments were henceforth to be meritocratic. In the words (written by Grolman) of an order of 6 August 1808: 'All social preference that has existed is henceforth and hereby terminated in the military establishment, and everyone, whatever his background, has the same duties and the same rights.'[28] The psychological impact of this and other innovations was heightened by the fact that they coincided with an unprecedented purge of the Prussian military leadership. In all, some 208 officers were removed from service following a forensic analysis of the defeat carried out by a committee of the Military Reorganization Commission. Of 142 generals, seventeen were simply dismissed and a further eighty-six received honourable discharges; only just over a quarter of all Prussian officers survived the purge.

The immediate objective of the order of 6 August 1808 was to ensure a better command cadre in the future. The reformers also had wider objectives. They aimed to overcome the caste-like exclusiveness of the officer corps. The army was to become the repository of a virtuous patriotism, which in turn would infuse it with the *élan* and commitment that had been so manifestly lacking in 1806. The objective was, in Scharnhorst's words, 'to raise and inspire the spirit of the army, to bring the army and the nation into a more intimate union . . .'[29] To effect an all-embracing consummation of this new relationship between the army and the Prussian 'nation', the reformers argued for universal military service; those who were not called up directly into the army should be liable for service in a territorial militia. The exemptions that had kept substantial parts of Prussian society (especially in the towns) out of the army should now be dismantled. Orders were also issued phasing out the more draconian corporal punishments for disciplinary infractions, most importantly the infamous 'running of the gauntlet', because these were felt to be incompatible with the dignity of a bourgeois recruit. The task of an officer was not to beat or insult his charges, but to 'educate' them. It was the culmination of a long process of change; military punishments had been under intermittent review since the reign of Frederick William II.[30]

The most influential expression of this sea-change in values was Clausewitz's *On War*, an encompassing philosophical treatise on military conflict that remained unfinished when the author died of cholera in 1831. In Clausewitz's typology of military engagements, soldiers were not cattle to be herded across the battlefield, but men subject to the vicissitudes of mood, morale, hunger, cold, weariness and fear. An army should not be conceptualized as a machine, but as a conscious willed organism with its own collective 'genius'. It followed that military theory was a soft science whose variables were partly subjective. Flexibility and self-reliance, especially among junior commanders, were vital. Coupled with this insight was an insistence on the primacy of politics. Military engagements must never be allowed, Clausewitz argued, to become an end in themselves – an implicit critique of Napoleon's ceaseless warmaking – but must always serve a clearly defined political objective. *On War* thus represented a first attempt to acknowledge and theorize the new and unpredictable forces unleashed by Napoleonic 'big war', while at the same time binding them to the service of essentially civilian ends.[31]

LAND REFORM

'The abolition of serfdom has consistently been my goal since the beginning of my reign,' Frederick William III told two of his officials shortly after the Peace of Tilsit. 'I desired to attain it gradually, but the unhappy condition of our country now justifies and indeed demands speedier action.'[32] Here again, the Napoleonic shock was the catalyst, not the cause. The 'feudal' system of land tenures had long been under growing pressure. Some of it was ideological, and resulted from the percolation of physiocratic and Smithian liberal ideas into the Prussian administration. But the economic rationale for the old system was also wearing thin. The growing use of waged employees, who were plentiful and cheap in an era of demographic growth, emancipated many estate owners from dependence on the labour services of subject peasants.[33] Moreover, the late eighteenth-century boom in grain prices produced new imbalances within the system. The better-endowed peasants took their grain surpluses to market and rode the boom while paying wage-labourers to perform their 'feudal' services for them. Under these conditions, the existence of a large subject peasantry whose secure land tenures were paid for with labour rents came to seem economically counter-productive. Labour dues, once a highly valued attribute of Junker manorial governance, now functioned like fixed rents within a system that benefited the better endowed peasants as 'protected tenants'.[34]

Two Stein associates, Theodor von Schön and Friedrich von Schroetter, were entrusted with the task of preparing a draft law outlining reforms to the agrarian system. The result was the edict of 9 October 1807, sometimes called the October Edict, the first and most famous of the legislative monuments of the reform era. Like so many of the reform decrees, it was more a declaration of intentions than a law as such. The edict heralded fundamental changes to the constitution of Prussian rural society, but there was a bombastic vagueness about many of its formulations. Essentially, it aimed to achieve two objectives. The first was the liberation of latent economic energies – the preamble declared that every individual should be free to achieve 'as much prosperity as his abilities allow'. The second was the creation of a society in which all Prussians were 'citizens of the state' equal before the law. These objectives were to be achieved through three specific measures. First, all restrictions on the purchase of noble land were abandoned. The state at last gave up its futile struggle to maintain the noble monopoly in privileged land and created for the first time something approximating a free land market. Second, all occupations were henceforth to be open to persons of all classes. For the first time there was to be a free market in labour, untrammelled by guild and corporate occupational restrictions. This too was a measure with a long prehistory: since the early 1790s, the abolition of guild controls had been the subject of repeated discussions between the General Directory and the Factory Department in Berlin.[35] Thirdly, all hereditary servitude was abolished – in a hugely suggestive but tantalizingly imprecise formulation, the edict announced that 'from Saint Martin's Day [11 November] 1810, there will only be free people' in the Kingdom of Prussia.

This last stipulation sent an electric shock through the rural communities of the kingdom. It also left many questions open. The peasants were to be officially 'free' – did this mean they were no longer obliged to perform their labour services? The answer was less obvious than it might seem, since most labour services were not attributes of personal servitude but forms of rent payable for land tenure. Nevertheless, landlords in many districts where the edict became common knowledge found it virtually impossible to persuade the peasants to perform their services. Efforts by the authorities in Silesia to prevent the news from reaching the villages failed, and in the summer of 1808 a rebellion broke out among peasants who believed they were now being held in unlawful subjection.[36]

A further vexing question was that of the ultimate ownership of peasant land. Since the edict made no reference to the principle of peasant protection that had traditionally informed Prussian agrarian policy, some noble landlords regarded it as a carte blanche for the seizure – or reclamation, as they saw it – of land under peasant cultivation, and there were a number of wildcat appropriations. A degree of clarity was achieved through the Ordinance of 14 February 1808, which stated that the ownership of land depended on the prior conditions of tenure. Peasants with strong ownership rights were secure against unilateral appropriation. Those with temporary leases of various kinds were in a weaker position; their lands could be appropriated, though only with the permission of the authorities. But many details of interpretation were still contested and it was only in 1816 that the questions of land ownership and the compensation of landlords for the services and land they had lost were settled.

The final position, as set out in the Regulation Edict of 1811 and the Declaration of 1816, defined a range of hierarchically graded prior peasant tenures and allotted them correspondingly differentiated rights. Broadly speaking, there were two options. The land could be partitioned, in which case peasants with hereditary tenures retained use rights to two-thirds of the land they had traditionally worked (one-half in the case of non-hereditary tenures), or the peasant might buy it outright, in which case the seigneurial portion had to be paid off. The payment of compensation by peasants for land, services and natural rents dragged on in many cases for over half a century. Peasants at the bottom end of the range were not entitled to convert the land they worked to freehold titles and their lands were vulnerable to enclosure.[37] These measures were in tune with then fashionable late-enlightenment physiocratic doctrine that freeing peasants from labour dues and other irksome 'feudal' duties ought to make them more productive. And the writings of Adam Smith, whose works were held in high esteem among the younger cohorts of the Prussian bureaucracy (including Schroetter and Schön), suggested that it might be best to let the weakest of the peasants lose their land, since they would in any case be unviable as independent farmers.[38]

Some noblemen resented bitterly this tampering with the agrarian constitution of old Prussia. For the conservative neo-Pietists around the Gerlach brothers in Berlin the years of reform brought the realization that the monarchical state posed as potent a threat to traditional life as the revolution itself. The growing pretensions of the central bureaucracy, Leopold von Gerlach believed, supplemented the personal power of the monarch with a new 'administrative despotism that eats away at everything like vermin'.[39] The most trenchant and memorable spokesman for this point of view was Friedrich August Ludwig von der Marwitz, an estate owner at Friedersdorf near Küstrin on the edge of the Oder floodplain, who denounced the reforms as an assault on the traditional patriarchal structure of the countryside. Hereditary subjecthood, he argued, was not a residue of slavery, but the expression of a familial bond that joined the peasant to the nobleman. To dissolve this bond would be to undermine the cohesion of the society as a whole. Marwitz was a melancholy character to whom nostalgia came naturally; he articulated his reactionary views with great intelligence and rhetorical skill, but he remained an isolated figure. Most noblemen saw the advantages of the new dispensation, which gave relatively little to most peasants and allowed the estate owner to intensify the agrarian production process using cheap wage labour on land unencumbered by complex hereditary tenures.[40]

CITIZENSHIP

By scouring the legal residue of 'feudalism' from the noble estates, the October Edict aimed to facilitate the emergence of a more politically cohesive society in Prussia. 'Subjects' were to be refashioned into 'citizens of the state'. Yet the reformers understood that more positive measures would be needed to mobilize the patriotic commitment of the population. 'All our efforts are in vain,' Karl von Altenstein wrote to Hardenberg in 1807, 'if the system of education is against us, if it sends half-hearted officials into state service and brings forth lethargic citizens.'[41] Administrative and legal innovations alone were insufficient; they had to be sustained by a broad programme of educational reform aimed at energizing Prussia's emancipated citizenry for the tasks that lay ahead.

The man entrusted with renewing the kingdom's educational system was Wilhelm von Humboldt, descendant of a Pomeranian military family who had grown up in the enlightened Berlin of the 1770s and 1780s. His tutors had included the emancipationist Christian Wilhelm von Dohm and the progressive jurist Ernst Ferdinand Klein. On the urging of Stein, Humboldt was appointed director of the Section for Religion and Public Instruction within the interior ministry on 20 February 1809. He was something of an odd-man-out among the senior reformers. He was not by nature a politician, but a scholar of cosmopolitan temperament who had chosen to spend much of his adult life abroad. In 1806, Humboldt was living with his family in Rome, hard at work on a translation of Aeschylus's *Agamemnon*. Only after the collapse of Prussia and the plundering by French troops of the Humboldt family residence in Tegel to the north of Berlin did he resolve to return to his beleaguered homeland. It was only with great reluctance that he agreed to accept a post in the new administration.[42]

Once installed, however, Humboldt unfolded a profoundly liberal reform programme that transformed education in Prussia. For the first time, the kingdom acquired a single, standardized system of public instruction attuned to the latest trends in progressive European pedagogy. Education as such, Humboldt declared, was henceforth to be decoupled from the idea of technical or vocational training. Its purpose was not to turn cobblers' boys into cobblers, but to turn 'children into

30. Wilhelm von Humboldt, *drawing by Luise Henry, 1826*

people'. The reformed schools were not merely to induct pupils into a specific subject matter, but to instil in them the capacity to think and learn for themselves. 'The pupil is mature,' he wrote, 'when he has learned enough from others to be in a position to learn for himself.'[43] In order to ensure that this approach percolated through the system, Humboldt established new teachers' colleges to train candidates for the kingdom's chaotic primary schools. He imposed a standardized regime of state examinations and inspections and created a special department within the ministry to oversee the design of curricula, textbooks and learning aids.

The centrepiece – and most enduring monument – of the Humboldt reforms was the Friedrich-Wilhelms-Universität founded in Berlin in 1810 and installed in the vacated palace of Prince Henry, the younger brother of Frederick the Great, on Unter den Linden. Here too, Humboldt strove to realize his Kantian vision of education as a process of self-emancipation by autonomous, rational individuals.

> Just as primary instruction makes the teacher possible, so he renders himself dispensable through schooling at the secondary level. The university teacher is thus no longer a teacher and the student is no longer a pupil. Instead the student conducts research on his own behalf and the professor supervises his research and supports him in it. Because learning at university level places the student in a position to apprehend the unity of scholarly enquiry and thereby lays claim to his creative powers.[44]

From this it followed that academic research was an activity with no predetermined end-point, no objective that could be defined in purely utilitarian terms. It was a process whose unfolding was driven by an immanent dynamic. It was concerned less with knowledge in the sense of accumulated facts than with reflection and reasoned argument. This was homage to the pluralist scepticism of Kant's critique of human reason, and also a return to that vision of an all-embracing conversation that had animated Prussia's enlightenment. Essential to the success of this enterprise was that it should be free from political interference. The state should abstain from intervening in the intellectual life of the university, except as a 'guarantor of liberty' in cases where a dominant clique of professors threatened to suppress academic pluralism within their own ranks.[45]

The Friedrich-Wilhelms-Universität (renamed Humboldt-Universität in 1949) quickly secured pre-eminence among the universities of the Protestant German states. Like the University of Halle in the age of the Great Elector, the new institution served to broadcast the cultural authority of the Prussian state. Indeed its foundation was partly motivated by the need to replace Halle, which had been lost to the Prussian Crown in the territorial settlement imposed by Napoleon. In this sense, the new university helped, as Frederick William III put it, to 'replace by intellectual means what the state had lost in physical strength'. But it also – and herein lies its true significance – lent institutional expression to a new understanding of the purpose of higher education.

The emancipated citizens who emerged from every level of Humboldt's educational system were expected to take an active part in the political life of the Prussian state. Stein hoped to achieve this through the creation of elected organs of municipal self-government that would encourage more active participation in matters of public interest. Shortly before his departure from office, the ministry enacted the Municipal Ordinance (*Städteordnung*) of November 1808. The category of 'citizen' (*Bürger*), once largely confined to the privileged members of corporate bodies such as guilds, was enlarged to include all persons owning a house (including single women) or practising a 'municipal trade' within the city limits. All male citizens who satisfied a modest property qualification were entitled to vote in town elections and to hold municipal office. The equivalence asserted here between ownership (*Teilhabe*) and participation (*Teilnahme*) would form an enduring theme in the history of nineteenth-century liberalism.

The same project – the engagement of citizens as active participants in public affairs – was mapped on to the kingdom as a whole during Hardenberg's period in office. The background to this remarkable experiment in popular participation, which went beyond the programmes envisaged by most of the pre-1806 enlightened reformers, was a major fiscal crisis. In 1810, Napoleon renewed his demand for payment of the war indemnity and offered the Dohna-Altenstein ministry the choice between paying up and ceding a chunk of Silesia. When the ministers considered taking the latter course, Frederick William III relieved them of their duties and appointed Hardenberg who promised to meet the French bill through radical fiscal reform. State debt was rising fast, from 35 million thalers in 1806 to 66 million in 1810, and the debasement of the coinage, the issue of new paper money and the raising of loans at high rates of interest were feeding an inflationary spiral.

To prevent a further deterioration, Hardenberg fired off a salvo of edicts announcing major fiscal and economic reforms. Tax burdens were to be equalized through the imposition of a 'territorial consumption tax', the freedom of enterprise heralded in the October Edict and the Municipal Ordinance was to be put into effect across the kingdom, church and state properties were to be sold off and the tariff and toll systems were to be thoroughly overhauled and rationalized. In order to ease these controversial proposals through the system, in February 1811 the chancellor convened an Assembly of Notables comprising sixty persons nominated by various regional and local elites, and informed them that they were to regard themselves as 'representatives of the whole nation' whose help would be needed in the establishment of a free and equal Prussian society.[46] The aim, as Hardenberg had put it in a memorandum of March 1809, was to find a way of extracting the needed funds without damaging 'the bond of love and trust between the government and the people'. By imposing new taxes, as it were, upon themselves, the assembly would 'spare the monarch the pain of demanding a grievous sacrifice, diminish ill-feeling among the citizens of the state, give these a degree of control over the details of implementation, prove their patriotism and enliven the necessary commitment to the common good'.[47]

In the event, the assembly – like so many historic assemblies convened for the same purpose – was a disappointment. Hardenberg had hoped that the public-spirited members of this gathering would offer constructive advice on how to implement the necessary changes and develop further innovations, before packing their bags and returning to their provinces as propagandists for the government. Instead the representatives loudly voiced their objections to Hardenberg's plans and the assembly became a forum for anti-reformist opinion. It was quickly dissolved. The same problem dogged the modestly named 'interim national representations' elected by local government assemblies and convened by the chancellor in 1812 and 1814. In retrospect, it seems unlikely that Hardenberg could ever have made a success of these pseudo-democratic assemblies. He had no intention in the first instance of allowing them to assume the powers of a fully fledged parliament; their function was to be consultative. They were to be conduits of understanding between the government and the nation. Here was the enlightenment dream of a reasoned 'conversation' between state and civil society writ large.

However, as the assembly and the two interim representations revealed, this congenial vision did not provide suitable mechanisms for the public conciliation of opposed social and economic interests in a period of heightened conflict and crisis. Hardenberg's experiments with representation illustrated a problem at the heart of the reform project, namely that where government action was controversial, the rituals of participation tended to focus and reinforce opposition rather than building consensus. The same problem could be observed in the cities, where the assemblies created by Stein often emerged as opponents of reforming measures.[48]

Among those who benefited from the efforts to create a more free, equal and politically coherent society of citizens were the Jews of the Prussian lands. Despite a partial easing of controls for the most privileged strata under Frederick William II, the Prussian Jews were still subject to many special restrictions and their affairs were administered under a particular jurisdiction. The first signals of a more comprehensive reform came with the cities ordinance of 1808, which allowed 'protected, property-owning Jews' to vote and hold municipal offices as members of town and city councils. It was thanks to this liberalizing measure that David Friedländer, a disciple of Mendelssohn, became the first Jew to hold a seat on the Berlin council. Yet the idea of a comprehensive emancipation remained controversial within the administration.[49] In 1809, the task of drafting a proposal on the future status of the Jews was entrusted to Friedrich von Schroetter. Schroetter suggested a gradualist approach, beginning with the piecemeal removal of restrictions and proceeding by slow stages to the concession of full citizenship rights. His draft was circulated to the various government departments for comments.

Responses from within the administration were mixed. The conservatives who controlled the ministry of finance insisted that emancipation must be conditional upon the abandonment of all ritual observance and the cessation of Jewish trading activity. Far more liberal was the reply from Wilhelm von Humboldt. He pleaded for a clean separation of church and state; in a state organized along secular lines, he argued, the religion of the individual citizen must be a purely private affair without consequences for the exercise of citizenship rights. Yet even Humboldt took the view that emancipation would eventually lead to the voluntary self-dissolution of Judaism. 'Since they are driven by an innate human need for a higher faith', he argued, the Jews will 'turn of their own free will to the Christian [religion]'.[50] Both viewpoints presumed – much as Dohm had done over twenty years before – that emancipation would entail the 'education' of the Jews away from their faith and habits towards a higher social and religious order. The difference was that Humboldt imagined this process as a voluntary consequence of emancipation, while the officials of the ministry of finance saw it as a state-imposed precondition.

The emancipation proposal might well have mouldered away in the archives until after the Napoleonic Wars if Hardenberg had not taken the matter up following his appointment as chancellor on 6 July 1810.

Hardenberg was favourable in principle to a general emancipation, but there was also a personal dimension to his advocacy. He had been a frequent guest at the Jewish salons of the 1790s and early 1800s and counted many Jews among his friends and associates. When Hardenberg had fallen into debt at the time of his divorce from his first wife, it was the Westphalian court banker Israel Jacobson – a passionate advocate of Jewish religious reform and of emancipation – who bailed him out with a low-interest loan. David Friedländer, who had moved in the same circles as Hardenberg, was asked to submit a memorandum setting out the community's case for emancipation – it was the first time a Jew had been involved in official consultations over a Prussian matter of state. The result of Hardenberg's canvassing and deliberation was the Edict Concerning the Civil Condition of the Jews in the Prussian State of 11 March 1812, which declared that all Jews resident in Prussia and in possession of general privileges, naturalization certificates, letters of protection, or special concessions should henceforth be regarded as 'natives' (*Einländer*) and 'citizens' (*Staatsbürger*) of the state of Prussia. The edict lifted all prior restrictions on Jewish commercial and occupational activity, swept away all special taxes and levies, and established that Jews were free to live where they wished and to marry whom they chose (although mixed marriages between Jews and Christians remained inadmissible).

These rulings certainly amounted to a major improvement, and they were duly celebrated by an enlightened Jewish journal based in Berlin as the inauguration of a 'new and happy era'.[51] The Jewish Elders of Berlin thanked Hardenberg for his good works, expressing their 'deepest gratitude' for this 'immeasurable act of charity'.[52] However, the emancipation made available by the edict was limited in several important respects. Most importantly, it postponed judgement on the question of whether positions in government service would be made available to Jewish applicants. It thus fell crucially short of the French emancipation of 1791, which had embedded Jewish entitlements in a universal endorsement of citizenship and political rights. By contrast, the language of the Prussian edict, which warned that the 'continuation of their allotted title of inhabitants and citizens of the state' would depend on the fulfilment of certain prior obligations, made it clear that the edict was about the concession of status rather than the recognition of rights.[53] In this respect, it echoed the ambivalence of Dohm's famous tract on the 'civil improvement' of the Jews. The majority of the reformers shared Dohm's view that it would take time before the negative effects of discrimination wore off and the Jews were ready to take their place as equal participants in the public life of the nation. As one Prussian official put it: 'repression had made the Jews treacherous' and the 'sudden concession of liberty' would not suffice to 'reconstitute all at once the natural human nobility within them'.[54] The edict thus stripped away much ancient discriminatory law without completing the work of political emancipation, which was seen as a process that would take a generation or so to accomplish.

WORDS

In the course of the nineteenth century, a nimbus of myth shrouded the era of Prussian reform establishing Stein, Hardenberg, Scharnhorst and their colleagues as the authors of a momentous revolution from above. If we look more closely at what was actually accomplished, however, the achievements of the reformers look rather modest. Subtract the propagandistic sound and fury of the edicts, and we might merely be looking at one energetic episode within a *longue durée* of Prussian administrative change between the 1790s and the 1840s.[55]

The reforms were not directed towards a single agreed objective, and many of the most important proposals were muted, held up or blocked altogether by bitter contention among the reformers themselves.[56] Take, for example, the plan to abolish patrimonial powers on the manorial estates. Stein and his ministers were determined from the very beginning to do away with these jurisdictions, on the grounds that they were 'out of tune with the cultural condition of the nation' and thus undermined popular attachments to 'the state in which we live'.[57] Hardenberg and his associate Altenstein, by contrast, took the view that the government must consider the interests of the landowners. And so the issue remained in contention, losing much of its urgency after Napoleon forced Stein's dismissal in 1808. Determined opposition from the nobility, especially in East Prussia, where corporate identities remained strong, helped to slow the process further, as did peasant unrest, a sobering reminder of the need for flexible and authoritative judicial organs on the land.[58] Then there was the fiscal crisis of 1810; the desperate shortage of cash was yet a further reason for avoiding a costly 'total revision' of rural justice – an example of how the burdens of war and occupation could interrupt as well as motivate the work of reform.[59] These factors in combination sufficed to drive the abolition of the patrimonial courts off the government's agenda.

The same fate befell the Gendarmerie Edict of 30 July 1812, which foresaw the imposition of a bureaucratized system of rural government on the French model and the creation of a paramilitary state police for all rural areas. The plan was first sketched out during Stein's period in office. Pressed to act by the director of the General Police Department in Berlin, Hardenberg entrusted the drafting of a law to his old Franconian protégé Christian Friedrich Scharnweber. Scharnweber embedded the formation of a new state police force within a thorough transformation of the Prussian administration. Under the terms of the edict, the entire surface of Prussia (with the exception of the seven largest cities) was to be divided into districts (*Kreise*) of even size with a uniform administration incorporating an element of local representation.[60] The Gendarmerie Edict was one of the most uncompromising reformist statements of the Hardenberg era; had it succeeded, it would have swept away much of the lumpy, cellular, old-regime structure of rural governance in the kingdom.

In fact, however, the edict met with a storm of protest and widespread civil disobedience from the rural nobility (especially in East Prussia) and from conservative members of the administration. The noble-dominated interim national representation meeting in Berlin during 1812 saw the Gendarmerie Edict as yet another attempt to rob the landowning nobility of its traditional rights and passed a motion rejecting any suspension of patrimonial jurisdictions – a copy book example of how participation and reform were not always compatible.[61] Two years later, after further arguments within the administration, the Gendarmerie Edict was suspended. Further efforts to subordinate all forms of rural local government to centralized state authority during the last years of the Hardenberg administration foundered, with the result that right up into the early years of the Weimar Republic, Prussia's arrangements for rural administration remained among the most antiquated in Germany.[62]

Fear of a political backlash from the nobility also discouraged the reformers from attempting a more radical overhaul of the taxation system. Hardenberg had promised to equalize the land tax and remove the many exemptions that still benefited the rural nobility. He had also spoken of introducing a permanent income tax. But these plans were renounced in the face of corporate noble protests. Instead the Prussians were saddled with an array of consumption taxes that weighed most heavily on the poorest strata. The government returned to the question of land tax reform in 1817 and again in 1820, but the promised reform never materialized.[63]

Perhaps the greatest disappointment was the failure of the reformers to establish an organ of all-Prussian representation for the kingdom. Hardenberg's finance edict of 27 October 1810 announced that the king intended to establish an 'appropriately constituted representation both in the provinces and for the whole [of the kingdom], whose advice we will gladly use'.[64] Under pressure from his ministers, the king renewed this promise in the Ordinance Concerning the Future Representation of the People, published on 22 May 1815. The ordinance reiterated that the government intended to establish 'provincial estates' (*Provinzialstände*) and to form out of these a 'Territorial Representation' (*Landes-Representation*), whose seat would be in Berlin. Yet no national parliament was forthcoming. Instead the Prussians had to make do with provincial diets established after Hardenberg's death under a General Law published on 5 June 1823. These were not the robust modern representative bodies the most radical among the reformers had wished for. They were elected and organized along corporate lines and their areas of competence were very narrowly defined.

One way of casting the specificity of Prussian developments into sharper relief is to set them in the broader context of reformist activity in the German states during the Napoleonic era. Baden, Württemberg and Bavaria all passed through a period of intensified bureaucratic reform during these years, yet the result was a substantially greater measure of constitutional reform: all three states received constitutions, territorial elections and parliaments whose assent was required for the passage of legislation. Seen in this company, the neo-corporate provincial diets established in Prussia after 1823 look decidedly unimpressive. On the other hand, the Prussians were far more radical and consistent in their modernization of the economy. While the reformers in Munich and Stuttgart remained wedded to the protectionist mechanisms of old-regime mercantilism, the Prussians aimed at deregulation – of commerce, of manufacture, of the labour market, of internal trade – eloquent testimony to the cultural and geoeconomic effects of Prussia's relative proximity to the markets of industrializing Britain. Baden, Württemberg and Bavaria launched reforms of comparable scope only in 1862, 1862 and 1868 respectively. The momentum of Prussian economic reform carried on long after 1815 into the great customs unions of the post-war era. Prussia thus emerged from the Napoleonic era with a rather less 'modern' constitutional system than the three southern states, but a rather more 'modern' political economy.[65]

How we judge the achievement of the reformers depends upon whether we emphasize what was accomplished, or whether we focus instead upon the still unmastered legacy of the past. One can highlight the ways in which estate-owners benefited from the compensation arrangements imposed by Hardenberg's various revisions to Stein's Emancipation Edict. Alternatively, one can point to the size and prosperity of the peasant small- and middle-holding class that emerged from the partitioning of the landed estates.[66] The liberal Humboldtian pedagogy of the Prussian primary schools was diluted after 1819, yet the Prussian school system was internationally admired for the humanity of its ethos and the quality of its output. The Friedrich-Wilhelms-Universität, with its powerful institutional commitment to the freedom of research, became a model admired across Europe and widely emulated in the United States, where Humboldt's prescriptions helped to establish the idea of a modern academy.[67] It is perfectly legitimate to underline the limits of what was on offer in the Jewish Emancipation Edict of 1812, but important, too, to acknowledge its central place in the history of Jewish emancipation in nineteenth-century Germany.[68] One can lament the failure of the reformers to do away with patrimonial jurisdictions in the countryside, or one can focus instead on the societal forces that transformed the patrimonial courts into legal instruments of the state during the decade after 1815.[69]

In other ways, too, the reformers endorsed and reinforced a momentum for change that would prove irreversible after 1815. The Council of State (*Staatsrat*) established in 1817 may not have enjoyed the fullness of power Stein had once envisaged for it, but it did come to play a crucial role in the formulation of laws. The resulting ministerialization of government tended, in practice if not in theory, to limit the independence of the monarch and reinforce the power of the ministerial bureaucracies.[70] Ministers were far more authoritative figures after 1815 than they had been in the 1780s and 1790s. The provincial diets, despite their limitations, ultimately became important platforms for political opposition.

No single edict better illustrates the long-term impact of the reforms than the State Indebtedness Law of 17 January 1820, one of Hardenberg's last and most important legislative achievements. The text of the law began by declaring that the current Prussian state debt (of just over 180 million thalers) was to be regarded as 'a closed [account] for all time' and went on to announce that if the state should in future be obliged to raise a new loan, this could take place only with the 'involvement and co-guarantee of the future national assembly'. By means of this law, Hardenberg planted a constitutional time-bomb within the fabric of the Prussian state. It would tick away quietly until 1847, when the unforeseen financial demands of the dawning railway age would force the government to summon a United Diet in Berlin, opening the door to revolution.

The reforms were above all acts of communication. The propagandistic, exalted tone of the edicts was something new; the October Edict in particular was a remarkable piece of plebiscitary rhetoric. Prussian governments had never spoken to the public in this way before. The most innovative figure in this domain was Hardenberg, who adopted a pragmatic but respectful attitude to public opinion as a factor in the success of government initiatives. During his ministry in Ansbach and Bayreuth, he did his best to meet security needs without undermining 'the freedom to think and to express one's opinions publicly'. His famous Riga Memorandum of 1807 stressed the value of a cooperative, rather than antagonistic, relationship between the state and public opinion, and argued that governments should not shrink from 'winning over opinion' through the use of 'good writers'. It was Chancellor Hardenberg who in 1810–11 pioneered the regular, annotated publication of new legislation, arguing that this departure from the secretive practice of earlier governments would strengthen trust in the administration. Particularly innovative was his engagement of freelance writers and editors as propagandists in the service of the state.[71]

One little-known but highly emblematic initiative in which Hardenberg was involved was the reform of the old chancellery style in official communications. This issue first came to the fore in March 1800, when it was proposed that the long-winded *nomine regis* starting with the words 'We Frederick William III' and listing all the king's titles in descending order of importance, should be omitted from the header of government documents. When the matter was discussed in the state ministry on 7 April 1800, virtually all of the ministers were opposed, arguing that removal of the full title would diminish the authority of utterances stemming from the government. But on the following day Hardenberg submitted a separate judgement expressing his support for a much more radical reform to the language of public and official communications. The chancellery style that was currently used, he wrote, was that of a 'bygone age'; but whereas the age had changed, '[the style] has remained'. There was thus no reason why the state authority should maintain the 'barbaric written style of an uneducated era'. Little came of this spirited intervention in 1800, but ten years later, the *nomine regis* was abolished by a law of 27 October 1810 that carried Hardenberg's and the king's signatures.[72]

This apparently trifling innovation takes us to the heart of what Hardenberg's reform project was about. What concerned him above all – and the same is true for many of the older reformers – was transparency and communication. In this sense, Hardenberg was not a liberal, but a man of the enlightenment. He did not recognize public opinion as an *autonomous* force whose role was to check or oppose the state. Nor did he (or Stein, for that matter) have any intention of consolidating the 'liberal public sphere' as a domain of critical discourse.[73] He wanted to make such opposition unnecessary and unthinkable by opening the channels of understanding, by embracing the educated public in a harmonious conversation about the general good. This was the logic behind the Assembly of Notables and the national interim representations, the exalted, captivating language of the decrees and the endless government publications. It also explains his willingness to apply censorship when he deemed it necessary.[74]

What Hardenberg overlooked was that words have a life of their own. When he said 'representation', he had in mind compliant and virtuous bodies of worthies conveying information and ideas between the province and the metropolis, but others were thinking of corporate interests, or of parliaments and constitutional monarchy. When he said 'participation', he meant co-option and consultation, but others meant co-determination and the power to check government. When he said 'nation', he meant the politically conscious people of Prussia, but others were thinking of a wider German nation, whose interests and fate were not necessarily identical with those of Prussia. This is one of the reasons why the reform era seems at once so rich in promise and so poor in achievements. There are parallels here with another beleaguered historical figure, Mikhail Gorbachev. Gorbachev was a man of reform and transparency (*glasnost*), not of revolutionary transformation. His aim, and Hardenberg's, was to adjust the state system to the needs of the present. But it would be churlish to deny either man his part in the changes that lay ahead.

I I

A Time of Iron

FALSE DAWN

In the spring of 1809, it seemed that the tide might at last be turning against Napoleon. The news that bands of freedom fighters were harrying the French armies in the Iberian Peninsula stirred excitement throughout Prussia. In the second week of April came reports that Emperor Francis I of Austria, goaded into action by the installation of Joseph Bonaparte on the Bourbon throne of Spain, had gone to war against Napoleon. The Emperor's chief minister Count Stadion hoped to enlist German popular support, and Austrian campaign propaganda duly exhorted Germans in all states to rise up against the French. On 11 April, a massive peasant uprising in the Tyrol under the leadership of the wine merchant Andreas Hofer succeeded in driving out the Bavarians, allies of the French, who had presented them with the formerly Austrian Tyrol only four years earlier.

To many Prussians, it seemed that the moment was right for Prussia, too, to rise up against the invader. 'The general mood,' Provincial President Johann August Sack reported from Berlin, 'is that now or never is the moment when salvation from dependence and subjection is possible.'[1] Once again, the king was confronted with impossible choices. Vienna pressed for Prussian support, urging that the two states coordinate their military planning and strike against France together. Meanwhile, the French reminded Frederick William that under the terms of the Franco-Prussian treaty of 8 September 1808, Prussia was obliged to support France with an auxiliary corps of 12,000 men. The Russians were noncommittal. They seemed unenthusiastic about the Austrian campaign and unwilling to offer assurances. The king quickly gravitated towards his default position: even before the hostilities had begun,

345

he had concluded that it was best for Prussia to 'sit tight in the first instance'.[2]

As in 1805–6, the foreign-policy dilemma facing the state polarized the most influential figures around the monarch. Some argued that it would be suicidal for Prussia to undertake any initiative against France without Russian support. Others, including the leading military reformers, Foreign Minister August Friedrich Ferdinand von der Goltz and Minister of Justice Karl Friedrich Beyme, pressed for an alliance with Austria.[3] But the king clung stubbornly to a policy of inaction. His strategy was to avoid any move that might incur the complete extinction of his state. Reputation and honour were unaffordable luxuries; survival was all. 'A political existence of some kind, no matter how small it be, is better than none, and then [. . .] at least some hope remains for the future, but none would remain if Prussia disappeared entirely from the community of states, which will very likely be the case if it shows its hand before the time is right.'[4]

In retrospect, Frederick William's seems the wisest course. The opponents of war were doubtless right when they observed that full Russian support was essential to any successful strategy against Napoleon. It seems highly unlikely that Prussia and Austria, had they joined forces in the spring of 1809, could have prevailed over Napoleon. Yet to many contemporaries, the cautious, waiting stance of the Königsberg court seemed ignoble, culpable. Rumours circulated at court that a plan was afoot to depose Frederick William and replace him with his supposedly more energetic younger brother William. Police and other official reports spoke of widespread frustration and restlessness within the officer corps. A wildcat insurrection by Pomeranian officers was foiled at the beginning of April; on the western boundary of the Altmark, the former Prussian lieutenant von Katte (presumably a distant relative of Frederick the Great's companion) led an armed band into the neighbouring Kingdom of Westphalia, seized control of the formerly Prussian town of Stendal and commandeered the cash chests.[5] It appeared that the majority of Prussian officers favoured a war at Austria's side. On 18 April, Friedrich Ludwig von Vincke, president of the Kurmark regional government, reported from Berlin that opinion within the army was highly critical of the royal government's policy and that if the king did not take the initiative, all the young officers were determined to leave 'and it would scarcely be possible to maintain order'. Vincke concluded with a warning that if the king did not come immediately to Berlin, general dissolution would be the result, 'for if [the dissolution] emanates from the army, who can resist it?' Lieutenant-General Tauentzien, a close associate of Scharnhorst, declared that he could not vouch for the loyalty of his troops if Prussia were to remain neutral, and the king's cousin Prince August warned Frederick William that the 'nation' would act without him if necessary.[6]

There was further excitement at the end of April when it became known that a Prussian officer had led his regiment out of Berlin with the intention of heading a patriotic insurrection against the French. Major Ferdinand von Schill was famous as a veteran of guerrilla warfare against the French.[7] In 1806, he had commanded a corps of volunteers and carried out raids against the French supply lines in the area surrounding the fortress of Kolberg. Such was his success as a raider that in January 1807 he was promoted to captain by Frederick William III and entrusted with forming a free corps. In this capacity, Schill mounted various successful actions against French forces during the spring and early summer of 1807. Following the Peace of Tilsit on 9 July, the Schill Free Corps was dissolved. Schill himself was promoted to major and awarded the 'Pour le mérite', Prussia's highest decoration for bravery. He was soon a celebrated figure. In the summer of 1808, the patriotic Königsberg weekly Der Volksfreund published a biographical essay outlining his exploits and praising him as the ideal of Prussian patriotic manhood. A portrait of the hero, published as a supplement to the Volksfreund, depicted a dark-haired, rather louche man with drooping black moustaches and a hussar's shako tilted rakishly to one side.

In the autumn of 1808, Schill's regiment was the first unit of Prussian troops to enter Berlin since the defeats of 1806. 'The jubilation,' his adjutant later recalled, 'was indescribable. Crowns of laurels and bunches of flowers rained down upon us; from every window, prettily adorned women and girls welcomed us. Wherever Schill was seen, jubilant crowds surrounded him.'[8] Perhaps the excitement turned his head. Schill began to believe that Germany was ripe for a mass insurrection against the French, and that he was the man to lead it. This delusion was nourished by his contacts with the various clandestine networks of patriots that had sprung up across Prussia – the League of Virtue based in Königsberg, over 80 per cent of whose members were military men of all ranks, and the Society of the Fatherland, based in Pomerania,

31. Anon., Major von Schill

whose agents urged him to take over the leadership of the patriot movement. In January and February 1809, there were even secret messages from patriot circles in the Kingdom of Westphalia beseeching him to command an insurrection in western Germany. The clandestine network of the German patriots may have been numerically small, but it was zealous, well connected and emotionally intense. Once inside, it was easy to lose touch with reality, to believe that the people were behind you, that victory was certain and liberation imminent. In April 1809, Schill agreed to lead the planned Westphalian insurrection. A proclamation was drawn up and sent to Westphalia urging all patriots to rise against the occupiers, but it was intercepted by the French. On 27 April Schill learned that his own arrest was imminent and decided, without consulting his superiors, to take his men out of Berlin on the following day and launch an insurrectionary campaign.

The news of his departure caused an immense sensation. In a report of 1 May to Interior Minister Count Dohna, the provincial president of Brandenburg, Johann August Sack, observed that the agitation in the capital could scarcely be described; throughout the city the talk was of nothing but Schill; a Prussian declaration of war against Napoleon was felt to be imminent. In order to forestall the impression that the king was no longer in control of the country, the city authorities decided to encourage, for the time being, the belief that Schill was acting with official sanction.[9] On 7 May, the king was presented in Königsberg with a report from the Berlin Police President Justus Gruner warning him that he could rescue his own authority in the kingdom only by entering immediately into an alliance with Austria or by coming to Berlin and personally endorsing a policy of peace at the side of France.

For the army is teetering – and what good is the authority of the administration then? [...] All the tireless zeal of individuals [on the king's behalf] will be swallowed up in a sea of restlessly agitated passions, unless the venerable pilot Himself grasps the tiller to calm the masses. The throne of the Hohenzollerns is at stake.[10]

Gruner was exaggerating. Schill's venture ended in abject failure. On 31 May 1809, he was sabred by a Dane and shot dead by a Dutchman, both fighting with the French, in the city of Stralsund. The Dutchman, according to one account, cut off his head, preserved it in 'spirits of wine' and placed it on display in the public library at Leyden, where it remained until 1837, when it was buried in Brunswick. Twenty-eight of his surviving officers and men were subsequently executed by firing squad on Napoleon's orders for their role in the uprising.[11] Although there were many Prussian officers who sympathized with Schill and the patriot networks, there were few who were willing to break their oath of obedience to the king. The great majority of ordinary subjects in Prussia – as in the rest of Germany – were content to be passive observers of the patriots' exploits. Schill's experience, like the failed and almost simultaneous revolt of Colonel Ferdinand Wilhelm Caspar Freiherr von Dörnberg against King Jerôme in Westphalia, revealed that the patriotic zeal of the German masses, such as it was, could not be converted into political action.

Yet this moment of panic among the Prussian authorities is revealing none the less. It demonstrated how much had changed in the relationship between the monarchy and its public since the reign of Frederick the Great. What was remarkable about the reports from Tauentzien, Gruner, Sack and Vincke was their plebiscitary logic. For the first time in the history of the dynasty, we find senior Prussian officials and high-ranking officers invoking public opinion in order to force the hand of the monarch. Phlegmatic as ever, Frederick William kept a calm head, insisting that things were not as bad as the alarmists claimed. 'I do not fear illegal disturbances from my people,' he told Foreign Minister von der Goltz on 9 May, adding inconsequentially that he had no intention of going to Berlin, where 'anarchical explosions' might distract him from devoting his time and energy to more important questions.[12]

But Frederick William himself seems at some points to have internalized the arguments of his officials. In an extraordinary undated handwritten note, composed some time during the crisis of 1809, he reflected on the possibility of a forced abdication, observing morosely that if he were to be deposed in favour of another individual 'more favoured by opinion', then he would not protest, but readily 'hand over the reins of government to him whom the nation believes worthier'.[13] This was partly just sulking, but it also conveys a fleeting sense of how the upheavals of the revolutionary era were transforming the self-understanding of traditional monarchy.

PATRIOTS AND LIBERATORS

What was at stake in the crisis of 1809 was not simply the question of whether and when to strike against the French, but also the nature of the war that Prussia would ultimately wage against Napoleon. Frederick William and the more conservative figures among the military leadership continued to think in terms of a traditional *Kabinettskrieg* in which the key weapons were dynastic diplomacy and a well-trained regular army. By contrast, the reformers envisaged a new insurrectionary mode of warfare involving armed masses of citizen-soldiers inflamed by love of their fatherland. 'Why should we believe ourselves inferior to the Spaniards and Tyroleans?', General Gebhardt Leberecht von Blücher asked Frederick William in October 1809, as he urged him to embrace the risk of war at Austria's side. 'We are better equipped than they!'[14]

The issue lost some of its urgency after the war crisis passed, but it resurfaced in 1811, as the prospect loomed of a major war between France and Russia. In a memorandum submitted to the king on 8 August 1811, Gneisenau set out a detailed plan for a popular partisan war in the Spanish manner that would be unleashed on the French army from behind the front lines. This mass uprising (*Aufstand in Masse*) would harry French units, disrupt supply routes and destroy resources that might otherwise fall into the enemy's hands. Gneisenau had observed the débâcle of his sometime subordinate Schill and was aware that ordinary Prussians might need some additional encouragement before they risked life and limb against the French. To ensure that the necessary patriotic commitment was not lacking, Gneisenau suggested, the state should employ clergymen to mobilize local communities.[15] Stein (now in exile in Prague) and Clausewitz arrived at similar proposals, though they placed more emphasis on the need for clear leadership from the monarchical executive.

The concept of an insurrectionary war against the French never enjoyed wide support within the officer corps. Only a minority of officers was comfortable with an approach to warfare that risked unleashing forces beyond the control of the regular army. But beyond the army itself, in the educated circles of the Prussian patriot intelligentsia, there were many who found the idea exhilarating. In a poem composed in 1809 and inspired by the Austrian campaign against Napoleon, the sometime Prussian guardsman Heinrich von Kleist imagined Germans from all corners of the old Reich rising against the French and evoked in remarkably uncompromising language the brutality of an all-out war:

> Whiten with their scattered bones
> Every hollow, every hill;
> From what was left by fox and crow
> The hungry fish shall eat their fill;
> Block the Rhine with their cadavers;
> Until, plugged up by so much flesh,
> It breaks its banks and surges west
> To draw our borderline afresh![16]

Perhaps the quirkiest expression of the insurrectionary idea was the *Turnbewegung*, or gymnasts' movement, founded by Friedrich Ludwig Jahn in 1811 in the Hasenheide park in what is now the Berlin suburb of Neukölln. The aim of the movement was to train young men for a coming war against the French. The objective was not to train paramilitaries, but to evolve specifically civilian forms of bodily prowess and patriotic commitment in preparation for a struggle in which the people as a whole would be pitted against the enemy. The gymnasts were not 'soldiers', a term that Jahn despised for its mercenary associations ('*Sold*' is the German word for wage), but citizen-fighters whose participation in the struggle was entirely voluntary, because it was motivated by love for the fatherland. Gymnasts did not 'march', Jahn pointed out in *The Art of German Gymnastics*, the official catechism of the early movement, because marching killed the autonomous will and was intended to degrade the individual to the mere tool of a higher authority. Instead they 'walked', swinging their legs in a flowing, natural motion, as befitted free men. The art of the gymnast, Jahn wrote, 'is an enduring site [*eine bleibende Stätte*] for the building of fresh sociable virtues [. . .] of a sense of decency and law and [of a feeling for] cheerful obedience without prejudice to freedom of movement and high-spirited independence'.[17]

In order to facilitate this freedom of movement, Jahn developed a special costume, whose loose jacket and wide-legged trousers of grey unbleached linen were designed to accommodate and encourage the free forms of bodily movement so prized by the gymnasts. Here again, there was an antimilitary dimension: 'The light and austere, unpretentious and thoroughly functional linen costume of the gymnast,' Jahn wrote, 'is unsuited to [. . .] braids, aiguillettes, armbands, dress swords and gauntlets on the leaders of processions etc. The earnest spirit of the fighter (*Wehrmannsernst*) is thereby transformed into idle play.'[18] Coupled with this hostility to the hierarchical order of the traditional military was an implicit egalitarianism. Jahn's followers were encouraged to address each other as '*du*', and their distinctive costume helped to dissolve barriers of status by removing the outward signs of social difference.[19] The gymnasts were even known to sing songs proclaiming that all members were 'equal in estate and rank' ('*An Rang und Stand sind alle gleich*').[20] Jahn's outdoor displays, in which young men swung, twirled and twisted on raised bars that were the prototypes of today's gymnastic equipment, attracted huge crowds. Here was a clear demonstration of how patriotism could provide the key to a reconceptualization of political culture as rooted in voluntary allegiances rather than hierarchical structures of authority.

It was precisely the subversive potential in patriotic discourses that alienated the monarch from the more radical prescriptions of the military reformers. On 28 December 1809, Frederick William at last returned to Berlin, where crowds cheered him through the city. But he remained opposed to patriotic experiments of any kind. Now that he was re-established in the capital, he was more completely under the eye of the French authorities than ever – indeed Napoleon had demanded that he leave Königsberg for this very reason. Moreover, after 1809, the position of the French seemed totally impregnable. By 1810, nearly all the German territories left over from the dissolution of the Holy Roman Empire had joined the Confederation of the Rhine, an association of states whose members were obliged to contribute military contingents in support of Napoleon's foreign policy. In the face of such might, resistance seemed hopeless.

Frederick William's reluctance to risk precipitate military action was further reinforced by personal tragedy. On 19 July 1810, the unexpected death of his wife Luise, at the age of only thirty-four, plunged him into a long depression in which his only comforts were seclusion and prayer. He had no faith in the idea of insurrectionary warfare; the reformers were allowed to proceed with various improvements to military administration and training but Frederick William blocked their efforts to mobilize a 'people's army' (*Volksarmee*) through the introduction of universal conscription. To Gneisenau's proposal that clergymen be employed to urge the people to rise up against their conquerors the king appended the laconic marginal note: 'One executed preacher and the whole thing will be over with.' On Gneisenau's proposals for a system of citizen militias he commented simply: 'Good – as poetry.'[21] Nevertheless, the king agreed one important concession to the war party. During the summer of 1811, he approved plans for the enlargement of the Prussian army and the reinforcement of key strongholds. There were also tactful feelers in the direction of Russia and England.

Fortunately for Frederick William, most of his senior advisers (including Hardenberg) supported his policy of wait-and-see. The king thus had little difficulty in resisting the entreaties of the 'war party'. But with the cooling of relations between France and Russia from 1810 onwards, the external pressures on the Berlin decision-makers gradually increased. It had always been difficult to imagine a European future in which Napoleon and Alexander I could get along as brothers. Tensions had been accumulating between the two for some time, but the breach came in December 1810, when Napoleon annexed the north-west German Duchy of Oldenburg, whose integrity had been guaranteed in the Peace of Tilsit and whose sovereign was Tsar Alexander's uncle. Alexander responded with the *ukaz* of 31 December, by which he closed Russian markets and ports to French products (except wines and silks). During the spring and summer of 1811 the two powers drifted apart, neither committing itself to war. By the winter of 1811–12, however, it was clear that a major French offensive was imminent. Napoleon reinforced his armies in eastern and central Germany, occupied Swedish Pomerania and transferred thirty-six battalions from Spain.[22]

Once again, the Prussians found themselves in danger of being ground under the wheels of great-power politics. Frederick William and his advisers – Hardenberg foremost among them – displayed the usual timidity and caution. The rearmament process that had been launched in the early summer was impossible to hide from the French. In August 1811, Napoleon demanded an explanation. Dissatisfied with Hardenberg's answer, he issued an ultimatum warning that if rearmament activity did not cease forthwith, the French ambassador would be withdrawn from Berlin and replaced by Marshal Davout at the head of his army. This announcement was greeted with consternation in Berlin. Gneisenau objected that to comply with such outright bullying would be political suicide, but Frederick William overruled him and orders went out that the recruitment drive and fortification works were to be stopped. There were also loud protests from the commanding officer of the Kolberg fortress, General Blücher, who would later play a key role in the campaigns against France. When Blücher urged that the king resist the French orders and remove himself from Berlin, he was recalled from his command and replaced by Tauentzien, a general acceptable to Napoleon.

The final humiliation came in the form of the offensive alliance treaty imposed by Napoleon on 24 February 1812. The Prussians undertook to quarter and supply the Grand Army as it tramped eastwards through Prussia on its way to invade Russia, to open all their munitions stores and fortresses to the French command and to provide Napoleon with an auxiliary corps of 12,000 men. This 'agreement' was extorted from Berlin in a manner that recalled the treaty negotiations of the Thirty Years War. Napoleon began by offering Krusemarck, the Prussian ambassador at the imperial headquarters, the choice of having the Grand Army enter Prussia as a friend or as a foe. In desperation, the ambassador provisionally accepted all conditions and forwarded the document to Berlin for ratification. But the French delayed the departure of the courier bearing the text, so that by the time it reached Frederick William a French army corps was already approaching the Prussian capital.

Prussia was now a mere instrument of Napoleon's military strategy, on a par with the German satellite states of the Rhenish Confederation. For those patriotic reformers who had striven so hard to prepare Prussia for the coming struggle with Napoleon, this was the ultimate disappointment. A group of prominent senior officials resigned from office in disgust. These included the sometime chief of police in Berlin, Justus Gruner, who made his way to Prague, where he joined a network of patriots dedicated to overthrowing the French through insurrection and sabotage (he was arrested by the Austrian government – also allied with France – in August). Scharnhorst, the driving engine behind the military reforms, went into 'inner exile', disappearing entirely from public life. Three of the most talented military innovators, Boyen, Gneisenau and Clausewitz, broke ranks with their colleagues and entered the service of the Tsar in the belief that only Russia now possessed the potential to break Napoleon's power. Here they were able to reconnect with Stein, who, having spent a period in Austrian exile, joined the imperial Russian headquarters in June 1812 at the express invitation of Tsar Alexander.

From March onward, the men of the Grand Army tramped through the Neumark, Pomerania, West and East Prussia, making their way eastwards to their assembly points. By June 1812, some 300,000 men – French, Germans, Italians, Dutch, Walloons and others – were gathered in East Prussia. It soon became clear that the provincial administration was in no position to coordinate the provisioning of this vast mass of troops. The previous year's harvest had been poor and grain supplies were quickly depleted. Hans Jakob von Auerswald, provincial president of West and East Prussia, reported in April that the farm animals in East and West Prussia were dying of hunger, the roads were strewn with dead horses, and there was no seed corn left. The provincial government's provisioning apparatus soon broke down under the pressure, and individual commanders simply ordered their troops to carry out independent requisitioning. It was said that those who still owned draft animals ploughed and sowed at night, so as not to see their last horse or ox carted off. Others hid their horses in the forest, though the French soon got wise to this practice and began combing the woods for concealed animals. Under these conditions, discipline rapidly broke down and there were numerous reports of excesses by the troops, especially extortion, plundering and beatings. One report from a senior official spoke of devastation 'even worse than in the Thirty Years War'. When no horses were to be had, the French commanders forced peasants into the harness. The average East Prussian farmer, Auerswald reported in August, found it impossible to understand how he could be so mistreated by the allies

355

of his king; indeed it was said the French behaved themselves worse as 'friends' in 1812 than they had as enemies in 1807. In the Lithuanian areas on the eastern margins of the province, the summer brought famine and the inevitable rise in deaths among children.[23] In the memorable words of the Hanoverian diplomat Ludwig Ompteda, the French had left the inhabitants of Prussia with 'nothing but eyes to weep with in their misery'.[24]

Throughout the Prussian lands, the mood gradually shifted from resentment to a simmering hatred of the Napoleonic forces. Vague early rumours of French setbacks in Russia were greeted with excitement and heartfelt *schadenfreude*. The first sketchy reports of the burning of Moscow (razed by the Russians to deny Napoleon winter quarters) arrived in the eastern provinces of Prussia at the beginning of October. There was particular interest in reports of the appalling damage done to the Grand Army by irregular forces of Cossacks and armed peasant partisans. On 12 November, when the newspapers reported the withdrawal of the Grand Army from Moscow, rumour gave way to near-certainty. The French diplomat Lecaro, stationed in Berlin, was shocked at the intensity of public emotion: in three and a half years of living in the city, he wrote, he had never seen its inhabitants display 'such intense hatred and such open rage'. Emboldened by the recent news, the Prussian people 'no longer concealed its desire to join with the Russians in exterminating everything that belongs to the French system'.[25] On 14 December, the 29th Bulletin of the Grand Army put an end to any further doubts about the outcome of the Russian campaign. Issued in the Emperor's name, the bulletin blamed the catastrophe on bad weather and the incompetence and treachery of others, announced that Napoleon had left his men in Russia and was hastening west towards Paris, and closed with a remarkably brutal expression of imperial self-centredness: 'The Emperor's health has never been better.' In Prussia, this news triggered further incidents of unrest. In Neustadt, West Prussia, local inhabitants fought with Neapolitan troops guarding a transport of Russian prisoners of war. There were spontaneous attacks on French military personnel, especially in taverns, where patriotic passions were inflamed by the consumption of alcohol.

But no rumour and no printed report could bring home the meaning of Napoleon's catastrophe as forcefully as the sight of the remnants of the once-invincible Grand Army limping westwards out of Russia.

The noblest figures had been bent and shrunken by frost and hunger, they were covered with blue bruises and white frost-sores. Whole limbs were frozen off and rotting [...] they gave off a pestilential stench. [...] Their clothing consisted of rags, straw mats, old women's clothing, sheepskins, or whatever else they could lay hands on. None had proper headgear; instead they bound their heads with old cloth or pieces of shirt; instead of shoes and leggings, their feet were wrapped with straw, fur or rags.[26]

The slow-burning malice of the peasantry now ignited into acts of revenge as the rural population took matters into their own hands. 'The lowest classes of the people,' District President Theodor von Schön reported from Gumbinnen, 'and especially the peasants, permit themselves in their fanaticism the most horrific mistreatment of these unhappy wretches [...] in the villages and on the country roads, they vent all their rage against them [...] All obedience to the officials has ceased.'[27] There were reports of attacks on stragglers by armed troops of peasants.

During the month of December 1812, the Prussian government, like those of the other German client states, remained committed to the French alliance. On 15 December, when Napoleon requested that the Prussians expand their military contingent, the government in Berlin meekly complied. As the year drew to an end, however, Frederick William came under increasing pressure to renege on the alliance of 24 February and join in Russia's struggle against Napoleon. Of three memoranda submitted to him by senior officials on Christmas day 1812, two (from Knesebeck and Schöler) urged him to seize the opportunity furnished by the collapse of the Russian campaign and turn against France. The third, from privy councillor Albrecht, was more circumspect and warned the king not to underestimate Napoleon's remaining potential.[28] Only when Austria's strength was fully engaged in the common cause should Prussia risk open aggression against the French forces.

Stolid, pessimistic and cautious as ever, the king was drawn to the third option. In an aide-mémoire written three days later, Frederick William set out his own views on Prussian foreign policy over the coming months. Its central theme was 'live and let live'; Austria should be entrusted with the mediation of a general European peace. Napoleon must be obliged to come to an understanding with Tsar Alexander on the basis of mutual respect, after which he would be permitted to retire unmolested into France and to hold on to his annexed German lands on the left bank of the Rhine. Only if he refused to be content with this arrangement would Prussia go to war, and then only at Austria's side. The king imagined that this might occur, if at all, in April of the coming year.[29]

TURNING POINT

By the time Frederick William penned these lines, events were already overtaking him. On 20 December 1812, the first advance parties of Russian troops crossed the border into East Prussia. Under the terms of the alliance with France, it now fell to the Prussian General Yorck, who had managed to extricate 14,000 of his men alive from the Russian campaign, to block the further progress of the Russians and thereby cover the retreat of what remained of the Grand Army. Yorck found himself bombarded with messages from both the French and the Russian commands. Marshal Alexandre Macdonald sent orders that he clear the way for his retreat and guard the French flank against Russian attack. From the Russian commander General Diebitsch there were entreaties to abandon Macdonald and let the Russians pass unhindered. On 25 December, Yorck and Diebitsch met and it was agreed that one of the Prussians attached to the Russian headquarters should be empowered to conduct further negotiations. The man entrusted with this task was none other than the reformer, patriot and military theorist Carl von Clausewitz, who had left the Prussian service earlier that year.

During a difficult discussion on the evening of 29 December, Clausewitz explained to Yorck that the Russians were close by and massed in very large numbers. Any attempt to reunite with Macdonald, whose small corps had come unstuck from the Prussian contingent, would be pointless. Impressed by the cogency of Clausewitz's arguments and the sincerity of his conviction, Yorck finally agreed: 'Yes. You have me. Tell General Diebitsch that we shall talk early tomorrow at Poscherun Mill [near the Lithuanian town of Tauroggen, forty kilometres east of the Prussian border] and that I have now firmly decided to separate from the French and their cause.'[30] The meeting was fixed for the next morning (30 December) at eight o'clock. Under the terms of the agreement drawn up there, known as the Convention of Tauroggen, Yorck undertook to

32. Anon., Johann David Ludwig
Count Yorck

neutralize his corps for a period of two months and allow the Russians to pass unhindered into Prussian territory.

It was a momentous decision. Yorck had no authorization whatsoever to countermand his government's policy in this way.[31] His defection was not merely disobedient; it was treasonable. This weighed very heavily with a man who was by background and nature a royalist and a conservative. Yorck attempted to justify his action in a remarkable letter he wrote to Frederick William on 3 January 1813:

Your Majesty knows me as a calm, cool-headed man who does not mix in politics. As long as everything went in the accustomed way, the loyal servant was bound to follow circumstances – that was his duty. But the circumstances have now brought about a new situation and duty likewise demands that this situation, which will never occur again, be exploited. I am speaking here the words of a loyal old servant; these words are almost universally the words of the Nation; a declaration from Your Majesty will breathe life and enthusiasm back into everything and we will fight like true old Prussians and the throne of Your Majesty will stand rock-solid and unshakeable for the future. [...] I now anxiously await an advisement from Your Majesty as to whether I should now advance against the true enemy, or whether political conditions demand that Your Majesty condemn me. I await both outcomes in a spirit of loyal dedication and I swear to Your Majesty that I shall meet the bullets as calmly at the place of execution as on the field of battle.[32]

Perhaps the most remarkable thing about this letter was the fact that it made – notwithstanding the superficial rhetoric of personal loyalty – so few concessions to the monarch's standpoint. Instead, Yorck offered Frederick William the choice of confirming his action or condemning him to death for his disobedience. Moreover, the reference to the 'true enemy', as opposed to the enemy projected by Berlin's foreign policy, made it clear that Yorck had arrogated to himself one of the constitutive attributes of sovereignty, namely the right to determine who is friend and who is foe. To make matters worse, Yorck justified this act of usurpation through an implicit appeal to the ultimate authority of the hard-pressed Prussian 'nation'.

These were surprisingly radical words from a man who had initially kept his distance from the military reformers. In 1808–9, Yorck had been a bitter opponent of armed insurrection, on the grounds that it posed too grave a threat to the political and social order. But as the pressure for action grew, he had begun to look less coldly on the populist designs of the patriots. The more he thought over the idea of a popular uprising, he told Scharnhorst in the summer of 1811, the more 'absolutely necessary' it seemed to be. In a memorandum submitted to the king at the end of January 1812, he set out a plan to use tightly focused insurrections in West Prussia to tie down French divisions and undercut the momentum of the main advance.[33] It is hard to imagine a better illustration of the potency of the ideas that animated the reformers than this belated conversion of a hard-boiled conservative to the cause of the nation.

By the end of the first week of February, the entire province of East Prussia had slipped beyond the direct control of the Berlin government. Stein, who entered the province as a functionary of the Russian administration, saw himself as empowered to exercise direct authority in the liberated areas, and he did so with his accustomed tactlessness. Various trade restrictions associated with the Napoleonic system of continental tariffs were lifted without local consultation, and the Prussian financial administration was obliged, despite bitter protests, to accept Russian paper money at a fixed rate of exchange. Flaunting his sovereign status as 'Plenipotentiary of the Russian Emperor', Stein even convened the East Prussian Estates in order to deliberate on arrangements for the coming war against France. 'Intelligence, honour, love of the fatherland, and revenge,' he told Yorck in a letter of early February, 'demand that we lose no time, that we call up a people's war [. . .] to break the chains of the insolent oppressor and wash away the dishonour we have suffered with the blood of his wicked bands.'[34] Stein wanted Yorck to open the first meeting of the Estates with a rousing speech, but Yorck was uncomfortable with any role that would make him appear to be the agent of Russian interests. However, he did agree to attend a session if the Estates themselves formally invited him.

On 5 February, the 'representatives of the nation', as they were widely called at the time, congregated in the meeting hall of the House of the Provincial Estates in Königsberg. At their head sat the president, to his right seven members of the Estates Committee, flanked by the deputies of the provincial nobility, the free peasants and the cities. Almost immediately, it was agreed that a delegation should be sent to invite Yorck to present his proposals to the assembly. The deputies were surely aware of the boldness of this step: by the beginning of February it was universally known that Yorck had been dismissed from office, that his arrest had been ordered and that he was out of favour with the king. The scope of the insurrection unfolding in East Prussia now widened to the point where it encompassed the political class of the province.

Yorck appeared only briefly before the assembly, urging that a committee be formed to oversee further preparations for war and closing with a characteristically pithy declaration: 'I hope to fight the French wherever I find them. I count on everyone's support; if their strength outweighs ours, we will know how to die with honour.' These words were greeted with thunderous cheers and applause, but Yorck raised his hand to silence the hall, saying: 'There is no call for that on a battlefield!' He then turned and left. On the same evening, a committee met in Yorck's apartment to agree the calling up of a provincial militia (*Landwehr*) of 20,000 men with 10,000 reserves. The exemptions allowed under the old cantonal system were abolished; all adult males up to forty-five years of age, excluding only school teachers and clergymen, were declared eligible to be called up, regardless of their social status or religion – the latter stipulation implied that Jews, for the first time, would be liable for conscription. The aim was to fill the troop quotas from volunteers in the first instance and only if this proved inadequate, to proceed to conscription by ballot. The ideal of the nation at arms rising against its foe had at last been realized. In the process, the authority of the monarchical state was almost totally displaced by the Estates, who now reactivated their traditional calling as organs of provincial governance.[35]

In Berlin, the government began during the January weeks to distance itself from the French alliance. On 21 January, after rumours to the effect that the French were planning to take him prisoner, Frederick William left Potsdam and transferred with Hardenberg and an entourage of some seventy persons to Breslau in Silesia, where he arrived four days later. During the first week of February, as the Estates prepared to meet in Königsberg, the king and his advisory circle remained in a state of uncertainty and indecision. To stay at the side of France seemed impossible in view of the events unfolding in the east, but the prospect of an open break with France brought the threat of total dependence upon Russia. The problem of Prussia's exposed position between the powers of east and west had never been so dramatically expressed. The western provinces remained vulnerable to French reprisals; East and West Prussia were already under what amounted to a Russian occupation. Faced with this fundamental dilemma, the Breslau court seemed paralysed; the king, Hardenberg observed in a private note on 4 February, appeared 'not to know what he actually wants'.[36]

At around the same time, however, the king began to approve decisions that pointed in the direction of a more energetic policy. Scharnhorst was recalled from his retirement, and on 8 February a general call went out for volunteers to form free corps of riflemen. On the following day, the service exemptions of the cantonal system were suspended, establishing, temporarily at least, universal male liability for military service. It was as if the government were hurrying to keep abreast of developments in its eastern provinces. But these measures did not suffice, in the short term, to arrest the collapse of public faith in the monarch and his advisers. By the middle of February, the spirit of insurrection had crossed the river Oder into the Neumark and there was talk of a revolution if the king did not immediately signal his solidarity with Russia. Even the Huguenot preacher Ancillon, one of the most cautious and ingratiating of the king's advisers, warned him in a memorandum of 22 February that it was the 'general will of the nation' that the king should lead his people in a war against France. If he failed to do so, Ancillon warned, he would be swept away by events.[37]

Only in the last days of February did the king finally decide to throw in his lot with the Russians and break openly with Napoleon. A treaty was signed with the Russians at Kalisch and Breslau on 27–28 February in which the Russians agreed to restore Prussia to the approximate borders of 1806. Under the terms of this treaty, Prussia would cede most of the Polish territories acquired through the second and third partitions to Russia, but retain a land corridor (in addition to West Prussia) between Silesia and East Prussia. The Russians in their turn agreed that Prussia would be compensated for these Polish concessions by the annexation of territory from the allies' joint conquests in Germany – informal discussions pointed to Saxony, whose king was still aligned with Napoleon, as the most likely victim.

Scharnhorst was despatched to Tsar Alexander's headquarters to begin discussions on a joint war plan. A formal announcement of the break with France followed on 17 March, and on 25 March the Russian and Prussian commands issued the joint Proclamation of Kalisch, in which the Russian tsar and the Prussian king sought to harness national enthusiasms by pledging their support for a united Germany. A committee was established under Stein's chairmanship to recruit troops from across the German territories and to plan for the future political organization of southern and western Germany. The Prussian government now made strenuous efforts to reclaim the ground that had been lost to the forces of insurrection. On 17 March the king issued the famous address 'To My People', in which he justified the government's cautious policy hitherto and called upon his people to rise up, province by province, against the French. Drafted by Theodor Gottfried Hippel, a native of Königsberg who had joined the chancellery under Hardenberg in 1811, 'To My People' steered a careful middle path between the insurrectionary rhetoric of the patriot radicals and the hierarchical order of traditional absolutism. Comparisons were drawn with the conservative uprisings of the Vendée (1793), Spain (1808) and the Tyrol (1808), but pointedly not with the revolutionary French *levée en masse* of 1793, and an effort was made to embed current events within a tradition of Hohenzollern dynastic leadership.[38] The edict of 21 April 1813 establishing the *Landsturm* (home army) was perhaps the most radical official utterance of these weeks – it stated that home army officers were to be elected, although eligibility to ascend to officer rank was restricted to certain social and professional groups.[39]

By early March, Breslau had become the centre of operations, not only for the Prussian and Russian army commands but also for the burgeoning volunteer movement. While Frederick William III, Scharn-horst, Gneisenau and Blücher met with their Russian counterparts in the royal palace to coordinate the coming campaign, crowds of volunteers converged on the Hotel Szepter only a short distance away to sign for service under Major Ludwig Adolf Wilhelm von Lützow. Lützow was a Prussian officer from Berlin who had served in Schill's regiment of hussars and was authorized by the king in 1813 to found a free corps of voluntary riflemen. The Lützow Rifles, also known as the 'Black Band' for their sombre, loose-cut uniforms, eventually numbered 3,000 men. Among those most actively involved in volunteer recruitment was Fried-rich Ludwig Jahn, who had come to Breslau with a flock of eager gymnasts and was already something of a cult figure. 'They goggle at him as if he were some kind of messiah,' a young regular army soldier noted, evidently with mixed feelings.[40] The young nobleman Leopold von Gerlach, who came to Breslau towards the end of February, was struck by the energy and exhilaration in the city. In the theatre of an evening, Gerlach wrote, Chancellor Hardenberg could still be seen chatting amiably with the French ambassador in order to keep up appearances. But the streets were agog with preparations for war. Sol-diers could be seen exercising on the ramparts, on the ring road and before the city gates; the lanes were crowded with horses being bought and sold, the streets lined with Jews selling muskets, pistols and sabres; 'virtually everyone, from tailors, swordsmiths, cobblers to harness makers, hatters and saddlers, is working for the war.'[41]

While the allied commanders laid their plans in Breslau, Napoleon too was preparing for war in Germany, building a new army from veterans and fresh untested recruits raised from the client states of the Confederation of the Rhine. Napoleon's history, charisma and repu-tation were still sufficient to dissuade most of the German sovereigns from defecting; their fear of his strength was reinforced by concern at the prospect of a national uprising against France that might sweep away German thrones as well as French garrisons. Even the beleaguered King of Saxony, who had momentarily wavered, returned to the French fold in May, partly because he recognized that the allies (and especially Prussia) posed a greater threat to the integrity of his kingdom than Napoleon. The allies thus faced a long and uncertain struggle against a foe who still controlled the resources and manpower of much of German Europe.

The Wars of Liberation, as they would come to be known, opened badly for the allies. It was agreed that the Prussian army would operate under a Russian supreme command – a telling indication of Prussia's junior status within the coalition – but it proved difficult at first to coordinate the two command structures. Having entered Saxony at the end of March, the allies were defeated at the battle of Lützen on 2 May. But Napoleon's victory was dearly bought: while the Prussians lost 8,500 and the Russians 3,000 in dead and wounded, the figure for the French and their client states was 22,000. This pattern was repeated at the battle of Bautzen on 20–21 May, where Napoleon forced the allies to withdraw, but lost another 22,000 men, twice as many as the Russo-Prussian forces. The allies were obliged to pull back out of Saxony into Silesia, but their armies remained intact.

It was not an encouraging start. Nevertheless, the ferocity of the allied resistance gave Napoleon pause. On 4 June, he agreed a temporary armistice with Tsar Alexander and Frederick William III. Napoleon later came to regard the ceasefire of 4 June as the error that undid his dominion in Germany. This was overstating the case, but it was certainly a serious failure of judgement. The allies used the respite afforded by it not only to enlarge and re-equip their forces, but also to put their war effort on a more solid financial footing by concluding alliance and subsidy treaties with Britain at Reichenbach on 8 June. In addition to direct subsidies totalling 2 million pounds, of which one-third (about 3.3 million thalers) would go to Prussia, Britain agreed to supply 5 million pounds in 'federal paper', a special currency underwritten by London that would be used by the allied governments for war-related costs and redeemed jointly by the three treaty partners after the end of the war.[42] In a war that had already plunged Britain into historically un-precedented levels of public debt, this was the biggest subsidy deal yet.

The most urgent objective of allied policy after 4 June was to persuade Austria to join the coalition. Clemens Wenzel von Metternich, the Aus-trian minister responsible for foreign policy, had kept his distance from the Russo-Prussian coalition during the early months of 1813. The Austrian government already viewed Russia as a threat in the Balkans and they had no wish to see Napoleon's control over Germany exchanged for Russian hegemony. But after the Treaty of Reichenbach was signed, followed by an alliance with Sweden on 22 July, it became clear that the future of Europe was in contention and Vienna could no longer afford to sit on the sidelines. During the summer, Metternich attempted to mediate a European peace that would be acceptable to Napoleon, while at the same time (at Reichenbach on 27 June) agreeing conditions for joint action with the allies in the event that mediation failed. When Metternich's efforts to broker peace foundered on Napoleon's intransigence, Austria resolved at last to join the allied coalition. The ceasefire of 4 June was allowed to expire on 10 August 1813; on the following day Austria formally entered the coalition and declared war against France.

The balance of power now tipped sharply against France. The Austrians contributed 127,000 men to the coalition war effort. The Russians had fielded an army of 110,000 during the spring campaign and this number was steadily rising as new waves of recruits arrived. Sweden contributed a further force of 30,000 men under the command of the former French marshal, now crown prince of Sweden, Jean Baptiste Jules Bernadotte. Under their new conscription laws, the Prussians were able to field a massive contingent of 228,000 infantry, 31,000 cavalry and 13,000 artillerymen. At the height of the fighting, about 6 per cent of the Prussian population were in active service. Against this imposing multinational force, Napoleon could muster 442,000 troops ready for combat, many of whom were ill-trained and poorly motivated new recruits.

Napoleon concentrated his forces around Dresden, on the territory of his loyal ally the King of Saxony, in the hope that an opportunity would arise to deal a devastating blow against one or other of the allied armies. The allies, for their part, adopted a concentric strategy: a Swedish-Prussian Northern Army under the command of Bernadotte moved southwards from Brandenburg, having retaken Berlin, while Blücher commanded the Silesian Army to Napoleon's east. Advancing from the south was the Army of Bohemia under Schwarzenberg. Closing in on Napoleon was not easy, despite the allied superiority in numbers. He enjoyed the advantage of internal lines and was still capable of mounting swift and destructive strikes. The allies suffered from the usual problem of coalition armies – relations between and within the Prussian, Swedish and Austrian commands were not harmonious and the widely dispersed forces faced the problem of tightening the ring around Napoleon without exposing themselves to a potentially devastating French attack. The third week of August brought three victories and a defeat. The Army of

Berlin, a force composed for the most part of Saxon, Franconian and other German contingents and commanded by the French General Oudinot, was beaten on 23 August in a battle near Grossbeeren as it approached the Prussian capital. A French corps of 10,000 men making its way into Brandenburg to assist Oudinot was subsequently attacked and destroyed near Hagelberg. In both these engagements, men of the Prussian Landwehr played a central role. On 26 August, Blücher's Silesian Army inflicted heavy losses on a 67,000-strong force of French and Rhenish Confederation troops under Macdonald; nearly half of Macdonald's army perished or was taken prisoner. But these successes were offset to some extent by a bitter engagement on the outskirts of Dresden on 26–27 August, in which Schwarzenberg's Army of Bohemia was driven back by Napoleon with over 35,000 casualties.

Encouraged by his success at Dresden, Napoleon initially focused on finding and destroying one of the allied armies on its route of approach, trusting that his advantage of internal lines would allow him to concentrate superior forces against any one of his adversaries. He drove his men through the broad wedge of territory between the rivers Saale and Elbe in search of either Bernadotte's Northern or Blücher's Silesian Army, both of which he knew to be in the area. But both evaded him by moving westward across the Saale.

By this point, Napoleon was starting to run out of options. He could not withdraw from the theatre without exposing himself to damaging attacks from irregulars and Cossacks, let alone his adversaries' armies, all of which were still intact and combat-ready. Domestic opinion in France was turning sharply against the prolongation of the conflict, and Napoleon's resources were running low. Pressed for time, he resolved to concentrate his forces around the Saxon city of Leipzig, await the arrival of his enemies and accept battle. The city thus became the setting for the greatest single military engagement to that date in the history of continental Europe, and probably of human warfare. The battle of Leipzig has justly been called the 'Battle of the Peoples' (*Völkerschlacht*), for the 500,000 men who took part included Frenchmen, Germans (on both sides), Russians, Poles, Swedes, nearly every one of the subject nationalities of the Austrian Empire and even a specialist British rocket brigade that had been formed only in the previous year and was to see its first action at Leipzig.

By the night of 14 October, Napoleon had concentrated 177,000

troops in and around the city. Early on the following day, Schwarzenberg's army, a mammoth corps numbering just over 200,000 men, made
contact with French forces under Murat to the south of the city. Much
of 15 October was spent in patrols and skirmishes as the two armies
felt out each other's positions. In the meanwhile, Blücher's Silesian
Army, whose exact position was unknown to Napoleon, advanced from
the north-west along the rivers Saale and Elster. The following day,
16 October, was dominated by ferocious fighting across a wide sweep
of land around the city as Schwarzenberg attacked from the south,
Blücher from the north and a small allied corps of 19,000 men pressed
through the wooded areas to the west of the city. At the end of the day,
Napoleon still held much of the line in the south, but had been pushed
back in the north-west, where his positions around Möckern had succumbed after a savage battle with the Prussians of the I Corps of the
Silesian Army under General Yorck, now restored to office, if not to
royal favour.

As night fell, the overall outcome still hung in the balance. The
casualties were prodigious: the French had lost nearly 25,000 men, and
the allies 30,000. Yet this augured well for the allies, for while Napoleon
could deploy only 200,000 men in all, including the remaining reserves,
the arrival of the Northern Army and the Polish Army under Bennigsen
would bring the allied forces concentrated around Leipzig to 300,000
men. Moreover, Napoleon's grip on his German allies was weakening.
During 16 October, news reached him that an army of 30,000 Bavarians
had defected to the Austrians and intended to intercept Napoleon's lines
of communication with France.[43]

The French Emperor considered the possibility of a retreat, but
decided ultimately to delay his withdrawal until the 18th, in the hope
that some fatal error by the allies might supply him with an opportunity
to tip the balance. He also attempted, in his accustomed manner, to
divide his enemies by offering a separate peace to Austria, but this
initiative merely had the effect of persuading his adversaries that he was
at the end of his resources. The following day (17 October) was quiet,
save for various skirmishes, as all the armies rested in preparation for
the decisive struggle and various gaps between the attacking forces were
closed. Meanwhile, the streets of Leipzig filled with wounded from both
sides. 'Since last night,' the Leipzig composer Friedrich Rochlitz noted
in his diary on 17 October, 'we have been working without pause to

bandage and house the wounded, and still there are many lying unattended to on the marketplace and in the nearby streets, so that at several places one is, quite literally, walking through blood.'[44]

On 18 October, the allies pushed forward towards the outskirts of Leipzig, tightening the noose around the French forces. An important role in this phase of the battle fell to the Prussian General Bülow, whose corps formed part of the Northern Army under Bernadotte. Bülow spearheaded its advance from the east across the river Parthe and bore the brunt of the fighting for the eastern approaches to the city. Once again, casualties on both sides were heavy. The allies lost a further 20,000 men; the French had remained for the most part on the defensive and lost perhaps half that number. There were also further defections, notably of 4,000 Saxons attached to Reynier's corps, who simply marched in closed ranks to the allies. Among those who observed this remarkable act of defection was Marshal Macdonald, who saw through his telescope how the Saxons, while leading a successful advance against the allies, simply turned about and trained their weapons on the Frenchmen following behind: 'In the most abominable and cold-blooded manner,' he later recalled, 'they shot down their unsuspecting fellows, with whom they had previously served in loyal comradeship of arms.'[45] Desperate attempts by Marshal Ney to close the line and mount a counter-attack were repelled by the British rocket brigade, whose Congreve rockets struck terror into the advancing column.

The outcome was now decided. Realizing that no hope remained of averting disaster, Napoleon ordered that the retreat of his forces begin under cover of darkness in the small hours of the morning. By eleven o'clock on the morning of 19 October, the French Emperor himself had left the city and was making his way back to the Rhine. A rearguard of 30,000 men stayed back to hold the city and cover the retreat. Yet the battle was still far from over, for the defenders, four of whom on average were manning each metre of the inner perimeter, had no intention of yielding without a fight. The allies pressed in along a wide arc from the north-west to the south of the city. As Bülow and his corps approached its eastern defences, they saw that the forward positions had been abandoned and hundreds of wagons overturned to impede their advance. There was a pause while a path was cleared using artillery fire. Entering the built-up area before the main wall, the vanguard of Bülow's corps was caught in intense fire from French marksmen on the roofs and upper

33. Johann Lorenz Rugendas, The Battle of Leipzig, *16–19 October 1813;
fighting before the Grimma Gate*

floors of the buildings on both sides of the narrow street. One thousand
of his Prussians were lost within the first few minutes of the fighting.
Artillery was virtually useless, since the men were locked in hand-to-
hand combat with defending troops as they fought their way from street
corner to street corner. Charging into a side street, a battalion of 400
East Prussian Landwehr were cut off and mauled by the defenders;
only half of them escaped with their lives. The fighting was especially
desperate at the Grimma Gate, where retreating French defenders found
themselves locked out of the city – the Badenese troops manning the
gate from within had received instructions to allow no one to pass.
The stranded Frenchmen were massacred by the approaching Prussians,
many of whom were Landwehr men attached to Bülow's vanguard.

By noon, the city had been breached in the east and the north and
was on the point of collapse. For the defenders, no option remained but
to flee westwards across the Elster bridge in the footsteps of the Grand
Army. Napoleon had ordered that the bridge be mined, held until the
retreat, and blown up after the last defenders had left the city. But the
hapless corporal who had been charged with this task panicked when

he saw Cossacks approaching and detonated the charges while the bridge was still choked with French soldiers and horses escaping the approaching allies. A thunderous explosion shook the entire city, destroying the only route of retreat and sending a macabre shower of human and equine body parts raining down into the waters of the fast-flowing river and on to the streets and housetops of the western perimeter. Trapped, the remaining defenders either drowned trying to cross the river, were cornered and killed, or gave themselves up.

The battle of Leipzig was over. It had cost Napoleon 73,000 men, of whom 30,000 had been taken prisoner and 5,000 had deserted. The allies had lost 54,000 men, of whom 16,033 were Prussians. During three days of fighting, an average of over 30,000 men had been killed or wounded each day. The epic struggle for control of the city did not end the war against Napoleon, but it did bring to a close his dominion in Germany. The road to the Rhine and to France itself now lay open.

The significance of these events for Prussia's re-emergence from the humiliation imposed at Tilsit in 1807 can scarcely be overstated. The Prussians played a crucial role in the campaign of 1813. Indeed, they were consistently the most active and aggressive element within the composite allied command. Although Bülow, as a corps commander within the Northern Army, was nominally subordinate to the cautious Bernadotte, he disregarded orders from his superior at several key points during the campaign to seek decisive engagements with French forces. Bülow's successful defence of Berlin, which changed the course of the war, was launched without support from Bernadotte. During the Northern Army's approach to Leipzig, it was Bülow who forced the pace. The impulsive Blücher likewise disregarded an order from the joint allied command to withdraw into Bohemia in September, choosing instead to march down the Elbe – had he complied with the command, it would have been impossible for the allies to concentrate their forces against Napoleon at the critical moment. A string of largely Prussian victories – at Dennewitz, Gross Beeren, on the Katzbach, Hagelberg and Kulm – helped to reverse the setback suffered by Schwarzenberg at Dresden and reinforced Prussia's claim to parity with Austria.[46]

The same pattern can be observed during the campaign of the following year. In February 1814, as the allies approached the borders of France, Schwarzenberg and Metternich argued that it was now time to sue for peace with a weakened Napoleon, who could safely be left on his throne. Once again, it was Blücher who pressed urgently for a continuation of the war, while Grolman persuaded the Prussian king and the Russian tsar to allow Blücher and Bülow to consolidate their forces and launch an independent offensive.[47] Whereas the Austrian command approached the struggle with Napoleon in the spirit of an eighteenth-century cabinet war, in which the purpose of military victories is to secure acceptable peace terms, the Prussian war-makers aimed at a more ambitious objective: the destruction of Napoleon's forces and of his capacity for making war. This was the outlook that would later be distilled in Clausewitz's *On War*.

In the decisive Flemish battles of 1815, too, the Prussian contribution was crucial. On 16 June, when the French launched the first major attack of the 1815 summer campaign at Ligny, it was the Prussians who did most of the fighting and took the heaviest losses. After receiving a battering at Ligny, where Wellington failed, for reasons that are still in dispute, to reinforce an exposed Prussian position, the Prussians regrouped with astonishing speed and concentrated around Wavre. From here they set out early on 18 June to link up with Wellington's forces at Waterloo. Marching through uneven ground still boggy from recent rain, the advance units of the Prussian 4th Army under Count Bülow reached the battlefield in the mid-afternoon and immediately charged the French right flank at Plancenoit, fighting bitterly for control of the village. Some hours later, at around 7.00 p.m., General Zieten's 1st Army corps arrived to reinforce Wellington's left flank. This was a crucial moment for the outcome of the battle. La Haye Sainte, a fortified farm close to the British lines, had fallen to the French an hour before, clearing the way for a potentially decisive strike against Wellington's battered centre. Napoleon seemed on the verge of victory. It was the arrival of Zieten's corps that allowed Wellington to transfer desperately needed forces to the most vulnerable parts of his line. Napoleon, conversely, had been forced to deploy men from his own centre to retake Plancenoit, where the Prussians threatened to open up the French rear. The Old Guard did briefly succeed in retaking Plancenoit, but between 8.00 and 8.30 p.m., after desperate house-to-house fighting, it fell once again to the Prussians, who now controlled the key to the French rear. Seeing the helter-skelter flight of French troops from Plancenoit, Wellington seized the moment and ordered a general advance. The French forces broke at last and fled.[48]

In the brief time at their disposal, the military reformers had done much to improve the performance of the Prussian army that had so signally failed in 1806. Particularly striking was the improvement in the quality of command. This was due in part to the excellence of a cohort of outstanding generals – Blücher, Yorck, Kleist, Bülow – who had emerged from the débâcle of 1806–7 with their reputations unscathed. The reformed command system was flexible enough to allow corps commanders a degree of autonomy on the battlefield. Lieutenant-General Zieten, for example, had been ordered by Blücher's head-quarters to reinforce the Prussian 4th Army corps at Plancenoit; only at the last moment did he resolve to disregard this instruction and support Wellington's left flank, an act of insubordination that may have saved the battle for the allies.[49] Even more significant was the integration of staff officers into the command structure. For the first time in the history of the Prussian army, responsible staff officers shadowed all senior commanders. Gneisenau was assigned to Blücher and the two formed an inspirational team, each recognizing the particular talents of the other. When Blücher was awarded an honorary doctorate by the University of Oxford after the war, he commented with characteristic diffidence: 'Well, if I am to become a doctor, you must at least make Gneisenau an apothecary, for we two belong always together.'[50] Not all such partnerships were as harmonious as this one, but throughout the Prussian armed forces, the new arrangements created a more responsive and cohesive fighting force.

It would be mistaken, however, to infer that the Prussian army of 1813–15 was a radically new instrument of war. The impact of the post-1807 reforms was rapidly diluted during 1813 and 1814 by casualties among veterans and a massive influx of recruits unschooled in the new methods. Little was done to heighten firepower through the technological improvement of weaponry, partly because the reformers tended – as one would expect – to focus above all on men, communication and motivation. The new Landwehr had been devised to provide the regular army with a highly motivated auxiliary force. However, while individual Landwehr units played an important supporting role in a number of engagements, their combat record was mixed and the Landwehr failed to fulfil the high expectations of its architects. The arrangements for training were still rudimentary, so that many Landwehr men lacked all but the most basic skills when they went to war.

The great majority were ignorant of the new regulations of 1812, which, in the spirit of the military reforms, emphasized skirmishing and marksmanship skills.[51] The Prussian military infrastructure also proved incapable of coping with the rapid proliferation of Landwehr units. As late as summer 1815, many of the men lacked coats, shoes and even trousers.[52] Uniforms and equipment were locally financed and often of inferior quality. There were correspondingly wide variations in fighting quality. Whereas the Landwehr of the Northern Army fought as effectively as the regular army units beside it, those attached to Blücher's Silesian Army proved unreliable under fire.[53]

The military reformers aimed above all to harness the war effort to the patriotic enthusiasm of the Prussian population. In this, too, they were only partly successful. Not all subjects of the Prussian Crown were equally moved by patriotic appeals. In parts of Silesia and West Prussia, the raising of Landwehr regiments prompted many to flee across the border into Russian-controlled Poland. Many merchants, landowners and innkeepers clung to the old system of exemptions and begged the authorities to overlook their sons or presented medical certificates of dubious authenticity suggesting that these were too sickly to serve. Patriotism was not only regionally, but also socially uneven. Educated males – high-school pupils, university students and men with academic qualifications – were over-represented in the volunteer contingents. They constituted 2 per cent of the population, but 12 per cent of volunteers. Even more remarkable are the figures for artisans, who accounted for 7 per cent of the population as a whole but 41 per cent of volunteers. Conversely, the peasants who made up nearly three-quarters of the kingdom's population supplied only 18 per cent of the volunteers, and most of these were either landless day-labourers or free farmers from outside the East-Elbian agrarian heartland of the Prussian state. The social constituency for patriotic activism had expanded greatly since the days of the Seven Years War, but it remained a predominantly urban phenomenon.[54]

Within these limitations, the Prussian public responded on an unprecedented scale to the government's call for help. The 'gold for iron' fund-raising campaign brought in 6.5 million thalers in donations and there was a flood of Prussian volunteers for the Landwehr and the free corps units of the volunteer riflemen. For the first time, young men from the Jewish communities, now legally eligible for military service and eager to demonstrate their patriotic gratitude for emancipation, flocked to join the colours, either in free corps or Landwehr units. There was a Jewish fund-raising campaign, in the course of which rabbis donated Kaddish cups and Torah-roll ornaments for the war effort.[55]

It was a mark of the modernity and inclusiveness of this war that women played a prominent role in supporting the state through organized charitable activity. For the first time in its history the dynasty expressly enlisted the support of its female subjects: the 'Appeal to the Women of the Prussian State', signed by twelve women of the Prussian royal family and published in March 1813, announced the foundation of a Women's Association for the Good of the Fatherland and urged 'noble-minded wives and daughters of all ranks' to assist in the war effort by donating jewellery, cash, raw materials and labour. Between 1813 and 1815, some 600 women's associations were created for these purposes. Here too, Jewish women were a conspicuous sub-group. Rahel Levin organized a circle of wealthy women friends to coordinate an ambitious fund-raising campaign and travelled to Prague in the summer of 1813 to oversee the creation of a medical mission dedicated to the care of the Prussian wounded. 'I am in touch with our commissariat and our staff surgeon,' she wrote to her friend and future husband Karl Varnhagen. 'I have a great deal of lint, bandages, rags, stockings, shirts; arrange for meals in several districts of the city; attend personally to thirty or forty fusiliers and soldiers every day; discuss and inspect everything.'[56]

Nothing better encapsulates the demotic quality of Prussian wartime mobilization than the new decorations created to honour distinguished service to the fatherland. The Iron Cross, designed and introduced on the initiative of the monarch, was the first Prussian decoration to be awarded to all ranks. 'The soldier [should be] on equal terms with the general, since people will know when they see a general and a soldier with the same decoration, that the general has earned it through merit in his capacity, whereas the soldier can only have earned it within his own narrower sphere . . .' Here, for the first time, was an acknowledgement that courage and initiative were virtues to be found alike in all classes of the people – the king personally overrode a proposal from his staff to exclude the ranks below sergeant-major. The new medal, formally introduced on 10 March 1813, was an austere object – a small Maltese cross fashioned in cast iron and decorated only with a sprig of oak leaves, the king's initials surmounted by a crown and the year of the campaign. Iron was chosen for both practical and symbolic reasons. Precious metals were in short supply and Berlin happened to possess excellent local foundries specializing in the decorative use of cast iron. Equally important was the metaphorical resonance of iron: as the king observed in a remarkable memorandum of February 1813, this was a 'time of iron' for the Prussian state, in which 'only iron and determination' would bring redemption. In an extraordinary gesture, the king ordered that all other decorations were to be suspended for the duration of the war and thereby transformed the Iron Cross into a campaign memorial. After the allies had reached Paris, the king ordered that the Iron Cross was to be incorporated into all Prussian flags and ensigns that had remained in service throughout the war. From its very inception, the Iron Cross was marked out to become a Prussian *lieu de mémoire*.[57]

On 3 August 1814, a complementary decoration was introduced for women who had made a distinguished contribution to the war effort. Its presiding spirit was the dead Queen Luise, well on her way to secular canonization as a Prussian Madonna. The Order of Luise resembled the Iron Cross in shape, but was enamelled in Prussian blue and mounted in the centre with a medallion bearing the initial 'L'. Eligible were Prussian women, born and naturalized, of all social stations, whether married or single. Among the women honoured for charitable and fundraising work was Amalia Beer, mother of the composer Giacomo Meyerbeer and one of the wealthiest women of Berlin's Jewish elite. The king saw to it that the medal, usually cast in the shape of a cross, was modified so as not to offend her religious sensibility.[58]

The creation of the *Luisenorden* reflected a broader public understanding of the forces mobilized in war than had been possible in the eighteenth century. For the first time, the voluntary initiatives of civil society – and particularly of its female members – were celebrated as integral to the state's military success. One consequence of this was a new emphasis on the activism of women. But this inclusiveness was attended by a heightened emphasis on gender difference. In the document inaugurating the Order of Luise, Frederick William III emphasized the specifically feminine and functionally subordinate character of women's contribution:

34. *The Iron Cross*   35. *The Order of Luise*

When the men of our brave armies bled for their Fatherland, they found refresh-
ment and relief in the comforting care of the women. The mothers and daughters
of this land feared for their loved ones fighting with the enemy and they grieved
for the fallen, but faith and hope gave them the strength to find peace in tireless
work for the cause of the Fatherland . . . It is impossible to honour all of those
who decorated their lives with these deeds of quiet service, but We think it fair
to honour those among them whose merit is recognised as especially great.[59]

What mattered about the new discourse of gender was not the emphasis
on difference, but the tendency to see in it a principle structuring civil
society. As conscription was expanded to encompass (in theory) all men
of serving age, it became possible to imagine the Prussian nation in
increasingly masculine and patriarchal terms. If, as the Prussian Defence
Law of 1814 put it, the army was 'the principal school for training the
whole nation for war', then it followed that the nation consisted only of
men. Women, by implication, were confined to an ancillary private
sphere defined by their special capacity for empathy and sacrifice.

It would be a mistake to see this solely as a consequence of the
campaigns against Napoleon. The patriot philosopher Fichte had been
arguing since the late 1790s that active citizenship, civic freedom and
even property rights should be withheld from women, whose calling
was to subject themselves utterly to the authority of their fathers and
husbands. The gymnastic movement founded by Jahn in 1811 was
centred on esteem for a putatively masculine form of physical prowess,

as was the aggressive patriotism of the poet and nationalist publicist Ernst Moritz Arndt.[60] In the same year, a circle of patriots gathered in Berlin to found a Christian-German Dining Society whose statutes explicitly excluded women (along with Jews and Jewish converts). Among the society's early cultural events was a lecture from Fichte on the 'almost unlimited subjection of the wife to the husband'. But the wars sharpened these distinctions and etched them more deeply in public awareness. The equivalence established here between masculinity, military service and active citizenship would become steadily more pronounced as the century progressed.[61]

THE 'MEMORY' OF WAR

On 18 October 1817, some 500 students from at least eleven German universities gathered at the Wartburg, a castle in the Thuringian hills where Luther had spent some time studying after his excommunication by Pope Leo X. They had come together to celebrate the 300th anniversary of the Reformation and the fourth anniversary of the battle of Leipzig. Both anniversaries recalled legendary moments of liberation in the history of the German nation; the former from 'papal despotism', the latter from the yoke of French tyranny. In addition to singing patriotic songs, the young men on the Wartburg solemnly burned the publications of a number of reactionary authors. Among the works consigned to the flames was a pamphlet published at the end of the Wars of Liberation by Theodor Anton Heinrich Schmalz, rector of the University of Berlin. In this pamphlet, Schmalz attacked the patriotic secret societies that had formed in Prussia during the occupation and forcefully rejected the view that the war against the French had been fuelled by a wave of popular enthusiasm in Prussia. Those Prussians who had joined the colours, Schmalz argued, had not done so out of enthusiasm for the cause, but rather out of a sense of duty, 'just as one hurries by when a neighbour's house is burning down'.[62] At the time of its appearance in 1815, the pamphlet prompted a storm of enraged protest from patriotic publicists. Schmalz himself was surprised and shocked at the vehemence of the public response.[63] Two years later, his description of a people wearily following its king into war still offended the students on the

Wartburg, many of them ex-volunteers, who had timed their meeting to fall on the fourth anniversary of the largest and most decisive military confrontation of the Wars of Liberation.

The symbolic *auto-da-fé* on the Wartburg reminds us of the controversy and emotion that accompanied public recollections of the Wars of Liberation in the immediate post-war years. The students on the Wartburg had adopted as their banner the black, red and gold colours of the Lützow volunteer corps. They were not commemorating a 'War of Liberation' but a 'War of Liberty'; not a war of regular armies, but a war of volunteers; 'not a war', as the fallen volunteer rifleman and poet Theodor Körner put it, 'that crowns know of', but rather 'a crusade', 'a holy war'.[64] They conceived of the war against the French as an 'insurrection of the people'.[65] These preoccupations contrasted crassly with conservative recollections of the war years. It was 'the princes and their ministers', wrote the publicist Friedrich von Gentz in the days following the Wartburg festival, who 'achieved the greatest [feats]' in the war against Napoleon.

Not all the demagogues and pamphleteers of the world and of posterity can take that away from them. [. . .] They prepared the war, founded it, created it. They did even more: they led it, nourished and enlivened it. [. . .] Those who today in their youthful audacity suppose that they overturned the tyrant [Gentz refers to the students on the Wartburg], couldn't even have driven him out of Germany.[66]

In part, these divergences in memory were grounded in the hybrid character of the struggle. The Wars of Liberation were wars of governments and monarchs, of dynastic alliances, rights and claims, in which the chief concern was to re-establish the balance of power in Europe. But they also involved – to an extent unprecedented in Prussia's history – militias and politically motivated volunteers. Of just under 290,000 officers and men mobilized in Prussia, 120,565 served in units of the Landwehr. In addition to the Landwehr regiments, which generally served under officers of the Prussian army, there were a variety of free corps, units of voluntary riflemen recruited from Prussia and other German states. Unlike their colleagues in the regular army, they swore oaths of loyalty not to the King of Prussia, but to the German fatherland. By the end of hostilities, free corps such as the famous Lützow Rangers accounted for 12.5 per cent of the Prussian armed forces, about 30,000 men in all.[67] The intense patriotism of many volunteers was tied up with potentially subversive visions of an ideal German or Prussian political order.

Yet it would be misleading to suggest that the divergence between dynastic and voluntarist recollections of the campaign was rooted solely or even primarily in distinctive modes of enlistment and combat experience. Not all post-war patriots had served in volunteer corps; many had served in the Landwehr militia and in regiments of the line, or not served at all. Nor were the officers and men of the regular army immune to the patriotic ferment of the war years. In January 1816, according to reports from the British envoy in Berlin, there were officers who had been 'infected' with 'revolutionary stirrings' in almost all regiments of the regular army.[68] The Volunteer Rangers (*freiwillige Jäger*), on the other hand, included noblemen (such as Wilhelm von Gerlach and the sons of Count Friedrich Leopold Stolberg) whose political orientation in the post-war period was conservative or corporate-aristocratic rather than liberal or democratic.[69] The controversies of the post-war period were fuelled not simply by diverse memories of wartime experience as such, but by the instrumentalization of memory for political ends.

Prussians found many ways of commemorating the Wars of Liberation in the years after 1815. The provincial archives – in particular the news reports (*Zeitungsberichte*) filed every month by the provincial governments – describe the ringing of church bells, target-shooting tournaments, processions involving men in militia costumes, and local theatrical events in commemoration of the battles of Leipzig and Waterloo.[70] 'Volunteer clubs' and 'funeral associations' were founded in Prussian towns during the 1830s and 1840s to collect funds for the ceremonial burial of deceased veteran volunteers. These groups not only paid the costs of burial, but also provided men in uniform for the funeral procession, thereby reminding the community of the special status of those – no matter how humble their social standing – who had served their king and fatherland in the wars against the French.[71] During the 1840s, according to a report in the Berlin-based *Vossische Zeitung*, veterans gathered almost every year in various locations to renew contact and remember fallen comrades. In June 1845, on the thirtieth anniversary of the battle of Waterloo, there were numerous meetings of veterans who had served in Landwehr and regular army regiments, as well as a gathering of surviving Lützow volunteers who congregated at the oak tree where the poet and volunteer rifleman Theodor Körner had been buried.[72]

Throughout the post-war decades, the volunteer, or *Freiwilliger*, continued to enjoy a special status; in Theodor Fontane's childhood memoirs for example, we find an account of a public execution that took place in 1826 while his family was living in Swinemünde. Because he was an '1813er', Fontane senior was selected to march at the head of the municipal procession to the place of execution and supervise the crowd around the scaffold. The condemned murderer, for his part, continued until his last breath to believe that he would be pardoned because of a letter of commendation he had received from the king after the battle of Jena.[73] General Yorck, too, remained under the spell of the war against France. His private memorial cult focused on the Convention of Tauroggen and his fall from royal favour. The Convention was never officially recognized as an act of state by the Prussian Crown; it was thus confined, for the short term at least, to the realm of private memory. Although Yorck was exonerated of any offence by a board of enquiry in March 1813, he remained convinced that he had been denied the honour he deserved for his part in the opening phase of the war against Napoleon. The original document bearing the text of the Convention was not returned for deposition among the state papers, but remained a revered heirloom in the Yorck family archive. The full-length free-standing statue that adorned the general's tomb on the family's estate was commissioned by Yorck himself; it shows him holding a stone scroll engraved with the words 'Convention of Tauroggen'.[74]

This disparate evidence reveals a memory of the Wars of Liberation that was anchored in specific social contexts.[75] One can speak, for example, of a distinctively Jewish memory of the Wars of Liberation, in which the story of volunteer enlistment was closely intertwined with the narrative of emancipation. Certainly, when the rabbis of Breslau blessed the weapons of Jewish volunteers on 11 March 1813, dispensing them at the same time from the stricter forms of observance for the duration of the campaign, they did not neglect to point out that the ceremony marked the first anniversary of the Prussian Edict of Emancipation.[76] Jewish participation in the campaign could be and was invoked as an argument against discriminatory legislation.[77] In 1843, when the *Militärwochenblatt* printed statistics from the Wars of Liberation substantially understating the numbers of Jewish volunteers, there were

36. Return of the Jewish Volunteer from the Wars of Liberation to his family still living by the Old Custom. *Oil painting by Moritz Daniel Oppenheimer 1833–34.*

indignant protests and corrections from Jewish journals such as *Der Orient* and *Allgemeine Zeitung des Judentums.*[78] This Jewish memory of the Wars of Liberation found pictorial expression in the paintings of Moritz Daniel Oppenheimer, the 'first modern Jewish artist'[79], known for his portraits of converts and assimilated Jews. In a painting of 1833–4 entitled *Return of the Jewish Volunteer from the Wars of Liberation to his Family Still Living by the Old Custom*, Oppenheimer depicted a young man in military uniform surrounded by his family in a room strewn with symbols of domesticity and Jewish worship. Light pours in through the windows of the room, illuminating the braid on his jacket. There could be no clearer illustration of the relationship between the drawn-out processes of assimilation and emancipation and the 'memory of 1813'.[80]

The war was also commemorated through the erection of monuments. A splendid war memorial was designed by Karl Friedrich Schinkel, greatest of the Prussian architects, and placed on the summit of the

Tempelhofer Berg, later known as the Kreuzberg, in 1821. Perched on the highest point in Berlin's otherwise flat cityscape and resembling a miniature gothic church tower, it was well placed to become a shrine for the sacralized memory of war. But Schinkel's monument bore an inscription which made it clear that it spoke for one memory in particular: the dynastic memory of war which placed the king at the head of his people. 'From the king to the people who, at his call, nobly sacrificed their blood and chattels to the Fatherland'. The message was reinforced by the twelve figures placed in niches around the monument. Initially intended as 'genii' representing the great battles of the Wars of Liberation, they were altered to function as portraits of generals and members of the Prussian and Russian ruling houses.[81] Commemorative tablets in the churches of Prussia likewise bore the inscription: 'For king and fatherland'.[82] The monuments to the Prussian fallen on the battlefields of Gross-Görschen, Haynau, an der Katzbach, Dennewitz and Waterloo carried the legend: 'King and fatherland honour the fallen heroes. They rest in peace.'[83]

By contrast, it seemed that the patriotic-voluntarist memory of war would have to remain without its remembrance in stone. Among those who felt this problem most keenly were the painter Caspar David Friedrich, a patriot and political radical who had grown up in Greifswald (Mecklenburg), but was now living in the Saxon city of Dresden, and Ernst Moritz Arndt, who hailed from the island of Rügen in that portion of the old Duchy of Pomerania that passed from Sweden to Prussia in 1815. Arndt and Friedrich collaborated on a statue of Scharnhorst but received no official support for the project. Both men viewed the Prussian war against Napoleon as a German 'national' undertaking and for both the memory of that conflict was intimately bound up with radical politics. 'I am not at all surprised,' Friedrich wrote to Arndt in March 1814, 'that no memorials are being erected, neither to mark the great cause of the *Volk*, nor to the magnanimous deeds of great German men. As long as we remain manservants to the princes, nothing of this sort will ever happen.'[84] The absence of an adequate monument to the 'people's' Wars of Liberation was a theme to which Friedrich repeatedly returned in the paintings he produced during the years after 1815. Not only the voluntarist patriots, but also reformers within the military and bureaucratic establishment were sensitive to the way in which public remembrance of the Wars of Liberation had been weighted in favour of the dynastic-military tradition. In 1822, when Theodor von Schön, the liberal provincial president of East Prussia and a former close associate of Stein, heard that there were plans to erect a monument to the conservative General von Bülow, he proposed a statue be raised instead to the militiaman who had reportedly shouted 'lick my arse' when Bülow blew a call for retreat during the advance on Leipzig.[85]

How does one publicly commemorate a war without monuments? This was one of the problems addressed by Friedrich Ludwig Jahn and his gymnasts. Within a few years of its foundation in the Hasenheide park on the outskirts of Berlin, the movement had spread beyond the borders of the kingdom, attracting new adherents across Protestant central and northern Germany. By 1818, Jahn estimated that there were 150 gymnastic clubs in all, encompassing a membership of around 12,000.[86] While the public representation of the past in stone after 1815 remained subject, as it were, to a dynastic monopoly, the gymnasts developed new ways of perpetuating a remembrance of war inflected with their own voluntarist nationalism. They made pilgrimages to the battlefields of the Wars of Liberation. They designed and celebrated memorial feast days, the most important being the anniversary of the battle of Leipzig. The first of these memorial events took place in the Hasenheide on 18 October 1814 and attracted some 10,000 spectators. With its symphony of bodies in disciplined motion, its songs, flaming beacons and torch-lit processions, it set the pattern for subsequent anniversaries until the suppression of the gymnastic movement in 1819.

The gymnastic festival was a high holiday in the gymnastic year, and its function as a populist memorial of the Wars of Liberation could hardly escape the notice of contemporaries. But the gymnastic art itself was a kind of memorial enactment. It was more than a fitness programme; it was the disciplined maintenance of readiness for struggle and conflict. In the early post-war period, this posture of preparedness could not fail to evoke the years of the French occupation. It was not, as we have seen, the stance of the soldier, but that of the civilian volunteer. The uniforms worn by the gymnasts, and designed by Jahn himself, further reinforced these commemorative associations. The gymnastic uniform belonged within an early nineteenth-century sartorial code that linked the patriotic 'Old German costume' (*altdeutsche Tracht*) popularized by Jahn around the turn of the century with the loose jackets worn by the volunteer riflemen, and connected both with the student garb of the *Burschenschaften* (nationalist student fraternities), in whose early history Jahn had also played a role.

The fraternity students, whose membership overlapped with that of the gymnastic movement, were a memorial cult, preoccupied by the great deeds of the recent past. Through their networks, the Prussian war against Napoleon was woven into the fabric of a broader German memory. When, in December 1817, the *Burschen* of Jena set out to explain in writing the meaning of their movement, they reminded their public of the remembered experiences that still held them together. 'For we have all seen the great year 1813', they wrote, recalling wounds suffered and friends lost on the field of battle. 'And would we not be contemptible before God and the world if we had not tended and sustained such thoughts and feelings? We have tended and sustained them and [we] return to dwell on them again and again and will never forsake them.'[87]

Wrapped up within this cult of memory was the possibility of a new kind of politics. The emphasis of the post-war patriots upon lived experience as a force capable of binding human beings together and endowing their bonds with meaning may appear transparent and unremarkable to us; it was, however, an invention of the period that bore all the marks of early nineteenth-century romanticism.[88] The festival on the Wartburg was 'a new form of political action',[89] not least because it represented the quest of the inward-looking 'bourgeois self' imagined by the language and thought of romanticism for a new kind of political community, welded together by a shared emotional commitment. To remember was to forge bonds with one's fellows; forgetfulness was betrayal. The appeal to a past held in common did not exclude those who had never been volunteers, since the very purpose of festivals and rituals was to enable people to 'remember' events, even if they had never experienced them. The result was a form of public spectacle that could release powerful emotions in spectators and participants alike. Its politics were not rational and argumentative, but symbolic, cultic and emotional.[90]

PRUSSIANS OR GERMANS?

Since its inception as a largely literary phenomenon within the educated middle classes during the Seven Years War, Prussian patriotism had always signified more than just a willingness to defend one's fatherland. It had blended emotional commitments with political aspirations. This was much more threateningly the case in the Napoleonic era than it had been during the Seven Years War, partly because the social constituency capable of sustaining patriotic enthusiasms was far larger, and partly because the rhetorical environment in which these were articulated had been radicalized by the French Revolution and the controversy over reform. 'One thing is now clear,' the young Leopold von Gerlach wrote as he observed the frantic preparations for war in Breslau in February 1813. 'The prevalent outlook among the most independent men is extremely Jacobin and revolutionary. Anyone who talks of the need for a future built upon historical foundations, anyone who seeks to graft the shoots of the new on to the still-healthy stems [of the past], is laughed at, so that even I feel myself wavering in my convictions.'[91]

The problem was not simply that patriotism sometimes went hand-in-hand with radical politics, but also that it could flow seamlessly into a nationalist commitment that threatened to unsettle the legitimacy of the particular German dynasties. The word 'nation' was used for both Prussia and Germany. Hardenberg and Yorck may have been at opposite ends of the political spectrum, but they were both Prussian loyalists (even if Yorck found it difficult on occasion to reconcile his loyalty to Prussia with obedience to its reigning monarch). By contrast, Fichte, Boyen, Grolman and Stein were unambiguous German nationalists. For Stein, this came to imply the complete abandonment of any commitment to a specifically Prussian interest: 'I have but one Fatherland, which is called Germany, and I am devoted with my whole heart to it alone and to no particular part of it,' he declared in a letter of November 1812. 'To me, in this great moment of transition, the dynasties are completely indifferent [. . .] Put what you will in the place of Prussia, dissolve it, strengthen Austria by Silesia and the Electoral Mark and North Germany, excluding the banished princes . . .'[92]

The intimate tension between Prussian patriotism and German nationalism contained a threat and a promise. The threat was that nationalist agitation would become a force capable of challenging dynastic authority across the German states, that it would substitute a new horizontal culture of loyalties and affinities for the hierarchical order of the *ancien régime* and thereby sweep away the particularist heritage that had endowed Prussia with a distinctive history and significance. The promise was that Prussia might find a way of harnessing national enthusiasms to its own interests, of riding the nationalist wave without surrendering its particularist identity and institutions. In the short term, the threat overshadowed the promise as Frederick William III joined with other sovereigns in suppressing nationalist 'demagoguery' and silencing public memory of the war of volunteers. But in the longer term, as we shall see, Prussian political leaders became adept at discerning and exploiting the synergies between nationalist aspirations and territorial interest. In the process, the divided memory of the post-war years made way for an irenic synthesis in which popular and dynastic elements were juxtaposed and seen as complementary. Purged of its political ambiguities, the Prussian war against Napoleon would ultimately be refashioned – however incongruously – as a mythical war of German national liberation. Gymnastics, the Iron Cross, the cult of Queen Luise, even the battle of Jena would all mutate with time into German national symbols, legitimizing Prussian claims to political leadership within the community of German states.[93]

12

God's March through History

The territorial settlements agreed at the Vienna Peace Congress of 1814–15 created a new Europe. A Dutch-Belgian composite state, the United Kingdom of the Netherlands, appeared in the north-west. Norway was transferred from Denmark to Sweden. Austria struck deep inroads into Italy with the acquisition of Lombardy-Venetia and the installation of Habsburg dynasts on the thrones of Tuscany, Modena and Parma. The borders of the Russian Empire, redrawn to encompass the bulk of eastern and central Poland, extended further westwards than at any time in European history.

THE NEW DUALISM

For Prussia, too, this was a new beginning. There was no return to the pre-1806 borders. Much of the Polish territory seized in the 1790s (excepting the Grand Duchy of Posen) was transferred to Russian control, and East Frisia (Prussian since 1744) was ceded to the Kingdom of Hanover. In return, the Prussians acquired the northern half of the Kingdom of Saxony, the Swedish-ruled rump of western Pomerania and a vast tract of Rhenish and Westphalian territory reaching from Hanover in the east to the Netherlands and France in the west.[1] This was no triumph of the Prussian will. Berlin failed to get what it wanted and got what it did not want. It wanted the whole of Saxony, but this was blocked by Austria and the western powers and the Prussians were forced to make do with the Saxon partition of 8 February 1815. Under this arrangement, Prussia acquired about two-fifths of the kingdom, including the fortress town of Torgau and the city of Wittenberg, where

Luther had launched the Reformation in 1517 by nailing his theses to the cathedral door. The creation of a large western wedge of Prussian territory along the river Rhine was a British, not a Prussian, idea. British policy-makers had long been concerned at the power-vacuum created by the withdrawal of the Habsburgs from Belgium and they wanted Prussia to replace Austria as the German 'sentinel' guarding the north-eastern frontier of France.[2] This suited the Austrians; they were happy to be rid of the obstreperous Belgians, who now entered a brief and unhappy period of rule by the Dutch.

The Prussians also failed to get their way in the complex negotiations over the future organization of the German states. What the Prussians (whose delegation was led by Hardenberg and Humboldt) wanted was a Germany with strong central executive organs through which Prussia and Austria could share power over the lesser states – in short, a 'strong dualist hegemonic solution'.[3] The Austrians, by contrast, pleaded for a loose association of independent states with the minimum in central institutions. The German Confederal Treaty signed on 5 June 1815 (revised in the Final Act of the Treaty of 1820) represented a victory for the Austrian over the Prussian conception. The new German Confeder-ation, encompassing thirty-eight (later thirty-nine) states, had only one statutory central body, the Federal Diet (*Bundesversammlung*), which met in Frankfurt and was in effect a permanent congress of diplomatic representatives. These arrangements were a setback for those Prussian policy-makers who had hoped for a more cohesive organization of the German territories.

None of this diminishes the significance of the post-Napoleonic settle-ment for the future of the Prussian state. The western compensation package created a block of Prussian Rhenish territory as large as Baden and Württemberg combined. Enclosed within the new territory, more by accident than design, were those apples of the Great Elector's eye, the principalities of Jülich and Berg. The Hohenzollern kingdom was now a colossus that stretched across the north of Germany, broken only by one gap, forty kilometres wide at its narrowest point, where the territories of Hanover, Brunswick and Hesse-Kassel separated the Prussian 'Province of Saxony' from the Prussian 'Province of West-phalia'. The consequences for Prussia's (and Germany's) nineteenth-century political and economic development were momentous.

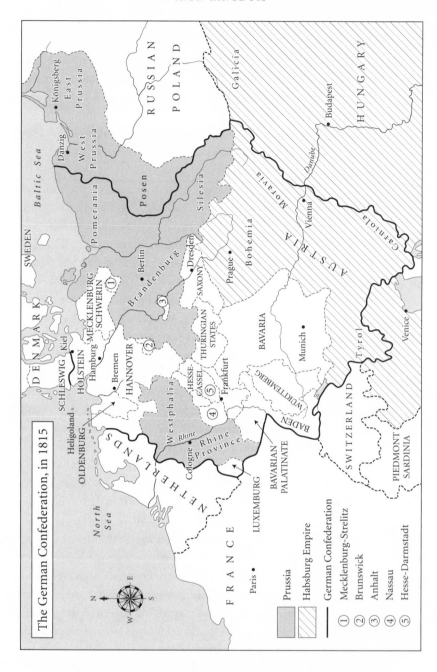

The German Confederation, in 1815

The Rhineland was destined to become one of the powerhouses of European industrialization and economic growth, a development entirely unforeseen by the negotiators at Vienna, who assigned little weight to economic factors when they redrew the map of Germany. The settlement of 1815 also had far-reaching geopolitical implications. In relinquishing its claims to much of the Polish territory acquired in the 1790s and accepting compensation in the centre and west, Prussia reinforced its presence within German Europe. At the same time, Austria relinquished for ever its place in the north-west (Belgium) and accepted substantial new territories in northern Italy. For the first time in its history, Prussia occupied more 'German' territory than Austria.

The Confederation did not provide Berlin with the strong executive institutions it would have needed in order to exercise formal dominance over northern Germany, but it was open-ended enough to allow Prussia to pursue an informal and limited hegemony without putting the system as a whole in jeopardy. Precisely because the Confederation failed to establish trans-territorial institutions of its own, the door remained open for Prussia to seize the initiative. Two areas in particular commanded the attention of Prussian administrations after 1815: customs harmonization and federal security policy. These were the domains in which Prussia evolved what we could describe as a 'German policy' during the decades before the 1848 revolutions.

The ministers in Berlin were slow to embrace an expansionist customs policy. When the government of Hesse-Darmstadt approached Berlin in June 1825 with a view to negotiating a customs agreement, they were turned down on the grounds that the potential financial advantage was too slight. The danger that the Hessians might opt to join the newly founded Bavarian-Württemberg customs union instead seems to have carried no weight whatsoever with the Prussians. Only from around 1826 did the Berlin administration begin to think in broader strategic terms. This was partly a function of the state's improving financial health, which did away with the need to prioritize financial over all other considerations. At around the same time, the foreign ministry began to insist that customs negotiations be seen as an arm of Prussian foreign policy. In 1827, when Hesse-Darmstadt appealed once again for a union with Berlin, it was welcomed with open arms.

The Austrians reacted with alarm to news of the new customs agreement. The Prussian-Hessian treaty, Metternich observed in a letter to

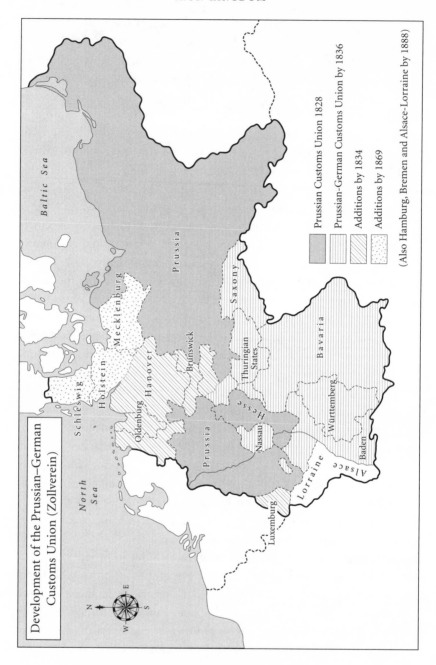

Development of the Prussian–German Customs Union (Zollverein)

Prussian Customs Union 1828

Prussian–German Customs Union by 1836

Additions by 1834

Additions by 1869

(Also Hamburg, Bremen and Alsace-Lorraine by 1888)

Baltic Sea

North Sea

Prussia

Mecklenburg

Schleswig

Holstein

Oldenburg

Hanover

Brunswick

Saxony

Thuringian States

Hesse

Nassau

Bavaria

Württemberg

Baden

Prussia

Luxemburg

Lorraine

Alsace

the Austrian ambassador in Berlin, 'engenders the most anguished and certainly justified concern of all the German governments. Henceforth all of Prussia's efforts will be focused on entangling the remaining states in its net . . .'[4] The Austrian chancellor did what he could to dissuade further German courts from joining the Prussians; he also encouraged the growth of a competing customs association, the Central German Commercial Union, whose members included Saxony, Hanover, Electoral Hesse and Nassau and whose territory ran up between the two separate territorial blocks of the post-Napoleonic Prussian state. But these were temporary triumphs. Berlin proved adept at combining friendly appeals to enlightened self-interest with arm-twisting and naked blackmail. Small adjacent states that refused to enter the Prussian-Hessian union were subjected to hard-hitting counter-measures, including 'road wars', in which new transport routes were used to suck the flow of trade away from target territories. Finally, on 27 May 1829, an agreement signed with Bavaria and Württemberg allowed Prussia and its partners to encircle some of the smaller states of the Central German Union. The way was now open to the amalgamation of the two customs zones.

The German Customs Union (*Zollverein*) that came into effect on 1 January 1834 incorporated the majority of Germans outside Austria. Baden, Nassau and Frankfurt joined in the following year, to be followed in 1841 by Braunschweig and Lüneburg. Nearly 90 per cent of the German population now lived in member states of the *Zollverein*.[5] No one who looks at a map of the *Zollverein* states in 1841 can fail to be impressed by its close resemblance to the Prussian-dominated German state that emerged from the wars of 1864–71. Yet this outcome still lay far beyond the mental horizons of those who made policy in Berlin. They aimed above all to extend Prussian influence within a more cohesive association of German states. Customs harmonization became a new arena for the old competition between Prussia and Austria for influence and prestige among the German territories.

With hindsight, it seems clear that both sides overestimated the significance of Prussia's success. The Customs Union never became an effective tool for the exercise of Prussian political influence over the lesser states. Indeed it may have had a small contrary effect, since it provided enlarged annual revenues to conservative territorial governments jealous of their autonomy.[6] For the lesser states, membership of the Customs Union was a matter of fiscal expediency; it did not – as the events of 1866 would show – translate into political loyalty to Berlin.[7] It does not even appear to have laid the ground for Prussian economic primacy in Germany, as is widely asserted in the older literature on the economic prehistory of German unification.[8] There is no evidence to suggest that the Customs Union decisively accelerated Prussian industrial investment, or did much to reverse the overwhelming preponderance of agriculture within the kingdom's economy.[9] The Zollverein's contribution to the later emergence of a Prussian-dominated German Empire was thus less straightforward than has often been assumed.

Customs policy was important, but for different reasons: it was for a time the pre-eminent domain of Berlin's 'German policy'. It was here that ministers and officials learned to think in an authentically German compass and to combine the pursuit of specifically Prussian benefits with the building of consensus and the mediation of interests among the other German states. The long, painstaking work towards a German Customs Union reinforced Berlin's moral authority; it demonstrated to liberal and progressive opinion in the lesser states that Prussia, for all its flaws, might stand for a more modern and rational order of things. Finance Minister Friedrich von Motz and Foreign Minister Christian Count von Bernstorff, the two statesmen most closely associated with Prussian customs policy in the 1820s and 1830s, understood this and they worked consistently to establish Prussia's reputation as a progressive force in German affairs.[10]

The coordination of German security arrangements provided another outlet for competitive pressures within the Confederal system. From the outset, this was an area where Prussian and Austrian interests clashed. Prussian negotiators tried in 1818–19 to establish a more cohesive and 'national' federal military force (under Berlin's leadership), but a lobby of lesser states supported by Austria refused to countenance any arrangement that might compromise the military autonomy of the minor German powers. These states won the day, with the result that Germany was left with no federal military apparatus. This suited the Austrians, who believed that a strong federal structure would ultimately play into Prussia's hands.

The first chance to test the waters of Confederal military policy came with the French July Revolution of 1830.[11] The memory of the revolutionary and Napoleonic invasions was still vivid and many contemporaries, especially in the south, feared that the upheaval of summer 1830 would be followed (as in the 1790s) by an invasion of western Germany. Prussian policy-makers were quick to see how the French war scare could be exploited to Prussia's advantage. In a letter of 8 October 1830 to the king, Bernstorff pressed for military consultations with the southern courts, with a view to formulating a joint security policy. This would not only meet immediate Prussian security needs, Bernstorff argued, but would also 'create a general trust in Prussia, so that one will depend upon her advice, her suggestions and her beneficial influence'.[12]

In the short term, his policy was a success. In the spring of 1831, the Prussian General August Rühle von Lilienstern was sent on a mission to southern Germany. There were cordial conversations with the Bavarian king, Ludwig I, who expressed doubts about the idea of a Prussian supreme command of the joint federal forces, but was enthusiastic about close cooperation. 'I know of no north and no south Germany, only Germany,' the Bavarian monarch wrote to Frederick William III on 17 March 1831. Bavaria, like Prussia, had acquired a tract of exposed Rhenish territory in 1815 (the Palatinate, opposite Baden on the west bank of the Rhine) and thus stood sorely in need of a coordinated defence policy. 'Safety', as the king himself put it, was 'only to be found in a firm connection with Prussia'.[13] Rühle von Lilienstern was also partly right when he reported that Prussia's 'sure, wise, magnanimous and prudent attitude' and the beneficial impact of its customs policy had earned the 'respect, trust and sympathy' of Bavarian political circles.[14] The reception in Stuttgart (Württemberg) and Karlsruhe (Baden) was less warm, but here too there was general agreement on the necessity of federal military restructuring and closer collaboration with Prussia.

In the event, it proved easy for the Austrians to block these Prussian initiatives. After all, the southern states, though they distrusted Austria and had little confidence in Vienna's commitment to the defence of western Germany, were also wary of further reinforcing the pre-eminence of Berlin. As the direct threat from France waned, their readiness to exchange independence for security declined. The most crucial Austrian asset was simply the fissured structure of the Prussian political elite. Clam-Martinitz, the devious Austrian envoy sent to sort things out in Berlin in September 1831, soon realized that the powerhouse behind the new federal military policy was the politically progressive Prussian-German faction around Bernstorff, Eichhorn and Rühle von Lilienstern. Opposed to these was the conservative 'independent Prussian faction' around Duke Charles of Mecklenburg, Prince Wilhelm Ludwig Sayn-Wittgenstein and the Huguenot preacher and royal confidant Ancillon (who intrigued with Clam although, as a foreign office bureaucrat, he was Bernstorff's subordinate). Clam thus found it relatively easy to prise the Prussian decision-making establishment apart by playing different interests against each other. Once he had secured the support of the anti-Bernstorff faction and enjoyed direct access to the king, he was able to undercut the foreign minister and shut him out of the remaining Austro-Prussian negotiations.[15]

The issue of federal security resurfaced during the French invasion scare of 1840–41. In the wake of international tensions over the Eastern Question, there was loose talk by Prime Minister Adolphe Thiers in Paris of a French attack on the Rhine. Across Germany, the 'Rhine crisis' unleashed a wave of nationalist outrage. Once again, a group within the Prussian administration looked to exploit the moment. A senior Prussian emissary was despatched to the south German courts to discuss closer military cooperation. Again there was a warm welcome, at least at first. The Austrian envoy in Berlin was quick to sound the alarm, reporting that the Prussian cabinet was working to found 'if not in name, then at least de facto, a Prussian Germany'.[16] The south German states played both angles, confiding to the Prussians that they distrusted the Austrians and to the Austrians that they feared the Prussians. An Austrian envoy shadowed the Prussian mission, working on the south German courts to undo the damage. Once again, it was the Austrians who ultimately won the diplomatic battle, obliging Prussia to forsake any unilateral initiatives and work in close concert with Vienna towards a negotiated settlement.

The Prussians thus gained little for their efforts. One reason for this was simply that the southern states viewed all such initiatives with profound distrust, especially if they stemmed from Prussia. The Austrians, who had established themselves early on as the guarantors of German small-state autonomy, could play on these fears to great effect. Then there was the fact that Berlin did not yet possess a unitary governmental policy-making apparatus. Ministers and other senior political figures were still not bound by collective responsibility – the reformers had seen this problem but had failed to impose a durable remedy for it. Instead, ministers, royal advisers, courtiers and even subordinate officials jockeyed for influence against each other, creating openings that the Austrians found it easy to exploit. The logic of the 'antechamber of power' continued to unsettle Prussian high politics. Not until the 1850s and 1860s would this problem be eliminated through the gradual concentration of authority in the hands of the first minister.

The men in Berlin, for their part, had no intention of risking an open break with Vienna. There was still a need for Austro-Prussian solidarity in the face of internal disorder and subversion. The prospect of political upheaval was still fearful enough to bring the conservative leaderships in Berlin and Vienna periodically back into collaboration. This is what happened in the spring of 1832, when, in the aftermath of the federal army crisis, a wave of radical agitation broke out in the south-west of Germany. Berlin and Vienna quickly reverted to cooperative mode, working together with representatives of other German states to reinforce the Confederation with new powers of censorship, surveillance and repression. Only with the marginalization of radical politics after the revolutions of 1848–9 would this constraint be overcome.

In any case, the men in Berlin still laid their plans within the mental horizons of a politically divided Germany under the captaincy of the Austrian imperial throne. When the Austrian envoy General Heinrich von Hess was granted an audience with Frederick William IV in Berlin at the height of the French war scare of 1840, he was surprised and slightly bewildered by the strength of the new monarch's sentimental attachment to Austria: 'Oh how I love Vienna,' the king told him. 'What I would not give to live there for some time as a private person! The Imperial Court is so gracious and a unique humanity shines from every one of its members.'[17] The king's advisers still saw (according to the Austrian envoy) 'the salvation of Germany not in a one-sided Prussiandom, but in close union with Austria'.[18] The unitary designs of radical nationalists held no attraction for Prussia's statesmen, or for the Hohenzollern dynast on its throne. Prussia thus continued to operate – as the British envoy to Berlin put it in 1839 – 'within that timid and passive system which marks Her political course'.[19] Austria remained – the Customs Union of 1834 notwithstanding – in a position of fragile hegemony. It could still play impressively upon the complicated registers of the German Confederation.

To a surprising degree, then, Prussia remained an object, rather than a subject, of the international system after 1815. It was by some margin the least of the European great powers. Indeed, given the very limited room for an autonomous Prussian initiative, even within Germany, there are grounds for supposing that Prussia occupied a lesser category, somewhere between the concert of the real great powers and the lesser continental states. Prussia's leaders acquiesced in this state of affairs and the kingdom entered another of its long phases of foreign-political passivity. Throughout the forty years of European peace between the Vienna Congress and the Crimean War, Berlin strove to be on the best possible terms with all the powers. It sought consensus wherever possible. It avoided irritating the British by staying on the sidelines of every major international crisis. It steered away from direct conflict with Austria. It was Berlin's established policy, the British envoy reported in 1837, 'to satisfy all parties by conciliation and thus preserve the peace of Europe'.[20]

Above all, Prussia appeased and propitiated Russia. During the Napoleonic Wars, Russia had mobilized an army of over one million men, establishing itself as the eastern hegemon of the European continent. The Polish territorial settlement of 1815 pushed the western salient of the Russian Empire deep into Central Europe. In the post-war years, the uncomplaining acceptance of Russian hegemony became an axiom of Prussian foreign policy. The memory of 1807 and 1812–13, when Prussia's future had rested in Russian hands, was still vivid. The relationship between Prussia and its eastern neighbour deepened in 1817 with the marriage of Frederick William III's daughter Princess Charlotte to Grand Duke Nicholas, heir to the Romanov throne. After his accession in 1825, Tsar Nicholas I exercised a profound influence on his Prussian relatives. He was involved in efforts to block constitutional reform and to bind the Hohenzollern monarchy to an absolutist system.[21] The merest hint of his displeasure was enough to deter the Prussians from any course of action that would conflict with Russian interests.[22]

THE CONSERVATIVE TURN

At five o'clock in the afternoon of 23 March 1819, the 24-year-old Karl Sand, son of an official from the formerly Prussian principality of Bayreuth and a sometime student of theology, rang the doorbell of the playwright August von Kotzebue in Mannheim.[23] Frau Kotzebue was receiving some female guests, so Sand waited near the stairs until he was invited into the living room by the playwright, who greeted him cordially. The two struck up a conversation. Suddenly Sand drew a dagger from the sleeve of his jacket and declared: 'I take no pride in you at all. Here, you traitor to the fatherland!' He stabbed his 57-year-old host twice in the chest and slashed him across the face. Kotzebue collapsed and was dead within minutes. As commotion filled the household, Sand staggered back to the front steps, drew a second dagger from his jacket and stabbed himself twice in the abdomen, saying 'Thank you God for the victory!' before he too collapsed.

The murder of Kotzebue by Sand was the single most sensational political act of the post-war decades in Germany. This was exactly what Sand had wanted. He had planned the murder long in advance and took care to endow it with the maximum symbolic charge. When he arrived at Kotzebue's door, he was dressed in the exotic 'Old German Costume' designed and popularized by Friedrich Ludwig Jahn and associated after 1815 with the aspirations of the radical nationalist movement. A contemporary engraving shows him taking leave of his hilly Franconian homeland, his features composed in seraphic tranquillity, with long blond hair falling artlessly from beneath the soft 'German cap', and the handle of a dagger peeping ominously out from under the lapel of his jacket. Sand fashioned the murder weapon himself from a French hunting knife he had picked up on the battlefield at Leipzig. His victim, too, was carefully chosen. Kotzebue had long been a hate figure for the fierce young men of the patriotic movement. His popular sentimental melodramas featured women in prominent roles, attracted numerous female spectators and often played teasingly on ambiguities in the prevailing code of bourgeois sexual morality. The nationalists viewed his plays as effeminate and immoral, and denounced him as a 'seducer of German youth'. Kotzebue, for his part, was critical of the chauvinism and coarseness of the young patriots. In an article he published in March

*37. An idealized portrayal of Karl Sand on his way to Mannheim
to murder Kotzebue*

1819 – one of the last things he wrote – he ridiculed the philistinism and
unruliness of the student fraternity movement, with whose radical wing
Sand was closely affiliated.

Thanks to these sharp symbolic polarities, the brutality of the murder
was eclipsed in the awareness of many contemporaries by profound
excitement at the radicalism of Sand's action and the purity of his
motivation. Having recovered from his self-inflicted wounds, Sand con-
valesced in prison, where, it was said, the other inmates lifted their
chains as they passed his cell in order to spare the sleeping hero. By the
time of his execution by beheading at five o'clock in the morning on
20 May, Sand was a celebrity. Crowds lined the streets as he made his
way to the scaffold. After his decapitation, spectators surged forward
to drench their handkerchiefs in his blood, a new patriotic twist on
the traditional practice of collecting the blood of the condemned for
medicinal and magical purposes. Relics, including locks of his famed
blond hair, circulated within the nationalist networks. It was even
reported that the executioner, having dismantled the blood-stained
scaffold, used the wood to build a small shed on his vineyard, where he

later welcomed pilgrims who had come to honour the memory of the dead patriot.

In the aftermath of the assassination, a mood of paranoia gripped the Prussian political authorities. Sand's act seemed to have laid bare the implacable core of the emergent nationalist movement. Even more alarming was the unwillingness of many contemporaries sympathetic to the patriot cause to come out with ringing denunciations of the murder. The most famous case of such equivocation was that of a professor of theology at the University of Berlin, Wilhelm de Wette. One week after the assassination, he wrote a letter of condolence to the murderer's mother, copies of which were read widely within the fraternity movement. De Wette acknowledged that Sand had committed a criminal act that was 'punishable by the worldly magistrate', but argued that this was not the yardstick by which his deed should be judged.

Error is excused by steadfastness and sincerity of conviction, and passion is sanctified by the good course from which it flows. I am firmly convinced that both of these were the case with your pious and virtuous son. He was certain of his cause; he believed it was right to do what he did, and so he was right.

In an oft-quoted passage the professor concluded that Sand's act was 'a beautiful sign of the times'.[24] Unfortunately for de Wette, a copy of his letter found its way into the hands of Prince Wilhelm Ludwig Georg von Wittgenstein, head of the Prussian police. On 30 September 1819, de Wette was dismissed from his professorial post. There was a wave of arrests, as suspects were rounded up in the police action known as the 'persecution of the demagogues' (Demagogenverfolgung). New and tougher censorship and surveillance measures were introduced under the Carlsbad Decrees drafted by Metternich with Prussian support and ratified by the entire Confederation in Frankfurt on 20 September.

Among the victims of the conservative turn was Ernst Moritz Arndt, now a professor of history at the University of Bonn. During an early-morning raid of Arndt's house, a crowd of fraternity students gathered to shower the police with whistles and catcalls as they left the patriot's home with armfuls of confiscated papers. Despite the objections of Provincial Governor Solms-Laubach, Arndt was suspended from his post in November 1820.[25] Friedrich Ludwig Jahn was another suspect. His gymnastic societies were closed, the elaborate stadium established on the Hasenheide was dismantled, and the wearing of the gymnastic uniform and of the 'Old German Costume' was made illegal. Jahn himself would later be imprisoned in Kolberg fortress.

A less prominent victim of the crackdown was the excitable young nobleman Hans Rudolf von Plehwe, a lieutenant in the Guards and a passionate disciple of Jahn. Plehwe had attended the festivities on the Wartburg in 1817 and was often to be seen in the streets of Berlin sporting his Old German Costume. He was renowned among his contemporaries for the rigour and regularity of his exercising – an early pioneer of jogging, he was in the habit of running all the way from the centre of Berlin to Potsdam and back; when this became too easy he took to running the same route with cobblestones packed in the pockets of his gymnastic jacket. After taking part in a rally in support of Jahn, he was arrested and transferred to garrison duty at Glogau in Silesia.[26]

The Prussian crackdown of 1819 was the work of a conservative camarilla that had coalesced around the monarch during the French occupation. After the death of Queen Luise in 1810, Frederick William III had fallen under the influence of a 'substitute family' of courtiers. Among them was the Huguenot preacher Ancillon, who became one of the first advisers to provide the monarch with consistent arguments against the constitutional designs of the reformers. Any form of national representation, Ancillon warned, would inevitably curtail the powers of the monarch. The dangers implicit in such a scheme were illustrated by the course of the French Revolution, which had begun with a national assembly, and then proceeded via the abolition of monarchy to the dictatorship of an illegitimate usurper. Another figure who loomed large after Luise's death was Countess Voss, a kindly older woman of conservative views whose company was important to the king during the raw early months of his bereavement. It was Countess Voss who brought her family friend, Prince Wittgenstein, into the king's inner circle.[27]

This curious trio, an 81-year-old countess and an aristocrat and a preacher both in their forties, formed the core of an influential court faction. Their indispensability to the king, and thus their power, derived from the fact that they provided him with a counterweight to the growing power of Hardenberg. The king had become deeply dependent on his chancellor and he sought, in characteristic fashion, to compensate by balancing Hardenberg with his own advisory clique. When Hardenberg submitted proposals painstakingly drawn up by his subordinates in the chancellery, these were passed to the intimate circle for comment. It was a return, in effect, to the 'cabinet government' that the reformers had set out to abolish in 1806.

The men of the camarilla worked at many levels to secure their political influence and neutralize that of their opponents. Prince Wittgenstein, Ancillon, and the cabinet councillor Daniel Ludwig Albrecht acted as informal intermediaries between Metternich and Frederick William III, driving a wedge between the king and Hardenberg and exploiting the increasingly conservative international climate for their own ends. They also launched a *sotto voce* campaign of denunciations within the Prussian administration, in which politically moderate senior figures were accused of having harboured, sympathized with or even encouraged political subversion. Among those singled out for suspicion by Wittgenstein and his energetic deputy Karl Albert von Kamptz were Justus Gruner, now a senior civil servant in the Prussian Rhineland, the military reformer General Neidhardt von Gneisenau and the provincial president of Jülich-Kleve-Berg, Count Friedrich zu Solms-Laubach, an old friend of Stein.

In the hawkish atmosphere that now prevailed in Berlin, anyone who did not zealously toe the new line was suspect. In the first week of October 1819, when the ministry of state met to discuss the implications of the Carlsbad decrees, Wilhelm von Humboldt, one of the most progressive figures of the reform era, presented his colleagues with a draft resolution objecting to the decrees. Humboldt argued that by vesting new repressive powers in the Confederation, the decrees compromised the sovereignty of the Prussian monarchy. That this liberal-minded minister should have chosen to argue the case in this way shows how difficult it had become to invoke progressive principles of governance in the new climate. Humboldt failed to win a majority in the ministry, but he was supported by two weighty figures, Minister of Justice Karl Friedrich von Beyme and Minister of War Hermann von Boyen. All three men had been deeply implicated in the reforms implemented after 1806. Humboldt and Beyme were both dismissed on the last day of 1819, although the king stipulated that they were to keep their ministerial salaries of 6,000 thalers (Humboldt turned this offer down in disgust). Hermann von Boyen was also dismissed after a bitter quarrel over the declining status of that fetish of the military reformers, the Prussian Landwehr. Among those who also left their posts over this issue were the reformers Grolman and Gneisenau.

Hardenberg himself cannot be absolved entirely from co-responsibility for the conservative turn. His obsessive concern with the consolidation of his own power as chancellor and senior minister alienated colleagues and subordinates, driving them into opposition and thus strengthening the hand of the conservatives. Humboldt's departure in 1819, for example, was as much the work of Hardenberg, who saw him as a rival and opponent, as it was of the conservative faction. By struggling so nakedly for power and attempting to suppress the independence of those around him, Hardenberg ensured that ideological tensions were amplified by bitter personal rivalries. Tactically, too, Hardenberg played into the hands of the camarilla, by supporting the censorship and surveillance measures ordered by Wittgenstein. He had always been an exponent of authoritarian enlightenment, rather than a 'liberal' in the present-day sense, and thus favoured the use of illiberal means to achieve progressive ends. He was also genuinely alarmed at the spread of subversion within Prussia.[28] He may have calculated that repressions would produce a more stable political climate and that this in turn would be favourable to the achievement of his most cherished objective, the creation of a 'national' representation of the Prussian people.

If this was his hope, it was deluded. The conservatives had long been warning against the concession of a 'national' representation of any kind. In their view, any workable form of representation had to be tailored to the interests and privileges of the existing, historically grounded corporate bodies within society. By contrast, a constitution that aimed to represent the Prussian nation as an undifferentiated whole was guaranteed to produce insurrection and disorder. For this reason, Metternich advised Wittgenstein in November 1818 that the King of Prussia should 'never go further than the establishment of provincial Diets'.[29] Encouraged by the camarilla and by his own fears and uncertainties, the king distanced himself from the beleaguered Hardenberg. A committee established to resolve the constitutional question in December 1820 was stocked with conservatives and the chancellor was sent away on a foreign mission early in 1821 to ensure that he did not interfere with its work. He died on 26 November 1822, having lived for long enough to see his project ruined. By the General Law of 5 June 1823, the government announced its intentions to the public. Prussia was to receive no written constitution and no national parliament. Instead, the king's subjects would have to make do with provincial diets.

The diets convened under the General Law were elected and organized along corporate lines, with the nobility, the cities and the peasantry separately represented, a measure intended to suggest continuity with the traditional estate representations of the old regime. Corporate quotas ensured that the regional nobilities enjoyed numerical preponderance, though the precise numbers varied from province to province. Together, the noble deputies could veto any proposal from the assembly. To ensure that they would not pose a challenge to the central administration, the responsibilities of the diets were very narrowly defined. They were convened only once every three years and they were granted no legislative or revenue-approving powers. Their deliberations were secret in order to prevent their becoming focal points for political agitation, and it was illegal to publish their proceedings. In short, they were not intended to function as representative organs in a present-day sense, but rather as advisory bodies that would also take on various administrative chores, such as the supervision of major publicly funded institutions in the regions.[30]

In the eyes of an even moderately progressive observer, the diets appeared outlandishly retrograde. They failed, among other things, to reflect the structure and power relations of provincial society. This was particularly the case in the Rhineland: the nobility, which had traditionally played a marginal role in most of the region, was grossly over-represented, a fact that grated with a society in which bourgeois values and cultural preferences were dominant. Deputies from the major industrial and commercial cities found themselves representing 120 times as many constituents and thirty-four times as much taxation revenue as their colleagues from the noble Estate. The whole process was further encumbered by the indirect election of deputies for the third and fourth estates. Voters from the respective social groups were required to nominate electors, who in turn elected district electors, who in turn elected the deputies who sat in the diet. It was a system designed to shield the assembly as far as possible from the currents and conflicts of provincial society.[31] An effort was also made to prevent the diets from becoming a forum for politicization: deputies were assigned to seats by lot, so that like-minded factions could not form partisan blocks within the assembly.[32] By contrast with Baden, Württemberg and Bavaria, Prussia thus remained a pre-parliamentary state.

*

The conservatives had won the day. But their victory was less fundamental, less final, than it appeared. A process of political change was under way that could no longer be reversed.[33] The acquisition of the Rhineland in 1815 irrevocably altered the political chemistry of the kingdom. With its large and confident urban middle class, the Rhineland introduced an element of dissent and turbulence that energized Prussian politics throughout the post-war decades. The Rhenish elites were sceptical of the 'Lithuanian' administration in Berlin and they strenuously resisted wholesale integration into the kingdom. Rhenish Catholics looked with suspicion on the new Protestant administration and Rhenish Protestants fought a twenty-year battle with Berlin in defence of their (relatively democratic) synodal constitution.[34] There was also a struggle over the Napoleonic legal system, whose egalitarian social presumptions and powerful endorsement of private property rights were far better suited to conditions in the Rhineland than the Prussian General Code. The efforts of the conservatives to impose Prussian law in the west met with determined local opposition and the idea was ultimately abandoned. The Rhineland thus remained a foreign country in legal terms, with regulations, institutions – including, for example, jury service – and judicial training facilities of its own. Indeed, as the Rhenish Napoleonic system gained adherents among jurists from the East-Elbian provinces, it became an important force for change. The new law code introduced in the Kingdom of Prussia after 1848 was modelled on the Rhenish system, rather than the old Frederician code.[35]

The same progressive momentum can be observed in the domain of customs reform. The process of economic deregulation and customs harmonization continued after 1815 with the customs law of 26 May 1818, which established Prussia's first homogeneous territorial customs regime (the eastern and western provinces initially received different schedules but these were unified in 1821). From the late 1820s, the same process of customs harmonization was projected beyond the borders of the kingdom as ministers and officials worked to create a German customs union under Prussian auspices. Here was a policy domain that engaged the interest of some of the most resourceful individuals within the senior administration.

Education was another area in which improvement and modernization continued after 1815. The expansion and professionalization of teacher training proceeded apace and by the 1840s, over 80 per cent of Prussian children between six and fourteen were attending primary schools, a figure unmatched anywhere in the contemporary world except for Saxony and New England. Literacy rates were correspondingly high.[36] Prussian education was noted and admired abroad not just for its effectiveness and near-universality of access, but also for the liberal tone of its institutions. The appointment in 1821 of Ludolf von Beckedorff as director of the Prussian public school system looked at first as if it might herald a reactionary turn in Prussian education policy – Beckedorff was an opponent of the liberal Pestalozzian pedagogy that had informed the designs of the reformers. But he was unable to halt the process of bureaucratic reform, because the responsible minister, Karl von Altenstein, still supported the progressives within the education system. In any case, Beckedorff was, like many conservatives of the era, an essentially pragmatic figure who was prepared to work with and expand the structures he had inherited from his predecessors. In the 1840s, when the American educational reformer Horace Mann visited Berlin, he was surprised to observe that school children in Prussia were taught to exercise their mental faculties for themselves by teachers whose techniques were anything but authoritarian. 'Though I saw hundreds of schools and [. . .] tens of thousands of pupils,' Mann wrote, 'I never saw one child undergoing punishment for misconduct. I never saw one child in tears from having been punished, or from fear of being punished.'[37] Liberal visitors from Britain frequently expressed their surprise that such a 'despotic' political arrangement should have produced such a progressive and open-minded educational system.[38]

As Beckedorff's case suggests, conservatism did not imply an implacable opposition to all that had changed since the crisis of 1806. It was far too fluid, unfocused and open-ended to attempt a comprehensive restoration of the pre-reform status quo, or even to halt the reforming state in its forward path. Moreover, the conservatives themselves gradually adopted and internalized many of the ideas central to the reform project, such as the notion that the Prussian 'nation' constituted a single coherent entity (rather than an assembly of distinct and privileged orders).[39] There were in any case still significant progressive power centres within the administration, not only in the departments of finance and foreign affairs, but also in the ministry of education, health and religious affairs, itself a product of the reform era. Its presiding minister after 1815 was the enlightened rationalist Karl von Altenstein, a friend, collaborator and sometime protégé of Hardenberg. The king – himself in many respects a child of the enlightenment – was never especially consistent in his appointments policy and no effort was made to impose a uniform ideological approach on the various branches of government.

THE POLITICS OF CHANGE

The provincial diets created in 1823 may not have been the robust organs of representation the radicals had wished for, but as they grew into their role, they became important focal points of political change. Although they looked like traditional Estate bodies, they were in fact representative institutions of a new type. Their legitimacy derived from a legislative act by the state, not from the authority of an extra-governmental corporate tradition. The deputies voted by head, not by Estate, and deliberations were held in plenary session, not in separate caucuses as in the corporate assemblies of the old regime. Most import-antly of all: the 'noble Estate' (*Ritterschaft*) was no longer defined by birth (with the exception of the small contingent of 'immediate' nobles in the Rhineland), but by property. It was the ownership of 'privileged land' that counted, not birth into privileged status.[40] The bourgeois estate buyers whose purchasing power had been transforming the social landscape of the Prussian lands since the mid eighteenth century were now admitted into the dress circle of the political nation (provided they were not Jewish, in which case they had to depute a proxy to represent them).

This was a point where forces for social and political change inter-sected, for the transfer of formerly noble estates into middle-class hands continued at an even greater pace after the reformers deregulated the market in rural land. In 1806, 75.6 per cent of noble estates in the rural hinterland of Königsberg were still in noble hands. By 1829, this figure had fallen to 48.3 per cent. The decline was even more extreme in the East Prussian district (*Departement*) of Mohrungen, where the pro-portion sank from 74.8 per cent to 40.6 per cent. East Prussia was a relatively extreme case, because of the devastating impact of the crises of 1806–7 and the Napoleonic blockade on the grain economy of the province, but the figures for Prussia as a whole bear out the general trend: by 1856 only 57.6 per cent of noble land remained in the hands of noble landowners. The diets, then, were more plutocratic than they looked. Their elaborate estatist trappings concealed the beginnings of a property-based franchise.

From the outset, tentatively at first and later more emphatically, the diets sought to expand the role assigned to them. The draft resolutions submitted by deputies were often openly political in character and aimed to test the boundaries the state had set for the work of the diet. There were calls for the circulation of printed transcripts of the diet's proceedings – a measure forbidden by the government's censorship regulations – petitions demanding that the diet's remit be widened to encompass an 'ever more diverse and comprehensive' range of affairs, and calls for a general (i.e. all-Prussian) assembly.[41] Freedom of the press was another recurrent theme frequently broached in the diets. They began, in other words, to channel liberal political pressures in the provinces. They performed this role not only for the deputies themselves, but also for a broader politically literate public. From the late 1820s, there were numerous petitions to the diet from the towns of East Prussia. One submission presented in January 1829 by signatories from the town of Mohrungen in the south-west of the province, criticized the administration in Berlin for neglecting the economic problems of the region, rebuked the impotence of the diet, and proposed that the Estates should ask the monarch to honour his promise to grant a constitution. Another from the sleepy little town of Stallupönen, due east from Königsberg and not far from the Polish border, reiterated the demand for a constitution and a national assembly, and backed up its plea with a reference to the province's contribution to the war of liberation against Napoleon.[42]

The striking thing about these petitions, which grew increasingly numerous in the 1830s and 1840s, is not simply that they hailed from all over the province, including the conservative, noble-dominated Oberland area in the west, but also that they represented a relatively broad social constituency. The signatories to a submission of 1843 from Insterburg, an administrative town in the centre of the province, included not just merchants and communal officials but a very substantial contingent of craftsmen: carpenters, stonemasons, locksmiths, bakers, belt makers, a furrier, a glass-blower, a bookbinder, a butcher, a soap maker and others. This diverse group requested not just a national assembly and public proceedings, but also a 'different mode of representation' that would give less weight to landed property.[43] In other words, the government's efforts to shut the diets off from their social and political hinterland were not successful. A multitude of informal connections between deputies and the political milieus of urban and small-town society ensured that the deliberations of the diet resonated across the province. These networks were supported by a modest but growing provincial press.

The diets also became a focal point for political aspirations and dissent in the Grand Duchy of Posen, the segment of Poland transferred to Berlin after 1815. In this region, constitutional issues were overshadowed by the question of Prussian policy *vis-à-vis* the Polish nationality. In a proclamation issued on 15 May 1815 and frequently cited thereafter, Frederick William III assured his Polish subjects that they, too, had a fatherland, and that they would be incorporated in the Prussian monarchy without having to relinquish their nationality. Their language, together with German, would be used in all public functions.[44]

In the early post-war years an effort was made to appease the Polish elite in the region. A viceroy (*Statthalter*) was appointed to mediate between the central executive and the local gentry (an arrangement unique to the Grand Duchy), and a credit society was founded in 1821 to alleviate the burden of gentry debt. Polish remained an official language for communications with the bureaucracy and in court proceedings, and Polish was the language of instruction in elementary and secondary schools, except for the final years of Gymnasium, when German was introduced to prepare students for university. The aim was not to 'Germanize' the Poles, but to ensure that they became loyal Prussian subjects.[45] Yet by the later 1820s, disappointment had already accumulated over developments in the Grand Duchy. There was unhappiness over the government's failure to form a separate Polish division of the Prussian army – a scheme warmly supported by the Posnanian gentry. At the first session of the diet in 1827, petitions were presented protesting against the use of German in the upper years of secondary school and objecting to the fact that many Prussian officials in the region could neither speak nor understand Polish. So strong were the emotions aroused by these issues that the supporters of one petition challenged the opposing deputies to duels.

Conditions deteriorated considerably after 1830. The Polish rising of that year was concentrated in the Russian, not the Prussian, area of Poland, but it awakened the enthusiasm of liberals across the kingdom.

The Königsberg professor Burlach later recalled how he secretly crossed the border in order to 'dream of [Poland's] liberation and bring the flowers of Polish liberty back to our homeland'.[46] The Polish rising also had a predictably disturbing effect on politics within the Grand Duchy, as thousands of Poles crossed the border to fight in support of the national cause, including over 1,000 absconders from Prussian military service. Alarmed at the prospect of a nationalist mobilization, the Berlin government abandoned the policy of conciliation. The Grand Duchy was demoted to the mere 'province' of Posen. The Polish viceroy, whose office signified the special status of Posen within the Prussian composite state, was dismissed without a replacement. Eduard Heinrich Flottwell, the new provincial president appointed in December 1830, was a hardliner who saw little point in appeasing the Polish gentry. 'Most of the male youth of this nobility,' he declared, 'have been duped by the academic swindles of fatherland and freedom, which united in the illogical head of a Pole with the proud insolence of a Sarmatian magnate in the most marvellous way.'

The notion that Posen constituted a Polish fatherland and the Poles a separate nationality was put aside in favour of a policy of outright assimilation. The Slavic inhabitants of the province were not 'Poles', Flottwell claimed, but 'Prussians'. All pretence of neutrality was abandoned as Flottwell launched a policy encouraging German peasant settlement, strengthened the organs of urban self-government so as to give a stronger voice to the substantially German burgher elites, and extended the use of German in school instruction. Bankrupted Polish estates were bought up and sold off to German buyers. These changes prompted a swift radicalization of Polish opinion in the province. At the diets of 1834 and 1837, there were bitter protests at the advancing use of German. Poles resigned in droves from Prussian civil service posts. In the mid-1830s, patriotic activists among the Polish gentry became involved in the Organic Work movement, a network of gentry clubs that aimed to enhance Polish cultural and social life in the province through the gradual improvement of agricultural methods and the creation of a Polish cultural infrastructure.[47]

In the Rhineland, too, the provincial diets became important focal points for liberal (and conservative) mobilization. Political activists in the west could draw on a living memory of corporate co-determination that reached back into the eighteenth century.[48] Here too, the diets were used after 1830 to confront the government with the demand for a general Estates assembly and fulfilment of the constitutional promise.[49] And in the Rhineland, as in the east, the diet was the focus for numerous petitions. In the Rhineland, as in East Prussia, the quickening of political expectations in provincial society bestowed a heightened status upon the diet and its members: in December 1833, the exclusive Casino Club in Trier even held a banquet to welcome the town's returning deputies.[50] Slowly but surely, this energizing commerce around the diets was bound to expand their pretensions. As the nineteenth-century liberal historian Heinrich von Treitschke put it: 'Diets that abandoned themselves to the judgement of public opinion could not long remain content to submit unbinding recommendations; they had to demand that they be given some power of decision.'[51]

CONFLICTS OF FAITH

In religion as in politics, this was an era of differentiation, fragmentation and conflict. Revivalist movements mobilized the faithful in ways that unsettled the equilibrium of the religious communities. The state intervened more aggressively in the confessional life of the kingdom than at any time since the reign of the Great Elector, so that the boundaries between religious nonconformity and political dissent were blurred. Confessional networks became incubators for partisan political affiliations. Religion was more than a reservoir for the language and arguments of political discourse; it was a powerful motive for action in its own right. Its dynamism as a social force was greater in this era than at any time since the seventeenth century.

In December 1827, an Englishman returned from Berlin to London with 'pleasing testimonies to the increase in religion amongst influential persons in the Prussian dominions'. This evangelical traveller told a prominent London missionary society of a prayer meeting in Berlin where he had met '30 persons of the first rank'. He reported that the king and his ministers were at one in the pursuance of pious projects and told of numerous meetings with army officers of 'truly Christian spirit'.[52] The English traveller had witnessed in Berlin one of the centres of the 'Awakening', a socially diverse movement of religious revival that swept across the Protestant north of Germany during the first decades of the nineteenth century. Awakened Christians emphasized the emotional, penitential character of their faith. Many of them experienced the transition from unbelief or a merely nominal Christian commitment to the fullness of awakened religious awareness as a traumatic moment of 'rebirth'. One participant in a nocturnal prayer meeting that took place in Berlin in 1817 recalled that at the stroke of midnight 'the Lord appeared, living and personal, as never before or since, in front of my soul. With a deep inward shock and hot stream of tears, I recognised my sinfulness, which stood before my eyes like a mountain.'[53]

This kind of religious commitment was personal and practical rather than ecclesiastical; it expressed itself in an astonishing range of social initiatives: voluntary Christian societies sprang up dedicated to the distribution of charity, the housing and 'betterment' of 'fallen women', the moral improvement of prisoners, the care of orphans, the printing and distribution of Bibles, the provision of subsistence labour for paupers and vagrants, the conversion of Jews and heathens. The Silesian nobleman Hans Ernst von Kottwitz, for example, a central figure in the early Awakening, set up a 'spinning institute' for the city's unemployed; a new mission to the Jews was founded in Berlin in 1822 and patronized by key figures within the elite, including close associates of the monarch himself.

To the west, in Prussian Westphalia, the pious Count Adalbert von der Recke founded the Düsselthal Salvation Institute in 1817 to provide a refuge for the orphaned and abandoned children whose numbers had risen after the Napoleonic Wars; he later added a workhouse for Jews seeking conversion to Christianity. Like many awakened Christians, the count was driven in part by a sense of millenarian expectation – he believed that he was working to build God's kingdom on earth. Sin and vice were given no quarter. An entry from Recke's own orphanage diary dated January 1822 relates that a young girl called Mathilde had to be 'slapped some forty times' before she would follow Recke in reciting a prayer.[54] Two weeks later a deaf mute boy who had been apprenticed out to a master blacksmith had to be 'thrashed thoroughly' for having defended himself while being beaten by his master.[55] On a Sunday morning in March, the boys of Düsselthal were treated to the public whipping of Jakob, who had bored a hole into a barrel of the brandy brewed on the premises in order to drink the contents. He was urged between strokes to repent of his misdeed, but remained 'unconverted' and had to be imprisoned for a week with his legs shackled into a pair of 'wooden boots'. Meals, school lessons and bedtime were signalled by trumpet blasts and inmates were marched to their respective tasks in military order. The Salvation Institute was a grim place for those who fell foul of its Dickensian discipline, but, like many other such voluntary foundations, it provided an indispensable supplement to the minimal social provision of the state authorities. By 1823, it had become an official clearing house for abandoned children in the area around the city of Düsseldorf.

The Protestant missions, institutes and pious societies of the post-war era represented a diverse social constituency. Wealthy individuals from the social (and often the political) elite loomed large among the founding fathers, mainly because they alone had the capital to acquire premises and equipment and the influence to secure privileges from the authorities. There was also a far-flung network of supporters in the lesser towns and villages of the Prussian provinces, in which artisans formed the overwhelming majority. They organized themselves in auxiliary societies that met for prayer, Bible-reading, discussion and the collection of donations for Christian purposes. The prominence of voluntary associations – *Vereine* – in the landscape of nineteenth-century evangelical Protestantism was something new and significant. This may not have been the sceptical, critical, contentious, bourgeois 'public sphere' idealized by Jürgen Habermas, but it did represent an impressive self-organizing impulse capable of feeding into proto-political networks and affiliations. It was part of that broader unfolding of voluntary energies that transformed nineteenth-century middle- and lower-middle-class society.

Protestant revivalism in Prussia tended to seek expression outside the confines of the institutional church. The church service was esteemed as one possible route to edification, but Awakened Christians preferred, in the words of one of their number, 'the private devotional meeting, the sermon in the house, the barn or the field, the conventicle'.[56] Some Awakened Protestants openly disparaged the official confessional structures, dismissing church buildings as 'stone houses' and church pastors as 'men in black gowns'.[57] In some Prussian rural areas, local populations refused to patronize the services of the official clergy, preferring to congregate in prayer meetings. On the noble estate of Reddenthin in Pomerania, prayer meetings of this kind began in 1819, where they were encouraged by the landlords, Carl and Gustav von Below. Among the participants was a shepherd by the name of Dubbach, who became famous for his impromptu sermons. Dubbach is reported to have leapt into the audience after one sermon and kicked the kneeling faithful – the lord of the estate included – in the napes of their necks, crying 'Get deeper down into humility!'[58] These charismatic occasions were intended not merely to supplement, but to replace the services provided by the official church; Awakened Christians on the estate were urged not to attend the sermons of the local clergyman or to seek his pastoral advice. In its more radical guise, in other words, revivalist evangelical Protestantism was driven by an open hostility to the structures of official religion. 'Separatist' revivalists were those who wished to sever themselves entirely from the body of the official church and refused to allow it any involvement in their lives, even in such areas as the baptism of infants, where clerical officiation was compulsory by law.

There was abundant potential here for conflict with the secular authorities. After 1815, the Prussian state began to intervene more aggressively in the religious life of the kingdom. On 27 September 1817, Frederick William III announced his intention to merge the Lutheran and Calvinist confessions into a single Prussian 'evangelical-Christian church', later known as the Church of the Prussian Union. The king himself was the chief architect of this new ecclesiastical entity. He designed the new United liturgy, cobbling together texts from German, Swedish, Anglican and Huguenot prayer books. He issued regulations for the decoration of altars, the use of candles, vestments and crucifixes. The aim was to create a composite that would resonate with the religious sensibilities of both Calvinists and Lutherans. It was a further, final chapter in the long history of efforts by the Hohenzollern dynasty to close the confessional gap between the monarchy and the people. The king invested immense energy and hope in the Union. This may in part have been a function of private motivations: the confessional divide had prevented the king from taking communion together with his late Lutheran wife, Luise. Frederick William also believed that the Union would stabilize the ecclesiastical fabric of Protestantism in the face of the greatly enlarged Catholic minority in the post-war Prussian state.[59]

The pre-eminent motive was the desire to bring order and homogeneity into the religious life of the kingdom and to forestall the potentially anarchic effects of religious revival. Frederick William III had an instinctively neo-absolutist aversion to the proliferation of sects. Throughout the

1820s, Altenstein, chief of the new *Kultusministerium* (the ministry of religion, health and education founded in the same year as the Church Union), kept a close eye on sectarian developments both within and beyond the borders of the kingdom. Of particular interest were the Swiss valley sects of Hasli, Grindelwald and Lauterbrunn, whose adherents were said to pray naked in the belief that clothes were a sign of sin and shame. The ministry assembled lists of sectarian publications, subsidized the dissemination of counter-sectarian texts and closely monitored religious groups and associations of all kinds.[60] Frederick William expected the edifying and accessible rituals and symbolic culture of the Prussian Union to arrest the centrifugal pull of sectarian formations, just as Napoleon had hoped that the Church of the French Concordat founded in 1801 would close the rifts that had opened among French Catholics since the Revolution.[61]

One finds at the heart of the unionist project an obsessive concern with uniformity that is recognizably post-Napoleonic: the simplification and homogenization of vestments at the altar as on the field of battle, liturgical conformity in place of the plurality of local practices that had been the norm in the previous century, even modular *Normkirchen* (standardized churches), designed to be assembled from pre-fabricated parts and available in different sizes to suit villages and towns.[62] The king appears to have seen the restoration of religious life in the kingdom as inextricably connected with the elimination of ecclesiastical pluralism: 'If every mindless priest wants to come to market with his unwashed ideas . . .' he told his confidant and collaborator Bishop Eylert, 'what will – or can – come of it?'[63]

The early consolidation of the Union Church proceeded harmoniously enough, but opposition increased dramatically in the 1830s. This was partly because the Prussian administration gradually extended the scope of the Union to the point where its liturgical regulations became binding for all Protestant public worship across the kingdom. Many Protestants objected to this element of compulsion. A more important factor was the changing character of Protestant revivalism. Having begun as an ecumenical movement, Protestant revivalism tended from around 1830 to develop a more sharply confessional profile. Lutheranism in particular experienced a major efflorescence, triggered in part by the 300th anniversary celebrations of the Augsburg Confession of 1530, the key doctrinal text of Lutheranism. Under the pressure of this Lutheran confessional revival, an Old Lutheran movement formed which demanded the right to secede from the church of the Prussian Union.

The emotional core of the movement was a deep attachment to the traditional Lutheran liturgy that had been modified under the auspices of the Prussian Union. At the height of the Old Lutheran agitation in the Kingdom of Prussia, some 10,000 active separatists were known to the police authorities, most of them concentrated in Silesia, where the influence of neighbouring Saxony, the heartland of Lutheranism, was especially strong. The king was enraged and genuinely bewildered by this resistance. He had conceived his Church Union as a broad church in which all Protestant Christians could find a comfortable home – how could anyone object to that? Urged on by their monarch, the Prussian authorities made all the usual mistakes. They presumed, above all, that the Old Lutherans were merely the hapless dupes of malevolent agitators. A report of June 1836 described the 600 separatists in the Züllichau district as persons 'of limited mental capacity' who had 'nothing to lose in the way of material goods', and were thus vulnerable to the 'exertions of a fanatical preacher'.[64]

Convinced that the Old Lutheran movement would subside once its ringleaders had been neutralized, the Prussian authorities bore down heavily on separatist preachers, imposing draconian fines and terms of imprisonment, and quartering troops on areas where congregations refused to see the government's sense. These measures were predictably futile. Silesian separatism was a movement with deep roots in the religiosity of the populace. The petitions submitted during the early and mid-1830s by groups of Lutherans, inscribed with the jagged signatures of crofters and day labourers, reveal a profound attachment to the words and spirit of local Lutheran tradition: 'what we seek is nothing new; we hold steadfastly to the teachings of our fathers.'[65] Repression merely stimulated sympathy for the beleaguered Lutherans, so that the movement steadily spread during the 1830s from Silesia into the neighbouring provinces of Posen, Saxony and Brandenburg. As the pressure increased, the Old Lutherans went underground, holding secret synods at which the rules and procedures were drawn up for an illegal church administration. In 1838, the dismissed separatist pastor Senkel was still travelling up and down Silesia in a variety of disguises performing illegal sacramental acts for his followers. The *Neue Würzburger Zeitung* reported in June 1838 that Senkel had recently been in Ratibor dressed as a woman in order to administer communion to some Lutherans in a cellar.[66]

In addition to difficulties of enforcement, the government faced a far more fundamental obstruction: uncertainty about the legal basis for anti-separatist measures. Prussian administrators in the late eighteenth century had generally been concerned to uphold the autonomy of the existing confessional communities. Wöllner's Edict of Religion of 9 July 1788 affirmed the right of 'the three main confessions of the Christian religion' to the protection of the monarch. Under the General Code of 1794, there was no explicit provision for an initiative by the state in religious affairs. The inviolability of conscience and the freedom of belief were defined as fundamental and inalienable rights; the state renounced any role in influencing the religious convictions of the individual. The tolerated 'religious parties', as they were called in the General Code, stood equally under the protection of a state that was, in theory at least, confessionally impartial. It followed that the state had no right to 'impose symbolic books as binding doctrine' or to take the initiative in dismissing preachers on the grounds of doctrinal unsoundness. As the jurist Carl Gottlieb Svarez had explained to the future Frederick William III in 1791–2, the authority for such action rested not with the state, but with the individual religious community. Codified Prussian law thus provided no foundation for the action taken by the Prussian state against the Lutheran separatists in the 1830s.

The foundation of *new* sects did require official permission under Prussian law, but the Lutherans could hardly be accused of founding a new sect. From the standpoint of the separatists, it was the state, not the Lutheran dissenters, that had created a new confession in Prussia. Lutheranism had been a recognized and publicly tolerated confession in the German states since the Peace of Augsburg. The right of Lutherans to tolerance in the province of Silesia had been guaranteed by Frederick the Great in 1740 and confirmed by Frederick William III in 1798. The separatists were well aware that the legality of government repression was questionable. Separatist petitions frequently cited key passages in the General Code defining the rights and legal autonomy of publicly tolerated religious organizations. They presented their oppositional stance as grounded in the dictates of conscience (*Gewissen*), thereby laying claim to the fundamental guarantees furnished by the code.

For all these reasons, the efforts of Interior Minister von Rochow and his colleagues to put an end to the Old Lutheran movement were a

38. Old Lutheran settlement at Klemzig, South Australia, *by George French Angas, 1845*

failure, although they did cause several thousand separatists to seek their fortunes in North America and Australia. Prussians living along the banks of the river Oder were thus treated to an astonishing sight: barges full of law-abiding, hymn-singing Lutherans on their way to Hamburg for transfer to London and thence to South Australia, fleeing the religious persecution of the Prussian authorities. It was as if the great drama of the Salzburg Protestants (also Lutherans!) were being played out in reverse. The exodus was widely reported in the German press. It was all deeply embarrassing. The conflict was defused only in 1845 when Frederick William IV offered a general amnesty and granted the Lutherans the right to establish themselves within Prussia as an autonomous church association.

The sharpening of confessional identities also unsettled relations between the state and its Catholic subjects, whose numbers were greatly increased by the territorial settlement of 1815. Catholicism, like Protestantism, was transformed by revival. The rationalism of the enlightenment made way for a heightened emphasis on emotion, mystery and revelation. There was a surge in popular pilgrimages – the most famous occurred in 1844, when half a million Catholics converged on the city of Trier in the Rhineland to view a garment believed to have been the robe Christ wore on the way to his crucifixion. Closely associated with Catholic revival was the rise of 'ultramontanism' – the term referred to the fact that Rome lies *ultra montes* or beyond the Alps. Ultramontanes perceived the church as a strictly centralized and transnational body focused firmly on the authority of Rome. They saw the strict subordination of the church to papal authority as the surest way of protecting it from state interference. This was a novelty in the Rhineland, whose bishoprics had traditionally been proud of their independence and sceptical of Rome's claims. The ultramontanes strove to bring the diverse devotional cultures of the Catholic regions into closer conformity with Roman norms. Thus the ancient liturgies of Rhenish episcopal cities such as Trier, with their passages of local dialect, were phased out and replaced with standardized Roman Latin substitutes.

The potential for conflict in this new 'Romanized' Catholicism became apparent in 1837, when a major fight broke out in the Rhineland over the education of children in Catholic-Protestant mixed marriages. Under Catholic doctrine, the priest officiating at the marriage of a mixed couple was obliged to obtain a signed undertaking from the Protestant partner to the effect that the children would be educated as Catholics before he could administer the sacrament of marriage. This practice was at variance with Prussian law, which stipulated (in the spirit of interconfessional parity) that in such marriages the children were to be educated in the religion of the father. In the early post-war years the state authorities and the Rhenish clergy agreed on a compromise arrangement: the officiating clergyman would merely urge the Protestant spouse to educate any future children as Catholics without requiring a signed contract. In 1835, however, the appointment of an ultramontane hardliner to the archbishopric of Cologne made further compromise impossible. Supported by Pope Gregory XVI, the new archbishop, Clemens August Count Droste-Vischering, unilaterally reintroduced the mandatory education contract for non-Catholic spouses in mixed marriages.

As the head and 'supreme bishop' of the Prussian Union Church, Frederick William III interpreted this change of policy as a direct challenge to his authority. After efforts to negotiate a settlement had failed, the monarch ordered Droste-Vischering's arrest in November 1837 – it was a matter, as his ministers put it, of 'demonstrating the fullness of the royal power in the face of the power of the Catholic church'.[67] Additional troops were secretly transferred to Cologne to handle any local unrest and the archbishop was escorted from his palace to an apartment within the walls of the fortress of Minden, where he remained under house arrest, forbidden to receive official guests or to discuss ecclesiastical issues. After royal decrees were issued criminalizing the practice of requiring the contract, the Prussian hierarchy hardened its position. On the eastern periphery of the Prussian dominions, where there was also a large Catholic population (including many Poles), the archbishop of Gnesen and Posen, Martin von Dunin, formally reintroduced the marital education contract; he too was arrested and incarcerated in the fortress of Kolberg.

In the course of these dramatic interventions, there were demonstrations in the streets of the major Catholic towns and clashes between Prussian troops and Catholic subjects. After the publication of an official papal declaration condemning the Prussian government, resistance to the new measures quickly spread to Paderborn and Münster, whose bishops likewise announced that they would return to demanding the marital contract. By the early months of 1838, a major controversy had blown up over the issue. There was extensive press coverage throughout the German states (and across Europe) and a flood of pamphlets, of which the best known and most widely read was the polemical *Athanasius*, a hard-hitting denunciation of the Prussian government by the sometime Rhenish radical and ultramontane Catholic Joseph Goerres. Across the western provinces, the events of 1837–8 produced a lasting radicalization of Catholic opinion. One Protestant contemporary who observed this struggle with mingled fascination and indignation was Otto von Bismarck, the future Prussian statesman, now in his early twenties.

The official churches and the various sectarian or separatist movements did not entirely monopolize the spiritual life of Prussians. On the margins of the churches, and in the numerous interstices of religious belief and practice there flourished a rich variety of eccentric variations on the norm, in which the tenets of licensed dogma blended seamlessly with folk belief, speculative natural philosophy and pseudo-science. These were the hardy weeds that shot up ceaselessly between the paving stones of official religion. They fed to some extent upon the energies released by the religious revivals. In Catholic rural or small-town communities, the post-war turn towards mystery and miracle could easily tip over into credulity and superstition. Late in the summer of 1822, there were reports of a 'miraculous fiery light' over an image of Mary in the little Catholic church of Zons, a small town on the banks of the Rhine between Cologne and Düsseldorf. When pilgrims began descending on the town, the church authorities in Cologne and Aachen mounted an investigation, which found that the light was due to refraction of the sun's rays through a window, and efforts were made to dissuade further pilgrims from congregating in the church. Such unruly local enthusiasms demanded constant vigilance on the part of the church authorities.[68]

The Catholic ecclesiastical and the Protestant secular authorities found it easy to agree on the case of the Zons 'fiery light'; other forms of miraculous belief were more problematic, because they lay in the grey zone between folk magic and popular piety. The practice – well established in the Prussian Rhineland – of 'healing' persons stricken with rabies by laying a thread from the shrine of St Hubertus into an incision on the forehead was deplored by the state authorities but tolerated by (most of) the local church leadership. One characteristic feature of the awakened Rhenish Catholicism of the 1820s and 1830s was an aspiration to build bridges between theology and the more *outré* varieties of contemporary speculative science and natural philosophy, including mesmerism and animal magnetism.[69]

On the Protestant side, too, religious belief could interact with folk magic in ways that the authorities found unsettling. In 1824, it was reported that the former stable-boy Johann Gottlieb Grabe in Torgau (in Prussian Saxony) was 'healing' over 100 'patients' per day through a combination of prayers, incantations, magical movements and animal magnetism. A government investigation at the Charité Hospital in Berlin refuted Grabe's claim to possess healing powers, but this did nothing to diminish his charisma as a healer. One Torgau merchant was even reported to have purchased Grabe's leather trousers, so that he might strengthen himself with the residual magnetism still inhabiting them.[70] In 1842, intense public controversy surrounded the Rhenish Catholic shepherd Heinrich Mohr of Neurath, whose feats of healing attracted as many as 1,000 persons per day, many of whom crossed the region to be seen by him. Figures such as Mohr filled a need that was not satisfied by contemporary medical practice, which stood helpless in the face of most chronic illnesses. But it was his 'blessing' above all that patients were after, a detail that particularly alarmed the Catholic church authorities because it implied the usurpation of one of the ordained clergy's definitive powers.[71]

Harder to place is the 'sect' that gathered in Königsberg around the maverick preachers Johann Wilhelm Ebel and Heinrich Diestel in the late 1830s. These two provided what we would now call marital counselling based upon an eclectic practical theology in which ideas drawn from pre-Christian natural philosophy were cobbled together with chiliastic expectation, humoral theory and mid nineteenth-century preoccupations with marriage and sexuality. Drawing on the teachings of the East Prussian millenarian mystic Johann Friedrich Schoenherr, Ebel and Diestel posited that the act of coitus between a man and a woman was essentially a re-enactment of the moment of creation, when two vast balls, one of fire and one of water, had collided to form the universe.[72] The sexual act between man (fire) and woman (water) thus had an intrinsic cosmic significance and value and should be accepted and cultivated as an essential feature of any harmonious marital relationship. Male participants in the circle were advised to make love to their wives with the lamp lit, rather than in darkness, so that erotic fantasies were banished and 'blind lust' was transformed into 'conscious affection for the spouse'.[73] Members of the circle – including the women – were urged to take positive pleasure in the sexual act. The two clergymen attracted a circle of high-status Königsbergers, including men and women from some of the city's leading families.

What with all the colliding of fire and water, the mood within the circle grew rather steamy, there was an unexpected pregnancy and rumours spread that the preachers were encouraging licentiousness and extra-marital sex. It was claimed – fancifully – that men and women attended the 'conventicles' of the sect in a state of nudity, that initiates received something called the 'seraphic kiss', 'with which the most abominable excesses were connected', and that 'two young ladies had died from the consequences of excessive libidinous excitement'.[74] To his great embarrassment, Theodor von Schön, who knew several of the participants personally, was obliged to mount an investigation. The resulting trial, known across Protestant Germany as the 'Muckerprozess' (trial of the fanatics) received intense and controversial press coverage.[75] We are used to thinking of religion as an ordering force but the boundary

between the collective, external canonized identity of the official confessional parties and that untidy package of private human needs and
inclinations that we call 'religiosity' became highly unstable during the
decades between the revolutions.

MISSIONARY STATE

The close identification of the secular authority with the religious life
and practice of the Protestant majority had far-reaching consequences
for the Prussian Jews. In the debate triggered by Dohm's famous emancipationist essay *Concerning the Civic Betterment of the Jews* (1781),
most commentators had shared the author's secular conception of the
state's tasks and responsibilities; none was prepared to argue that
religion provided adequate grounds for civic discrimination against the
Jews, and none saw conversion as either the sole or a necessary means
of resolving the problem of Jewish status. Hardenberg's Edict of Emancipation had likewise been conceived in a secular spirit. What the
reformers sought in 1812 was not the religious conversion of the Jews
(to Christianity), but their secular conversion to an unconditional
membership of the Prussian 'nation'. Things changed thereafter. Thanks
to the edict, the Jews of the core provinces were no longer 'foreigners'
dwelling on Prussian soil on His Majesty's sufferance, but 'citizens of
the state' along with their fellow citizens of Christian faith. The question
now was: should the Jews, having already been allowed to participate
on an equal footing as private individuals in the sphere of the economy
and society, be admitted to participation in the public life of the state?
Answering this question involved making claims about the purposes for
which the state and its organs existed.

The most striking feature of Prussian Jewish policy after 1815 – and
it sets Prussian developments apart from those in most of the other
German states – was a new emphasis on religion as the key to the
question of Jewish status. In the course of debate over these matters
within the council of ministers in 1816, the ministry of finance submitted
a long memorandum that opened with some general reflections on the
role of religion as the only true foundation for a confident and independent state: 'A cohesive, independent people', it argued, should consist
of members who share the same 'basic ideas that are most dear to them';

religion was the only bond powerful enough to transform a people into a 'unanimous whole' capable of unified and determined action in 'times of external threat'. The report went on to recommend that 'the conversion of Jews to Christianity should be made easier and should entail the granting of all civil rights', but that 'as long as the Jew [remained] a Jew, he must not be permitted to take up a position in the state'.[76] The same theme was taken up in the provinces: in a report of 1819, the district government of Arnsberg in the Rhineland affirmed that religion was the main hindrance to emancipation and proposed that the state should introduce measures to encourage Jewish conversions. A report of 1820 from the district magistrates of Münster recommended mandatory Christian adult education for Jews and special benefits for converts to Christianity.[77]

Frederick William III endorsed these views. When the Jewish mathematician David Unger, a citizen of Prussia, applied for a teaching position at the Berlin Bauakademie (a position in the pay of the Prussian state), he was advised by the monarch personally that his application would be reconsidered after his 'conversion to the Evangelical Church' (i.e. the Prussian Union). A similar case was that of the Jewish Lieutenant Meno Burg, who had joined the Grenadier Guards in 1812 as a volunteer rifleman and had performed with distinction ever since. In 1830, when Burg was due to be promoted to the rank of captain, the king issued a cabinet order in which he expressed his conviction that, in view of his education and experience of life among Prussian officers, Burg would have the sense to recognize the truth and redeeming power of the Christian faith, and thereby 'clear away any obstacle to his promotion'.[78] In addition to such ad hoc interventions, Frederick William III actively encouraged conversion by introducing a royal bounty for Jewish converts who had the name of the sovereign entered in the church baptismal records as their nominal 'godfather'. A concerted effort was also made by the state authorities to prevent women who were planning to marry Jewish partners from converting to Judaism, although the legal basis for such action was very fragile, given that the Prussian General Code permitted conversion from or to any tolerated 'religious party' after the age of fourteen.[79]

Other related initiatives included an order forbidding Christian clergymen from attending Jewish festivities (such as weddings and bar mitzvahs) and repeated attempts (in 1816, 1836 and 1839) to prevent

Jews from carrying Christian first names, so as not to blur the socio-legal boundaries between the two communities. Finally, the king supported the work of the Berlin Society for the Propagation of Christianity among the Jews, its daughter-societies in Königsberg, Breslau, Posen, Stettin and Frankfurt/Oder and the network of auxiliary groups in lesser towns. Missionary free schools in Posen – the area of densest Jewish settlement – exploited the new laws on elementary education to lure Jewish children into the classrooms of the missionaries. The Prussian state had become a missionary institute.[80]

The trend in his policy after 1815 suggests that Frederick William III gradually moved away from the functional conception of religion he had imbibed from the enlightened tutors of his youth towards a belief that the state might exist to pursue ends defined by religion. 'However strong the claim to tolerance may become,' he observed in 1821, 'a borderline must be drawn wherever this implies a step backwards on the road to the redemption of mankind.'[81] By the 1840s, the term 'Christian state' was in wide use; in 1847, following a debate in the United Diet over the admission of Jews to state office, Friedrich Julius Stahl, a conservative professor of law at the University of Berlin and a convert from Judaism, attempted to endow the idea with a measure of theoretical coherence. His book, *The Christian State*, argued that, since the state was 'a revelation of the ethical spirit of the nation', it must itself express the 'spirit of a Christian people'. It was thus unthinkable that Jews (and other non-believers) should occupy state office.[82]

Understandably enough, Jewish journalists denounced 'the phantom of the Christian state' as merely 'the very latest pretext for denying us our rights'.[83] Yet there was more to it than that. The Christian statism of the post-war era took root because it provided an outlet for the activist, utopian, evangelizing strand in contemporary Protestantism. Moreover, it generated an account, however limited, of the state's ultimate moral purpose. It invoked an identity between state and society that was religious, rather than ethnic and thus offered an alternative to nationalism, whose arguments were so threatening to the territorial sovereignty of the German princes after 1815. For pursuing these elusive benefits, the Prussian monarchy paid a heavy price. The aggressive confessional statism of the post-war era blurred the boundaries between religious and political dissent. Theological debates and affiliations were politicized. Political dissent acquired a theological flavour – it became both more absolute and more diffuse.

APOTHEOSIS OF THE STATE

In 1831, there were 13,151,883 subjects in the Kingdom of Prussia. Of these, about 5,430,000 (or roughly 41 per cent) lived in the provinces of Saxony, the Rhineland and Westphalia, areas that had been Prussian only since 1815. If we add the inhabitants of the Grand Duchy of Posen, annexed by Prussia following the second Polish partition of 1793, incorporated into the Napoleonic Duchy of Warsaw after the Peace of Tilsit in 1807 and only 'returned' to Prussia in 1815, then the proportion of new Prussians rises to nearly 50 per cent. The task of making Prussians had to begin anew. This problem was not unique to Prussia – Baden, Württemberg and Bavaria also emerged from the upheavals of the Napoleonic era with substantial new territories. In these states, however, the integration of new subjects was facilitated by the creation of territorial parliaments and the imposition of a unitary administrative and judicial structure. Prussia, by contrast, acquired no 'national' parliament and no 'national' constitution.

The kingdom also remained fragmented in an administrative sense. There was still no unitary legal fabric. The Berlin administration attempted to homogenize the system piecemeal in the 1820s, but Rhenish (i.e. Napoleonic) law remained valid in the western provinces, with the result that candidates for the judiciary there had to be trained within the Rhineland or Westphalia. Throughout the first half of the nineteenth century, there were, in addition to the *Geheime Obertribunal* in Berlin, four other supreme courts, including one for the Rhineland, one for Posen and one in Greifswald for formerly Swedish Pomerania.[84] The formerly Swedish part of Pomerania kept its own traditional legal code, its own institutions of communal and urban self-government, and its own distinctive municipal constitutions.[85] The Rhineland, too, retained the relatively liberal system of local governance introduced by the French.[86] The use of the Prussian General Code in most of the other provinces concealed the great variety of local laws and regulations. The Emancipation Edict of 11 March 1812 was not extended to the provinces acquired in 1815, so that the Jews of the kingdom lived under no fewer than thirty-three different legal codes. One district authority spoke of the state's having capitulated – in this sphere at least – to the provinces and localities.[87]

Prussia was therefore less juridically homogeneous in 1840 than it had been in 1813. It is worth emphasizing this fragmentation, because Prussia has often been perceived as the very model of a centralized state. Yet the thrust of the Stein municipal reforms had been precisely to devolve power upon what became a widely admired system of urban self-government. Even the more conservative Revised Municipal Law introduced in Westphalia in 1831 provided the towns with more autonomy than they had enjoyed under the Napoleonic system.[88] Throughout the post-war era, the organs of the central state adopted a deferential attitude to the grandees of the Prussian provinces, and the provincial elites remained strongly aware of their distinctive identities, especially in the peripheral areas of east and west. This tendency was amplified by the fact that whereas each province had its own diet, the kingdom as such had none. One effect of the constitutional settlement of 1823 was thus to magnify the significance of the provinces at the expense of the Prussian commonwealth. East Prussia was not 'merely a province', one visitor to Königsberg was told in 1851, but a *Land* in its own right. Prussia was in this sense a quasi-federal system.[89]

A devolved, pragmatic approach to government went hand in hand with an implicit acceptance of cultural diversity. Early nineteenth-century Prussia was a linguistic and cultural patchwork. The Poles of West Prussia, Posen and Silesia accounted for the largest linguistic minority; in the southern districts of East Prussia, the Masurians spoke various agrarian dialects of Polish; the Kashubians of the Danzig hinterland spoke another. Until the mid nineteenth century, the Dutch language was still widely used in the schools of the former Duchy of Kleve. In the Walloon districts of Eupen-Malmédy – a small east-Belgian territory that was transferred to Prussia in 1815 – French remained the language of schools, courts and administration until 1876.[90] The 'Philipponen', communities of Old Believers who settled in Masuria as refugees from Russia in 1828–32, spoke Russian – traces of their distinctive wooden churches can still be seen in the area today. There were communities of Czechs in Upper Silesia, Sorbs in the Cottbus district, and speakers of the ancient Slavic dialect of the Wends scattered across villages in the Spreewald near Berlin. Eking out an existence on the long spit of Baltic coastal land known as the Kurische Nehrung were the Kuren, inhabitants of one of the barest and most melancholy landscapes of northern Europe. These hardy fishermen spoke a dialect of Latvian and were known for supplementing their monotonous diet with the flesh of crows they caught and killed with a bite to the head. Some areas, such as the district of Gumbinnen in East Prussia, were trilingual, with substantial communities of Masurian, Lithuanian and German speakers living in close proximity.[91]

Prussian policy in the eastern provinces had traditionally been to treat these settlements as 'colonies' with their own distinctive cultures; indeed, the Prussian administration helped to consolidate provincial vernaculars by supporting them as the vehicle of religious instruction and elementary education. Protestant clerical networks were also important. They disseminated hymn books, Bibles and tracts in a range of local languages and offered bi-lingual services in minority language areas. The first Lithuanian-language periodical in the kingdom, *Nusidavimai*, was a missionary journal edited by a German-speaking pastor working among the Lithuanians.[92] German-speaking Prussians, such as the statesman and scholar Wilhelm von Humboldt and the Königsberg theology professor Martin Ludwig Rhesa, played a crucial role in establishing Lithuanian and its folk heritage as an object of wider cultural interest.[93] Not until 1876 did a general law define German as the official language of all parts of Prussia.

Prussia thus remained, in the words of a Scottish traveller who toured the Hohenzollern provinces in the 1840s, a 'kingdom of shreds and patches'. Prussia, Samuel Laing observed, 'has, in ordinary parlance, only a geographical or political meaning, denoting the Prussian government, or the provinces it governs – not a moral or social meaning. The Prussian nation is a combination of words rarely heard, of ideas never made [...]'[94] Laing's comment, though hostile, was insightful. What exactly did it mean to be 'Prussian'? The Prussia of the restoration era was not a 'nation' in the sense of a people defined and bound together by a common ethnicity. There was not, and never had been, a Prussian cuisine. Nor was there a specifically Prussian folklore, language, dialect, music or form of dress (leaving aside the uniforms of the military). Prussia was not a nation in the sense of a community sharing a common history. Moreover, 'Prussianness' had somehow to define itself on grounds that had not already been occupied by the powerful competing ideology of German nationalism. The result was a curiously abstract and fragmented sense of identity.

For some, Prussia meant the rule of law; hence the confidence with which Old Lutheran separatists in Silesia cited the Prussian General Code in their defence against arbitrary action by the state authorities.[95] To these humble subjects of the Prussian Crown, the code was a safeguard for freedom of conscience, a 'constitution' curtailing the state's right to intervene in the life of the subject. The law that guaranteed certain individual liberties also held out the promise of public order, another cherished feature of Prussian governance. In a Protestant song that circulated during the 'Cologne events' of the late 1830s, the anonymous author contrasted the arrogance and despotism of the Catholic clergy with the orderliness of the Prussian way of life:

> For us who live in Prussia's land
> The King is always lord;
> We live by law and the bonds of order,
> Not like some bickering horde.[96]

'Prussianness' thus came to imply commitment to a certain order of things. The 'secondary virtues' of Prussophile cliché – punctuality, loyalty, honesty, thoroughness, precision – were all attributes of service to a higher ideal.

To what ideal precisely? The time was past for the kind of king-cult that had thrived after the reign of Frederick the Great. The government did its best to propagate monarchist patriotism in the 1830s, but with limited success. The 'Prussia Song', adopted by the government as a kind of territorial anthem in the later 1830s, articulated an officially condoned version of Prussian patriotic sentiment. Written by Bernhard Thiersch, a teacher at the Halberstadt Gymnasium, and set to a jaunty marching tune by Heinrich August Neithard, director of music of the II Grenadier Guards Regiment, the song opened strongly with the words 'I am a Prussian, do you know my colours?' but soon lost itself in servile monarchist effusions. An imaginary Prussian – stoical, reserved and masculine – approaches the throne 'with love and loyalty' and hears from it the mild voice of a father. He swears filial allegiance; he feels the king's call vibrating in his heart; he observes that a people can really flourish only as long as the bonds of love and loyalty between king and subjects remain intact etc. etc. The '*Preussenlied*' was a good marching ditty, but it never took off as a popular song, and it is not difficult to see why.[97] Its field of reference was too narrowly military, the monarch at its centre too disembodied, the tone too grovelling to capture the boisterous aspirations expressed in popular patriotism.

The one institution that all Prussians had in common was the state. It is no coincidence that this period witnessed an unprecedented discursive escalation around the idea of the state. Its majesty resonated more compellingly than ever before, at least within the milieu of academia and senior officialdom. No individual did more to promulgate the dignity of the Prussian state after 1815 than Georg Wilhelm Friedrich Hegel, the Swabian philosopher who took up Fichte's vacant chair at the new University of Berlin in 1818. The state, Hegel argued, was an organism possessing will, rationality and purpose. Its destiny – like that of any living thing – was to change, grow and progressively develop. The state was 'the power of reason actualising itself as will';[98] it was a transcendent domain in which the alienated, competitive 'particular interests' of civil society merged into coherence and identity. There was a theological core to Hegel's reflections on the state: the state had a quasi-divine purpose; it was 'God's march through the world'; in Hegel's hands it became the quasi-divine apparatus by which the multitude of subjects who constituted civil society was redeemed into universality.

In adopting this approach, Hegel broke with the view prevalent among Prussian political theorists since Pufendorf and Wolff that the state was no more than a machine engineered to meet the external and internal security needs of the society that fashioned it.[99] Hegel vehemently rejected the metaphorical machine-state favoured by theorists of the high enlightenment, on the grounds that it treated 'free human beings' as if they were mere cogs in its mechanism. The Hegelian state was not an imposed construct, but the highest expression of the ethical substance of a people, the unfolding of a transcendent and rational order, the 'actualization of freedom'. From this it followed that the relationship between civil society and the state was not antagonistic, but reciprocal. It was the state that enabled civil society to order itself in a rational way, and the vitality of the state depended in turn upon each of the particular interests that constituted civil society being 'active in its particular function – equipping itself for its particular sphere and thereby promoting the universal'.[100]

Hegel's was not a liberal vision – he was not a champion of unitary national legislatures, having seen what they were capable of in Jacobin France. But the progressive orientation of his vision was undeniable. For all his misgivings about the Jacobin experiment, Hegel celebrated the French Revolution as a 'splendid dawn' that had been greeted with joy by 'all thinking people'. Hegel's Berlin students were told that the Revolution represented an 'irreversible achievement of the world spirit' whose consequences were still unfolding.[101] The centrality of reason and a sense of forward momentum suffuse his reflections on the state at every point. There was no place in the Hegelian polity for privileged castes and private jurisdictions. And by elevating the state above the plane of partisan strife, Hegel brought into view the exhilarating possibility that progress – in the sense of a beneficent rationalization of the political and social order – might simply be a property of the unfolding of history, as embodied in the Prussian state.[102]

It is difficult, from a present-day standpoint, to appreciate the intoxicating effect of Hegel's thought on a generation of educated Prussians. It was not a question of Hegel's pedagogical charisma – he was notorious for standing hunched over the lectern reading out his text in a halting and scarcely audible mumble. According to an account by his student Hotho, who attended Hegel's lectures at the University of Berlin, 'his features hung pale and loose upon him as if he were already dead.' 'He sat there morosely with his head wearily bowed down in front of him, constantly leafing back and forth through his compendious notes, even as he continued to speak.' Another student, the future Hegel-biographer Karl Rosenkranz, recalled laborious paragraphs punctuated by constant coughing and snuff-taking.[103]

It was the ideas themselves and the peculiar language Hegel invented to articulate them that colonized the minds of disciples across the kingdom. Part of the explanation lies in the context. Hegel's appointment was the work of the sometime Hardenberg protégé, enlightened reformer and Minister of Education Karl von Altenstein. The philosopher's writings provided an exalted legitimation for the Prussian bureaucracy, whose expanding power within the executive during the reform era demanded justification. Hegel steered a path between doctrinaire liberalism and restorationist conservatism – in an era of deepening political uncertainty, many found this *via media* enormously attractive. His writing balanced opposing standpoints, often with dazzling virtuosity. His

39. *Hegel at the lectern, surrounded by students. Lithograph from 1828 by Franz Kugler.*

dialectical wizardry, combined with an oracular and sometimes obfuscating mode of delivery, opened the work to diverse interpretations, enabling Hegelian language and ideas to flow seamlessly into the political ideologies of both right and left.[104] Finally, Hegel appeared to offer a means of reconciling the fact of political and social conflict with the hope for an ultimate harmony of interests and purposes.

'Hegelianism' was not the stuff that popular identities are made of. The master's work was notoriously difficult to read, let alone understand. Richard Wagner and Otto von Bismarck were among those who attempted without success to make sense of him. Moreover, his appeal was confessionally coloured. Hegel hailed from a Protestant Pietist milieu, whose imprint can be discerned in his attempts to assimilate the earthly to the divine order. Catholic students responded ambivalently to his teachings. In 1826, a group of Catholic students at the University of Berlin even made a formal complaint to the ministry of education: it seems that Hegel had made light of Catholic doctrine, observing that if a mouse were to nibble at a eucharist wafer after its consecration, then, by virtue of the sacramental miracle of transubstantiation, 'God would exist in the mouse and even in its excrement.'[105] Asked by the ministry to explain himself, Hegel invoked the principle of academic freedom

433

and added that Catholics were free to stay away from his lectures if they so wished. Even without such irritations, it was clear that Hegel's sacralization of the state held a more immediate appeal for Protestant adherents of the Prussian state church than for Catholics, whose relationship with the Protestant secular authority was more problematic.

Within the Protestant mainstream, however (not to mention assimilated Jewish circles), Hegel's influence was profound and lasting. His arguments diffused swiftly into the culture, partly through the students who crowded into his lectures and partly through the patronage of Culture Minister Altenstein and his privy councillor Johannes Schulze, a sometime Hegel student, who supported the candidacy of Hegelians for key academic posts, especially at the universities of Berlin and Halle. Hegelianism – like post-modernism – became ambient, infiltrating the language and thinking even of those who had never read or understood the master's work.

Hegel's influence helped to establish the modern state as a privileged object of enquiry and reflection. No one better exemplifies the discursive escalation that took place around the concept of the state during the years of realignment that followed the French Revolution. The state was no longer just the site of sovereignty and power, it was the engine that makes history, or even the embodiment of history itself. This distinctively Prussian intimacy between the idea of the state and the idea of history left abiding traces on the emergent cultural disciplines of the universities, not least history itself. Leopold von Ranke, the founder of history as a modern scholarly discipline, was no enthusiast of Hegel, whose philosophical system he denounced as unhistorical. Worlds lay between Hegel's metaphysical understanding of the 'history of human consciousness and spirit' and the obsessive quest for authentic sources and the insistence upon accurate description that were the hallmark of the nascent Prussian historical school. Yet the young Ranke, a Saxon who came to Prussia in 1818 at the age of twenty-three and was appointed to an academic post at the University of Berlin in 1825, did not entirely escape the contagion of Prussia's statist idealism. In essays published in 1833 and 1836, Ranke declared that the state was a 'moral good', and an 'idea of God', an organic being with its 'own original life', which 'penetrates its entire environment, identical only with itself'. Throughout the nineteenth and well into the twentieth century, the 'Prussian school' of history would remain overwhelmingly focused on the state as the vehicle and agent of historical change.[106]

After the philosopher's death during the cholera epidemic of 1831, Hegelianism disintegrated into warring schools and passed through swift ideological mutations. Among the raucous 'Young Hegelians' who coalesced in Berlin in the late 1830s was the youthful Karl Marx, a new Prussian from the Rhineland and the son of a Jewish convert to Christianity, who had moved to Berlin in 1836 to continue his studies in jurisprudence and political economy. For Marx, the first true encounter with Hegel's thought was a revelatory shock akin to a religious conversion. 'For some days', he told his father in November 1837, his excitement made him 'quite incapable of thinking'; he 'ran about madly in the garden by the dirty water of the Spree', even joined his landlord on a hunting excursion, and found himself overpowered by the desire to embrace every street corner loafer in Berlin.[107] Marx would later reject Hegel's understanding of the state bureaucracy as the 'general estate', but it stayed with him none the less. For what else was Marx's idealization of the proletariat as the 'pure embodiment of the general interest' than the materialist inversion of the Hegelian concept? Marxism, too, was made in Prussia.

13

Escalation

In the 1840s, political dissent across the European continent became better organized, more confident and socially more diverse. Popular cultures acquired a harder critical edge. An intensifying social crisis generated conflict and violence, confronting administrative and political establishments with problems they seemed unable to solve. This was the most turbulent phase of the post-Napoleonic 'age of flux and hiatus'.[1] In Prussia, these trends were amplified by a regime change. The death of Frederick William III on 7 July 1840 left an oppressive residue of unfinished business. The political predicaments of the previous reign were still unresolved. Above all, Frederick William III's 'solemn and famous promise' to grant a constitution remained, at his death, 'an unredeemed pledge'.[2] The hopes and expectations of liberals and radicals across the kingdom were focused on his successor.

A POLITICAL ROMANTIC

The new king, Frederick William IV, was already forty-five years old when he ascended the throne. He was something of a puzzle, even to those who knew him well. His predecessors, Frederick William III, Frederick William II and Frederick the Great, had all been educated in the spirit and values of the enlightenment. The new king, by contrast, was a product of the Romantic era. He had grown up on a diet of romantic historic novels – a favourite was the Prussian writer Friedrich de la Motte Fouqué, a descendant of the Huguenot colony in Branden-burg whose historical romances featured high-minded knights, damsels in distress, windswept crags, ancient castles and gloomy forests. Fred-erick William was a romantic not only in his tastes, but also in his personal life. He wept frequently. His letters to intimates and siblings were long unbosomings copiously sprinkled with batches of up to seven exclamation marks.[3]

Frederick William IV was the last Prussian – perhaps the last European – monarch to place religion at the centre of his understanding of kingship. He was a 'lay theologian on the throne', for whom religion and politics were inseparable.[4] At times of stress and high drama, he turned instinctively to biblical language and precedents. But his Christianity was not merely a matter of images and formulations; it shaped his policies and affected his choice of advisers.[5] Long before the death of his father in 1840, the crown prince surrounded himself with like-minded Christian friends. For his sceptical younger brother Prince William, writing in 1838, it was clear that the heir to the throne had fallen into the hands of a 'sect of enthusiasts'. Prince William complained that these 'fanatics' had been able to 'gain complete control of his entire person and his labile imagination'. The ethos of awakened Christianity had established itself so securely in the crown prince's following, Prince William argued, that ambitious courtiers with an eye on the future sovereign had merely to master the behavioural reflexes of Pietistic devotion in order to assure their advancement. The accession brought many of the crown prince's Christian friends – Leopold von Gerlach, Ludwig Gustav von Thile (known to his detractors as 'Bible Thile'), Count Anton von Stolberg-Wernigerode and Count Karl von der Groeben – into positions of political influence. These were men who had been involved with the Protestant awakening of the 1810s; some of them had close ties with the Pietist and Lutheran separatist movements on the fringes of the Prussian state church.

For Frederick William IV, as for his father, the Prussian state was a Christian institute. However, whereas Frederick William III had set out to impose his own eclectic brand of Calvino-Lutheranism on the Protestant congregations of Prussia and antagonized Prussia's Catholics by seeking a confrontation over the issue of mixed marriages, his son's Christianity was broader and more ecumenical. To the consternation of his father, Frederick William IV chose to marry a Catholic princess, Elisabeth of Bavaria, and insisted that she be allowed to convert in her own time (as indeed she duly did). His outspoken support for the refurbishment and completion of the great cathedral at Cologne reflected not only a characteristically romantic taste for the Gothic style, but also his determination to acknowledge Catholicism as a religion with historic and cultural claims to equality within the Prussian state.

The Anglo-Prussian bishopric in Jerusalem, founded in 1841 with the intention of evangelizing the Jews of the Holy Land and building contacts with the eastern Christians, was a uniquely ecumenical institution occupied in alternation by clergymen of the Church of England and the Prussian Union. Its chief architect was the king's close friend Carl Josias Bunsen, an expert on liturgical history who shared Frederick William's enthusiasm for the early Christian church.[6] Already as crown prince, Frederick William had been critical of the heavy-handed measures taken by his father's administration against the Lutheran dissidents in Silesia and Pomerania. One of his earliest acts as king was to order the release of those Old Lutheran clergymen who had been imprisoned during the confrontations of the late 1830s. The obstacles to the creation of a separate Lutheran territorial church were gradually removed and the flow of Lutheran emigrants to North America and Australia came to an end.

Frederick William was not a liberal. Nor, on the other hand, was he an authoritarian statist conservative in the Kamptz-Rochow-Wittgenstein mould. The governmental conservatism of the Restoration era was rooted in the authoritarian strand of the Prussian enlightenment. By contrast, Frederick William was steeped in the corporatist ideology of the romantic counter-enlightenment. He was not opposed to representative bodies as such, but they had to be 'natural', 'organic', 'grown'; in other words, they had to correspond to the natural and god-given hierarchy of human status and accomplishment, as exemplified in the medieval 'society of orders'. Underlying his vision of politics and history was an emphasis on continuity and tradition – a response, perhaps, to the trauma he experienced in 1806 as he fled eastwards with his mother from the advancing French and to his mother's sudden death in 1810, during Prussia's 'time of iron'. Frederick William's attitude to the modern bureaucratic Prussian state was ambivalent. The state did not in his view embody the living forces of historical continuity; it was an artificial thing whose claim to universal authority violated the older and more sacred authority of the locality, the congregation, the corporation. The king was thus more than a supreme administrator, and certainly more than the first servant of the state. He was a sacred father, bound to his people in a mystical union and gifted by God with a peerless understanding of his subjects' needs.[7]

The king articulated these commitments in a language that could sound almost liberal. It was a feature of the idiom of political romanticism that it tended at least superficially to blur the differences between progressive and conservative positions. Frederick William spoke admiringly of Britain and its 'ancient constitution'. He was open – like his romantic Bavarian colleague Ludwig I – to the appeal of German cultural nationalism. He invoked the buzzwords 'renewal', 'revitalization' and 'development' and denounced the evils of 'bureaucracy' and 'despotism' in a way that seemed to speak to liberal aspirations. One of the king's closest friends recognized that he expounded a diffuse combination of 'Pietism', 'medievalism' and 'aristocratism' with 'patriotism', 'liberalism' and 'Anglomania'.[8]

All this made Frederick William IV a difficult man to read. Hyperbolic expectations of political change often attend a change of regime. They were encouraged in this case by early signs of a more liberal course. The new monarch immediately announced that all the Prussian provincial diets were to meet at the beginning of 1841 and thereafter every two years (under his father they had met every three years); he also spoke of the 'reinvigoration' of representative politics.[9] In September 1840, when the Königsberg Diet presented a memorandum begging the monarch to grant a 'representation of the entire land and of the people', Frederick William replied that he intended 'to continue cultivating this noble work' and to oversee its further 'development'.[10] What exactly the king meant by these words was unclear, but they aroused huge excitement. Political offenders were released from confinement, and Ernst Moritz Arndt was permitted to resume his teaching post at the University of Bonn. Censorship restrictions were relaxed. There were also concessions to the Poles in the province of Posen. On 19 August 1840, there was a general amnesty for Poles who had taken part in the November uprising of 1830. The provocative Eduard Flottwell was removed in 1841, political émigrés from Russian Poland were permitted to take up residence in the province, the German settlement policy was abandoned, and a new school language ordinance met the basic demands of the Polish activists.[11]

The new minister of education, health and religious affairs, Johann Albrecht Friedrich Eichhorn, who took up his post in October 1840, was a former collaborator of Stein and one of the architects of the Customs Union; his entry into the ministry of state kindled liberal hopes.[12] Another hopeful sign was the political rehabilitation of Hermann Boyen, the veteran champion of military and political reform, who had been forced out of public life by the conservative ministers in 1819. Now seventy-one years old, Boyen was recalled to Berlin and appointed minister of war. The new king fêted the elderly warrior, assigning him the first place in the ministry of state (on grounds of his seniority) and appointing him to the command of the I Infantry Regiment. At the unveiling of a monument to Gneisenau, Frederick William presented Boyen with the Order of the Black Eagle – eloquent testimony to the king's determination to close the gap between patriotic and dynastic memories of the war against Napoleon. Boyen's dramatic rehabilitation sent out clear political signals – the old man had only recently offended conservative opinion with a polemically partisan biography of the great patriot and military reformer Scharnhorst.

The accession of the new monarch also brought an end to the career of Police Chief Karl Christoph Albert Heinrich von Kamptz, that zealous hunter of demagogues who had worked with Wittgenstein to shut down political dissent in the post-war years. In the 1830s, Kamptz had become a hate figure whose name often cropped up in the songs and poems of the radical opposition. He was shocked to receive, while taking the waters in Gastein in the summer of 1841, a note from Berlin informing him that the 'vitality and spiritual energy' of His Majesty called for younger and more vigorous servants.[13] The impact of such signal interventions was enhanced by the vibrant personal style of the new monarch. Frederick William IV received the homage of the Prussian Estates in Königsberg and Berlin, as his predecessors had done, but he was the first of his dynasty to follow up the formal part of the proceedings with an impromptu public address to the crowds gathered before the palace. These two speeches, delivered in a passionate, evangelical, plebiscitary idiom, had an electrifying effect on spectators and public opinion.[14]

The exhilaration and optimism generated by the inaugural ceremonies and the king's speeches quickly dissipated, however. Alarmed by the intensity of liberal speculation, the king took steps to quash press discussion of his constitutional plans. In a cabinet order of 4 October, Interior Minister Gustav von Rochow was ordered to announce that the king regretted any misunderstandings that had arisen from his reply to the Königsberg diet and wished it to be known that he had no intention of granting its request for a national assembly. This announcement met with disappointment and bitterness, compounded by the fact that the bad news came from the desk of Rochow, a hardliner from the previous reign who was loathed by liberals throughout the kingdom.[15]

Among those who found themselves at loggerheads with the new regime was the long-serving provincial president in Königsberg, Theodor von Schön. Schön was an emblematic figure, even for his contemporaries. He had made repeated journeys to England in his youth; throughout his life he remained a Smithian economic liberal and an admirer of the British parliamentary system. He had been a close associate of Stein, indeed he had drafted Stein's Political Testament of 1808, which called for a 'general national representation'. Only through the 'participation of the people in the operations of the state', Schön had written, could the 'national spirit be positively aroused and animated'.[16] During the early post-war years he worked with considerable success to develop the basis for a constructive interplay between the regional government and corporate assemblies in West Prussia. Like many moderate reformers, he was aware of the limitations of the provincial diets established in 1823, but welcomed them none the less as a platform for further constitutional development.[17] As the provincial president of East Prussia, he was a powerful local boss who held one of the pivotal offices in the post-Napoleonic Prussian state. He also stood at the head of an influential party of liberal East Prussian noblemen, including the Lord Mayor of Königsberg, Rudolf von Auerswald.

During the press debate that followed the homage of the Estates in September 1840, Schön composed the essay *Where Are We Headed?* in which he celebrated the era of reform, lamented the 'bureaucratic [. . .] reaction' that followed and called for the establishment of a general Estates assembly: 'Only with national representative institutions,' he argued, 'can public life begin and develop in our state.' Published in a limited edition of only thirty-two copies, *Where Are We Headed?* circulated privately among the Provincial President's closest friends and associates. Schön also presented a copy to the king, presumably in the belief that he and the new monarch, whom he knew well, were essentially in agreement on the constitutional question. Frederick William's reply to Schön's tract was sharp and unequivocal. He would never allow a 'piece of paper' (constitution) to come between him and his subjects. It was his sacred duty, he declared, to continue ruling Prussia in 'patriarchal' fashion; 'artificial' organs of representation were unnecessary.[18]

Relations between Berlin and Königsberg quickly cooled and the conservatives in Berlin seized the opportunity to reaffirm their control over the government's policy.[19] Interior Minister Gustav von Rochow raised the stakes by sending Schön the text of a radical song that had been passed to the Berlin police, in which the East Prussian provincial president was lauded as a 'teacher of liberty'. Schön responded to this provocation with undisguised disdain, rebuking the minister and denouncing him as a danger to the state he served. A bitter press feud broke out; Schön's friends launched salvos against the interior minister in the East Prussian liberal newspapers, while Rochow ordered his subordinates in the ministry to plant poison-pen pieces, not only in Prussian journals, but also in the Leipzig and the Augsburg *Allegemeine Zeitungen* – such was the importance Prussian officials attached to the state of public opinion in the other German territories. The clash came to a head in May 1842, when *Where Are We Headed?* was republished without Schön's permission by a radical in Strasbourg. The new edition included a long afterword attacking the king. Schön's dismissal was announced on 3 June, followed by that of Rochow ten days later; Frederick William IV wished to avoid the appearance of partisanship that might have been conveyed by removing only one of the two antagonists.

What was significant about the Schön–Rochow showdown was not the enmity between two powerful servants of the Prussian Crown, for this was nothing new, but the extraordinary public resonance of the struggle. In October 1841, when he returned to Königsberg from a sitting of the state ministry in Berlin, Schön was welcomed like a hero: boats flying festive pennants sailed out to meet him as he entered the harbour and the windows of his many Königsberg supporters were illuminated that evening. On 8 June 1843, a year after his removal from office, the liberals in Königsberg orchestrated festivities to celebrate the fiftieth anniversary of the former president's entry into state service. A collection was organized, and so widely had Schön's fame spread across Germany that contributions flowed in from sympathetic liberals as far afield as Baden and Württemberg. The amount collected sufficed to liquidate the remaining debt on the Schön family estate at Arnau, with enough left over to finance the erection of a memorial obelisk in the city. For the first time in Prussian history, a senior state official had allowed himself to be celebrated as the figurehead of a dissident political movement.

The political frustrations that attended the accession of Frederick

William IV were no passing storm; they signalled an irreversible elevation in the political temperature. There was a dramatic sharpening
and refinement of critical politics. The radical Jewish physician Johann
Jakoby was a member of a group of like-minded friends who met for
political discussions at Siegel's Café in Königsberg. His pamphlet, *Four
Questions, Answered by an East Prussian*, published in 1841, demanded
'lawful participation in the affairs of state', not as a concession or favour,
but as an 'inalienable right'. Jakoby was subsequently arraigned on
charges of treason but was acquitted after a chain of trials by an appeals
court; in the process he became one of the most celebrated figures of the
Prussian opposition movement. By contrast with the genteel Theodor
von Schön and his noble circle, Jakoby represented the more impatient
activism of the urban professional classes. The radicalized intellectuals
of the urban elites found a forum in the new political associations that
proliferated across the major Prussian cities – the *Ressource* in Breslau,
the Citizens' Club in Magdeburg and the Thursday Society in Königsberg, which was a more formally constituted version of the Siegel's Café
group.[20] But political participation could unfold in many other contexts
as well – in the Cathedral Building Society of Cologne, for example,
which became an important meeting place for liberals and radicals, or
at the lectures given by visiting speakers in the wine gardens of the city
of Halle.[21]

Within the provincial diets, too, there was an unmistakable change in
tone. The demands articulated here and there by individual assemblies
during the 1830s now merged into an all-Prussian chorus. In 1841 and
1843, virtually all the diets passed resolutions calling for freedom of
the press. In 1843, the Rhenish Diet – supported by a broad swathe
of middle-class opinion – rejected a new and in many respects quite
progressive Prussian penal code because it breached the principle of
equality before the law by incorporating penalties that varied in accordance with a person's corporate status.[22] The campaigns mounted in
support of petitions to the diet grew dramatically in size and public
resonance.[23] The Polish national movement in the province of Posen was
initially reluctant to support liberal calls for a national parliament, on
the ground that this would further integrate the province into the fabric
of the kingdom. But by 1845, Polish patriots and German liberals among
the deputies to the diet were ready to join forces in demanding a wide
range of liberal measures.[24]

If the liberals had begun to coalesce into a 'party of movement' by the 1840s, the same could not be said of conservatives. Conservatism (a retrospective construct, since the term was not yet in use) remained a diffuse, fragmented phenomenon whose diverse threads had not been woven into a coherent fabric. The nostalgic rural paternalism so eloquently expressed by the estate owner Friedrich August Ludwig von der Marwitz remained a minority taste, even among the landed nobility. The 'historical school', formed by opponents of Hegelian philosophy at the University of Berlin, embraced too many conflicting perspectives, not all of which were 'conservative' in any straightforward sense, to furnish the basis for an abiding coalition. Those conservatives whose outlook was rooted in the neo-Pietist commitment of the Awakening found it difficult to see eye to eye with those who were inspired by the secular authoritarian statism of the late eighteenth century. The ambivalent attitude of many conservatives towards the bureaucratic state also made collaboration with the authorities difficult. The *Berliner Politisches Wochenblatt*, formed by ultraconservatives in 1831, conceived of itself as a loyalist organ directed against the forces unleashed by the July Revolution in France, but this newspaper soon fell foul of the Prussian censorship authorities, whose officials, according to the paper's disgruntled sponsor, were men of 'liberalistic' temperament. After struggling to acquire a secure readership, the paper went under in 1841.[25]

Conservatives were thus in no position to coordinate a response to the expansion of liberal dissent. Most either fished around for compromises or lapsed into a resigned awareness of the inevitability of change. Even within the Cabinet, there was little sign of a unified conservative bloc. The political discussions among ministers were surprisingly speculative, conflictual and open-ended, a feature that was encouraged – or at least tolerated – by the king himself.[26] In October 1843, Leopold von Gerlach, commander of the I Guards *Landwehrbrigade* in Spandau on the outskirts of Berlin and a close personal friend of the king, reflected on the political situation in Prussia. What worried him was not just the pressure building behind demands for constitutional reform, but also the failure of the conservatives – even within the government – to form a united front against it. Several of the ministers – including the supposedly archconservative 'Bible Thile' – had begun to talk 'quite uninhibitedly' of conceding a Chamber of Deputies. The ship of state,

Gerlach observed, was sailing in the direction of Jacobinism, driven by the 'always freshly blowing wind of the Zeitgeist'. He listed various steps that might help to arrest the process of liberalization, but he was under no illusions about the prospects of success. 'What can these little manoeuvres possibly achieve,' he concluded, 'against the onward pressing Zeitgeist, which, with satanic cleverness, wages an unceasing and systematic war against the authority established by God?'[27]

In these circumstances, it was inconceivable that the king would be able to re-sculpt society in the image of his neo-corporate ideology. He made an unsuccessful attempt to do so in 1841, when he declared in a cabinet order that the Jews of Prussia should be organized for administrative purposes into *Judenschaften* (Jewries), whose elected deputies would represent the interests of the Jewish communities before the local authorities. The order also stated that Jews were to be absolved of the obligation to perform military service. Neither of these measures was ever carried out. The king's own ministers opposed them – Interior Minister Rochow and the new minister for religious and educational affairs, Karl Friedrich Eichhorn, objected that the proposals ran counter to the recent development of Prussian society. A survey of district governments revealed that these, too, were opposed to the king's plan. Local administrations were prepared to bestow corporate legal status upon Jewish religious institutions, but they were strongly opposed to the imposition of corporate status in the broader political sense favoured by Frederick William, which they saw as hindering the all-important process of societal assimilation. Indeed the vehemence and candour with which they rejected this royal hobby-horse are remarkable. The district government of Cologne even pressed for full and unconditional emancipation of the Jewish minority, pointing out the success of this policy in France, Holland, Belgium and England. The officials of the 1840s were not servile *Untertanen* (subjects) bent on 'working towards' their king. They viewed themselves as autonomous participants in the policy-making process.[28]

As the Jewish initiative suggests, Frederick William's neo-corporatist vision was out of tune, not only with public opinion in the broadest sense, but even with the prevalent ethos of the administration itself, which found it increasingly difficult to reach consensus on the great political questions of the day. To liberals and radicals, and even to some conservatives, the politics of the new reign seemed fundamentally incoherent, 'a deranged mixture of the extremes of our time'.[29] No one captured the resulting sense of disconnection better than the radical theologian David Friedrich Strauss, whose pamphlet *A Romantic on the Throne of the Caesars* was published in Mannheim in 1847. Strauss's tract purported to be about the Emperor known as Julian the Apostate, but was in fact a caricature of the Prussian king, who was depicted as an unworldly dreamer, a man who had turned nostalgia for the ancients into a way of life and whose eyes were closed to the pressing needs of the present.[30]

POPULAR POLITICS

The expansion of political activism around the diets took place against the background of a broader process of politicization that reached deep into the hinterlands of the Prussian provinces. In the Rhineland in particular the 1840s saw dramatic growth in the popular consumption of newspapers. Rates of literacy were very high in Prussia by European standards, and even those who could not read for themselves could hear newspapers being read aloud in taverns. Beyond the newspapers, and far more popular with the general public, were 'people's calendars' (*Volkskalender*), a traditional, cheap, mass-distributed print format that offered a mixture of news, fiction, anecdotes, and practical advice. By the 1840s, the market in calendars had become highly differentiated, catering to a range of political preferences.[31] Even the traditional commerce in popular printed prophecy acquired a sharper political edge in the 1840s. Of particular concern to the Prussian authorities was the 'Prophecy of Lehnin', a text of obscure origin that appeared to divine the future of the House of Hohenzollern. The Prophecy of Lehnin, which circulated widely in the Rhineland, had traditionally foretold the imminent conversion of the royal house to Catholicism – reason enough in itself to attract the hostile attention of the authorities – but the early 1840s saw the appearance of a more radical version predicting that the 'infamous king' would be punished with death for his role in an 'atrocity'.[32]

This creeping politicization of popular culture was not confined to the print media. Song was an even more ubiquitous medium for the articulation of political dissent. In the Rhineland, where memories of the French Revolution were especially vivid, the records of the local police are full of references to the singing of forbidden 'liberty songs', including endless variations on the *Marseillaise* and the *Ça ira*. Liberty songs recalled the life and deeds of Kotzebue's assassin Karl Sand, celebrated the virtuous struggles of the Greeks or the Poles against Ottoman and Russian tyranny and commemorated moments of public insurrection against illegitimate authority. No fair or public festivity was complete, moreover, without travelling ballad-singers (*Bänkelsänger*), whose songs were often irreverently political in content. Even the 'peep-show men', travelling performers who exhibited *trompe-l'oeil* scenes, were adept at weaving witty political critiques into their commentaries, so that even ostensibly harmless landscape views became pretexts for satire.[33]

From the 1830s, carnivals and other popular traditional festivities such as Maypole ceremonies and charivaris also tended increasingly to carry a (dissenting) political message.[34] By the 1840s, the carnivals of the Rhineland – especially the elaborate processions orchestrated on the Monday before Ash Wednesday – had become a focal point for political tension between locals and the Prussian authorities. With its anarchic, twelfth-night atmosphere, in which conventional social and political relationships were inverted or satirized, the carnival was suited to become an eloquent medium of political protest. It was precisely in order to discipline the unruly energies of the street festival that carnival societies were founded in the Rhineland in the 1820s and 1830s. By the early 1840s, however, these too had been infiltrated by the spirit of dissent. In 1842, the Cologne carnival society split when radical members declared that 'the republican carnival constitution' was the only one 'under which true foolishness could flourish'. They intended to enthrone a 'carnival king' whose authority was to be defended by a 'standing army of fools'. The unusually radical Düsseldorf carnival society was also known for its harsh satires of the monarch.[35]

Ridicule of the king was an increasingly prominent feature of dissenting utterances in Prussia during the 1830s and 1840s. Although only 575 cases of *lèse-majesté* were actually investigated during the decade between 1837 and 1847, the records suggest that a multitude of other such misdemeanours went unprosecuted, and we can presume that many more again never came to the attention of the police at all. Yet such cases as did come before the courts were generally treated seriously.

When the tailor Joseph Jurowski from Warmbrunn in Silesia declared in a drunken moment 'our Freddy is a scoundrel; the king is a scoundrel and a swindler', he received the remarkably harsh sentence of eighteen months in jail. The judicial official Balthasar Martin, from near the city of Halberstadt, was sentenced to six months of imprisonment for stating, while sitting in a tavern, that the king 'drank five or six bottles of champagne a day'. 'How can the king take care of us?', Martin asked his listeners, presumably unaware that a police informer was sitting among them. 'He's a lush, the lush of lushes, he only drinks the really potent stuff.'[36]

These calumnies referred to an image of the king that by the mid-1840s had established itself ineradicably within the popular imagination. Frederick William IV, a plump, plain, unmilitary man who was known as 'fatty flounder' to his siblings and close friends, was the least physically charismatic individual to occupy the Hohenzollern throne since the reign of the first king. He was also the first Prussian king ever to be lampooned in numerous satirical images. Perhaps the most famous contemporary depiction, produced in 1844, portrays the monarch as a portly, drunken puss-in-boots clutching a bottle of champagne in his left paw and a foaming glass in his right, pathetically attempting to ape Frederick the Great against the backdrop of the palace complex at Sans Souci. Having relaxed literary censorship shortly after his accession to the throne, Frederick William reimposed the censorship of images, but it proved impossible to prevent grotesque visual satires of the monarch from circulating widely across the kingdom.[37]

Perhaps the most extreme expression of disregard for the person of the sovereign was the *Tschechlied*, a song that recalled the attempted assassination of the king by the mentally disturbed former village mayor Heinrich Ludwig Tschech. Tschech had failed to secure official support for a crusade against local corruption in his native Storkow and fell under the delusion that the monarch was personally to blame for his misfortune. On 26 July 1844, having had himself photographed in a theatrical pose by a daguerreotypist in Berlin, Tschech walked up to the royal carriage and fired two shots at close range, both of which missed. The public initially responded with a wave of sympathy for the king, although it was also widely expected that Tschech would be spared the death penalty in view of his abnormal mental condition. Frederick William was at first inclined to grant him clemency, but his ministers

*40. Frederick William IV as a tipsy Puss-in-Boots trying vainly
to follow in the footsteps of Frederick the Great.
Anonymous lithograph.*

insisted that he be made an example of. When it became known in
December that Tschech had been executed in secret, public sentiment
swung against the king.[38] Over the following years a range of Tschech
songs circulated in Berlin and across the German states. Their irreverence
is captured in the following stanza:

> A fortune ill beyond compare
> Befell poor Tschech the village mayor,
> That he, though shooting close at hand,
> Could not hit this bloated man![39]

THE SOCIAL QUESTION

In the summer of 1844, the Silesian textile district around Peterswaldau and Langenbielau became the scene of the bloodiest upheaval in Prussia before the revolutions of 1848. The trouble began on 4 July, when a crowd attacked the headquarters of Zwanziger Brothers, a substantial textile firm in Peterswaldau. The firm was regarded in the locality as an inconsiderate employer that had exploited the region's oversupply of labour to depress wages and degrade working conditions. 'The Zwanziger Brothers are hangmen,' a popular local song declared.

> Their servants are the knaves.
> Instead of protecting their workers,
> They crush us down like slaves.[40]

Having broken into the main residence, the weavers smashed everything they could lay their hands on, from tiled ovens and gilt mirrors to chandeliers and costly porcelain. They tore to shreds all the books, bonds, promissory notes, records and papers they could find, then stormed through an adjacent complex of stores, rolling presses, packing rooms, sheds and warehouses, smashing everything as they went. The work of destruction continued until nightfall, bands of weavers making their way to the scene from outlying villages. On the next morning, the weavers returned to demolish the few structures that remained intact, including the roof. The entire complex would probably have been torched, had someone not pointed out that this would entitle the owners to compensation through their fire insurance.

Armed with axes, pitchforks and stones, the weavers, by now some 3,000 in number, marched out of Peterswaldau and found their way to the house of the Dierig family in Langenbielau. Here they were told by frightened company clerks that a cash payment (five silver groschen) had been promised to any weaver who agreed not to attack the firm's buildings. Meanwhile two companies of infantry under the command of a Major Rosenberger had arrived from Schweidnitz to restore order; these formed up in the square before the Dierig house. All the ingredients of the disaster that followed were now in place. Fearing that the Dierig house was about to be attacked, Rosenberger gave the order to fire. After three salvos, eleven lay dead on the ground; they included a woman

Hunger und Verzweiflung

41. *How the weavers suffered; and how the state responded. This woodcut published in the radical journal* Fliegende Blätter *in 1844 refers to the Silesian uprising of that year and bears the caption:* Hunger and Desperation.

and a child who had been with the crowd, but also several bystanders, including a little girl who had been on her way to a sewing lesson and a woman looking on from her doorway some 200 paces away. Eye-witnesses reported that one man's head had been smashed by the shot; the blood-flecked pan of his skull was thrown several feet from his body. The defiance and rage of the crowd now knew no bounds. The troops were driven away by a desperate charge and during the night the weavers rampaged through the Dierig house and its attached buildings, de-stroying eighty thousand thalers worth of goods, furnishings, books and papers.

The worst was over. Early on the following morning troop reinforce-ments, complete with artillery pieces, arrived in Langenbielau and the crowd of those who remained in or around the Dierig buildings was quickly dispersed. There was some further rioting in nearby Fried-richsgrund, and also in Breslau, where a crowd of artisans attacked Jewish houses, but the troops stationed in the city managed to prevent any further tumults. About fifty persons were arrested in connection with the unrest; of these eighteen were sentenced to terms of imprison-ment with hard labour and corporal punishment (twenty-four lashes).[41]

There were many tumults and hunger riots in the Prussian lands during the 1840s, but none resonated in public awareness like the Sile-sian weavers' revolt. Despite the best efforts of the censors, the news of the revolt and its suppression spread across the kingdom within days. From Königsberg and Berlin to Bielefeld, Trier, Aachen, Cologne, Elber-feld and Düsseldorf, there were extensive press commentaries and public discussion. There was a flowering of radical weaver poems, among them Heinrich Heine's apocalyptic incantation of 1844, 'The Poor Weavers', in which the poet invokes the misery and futile rage of a life of endless work on a starvation wage:

> The crack of the loom and the shuttle's flight;
> We weave all day and we weave all night.
> Germany, we're weaving your coffin-sheet;
> Still weaving, ever weaving!

Numerous essays appeared over the following months analysing the uprising from every possible angle.

The Silesian events caused a sensation because they spoke to a fashion-able contemporary obsession with what was coming to be known as 'the Social Question' – there are parallels with the almost contemporary British debate that greeted the appearance of Carlyle's essay of 1839 on the 'Condition of England'. The Social Question embraced a complex of issues: working conditions within factories, the problem of housing in densely populated areas, the dissolution of corporate entities (e.g. guilds, estates), the vicissitudes of a capitalist economy based on compe-tition, the decline of religion and morals among the emergent 'prole-tariat'. But the central and dominant issue was 'pauperization', the progressive impoverishment of the lower social strata. The 'pauperism' of the pre-March era differed from traditional forms of poverty in a number of important ways: it was a mass phenomenon, collective and structural, rather than dependent upon individual contingencies, such as sickness, injury or crop failures; it was permanent rather than seasonal; and it showed signs of engulfing social groups whose position had previously been relatively secure, such as artisans (especially apprentices and journeymen) and smallholding peasants. 'Pauperism,' the *Brockhaus Encyclopaedia* noted in 1846, 'occurs when a large class can subsist only as a result of the most intensive labour . . .'[42] The key problem was a decline in the value of labour and its products. This affected not only unskilled labourers and those who worked in the craft trades, but also the large and growing section of the rural population who lived from various forms of cottage industry.

The deepening misery was reflected in patterns of food consumption: whereas the inhabitants of the Prussian Rhine province consumed on average forty-one kilos of meat per annum in 1838, this figure had fallen to thirty by 1848.[43] A statistical survey of 1846 suggested that between 50 and 60 per cent of the Prussian population were living on or near the subsistence minimum. In the early 1840s, the deepening of poverty across the kingdom triggered a moral panic among the Prussian literary classes. Bettina von Arnim's *This Book Belongs to the King*, published in Berlin in 1843, opened with an emotive essay by Arnim imploring the new monarch, Frederick William IV (r. 1840–59), to inaugurate a 'social monarchy' dedicated to alleviating the social crisis in the kingdom.[44] Included in the text was a detailed appendix recording the observations of Heinrich Grunholzer, a 23-year-old Swiss student, in the slums of Berlin. Over the three decades between 1816 and 1846, the population of the capital had risen from 197,000 to 397,000. Many of the poorest immigrants – wage labourers and artisans for the most part – settled in the densely populated slum area on the northern outskirts of the city known as the 'Vogtland' because many of the earliest arrivals hailed from the Vogtland in Saxony. It was here that Grunholzer recorded his observations for Arnim's book.

In an era that has become inured to the authenticity-effect of documentary, it is hard to recapture the fascination of Grunholzer's bald descriptions of life in the most desolate corners of the capital. He spent four weeks combing through a few selected tenements and interviewing their occupants. He recorded his impressions in a spare prose that was paced out in short, informal sentences, and integrated the brutal statistics that governed the lives of the poorest families in the city. Passages of dialogue were woven into the narrative and the frequent use of the present tense suggested notes scribbled *in situ*.

In basement room no. 3, I found a woodchopper with a diseased leg. When I entered, the wife grabbed the potato peelings from the table and a sixteen-year-old daughter withdrew embarrassed into a corner of the room while her father began to tell me his tale. He had been rendered unemployable while helping to construct the new School of Engineering. His request for assistance was long ignored. Only when he was economically completely ruined was he granted a monthly allowance of 15 silver groschen [half a thaler]. He had to move back into the family apartment, because he could no longer afford an apartment in the city. Now he receives two thalers monthly from the Poor Office. In times when the incurable disease of his leg permits, he can earn one thaler a month; his wife earns twice that amount, his daughter can bring in an additional one-and-a-half thalers. But their accommodation costs two thalers a month, a 'meal of potatoes' one silver groschen and nine pennies; at two such meals a day, this comes to three-and-a-half thalers per month for the staple nourishment. One thaler thus remains for the purchase of wood and for all that a family needs, aside from raw potatoes, in order to survive.[45]

Another work in the same vein was Friedrich Wilhelm Wolff's widely read article on the 'vaults of Breslau', a shanty-town area of former barracks and military stores on the outskirts of the Silesian capital, which appeared in the *Breslauer Zeitung* in November 1843. Wolff, the son of a poor Silesian farmer who became a renowned radical journalist, claimed to describe a world that was both close and remote, a world that lay, as he put it, like an 'open book' before the walls of the city but was invisible to most of its better-off inhabitants. There was doubtless an element of voyeuristic pleasure in the consumption of such texts by bourgeois readers – an important influence on the burgeoning literature of social thick description was Eugène Sue's remarkable blockbusting ten-volume novel of the Parisian underworld, *Les Mystères de Paris*, which appeared in instalments during 1842–3 and was widely imitated across Europe. If readers were prepared to lose themselves in Sue's colourful *demimonde*, Wolff declared, then they should take all the more interest in the real 'mystères de Breslau' before their own doorstep.[46] In almost identical language August Brass, author of *Mysteries of Berlin* (1844), insisted that anyone could observe the misery of the underworld in the capital if they merely 'took the trouble to cast off the convenient veil of selfish comforts' and cast their gaze outside their 'usual circles'.[47]

By the early months of 1844, all eyes were fixed on the mountainous textile districts of Silesia, where years of falling prices and slackening demand had driven entire communities of weavers into grinding poverty. There were collections for the Silesians in the textile towns of the Rhineland. During March, the poet and radical literary scholar Karl Grün toured from town to town holding popular lectures on Shakespeare, the proceeds from which were sent via the provincial government to help the weavers of the Liegnitz district. In the same month, the Association for the Alleviation of Need among the Weavers and Spinners of Silesia was founded in Breslau. During May, on the eve of the uprising, Alexander Schneer, an official in the provincial administration and a member of the Breslau association, walked from house to house in some of the most affected areas, meticulously documenting the circumstances of weaver families in the manner pioneered by Grunholzer.[48] In this sensitized environment, it is hardly surprising that contemporaries viewed the uprising of June 1844 not as an inadmissible tumult, but as the inevitable expression of an underlying social malaise.

The apparent correlation between rising population and mass poverty may lead us to suspect that the social crisis of this era was the result of a 'Malthusian trap', in which the needs of the population exceeded the available supply of food.[49] This view is misleading, at least for Prussia. During the post-war decades, technical improvements (artificial fertilizers, modernized animal husbandry and the three-field rotation system) and an increase in land under cultivation doubled the productivity of agriculture. As a result, the food supply increased at about twice the rate of population growth. The problem was not, therefore, chronic underproduction. Large agricultural surpluses could also have a harmful effect on manufacturing, however, since they depressed the prices of agricultural produce. The resulting collapse in agrarian incomes entailed a corresponding decline in the demand for goods from the overcrowded manufacturing sector.

More importantly, food supplies remained vulnerable despite the impressive growth in total agricultural production, because natural catastrophes – poor harvests, cattle epidemics, crop diseases – could still turn the surplus into a drastic shortfall. The crisis that unfolded from the winter of 1846, when harvest failures sent food prices up to double and even triple the normal average, was a case in point. The crisis of 1846–7 was compounded by a downturn in the business cycle and a crop disease that wiped out the potato harvests upon which the poor in many areas had become dependent (Grunholzer, for example, had found in 1842 that potatoes were the main – and indeed virtually the only – food-stuff consumed by the poorest families he visited in the Vogtland in Berlin).

The pressure exerted by subsistence crises produced waves of unrest. In Prussia, 158 food riots – including marketplace disturbances, attacks on stores and shops, and transportation blockades – took place during April–May 1847 alone, when food prices were at their highest. On 21–22 April, the population of Berlin stormed and plundered market stalls and shops and attacked potato merchants.[50] Interestingly enough, the geography of food riots did not coincide with that of the most acute shortage. Tumults were more likely to occur in areas that produced food for export, or in transit areas with high levels of food transportation. The Prussian territories bordering on the Kingdom of Saxony were thus particularly riot-prone, because the demand generated by the relatively industrialized Saxon economy ensured that grain exports passed through these areas.

Far from being politically subversive, such protests were generally pragmatic attempts to control the food supply, or to remind the authorities of their traditional obligation to provide for afflicted subjects, along the lines of the 'moral economy' famously theorized by E. P. Thompson in his study of the eighteenth-century English crowd.[51] Rioters did not act as members of a class, but as representatives of a local community whose right to justice had been denied. The human targets of their wrath were likely to be outsiders: merchants who dealt with distant markets, customs officials, foreigners or Jews. There was thus no automatic or necessary link between subsistence rioting in 1846–7 and revolutionary activism in 1848. Many of the most riotous areas of 1846–7 remained quiescent during the revolutions and the most politically active group in Silesia during the revolutions of 1848 was not the Silesian weavers who had risen in 1844, but the better off among the peasants. Of the peasants, it was the most upwardly mobile who became active, forming associations and cooperating with the urban middle-class democratic intelligentsia.

Even if they were often spontaneous or apolitical in motivation, however, subsistence riots were certainly highly political in their effect. They accelerated processes of politicization that extended far beyond the milieu of the participants. Conservatives and protectionists blamed price rises and mass impoverishment upon government inaction or the deregulatory reforms introduced by liberal bureaucrats. Some conservatives blamed the 'factory system'. On the other hand, liberals argued that industrialization and mechanization were the cure for, not the cause of, the social crisis, and called for the removal of government regulations that hindered investment and obstructed economic growth. Alarmed by the social emergency of 1844–7, conservatives experimented with prescriptions anticipating the German welfare state of the later nineteenth century.[52] For radicals in particular, subsistence riots provided the opportunity to focus and sharpen their rhetoric and theory. Some left Hegelians argued, like the 'social conservatives', that the responsibility for arresting the polarization of society must lie with the state as the custodian of the general interest. The Silesian events of 1844 prompted the writer Friedrich Wilhelm Wolff to elaborate and refine his socialist analysis of the crisis. Whereas his report of 1843 on the Breslau slums was structured around loose binary oppositions such as 'rich' and 'poor', 'these people' and 'the rich man', or 'a day-labourer' and 'the independent bourgeoisie', his detailed article on the Silesian uprising, written seven months later, was far more theoretically ambitious. Here 'the proletariat' is opposed to 'the monopoly of capital', 'those who produce' to 'those who consume' and 'the labouring classes of the people' to the domain of 'private ownership'.[53]

The debate between Arnold Ruge and Karl Marx over the meaning of the Silesian revolt provides a further illustration of the same process. In a rueful piece for *Vorwärts!* (Forwards), the journal of the German émigré radicals in Paris, Ruge argued that the weavers' uprising had been a mere hunger riot that posed no serious threat to the political authorities in Prussia. Karl Marx responded to his former friend's reflections with two long articles in which he put the contrary case, arguing, with what almost sounds like Prussian patriotic pride, that neither the English nor the French 'worker uprisings' had been as 'theoretical and conscious in character' as the Silesian revolt. Only 'the Prussian', Marx announced, had adopted 'the correct point of view'. In burning the company books of the Zwanzigers and the Dierigs, he suggested, the weavers had directed their rage at the 'titles of property' and thereby struck a blow not only at the industrialist himself, but against the system of finance capital that underpinned him.[54] This dispute, which ultimately turned on the issue of the conditions under which an oppressed population can be successfully revolutionized, marked an irrevocable parting of the ways for the two men. The bitter social conflict over resources gave off a negative energy that quickened the pace of political differentiation in Prussia.

HARDENBERG'S TIME-BOMB

By the 1840s, the Prussian political system was living on borrowed time. This was not just a matter of rising popular political expectations, but of financial necessity. Under the terms of the State Indebtedness Law of 17 January 1820, the Prussian government was prevented from raising loans unless these could be cleared through a 'national Estates assembly'. By this means, the reformers (the drafter was Christian Rother, chief of the central directory of the ministry of finance and a close associate of Hardenberg) tied the hands of the government until such time as it should see its way to conceding further constitutional reform. This was the time-bomb that Hardenberg planted at the heart of the Prussian state. It ticked away quietly during the 1820s and 1830s, while successive finance ministers focused on raising loans indirectly through the nominally independent Seehandlung and keeping overall borrowing to a minimum. As a result, Prussia borrowed less in the 1820s and 1830s than any other German government.[55]

This could not continue for ever, as Frederick William IV well knew. The king was a passionate railway enthusiast at a time when the economic, military and strategic importance of the revolutionary in transport technology was becoming increasingly apparent.[56] 'Every new development in railways is a military advantage,' the young Helmut von Moltke observed in 1843, 'and for the national defence a few million on the completion of our railways is far more profitably employed than on our fortresses.'[57] Since this was an area too important to be left to the private sector, it was clear that the Prussian state would soon face infrastructural expenditures it could not cover without raising substantial loans.

Yet the king was slow to accept the inevitability of a united national diet. There was a danger, as one of his closest associates observed, that a national assembly 'would not stop at consultation over the state loan, but would act on anything it considered urgent'.[58] In 1842, the king convened a United Committee composed of twelve delegates from each of the provincial diets, in the hope that this body would engage in consultations on matters such as the need for state railway finance without attempting to expand its own constitutional role. Petitions to the United Committee were forbidden, the issues for discussion were narrowly defined, and the rules of discussion ensured that genuine debate was out of the question – delegates were called upon to speak in alphabetical order and once only on each issue. This modest gathering could not achieve anything of substance; most importantly, as one Rhenish delegate had the temerity to point out during a discussion of railway finance, it lacked the authority to approve a state loan.[59] By the end of 1844, Frederick William had resigned himself to convening a national meeting of the provincial diets within the next three years.

By the mid-1840s, the railway question was coming to a head. The Prussian railway network had grown impressively in recent years, from 185 kilometres in 1840 to 1,106 kilometres by 1845.[60] But this growth had been concentrated in areas where private investors stood to make profits; entrepreneurs understandably had little interest in unprofitable major projects geared to macro-economic and military needs. In the autumn of 1845, however, news reached Berlin that the French government had embarked upon the construction of a strategic rail network whose eastern terminals posed a potential threat to the security of the German Confederation. Berlin's calls for a coordinated all-German strategic railway policy were in vain: the Confederation failed to secure a consensus among the member states, even on the question of the appropriate gauge for an integrated network. It was clear that Prussia would have to see to its own needs.[61] At the centre of the programme that crystallized during 1846 was the *Ostbahn*, a railway artery that would link the Rhineland and the French frontier with Brandenburg and East Prussia.

Hardenberg's time-bomb was now primed to explode. The king's Patent of 3 February 1847, which announced the convocation of a United Diet, stated clearly that this was the body envisaged in the State Indebtedness Law of 1820. It was not a new constitutional instrument, but merely the combination of all the provincial diets into a single body. It thus inherited the awkward hybrid identity of its predecessors: delegates were seated by province and estate, but voting was by head and the assembly operated as a single body, like a national parliament, for most of its business. There was an upper house, composed of princes, counts, mediatized nobles and members of the royal family. The rest of the delegates, representing the landed nobility, the towns and the peasants, sat in the Curia of the Three Estates. Complex voting arrangements ensured that the individual provinces retained the power to veto proposals damaging to their interests – in this respect the diet reflected the 'federal' structure of the Prussian state after 1815. The text of the Patent made it clear that the main business of the diet would be the introduction of new taxes and the approval of a state loan for railway construction.[62]

The United Diet was controversial even before it met. There was a small chorus of moderate conservative enthusiasts, but they were drowned out by the roar of liberal critique. Most liberals felt that the arrangements outlined in the Patent fell far short of their legitimate expectations. 'We asked you for bread and you gave us a stone!' thundered the Silesian liberal Heinrich Simon in a polemical essay published – to avoid the Prussian censors – in Saxon Leipzig. Theodor von Schön took the view that the delegates should use the opening session to declare themselves incompetent to act as a general diet and demand a new election. If the Patent was offensive to liberals, it also alarmed the hardline conservatives, who saw it opening the door to a full-blown constitutional settlement. Many lesser landowning noblemen – even conservative ones – were put off by the special status accorded to the higher nobility; the preponderance of Silesian and Westphalian family names in the upper house also irritated the provincial deputies of the older provinces.[63] And yet, at the same time, the announcement of the United Diet triggered a further expansion of political expectations.

On Sunday 11 April 1847 – a cold, grey, rainy Berlin day – a crowd of provincial delegates numbering over 600 was herded into the White Hall of the royal palace for the inaugural ceremony of the United Diet. The king's opening speech, delivered without notes over more than half an hour, was a warning shot. Infuriated by the reception of his Patent, the king was in no mood for compromise. 'There is no power on earth,' he announced, 'that can succeed in making me transform the natural relationship between prince and people [...] into a conventional constitutional relationship, and I will never allow a written piece of paper to come between the Lord God in Heaven and this land.' The speech closed with a reminder that the diet was no legislative parliament. It had been convened for a specific purpose, namely to approve new taxes and a state loan, but its future depended upon the will and judgement of the king. Its task was emphatically not to 'represent opinions'. He would reconvene the diet, he told the deputies, only if he considered it 'good and useful, and if this Diet offers me proof that I can do so without injuring the rights of the crown'.[64]

In the event, the deliberations of the diet were to prove the hard-line conservatives right. For the first time, Prussian liberals of every stripe found themselves performing together on the same stage. They mounted a campaign to transform the diet into a proper legislature – by securing the right to reconvene at regular intervals, by demanding the power to approve all laws, by protecting it against arbitrary action on the part of the state authorities, by sweeping away what remained of corporate discrimination. Unless these demands were granted, they insisted, the diet could not approve the government's spending plans. For liberal politicians from the regions, this was an exhilarating chance to socialize and exchange ideas with like-minded colleagues from across the kingdom. A liberal partisan culture began to emerge.

The Rhenish industrialist and railway entrepreneur David Hansemann had been a deputy in the Rhenish provincial diet since 1843 and was a leading figure in Rhenish liberal circles. He took care to procure a large apartment near the royal palace, where he hosted meetings with liberal delegations from other provinces. Parties of liberals also congregated at the hotel Russischer Hof for political discussions, debates and general conviviality. Liberal deputies were urged to arrive in the capital at least eight days in advance of the first session, so that there would be time for preliminary meetings. The importance of this experience in a state where the press and political networks were still fragmented along regional lines can scarcely be overstated. It fired liberals with a sense of confidence and purpose; it also taught them a first intense lesson in the virtues of political cooperation and compromise. As one conservative ruefully observed, the liberals regularly worked 'late into the night' coordinating their strategy for key political debates.[65] By this means they succeeded in retaining the initiative in much chamber debate.

The conservatives, by contrast, were something of a shambles. Throughout much of the proceedings they seemed on the defensive, reduced to reacting to liberal proposals and provocations. As the champions of provincial diversity and local autonomy, they found it harder to work together on an all-Prussian plane. For many conservative noblemen, their politics was inextricably bound up with elite corporate status – this made it difficult to establish a common platform with potential allies of more humble station. Whereas the liberals could agree on certain broad principles (constitutionalism, representation, freedom of the press), the conservatives seemed worlds away from a clearly defined joint platform, beyond a vague intuition that gradual evolution on the basis of tradition was preferable to radical change.[66] The conservatives lacked leadership and were slow to form partisan factions. 'One defeat follows another,' Leopold von Gerlach remarked on 7 May, after four weeks of sessions.[67]

In purely constitutional terms, the diet was a non-event. It was not permitted to transform itself into a parliamentary legislature. Before it was adjourned on 26 June 1847, it rejected the government's request for a state loan to finance the eastern railway, declaring that it would cooperate only when the king granted it the right to meet at regular intervals. 'In money matters,' the liberal entrepreneur and deputy David Hansemann famously quipped, 'geniality has its limits.' Yet in terms of political culture the United Diet was of enormous importance. Unlike its provincial predecessors, it was a public body whose proceedings were recorded and published, so that the debates in the chamber resounded across the political landscape of the kingdom. The diet demonstrated in the most conclusive way the exhaustion of the monarch's strategy of containment. It also signalled the imminence – the inevitability – of real constitutional change. How exactly that change would be brought about, however, remained unclear.

PRUSSIA ON THE EVE OF REVOLUTION

In his verse satire *Germany – a Winter's Tale*, the poet, essayist, wit and radical satirist Heinrich Heine described his return to Prussia after thirteen years in Parisian exile. Heine hailed from a modest Jewish mercantile family in Düsseldorf, attended lectures by Hegel in Berlin, and converted to Christianity as a young adult in order to clear any obstacles to a career in the bureaucracy, a reminder of the assimilatory pressure exerted on Jewish subjects by Prussia's 'Christian state'. In 1831, having abandoned his ambition to enter state employment and acquired a considerable reputation as a poet and writer, he left Prussia to work as a journalist in Paris. In 1835, thanks to his outspoken critical commentaries on contemporary German politics, the Confederal Diet issued a nationwide ban on the publication and circulation of his books. A literary career inside the Confederation was now out of the question. *Germany – A Winter's Tale* was published in 1844, following a brief and unhappy visit to his native Rhineland. The first Prussians to welcome him home were of course the customs officials, who made a thorough search of his luggage. In a sequence of sparkling quatrains, Heine evokes his experience at the Prussian border:

> They snuffled and burrowed through trousers and shirts
> And handkerchieves – nothing was missed;
> They were looking for pen-nibs and trinkets and jewels
> And for books on the contraband list.

> You fools! If you think you'll find anything here
> You must have been sadly misled!
> The contraband that travels with me
> Is stored up here, in my head!
> [. . .]

> So many books are stacked in my head –
> A number beyond estimation!
> My head is a twittering bird's nest of books
> All liable to confiscation!

It would be absurd to deny that these verses captured something real about the Prussian state. The oppressive, humourless and pettifogging engagement of the Prussian censorship authorities with political dissent was widely lamented by freethinkers across the kingdom. In the diary of the Berlin liberal Karl Varnhagen von Ense, the burdens of censorship are a constant theme. He writes of the 'misery of small-minded, mischievous, obstructive surveillance', the inventiveness of the censors in devising 'ever new provocations', the frustrations of running a critical literary journal under the arbitrary rule of the censorship office.[68]

On the other hand, as even Varnhagen was aware, Prussian censorship was laughably ineffective. Its real purpose, he observed in August 1837, was not to police popular reading habits, but to justify itself to the rest of the royal administration: 'The people can read what it wishes, regardless of the content; but everything that might come before the king is carefully vetted.'[69] It was virtually impossible, in any case, to control the traffic in contraband print. The political fragmentation of German Europe was a disadvantage from the censors' point of view, for it meant that works banned in one state could easily be printed in another and smuggled across the lightly guarded borders. The radical Württemberg card seller Thomas Beck frequently crossed the border into the Prussian Rhineland with sheaves of his forbidden publications concealed within his hat.[70] 'I am now a large-scale importer of banned books into Prussia,' Friedrich Engels, the radical son of a pious Barmen textile manufacturer, wrote to his friend Wilhelm Graeber from the city of Bremen in November 1839. 'Börne's *Francophobe* in four copies, the *Letters from Paris* by same, six volumes, Venedey's *Prussia and Prussianism*, most strictly prohibited, in five copies, are lying ready for dispatch to Barmen.'[71] Confederal bans on books such as Jakob Venedey's *Prussia and Prussianism*, an angry tract against the Prussian administration by a Rhenish liberal, were ineffective because German booksellers routinely concealed their contraband stocks from the authorities.[72] Songs were even harder to pin down, since they took up so little paper and could circulate without printed text. The politicization of popular culture confronted government with a mode of dissent that could never be effectively policed, because it was informal, protean, omnipresent.

The figure of the Prussian soldier, with his arrogant, affected, supercilious pose, symbolized for many, especially in the radical milieu, the worst features of the polity. It was in the city of Aachen, once the ancient capital of Charlemagne, now a sleepy Rhenish textile centre, that the returning Heinrich Heine caught his first glimpse of the Prussian military:

> I wandered about in this dull little nest
> For about an hour or more
> Saw Prussian military once again
> They looked much the same as before.
> [...]
>
> Still the same wooden, pedantic demeanour
> The same rectangular paces
> And the usual frozen mask of disdain
> Imprinted on each of their faces.

They still strut so stiffly about the street
So groomed and so strictly moustached,
As if they had somehow swallowed the stick
With which they used to be thrashed.

Popular antipathy to the military varied in intensity across the kingdom. It was strongest in the Rhineland, where it fed on local patriotic resentment of Protestant Berlin. In many Rhenish towns, tension between solders and civilians – particularly young male civilians of the artisan and labouring classes – was a part of day-to-day life. Soldiers standing watch before public buildings made easy targets for young men on a night out; many chance violent encounters between soldiers and civilians occurred in or near taverns.[73] Troops were also hated for their role in law enforcement. Prussian towns were very lightly policed by tiny contingents of ill-trained constables whose official duties included a wide range of tasks, such as attending to the orderly disposal of 'raw materials and waste', the cleaning of 'streets and drains', the clearing of obstacles, the removal of dung, the delivery of summonses, the 'notification of official announcements by hand-bell', and so on.[74] The feebleness of civilian policing meant that the Prussian authorities were often forced to fall back on the military as a means of restoring order. In cases of serious tumult, the few local gendarmes generally made themselves scarce and waited for military assistance while the crowd, sensing its power, took the initiative – this is precisely what happened at Peterswaldau and Langenbielau in 1844. Lacking nuanced techniques of crowd management, military commanders tended to progress abruptly from verbal warnings to mounted charges with sabre blows or even gunfire. But this was not a specifically Prussian problem. In England and France too, the use of military units to restore order remained the norm. And the extreme violence meted out at Langenbielau in 1844 was no more typical of Prussian conditions than the Peterloo massacre of 1819 was of policing methods in Great Britain.

Britain was of course – as British travellers were forever pointing out – an incomparably more liberal polity, but it was not necessarily a more humane one. Britons tolerated levels of state violence that would have been unthinkable in Prussia. The number of condemnations to death in Prussia during the years from 1818 to 1847 fluctuated between twenty-one and thirty-three per annum. The number of actual executions was much lower – it varied between five and seven – thanks to the intensive use of the royal pardon, which became an important mark of sovereignty in this period. By contrast, 1,137 death sentences were handed down every year on average over the period 1816–35 in England and Wales, whose combined population (around 16 million) was comparable to Prussia's. To be sure, relatively few (less than 10 per cent) of these sentences were actually carried out, but the number of persons executed still exceeded the Prussian figure by a factor of sixty-to-one. Whereas the great majority of English and Welsh capital sentences were passed for property crimes (including quite minor ones), most Prussian executions were for crimes of homicide. The only 'political' execution of the pre-revolutionary era was that of the village mayor Tschech, who was found guilty of high treason for having attempted to murder the king.[75] In short: there was no Prussian parallel to the routine slaughter perpetrated at the gallows under England's 'bloody code'.

Terrible as the extremes of poverty were in the 'hungry forties', they pale in comparison to the hunger catastrophe that ravaged British-administered Ireland. Today we blame this disaster on a combination of administrative error with the dynamics of the free market. Had such a mass famine been visited upon the Poles in Prussia, we would perhaps now be discerning in it the antecedents of post-1939 Nazi rule. It is also worth remembering that the Prussians faced constraints in Poland that had no counterpart in Ireland. Poland was the unquiet frontier between Prussia and the Russian Empire, and Prussian policy in the region had to take account of Russian interests. The Prussian Crown did not, of course, accept the legitimacy of Polish nationalist strivings. It did, however, accommodate the aspiration of its Polish subjects to cultivate their distinctive nationality. Indeed, the government's promotion of Polish-language elementary and secondary schooling led to a dramatic rise in Polish literacy rates in the Prussian-occupied sector of the old Polish Commonwealth. There was, to be sure, a ten-year period when Provincial Governor Flottwell switched to a policy of assimilation through 'Germanization' – an ominous foretaste of later developments. But this was very inconsistently pursued, came to an end with the accession of the romantic Polonophile Frederick William IV and was in any case a response to the Polish revolution of 1830, which had raised serious doubts about the political loyalty of the province.

In the early 1840s, when Heine departed Prussia for literary exile in

Paris, Prussian Poland remained an attractive refuge for Polish political exiles from east of the Poznanian border. Russian dissidents, too, found their way to Prussia. The radical literary critic Vissarion Grigorevich Belinskii was living in Salzbrunn, Silesia in 1847 when he wrote his famous *Letter to Gogol* denouncing the political and social backwardness of his homeland, a crime for which he was condemned to death *in absentia* by a Russian court. So resonant was this cry of protest within Russian dissident circles that Turgenev, who visited Belinskii in Silesia, chose to sign 'Bailiff', the savage pen-portrait of a tyrannical landlord in *Sketches from a Hunter's Album*, with 'Salzbrunn, 1847', a coded indication of his support for Belinskii's critique. In the same year, another exile, the Russian radical Alexander Herzen, crossed the Prussian border from the east. Arriving in Königsberg, he expressed a profound sense of relief: 'The unpleasant feelings of fear [and] the oppressive sense of suspicion were all dispelled.'[76]

14

Splendour and Misery of the
Prussian Revolution

BARRICADES IN BERLIN

By the end of February 1848, the population of Berlin was growing accustomed to the news of revolution. In the winter of 1847, Protestant liberals in Switzerland had fought – and won – a civil war against the conservative Catholic cantons. The result was a new Swiss federal state with a liberal constitution. Then, on 12 January 1848, after reports of unrest in the Italian peninsula, came the news that insurgents had seized power in Palermo. Two weeks later, the success of the Palermitan revolution was confirmed when the King of Naples became the first Italian monarch to offer his people a constitution.

It was above all the news from France that electrified the city. During February, a liberal protest campaign gained momentum in the French capital, culminating in bloody clashes between troops and demonstrators. On 28 February, an extra edition of Berlin's *Vossische Zeitung* featured a 'telegraphic despatch' reporting that King Louis Philippe had abdicated. In view of the 'current state of France and of Europe', the editors declared, 'this turn of events – so sudden, so violent and so utterly unexpected – appears more extraordinary, perhaps more momentous in its consequences than even the July Revolution [of 1830].'[1] As the news from Paris broke in the Prussian capital, Berliners poured on to the streets in search of information and discussion. The weather helped – these were the mildest and brightest early spring days that anyone could remember. Reading clubs, coffee-houses and public establishments of all kinds were crammed to bursting. 'Whoever managed to get his hands on a new paper had to climb on to a chair and read the contents aloud.'[2] The excitement grew as word arrived of events closer to home – large demonstrations in Mannheim, Heidelberg, Cologne and other German cities, the concession of political reforms and civil liberties by King Ludwig I of Bavaria, the dismissal of conservative ministers in Saxony, Baden, Württemberg, Hanover and Hesse.

One important focal point for debate and protest was the Municipal Assembly, where elected members of the burgher elite regularly met to discuss the affairs of the city. After 9 March, when a crowd forced its way into the City Hall, the usually rather stolid assembly began to mutate into a protest rally. There were also daily political meetings at the 'Tents', an area of the Tiergarten just outside the Brandenburg Gate reserved for outdoor refreshments and entertainments. These had begun as informal gatherings, but they soon took on the contours of an im-provised parliament, with voting procedures, resolutions and elected delegations, a classical example of the 'public meeting democracy' that unfolded across the German cities in 1848.[3] It was not long before the Municipal Assembly and the Tents began to work together; on 11 March, the assembly discussed a draft petition from the Tents demanding a long list of political, legal and constitutional reforms. By 13 March, the gathering at the Tents, now numbering over 20,000, had begun to hear speeches from workers and artisans whose chief concern was not legal and constitutional reform, but the economic needs of the working populace. A gathering of workers at one corner formed a separate assembly and drew up a petition of its own pressing for new laws to protect labour against 'capitalists and usurers' and asking the king to establish a ministry of labour. Distinct political and social interests were already crystallizing within the mobilized crowd of the city.

Alarmed at the growing 'determination and insolence' of the crowds circulating in the streets, the President of Police, Julius von Minutoli, ordered new troops into the city on 13 March. That night, several civilians were killed in clashes around the palace precinct. The crowd and the soldiery were now collective antagonists in a struggle for control of the city's space. Over the next few days, crowds flowed through the city in the early evenings. They were, in Manzoni's memorable simile, like 'clouds still scattered and scudding about a clear sky, making every-one look up and say that the weather has not yet settled'.[4] The crowd was afraid of the troops, but also drawn to them. It cajoled, persuaded and taunted them. The troops had their own elaborate rituals. When confronted by unruly subjects, they were required to read out the riot

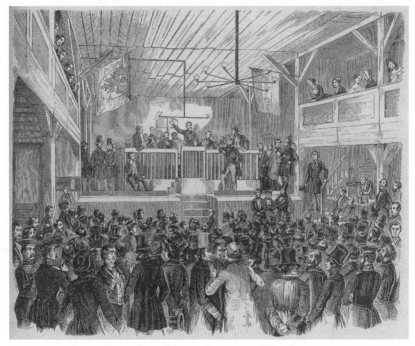

42. From the club life of Berlin in 1848. *Contemporary engraving.*

act of 1835 three times, before giving three warning signals with the drum or the trumpet, after which the order to attack would be given. Since many of the men in the crowd had themselves served in the military, these signals were almost universally recognized and understood. The reading of the riot act was generally greeted with whistling and jeers. The beating of the drum, which signalled an imminent advance or charge, had a stronger deterrent effect but this was generally temporary. On a number of occasions during the struggles in Berlin, crowds forced troops standing guard to run through their warning routines over and over again by provoking them, melting away when the drum was sounded, then reappearing to start the game again.[5]

So poisonous was the mood in the city that men in uniform walking alone or in small groups were in serious danger. The liberal writer and diarist Karl August Varnhagen von Ense watched with mixed feelings from his first-floor window on 15 March as three officers walked slowly along the footpath of a street adjoining his house followed by a shouting crowd of about 200 boys and youths. 'I saw how stones struck them, how a raised staff crashed down on one man's back, but they did not flinch, they did not turn, they walked as far as the corner, turned into the Wallstrasse and took refuge in an administrative building, whose armed guards scared the tormentors away.' The three men were later rescued by a troop detachment and escorted to the safety of the city arsenal.[6]

The military and political leadership found it difficult to agree on how to proceed. The mild and intelligent General von Pfuel, governor of Berlin, with responsibility for all troops stationed in and around the capital, favoured a mix of tact and political concessions. By contrast, the king's younger brother, Prince William, urged the monarch to order an all-out attack on the insurgents. General von Prittwitz, commander of the King's Lifeguards and a hard-line supporter of Prince William, later recalled the chaotic atmosphere that reigned at the court. The king, Prittwitz claimed, was buffeted about by the conflicting advice of a throng of advisers and well-wishers. The tipping point came with the news (breaking in Berlin on 15 March) that Chancellor Metternich had fallen, following two days of revolutionary upheaval in Vienna. Deferential as ever to Austria, the ministers and advisers around the king read this as an omen and resolved to offer further political concessions. On 17 March, the king agreed to publish royal patents announcing the abolition of censorship and the introduction of a constitutional system in the Kingdom of Prussia.

By this time, however, plans had already been laid for an afternoon rally to take place on the following day, 18 March, in the Palace Square. On that morning the government broadcast the news of its concessions across the city. Municipal deputies were seen dancing in the streets with members of the public. The city government ordered the illumination of the city that evening as a token of its gratitude.[7] But it was too late to stop the planned demonstration: from around noon, streams of people began to converge upon the Palace Square, including prosperous burghers and 'protection officers' (unarmed officials recruited from the middle classes and appointed to mediate between troops and crowds), but also many artisans from the slum areas outside the city boundaries. As the news of the government's decisions circulated, the mood became festive, euphoric. The air was filled with the sound of cheering. The crowd, ever more densely packed in the warm sunlit square, wanted to see the king.

The mood inside the palace was light-hearted. When Police Chief Minutoli arrived at around one in the afternoon to warn the king that he believed a major upheaval was still imminent, he was met with indulgent smiles. The king thanked him for his work and added: 'There is one thing I should say, my dear Minutoli, and that is that you always see things too negatively!' Hearing the applause and cheering from the square, the king and his entourage made their way in the direction of the people. 'We're off to collect our hurrahs,' quipped General von Pfuel.[8] At last the monarch walked out on to a stone balcony overlooking the square, where he was greeted with frenetic ovations. Then Prime Minister von Bodelschwingh stepped forward to make an announcement: 'The king wishes freedom of the press to prevail! The king wishes that the United Diet be called immediately! The king wishes that a constitution on the most liberal basis should encompass all the German lands! The king wishes that there should be a German national flag! The king wishes that all customs turnpikes should fall! The king wishes that Prussia should place itself at the head of the movement!' Most of the crowd could hear neither the king nor his minister, but printed copies of his recent patents were being passed through the throng and the wild cheering around the balcony soon spread across the square in a wave of elation.

There was only one dark cloud on the crowd's horizon: under the arches of the palace gates and in the courtyards behind them, lines of troops could be seen. At the sight of this familiar enemy, the mood began to sour. There was some panic on the edges, where people feared to be pushed up against the soldiers. The chanting began: 'Soldiers out! Soldiers out!' The situation in the square seemed about to slip out of control. At this point – it was around two in the afternoon – the king transferred the command over the troops in the capital from Pfuel to the more hawkish Prittwitz and ordered that the square be cleared immediately by soldiers and 'an end be put to the scandalous situation prevailing there'. Bloodshed was to be avoided: the cavalry should advance at marching pace without drawing swords.[9] A scene of utter confusion followed. A squadron of dragoons pushed slowly forward into the crowd, but failed to disperse it. Controlling the men was difficult, because the noise was so intense that no orders could be heard. Some of the horses took fright and began to pace backwards. Two men fell when their mounts lost their footing on the cobbles. Only when the dragoons raised their sabres and made to charge did the crowd flee the centre of the square.

Since substantial numbers of people were still concentrated on the eastern edge of the palace precinct between the Langenbrücke and the Breitenstrasse, a small contingent of grenadiers was sent to clear them. It was during this action that two weapons were accidentally discharged. Grenadier Kühn's musket caught on the handle of his sabre; warrant officer Hettgen's gun went off when a demonstrator struck it on the hammer with a stick. Neither shot caused an injury, but the crowd, thinking with its ears, was convinced that the troops had begun to shoot civilians. Word of this outrage passed swiftly through the city. The rather surreal attempt of the palace to correct this misinformation by employing two civilians to walk the streets with a massive linen banner bearing the words: 'A misunderstanding! The king has the best intentions!' was predictably futile.

Barricades sprang up across Berlin, improvised from materials to hand. These makeshift barriers became the focal points of most of the fighting, which followed a similar pattern across the city: infantry advancing on a barricade came under fire from the windows of buildings in the vicinity. Tiles and stones rained down from the roofs. The houses were entered and cleared by troops. Barricades were demolished with artillery shot or dismantled by soldiers with the aid of prisoners taken during the fight. Varnhagen von Ense described how the defenders of a barricade near his house responded to the sound of approaching troops: 'The fighters were instantly ready. You could hear them whispering, and upon the order of a youthful sonorous voice: "Gentlemen, to the roofs!" each went to his post.'[10] A Private Schadewinkel who took part in the storming of a barricade in the Breitenstrasse later recalled his role in the action. After the man beside him had been killed by a shot to the head, Schadewinkel joined a handful of soldiers who broke into a building where protesters had been seen. Fired with murderous rage, the men charged up stairways and into apartments, 'cutting down anyone who resisted'. 'I am unable to give any precise account of events inside the house,' Schadewinkel declared. 'I was in a state of agitation such as I have never been in before.'[11] Here, as in many parts of Berlin, innocent bystanders and the half-involved were killed along with the combatants.

It proved much harder to take control of the city than the military commanders had imagined. At around midnight on 18 March,

43. The Barricade on the Krone and Friedrichstrasse *18 March 1848, as seen by an eyewitness; lithograph by F. G. Nordmann, 1848*

when General Prittwitz, the new commander-in-chief of the counter-insurrectionary forces, reported to Frederick William IV in the palace, he had to acknowledge that while his troops controlled the area between the river Spree, the Neue Friedrichstrasse and the Spittelmarkt, a further advance was currently impossible. Prittwitz proposed that the city be evacuated, encircled and bombarded into submission. The king responded to this grim news with an almost other-worldly calm. Having thanked the general, he returned to his desk, where Prittwitz observed 'the elaborately comfortable way in which His Majesty pulled a furry foot-muff over his feet after taking off his boots and stockings, in order, as it seemed, to begin writing another lengthy document'.[12] The document in question was the address 'To My Dear Berliners', published in the small hours of the following day, in which the king appealed to the residents of the city to return to order: 'Return to peace, clear the barricades that still stand [. . .], and I give you my Royal Word that all streets and squares will be cleared of troops, and the military occupation reduced to a few necessary buildings.'[13] The order to pull the troops out of the city was given on the next day shortly after noon. The king had placed himself in the hands of the revolution.

This was a momentous decision, and a controversial one. The forced withdrawal from Berlin was the most vexing challenge the Prussian army had faced since 1806. Had the king simply lost his nerve? This was certainly the view taken by the hawks within the military.[14] Prince William of Prussia, whose preference for hard measures had earned him the sobriquet 'the shrapnel prince', was the most furious hawk of all. Having heard the news of the withdrawal, he marched up to his elder brother and spat out the words: 'I have always known that you were a babbler, but not that you are a coward! One can no longer serve you with honour' before flinging his sword at the king's feet. With tears of rage in his eyes, the king is said to have replied: 'This is just too bad! You can't stay here. You will have to go!' William, by now the most hated figure in the city, was at length persuaded to leave Berlin in disguise and cool down in London.[15]

In retrospect, there is much to be said for the king's decision. The early departure of the troops prevented further bloodshed. This was an important consideration, given the ferocity of the fighting during the night of 18–19 March. With a toll of over 300 dead protesters and around 100 dead soldiers and officers, Berlin saw some of the bloodiest urban fighting of the German March revolution. By contrast, the death toll for the March days in Vienna was around fifty.[16] Frederick William's decision also preserved Berlin from artillery bombardment, a fate that was visited upon several European cities during that year. And it allowed the king to emerge as a public figure with his reputation untarnished by the violent confrontations in the capital, a matter of some weight if he intended to seize the opportunity offered by the revolution to reassert Prussia's leadership role among the German states.

THE TURNING OF THE TABLES

The impact of the Berlin events was reinforced by the news of unrest and rebellion across the kingdom. Since the beginning of March there had been a crescendo of unlicensed rallies and mass meetings, riots, violence and machine-breaking. Some protests (mainly in cities) focused on the articulation of liberal political demands such as the call for a constitution, civil liberties and legal reform. Others were directed against factories, warehouses or machines that were seen as undermining the welfare of districts suffering from high unemployment. Around the Westphalian town of Solingen, for example, cutlery workers attacked and demolished foundries and factories on 16 and 17 March.[17] In Warendorf, a textiles town, unemployed weavers and tanners protested against factories using mechanized production methods.[18] Along the riverbank towns of the Rhine there were protests against the use of steamers that rendered the small river ports and the services they provided redundant; in some places protesters even fired guns and small cannon at passing boats.[19]

Sometimes liberals and radicals competed for control of the process of mobilization. In Cologne, for example, on 3 March, a meeting of city deputies who had gathered together to discuss a liberal petition to the monarch was broken up by a large crowd demanding universal manhood suffrage and abolition of the standing army. The deputies fled the chamber, one of them breaking his leg as he leaped from a window. In Silesia, where less had been achieved in the way of agrarian emancipation than in any other province, it was the peasants who took the lead, marching en masse to administrative offices and demanding the total abolition of the 'feudal' system.[20] The towns were focal points for the labile street politics of the revolution. In Berlin alone there were 125 episodes of public unrest; forty-six were recorded in Cologne, forty-five in Breslau and twenty-one in liberal Königsberg. Smaller towns – especially in the Rhineland and Westphalia – also witnessed intense tumults and conflict.[21] The simultaneity and force of this wave of protest, not only across the Kingdom of Prussia, but also across the German states and the continent of Europe, were overwhelming.

In Berlin, the king was now at the mercy of the citizens. The meaning of this was brought home to him on the afternoon of 19 March, when he and his wife consented to stand on the palace balcony while the corpses of those insurgents who had fallen during the night's fighting were carried across the square laid out on doors and pieces of wood, decorated with leaves, their clothes peeled back to reveal the wounds struck by shot, shrapnel and bayonet. The king happened to be wearing his military cap; 'Hat off!' roared an elderly man near the front of the crowd. The monarch doffed his cap and bowed his head. 'The only thing missing now is the guillotine,' murmured Queen Elisabeth, white with horror. It was a traumatic ritual humiliation.[22]

And yet within days the king began to inhabit his new role with a certain gusto. On the morning of 21 March, after placards had appeared in the city calling upon him to take up the cause of the German national movement, Frederick William announced that he had decided to support the formation of an all-German parliament. He then engaged in a spectacular public relations exercise. Mounting his horse in the palace courtyard, he rode out into the city behind a civil guardsman carrying the German tricolour, much to the surprise and horror of his courtiers. The little procession moved slowly through packed and cheering crowds, stopping here and there so that the monarch could deliver short impromptu speeches expressing his support for the German national cause.[23]

Four days later, the king travelled out to Potsdam to see the commanders of the army, still furious over their removal from Berlin. 'I have come to speak to you,' he told the assembled officers, 'in order to prove to the Berliners that they need expect no reactionary strike from Potsdam.' The climax came with the king's extraordinary declaration that he had 'never felt freer or more secure than under the protection of his citizens'.[24] According to one eyewitness, Otto von Bismarck, these words were greeted by 'a murmuring and clattering of sabre-scabbards such as a king of Prussia in the midst of his officers has never heard and will hopefully never hear again'.[25] Few episodes convey more succinctly than this one the complexity of the king's position in the early days of the revolution. He suspected – rightly, as it turns out – that reactionary conspiracies were beginning to circulate among his alienated commanders and he intended to nip these in the bud by securing a renewed assurance of their loyalty to his person.[26] But the meeting also had a broader public function: texts of the king's address were published almost immediately in the *Vossische* and the *Allgemeine Preussische Zeitung* in Berlin with a view to assuring the city that the king had separated himself (at least for now) from his military, that his commitment to the revolution was genuine.

Over the next few weeks, a new political order began to unfold in Prussia. On 29 March, the distinguished Rhenish businessman Ludolf Camphausen, a leading liberal at the United Diet of 1847, was appointed prime minister. The new cabinet included as finance minister the liberal Rhenish entrepreneur and provincial delegate David Hansemann. Within a few days of its opening session at the beginning of April, the

Second United Diet passed a law providing for elections to a constituent Prussian National Assembly. The franchise was indirect – the voters elected a college of electors, who in turn voted for deputies. Otherwise it was a remarkably progressive arrangement: all adult males were eligible to vote, providing they had resided in the same place for at least six months and were not receiving poor relief. The May elections returned a predominantly liberal and left-liberal assembly. About a sixth of the deputies were artisans and peasants – a higher proportion than could be found in the Frankfurt or Viennese revolutionary assemblies. Conservatives were few and far between; only 7 per cent of the deputies in the new National Assembly were landowners.[27] The assembly was correspondingly robust in its handling of key symbolic issues. Over the summer and early autumn of 1848 it passed resolutions proposing narrower limits to the power of the monarchical executive, demanded the subordination of the army to the authority of the constitution and called for the abolition of seigneurial hunting rights without compensation – hunting policy was a potent weapon of class warfare.

The Camphausen government made valiant efforts to ensure that the new Prussia was run on liberal principles. There were bitter struggles with the king and his conservative advisers over the policy to be adopted *vis-à-vis* the Poles – Camphausen's foreign minister, Baron Heinrich Alexander von Arnim-Suckow, a liberal who had served as the Prussian minister to Paris until March 1848, favoured making concessions to the Polish national movement, whereas the king and his advisers were reluctant to alienate Russia by appearing to encourage the Poles. Predictably, the foreign minister was forced to yield on this question and the Prussian army was sent into Posen to suppress the unrest there in May. There was also strife over the sensitive issue of ministerial co-responsibility for the conduct of military affairs. Frederick William, like his predecessors, regarded the Prussian monarch's personal command over the army, the so-called *Kommandogewalt*, as an essential attribute of his sovereignty and was unwilling to make any concessions in this area; to do so, he informed the cabinet in characteristically extravagant terms, would be 'incompatible with my honour as a human being, a Prussian, and a king, and would lead me directly to abdication'.[28] Here again it was the ministry that backed down.

Unsurprisingly, there was also much contention over the new draft constitution, prepared in great haste by the Camphausen government in the hope that it would be ready for presentation to the National Assembly after its opening on 22 May. Frederick William was unhappy with many aspects of this document and later described his constitutional discussions with the ministers as 'the most ghastly hours of my life'. The amended draft duly included revisions asserting that the monarch was king 'by the grace of God', that he exercised exclusive control over the army and that the constitution was to be understood as an 'agreement' (*Vereinbarung*) between himself and his people (as opposed to a basic law imposed upon the sovereign by the popular will).[29]

By the time this much-discussed document came before the National Assembly in June, the mood in the city and in the assembly itself had begun to sour. In Berlin, as in many parts of Prussia and Germany, the radical left was growing in numbers and confidence. Organizations and newspapers emerged to articulate the aspirations of those who rejected the elitism of the liberal programme. On the streets, too, there were signs that the liberal government was losing its grip on popular opinion. There were bitter disagreements over how to manage the legacy of the March uprising. Should the insurrection be retrospectively decriminalized? There was bitter debate over this question in the Berlin National Assembly. When the majority of deputies refused to accept the legality of the uprising, the radical deputy Julius Berends delivered a thundering oration in which he reminded the deputies that the assembly owed its very existence to the barricade fighters of 18–19 March. At around the same time, the democratic newspaper *Die Lokomotive* accused the National Assembly of denying its origins 'like a badly brought up boy who does not respect his father'.[30] A memorial procession in honour of the 'March fallen' attracted well over 100,000 people, but these were virtually all labourers, working women and journeymen, or to put it more pointedly, people from the same social stratum as the dead barricade fighters themselves. Middle-class burghers of the kind who predominated in the National Assembly were conspicuous by their rarity.

In this increasingly troubled climate, the chances of securing a majority in the National Assembly for the compromises enshrined in the first draft constitution were slim. When he failed to do so, Camphausen resigned on 20 June and Hansemann was asked to form a new government. Prime minister of the new cabinet was the liberal East Prussian nobleman Rudolf von Auerswald (Hansemann remained finance minister). Over the following month, the assembly's constitutional committee, chaired by the distinguished democrat Benedikt Waldeck, presented a counter-proposal for the assembly's consideration. The new draft constitution limited the monarch's power to block legislation, provided for a genuinely popular national militia (a throw-back to the programme of the radical military reformers), proposed the introduction of civil marriage and removed the last traces of patrimonial privilege in rural areas.[31] This draft was as contentious as the previous one. The resulting debates further polarized the assembly and no agreement was reached. The constitution remained in limbo.

It was the question of the relationship between the civilian and military authorities – a problem that would revisit Prussia in generations to come – that did most to undermine the fragile political compromise in Berlin. On 31 July, a violent clash over the arbitrary orders of a local army commander in the Silesian town of Schweidnitz resulted in the death of fourteen civilians. There was a wave of outrage, in the course of which the Breslau deputy Julius Stein presented a motion to the National Assembly proposing that measures be introduced to ensure that officers and soldiers acted in conformity with constitutional values. By this he meant that all army personnel should 'distance themselves from reactionary tendencies' and fraternize with civilians as proof of their commitment to the new political order.

Stein could be faulted in retrospect for his diffuse formulations, but he expressed the understandably deepening alarm of the new political elite over the unbroken power of the military. If the army remained the compliant tool of interests opposed to the new order, then it might be said that the liberals and their institutions were living on sufferance, that their debates and law-making amounted to little more than a farcical performance. The Stein motion tapped a deep vein of nervousness in the Assembly and was passed with a substantial majority. Sensing that the king would not yield to pressure on the military issue, the Auerswald-Hansemann government did its best to avoid taking actions that would precipitate a confrontation. But the patience of the assembly soon ran out and on 7 September it passed a resolution demanding that the government implement Stein's proposals. Frederick William was enraged and talked of restoring order in his 'disloyal and good-for-nothing' capital by force. In the meanwhile, the controversy over the Stein proposals forced the government to resign.

The new prime minister was General Ernst von Pfuel, the very man who had commanded the forces in and around Berlin on the eve of 18 March. Pfuel was a good choice – he was not a hard-line conservative, but a man formed by the enthusiasms and political ferment of the revolutionary era. His youth had been consumed by an intense homoerotic friendship with the romantic dramatist Heinrich von Kleist. Pfuel was among those who had emigrated in a spirit of injured patriotism during the French occupation. A popular figure at the Jewish salons and a friend of Wilhelm von Humboldt, he was widely admired by liberal contemporaries for his tolerance and erudition. But not even the mild-mannered Pfuel could mediate successfully between a recalcitrant king and an obstreperous assembly, and on 1 November, he too resigned.

The announcement that his successor would be Count Friedrich Wilhelm von Brandenburg was greeted with dismay in the liberal ranks. Brandenburg was the king's uncle and the former commander of the VI Army Corps in Breslau. He was the favoured candidate of the conservative circle around the king and the purpose behind his appointment was straightforward. His task, according to Leopold von Gerlach, one of the king's most influential advisers, would be to 'show in every possible way that the king still rules in this country and not the assembly'.[32] The assembly sent a delegation to Frederick William on 2 November to protest against the new appointment, but it was brusquely dismissed. One week later, on the foggy morning of 9 November, Brandenburg presented himself before the assembly in its temporary home on the Gendarmenmarkt and announced that it was adjourned until 27 November, when it would meet in the city of Brandenburg. A few hours later, the new military commander-in-chief, General Wrangel, entered the capital at the head of 13,000 troops and rode to the Gendarmenmarkt to inform the deputies in the assembly personally that they would have to disperse. The assembly responded by calling for 'passive resistance' and announcing a tax strike.[33] On 11 November martial law was declared, the Civil Guards were disbanded (and disarmed), political clubs were closed down, and prominent radical newspapers were banned. Many of the deputies did attempt to congregate in Brandenburg on 27 November, but they were soon dispersed and the assembly was formally dissolved on 5 December. On the same day, in an astute political move, the Brandenburg government announced the promulgation of a new constitution.

The revolution was over in the capital, but it smouldered on in the

Rhineland, where the exceptionally well-organized political networks of the radicals were successful in mobilizing mass opposition to the counter-revolutionary measures of the Berlin government. There was strong support throughout the Rhine province for the tax boycott pronounced by the National Assembly in its dying hours. Every day for a month, the *Neue Rheinische Zeitung*, organ of the socialist left, ran the words 'No more taxes!' on its masthead. 'People's committees' and 'citizens' committees' sprang up to support the boycott in Cologne, Koblenz, Trier and other towns. Outrage over the dissolution of the assembly blended with provincial hostility to Prussia, confessional resentments (especially among Catholics) and the discontents associated with the patterns of economic stress and deprivation in the region. In Bonn, angry crowds insulted and beat tax officers and defaced or removed the Prussian eagles fixed to public buildings. In Düsseldorf on 20 November, there was a parade of the (now illegal) Civil Guard that culminated in a public oath to fight to the bitter end for the National Assembly and the rights of the people. The tax boycott campaign revealed the strength and social depth of the democratic movement in the Rhineland, and it certainly alarmed the Prussian authorities in the area. But the formal dissolution of the assembly in Brandenburg on 5 December deprived the democrats of a political focus. The arrival of troop reinforcements, coupled with the imposition of martial law in some hotspots and the disarmament of makeshift leftist militias sufficed to restore state authority.[34]

How had this happened? Why was the revolution that unfolded with such force in March so easily checked in November? It has often been noted that the overwhelmingly proletarian fighters who died on the barricades in Berlin and the wealthy liberal businessmen who occupied ministerial posts in the 'March ministry' represented utterly different social worlds and correspondingly opposed political expectations. The resulting divide ran right through the history of the revolution. The inability of liberals and radicals to agree on joint candidates for the May National Assembly elections, for example, meant that conservative and right-liberal candidates won instead.[35] In the National Assembly in Berlin, the liberals consistently marginalized and stigmatized the social issues at the centre of the radical programme. As for the democratic left, it was successful in mobilizing mass support, especially in the Rhineland – a process facilitated by the politicization of popular culture in the

1840s. But the left, too, was divided. In May 1849, when a democratic uprising was organized in the Rhineland in support of the imperial constitution drawn up by the Frankfurt Parliament, the movement split between 'constitutional' and 'Marxist' or Communist democrats, who abstained on the grounds that the fate of a 'bourgeois' constitution ought to be a matter of indifference to the working class.[36]

What really tipped the scales in Prussia was the underlying strength of the traditional authority. In this connection, it is worth noting that Frederick William IV, the 'romantic on the throne', acted with more intelligence and flexibility during the crisis than he has often been given credit for. Indeed he performed his new role with surprising aplomb. Remaining in the capital after the troops had left and consenting in principle to the constitutionalization of the monarchy, he locked the liberals into an arduous process of negotiation while biding his time and looking for an opportunity to regain his freedom of manoeuvre. Behind the scenes, he gathered about him a cabal of conservatives determined to end the revolution at the earliest opportunity. By associating himself with the unionist objectives of the German national movement, he even secured a degree of popular legitimacy. In August 1848, when he visited the Rhineland, the popular enthusiasm was so intense that Karl Marx's *Neue Rheinische Zeitung* had to cancel an issue after the workers in the press-room took the day off to cheer the king. Frederick William IV may have suffered from a 'psychopathic' fear of revolutionary upheaval, but his actions during the months of upheaval showed a sound tactical instinct.[37]

Then there was the fact that the revolution remained confined to particular areas of the kingdom. It was above all an urban event. There was certainly widespread rural protest, but with the exception of parts of the Rhineland, rural disorder tended to be very locally focused; urban politicians found it difficult to win the interest and support of people in the countryside, and protesters there rarely mounted a principled challenge to the authority of the king or of the state and its organs. For the most part, the countryside, especially in the East-Elbian provinces, continued to support the crown. It was here that conservative opposition to the revolution began to organize itself as a mass movement. During the summer of 1848, a range of conservative associations – veterans' societies, patriotic leagues, Prussian leagues and peasants' associations – proliferated across Brandenburg and Pomerania, the old core provinces where attachment to the Hohenzollern monarchy ran deepest. By May 1849, organizations of this kind encompassed a membership of over 60,000. It was a movement of artisans, peasants and shopkeepers – the people who had traditionally supported the evangelical voluntarism of the missionary societies.[38]

Another sign of the vitality of popular conservatism was the proliferation of 'military clubs' for patriotic veterans. Groups of this kind had existed since the 1820s, but they generally catered specifically to veterans of the Wars of Liberation and there were few of them. Their numbers rocketed from the summer of 1848; in Silesia, where there were eight military clubs before 1848, a further sixty-four were founded in the immediate aftermath of the revolution. In all, it is estimated that around 50,000 men in Brandenburg, Pomerania and Silesia joined such associations during the years 1848 and 1849.[39] In this sense it could be said that the revolution of 1848 represented a coming of age for Prussian conservatism, which began to find its way towards a practical partisan articulation of conservative interests as well as ways of incorporating the voices and aspirations of ordinary people.

Most important of all was the continuing loyalty and effectiveness of the Prussian army. It hardly needs saying that the army played a crucial role in the suppression of the revolution. It marched into Posen in May 1848 to put an end to the Polish uprising there; it expelled the National Assembly from its Berlin premises in November and closed down its successor in Brandenburg a few weeks later; it was called in to deal with countless local tumults across the country. Yet the loyalty of the army was a less straightforward phenomenon than we might imagine. It was, after all, an army of Prussian citizens. The majority of soldiers were drawn from the very social strata that supported the revolution. Moreover, many of them were recalled at short notice from leave during the summer, which meant that they went directly from participating in the revolution to assisting in its suppression.[40]

It thus makes sense to ask why more men of the ranks did not defect or refuse to serve, or form revolutionary cells within the armed forces. Some did, of course. The radicals in particular made strenuous efforts to woo soldiers into crossing the picket line, and they were sometimes successful. Some local Landwehr units split into opposing democratic and loyalist factions – in Breslau, a radical Landwehr Club succeeded in attracting a membership of over 2,000.[41] Despite the worst fears of the military leadership, however, the great majority of troops remained loyal to the king and their commanders. This was true not only of the East-Elbian troops (though it was especially true of them), but also of most of those who hailed from hotspots such as Westphalia and the Rhineland. The motivations for their compliance obviously varied according to local conditions and individual circumstances, but one factor stands out. This is the widespread belief among soldiers entrusted with the repression of local insurgencies that they were not closing down, but on the contrary *protecting* the revolution, safeguarding the constitutional order against the anarchy and disorder of the radicals. Soldiers did not, on the whole, see themselves as the shock troops of counter-revolution, but as the preservers of the 'March achievements' against the threat posed by radical tumult. Indeed, so strong was the identification of some units with the struggle of the Prussian state to restore order that it could temporarily sweep aside the particularism of local and regional identities. So it was that the tax boycott campaign supported by radicals in Düsseldorf was brought to an end in November 1848 by two companies of the XVI Westphalian Infantry Regiment, who marched into the city singing the 'Prussia Song': 'I am a Prussian, do you know my colours?'[42]

This perspective acquired a certain plausibility from the fact that the focus of initiative within the revolution did indeed pass swiftly to the radical left. From mid-April until July 1849, the German states were rocked once again by a wave of insurrections that extended from Saxony and the Prussian Rhineland to Baden, Württemberg and the Bavarian Palatinate. Although the insurgents involved in this second revolution claimed to be rising in support of the Frankfurt Parliament and its national constitution, they were essentially social revolutionaries whose programme recalled the politics of Jacobin radicalism. The position was especially critical in Baden, where the collapse of morale within the army opened the way to the establishment of a Committee of Public Safety and a revolutionary provisional government. Prussian troops, working beside contingents from Württemberg, Nassau and Hesse, played a crucial role in suppressing this last radical spasm of the revolution: they assisted the Saxon army in putting down the insurrection in the city of Dresden (in which Richard Wagner and the anarchist Mikhail Bakunin both participated) and then marched south to retake the Palatinate. On 21 June, Confederal forces defeated an insurgent army at

Waghäusel and ended the revolution in the Grand Duchy of Baden. These were bitter and deadly encounters: unlike in 1848, the revolutionaries of the second phase formed an armed force numbering over 45,000 men and fought pitched battles with the enemy, in which they defended themselves with courage and desperation.

The campaign in the south ended only with the capitulation of the hungry and demoralized remainder of the revolutionary army at the fortress of Rastatt on 23 July 1849. Under a Prussian occupation administration, three special courts were established in Freiburg, Mannheim and Rastatt to try the leading insurrectionists. Staffed by Badenese jurists and Prussian officers and operated in accordance with Baden law, these tribunals issued verdicts against sixty-four civilians and fifty-one military personnel. There were thirty-one death sentences, of which twenty-seven were actually carried out – executed by Prussian troops. According to one eyewitness, who saw the firing squads at work inside the walls of Rastatt fortress, the Prussians obeyed their orders to a man, though they returned from the execution grounds with faces 'as white as chalk'.[43]

GERMANY CALLING

1848 was the year of the nationalists. Across Europe, the political and social upheavals of the revolution were intertwined with national aspirations. Nationalism was contagious. German and Italian nationalists were inspired by the example of the Swiss liberals, whose conquest of the conservative *Sonderbund* in 1847 paved the way to the creation of the first Swiss federal state. In the southern German states, republican nationalists even formed volunteer brigades to fight alongside the Protestant Swiss cantons. Italian revolutionary nationalism in turn stirred the ambitions of the Croats, whose chief nationalist organ, in the absence of an agreed Croatian literary idiom, was the Italian-language *L'Avventura* in Dubrovnik. German nationalism stimulated the Czech patriotic movement. So powerful was the spell cast by the national idea that Europeans could derive vicarious excitement from each other's national causes. Liberals in Germany, France and Britain became enthusiasts of Polish, Greek and Italian liberty. Nationalism was a potentially radical force for two reasons. Firstly, nationalists, like liberals and radicals, claimed to speak for 'the people' rather than the crown. For liberals, 'the people' was a political community composed of educated, tax-paying citizens; for the nationalists it denoted an ethnicity defined by a common language and culture. In this sense, liberalism and nationalism were ideological cousins. Indeed nationalism was in some respects more inclusive than liberalism, whose horizons were confined to a wealthy, educated and largely urban elite. Nationalism by contrast, in theory at least, embraced every last member of the ethnic community. There was a close affinity here with the democratic orientation of mid-century radicalism; it is no coincidence that many German radicals became uncompromising nationalists. Secondly, nationalism was subversive because in many parts of Europe, the realization of the national vision implied fundamental transformations of the political map. Hungarian nationalists sought to separate themselves from the commonwealth of peoples under Habsburg rule; Lombard and Venetian patriots chafed under Habsburg rule; the Poles dreamed of a reconstituted Poland within the borders of 1772 – some Polish nationalists even called for the 'return' of Pomerania. Greek, Romanian and Bulgarian nationalists dreamed of throwing off the yoke of Ottoman imperial power.

If nationalism implied the political disintegration of the Habsburg monarchy, in Germany its thrust was integrative, it aimed to solder together the sundered parts of a putatively single German fatherland. How exactly the new Germany would look in practice was unclear. How would the unity of the new nation be reconciled with the rights and powers of the traditional monarchies? How much power would be concentrated in the central authority? Would the new German union be led by Austria or by Prussia? Where would its borders lie? These were questions that prompted endless contention and debate as the revolution unfolded. The national question was discussed in all the chancelleries and legislatures of the German states, but the pre-eminent theatre of public debate was the national parliament that opened on 18 April 1848 in St Paul's Church in Frankfurt/Main. This assembly, comprising deputies from all over the German states elected under a national franchise, set itself the task of drawing up the constitution for a new united Germany. The interior of the parliamentary chamber, an elegant elliptical rotunda, was draped in the national colours and dominated by a huge painting of *Germania* by the artist Philip Veit. Veit's monumental allegorical work, which was painted on to canvas and hung in front of the organ loft in the main chamber, showed a standing female figure crowned in oak leaves, a cast-off manacle at her feet; behind her the rising sun loosed darts of light through the tricolour fabric of the national flag.

The attitude of the Prussian authorities to the national project was of necessity ambivalent. Inasmuch as nationalists posed a principled challenge to the authority of the German territorial crowns, they were recognized as a subversive and dangerous force. This was the logic behind the campaign waged against the 'demagogues' in the post-war years. On the other hand, Prussian governments had no objection in principle to the creation of a tighter and more cohesive political organization of the German states, so long as this process served Berlin's power-political interests. This was the logic at work in Prussia's sponsorship of the Customs Union and its support for stronger Confederal security arrangements. By the 1840s, this consistent and self-interested pursuit of greater inter-territorial cohesion implied a more nuanced response to nationalism than had been possible in the immediate post-war years: if national sentiment could be managed, if it could be co-opted into some kind of partnership with the Prussian state, then national enthusiasm was a force that might be cultivated and exploited. This policy could bear fruit, of course, only if the nationalists in question could be persuaded that Prussia's interest and that of Germany as a whole were one and the same.

During the 1840s, the idea of an alliance between Prussia and the liberal nationalist movement came to appear increasingly plausible. In the aftermath of the war scare of 1840–41 and the crisis in 1846 over the future of the ethnically mixed duchies of Schleswig and Holstein on the border with Denmark, moderate liberals throughout Germany looked increasingly to Prussia as a surrogate for the underdeveloped security arrangements of the Confederation. 'Prussia must place itself at the head of Germany,' the Heidelberg professor Georg Gottfried Gervinus told Friedrich Engels in 1843, though he added that Berlin would first have to enact constitutional reform. The *Deutsche Zeitung*, a liberal journal founded in May 1847, explicitly advocated the pursuit of German unity through an active foreign policy, to be achieved through an alliance between the Prussian state and the nationalist movement.[44]

The appeal to national aspirations featured prominently in the Prussian king's early reactions to the revolutionary upheaval of March 1848. On the morning of 21 March, two days after the uprising and the departure of the army from the capital, a poster authorized by the king broadcast the following oracular announcement:

A new and glorious history is beginning for you today! You are henceforth once again a single great nation, strong free and powerful in the heart of Europe! Trusting in your heroic support and your spiritual rebirth, Prussia's Frederick William IV has placed himself at the head of the movement for the redemption of Germany. You will see him on horseback today in your midst with the venerable colours of the German nation.[45]

Sure enough, the Prussian king appeared at midday, sporting a tri-colour armband (some accounts speak of a sash in the national colours), with the national flag behind him, held aloft by a member of a Berlin shooting club. Throughout this curious royal perambulation through the capital the talk was of the nation. Students hailed the passing king as the new German Emperor, and Frederick William halted at intervals to address onlookers on the great importance of current developments for the future of the German nation. To drive the message home, the red, black and gold flag was flown that evening from the dome of the royal palace. A cabinet order despatched to the ministry of war announced that since the king would henceforth be devoting himself entirely to the 'German question' and expected Prussia to play a role in the resolution of the same, he wished the troops of his army to wear the 'German cockade as well as the Prussian one'.[46]

Most astonishing of all was the declaration issued on the evening of 21 March under the title 'To My People and to the German Nation'. The address began by recalling the dangerous days of 1813, when King Frederick William III had 'rescued Prussia and Germany from shame and humiliation' and went on to argue that in the current crisis, the collaboration of Germany's princes under a unified leadership was essential:

Today I assume this leadership [. . .]. My people, which does not fear danger, will not forsake me, and Germany will join me in a spirit of trust. I have today taken up the old German colours and have placed myself and my people under the venerable banner of the German Reich. Prussia is henceforth merged in Germany.[47]

It would be a mistake to see these extravagant gestures simply as an opportunist attempt to rally mass support around a beleaguered monarchy. Frederick William's enthusiasm for 'Germany' was entirely authentic and long predated the outbreak of the 1848 revolutions. Indeed there is something to be said for the view that he was the first truly German-minded monarch to occupy the Hohenzollern throne. Frederick William was deeply involved in the project to resume the construction of Cologne Cathedral, an imposing Gothic structure begun in 1248 but unfinished since work had ground to a halt in 1560. There had been talk of completing the cathedral since the turn of the century and Frederick William became an enthusiastic advocate and supporter of the idea. In 1842, two years after his accession, the king travelled to the Rhineland to take part in celebrations inaugurating the building works. He attended Protestant and Catholic services and presided over a cornerstone ceremony at which, to the astonishment and delight of the onlookers, he delivered a sparkling impromptu speech praising the 'spirit of German unity and strength' embodied in the cathedral project.[48] At around the same time, he wrote to Metternich that he had decided to devote himself to 'ensuring the greatness, power and honour of Germany'.[49]

When Frederick William spoke of German 'unity', he was not referring to the political unity of a nation-state, but to the diffuse, cultural, sacral unity of the medieval German Reich. His speculations did not, therefore, necessarily imply a challenge to Austria's traditional captaincy within the community of German states. Even during the war crisis of 1840–41, when Frederick William supported efforts to extend Prussia's influence over the security arrangements of the south German states, he was reluctant to contemplate a direct confrontation with Vienna. In the spring months of 1848, the Prussian king's vision of the German future was still in essence a vision of the past. On 24 April, Frederick William told the Hanoverian liberal and Frankfurt deputy Friedrich Christoph Dahlmann that his vision for Germany was a kind of reinvigorated Holy Roman Empire, in which a 'King of the Germans' (a Prussian, perhaps) would be chosen by a revived College of Electors and wield executive power under the honorary captaincy of a Habsburg 'Roman Emperor'.[50] As a romantic monarchical legitimist, he deplored the idea of a unilateral bid for power that would injure the historic rights of the other German crowns. He thus professed to be horrified when his new liberal foreign minister (Heinrich Alexander von Arnim-Suckow, appointed 21 March) proposed that he should accept the crown of a new 'German Empire'. 'Against my own declared and well-motivated will,' he complained to a close conservative associate, '[Arnim-Suckow] wants to present me!!!!!! with the imperial title . . . I will *not* accept the crown.'[51]

Yet the king's objection to a Prussian imperial title was by no means categorical. It would be another matter entirely if the other German princes voluntarily elected him to a position of pre-eminence and the Austrians were willing to renounce their ancient claim to leadership within the German Commonwealth. Under these circumstances, he told King Frederick August II of Saxony during the first week of May, he would be willing to consider accepting the crown of a new German Reich.[52] These were highly speculative reflections at the time, but as events unfolded over the summer and autumn of 1848, they came to seem increasingly plausible.

Within a month of the outbreak of the revolution, Prussia had an opportunity to demonstrate its willingness to show leadership in the defence of the German national interest. A crisis was brewing over the future of the duchies of Schleswig and Holstein, predominantly agrarian principalities that straddled the frontier between German- and Danish-speaking northern Europe. The complex legal and constitutional status of the two duchies was defined by three awkward facts: firstly, a law dating back to the fifteenth century forbade the separation of the two principalities; secondly, Holstein was a member of the German Confederation but Schleswig to the north was not; thirdly, the duchies operated under a different law of succession from that of the Kingdom of Denmark – succession through the female line was possible in the kingdom but not in the duchies, where the Salic law prevailed. The inheritance issue began to cause consternation in the early 1840s, when it became clear that the Danish crown prince, Frederick VII, was likely to die without issue. For the government in Copenhagen, the prospect loomed that Schleswig, with its numerous Danish speakers, might be separated for ever from the Danish state. In order to guard against this eventuality, Frederick's father, Christian VIII, issued the so-called 'Open Letter' of 1846, in which he announced the application of Danish inheritance law to Schleswig. This would permit the Danish Crown to retain its rights in the principality through the female line, should the future king die childless. The crisis triggered in the German states by the Open Letter brought about a dramatic intensification of nationalist sentiment; as we have seen, it also prompted many moderate liberals to look to Prussia for leadership in the face of the threat posed to the German interest (and specifically the German minority in Schleswig) by the Danish government.

Shortly after his accession to the Danish throne on 20 January 1848, Frederick VII brought the issue to a head by announcing the imminent publication of a national Danish constitution and stating that the king intended to integrate Schleswig into the Danish unitary state. A process of escalation was now under way on both sides of the border: in Copenhagen, Frederick VII's hand was forced by the nationalist Eiderdane movement; in Berlin, Frederick William IV was pressured into responding by Arnim-Suckow, a beneficiary of the March uprising. On 21 March, the new Danish government annexed Schleswig. The Germans in the south of Schleswig responded by forming a revolutionary provisional government. Outraged by the Danish annexation, the Confederal authorities voted to make Schleswig a member of the German Confederation. Acting with the official endorsement of the German Confederation, the Prussians assembled a military contingent, reinforced by small units from several other northern German states, and marched into Schleswig on 23 April. The German troops quickly overran the Danish positions and pressed northward into Danish Jutland, though they found it impossible to break the superiority of the Danish forces at sea.

There was jubilation among the nationalists, especially in the Frankfurt Parliament, where several of the most prominent liberal deputies – including Georg Beseler, Friedrich Christoph Dahlmann and the historian Johann Gustav Droysen – had close personal connections with the duchies. What the nationalists failed adequately to appreciate was the fact that the Schleswig-Holstein question was swiftly becoming an international affair. In St Petersburg, Tsar Nicholas was furious to find his Prussian brother-in-law working, as he saw it, hand-in-hand with the revolutionary nationalists. He threatened to send in Russian troops if Prussia did not withdraw from the duchies. This energetic Russian démarche in turn aroused the disquiet of the English government, which feared that the Schleswig-Holstein question might serve as a pretext for the creation of a Russian protectorate over Denmark. Since the Danes controlled access to the Baltic Sea (the Danish straits of Sund and Kattegat were known as the 'Bosporus of the North'), this was a matter of great strategic concern to London. The pressure for a Prussian with-drawal began to mount. Sweden soon joined the fray, along with France, and Prussia was forced to agree to a mutual evacuation of troops under the terms of the Armistice of Malmø, signed on 26 August 1848.[53]

The armistice came as a profound shock to the deputies in Frankfurt. The Prussians had signed it unilaterally, without the slightest reference to the Frankfurt Parliament. Nothing could better have demonstrated the impotence of this assembly, which was headed by a provisional 'imperial government', but had no armed force of its own and no means of obliging territorial governments to comply with its will. It was a serious blow to the legitimacy of the parliament, which had already begun to lose its grip on public opinion in the German states. In the initial mood of outrage that greeted the news of the armistice, a majority of the deputies voted on 5 September to block its implementation. But this was mere posturing, since the executive in Frankfurt had no means of controlling the situation in the north. On 16 September, the members voted again; this time they capitulated to power-political realities and accepted the armistice. During the riots that followed in the streets of Frankfurt, two conservative deputies were slain by an angry mob. Prussia thus demolished the hopes of the German nationalists. And yet this setback paradoxically helped to reinforce the Prussophilia of many moderate nationalist liberals, for it confirmed the centrality of Prussia to any future political resolution of the German question.

In the meanwhile, the Frankfurt Parliament was struggling to resolve the matter of the relationship between the Habsburg monarchy and the rest of Germany. Towards the end of October 1848, the deputies voted to adopt a 'greater-German' (*grossdeutsch*) solution to the national question: the Habsburg German (and Czech) lands would be included in the new German Reich; the non-German Habsburg lands would have to be formed into a separate constitutional entity and ruled from Vienna under a personal union. The problem was that the Austrians had no intention of accepting such an arrangement. Austria was by now recovering from the trauma of the revolution. In a vengeful crusade that took 2,000 lives, Vienna was retaken by government troops at the end of October. On 27 November, Prince Felix zu Schwarzenberg, chief minister in Vienna's new conservative government, exploded the greater-German option by announcing that he intended the Habsburg monarchy to remain a unitary political entity. The consensus at Frankfurt now shifted in the direction of the 'lesser-German' (*kleindeutsch*) solution favoured by a faction of moderate Protestant liberal nationalist deputies. Under the terms of a lesser-German option, Austria would be excluded from the new national polity, pre-eminence within which would pass (by default if not by design) to the Kingdom of Prussia.

Frederick William's speculations on a Prussian-imperial Crown were drifting from dream into reality. Late in November 1848, Heinrich von Gagern, the new minister-president (prime minister) of the provisional Reich government in Frankfurt, travelled to Berlin to attempt to per-suade Frederick William to accept – in principle – a German-imperial Crown. Frederick William initially refused, observing famously that the imperial title on offer was 'an invented crown of dirt and clay', but he also kept open the option of an acceptance, should the Austrians and the other German princes be in agreement. The signals broadcast by the government in Berlin were sufficiently encouraging to keep the small-German option afloat for the next few months. On 27 March 1849, the Frankfurt assembly voted (by a narrow margin) to approve a monarchi-cal constitution for the new Germany and, on the following day, a majority voted for Frederick William IV as German Emperor. In one of the famous set-pieces of German history, a delegation from the assembly, led by the Prussian liberal Eduard von Simson, travelled to Berlin to make a formal offer. The king received them on 3 April, thanked them warmly for the trust that they, in the name of the German people, had placed in his person, but refused the crown, on the grounds that Prussia could accept such an honour only on terms agreed with the other legitimate princes of the German states. In a letter addressed to his sister Charlotte – officially known as Tsarina Alexandra Federovna – but intended for the eyes of her husband, he spoke a different language: 'You have read my reply to the man-donkey-dog-pig-and-cat delegation from Frankfurt. It means in simple German: "Sirs! You have not any right at all to offer me anything whatsoever. Ask, yes, you may ask, but give – No – for in order to give, you would first of all have to be in possession of something that can be given, and this *is not the case*!" '[54]

With Frederick William's rejection of the crown, the fate of the great parliamentary experiment in Frankfurt was sealed. Yet the idea of a Prussian-led German union was not yet dead. During April, the Berlin government made it clear through a sequence of announcements that Frederick William IV was still willing to lead a German federal state

44. Frederick William IV receives a delegation from the Frankfurt Parliament. *Addressing the king is the deputy Eduard von Simson. Standing beside the monarch is Count Brandenburg.*

of some kind. On 22 April, the king's old friend Joseph Maria von Radowitz, who had been serving as a deputy to the Frankfurt Parliament, was recalled to Berlin to coordinate policy on a German union. Radowitz aimed to disarm the objections of Vienna by proposing a system of two concentric unions. Prussia would lead a relatively cohesive 'narrower union', which in turn would be loosely linked to Austria through a broader union. During May 1849, there were arduous negotiations with representatives of the lesser German kingdoms, Bavaria, Württemberg, Hanover and Saxony. At the same time, it was recognized that the new entity would not succeed unless it possessed some degree of legitimacy in public opinion. To this end, Radowitz rallied liberal and conservative advocates of the small-German idea at a widely publicized meeting in the city of Gotha. Amazingly, the Austrians seemed willing to consider the Radowitz plan; the Austrian envoy in Berlin, Count Prokesch von Osten, was much less hostile than might have been expected.

Despite these positive signs, the union project soon ran into serious trouble. It proved extraordinarily difficult to forge a compromise acceptable to all the key players. Twenty-six lesser territories expressed their willingness to join, but Bavaria and Württemberg, as ever, remained suspicious of Prussian intentions and stayed out. By the winter of 1849, Saxony and Hanover had also pulled back, followed by Baden. The Austrians, for their part, turned decisively against the idea, and began insisting first (from late February 1850) upon the inclusion in any proposed union of the entire Habsburg monarchy and later (from early May) upon the reinstatement of the old German Confederation. In this they were supported by the Russians, who heartily disapproved of Radowitz and his programme and intended to assist Austria against any serious challenge to its position in Germany.

The accumulating tension between Berlin and Vienna came to a head in September 1850. The flashpoint was a political conflict in the Electorate of Hesse-Kassel, a small territory that straddled the network of Prussian military roads linking Rhineland and Westphalia with the East-Elbian core provinces. The Elector of Hesse-Kassel – a notoriously reactionary figure – had attempted to force through counterrevolutionary measures against the will of the territorial diet, or *Landtag*. When influential elements within the army and the bureaucracy refused to comply, he called upon the aid of the revived German Confederation (the diet had been reinstated in Frankfurt, albeit without delegates from the union territories, on 2 September). Schwarzenberg immediately saw his opportunity: the deployment of Confederal troops in Hesse-Kassel would force the Prussians to back away from their unionist plans and to accept the resurrected Confederal Diet, with its Austrian presidency, as the legitimate political organization of the German states. Steered by the Austrians, the diet accordingly voted to restore the Elector's authority in Hesse-Kassel through a 'federal execution'. Enraged by this provocation, Frederick William IV appointed Radowitz foreign minister, with a view to signalling that Prussia had no intention of backing down.

A German civil war now seemed imminent. On 26 October, the diet in Frankfurt authorized Hanoverian and Bavarian forces to intervene in Hesse-Kassel. The Prussians deployed their own forces to the Hessian frontier, ready to resist a Confederal incursion. There followed a chain of stops and starts. On 1 November, news reached Berlin that the federal execution had begun – Bavarian troops had crossed the Hessian border. The Prussian cabinet was initially inclined to stop short of a full mobilization and seek a negotiated settlement, but this changed four days later when Schwarzenberg, pressing for an outright humiliation, demanded that Berlin remove the small troop contingents guarding the key Prussian military routes across Hesse-Kassel. Frederick William and his ministers now reluctantly resolved to order a full mobilization. On 24 November, Schwarzenberg, supported by Russia, served an ultimatum to Berlin demanding a complete Prussian withdrawal from Hesse-Kassel within the next forty-eight hours. Just as time was running out, Prussia agreed to further negotiations and everyone backed away from war. At a conference in Olmütz, Bohemia on 28–29 November, the Prussians stood down. Under the terms of the agreement known as the Punctation of Olmütz, Berlin undertook to participate in a joint federal intervention against Hesse-Kassel and to demobilize the Prussian army. Prussia and Austria also agreed to work together as equals in negotiating a reformed and restructured Confederation. These negotiations duly took place, but the promise of reform was not fulfilled; the old Confederation was restored, with some minor modifications, in 1851.

THE LESSONS OF FAILURE

Through the shouting and gunfire of the March days, Frederick William IV had heard German music. Among the many German sovereigns who feared for their thrones in that tumultuous year, he was the only one to drape himself in the colours of the nation. While the Habsburg monarchy turned inward to confront its multiple domestic revolutions, Prussia began to play a leading role in German affairs, confronting the Danes over Schleswig and leading the effort to repress the second revolution of 1849 in the southern states. With some success, Berlin cultivated the pro-Prussian faction emerging within the German liberal movement, creating a degree of public legitimacy for its hegemonial designs. Prussia pursued the union project in a spirit of flexibility and compromise, hoping thereby to build a German entity that would be both popular (in the elitist, liberal sense) and monarchical without alienating Vienna. But the union project failed, and with it the king's hopes of placing Prussia at the head of a united Germany. What light does this failure shed on the condition of Prussia and its place in the commonwealth of German states after the revolutions of 1848?

The events of 1848–50 revealed, among other things, how very disjointed the Prussian executive still was. Because the monarch – rather than the cabinet or ministry of state – was still at the centre of the decision-making process, factionalism and rivalry within the antechamber of power remained a serious problem. Indeed, in some respects, this tendency was reinforced by the revolutions, which forced the king into the arms of the conservative circles at court. This was a source of endless problems for Radowitz, who was loathed by the court camarilla and lived in constant fear of conspiracies against him. It also meant that Berlin's support for the unionist initiative at times appeared half-hearted, as powerful ministers and advisers close to the king let it be known to compatriots and foreign emissaries alike that they did not support the Radowitz policy. Even Frederick William IV himself, who liked to peer at questions from every possible angle, occasionally gave signs of wavering in his support for his beloved favourite. This systemic irresolution in Berlin in turn reinforced Schwarzenberg's determination to press the Prussians hard over Hesse-Kassel. His ultimate aim was not to wage war against Prussia, but to 'get rid of the radical leadership' there, and 'strike an agreement with the conservatives, with whom one could safely share power in Germany'.[55] The Austrians could still, in other words, exploit the divisions within the Prussian executive, just as they had done in the 1830s and 1840s. Here was a problem that would be resolved only when a powerful prime minister succeeded in suppressing the antechamber and imposing his authority on the government.

The particularism of the lesser states was a further obstacle. Bavaria refused to join the Prussian union; Baden and Saxony refused to stay in it. This was a poor reward for the bloody work the Prussians had done in restoring monarchical authority in all three states. In Baden, the Grand Duke owed his very existence as sovereign to the intervention of the Prussians, who remained in occupation until 1852. It was as if the treasury of merits the Prussians had worked so hard to accumulate through the Customs Union, German security policy and the suppression of revolution counted for nothing. The irony did not escape the notice of those two percipient contemporary Prussians, Karl Marx and Friedrich Engels, who wrote from London in October 1850:

Prussia had restored the rule of the forces of reaction everywhere and the more these forces re-established themselves, the more the petty princes deserted Prussia to throw themselves into the arms of Austria. Now that they could again rule as they had done before March [1848], absolutist Austria was closer to them than a power whose ability to be absolutist was no greater than its desire to be liberal.[56]

The débâcle of 1850 thus conformed to a time-honoured pattern. The Habsburgs would never be able to sound the bright trumpets of German unity, but they could still play masterfully upon the wheezing organ of the Confederation. In the ears of the lesser German dynasties, this was still the more congenial music.

Schwarzenberg's success in facing down the Prussians over Hesse-Kassel would have been unthinkable without the advantages of an international setting that favoured Vienna against Berlin. Here was another lesson that Prussian sovereigns had had to learn at intervals throughout the history of the kingdom. The German question was ultimately a European question. It could not be addressed (let alone resolved) in isolation. Russia, France, Britain and Sweden all joined in pressing Berlin to back down in the war with Denmark in the summer of 1848, and Russian aid was essential in restoring Vienna to a position where it could respond forcefully to the challenge from Berlin. It was the Russians who tipped the balance in the struggle between Habsburg forces and the Hungarian revolution, the largest, best organized and most determined insurrection of 1848 anywhere in Europe. Behind Schwarzenberg at Olmütz stood the incalculable power of the Russian Tsar. 'At the Tsar's command,' Marx and Engels predicted in October 1850, 'rebellious Prussia will finally give way without a drop of blood being spilled.'[57] From the perspective of November 1850, it was clear that a successful bid for German unity by Prussia would require a fundamental change in the power-political constellation of Europe. How this transformation might come about and what consequences it would entail were matters beyond the horizons of even the most imaginative contemporaries.

For the enthusiasts of the unionist project, the Punctation seemed a shocking defeat, a humiliation, a stain on the kingdom's honour that called out for vengeance. The liberal nationalist historian Heinrich von Sybel, who had studied with Leopold Ranke in Berlin, later recalled the mood of disappointment. The Prussians, he wrote, had cheered their king as he took up the national cause against the Danes and defended the worthy people of Hesse-Kassel against their tyrannical Elector. 'But now came a change: the dagger slipped from the trembling fist, and many a doughty warrior shed bitter tears into his beard. [. . .] From a thousand throats rang a single cry of pain: for the second time the work of Frederick the Great had been annihilated.'[58] Sybel was exaggerating. There were many who welcomed the news of Olmütz, including of course the conservative enemies of Radowitz. One of these was Otto von Manteuffel, who had long been pressing for a negotiated settlement with Austria and was appointed minister-president and foreign minister on 5 December 1850 – he was to remain in both posts for most of the following decade. Another was the conservative deputy Otto von Bismarck. In a famous speech to the Prussian parliament on 3 December 1850, Bismarck welcomed the Olmütz agreement, adding that he did not think it lay in Prussia's interest 'to play Don Quixote all over Germany on behalf of disgruntled parliamentary celebrities [*gekränkte Kammerzelebritäten*]'.[59]

And even those national-minded Protestant liberals who had supported the unionist project conceded that Olmütz was also a moment of sobriety and clarification after the rhetorical excesses of the revolution. 'Realities,' wrote the small-German nationalist and historian Johann Gustav Droysen in 1851, 'began to triumph over ideals, interests over abstractions [. . .] Not through "freedom", not through national resolutions would the unity of Germany be achieved. What was called for was one power against the other powers.'[60] Far from undermining Droysen's belief in Prussia's German vocation, the setbacks of 1848–50 actually reinforced it. In an essay published in 1854 on the eve of the Crimean War, he expressed the hope that a determined Prussia would one day emerge to assert its leadership over the other German states and thereby found a unified, Protestant German nation. 'After 1806 came 1813, after Ligny, Waterloo. In truth, we only need the cry "Forward", and everything will spring into motion.'[61]

THE NEW SYNTHESIS

Historical narratives of the 1848 revolutions across Europe commonly end with an elegiacal reflection on the failure of revolution, the triumph of reaction, the execution, imprisonment, persecution or exile of radical activists and the concerted efforts of subsequent administrations to erase by force the memory of insurrection. It is a commonplace that the restoration of order in 1848–9 ushered in an era of reaction in Prussia. There was a concerted effort to erase the memory of insurrection from public awareness. Ceremonies in honour of the 'March fallen' and processions to their graves in the Friedrichshain cemetery were strictly forbidden. The police force was consolidated, enlarged and its sphere of responsibility extended.

The democratic suffrage conceded by the Prussian authorities under the constitution of December 1848 was rescinded in April 1849. Under the new franchise, nearly all male inhabitants of the kingdom were entitled to a vote, but their votes differed in value, since they were divided into three 'classes' according to their taxable income. Each class voted for one third of the electors who in turn elected the deputies to the parliament. In 1849, the steep income differentials across the kingdom's population meant that the first class, representing the wealthiest 5 per cent of the electorate, voted for as many electors as the second (12.6 per cent) and the third (82.7 per cent).[62] The parliament was saddled in 1855 with a new upper house, the *Herrenhaus*, loosely modelled on the British House of Lords and containing not a single elected member. The revived German Confederation returned to its time-honoured role as an organ of domestic repression throughout the German states and issued the Confederal Act of 6 July 1854, which, coupled with supporting legislation in the individual states, introduced a range of instruments to inhibit the circulation of subversive publications. Even more significant was the Confederal Act on Associations, passed just over a week later, which subjected all political associations to police supervision and forbade them to maintain relations with each other.[63]

Yet there was no return to the conditions of the pre-March era. Nor should we think of the revolutions as a failure. The Prussian upheavals of 1848 were not, to borrow A. J. P. Taylor's phrase, 'a turning point' where Prussia 'failed to turn'. They were a watershed between an old world and a new. The decade that began in March 1848 witnessed a profound transformation in political and administrative practices, a 'revolution in government'.[64] The upheaval itself may have ended in failure, marginalization, exile or imprisonment for some of its protagonists, but its momentum communicated itself like a seismic wave to the fabric of the Prussian (and not only the Prussian) administration, changing structures and ideas, bringing new priorities into government or reorganizing old ones, reframing political debates.

Prussia was now – for the first time in its history – a constitutional state with an elected parliament. This fact in itself created an entirely new point of departure for political developments in the kingdom.[65] The Prussian constitution of 1848 was promulgated by the crown, rather than drawn up by an elected assembly. Yet it was popular with the great majority of liberals and of the moderate conservatives.[66] The leading liberal newspapers welcomed the constitution and even defended it against its detractors on the left, on the grounds that it incorporated most of what the liberals had demanded and was thus 'the work of the people'. The fact that the government had broken with liberal principle by issuing it without parliamentary sanction was widely overlooked.[67] Over the years that followed, the constitution became 'a part of Prussian public life'.[68] Moreover, the unwillingness of the moderate liberals to risk a return to open confrontation and revolution on the one hand, and the readiness of the government to persevere with a policy of reform on the other, furnished the basis for a governmental coalition of factions that could generally muster a majority in the lower chamber.[69]

By contrast with the old provincial Estates of the pre-March era, which were dominated by the regional nobilities, the new representative system, centred on the Landtag in Berlin, had the effect of gradually pruning back the political dominance in rural areas of the old land-owning class and thereby altered in a lasting way the balance of power within Prussian society.[70] This effect was amplified by the Commutation Law of 1850, which completed the work begun by the agrarian reformers of the Napoleonic era and finally eliminated patrimonial juris-dictions in the countryside.[71] Otto von Manteuffel, minister-president of Prussia from 1850 until 1858, was thus not wrong in seeing himself as overseeing the advent of a new age for Prussia. The basis for what would later be called the 'new era' of liberal resurgence after 1858 could already be discerned within the constitutional system forged by the revolution.

The tone was set after 1848 by a loose post-revolutionary coalition that answered to the aspirations both of the more statist and moderate elements of liberalism and of the more innovative and entrepreneurial elements among the old conservative elites – there were parallels here with the 'marriage' (*connubio*) between right-liberal and reform-conservative interests that dominated the new parliament in post-revolutionary Piedmont and with the trans-partisan coalitions of the *Regeneração* in Portugal and the *Unión Liberal* in Spain.[72] This informal coalition was not confined to parliament and the bureaucracy, but also embraced parts of civil society. New channels of communication opened up between the administration and powerful lobby groups of liberal entrepreneurs who found ways of making themselves heard and influencing the formulation of policy. The result was an amalgamation of old and new elites based not on an identity of interest, but on a 'negotiated settlement', from which both sides could draw benefits.[73]

So effective was this new politically and socially composite elite in controlling the middle ground of politics that it successfully marginalized both the democratic left and the old right. The 'Old Conservatives' found themselves on the defensive, even at court, where they were outmanoeuvred by those less doctrinaire conservatives who were willing to work within the new political constellation and to orient themselves pragmatically towards the state. It is remarkable how quickly the king himself and many of the conservatives around him came to accept the new constitutional order. The monarch who had once vowed in public that he would never allow a 'written piece of paper' to come between his Lord God in heaven and his country, soon made his peace with the new regime, though he continued to look for ways of shoring up his own authority within it. An important figure in the process of conservative accommodation was the new minister-president, Otto von Manteuffel, a sturdy and unexcitable career bureaucrat who took the view that the purpose of government was to mediate between the conflicting interests of the entities that constitute civil society.[74] The conservative university professor Friedrich Julius Stahl was another important modernizer; he led the way in reconciling conservative objectives with modern representative politics.

Even Prince William of Prussia, initially a more vehemently conservative figure than Stahl had ever been, was quick to adapt to the demands of the new situation. 'What is past is past!' he wrote in a remarkable letter to the Camphausen government only three weeks after the March events. 'Nothing can be brought back; may every attempt to do so be abandoned!' It was now the 'duty of every patriot' to 'help build the new Prussia'.[75] The former 'grape-shot prince' returned from Britain in the summer of 1848 ready to work within the post-revolutionary order. The politics of the traditional conservatism, with its pious legitimism and its attachment to corporatist structures now appeared narrow, self-interested and retrograde. It was unthinkable, Prussian Minister-President Otto von Manteuffel pointed out to the conservative rural opponents of fiscal reform, that the Prussian state should continue to be run 'like the landed estate of a nobleman'.[76] In their unwillingness to embrace the new order, the exponents of an unreconstructed pre-March conservatism risked acquiring the taint of opposition, or even of treason.

The revolution also placed the Prussian state on a new fiscal footing. Among other things, it enabled the administration to escape from the shackles of Hardenberg's State Indebtedness Law, which had limited public spending in the Restoration era. As one deputy of the Prussian parliament declared in March 1849, the previous administration had 'stingily refused' to provide the sums necessary to develop the country. 'However,' he added, 'we now stand at the government's side and will always approve the funds required for the promotion of improved transport and for the support of commerce, industry and agriculture . . .'[77] Neither the new income tax introduced in 1851 (whose legitimacy was perceived as deriving from the suffrage) nor the long-awaited reform of the old land tax in 1861, would have been possible before the revolution.[78] Flush with new cash, the Prussian administrations of the 1850s could afford a substantial rise in public spending on commercial and infrastructural projects, not only in absolute terms, but also in relation to spending on defence, which had traditionally absorbed the lion's share of Prussian government budgets.[79] The problem of raising a loan for the Eastern Railway, which had forced the government to summon the United Diet in 1847, was solved by the new constitution; 33 million thalers were duly approved for this and two other unfinished arterial lines.[80]

This unaccustomed liberality was underwritten by a new emphasis on the right and obligation of the state to deploy public funds for the purpose of modernization.[81] Such arguments benefited from the congenial climate of contemporary German economic theory, which underwent a reorientation during the middle decades of the nineteenth century away from the stringently anti-statist positions of the German 'free trade school' towards the view that the state had certain macro-economic objectives to fulfil that could not be achieved by individuals or groups within society.[82] Closely linked with this holistic view of the state's economic competence was an insistence upon the need to develop administrative measures in accordance with an over-arching preconceived plan. During the business crisis of 1846–8, some prominent Prussian liberals had called upon the state to take over the administration of the kingdom's railways and unite them into 'an organic whole'.[83] But it was not until the 1850s that the Prussian finance minister, August von der Heydt, himself a liberal merchant banker from Elberfeld, presided over a gradual 'nationalization' of the Prussian railways, motivated by the conviction that only the state was capable of ensuring that the resulting system was rational in terms of the state as a whole – private interests alone would not suffice. In this he was fully supported by the lower house of the new parliament. A parliamentary railways commission formed to advise the government expressed the view that 'the transfer of all railways to the state's possession must remain the government's goal' and that the authorities must 'strive to reach it through every means available'.[84]

On the other hand, the implicit terms of the post-revolutionary settlement also required that the state at times step back and honour the autonomy of the business sector. This is what happened in 1856, when conservatives within the cabinet attempted to put a stop to the proliferation of 'commandite' banks in the Kingdom of Prussia. These banks were essentially private investment vehicles used by the business community to bypass the government's continuing reluctance to charter joint-stock banks. The conservatives (including the king himself) viewed these institutions as dubious French innovations that would encourage high-risk speculations and destabilize the social order. In 1856, therefore, the cabinet drew up a draft decree prohibiting the formation of commandite banks. Manteuffel, who had been approached by leading businessmen, was able to block this initiative and the government gradually relinquished its authority to control the flow of credit to financial institutions. Even in the coal and iron industries, which had traditionally been subject to close government supervision, entrepreneurs were successful in negotiating a loosening of state controls.[85]

Steps were also taken after 1848 to secure the unity and coherence of the central administration. In 1852, Minister-President Otto von Manteuffel elicited a cabinet order from the king establishing the minister-president as the sole conduit for formal communications between the ministry and the monarch. This important document signalled an attempt to realize at last the unity of administration that Hardenberg had struggled for in the 1810s, but it was also a reply to the challenge thrown up by the revolution which had pushed the king into the arms of his camarilla and thereby undermined the coherence of the supreme executive. In the short term, the cabinet order did not suffice to eliminate the influence of courtiers, intriguers and favourites. Manteuffel suffered, as all his predecessors had, from the incessant plotting of the ultra-conservatives who clustered around the king. The intriguing reached fever pitch in 1855, when the outbreak of the Crimean War split the political elite into the usual western and eastern factions. The ultras, who favoured an alliance with autocratic Russia against the west, did their utmost to dislodge the king from his commitment to neutrality.

Unsettled by these machinations and uncertain of the king's confidence in himself, Manteuffel kept abreast of the situation by employing a spy to secure copies of confidential papers from the apartments of key ultras, including the venerable Leopold von Gerlach, still faithfully serving his king as adjutant-general. There was profound embarrassment when the spy in question, a former lieutenant by the name of Carl Techen, was picked up by police and confessed under questioning that he had purchased them on behalf of the minister-president. The embarrassment deepened yet further when one of the stolen letters revealed that Gerlach had himself been employing a spy to watch the king's brother, Prince William, who was seen as a powerful opponent of a Russian alliance. This 'Prussian Watergate'[86] revealed that the problem of the antechamber of power remained unsolved. The Prussian central executive was still a loose assemblage of lobbies clustered around the king. The cabinet order of 1852 was an important start, nevertheless. In later years under the premiership of the far more ruthless and ambitious Otto von Bismarck, it would provide a mechanism for a concentration of power sufficient to ensure a measure of unity across cabinet and administration.

The years following the revolutions of 1848 also saw a renegotiation of the relationship between government and its public. The revolutions of 1848 triggered a transition towards a more organized, pragmatic and flexible handling of the press than had been the norm in the Restoration era. A central feature of this transition was the abandonment of censorship. Censorship – in the sense of the vetting of printed material for political content prior to publication – had been an important instrument of government power in the Restoration era and the call for its abolition was one of the central themes of liberal and radical dissent before 1848. In the course of the revolutions, censorship regimes across Germany were dismantled and the freedom of the press enshrined in laws and constitutions. To be sure, many of the permissive press laws issued in 1848 did not survive the reimposition of order. On the other hand, this did not imply – in most states – a return to pre-March conditions. In Prussia, as in a number of other German states, the focus of press policy shifted from the cumbersome pre-censorship of printed material to the surveillance of those political groups that produced it. A substantial component of the liberal programme thus survived the débâcle of the revolution.[87]

This was an important shift, because the transition from a preventive to a repressive policy brought governmental measures into the open. Newspapers and journals could be penalized only after they had begun to circulate, that is, after the 'damage', as it were, had been done. The administration was thus under increasing pressure to find other, less direct means of influencing the press. At the same time, differences between the police authorities, the judiciary and responsible ministers as to what constituted an illegal printed utterance meant that the efforts of the former were often thwarted. This problem was particularly pronounced under Minister-President von Manteuffel, who disagreed with the extremely conservative Interior Minister Ferdinand von Westphalen on what was permissible in print and what was not.[88] The fact that all citizens now enjoyed the right, in theory at least, to express their opinions in print provided the basis for all those involved with the production of political reading matter – booksellers and newsagents, publishers and editors-in-chief – to besiege the authorities with petitions, constitutional objections and appeal proceedings. In such cases, the governments found themselves confronting not merely an isolated journalist or editor, but the entire circle of those who supported a specific journal.[89]

In Prussia, as in most European states, the expansion of political print and of the politicized reading public that had taken place during the revolution proved irreversible. The government dealt with this problem by adopting a more supple and coordinated approach to the business of shaping public attitudes. Here as in so many other areas of administrative innovation, it was the experience of revolution that provided the impetus behind reform. In the summer of 1848, under the liberal government of Minister-President Auerswald, the Prussian administration established a Literary Cabinet in order to coordinate an official response both to liberal policy critiques and to the more fundamental anti-constitutional opposition of the Old Conservatives and their organ, the *Neue Preussische Zeitung.*[90] The first Literary Cabinet collapsed in November 1848 after the change of government, but it was reconstituted under Otto von Manteuffel in the following month, and its activities gradually broadened to encompass the strategic placement of government-friendly articles in key journals and the purchase of a semi-official newspaper, the *Deutsche Reform*, that would support the line of the Cabinet while retaining the appearance and credibility of an independent publication. On 23 December 1850, the coordination of press policy was at last given a secure institutional basis in the Central Agency for Press Affairs (*Zentralstelle für Pressangelegenheiten*). The agency's responsibilities included the administration of funds set aside for the purpose of subsidizing the press, the supervision of subsidized newspapers, and the cultivation of 'relationships' with domestic and foreign papers.[91] The *Zentralstelle* also ran its own newspaper, *Die Zeit*, which was known for its blistering attacks on the chief spokesmen of the conservative camp, including Otto von Bismarck, the Pietist Hans Hugo von Kleist-Retzow and even Interior Minister Westphalen himself.[92]

Manteuffel believed that it was time to move beyond the traditionally confrontational relationship between press and government that had been the norm before 1848. The administration would not enter directly into political debate, but through its press agency it would inaugurate 'an organic exchange [*Wechselwirkung*] between all arms of the state and the press'; it would work proactively to establish in advance the right attitude to governmental activity. The government would draw on privileged sources within the various ministries to promulgate news concerning the life of the state and important events abroad.[93] During the early 1850s, the Central Agency succeeded in building up a network of press contacts that penetrated deep into the provincial press. Cooperative editors were provided with privileged information or funding, and many local newspapers became financially dependent on the various perks that came with joining the system: fees for official announcements, subsidies, ministerial block subscriptions and so on.

Manteuffel's innovation thus heralded the transition from a system based on the filtering of press material through a cumbersome apparatus of censorship, to a more nuanced method of news and information management. All this was persuasive testimony to the irreversibility of the changes wrought by 1848. 'Every century has seen new cultural powers enter into the sphere of traditional life, powers which were not to be destroyed but to be incorporated [*verarbeitet*],' Manteuffel wrote in July 1851. 'Our generation recognizes the press as such a power. Its significance has grown with the expanded participation of the people in public affairs, a participation that is partly expressed, partly fed and directed by the press.'[94] Among those entrusted with disbursing Manteuffel's cash to friendly journalists and newspaper editors was none other than Otto von Bismarck, who took up his post as Prussia's representative at the Confederal Diet in 1851.

15

Four Wars

For nearly half a century after 1815, Prussia stood on the sidelines of European power politics, steering in the lee of the great powers, avoiding commitments and shying away from conflict. It avoided antagonizing its powerful neighbours. It acquiesced in Russian tutelage over its foreign policy. Prussia was the only major European power to remain neutral during the Crimean War (1854–6). To some, it even seemed that Prussia's status as a member of the concert of the great European powers was obsolete. Prussia, a *Times* leader article observed in 1860, was

always leaning on somebody, always getting somebody to help her, never willing to help herself [. . .] present in Congresses, but absent in battles [. . .] ready to supply any amount of ideals or sentiments, but shy of anything that savours of the actual. She has a large army, but notoriously one in no condition for fighting. [. . .] No one counts on her as a friend; no one dreads her as an enemy. How she became a great Power, history tells us; why she remains so nobody can tell.[1]

And yet, within eleven years of this blistering appraisal, the Kingdom of Prussia had reinvigorated its armed forces, driven Austria out of Germany, destroyed the military might of France, built a new nation-state and transformed the European balance of power in a burst of political and military energy that astonished the world.

THE ITALIAN WAR

It was no coincidence that the unifications of Italy and Germany were accomplished within a decade of each other. The cultural prehistory of the German nation-state extends back into and beyond the eighteenth century, but the chain of events that made its foundation a *political* possibility began with the second Italian war of unification. On 26 April 1859, the Austrian Empire declared war on the north Italian Kingdom of Piedmont. This was a conflict that had been planned in advance. During the summer of 1858, the Piedmontese Prime Minister Camillo di Cavour had negotiated a defensive alliance with Emperor Napoleon III of France. In the spring of 1859, Cavour provoked Vienna by massing Piedmontese troops near the border with Austrian Lombardy. The resulting Austrian declaration of war activated France's obligations under the secret treaty. French troops rushed southwards across the Alps in the first major mobilization by railway. Between the end of April and the beginning of July, the joint French-Piedmontese forces occupied Lombardy, winning two major victories against the Austrians at Magenta (4 June) and Solferino (24 June). Piedmont annexed the Duchy of Lombardy; the duchies of Parma, Modena and Tuscany and the papal territory of Romagna were coaxed into a union with Turin. Piedmont now controlled the north of the peninsula and things might have stayed that way, had it not been for an invasion of the south by a band of volunteers under the command of Giuseppe Garibaldi. The Kingdom of Naples quickly collapsed, clearing the way for the unification of most of the peninsula under the rule of the Piedmontese monarchy. An Italian kingdom was proclaimed in March 1861.

The Prussian monarch, William I, and his foreign minister, Alexander von Schleinitz, responded to these events with the usual Prussian circumspection. As the Franco-Austrian conflict loomed, Prussia stuck to the middle ground, adopting neither the 'conservative' option of an alliance with Vienna, nor the 'liberal' option of a partnership with France against Austria. There were the usual efforts to make incremental gains in Germany at Austria's expense. Berlin promised, for example, to assist Austria against France, but only on the condition that Prussia be placed in command of all the non-Austrian Confederal contingents. This proposal, which recalled the security initiatives of Bernstorff and Radowitz during the war scares of 1830–32 and 1840–41, was rejected on prestige grounds by the Austrian Emperor. At about the same time, Berlin deployed heavy troop concentrations to the Rhineland to deter Napoleon III from extending the sphere of his operations to western Germany. There was nothing particularly remarkable or unexpected about these measures. In responding thus to the Italian crisis (and the accompanying French war scare), the Prussian government worked within the well-worn grooves of a tentative dualist rivalry that sought to avoid direct confrontation while embracing the opportunity to expand Prussian influence at Austria's expense.

Yet it is clear in retrospect that the Italian war set Prussian national policy on a new footing. It was obvious to contemporaries that there were parallels between the Italian and the German predicament. In both cases a strong sense (within the educated elite) of historical and cultural nationhood coexisted with the fact of dynastic and political division (though Italy had only seven separate states to Germany's thirty-nine). In both cases, it was Austria that stood in the way of national consolidation. There were also clear parallels between Piedmont and Prussia. Both states were noted for their confident bureaucracies and their modernizing reforms, and both were constitutional monarchies (since 1848). Each had sought to suppress popular nationalism while at the same time manoeuvring to extend its own influence in the name of the nation over the lesser states within its sphere of interest. It was thus easy for small-German enthusiasts of a Prussian-led union to project the Italian events of 1859–61 on to the German political map.[2]

The Italian war also demonstrated that new doors had opened within the European political system. Most important of these was the estrangement between Austria and Russia. In 1848, the Russians had saved the Austrian Empire from partition at the hands of the Hungarian national movement. During the Crimean War of 1854–6, however, the Austrians had made the fateful decision to join the anti-Russian coalition, a move that was seen in St Petersburg as rank treachery. Vienna thereby irretrievably forfeited the Russian support that had once been the cornerstone of its foreign policy.[3] Cavour was the first European politician to show how this realignment could be exploited to his state's advantage.

The events of 1859 were instructive in other ways as well. Under Napoleon III, France emerged as a power prepared to challenge by force the European order established at Vienna in 1815. The Prussians now felt the ancestral threat from the west more keenly than ever. The shock effect of the French intervention in Italy was heightened by memories of the first Napoleon, whose ascendancy had begun with the subjugation of the Italian peninsula and continued with an invasion of the Rhineland. The Prussian mobilization of 1859 may not have been the disaster some historians have described, but it did nothing to allay the sense of vulnerability to a resurgent Bonapartist France.[4] As for the Austrians, they had fought bitterly to keep their Italian possessions, inflicting 18,000 casualties on the Franco-Piedmontese at Magenta and Solferino. Would they not also fight to defend their political pre-eminence within a divided Germany? Prussia's position was in some respects worse than Piedmont's, for it seemed clear that the middling states of the 'third Germany' (unlike the lesser north Italian principalities) would support Austria in any open struggle between the two potential German hegemons. 'Almost all Germany for the last forty years has [. . .] cherished a hostile spirit against Prussia,' William wrote to Schleinitz on 26 March 1860, 'and for a year this has decidedly been on the increase.'[5]

The Italian war was thus a reminder of the centrality of armed force to the resolution of entrenched power-political conflicts, and the view gained ground within the military leadership that Prussia would have to reform and strengthen its army if it was to meet the challenges facing it in the near future. This was not a new problem. Since the 1810s, financial constraints had meant that the size of the army had not kept pace with the growth in the Prussian population. By the 1850s, only about one-half of the young men of eligible age were being drafted. There were also concerns about the quality of the Landwehr militia created to fight Napoleon by the military reformers Scharnhorst and Boyen, as its officers were trained to much less exacting standards.

Leading the campaign for military reform was the new regent, Prince William of Prussia. William was already a 62-year-old man with an impressive spray of whiskers when he began in 1858 to deputize for his older brother, who had been incapacitated by a sequence of strokes. William's emotional attachment to the Prussian army was deeply rooted in his biography. He had worn a uniform since the age of six. On 1 January 1807, at the age of nine, he received his ensign's commission (together with promotion to lieutenant as a Christmas present). His earliest experiences in service were bound up with the memory of invasion and the flight of the royal family to East Prussia. Unlike his more mentally agile elder brother, William disliked his lessons and was never happier than when in the company of his fellow cadets and military tutors.[6] It is easy to imagine how important the companionable routines of service must have become after the trauma of his mother's death in 1810. William's devotion was focused on the regular army of the line, not on the auxiliary militias of the Landwehr. William was repelled by the civilian ethos of the Landwehr, which he regarded as both militarily ineffective and politically unreliable. Boyen and Scharnhorst had set out to forge a military establishment that would feel and engage the patriotic enthusiasms of the people. William and his military advisers wanted an armed force that was responsive only to the will of the sovereign.

It would be going too far to suggest that William already had in mind the unification of Germany by armed Prussian force – his thinking on the German question was much more open-ended than that. Yet there is no doubt that he was a consistent enthusiast for the idea of a closer German union of some kind, and that he envisaged this as occurring under Prussian captaincy. William had shared his brother's enthusiasm for the ill-fated Erfurt Union and was disappointed by the Prussian retreat at Olmütz. 'Whoever wants to govern Germany must conquer it first,' he had written in 1849. 'Whether the time for this unification has come, God alone knows; but that Prussia is destined to stand at the summit of Germany is an underlying fact of our history. But when and how? That is the question.' During his posting to the Rhineland as military governor in 1849, William cultivated contacts with 'small-German' liberal enthusiasts of a Prussian-led union. 'Prussia's historical development shows that it is destined to lead Germany,' he wrote in May 1850.[7]

In order to meet the challenges of a more aggressive German policy, Prussia needed a flexible and highly effective military instrument. William and his military advisers aimed to double the size of the Prussian army by raising the number of recruits in each annual levy, extending the period of basic training by six months to three years and lengthening the period of service in the regular army reserve from two to five years. The regent also proposed to draw a clearer line between the regular army and the Landwehr, which was to be separated from the front line and regular reserve units and relegated to a subordinate position at the rear.

The government's call for military reform was not in itself particularly controversial. Military expenditure had been in relative decline since 1848 and there was broad support across the liberal majority in the parliament for the idea that Prussia needed a stronger army if it was to remain capable of independent action. The events of 1859, moreover, produced a remarkable mobilization of liberal nationalist opinion across northern Germany, culminating in the foundation of the National

Society (*Nationalverein*) in September 1859. Led by the Hanoverian nobleman Rudolf von Bennigsen, this was an elite body of several thousand parliamentary deputies, university professors, lawyers and journalists, whose purpose was to lobby the Prussian government on behalf of the small-German cause.

The real problem lay in the question of the political relationship between the army and the parliament. Three aspects of the monarch's reform programme particularly antagonized the liberals. The first was the plan to do away with what remained of the Landwehr's independence. The military chiefs viewed the Landwehr as the defunct remnant of a bygone era, but for many liberals it remained a potent embodiment of the ideal of a people's army. The second bone of contention was the king's insistence on a three-year training period for soldiers of the line. Liberals rejected this in part because of the cost implications, and in part because they believed – with some justice – that the three-year period was intended less as a military than as a political measure, to ensure that soldiers were imbued with conservative and militarist values, as well as trained to make war. Underlying both these issues was the central question of the monarch's unique, extra-constitutional power of command – the *Kommandogewalt*.[8]

Conflict over the military was pre-programmed into the Prussian political system after 1848. The issue had both a constitutional and a broader cultural dimension. The constitutional problem was simply that the monarch and the parliament had potentially conflicting rights over the army. The monarch was responsible for command functions and in general for the composition and functionality of the military establishment. But it was the parliament that controlled funding. From the crown's point of view, the army was an organization bound in personal loyalty to the monarch and quite independent of the parliament. Liberal parliamentarians, by contrast, took the view that their budgetary powers implied a limited right to co-determine the character of the army. This implied not only policing expenditure, but also ensuring that the army reflected the values of the broader political culture – this latter issue was the tripwire that had precipitated the crisis of the Berlin parliament in 1848. On both sides, the issues involved were of constitutive importance. William insisted that the *Kommandogewalt* was an unalienable attribute of his sovereignty, while the liberals saw that the curtailment of their budgetary powers or the creation of a reactionary praetorian guard honed for the purpose of domestic repression would make a nonsense of the powers granted to parliament under the new constitution.

The military-constitutional conflict that resulted gradually brought the Prussian constitutional system created in 1848 to a standstill. Early in 1860, the government presented two bills to parliament, one outlining reforms and the other approving funds. William saw these bills as distinct in their constitutional status; it was permissible for the parliament to have a say in the question of financing, since budgetary powers were essential attributes of the assembly. On the other hand, he did not recognize the right of the deputies to tamper with the details of the proposed reform itself, which fell, as he saw it, within the sphere of his power of command. The parliament responded to this gambit by making only a provisional grant of extra monies – tactically an unwise step, as it turned out, since it permitted the government to go ahead with the first phase of the reforms, even though final approval had not yet been given.

A process of political radicalization set in among the liberals. In January, a group of seventeen deputies broke off from the main body of the liberal faction to become the core of the new Progressive Party (*Fortshrittspartei*). Thinking that a more conservative parliament might give the administration an easier ride, William dissolved the parliament and called for new elections. The new chamber returned at the end of 1861 was even more resolutely liberal than the old, with over 100 Progressive Party members. The conservative faction, who had ruled the roost in the 1850s, were cut back to a rump of only fifteen members. The new chamber was no more willing to approve the military reforms than its predecessor; in the spring of 1862 it too was dissolved. The new elections of May 1862 merely confirmed the intractability of the standoff. More than 230 of the 325 deputies belonged to liberal factions.

Among the men who ran Prussia's military establishment there were some who now favoured an all-out break with the constitutional system. Of these, the most influential was the chief of the military cabinet, Edwin von Manteuffel, cousin of the minister-president, whose conservative reformism had done so much to secure the new constitutional system after the 1848 revolutions. Edwin was both more charismatic and less politically flexible than his cousin. He was an army man of the old school who equated his relationship with the monarch with the fealty of a German tribesman to his chieftain. Contemporary prints show an upright, hyper-masculine figure with thick curling hair, the lower half of the face concealed behind a hedge of dense beard.[9] As a member of the military cabinet, a body attached directly to the person of the king, he stood completely outside the parliamentary/constitutional order.

Manteuffel could be ruthless in defence of his 'honour' and that of the Prussian army (which he appears to have seen as essentially the same thing). In the spring of 1861, when a liberal city councillor by the name of Karl Twesten published an article criticizing the proposed military reforms and attacking Manteuffel personally for seeking to alienate the army from the people, the general offered the councillor the choice between a full public retraction and a duel. Unwilling to endure the humiliation of a retraction, Twesten chose the duel, though he was no marksman. The councillor's bullet flew wide, while the general's drilled his opponent through the arm. The episode highlighted not just the polarization generated by the military question, but the increasingly raw style of public life in post-1848 Prussia.

There was a moment of collective paranoia in the early months of 1862 when Manteuffel's extreme views enjoyed a certain resonance among conservatives close to the monarch, but the post-revolutionary consensus held firm and the general's 'great hour' never arrived.[10] Neither King William (Frederick William IV had died in January 1861) nor the majority of his political and military advisers seriously contemplated an all-out break with the constitution. The minister of war, Albrecht von Roon, the chief architect of the proposed reforms, preferred to search for a compromise that would spare the system while preserving the essence of the reform programme.[11] Even King William found it easier to imagine his own voluntary departure from office than to contemplate a return to absolutism. By September 1862, he appeared to be on the point of abdicating in favour of his son, Crown Prince Frederick William, who was known to be sympathetic to the liberal position. It was Albrecht von Roon who persuaded the king to step back from the brink and adopt a measure of last resort: the appointment of Otto von Bismarck to the minister-presidency of Prussia.

45. Otto von Bismarck at the
age of thirty-two. *Woodcut,
after an anonymous drawing
from 1847.*

BISMARCK

Who was Otto von Bismarck? Let us begin with a letter he wrote in the spring of 1834, when he was just nineteen years old. His school-leaving certificate had been delayed; as a result, doubts arose about whether he would be able to matriculate in the University of Berlin. In this transitional moment, forced into idleness and full of uncertainty about what the future held, the young Bismarck was moved to reflect on what would become of him if he failed to gain entry to university. From the family estate at Kniephof he penned the following lines to his school friend Scharlach:

I shall amuse myself for a few years waving a sword at raw recruits, then take a wife, beget children, till the soil and undermine the morals of my peasantry by the inordinate distillation of spirits. So, if in 10 years' time you should happen to find yourself in the neighbourhood, I invite you to commit adultery with an easy and curvaceous young woman selected from the estate, to drink as much potato brandy as you fancy and to break your neck out hunting as often as you see fit. You will find here a fleshy home-guard officer with a moustache that curses and swears till the earth trembles, cultivates a proper repugnance to Jews and Frenchmen, and thrashes his dogs and domestics with egregious brutality when bullied by his wife. I shall wear leather trousers, make a fool of myself at the Stettin wool market and when people address me as baron I shall stroke my moustache benignly and knock a bit off the price; I shall get pissed on the king's birthday and cheer him vociferously and the rest of the time I shall sound off regularly and my every other word will be: 'Gad what a splendid horse!'[12]

This letter is worth citing at such length because it demonstrates how much ironic distance there was in the young Bismarck's perception of his own social milieu – the milieu of the East-Elbian Junkers. Bismarck often liked to play the part of the red-necked *Krautjunker* of the Prussian boondocks, but in reality he was a rather untypical example of the type. His father was the real thing: he was descended from five centuries of noble East-Elbian landowners. But his mother's family carried the imprint of a different tradition. Bismarck's mother, Wilhelmine Mencken, was the descendant of an academic family from Leipzig in Saxony. Her grandfather had been a professor of law who entered the employ of the Prussian state to serve as cabinet secretary under Frederick the Great.[13]

It was Wilhelmine Mencken who made the key educational decisions for her sons; Bismarck consequently received a rather uncharacteristic upbringing for a member of his class: he began, not with Cadet School, but with a classic bourgeois education as a boarder at the Plammann Institute in Berlin – a school for the sons of senior civil servants. From there he progressed to the Friedrich Wilhelm Gymnasium, and later to the universities of Göttingen (1832–3) and Berlin (1834–5). There followed a four-year period of civil service training in Aachen and Potsdam. Bored by the monotony and the lack of personal autonomy that were the hallmarks of civil service training, young Otto retired, to the astonishment and dismay of his family, to work on his own estate at Kniephof, where he stayed from 1839 to 1845. During this long interlude, he played the Junker in heroic style; these were years of heavy eating and drinking, with epic breakfasts of meat and ale. And yet a closer examination of life at home with Otto von Bismarck reveals some thoroughly unjunkerly pursuits, such as wide reading in the works of Hegel, Spinoza, Bauer, Feuerbach and Strauss.

These observations suggest themes that are important to an understanding of Bismarck's political life. His background and attitude help to explain the fractured relationship between Bismarck and the conservatives who were – in their own eyes at least – the natural representatives of the landed aristocracy. Bismarck was never really one of them, and they, sensing this, never really trusted him. He never shared the corporatism of the Old Conservatives; he had never been attracted to a world-view that saw the Junker interest as pitted in corporate solidarity against the state. He had little interest in championing the rights of the locality and the province against the claims of the central authority; he did not see revolution and the reforming state as two faces of the same satanic conspiracy against the natural historic order. On the contrary, Bismarck's remarks on politics and history were always informed by a deep respect for – and even at times a crude glorification of – the absolutist state, and above all of its capacity for autonomous action. 'When Prussia was invoked in his speeches, it was the Prussia of the Great Elector and of Frederick, never the backward-looking utopia of the corporative state that put a curb on absolutism.'[14]

Like his maternal ancestors, Bismarck would seek his fulfilment as an adult in service to the state. But he would serve the state without being a servant. The link to the Estate was not in itself a destiny – it was too narrow and boring for that – but it represented an assurance of independence. The tie to the Estate, with the sense of mastery and separateness that it brought, was a fundamental strut in Bismarck's concept of personal autonomy – as he explained in a letter to his cousin at the age of twenty-three, a man who aspired to play a role in public life must 'carry over into the public sphere the autonomy of private life'.[15] His concept of that autonomy of private life was emphatically not bourgeois; it derived from the social world of the landed estate, whose lord is responsible to none but himself.

The consequences of this understanding of his own place in the world can be observed in his demeanour as a public figure, and particularly in his tendency towards insubordination. Bismarck never behaved as if he had a boss. This was most glaringly apparent in his relations with William I. As chancellor, Bismarck frequently pushed policies through against the monarch's will; when the king created obstructions, Bismarck resorted to tantrums and fits of weeping, backed up by the threat – sometimes unspoken and sometimes explicit – to resign and return to the comfort and peace of his estate. When Bismarck wanted to consolidate his relationship with the monarch, he generally did so not by endearing himself directly to the sovereign, but by engineering crises that highlighted his own indispensability, like a helmsman who steers into the storm in order to demonstrate his mastery of the ship.

Bismarck appeared to stand outside the ideological prescriptions of any one interest. He was not an aristocratic corporatist; nor, on the other hand, was he, or could he be, a liberal. Nor, for all his civil service experience, did he ever identify with the 'fourth estate' of the bureaucrats (throughout his life he regarded the 'pen-pushers' (*Federfuchser*) of the administrative bureaucracy with a certain disdain). The result was a freedom from ideological constraints that made his behaviour unpredictable – one could call it realism, pragmatism or opportunism – an ability in any case to spring from one camp to the other, wrong-footing his opponents or exploiting the differences among them. Bismarck was not accountable. He could collaborate with the forces of liberalism against the conservatives (and vice versa), he could flourish the democratic franchise as a weapon against elitist liberalism, he could puncture the pretensions of the nationalists by seeming to take charge of the national cause.

Bismarck was perfectly conscious about all of this. He disparaged theory and principle as yardsticks for political life: 'Politics is no science, it is an art, and anyone without the knack for it should leave it alone.'[16] 'If I am to proceed through life on the basis of principles, it is as if I were to walk down a narrow path in the woods and had to hold a long pole in my mouth.' Bismarck's ability to toss away the pole when it became bothersome shocked those friends who believed they were his ideological soulmates. One of these was the conservative nobleman Ludwig von Gerlach (brother of Leopold) who fell out with Bismarck in 1857 over whether Napoleon III should be treated as a legitimate monarch despite the fact that he had been carried into power by a revolution. So Bismarck was not a man of principle; he is better described as the man of detachment from principle, the man who disconnected himself from the romantic attachments of an older generation to practise a new kind of politics, flexible, pragmatic, emancipated from fixed ideological commitments. Public emotion and public opinion were not authorities to be indulged or followed, but forces to be managed and steered.

Bismarck's post-romantic politics was also part of the broader transformation wrought by the revolutions of 1848. In this sense, Bismarck belongs in the company of Cavour, Field Marshal Saldanha, Pius IX and Napoleon III. The point has sometimes been made that Bismarck learned much from the populist authoritarianism of the French Emperor, and that his governance as German chancellor after 1871 amounted to a belated German version of 'bonapartism'.[17] However, the importance of the French model should not be overstated. Prussia itself, as we have seen, underwent a transformation in governmental practices after 1848. Like Otto von Manteuffel and the new king himself, Bismarck was a 'man of 1848', prepared to mix politics in new combinations. Like Manteuffel, he saw the monarchical state as the key actor in political life. It was during Manteuffel's period in office that Bismarck acquired his shrewd 'respect' for public opinion, not as the arbiter of the future but as a subordinate partner to be cajoled and manipulated into cooperation. As the Prussian representative at the headquarters of the German Confederation in Frankfurt, Bismarck was entrusted with the covert channelling of government funds to friendly newspaper editors and journalists. Governmental manipulation of the press was a device that Bismarck would later raise to a high art.

In the autumn of 1862, Bismarck was installed as minister-president in Berlin. His objective, as he explained in a letter to the crown prince, was to secure 'an understanding with the majority of the deputies', while at the same time safeguarding the powers of the crown and the proficiency of the army.[18] Bismarck opened play by concocting a modified military reform programme that would enlarge the army and secure government control in key areas while meeting the liberal demand for two-year service. This gambit foundered on the resistance of Edwin von Manteuffel, who succeeded in persuading the king to withhold his support. It was the old problem of the antechamber of power. Bismarck immediately understood that the key to remaining in office now lay in neutralizing all rivals for the king's confidence, and he altered his policy accordingly. The attempt at compromise was abandoned and Bismarck switched to a policy of open confrontation designed to assure the king of his absolute dedication to the crown and its interests. The military reforms were put in train and taxes collected without parliamentary approval, civil servants were informed that disobedience and political involvement with the opposition would be punished with immediate dismissal, and the parliament was baited into ineffectual and self-undermining expressions of outrage. All this sufficed to convince the king of Bismarck's skill and dependability and he soon began to overshadow the other competitors for influence over the monarch.

In other respects, however, Bismarck's position remained extremely fragile. A further election in October 1863 produced a chamber with only thirty-eight pro-government deputies. The battle for public opinion had evidently been lost. The king was so downcast by the election results that he reportedly sank into despondency and remarked, while looking down from a window above Palace Square: 'Down there is where they will put up a guillotine for me.'[19] The political paralysis in Berlin also appeared to be undermining Prussia's ability to make the running in the German question. In 1863, while Bismarck struggled with the chamber, the Austrians were busy drafting and proposing reforms that would breathe new life into the German Confederation.

Berlin seemed to be drifting. The Prussian minister-president's achievements in the realm of foreign policy appeared modest, to say the least: in 1863, he succeeded in blocking the Austrian reform project and continued to stave off Vienna's efforts to join the German Customs Union. More important was Bismarck's rapprochement with Russia, formalized in the Alvensleben Convention (8 February 1863). This agreement, by which Prussia and Russia undertook to collaborate in the suppression of Polish nationalism, secured the goodwill of St Petersburg, but it was deeply unpopular with Polonophile liberals and helped to make Bismarck a widely hated figure. After only eighteen months in office, the new minister-president had made a mark as an unusually energetic, ruthless and inventive political tactician. From a contemporary standpoint, however, it was still easy to imagine that he might struggle on for a year or two before being dismissed to make way for a compromise settlement with the lower house of parliament. It was the Danish war of 1864 that transformed Bismarck's fortunes.

THE DANISH WAR

In the winter of 1863, Schleswig-Holstein was in the news again. Frederick VII of Denmark had died on 15 November 1863, triggering a succession crisis. As there was no direct male heir (the Danish Crown passed instead via the maternal line to Christian of Glücksburg), a dispute arose over who had a legitimate hereditary claim to rule over the duchies. The details of the Schleswig-Holstein controversy have always been taxing to follow – the more so as nearly everyone involved in it was called either Frederick or Christian – and the following is a sketch of the salient points. A series of international treaties had established in the early 1850s that the new King of Denmark, Christian of Glücksburg, would succeed on the same terms as his predecessor, Frederick VII.[20] In 1863, however, the waters were muddied by the appearance of a rival claimant, Prince Frederick of Augustenburg. The Augustenburgs did have a longstanding claim to the duchies, but Prince Frederick's father, Christian of Augustenburg, had agreed to renounce it as part of the 1852 Treaty of London. In 1863, however, Frederick of Augustenburg declared himself unbound by the treaty of 1852 and defiantly adopted the title 'Duke of Schleswig-Holstein'. His claim was enthusiastically supported by the German nationalist movement.

It is worth reflecting for a moment on the distinctive quality of the Schleswig-Holstein crisis. Modern and pre-modern themes were interwoven. On the one hand, it was an old-fashioned dynastic crisis, triggered, like so many seventeenth and eighteenth-century crises, by the death of a king without male issue. In this sense, we might call the conflict of 1864 'the War of the Danish Succession'. On the other hand, Schleswig-Holstein became the flashpoint for a major war only because of the role played by nationalism as a mass movement. The galvanizing effect of the Schleswig-Holstein issue on the German national movement had already made itself felt in the Frankfurt Parliament of 1848; in 1863–4, German nationalist opinion demanded that the duchies be constituted jointly as a new German federal state under the rule of the Augustenburg dynasty. Nationalism was crucial on the Danish side as well: the Danish nationalist movement demanded that Denmark defend its claim to Schleswig, and it was supported in this by the mainstream of Danish liberal opinion. The inexperienced and ineffectual new king, Christian IX, thus faced an explosive domestic situation when he came to the throne. At one point, the demonstrations taking place outside the royal palace in Copenhagen were so turbulent that the city's chief of police warned of the imminent collapse of law and order in the capital. It was anxiety about the prospect of political upheaval that forced the hand of the new king. By signing the November Constitution of 1863, Christian IX announced his intention to absorb the Duchy of Schleswig into the Danish unitary state, a gesture denounced by the German nationalists as an unpardonable provocation.

There were now three conflicting positions on the duchies. The Danes insisted on the incorporation of Schleswig as set out in the November Constitution of 1863. The German nationalist movement and the majority of states in the Confederation favoured the Augustenburg claim and were prepared to support an armed intervention. The Prussians and the Austrians opposed the Augustenburg claim and insisted that the Danes (and the Augustenburgs) abide by the promises made in the international treaties of 1851 and 1852. After much horse-trading at the Confederal Diet in December, a resolution was passed (by just one vote) that an intervention could proceed on the basis of the London treaties. On 23 December 1863, a small Confederal task force crossed the Danish frontier and moved northwards without resistance to occupy most of Holstein south of the river Eider. The strains within the Confederation soon began to tell. The task force (with only 12,000 men) had been sufficient to take undefended Holstein, but Schleswig would be another matter. The Danes were expected to put up a vigorous defence and a much larger force would be required to ensure success. Still acting in concert, Prussia and Austria declared that they were prepared to invade Schleswig, but only in their own right as European powers and only on the basis of the treaties of 1851 and 1852, not as representatives of the German Confederation and not in support of the Augustenburg claim. In January 1864, the two powers presented their joint ultimatum separately to Denmark (without consulting the other Confederal states) and, when the Danes refused to comply, moved their combined forces across the river Eider and into Schleswig.

It was a remarkable turnaround. The Austro-Prussian rivalry of the 1850s and early 1860s seemed to have made way for a mood of sweet harmony and cooperation. But the apparent unity of purpose concealed a pandemonium of conflicting expectations. For the Austrian Chancellor Count Johann Bernhard Rechberg, the joint campaign was a chance to discredit the German nationalist movement while establishing an Austro-Prussian condominium over Germany and reinvigorating the trans-territorial institutions of the German Confederation. It was also a way of preventing Berlin from securing major unilateral gains (such as the annexation of Schleswig) at Denmark's (and Austria's) expense. At the back of Rechberg's mind was another threatening prospect: Napoleon III, who had begun to warm to his role as Europe's trouble-maker, had suggested to the Prussians that France would support the outright annexation of Schleswig-Holstein, along with the lesser states of northern Germany, to Prussia. It looked as if Paris was angling for another anti-Austrian war, with Prussia playing the role of Piedmont. Rechberg, who was kept fully informed by Bismarck of these initiatives, knew this was a war that the Austrian Empire could not afford to fight.

Bismarck's agenda could scarcely have been more different. The Confederation as such played no role in his planning. His ultimate objective was to annex the duchies to Prussia. The Prussian Chief of Staff Helmut von Moltke may well have been the key influence here. Moltke was strongly opposed to the transformation of the duchies into an independent principality, on the grounds that the new entity might become a satellite of the Habsburgs and open up a hole in Prussia's northern seaward flank. As Bismarck knew, however, a unilateral annexation would have exposed Prussia to the threat of combined reprisals from Austria, the rest of the Confederation, and possibly one or more European powers. The extra troops would also come in handy, especially if, as Moltke warned, the Danes succeeded in exploiting their superiority at sea to evacuate their troops from the mainland. The agreement to work with Austria was thus a temporary device to limit risk and ensure that all options remained open.[21]

The Danish war came to an end on 1 August 1864, when the Danes were forced to sue for peace. Three features of the conflict deserve emphasis. The first is that the Prussians did not outperform the Austrians militarily. One early mistake was to nominate the Prussian Field Marshal Count Friedrich Heinrich Ernst von Wrangel as overall commander of the allied forces. The eighty-year-old Wrangel was old for his years and, though popular with the conservatives at court, at best a mediocre general. All his combat experience had been acquired against civilian insurgents in the revolutions of 1848. While Wrangel lurched from blunder to blunder in Denmark, the Austrian units acquitted themselves with courage and skill. On 2 February 1864, one Austrian brigade charged and took the Danish positions at Ober-Selk with such panache that old Wrangel rushed to embrace and kiss its commander on the cheeks, to the embarrassment of his Prussian colleagues. Four days later, the Austrian Brigade Nostitz broke through heavily defended Danish fortifications at Oeversee, while a Prussian Guards division on their flank looked on almost inert. These were frustrating setbacks for an army that had not experienced war for half a century and desperately needed to prove its mettle, both to the international community and to

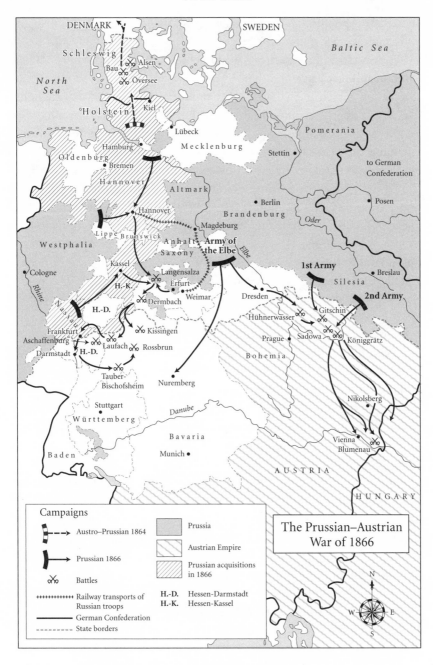

Campaigns

⚔ ⇢ Austro–Prussian 1864	▨ Prussia	
⚔ → Prussian 1866	▨ Austrian Empire	
✕ Battles	▨ Prussian acquisitions in 1866	
+++++ Railway transports of Russian troops	**H.-D.** Hessen-Darmstadt	
—— German Confederation	**H.-K.** Hessen-Kassel	
----- State borders		

The Prussian–Austrian War of 1866

a domestic population that had been following the political struggle over military reform.[22]

A second striking feature of the conflict was the primacy of the political over the military leadership. The Danish war was the first Prussian armed conflict in which a civilian politician exercised control. Throughout the war Bismarck ensured that the evolution of the conflict served the objectives of his diplomacy. He prevented the Prussian forces from pursuing the Danish army into Jutland during the early weeks of the war, so as to reassure the great powers that the joint campaign was not aimed at the territorial integrity of the Danish kingdom. There were slip-ups, to be sure – in mid-February, Wrangel sent an advance detachment of Guards north of the Jutland border despite instructions to the contrary. But Bismarck persuaded the war minister to send a sharp reprimand to the elderly general, and Wrangel was relieved of his command at Bismarck's insistence in mid-May. It was Bismarck who oversaw Prussian communications with Vienna, ensuring that the terms of the alliance evolved to Prussia's advantage. And in April it was Bismarck who insisted that the Prussian forces attack the Danish fortifications at Düppel in Schleswig, rather than mounting a protracted invasion of Denmark that might have dragged the other powers into the conflict.

The decision to attack Düppel was controversial. The Danish positions there were heavily fortified and manned, and it was clear that a Prussian frontal attack would succeed only – if at all – with numerous casualties. 'Is it supposed to be a political necessity to take the bulwarks?' asked Prince Frederick Charles, a brother of the king, who had been placed in charge of the siege. 'It will cost a lot of men and money. I don't see the military necessity.'[23] The case for engineering a showdown at Düppel was indeed political rather than military. A full-blown invasion of Denmark was undesirable for diplomatic reasons and the Prussians sorely needed a spectacular victory. There was much grumbling among the commanders, but Bismarck's will prevailed and the deed was done. On 2 April, the Prussians began a heavy bombardment of the defence works, using their new rifled field guns. On 18 May, the infantry went in under the command of Frederick Charles. It was no easy fight. The Danes offered fierce resistance from behind their battered defences and subjected the Prussians to heavy fire as they climbed the slopes before the entrenchments. Over 1,000 Prussians were killed or wounded; the Danes suffered 1,700 casualties.

46. Prussian troops storm the Danish entrenchments at Düppel, *18 April 1864*.
Contemporary engraving.

Bismarck's dominance throughout the conflict generated considerable
tension and ill-feeling. When the commanders protested, Bismarck was
quick to remind them that the army had no business interfering in the
conduct of politics – itself an extraordinary declaration in the Prussian
setting, and one which reveals how things had changed since the revolutions of 1848. The army, however, had no intention of accepting this
verdict, as War Minister Albrecht von Roon made clear in a memorandum of 29 May 1864:

There has been, and is now hardly any army that regarded itself and understood
itself to be *purely* a political instrument, a lancet for the diplomatic surgeon.
[. . .] When a government depends – and this is our situation – particularly upon
the armed part of the population [. . .] the army's views on what the government
does and does not do are surely not a matter of indifference.[24]

In the exhilaration of victory, these altercations were quickly forgotten,
but the issue underlying them would later resurface in more acrimonious
and menacing forms. Bismarck's assertion of control over virtually every
branch of the executive papered over but did not solve the structural

problem of civil–military relations at the apex of the Prussian state. The 1848 revolutions had parliamentarized the monarchy without demilitarizing it. At the heart of the post-revolutionary settlement lay an avoided decision that would haunt Prussian (and German) politics until the collapse of the Hohenzollern monarchy in 1918.

Prussia's victories in Denmark – Düppel was followed at the end of June by a successful amphibious assault on the island of Alsen – also transformed the domestic political landscape. The resulting wave of patriotic enthusiasm opened up latent divisions within the Prussian liberal movement. The Arnim-Boitzenburg petition of May 1864, which called for annexation of the duchies, attracted 70,000 signatures, not only from conservatives but from many liberals as well. Prussian military successes also had an unsettling effect more generally, since they seemed to demonstrate the effectiveness of the reform programme so bitterly opposed by the liberals. There was a growing desire for a settlement with the government, reinforced by the fear that if the conflict dragged on, the liberal movement would forfeit its purchase on public opinion.

During 1864 and 1865, Bismarck and 'his' ministers played skilfully with the parliament, confronting it with bills that divided the liberal majority or forcing it into unpopular positions. In the naval construction bill of 1865, for example, the government asked parliament to approve the building of two armed frigates and a naval base in Kiel, at a cost of just under 20 million thalers. The creation of a German navy was a fetish to the liberal nationalist movement, especially in the aftermath of the Danish war, where naval operations had played a prominent role. The overwhelming majority of the deputies strongly supported the proposed expenditures, but they were forced nevertheless to reject the bill on the grounds that, in the absence of a legal budget, no new funds could be approved by parliament. Bismarck seized his opportunity to deliver a tirade against the 'impotently negative' attitude of the chamber.[25]

The minister-president could afford to gamble in this way because the coffers of the Prussian government were full to overflowing. During the 1850s and 1860s, the Prussian economy experienced the transforming effects of the first world boom. Rapid growth in the railway network and in associated enterprises, such as steel smelting and machine-building, was supported by a phenomenal expansion in the extraction of fossil fuels. During the 1860s, the coalmines of the Ruhr district in the Prussian Rhineland grew at an average rate of 170 per cent per annum bringing economic and social change at a pace unparalleled in the history of the region. This growth was sustained by the convergence of change on many different levels: quality gains at every stage of production, savings through improvements to transport infrastructure, a highly liquid capital market (supported by the gold rushes in Australia and California), a favourable balance of trade and, as we have seen, the withdrawal of the Prussian government from various forms of regulation that had previously obstructed growth.

Although the boom slowed somewhat during the 'first world slump' of 1857–8, the 1860s saw a return to robust expansion, though on a broader sectoral basis than had been the case for the previous decade. By contrast with the 1850s, when growth was largely driven from within the heavy-industrial sector, the 1860s witnessed more coordinated expansion across heavy industry, textiles and agriculture. This was sustained by steadily growing investment through banks and in joint-stock companies that yielded increasingly high rates of return.[26]

The combination of this prolonged boom with the fiscal and financial improvements of the 1850s and the expansion of production in the state-owned mines had a predictable effect on government revenues. In March 1865 Bismarck boasted to a confidant that the Danish war had largely been financed out of budget surpluses for the previous two years; only 2 million thalers had had to be sourced from the state treasury. Nor did it seem likely that the money would run out in the near future. Obliging entrepreneurs, such as the Cologne banker Abraham Oppenheimer and his Berlin colleague Gerson Bleichröder, besieged the minister-president with lucrative offers to privatize government enterprises or buy out the state-owned shares of semi-public companies. 'The financiers are pressing loans on us without parliamentary approval,' Bismarck declared, 'but we could wage the Danish War twice over without needing one.'[27]

PRUSSIA'S WAR AGAINST GERMANY

On 1 August 1864, King Christian of Denmark ceded all rights to the duchies to Prussia and Austria and they passed under a joint Austro-Prussian military occupation, pending a decision concerning their future by the German Confederation. All of this looked rather like the inaugur-ation of an era of harmonious dual hegemony based on cooperation between the two German major powers. This was certainly what the Austrians were after and Bismarck did his best to encourage their hopes. In an instruction of August 1864 to the Prussian ambassador in Vienna, he offered the ingratiating observation that 'a true German policy is only possible when Austria and Prussia are united and take the lead. From this high standpoint, an intimate alliance of the two powers has been our aim from the outset. [...] If Prussia and Austria are not united, politically Germany does not exist.'[28] This was no more than eyewash. Bismarck's objective was still to annex both duchies to Prussia and neutralize Austrian political influence in Germany. He planned to do so, if necessary, by war. Already in 1863 he had suggested to the Russians that Prussia might soon mount a surprise attack on the Austrian Empire 'as under Frederick II in 1756'.[29] His tactic was to keep all options open by eking out the joint occupation while at the same time picking fights with the Austrians at every possible opportunity.

In the diplomatic struggle that ensued over the future of Schleswig-Holstein the Austrians were at a geopolitical disadvantage. The duchies were extremely remote from Vienna, and Austria's interest in main-taining a troop presence there was correspondingly lukewarm. In the autumn of 1864, the Austrians offered Berlin a choice between two courses of action: the Prussians could either (a) recognize the duchies as a separate state under the Augustenburg dynasty or (b) annex them to Prussia and compensate Austria with land along the Silesian border. Bismarck rejected both options, declaring that Silesia was not negotiable and adding rather mysteriously that Berlin had special rights in both duchies. This was followed up in February 1865 by a provocative declar-ation to the effect that Prussia intended to regard any form of 'indepen-dent' Schleswig-Holstein as a Prussian satellite. In the meanwhile, the Prussians in the duchies continued to extend their control, prompting furious complaints from the Austrians, who responded by taking the matter to the Confederal Diet and putting the Augustenburg succession back on to the table. By the summer, it looked as if war was imminent. The crisis was deferred when Francis Joseph sent an ambassador to negotiate a new agreement with King William.

The result was the Convention of Gastein signed on 14 August 1865. Based on a proposal by Bismarck, the Convention maintained joint

Austro-Prussian sovereignty in the duchies, while placing Schleswig under Prussian and Holstein under Austrian control. But Gastein was no more than an interim arrangement conceived by Bismarck as a means of gaining time. The Prussian provocations in Holstein continued and in January 1866, Berlin seized on a pro-Augustenburg nationalist meeting in Holstein to accuse Vienna directly of breaking with the terms of the treaty. On 28 February, a crown council in Berlin resolved that war between the two German powers was inevitable. The assembled generals, ministers and senior diplomats agreed that Austria had failed to honour the Gastein Convention and continued to treat Prussia as a rival and an enemy. There was general assent when Bismarck pointed out that Prussia's mission was to lead Germany and that this very 'natural and justified' ambition had been unjustly blocked by Austria. The crown prince was alone in pleading for a non-military resolution.[30]

Bismarck's next step was to seek an alliance with Italy. Negotiations began soon after the crown council and a treaty against Austria was signed on 8 April 1866. The two states were now committed to assist each other in the event of a war breaking out with Austria over the following three months. (Bismarck also revived the time-honoured Prussian tradition of the Hungarian fifth column, deployed by Frederick the Great during the Seven Years War and again in the 1790s by Frederick William II, but his contacts with the Hungarian revolutionary movement produced nothing of any consequence.) At the crown council of 28 February, Bismarck had announced as well that he intended to seek 'more definite guarantees' from France, and feelers were duly extended to Paris. These produced a chain of vague proposals and counter-proposals. Exactly what assurances Bismarck gave to Napoleon has been hotly disputed, but it seems likely that French neutrality was bought with the promise of compensations in Belgium, Luxembourg and possibly in the region between the Rhine and the Moselle (encompassing the Prussian Saarland and the Bavarian Palatinate). Since the Austrians secretly purchased French neutrality on very similar terms (including a French satellite state in the Rhineland!), Napoleon III had every reason to be confident that France would end up as a beneficiary of the Prusso-Austrian conflict, whoever emerged as the victor.[31]

Russia was the third power whose attitude was crucial to the success of Prussian designs. Russia had blocked the unionist designs of Frederick William IV and Radowitz in 1848–50, while helping to restore Austria's fortunes. By 1866, however, things had changed. Russia was locked into a process of fundamental domestic political reform. Relations with Austria were still cool (Russian strategic planning foresaw Austria and Britain – not Prussia – as the most likely opponents in a future war). The post-Crimean estrangement between the two eastern empires had already yielded dividends for Cavour in 1859. This lesson was not lost on Bismarck, who had just left his post at Frankfurt and happened to be stationed at the Prussian embassy in St Petersburg when the Italian crisis broke. Bismarck had cultivated relations with Russia with great care since coming to office as minister-president and there seemed little reason to fear intervention from this quarter.[32]

These diplomatic preparations were flanked with other measures intended to disorient the German liberal camp and unsettle public confidence in the German Confederation. On 9 March, Bismarck sprang a proposal on the diet calling for the creation of a German national parliament to be elected by direct universal male suffrage. The Confederal representatives were still mulling over this unexpected initiative when news of troop movements in Italy triggered a partial Austrian mobilization on 21 April. Now began a chain of troop deployments and counter-measures that culminated in a full-scale mobilization on both sides.

As the two German great powers prepared for a war, it became clear that most of the lesser states of the Confederation supported Austria. On 9 May, a majority of representatives to the diet voted in favour of a resolution demanding that Prussia explain its mobilization. At the end of the month, the Austrians formally passed responsibility for the duchies to the Confederation. During the first week of June, Prussian troops entered Holstein, encountering no resistance from the Austrians, who withdrew into Hanover. On 11 June, the Austrian ambassador to the diet denounced the Prussian occupation of Holstein as illegal and in breach of the terms of the Convention of Gastein and proposed a resolution calling for the mobilization of the Confederation against Prussia. On 14 June, at the last plenary meeting of the diet in Frankfurt, this resolution was passed by majority vote and the Prussian ambassador walked out, declaring that his government regarded the Confederation as dissolved. Five days later, the Italians declared war on Austria.[33]

With Russian and French neutrality virtually assured, Prussia went to war with Austria in the summer of 1866 under an auspicious great-power constellation. Yet the outcome was by no means a foregone conclusion. Most well-informed contemporaries – including Emperor Napoleon III, who had actually fought the Austrians in 1859 – predicted an Austrian victory.[34] The combat performance of the two armies in the Danish war had done nothing to dispel this view. It is true that Prussians had embarked on a programme of military reforms after 1859, but these were not as revolutionary as has often been claimed.[35] In any case, Austria too had responded to the disasters of 1859 with its own reform programme. Its artillery was sophisticated and deployed by well-trained battery teams. It was true that Prussia enjoyed a slight superiority in numbers in the Bohemian theatre of operations where the war would be decided: 254,000 Prussians faced the 245,000 troops of Austria's North Army. The situation would have been very different, of course, had the Italians not committed over 200,000 men to their offensive in Venetia, forcing the Austrians to divert an extra 100,000 troops to the south-western front.

Austria also enjoyed an important strategic advantage: in the diplomatic contest of 1866, most of the middling German states opted to side with Vienna against Berlin. The Prussians were thus obliged to mobilize not only against the Austrians but also against the other German combatant states, including, most importantly, Hanover and Saxony. In all, the Confederal armies of 1866 mustered some 150,000 men dispersed among a number of separate armies. This meant in turn that Prussia's Chief of the General Staff Helmut von Moltke had to break the Prussian army into four blocks small enough to be transported quickly by Prussia's widely separated rail lines to the Austrian, Saxon and Hanoverian frontiers. Austria, by contrast, could operate on a much more concentrated terrain and had the advantage of interior lines.

Why, then, did the Prussians win? Bismarck's famous invocation of 'blood and iron' has often been seen as a reference to the role of industry in consolidating Prussian power. Prussia, or at least parts of Prussia, had certainly experienced a dramatic growth in their industrial capacity during the later 1850s and 1860s. But this played a lesser role in Prussia's victory over Austria than we might suppose.[36] The figures we would need to make direct comparisons are not available, but there is little to indicate that a major qualitative gap separated the economies of the two antagonists in 1866. In some respects, indeed, the Prussian economy appears to have been more backward than the Austrian – a larger proportion of Prussians than Austrians worked in agriculture, for example. Of the various weapons that played a role in 1866, the ones requiring the most sophisticated manufacturing processes were the field guns of the artillery, and here it was the Austrians, with their accurate rifled cannon, who clearly had the advantage. In any case, this was not a war that pitted industrial economies against each other. It was a short, sharp fight in which both sides managed to get by on pre-stocked weaponry and munitions. It is true that Moltke attached great importance to the use of railways, but in the event his elaborate planning nearly brought disaster upon the Prussians, whose supply trains caught up with their armies only when the battle of Königgrätz had already been won. In the meantime, the Prussian armies lived off the land or paid their way, much as the armies of Frederick the Great had done. Industrial power thus mattered less than politics and military culture.

Although the army of the German Confederation disposed of some 150,000 men, these were hardly a formidable fighting force. They did not properly constitute an army, since they had never trained together and did not possess a unified command structure – here was the consequence of a half-century of particularism within the Confederation. Moreover, the armies of the middling states were unwilling to take the initiative against Prussia. Appealing to the stipulations of the Confederal constitution, which forbade the German states to settle their differences by force, they preferred to wait until Prussia had openly breached the peace. Bavaria, for example, which controlled the largest single contingent – the 65,000 men of the VII Federal Corps – informed Vienna early in June 1866 that the Austrians could rely on Bavarian support only if the Prussians actually invaded a fellow German state. They were thus unwilling to contemplate pre-emptive action of any kind.

Many of the other individual federal corps were hamstrung by internal political divisions that made swift and concerted action virtually impossible. In the case of the VIII Confederal Corps, for example, comprising troops from Württemberg, Baden and Hesse-Darmstadt, the commander, Prince Alexander of Hesse, was an Austrophile who favoured intervention on behalf of Austria, but the staff chief was a more cautious Württemberger. His orders from his sovereign were to slow the prince's deployment to a crawl and to do what he could to prevent movements east, so that troops would be available if necessary to defend the frontiers of Württemberg itself. In the face of the Prussian offensive, the Hanoverian army withdrew south in the forlorn hope that the Bavarians or the Austrians might march north to join them. After a small victory against a numerically inferior force at Langensalza, they were pushed out of their defensive positions by Prussian reinforcements, compelled to surrender on 29 June, and provided with free train tickets home. News of the Hanoverian defeat further reinforced the determination of the south German states to sit tight and guard their frontiers. The only truly effective contribution came from the Saxons, who abandoned their home territory to fight alongside the Austrian North Army in Bohemia.

The chief author of the Prussian victory of 1866 was the Chief of the General Staff, Helmut von Moltke. In Bohemia, to a much greater extent than in Denmark, Moltke was able to unfold an innovative strategic conception. His approach to the Austrian war was to break the Prussian forces up into groups small enough to be moved at the highest possible speed to the point of attack. The objective was to mesh the converging units wing-to-wing only at the last minute, in order to deliver the decisive blow in battle. The advantage of this approach was that it reduced the logistical strain on narrow country roads and one-track railways and thus saved on tailbacks and traffic jams. The increased speed and manoeuvrability of the forces in the field raised the likelihood that the Prussians rather than their enemies would be able to determine the timing and the setting of the decisive engagement. It was a conception of mobilization that required sophisticated use of the most modern infrastructural resources: of railways and roads in particular, and of telegraph, since the separate armies would be out of immediate contact with each other and would need to be rigorously coordinated from headquarters. The chief potential drawback of this approach was that it could, as we have seen, so easily go wrong. If the armies were forced off course or became seriously out of sync, there was the risk that the enemy might attack them individually with a superior force.

Complementing this aggressive strategic approach was a set of measures designed to make the Prussian infantryman the best in Europe. In the mid-1860s, Prussia was the only European great power to be armed with a breech-loading rifle, the Dreyse Zündgewehr, or needle-gun. This was essentially a rifle of the modern type, in which a cartridge consisting of a projectile mounted on a small cylindrical case of explosive charge was loaded into a metal chamber and detonated by a blow from a hammer (known as the 'needle' on account of its elongated shape). The needle-gun had one crucial advantage over the traditional muzzle-loading weapons still used by most European armies. It could be reloaded and fired between three and five times as fast. A man lying behind a tussock of grass, or standing behind a tree could reload, aim and fire his needle-gun without emerging from cover; there was no need to drop powder, wadding and shot down the barrel of the weapon. This allowed for a much more flexible and lethal application of infantry firepower at close quarters than had previously been possible.

There was nothing particularly mysterious about the needle-gun. The technology was widely known. Yet most military establishments chose not to introduce it as the general weapon of infantry warfare. There were good reasons for this. The early needle-gun prototypes were notoriously unreliable; the gas seals were sometimes faulty, so that the chamber exploded or emitted a searing spray of burning powder – not a feature that inspired enthusiasm in the average rifleman. Many soldiers trained with early-generation needle-guns found that the bolt action was prone to get stiff and sometimes had to be hammered open with a rock; there was also a tendency to jam during frequent fire. Another concern was that men provided with this sophisticated instrument would fire too fast, squander their costly ammunition and then toss away the now-useless gun and leave the field. By contrast, it was argued, the old muzzle-loaders with their slow rate of fire imposed a degree of discipline on infantry-lines. Perhaps the most important reason for rejecting the needle-gun was simply the widespread contemporary preference for what were known as 'shock tactics'. These were based on the notion – a kind of orthodoxy among the military thinkers of mid nineteenth-century Europe – that infantry firepower was ultimately of secondary importance in any serious military confrontation. It was the artillery that should focus on high-accuracy, high-impact fire. What counted in the front line was the ability to unseat the enemy from a coveted position, and this was best achieved by swift charges of massed infantry with mounted bayonets.

The Prussians overcame most of the practical objections to the new weapon by rigorously testing and modifying the Dreyse prototype, with the result that its specifications steadily improved over successive batches, while the costs of production and ammunition fell. At the same time, policies were set in place to improve the technical mastery and fire discipline of the men who used the weapon. Between 1862 and 1864, while the Austrians cut their annual expenditure on target practice, relying instead on shock tactics, the Prussians introduced an extensive regime of marksmanship: infantrymen were trained to use their weapons at all ranges, educated about how to use their sights to compensate for the arc of a bullet and required to keep a record of their success or failure in a 'shooting log'. Here, the military command could reap the rewards of Prussia's exemplary education system. Without the kingdom's exceptionally high rates of literacy and numeracy, a regime of this kind would have been impossible. All of this implied the cession of a much greater level of autonomy and self-governance to the rank-and-file soldier than was the norm in Europe's mid-century armies. The new Prussian infantry were – in theory at least – professionals, not cattle to be herded in the direction of the enemy by their officers. The Prussian army's ability to achieve technical innovation over a range of separate but interdependent domains owed much to the General Staff, which specialized in integrating weapons research with the evolution of strategy and tactical doctrine.

The result of these changes was a growing complementarity between Prussian and Austrian practices in the field. While the Austrians focused on refining their shock tactics – especially after the disasters of 1859 – the Prussians focused on 'fire tactics' centred on the needle-gun. Moltke was able to combine flexibility and speed in the offensive strategic deployment of large units with the controlled and defensive tactical deployment of infantry units on the battlefield. By contrast, the Austrians tended to be strategically defensive and tactically offensive. None of this made a Prussian victory inevitable. There was little reason, without hindsight, to suppose that fire would win the day over shock. The Austrians used shock tactics with great success against the Italians at Custozza on 24 June 1866, and the Prussians themselves had used them with effect against the Danes entrenched at Düppel. It also made sense, from the Austrian standpoint, to adopt a defensive strategic policy on the assumption that the attacking Prussians, with their separate armies and extended supply lines, would at some point expose themselves to a crippling Austrian strike. Nor was it obvious that the needle-gun would prove a decisive advantage – after all, the 1854 model muzzle-loader used by the majority of Austrian infantrymen was a more accurate weapon with a longer range.

In the event, however, the war in Bohemia showed that the advantages of speed outweighed those of range and that waves of infantrymen charging with bayonets mounted stood little chance against the shredding fire of well-placed infantry armed with breech-loaders. On 28 June, the Austrians were subjected to a painful early demonstration of the potency of fire tactics when General Clam-Gallas, commander of the Austrian I Corps, engaged two companies of Prussian riflemen on a bridge across the river Isar at the little town of Podol. The men of I Corps initially cleared the town with little difficulty. When Prussian reinforcements moved up, the Austrians launched a bayonet charge to repel them. But instead of running away, the Prussians stopped in their tracks, deployed their forward platoons and began firing rapidly into the mass of approaching Austrians. The shooting continued for thirty minutes. After the momentum of the Austrian attack had been broken, the Prussians combed through the town street by street, 'keeping touch by their rifle flashes as dusk turned to night'.[37] Of the 3,000 Austrians engaged in the battle for Podol, nearly 500 were shot; Prussian casualties were about 130. By two o'clock in the morning the Austrians had had enough and withdrew.

On the previous day, an encounter between units of the Prussian 2nd Army and the Austrian VI Corps on the Nachod plateau in Bohemia had produced similarly unbalanced casualty figures – 1,200 Prussians against 5,700 Austrians. In this bloody engagement, over one-fifth of the Austrians committed were either killed or wounded. Even in situations where the Austrians prevailed, as at Trautenau, where the Prussians were caught on the back foot and forced to withdraw out of Bohemia into the mountains, the scything fire of the needle-guns took 4,800 Austrian casualties to 1,300 Prussian.[38]

The victory of the Prussian armies cannot, of course, be ascribed solely to the needle-gun. Although it is difficult to gauge exactly the impact of such factors, there is evidence that the Austrians suffered from lower morale by comparison with their Prussian adversaries. Poles, Ukrainians, Romanians and Venetians figured prominently among those who deserted or were captured unwounded by the Prussians, suggesting that motivation among the non-German (though not the Hungarian) troops was lower than among Austrians proper. Italian subjects of the Habsburg Crown obviously had little reason to relish a war that was also being fought against their countrymen. One Prussian officer participating in the skirmish at Hühnerwasser on 26 June 1866, was surprised to come across three Venetian infantrymen sitting out the fire-fight in the tall corn around the village. At the sight of the approaching Prussian, they reportedly dropped their rifles, covered his hands in kisses and begged for mercy. There were also problems of communication: in many Austrian units, officers and men spoke different languages. Recalling the battle of Münchengrätz, the staff chief of the Austrian I Corps reported of the mixed Polish and Ukrainian XXX Regiment that it had fought bravely until dusk, when the men were no longer able to see their officers miming examples of what was needed.[39] By contrast, the Polish recruits to the Prussian army proved willing and reliable soldiers.

The Austrian command culture was a further factor in the defeat. While there were certainly misunderstandings, failures of communication and episodes of disobedience by Prussian subordinate commanders, the Austrians suffered from a systemic crossing of lines of command, so that the movement of armies was frequently dogged by inconsistent or conflicting orders; there was a tendency to lose time in debating the merits of instructions from above, and officers lacked a clear sense of the immediate and longer-term objectives of a given engagement. Supply trains failed to arrive, so that troops retired from protracted actions without food or drink. The Austrians also failed to maintain a staff organization with the power and cohesion of the Prussian General Staff. By the beginning of July, the staff of the North Army in Bohemia had degenerated into a loose gathering of couriers and order-drafters. Finally, the Austrian field commander General Ludwig Benedek made a number of serious errors, the most disastrous being the deployment of Austrian troops at the beginning of July around the fortress of Königgrätz – in a position where they could be pinned down by the Prussians with the river Elbe cutting them off at the back.

It was here that the decisive battle took place on 3 July 1866. For seventeen hours, nearly half a million armed men contested a front between the river fort of Königgrätz and the Bohemian town of Sadowa. This immense engagement was no triumph of military planning. Benedek had not originally intended to give battle at Königgrätz; he had been trapped there on his way to Olmütz, and initially hoped that the Emperor would let him off the hook by entering into peace negotiations with the Prussians. As for the Prussians, as late as 30 June their two separated main armies were still finding it difficult to stay in touch and there was confusion among the Prussian commanders about the precise location of the Austrian North Army. When battle opened on 3 July, it was partly by accident. Prince Frederick Carl, commander of the Prussian 1st Army, had encountered an Austrian force on the previous evening, became convinced that Benedek had decided to stand and fight, and launched an attack in the small hours of the morning without consulting his commander-in-chief. The odds were still with the Austrians, who held the high ground, were well entrenched and enjoyed a decisive advantage in heavy artillery. Yet it was the Prussians who won the day. After the Prussian 1st Army had engaged the Austrians for most of the morning, the 2nd Army under the command of Crown Prince Frederick moved up to attack the Austrian flank. As the noose tightened around the Austrian positions, Benedek failed to take full advantage of openings in the enemy line. He also made the error of committing forty-three battalions to a desperate fight in the Swiepwald, a patch of dense wood on the Prussian left flank, where infantrymen used needle-guns to cut down wave after wave of Austrian troops. By the end of the afternoon, the Austrians had been forced to withdraw. The Prussian victory was comprehensive. Over 40,000 men of the North Army had been killed or wounded. There remained not a single combat-effective Austrian infantry brigade on the field.

On 22 July 1866, Emperor Franz Joseph capitulated to the Prussians. The Austro-Prussian war was over, just seven weeks after it had begun. The Austrian Emperor was spared any annexations, but had to agree to the dissolution of the German Confederation and the creation of a new Prussian-dominated North German Confederation to the north of the river Main. Prussia secured carte blanche to exact annexations as it pleased in the north, with the exception of the Austrians' faithful ally, the Kingdom of Saxony. Schleswig and Holstein were annexed, along with part of Hesse-Darmstadt and the entirety of Hanover, Hesse-Kassel, Nassau and the city of Frankfurt. The unfortunate burghers of Frankfurt, the scene of Prussia's diplomatic humiliation on the eve of the Austrian war, were subjected to a punitive indemnity of 25 million guilders.

Bismarck had prevailed over his German enemies. He prevailed over his Prussian enemies too. At the end of February 1866, the Prussian liberals had formed a solid oppositional bloc, welded together by the tyrannical and provocative behaviour of the Bismarck administration. By contrast with Austria, where there was considerable enthusiasm for a war, Prussian public opinion was overwhelmingly hostile. An anti-war rally held in the industrial city of Solingen in the Rhineland on 25 March inaugurated a wave of oppositional meetings across the monarchy. There was a flood of petitions and anti-war manifestos. It looked very much as if the liberals had succeeded in mobilizing a genuine mass movement.

The news of Prussia's mobilization and victory transformed the situation utterly. The Prussian occupation of Hanover, Dresden and Kassel was greeted with a wave of jubilation. Cheering crowds mobbed Bismarck whenever he appeared in public. The political consequences made themselves felt in the first round of the Landtag elections on 25 June, when voting for the electoral college revealed a sharp turn towards the conservatives. On 3 July, as Prussian troops charged the Austrian positions near Königgrätz, the second round of voting returned a chamber with 142 conservative mandates (as opposed to twenty-eight in the previous chamber). Bismarck had foreseen this: 'At the moment of decision,' he told Count von der Goltz, the Prussian ambassador in Paris, 'the masses will stand by the monarchy.'[40]

The news of the victory at Königgrätz and the subsequent capitulation left the old liberal parliamentary bloc in an impossible position. They could no longer dispute the legitimacy of the military reforms. An Austrian indemnity of 40 million florins restored the government's liquidity and underscored its independence from the parliament. Moreover, many of the leading figures in the liberal camp were themselves profoundly moved by the scope of Prussia's success. A characteristic example was Gustav Mevissen, the former revolutionary minister of 1848, who watched the victory parade down Unter den Linden in a state of near intoxication: 'I cannot shake off the impression of this hour. I am no devotee of Mars; I feel more attached to the goddess of beauty and the mother of graces than to the mighty god of war, but the trophies of war exercise a magic charm upon the child of peace. One's eyes are involuntarily riveted on [. . .] the unending rows of men who acclaim the god of the moment – success.' Another such case was the industrialist Werner Siemens, for whom the news of the victory over Austria was a transformative moment. Within the space of a few months, he broke with his left-liberal friends and campaigned for a reconciliation with Bismarck, before withdrawing entirely from politics in order to focus on building his firm.[41]

To many liberals, it seemed obvious that the events of 1866 had created an entirely new point of departure. The defeat of neo-absolutist Austria (and the implicit defeat of Catholicism as a force in German affairs) appeared in the eyes of many to be an intrinsically liberal achievement. Bismarck's promise of a closer national union on a constitutional basis spoke to deeply ingrained liberal aspirations. The liberals saw national unity on the terms proposed by Bismarck as the basis for a more rational political order that would open the door to further political and constitutional progress. Underlying this sanguine vision was a belief in the essentially progressive character of the Prussian state, which in turn legitimated Prussia's dominant role in the new Germany. There was common ground here with elements of the military leadership. Moltke, too, a sometime student of Hegel, viewed Prussia as the model of a progressive, prejudice-free, rational state to which political leadership must necessarily fall because it stands at the forefront of historical development.[42] This consensus about the fundamentally progressive and virtuous quality of the state – whatever the designs of the current government – played a crucial role in healing the breach created by the constitutional crisis.

Bismarck recognized that the time had come to knit the Prussian political system back together. Liberalism was too important and potentially fruitful a political force to be marginalized for ever – in conceding this, Bismarck revealed himself a true executor of the post-revolutionary settlement of the 1850s. There was – much to the chagrin of the backwoods conservatives who wishfully claimed Bismarck as one of their own – no coup against the constitution. An indemnity bill was offered to the parliament; this amounted to an open acknowledgement that the government had acted illegally during the crisis years; it also provided a means of reaffirming the authority of parliament and getting the boat of the constitution back on to an even keel.[43] These and other shrewdly devised concessions sufficed to dissolve the already fragile unity of the liberal opposition. There was a growing stream of defections from the ranks of parliamentary progressives still holding out against Bismarck. Defectors such as Karl Twesten (he who had been shot in the arm only four years before by the chief of the military cabinet) were warmly welcomed by Bismarck, who disarmed any residual doubters by drawing them respectfully into consultations over further concessions to the liberal interest.[44]

Under the pressure of this accommodation between Bismarck and the moderate opposition, the liberal front that had coalesced during the constitutional crisis finally came undone. A cleavage opened between those National Liberals who saw in national unity the promise of a more rational political order and those progressives who focused instead on the issues of liberty and parliamentary powers that had been at the heart of the constitutional conflict. Interestingly enough, 'new Prussians' soon came to dominate the nascent National Liberal movement – its two most distinguished leaders, Rudolf von Bennigsen and Johannes Miquel, were both Hanoverians elected after the annexations of 1866 (many of the old Prussian liberals found it hard to shake off the antipathies of the crisis years).

A complementary rift opened up within the conservative ranks. Many of the conservatives had been hoping that the victory over Austria would usher in a final reckoning with the parliamentary-constitutional system, and they were bitterly disappointed by Bismarck's decision to propose an indemnity bill. The result was a schism between those 'free conservatives' who were willing to support the adventurous minister-president and those 'Old Conservatives' who deeply resented any attempt to conciliate the liberals through political concessions. At the centre of the political spectrum there now emerged that hybrid bloc of moderate liberals and flexible Bismarckian conservatives who would play a crucial role in providing a stable platform for government in the Prussian parliament and the new Reichstag of the North German Confederation. This was not just a consequence of Bismarck's statesmanship; it was a return to the post-revolutionary political settlement of the 1850s. It was the constitutional crisis that had forged the liberals into a unified bloc; once the pressure eased, they fell apart into fundamentalist and realist wings. On the conservative side too, the schism of 1866–7 ran along a well-established cleavage between those who had accepted the constitutional order of 1848–9 and those who had not. This was overlaid after Königgrätz by the divide between those (including a substantial contingent of Pietist East-Elbian landowners) who remained attached to a specifically Prussian state identity and those who were willing to embrace the broader cause of the German nation.

With the victory of 1866, the long history of Prussia's contest with Austria for hegemony over the German states came to an end. A solid block of Prussian territory now stretched between France and Belgium in the west and the flatlands of Russian Lithuania in the east. Prussia encompassed over four-fifths of the population of the new North German

Confederation, a federal entity comprising the twenty-three northern states and centred on Berlin. The southern states of Hesse-Darmstadt, Baden, Württemberg and Bavaria escaped annexation, but were made to sign alliances that placed them within Prussia's sphere of influence.

The North German Confederation may have looked a little like a continuation of the old Deutscher Bund (whose diet had obligingly voted itself out of existence on 28 July in the dining room of the Three Moors Hotel in Augsburg), but in reality the name was little more than a fig-leaf for Prussian dominance. Prussia exercised exclusive control over military and foreign affairs; in this sense, the North German Confederation was, as King William himself put it, 'the extended arm of Prussia'. At the same time, however, the new Confederation bestowed a certain semi-democratic legitimacy upon the power-political settlement of 1866. In constitutional terms, it was an experimental entity without precedent in Prussian or German history. It had a parliament representing the (male) populations of all the member states, whose deputies were elected on the basis of the Reich electoral law drawn up by the revolutionaries in 1849. No attempt was made to impose the Prussian three-class franchise; instead, all men of the age of twenty-five years and over acquired the right to a free, equal and secret ballot. The North German Confederation was thus one of the late fruits of the post-revolutionary synthesis. It blended elements of the old politics of princely cabinets with the new and unpredictable logic of national parliamentary representation.[45]

WAR WITH FRANCE

As early as August 1866, Bismarck confided to a close associate of the Grand Duke of Baden that he believed a union between the north and the south of Germany was only 'a matter of time'.[46] Yet in many respects, the conditions for such a union remained inauspicious after the Austrian war. France, which stood to lose most from a further extension of Prussian influence, would obviously oppose it. The Austrians still hoped to overturn the verdict of 1866. The new Austrian foreign minister, Friedrich Ferdinand von Beust, was a Prussophobe Saxon who hoped that the German southern states might serve – in collusion, perhaps, with France – as a lever to unsettle Prussian hegemony. In the south German states, and especially in Württemberg and Bavaria, public opinion was still vehemently opposed to a closer union. There was outrage in March 1867 when it was revealed that the south German governments had signed away their autonomy after the Austrian war in 'eternal' offensive-defensive treaties with the North German Confederation. In Bavaria and Württemberg, the parliamentary elections of 1869 produced anti-liberal majorities opposed to a small-German union. In Bavaria in particular, the Catholic clergy agitated from the pulpits against a closer union with the Prussian-dominated North German Confederation, circulating petitions that attracted hundreds of thousands of signatures. An anti-Prussian front began to crystallize, composed of particularist patriots, pro-Austrian Catholics and southern German democrats. Political Catholicism emerged as a formidable domestic obstacle to unionist objectives. Anti-unionist agitation depicted Prussia as anti-Catholic, authoritarian, repressive, militaristic and a threat to southern economic interests.

Bismarck remained flexible, as always, on the question of how and when German unification would be achieved. He soon abandoned his early hope that it would come about through a process of peaceful coalescence. For a time he took an interest in plans to create a 'southern confederation' (*Südbund*) linking Baden, Württemberg and Bavaria, but mutual distrust among the southern states (especially of Bavaria) made such an agreement impossible. Then there was a plan to integrate the southern states gradually through the creation of a 'customs parliament' (*Zollparlament*), to which members of the *Zollverein* outside the North German Confederation would be entitled to send deputies. But the south German elections for this body in March 1868 merely revealed the depth of opposition to closer union.

The notion that unification might be expedited by a security threat from France was another theme in Bismarck's thinking. In the summer of 1866, he had observed that 'in the event of war with France, the barrier of the River Main will be broken and the whole of Germany will be drawn into the struggle.'[47] This comment referred specifically to contemporary apprehensions that France might decide to use force to reverse Prussia's gains after Königgrätz, but it was also in line with Prussian policy since the 1820s, which had always tended to see French security threats as facilitating Prussian designs. There was certainly abundant potential for friction between the two powerful neighbours. Emperor Napoleon III was shocked at the scale of Prussia's success in

1866 and convinced that it posed a threat to French interests. He also resented the fact that France had received no 'compensation' in the traditional manner, despite the generous, if vague, undertakings given by Bismarck before the war. In the spring of 1867, Bismarck exploited these tensions in the set-piece known as the Luxembourg crisis. Having covertly encouraged Napoleon III to satisfy his expectations through the annexation of Luxembourg, Bismarck first leaked news of the Emperor's designs to the German press, knowing that these would prompt a wave of nationalist outrage, and then posed publicly as the German statesman bound by honour and conviction to execute the will of his people. The crisis was resolved by an international conference that guaranteed Luxembourg's status as an independent principality, but it could easily have led to a French declaration of war, as Bismarck himself was aware.[48] Here again, Bismarck showed himself to be the master of mixed registers, who could blend covert manoeuvre and public posturing, high diplomacy and popular politics, with consummate skill.

A further opportunity to exploit friction with France arose over the question of the Hohenzollern candidacy for the Spanish throne. After the deposition of Queen Isabella in the Spanish revolution of 1868, the new government in Madrid identified Prince Leopold of Hohenzollern-Sigmaringen, a Catholic south German relative of the Prussian reigning family, who had a Portuguese wife, as an appropriate figure to take her place. Bismarck recognized that this issue could be used to generate friction with France and became an ardent supporter of Prince Leopold's succession. Pressing the case for the prince was an uphill battle, since both William I and Leopold's father were at first strongly opposed. By the summer of 1870, however, he had managed, through patient persuasion and intriguing, to secure the consent of both men. In July, the news that the candidature had been formalized prompted a wave of nationalist outrage in France. In a bellicose speech to the French parliament, the inexperienced new foreign minister, Antoine Agénor, Duc de Gramont, promised the French nation that Leopold would never be permitted to ascend the 'throne of Charles V' – a reference to the sixteenth century, when the German dynasty of the Habsburgs had threatened to encircle France. The French ambassador to Berlin, Vincent de Benedetti, was despatched to Bad Ems, where William I was on summer vacation taking the waters, to sort the matter out with the Prussian king.

Since William I responded in a conciliatory manner to Benedetti's representations and eventually accepted that Leopold must renounce his claim to the Spanish throne, the matter might simply have ended there, with a diplomatic victory for Paris. But Gramont made a serious tactical error. Benedetti was sent back to the Emperor to demand a further and more far-reaching assurance that the Prussian king would never again support the candidacy. Demanding that the Prussian monarch tie his hands in perpetuity was a step too far and William responded with a polite refusal. When Bismarck received the king's telegram (immortalized as the 'Ems telegram') summarizing the substance of the meeting with Benedetti, he saw immediately that an opportunity had arisen to slap down the French without surrendering the moral high ground. On 13 July, he released a lightly edited version of the text (a few words were removed, but none was added), in which the refusal was made to appear as a brusque rebuff and the ambassador as an impertinent petitioner. French translations of the edited version were also leaked to the press. The French government, enraged and anticipating an explosion of national outrage, responded with mobilization orders on the following day.

Here, as in 1864 and 1867, was a political crisis made to measure for Bismarck, who understood better than anyone how to exploit the unstable relationship between dynastic mechanisms and the forces of mass nationalism. Yet Bismarck's skill and cunning, remarkable as they were, can also be deceptive. He was not in control of events. He had not planned the Hohenzollern candidacy, and although he pressed hard for it during the spring and summer of 1870, he was also prepared to step back when it looked as if the Prussian king had agreed to withdraw and was willing to accept a French diplomatic victory. Even to say that the French played into his hands partly misrepresents the situation, for France's readiness to risk war was not the outcome of Bismarck's actions as such, but expressed a principled refusal to countenance any diminution of its privileged place within the European international system. The French went to war in 1870 because they believed – reasonably enough – that they could win. It would thus be an exaggeration to say that Bismarck 'planned' the war with France. Bismarck was not an exponent of preventive war. It was, as he once remarked, equivalent to shooting yourself in the head because you are afraid to die.[49] On the other hand, war with France was certainly on his menu of political options, provided that the

French took the initiative and acted first. Throughout the Luxembourg and Spanish crises, Bismarck operated an open-ended policy that incorporated the *possibility* of war but also served other objectives, such as accelerating the integration of the south German states and challenging French pretensions.[50] Had the Ems despatch merely generated friction and threats from Paris, this too would have served Bismarck's objectives by reminding the south Germans that they would remain vulnerable until they entered into a union with the north.

The news of mobilization and the subsequent French declaration of war set off a wave of patriotic emotion in Prussia and the other German states. As he returned by train from Bad Ems, William I was mobbed at every station by cheering crowds. Even the South Germans were outraged by the bellicosity and arrogance of Gramont's speech to the French parliament and indignant over his insolent treatment of the Prussian king. The mood in the foreign office and the ministry of war was one of confidence, and with good reason. Plans were already in place to coordinate military operations with the south German states under the terms set out in their alliances with the North German Confederation. The diplomatic setting was also auspicious: Vienna was still struggling with the consequences of far-reaching domestic reforms and was reluctant to risk any joint action; a draft treaty of 1869 thus remained unsigned. As for the Italians, they were unlikely to help Paris while French troops continued to occupy what remained of the Papal States (thereby preventing the absorption of Rome and its hinterland into the Kingdom of Italy). Britain had already made its peace with the idea of a unified Germany dominated by Prussia, and the Russians were easily won over by Bismarck's promise that Prussia would support St Petersburg in revising the most burdensome stipulations of the Crimean peace settlement. There was thus little reason to fear that Russia would intervene in support of France.[51] The window of opportunity created by the Crimean conflict was still open.

In military terms, the Prussians were well placed – better indeed than most contemporaries were aware – to win. They had – at full force – a larger, fitter and more disciplined army than the French. They also outperformed them in tactics and infrastructure. As in the Austrian war, the superiority of Prussian military organization was crucial. By contrast with the Prussian-German General Staff, which reported directly to the king, the French General Staff was a mere department of the ministry of war; in matters of strategy, tactics and discipline it was always subject to political pressure from the left-leaning National Assembly. The Prussian General Staff, its reputation sealed by the victory of 1866, had continued in the aftermath of the Bohemian war to introduce improvements to transport and supply, with the result that Prussia mobilized much more swiftly than her adversary, transporting over half a million men to the frontier with France while the French army on the Rhine still numbered only 250,000. The antique smooth-bore field guns that had performed so lamentably against the Austrian artillery in 1866 were phased out and replaced by rifled cannon incorporating the latest technology. Enormous effort was expended on improving the tactical deployment of artillery in support of infantry, an area where the Prussians had fallen down in 1866.

None of this made a Prussian victory inevitable. For all the efforts of the General Staff, the weaponry of the two sides was more closely matched in 1870 than in the previous conflict. The decisive advantage bestowed by the needle-gun in Austria was cancelled out in 1870 by the excellent infantry rifle (known as the *chassepot*) of the French, not to mention the *mitrailleuse*, an early machine gun that sowed havoc wherever it came into action against Prussian troops. The Prussians were dogged by the usual misunderstandings and false steps. General Steinmetz once again distinguished himself by his blithe disregard of instructions from the General Staff, and the August engagements at Spicheren, Wissembourg and Froeschwiller were stumbled into rather than planned. Even Moltke made some serious errors, most notably at the outset of the campaign, when he route-marched more than 200,000 men across the French front, exposing his forces to a devastating flanking attack; fortunately for the Prussians, the French commander, General Bazaine, failed to seize the opportunity.

The Prussians also exploited their marginal superiority in artillery with increasing skill, using their field guns to draw French fire away from advancing Prussian infantry. Most importantly, perhaps, the Prussians made fewer mistakes than their opponents. At Mars-la-Tour, Bazaine, commander of the French Army of the Rhine, failed to mount an offensive, transforming a potential French victory into a disaster that left the strategic strongpoint at Verdun exposed to a German advance. By early September 1870, barely six weeks into the war, the French had lost a series of decisive battles and with them, an irreplaceable reservoir of weaponry, officers and experienced cadres. After the crushing defeat and capitulation of the French forces under General Patrice de MacMahon on 1 and 2 September at Sedan, Napoleon III himself was taken prisoner, along with 104,000 men. The war dragged on for many more weeks as the Germans took Strasbourg and Metz and dug in for a protracted siege of Paris, while *francs-tireurs* took a rising toll in casualties behind the lines. After arduous negotiations with the new republican prime minister, Adolphe Thiers (the very man whose loose talk of French annexations in 1840 had triggered the Rhine crisis), a provisional peace was signed at the end of February. It was not until 10 May 1871, after French government forces had crushed the uprising of the Commune in Paris, that a final treaty was agreed at Frankfurt. In the meanwhile, Bismarck had overcome the objections of the southern states and secured their agreement to a union. On 18 January 1871, a new German Empire was proclaimed in the Hall of Mirrors at the Palace of Versailles. Exactly 170 years to the day after the coronation of Frederick I as Prussian king, King William I accepted the title of German Emperor.

A NEW EUROPE

For centuries, Europe's German centre had been politically fragmented and weak. The continent was dominated by the states on its periphery, whose interest was to maintain the power vacuum at the centre. Now, however, for the first time, the centre was united and strong. Relations among the European states would henceforth be driven by a new and unfamiliar dynamic. Benjamin Disraeli, leader of the Conservative opposition in the House of Commons, saw this more clearly than most: 'This war represents the German revolution, a greater political event than the French,' he declared before the House. 'There is not a single diplomatic tradition that has not been swept away.'[52] How true these observations were would only gradually become clear.

The era of Austro-Prussian dualism – once the structuring principle of political life among the German states – was over. As early as May 1871, the Austrian foreign minister, Count Friedrich Ferdinand von Beust, recognized the futility of a policy of containment and advised Emperor Francis Joseph that Vienna should henceforth seek 'an agreement between Austria-Hungary and Prussia-Germany embracing all

47. *18 January 1871: King William I of Prussia is proclaimed German Emperor in the Hall of Mirrors at the Palace of Versailles; engraving after a drawing by Anton von Werner*

current affairs'.[53] Beust himself did not survive to oversee the new orientation – he was dismissed in November 1871 – but his successor, Count Gyula Andrássy, pursued the same general line. Its first fruit was the Three Emperors' League of October 1873 between Austria-Hungary, Russia and Germany; six years later, Bismarck negotiated the more comprehensive Dual Alliance of 1879 that transformed Austria-Hungary into Germany's junior ally. Henceforth, Austrian policy would aim to engage Berlin as deeply as possible in the security interests of Austria-Hungary, even if this meant accepting subordinate status within the relationship. The two states would remain bound to each other until 1918.

The war of 1870 also placed the relationship with France on an entirely new footing. The annexation of Alsace-Lorraine – strongly advocated by Bismarck – traumatized the French political elite and imposed a lasting burden on Franco-German relations.[54] Alsace-Lorraine became the holy grail of the French cult of *revanche*, providing the focus for successive waves of chauvinist agitation. Pressing for it may well have been the 'worst mistake' of Bismarck's political career.[55]

Even without the annexation, however, the very existence of the new German Empire would have transformed the relationship with France. German weakness had been one of the traditional mainstays of French security policy. 'It is easy to see,' French Foreign Minister Charles Gravier Count Vergennes wrote in 1779, 'what advantage [Germany] would have over us if this formidable power were limited by the form of its constitution. [. . .] We thus owe our superiority and our security to the forces of [German] disunity.'[56] After 1871, France was bound to seek every possible opportunity to contain the new power on its eastern border. A lasting enmity between France and Germany – despite intermittent efforts on both sides to achieve a rapprochement – was thus to an extent pre-programmed into the European international system after the wars of unification.

If we consider these two factors – the close bond with Austria-Hungary and the lasting enmity with France – as fixtures of the European scene in the post-unification decades, then it becomes easier to see why Prussia-Germany found it so difficult to avoid the drift into isolation that was such a striking feature of the decades before 1914. From Paris's perspective, the chief objective had to be to contain Germany by forming an anti-German alliance. The most attractive candidate for such a partnership was Russia. Berlin could prevent this only by attaching Russia to an alliance system of its own. But any alliance system incorporating both Russia and Austria-Hungary was bound to be unstable: having been shut out of Germany and Italy, Austro-Hungarian foreign policy focused increasingly on the Balkans, a region where Vienna's interests conflicted directly with those of Russia.[57]

It was tension over the Balkans that broke the Three Emperors' League in 1885. Bismarck managed to patch up German relations with Russia by negotiating the Reinsurance Treaty of 1887, but by 1889 it had become increasingly difficult to reconcile Berlin's commitments to Austria-Hungary with its obligations to Russia. In 1890, Bismarck's successor, Leo von Caprivi, allowed the Reinsurance Treaty to lapse. France promptly leapt in, offering St Petersburg generous loans and armaments subsidies. The result was the Franco-Russian military convention of 18 August 1892 and the fully fledged alliance of 1894, both of which clearly envisaged Germany as the future enemy. It was to compensate for this adverse development that Germany in turn moved closer to Turkey in the 1890s, freeing Britain from its traditional role as guardian of the Dardanelles and Bosporus Straits and allowing it (after 1905) to pursue a policy of appeasement *vis-à-vis* Russia.[58] The bi-polar Europe that would go to war in 1914 was now in place. This does not mean that the statesmen of united Germany should be cleared of blame for the epic blunders and omissions that did so much to undermine Germany's international standing during the last decade and a half before 1914. But it does suggest that the momentous drift into isolation can only partly be explained in terms of political provocation and response. It represents, at a deeper level, the unfolding of the structural transformation wrought by Prussia's 'German revolution' of 1866–71.

16

Merged into Germany

In the spring of 1848, as crowds thronged through the streets of revolutionary Berlin, King Frederick William IV declared that Prussia would 'henceforth be merged into Germany' (*Preussen geht fortan in Deutschland auf*). His words were premature, but prescient nevertheless. They hinted at the ambivalent portent of national unification for the Prussian state. Germany was unified under Prussian leadership, but the long-awaited consummation inaugurated a process of dissolution. With the formation of a German national state, the Prussia whose history we have traced in this book came to an end. Prussia was no longer an autonomous actor on the international stage. It had to learn to inhabit the large and ponderous body of the new Germany. The demands of German nationhood complicated the inner life of the Prussian state, amplifying its dissonances, disturbing its political equilibrium, loosening some bonds while reinforcing others, bringing at once a diffusion and a narrowing of identities.

PRUSSIA IN THE GERMAN CONSTITUTION

In formal terms, Prussia's place within the new Germany was defined by the imperial constitution of 16 April 1871. This remarkable document was the fruit of a complex historical compromise. A balance had to be struck between the ambitions of the sovereign entities that had come together to form the German Reich. Bismarck himself was mainly concerned with consolidating and extending Prussian power, but this was not a programme that held much appeal for the governments of Baden,

Württemberg or Bavaria. The constitution that resulted was emphatically devolved in character. Indeed, it was not so much a constitution in the traditional sense as a *treaty* among the sovereign territories that had agreed to form the German Empire.[1] This was made abundantly clear in the preamble, which opened with the words:

His Majesty the King of Prussia in the name of the North German Confederation, His Majesty the King of Bavaria, His Majesty the King of Württemberg, His Royal Highness the Grand Duke of Baden, His Royal Highness the Grand Duke of Hesse [. . .] for those parts of the Duchy of Hesse that are south of the River Main, conclude an everlasting federation [*Bund*] for the protection of the territory of the federation and the rights thereof – as well as to care for the welfare of the German people.

In accordance with the notion that the new Empire was a confederation of sovereign principalities (*Fürstenbund*), the member states continued to operate their own parliamentary legislatures and constitutions. The power to set and raise direct taxes rested exclusively with the member states, not with the Reich, whose revenues derived chiefly from indirect levies. There remained a plurality of German crowns and courts, all of which still enjoyed various privileges and traditional dignities. The larger German states even continued to exchange ambassadors with one another, as they had within the old German Confederation. Foreign powers, by the same logic, sent envoys not only to Berlin, but also to Dresden and Munich. There was no reference to the German nation and as yet no official German nationality, though the constitution also obliged the federal states to concede equal citizenship rights to all members of the new Empire.[2]

Perhaps the most striking aspect of the new political order – as the constitution defined it – was the weakness of the central authority. This aspect is cast more sharply into relief if we compare it with the abortive imperial constitution drawn up by the liberal lawyers of the Frankfurt Parliament in 1848–9. Whereas the Frankfurt constitution set down uniform political principles for the governments of all the individual states, the later document did not. Whereas the Frankfurt constitution envisaged the formation of a 'Reich Authority' distinct from those of the member states, the constitution of 16 April 1871 stated that the sovereign German authority was the Federal Council, consisting of 'representatives of the members of the Federation'.[3] The council determined what bills were to be brought before the Reichstag, its assent was required before bills could become law, and it was responsible for overseeing the execution of Reich legislation. Every member of the Federation had the right to propose bills and to have them debated in the council. The constitution of 1871 even announced (art. 8) that the Federal Council would form from its own members a range of 'permanent committees' with responsibility for a variety of spheres, including foreign affairs, the army and fortresses, and naval matters. An uninitiated reader of the constitution could thus be forgiven for drawing the conclusion that the Federal Council was the true seat, not only of sovereignty, but of political power in the German Empire. This fastidious accommodation of federal rights appeared to leave little room for the exercise of Prussian hegemony.

But constitutions are often unreliable guides to political reality – one thinks of the 'constitutions' of the Soviet-bloc states after 1945 with their pious allusions to freedom of the press and opinion. The *Reichsverfassung* of 1871 was no exception. The practical evolution of German politics over the following decades undermined the authority vested in the Federal Council. Although Chancellor Bismarck always insisted that Germany was and remained a 'confederation of principalities' (*Fürstenbund*), the constitutional promise of the Council was never fulfilled. The most important reason for this was simply the overwhelming primacy, in military and territorial terms, of Prussia. Within the federation, the state of Prussia, with 65 per cent of the surface area and 62 per cent of the population, enjoyed de facto hegemony. The Prussian army dwarfed the south German military establishments. The King of Prussia was also, as German Emperor under article 63 of the constitution, the supreme commander of the imperial armed forces, and article 61 stipulated that the 'whole Prussian military code' was to be 'introduced throughout the Reich without delay'.

This made a nonsense of any federal pretensions to regulate military affairs through a 'permanent committee'. Prussia's dominance also made itself felt within the Federal Council. With the exception of the Hanseatic city-states of Hamburg, Lübeck and Bremen, the lesser principalities in central and northern Germany formed a Prussian clientele upon whom pressure could always be applied if necessary. Prussia in its own right possessed only seventeen of the fifty-eight votes on the Council, a smaller portion than its size justified, but since only fourteen votes were needed to veto draft laws, Prussia was in a position to block unwelcome initiatives from other states. As Prussian minister-president, Prussian foreign minister and imperial chancellor, Bismarck ensured that the federal Committee for Foreign Affairs remained a dead letter, despite the provisions of the constitution under article 8. As a result, the Prussian foreign ministry became in effect the foreign ministry of the German Empire. In the sphere of domestic politics, the Federal Council lacked the bureaucratic machinery necessary for the drafting of laws. This left it dependent upon the large and well-trained Prussian bureaucracy, with the result that the Council came increasingly to function as a body of review for bills which had been formulated and debated by the Prussian ministry of state. The subordinate role of the Federal Council was reflected even in the political architecture of Berlin; lacking a building of its own, it was housed in the imperial chancellery.

The primacy of Prussia was further assured by the relative weakness of imperial administrative institutions. A Reich administration of sorts did emerge during the 1870s as new departments were established to deal with the growing pressure of Reich business, but it remained dependent upon the Prussian administrative structure. The heads of the Reich offices (foreign affairs, interior, justice, postal services, railways, treasury) were not ministers properly speaking, but state secretaries of subordinate rank who answered directly to the imperial chancellor. The Prussian bureaucracy was larger than the Reich's and remained so until the outbreak of the First World War. Most of the officials employed in the imperial administration were Prussians, but this was not a one-way process in which Prussians swarmed on to the commanding heights of the new German state. It would be truer to say Prussian and German national institutions grew together, intertwining their branches. It became increasingly common, for example, for non-Prussians to serve as imperial officials and even as Prussian ministers. The personnel of the Prussian ministries and the imperial secretariats grew ever more enmeshed.[4] By 1914, some 25 per cent of 'Prussian' army officers did not possess Prussian citizenship.[5]

Yet even as the membranes between Prussia and the other German states became more permeable, the residual federalism of the German system ensured that Prussia retained its distinctive political institutions. Of these, the most important in constitutional terms was Prussia's bicameral legislature. The German Reichstag was elected on the basis of universal manhood suffrage. By contrast, the lower house of the Prussian Landtag, as we have seen, was saddled with a three-class franchise whose powerful inbuilt bias in favour of property-owners ensured the predominance of conservative and right-liberal forces. Whereas elections to the national parliament were based on direct and secret ballots, the Prussian Landtag was constituted using a system of public ballots and an indirect franchise (voters elected a college of representatives, who in turn chose deputies).

This system had seemed a reasonable enough answer to the problems facing the administration in the aftermath of the revolutions of 1848, and it did not prevent the liberals from mounting a formidable campaign against Bismarck during the constitutional crisis of the early 1860s, but in the decades following unification it began to look increasingly problematic. The three-class system was, above all, notoriously open to manipulation, because the colleges of representatives with their public ballots were much more transparent and manageable than the general public.[6] In the 1870s, liberal grandees in the provinces exploited this system to great effect, using their control over local patronage to ensure that rural constituencies returned liberal deputies. But things changed from the late 1870s, when the Bismarck administration began systematically manipulating the electoral process in favour of conservative candidates: local bureaucracies were purged of politically unreliable elements and opened to conservative aspirants who were encouraged to play an active role in pro-government agitation; electoral boundaries were gerrymandered to safeguard conservative majorities; polling places were moved to conservative areas within swinging rural constituencies, so that voters from opposition strongholds had to trudge across kilometres of open country to place their votes.

The conservatives also benefited from a sea-change in political attitudes, as country voters, unnerved by the economic slump of the mid-seventies, abandoned liberalism to embrace protectionist, pro-agrarian sectoral politics. In rural areas the result was an almost seamless continuity between conservative landed elites, Prussian officialdom and the conservative contingent in the Landtag. The cohesion of this network was further reinforced by the Prussian upper house, an even more conservative body than the Landtag, in which hereditary peers and representatives of the landed interest sat beside ex officio delegates from the cities, the clergy and universities. Established in 1854 by Frederick

William IV (on the model of the British House of Lords) with a view to strengthening the corporate element in the new constitution, the upper house had helped to block liberal bills during the 'New Era' and remained thereafter – until its dissolution in 1918 – a weighty conservative 'ballast' within the system.[7]

The effects of this partial merging of the conservative rural interest with the organs of government and representation were far-reaching. The Prussian electoral system favoured the consolidation of a powerful agrarian lobby. This in turn meant that a substantial part of the rural population, which accounted for the great majority of mandates, came to see the three-class system as the best guarantor of agrarian interests. It was reasonable to assume that the introduction of a direct, secret and equal franchise in Prussia would undermine the conservative and national-liberal fractions and thereby jeopardize the fiscal privileges of the agrarian sector, which benefited from preferential tax rates and protectionist tariffs on imported foodstuffs. After 1890, when the Social Democrats emerged as the largest polling party in the German national (Reichstag) elections, it became possible to argue that the three-class system was the only bulwark protecting Prussia, its institutions and traditions, against revolutionary socialism. This was an argument that not only conservatives, but also many right-wing liberals and some rural Catholics found persuasive.[8] The three-class franchise thus had the baleful effect of reinforcing the influence of the conservative rural interest to the point where far-reaching reform of the system became impossible. Chancellors – or even a Kaiser – who attempted to tamper with the special entitlements of the rural sector risked vociferous and well-coordinated opposition from the agrarian *fronde*. Learning this lesson cost two chancellors (Caprivi and Bülow) their posts.[9]

The Prussian system thus immobilized itself; it became in constitutional terms the conservative anchor within the German system, just as Bismarck had intended.[10] There was nothing especially nefarious about the egotistical sector-politics of the agrarians – the left liberals were just as frank about their pro-business, low-tax policies, and the Social Democrats claimed to speak only for the German 'proletariat', whose future 'dictatorship' – in the raw Marxist rhetoric still favoured by the party – was assured. But it was the agrarians and their conservative allies who succeeded in imprinting their interests and, to an extent, their political culture, on the system itself, laying claim in the process to ownership of the very idea of a unique and independent Prussia. Between 1899 and 1911, while virtually every other German territory (excepting the Mecklenburgs and the tiny principality of Waldeck) underwent substantial electoral reform, Prussia remained ensnared in its increasingly anomalous electoral arrangements.[11] On the eve of the First World War, Prussian citizens were still being denied an equal, direct and secret ballot. Only in the summer of 1917, under the pressure of war and a growing domestic opposition, did the Prussian administration relinquish its commitment to the old franchise. But before there was a chance to find out how the monarchical system would fare under more progressive electoral arrangements, it was swallowed up in the defeat and revolution of 1918.

POLITICAL AND CULTURAL CHANGE

While the Prussian constitution remained frozen in time, Prussian political culture did not. The hegemony of the conservatives was impressive, but it was also limited in important ways. There was a fraught polarity between the Prussia whose deputies – many of them socialists and left liberals – sat in the Reichstag, and the rural Prussia whose representatives dominated the Landtag. Reichstag elections enjoyed remarkably high rates of voter participation – from 67.7 per cent in 1898 to a staggering 84.5 per cent in 1912, the last election before the end of the war, when the Social Democrats captured more than a third of all German votes. By contrast, Prussian voters in the poorer income brackets showed their contempt for the three-class system by simply staying away from the polls during Prussian state elections – in the elections of 1893, only 15.2 per cent of the third class of voters (encompassing the overwhelming majority of the population) actually bothered to cast their votes.

The extreme regional diversity of the Prussian lands also limited the scope of conservative politics. On the eve of the First World War, Prussian conservatism was almost exclusively an East-Elbian phenomenon. Of 147 conservative deputies in the Prussian Landtag of 1913, 124 were from the old provinces of Prussia; only one conservative deputy was returned from the Prussian Rhineland.[12] In this sense, the three-class system accentuated the divide between east and west, widening the emotional distance between the politically progressive industrial, commercialized, urban and substantially Catholic west and the 'Asiatic steppe' of Prussian East-Elbia.[13] And this socio-geographical separateness in turn hindered the emergence of the kind of bourgeois-noble 'composite elite' that set the tone in the south German states, ensuring that the politics of the Junker milieu acquired a flavour of intransigence and extremism that set it apart.[14]

Outside the conservative heartlands, however, and especially in the western provinces and the major cities, there flourished a robust and predominantly middle-class political culture. In many large towns, liberal oligarchies, sustained by limited urban franchises, oversaw progressive programmes of infrastructural rationalization and social provision.[15] Especially in the years after 1890, the dramatic expansion in the variety and mass consumption of newspapers across the Prussian cities released formidable critical energies, confronting successive administrations with an image problem they found it impossible to resolve. This was, as one senior political figure observed in 1893, 'an era of limitless publicity, where countless threads run here and there and no bell can be rung without everyone forming a judgement about its tone'.[16]

The 1890s were a turning point for the socialists too, whose most important strongholds lay in the industrial zone around Berlin and the growing conurbations of the Ruhr area. In the elections of 1890, the socialists emerged from a period of draconian repression as the largest-polling German party. A socialist sub-culture evolved, with specialist clubs and venues catering to an emergent constituency of industrial workers, labourers, tradesmen and low-wage employees. By the turn of the century, Prussia was the stamping ground of Europe's largest and best-organized socialist movement, a fitting tribute to its two Prussian grandfathers, Karl Marx and Friedrich Engels.

The strife and polarization so characteristic of European cultural life in the *fin de siècle* also left their mark on Prussia. Here was another world that quickly slipped beyond the control of the conservative elites. The biggest theatrical sensation of the early 1890s in Berlin was Gerhard Hauptmann's *Die Weber*, a sympathetic dramatization of the Silesian weavers' revolt of 1844. Conservatives denounced the play on political grounds as a socialist manifesto, but they were also appalled by the harsh naturalism of its idiom, which was seen as negating the essential values of theatre. The interior ministry in Berlin imposed a ban on public performances of the play, but could not prevent it from appearing before enthusiastic audiences in large private venues such as the Freie Bühne and the Neue Freie Volksbühne, a theatre with links to the Social Democrats. Further bans in the Prussian provinces failed to prevent *Die Weber* from becoming a huge public success. Even more worrying, from the government's standpoint, was the fact that a debate over the bans in the lower house of the Prussian Landtag revealed deep divisions around the question of whether the tradition of state theatre censorship was still legitimate in an era of 'artistic freedom'. Even within the ministry itself, there were doubts about the wisdom of the interior minister's heavy-handed approach.[17]

A gap opened up between the official culture of the court and the experimentation and anti-traditionalism of an increasingly fragmented cultural sphere. It can be seen, for example, in the divergence of courtly and popular dance cultures. Around the turn of the century, new North American and Argentinian steps flooded into the dance locales of the larger cities. The fashionable shelf life of individual styles grew shorter and shorter as the *jeunesse dorée* welcomed the Cakewalk, the Two-Step, the Bunny Hug, the Judy Walk, the Turkey and the Grizzly Bear. But while an increasingly broad public consumed these transatlantic imports, the court of William II saw a revival of pomp and old-world ceremony. All court balls were organized so as not to upstage members of the royal family: 'if a princess is participating in the dance,' the journal *Der Bazar* noted in 1900, 'only two other pairs apart from the one in which the princess finds herself may dance at the same time.' William II explicitly forbade members of the armed forces to perform the new steps in public: 'The Gentlemen of the Army and the Navy are hereby requested to dance neither Tango nor One-Step or Two-Step in uniform, and to avoid families in which these dances are performed.'[18]

The same widening cultural gap could be seen in architecture and the visual arts. Consider, for example, the contrast between the heavy, neo-baroque megalomania of the new Berlin Cathedral, completed in 1905 after ten years of construction works, and the graceful, austere proto-modernism of the new architects – such as Alfred Messel, Hans Poelzig and Peter Behrens, among others – whose works between 1896 and 1912 were emphatic rejections of the eclectic 'historical style' favoured by official Prussia.[19] The arbiters of public taste – from Emperor William II to the rectors and professors of the state-funded academies – held that art should edify by drawing its subject matter from medieval legend, mythology or stirring historical episodes, while remaining true to the eternal canons of the ancients. But in 1892 there was bitter controversy in Berlin over an exhibition staged by eleven artists who wanted to free themselves from the strictures of the official salon. The 'bleak and wild naturalism' (thus the words of one outraged critic) of Max Liebermann, Walter Leistikow and their associates ran directly against the grain of officially sanctioned art practice. By 1898, the rebellion had broadened and diversified into the 'Berlin Secession', whose first exhibition, held in 1898, showcased the wide range of styles and perspectives taking shape within the non-official art world and was a huge public success.

What was interesting about the Secessionists was not simply their oppositional relationship to the prevailing cultural authorities, but the specifically Prussian and local content of much of their work. Walter Leistikow, who hailed from Bromberg in West Prussia, was well known for his haunting images of the Mark Brandenburg: trees brooding in shadow beside lakes, flat landscapes pocked with still, luminous water. His painting *Der Grunewaldsee*, a dark, atmospheric view of a lake on the leafy south-western outskirts of Berlin, was rejected for exhibition by the official Berlin Salon in 1898 – indeed, it was the controversy over this decision that prompted the Secessionists to create their own forum in the following year. Leistikow's paintings and etchings disturbed contemporary sensibilities in part because they took possession of the Brandenburg landscape in the name of a new and potentially subversive sensibility. William II, who loathed Leistikow's work, registered this sense of displacement when he complained that the artist had 'ruined the entire Grunewald' for him (*'er hat mir den ganzen Grunewald versaut'*).[20] Käthe Kollwitz laid claim to a specifically Prussian tradition in a different sense: in a widely praised cycle of etchings inspired by Hauptmann's play, she invoked the Silesian weavers' revolt of 1844. These were scenes of bitter conflict and suffering, in which the epic canvas of history painting was subverted to serve a socialist vision of the past. Even the proto-modernist architects Messel, Poelzig and Behrens were engaged in a dialogue with the specificity of the Prussian setting: their airy and technically innovative architectural designs responded at many levels with the spare neo-classicism of the 'Prussian style' associated with Gilly and Schinkel.[21]

The last decades before the war witnessed a dramatic proliferation in

48. The Avenue of Victory (Siegesallee), *Berlin*

the erection of public monuments and statues. In Prussia, as across much of Europe, the public statuary of this era tended towards weightiness and magniloquence. Patriotic themes loomed large. A study published in 1904 found that in recent years, 372 monuments had been erected to Emperor William I alone, most of them in the Prussian provinces. Some of these were financed from state funds, but local 'monument committees' also played a role in many areas, securing the necessary permissions and raising donations. By the turn of the century, however, the public echo of such objects was ambivalent. A telling moment was the opening in 1901 of the *Siegesallee* (Avenue of Victory), a chain of monumental statues extending for 750 metres along one of the axial roads of the capital. Set into a long sequence of spacious alcoves lined with stone balustrades were freestanding figures on lofty pedestals representing the rulers of the House of Brandenburg, flanked by busts of generals and senior statesmen from the reign. Already at the time of its opening, this gargantuan project appeared out of touch with the times. In his hurry to complete the avenue on schedule, Emperor William II had commissioned sculptors of varied distinction to execute the statues – all were conventional and bombastic, many were clumsy and lifeless as well. The result

49. Advertisement for Odol mouthwash

was an expensive exercise in pomposity and monotony. With their usual irreverence, the Berliners dubbed the avenue the *Puppenallee*, or 'puppet alley', and numerous contemporary visual satires mocked the project as the Emperor's megalomaniacal folly. The *coup de grâce* was administered in 1903 when a famous advertisement for a brand of mouthwash featured the Avenue of Victory lined with gigantic bottles of Odol.

The increasingly polarized relationship between official and dissenting political cultures was – even in the German context – a specifically Prussian phenomenon. It was far less marked in the southern German states, where progressive coalitions succeeded in pushing through programmes of constitutional reform. The relationship between the 'governmental' parties and the Social Democrats was also less fraught in the south, partly because the established partisan groups were more open to collaboration with the left and partly because south German socialists were more moderate and less confrontational than their Prussian counterparts. In high-cultural terms, too, the polarization was less pronounced. By contrast with Kaiser Wilhelm II, who publicly denounced cultural modernism of all kinds, Grand Duke Ernst Ludwig of Hesse-Darmstadt was a well-known connoisseur and sponsor of modern art and sculpture. In this small federal state, the court was still an important centre of cultural innovation.

CULTURE WAR

By the end of 1878, more than half of Prussia's Catholic bishops were in exile or in prison. More than 1,800 priests had been incarcerated or exiled and over 16 million marks' worth of ecclesiastical property seized. In the first four months of 1875 alone, 241 priests, 136 Catholic newspaper editors and 210 Catholic laymen were fined or imprisoned, 20 newspapers were confiscated, 74 Catholic houses were searched, 103 Catholic political activists were expelled or interned and 55 Catholic associations or clubs were closed down. As late as 1881, a quarter of all Prussian parishes remained without priests. This was Prussia at the height of the *Kulturkampf*, a 'struggle of cultures' that would shape German politics and public life for generations.[22]

Prussia was not the only European state to see tension over confessional questions in this era. In the 1870s and 1880s, there was heightened conflict between Catholics and secular liberal movements across the European continent. But the Prussian case stands out. Nowhere else did the state proceed so systematically against Catholic institutions and personnel. Administrative reform and law were the two main instruments of discrimination. In 1871, the government abolished the 'Catholic section' in the Prussian ministry for church affairs, thereby depriving the Catholics of a separate representation within the senior echelons of the bureaucracy. The criminal code was amended to enable the authorities to prosecute priests who used the pulpit 'for political ends'. In 1872, further state measures eliminated the influence of ecclesiastical personnel over the planning and implementation of school curricula and the supervision of schools. Members of religious orders were prohibited from teaching in the state school system and the Jesuits were expelled from the German Empire. Under the May Laws of 1873, the training and appointment of clergy in Prussia were placed under state supervision. In 1874, the Prussian government introduced compulsory civil marriage, a step extended to the entire German Empire a year later. Additional legislation in 1875 abolished various allegedly suspect religious orders, choked off state subsidies to the church, and deleted religious guarantees from the Prussian constitution. As Catholic religious personnel were expelled, jailed and forced into hiding, the authorities imposed statutes permitting state-authorized agents to take charge of vacated bishoprics.

Bismarck was the driving force behind this unprecedented campaign. Why did he undertake it? The answer lies partly in his highly confessionalized understanding of the German national question. In the 1850s, during his posting to the German Confederal authority in Frankfurt, he had come to believe that political Catholicism was the chief 'enemy of Prussia' in southern Germany. The spectacle of Catholic revivalist piety, with its demonstrative pilgrimages and public festivities, filled him with disgust, as did the increasingly Roman orientation of mid-century Catholicism. At times, indeed, he doubted whether this 'hypocritical idolatrous papism full of hate and cunning', whose 'presumptuous dogma falsified God's revelation and nurtured idolatry as a basis for worldly domination' was a religion at all.[23] A variety of themes were bundled together here: a fastidious Protestant contempt (accentuated by Bismarck's Pietist spirituality) for the outward display so characteristic of the Catholic revival blended with a strain of half-submerged German idealism and political apprehensions (shading into paranoia) about the church's capacity to manipulate minds and mobilize masses.

These antipathies deepened during the conflicts that brought about the unification of Germany. The German Catholics had traditionally looked to Austria for leadership in German affairs and they were unenthusiastic about the prospect of a Prussian-dominated 'small Germany' excluding the 6 million (mainly Catholic) Austrian Germans. In 1866, the news of Prussian victory triggered Catholic riots in the south, while the Catholic caucus in the Prussian Landtag opposed the government on a number of key symbolic initiatives, including the indemnity bill, the Prussian annexation programme and the proposal to reward Bismarck and the Prussian generals financially for the recent victory. In 1867–8, the Prussian minister-president – now chancellor of the North German Confederation – was infuriated by the strength of Catholic resistance in the south to a closer union with the north. Particularly alarming was the Bavarian campaign of 1869 against the pro-Prussian policies of the liberal government in Munich. The clergy played a crucial role in mobilizing support for the Catholic-particularist programme of the opposition, agitating from pulpits and collecting petitions bearing hundreds of thousands of signatures.[24] After 1871, doubts about the political reliability of the Catholics were further reinforced by the fact that, of the three main ethnic minorities (Poles, Alsatians and Danes), whose representatives formed opposition parties in the Reichstag, two were emphatically Catholic. Bismarck was utterly persuaded of the political 'disloyalty' of the 2.5 million Catholic Poles in the Prussian East, and he suspected that the church and its networks were deeply implicated in the Polish nationalist movement.

These concerns resonated more destructively within the new nation-state than they had before. The new Bismarckian Reich was not in any sense an 'organic' or historically evolved entity – it was the highly artificial product of four years of diplomacy and war.[25] In the 1870s, as so often in the history of the Prussian state, the successes of the monarchy seemed as fragile as they were impressive. There was an unsettling sense that what had so swiftly been put together could also be undone, that the Empire might never acquire the political or cultural cohesion to safeguard itself against fragmentation from within. These anxieties may appear absurd to us, but they felt real to many contemporaries. In this climate of uncertainty, it seemed plausible to view the Catholics as the most formidable domestic hindrance to national consolidation.

In lashing out against the Catholics, Bismarck knew that he could count on the enthusiastic support of the National Liberals, whose powerful positions in the new Reichstag and the Prussian Chamber of Deputies made them indispensable political allies. In Prussia, as in much of Germany (and Europe), anti-Catholicism was one of the defining strands of late-nineteenth-century liberalism. Liberals held up Catholicism as the diametrical negation of their own world-view. They denounced the 'absolutism' and 'slavery' of the doctrine of papal infallibility adopted by the Vatican Council in 1870 (according to which the authority of the pope is unchallengeable when he speaks *ex cathedra* on matters of faith or morals). Liberal journalism depicted the Catholic faithful as a servile and manipulated mass (by implied contrast with a liberal social universe centred on male tax-paying worthies with unbound consciences). A bestiary of anti-clerical stereotypes emerged: the satires in liberal journals thronged with wily, thin Jesuits and lecherous, fat priests – amenable subjects because the cartoonist's pen could make such artful play with the solid black of their garb. By vilifying the parish priest in his confessorial role or impugning the sexual propriety of nuns, they articulated through a double negative the liberal faith in the sanctity of the patriarchal nuclear family. Through their nervousness about the prominent place of women within many of the new Catholic orders and their prurient fascination with the celibacy (or not) of the priest, liberals revealed a deep-seated preoccupation with 'manliness' that was crucial (though not always explicitly) to the self-understanding of the movement.[26] For the liberals, therefore, the campaign against the church was nothing less than a 'struggle of cultures' – the term was coined by the liberal Protestant pathologist Rudolf Virchow in a speech of February 1872 to the Prussian Chamber of Deputies.[27]

Bismarck's campaign against the Prussian Catholics was a failure. He had hoped that an anti-Catholic crusade would help to create a broad, Protestant liberal-conservative lobby that would help him to pass legislation consolidating the new Empire. But the integrating effect of the campaign was more fleeting and fragile than he had anticipated. Anti-Catholicism could not sustain a durable platform for government action, either in Prussia or in the Empire. There were many facets to this problem. Bismarck himself was less of an extremist than many of those whose passions were aroused by his policy. He was a religious man who sought the guidance of God in his administration of state affairs (and usually, as the left liberal Ludwig Bamberger sardonically noted, found the deity agreeing with him).[28] His religion was – in the Pietist tradition – non-sectarian and ecumenical. He was opposed to the complete separation of church and state sought by the liberals, and he did not believe that religion was a purely private affair. Bismarck did not share the left-liberal hope that religion would ultimately wither away as a social force. He was thus unnerved by the anti-clerical and secularizing energies released by the *Kulturkampf*.

The anti-Catholic campaign also failed because the confessional divide was cross-cut by the other fault-lines in the Prussian political landscape. As the *Kulturkampf* wore on, the rift between left liberals and right liberals proved in some respects even deeper than that between the liberals and the Catholics. By the mid-1870s, the left liberals had begun to oppose the campaign on the grounds that it infringed fundamental rights. The increasing radicalism of anti-church measures also prompted misgivings in many Protestants on the 'clerical' wing of German conservatism. The view gained ground that the real victim of the *Kulturkampf* was not the Catholic church or Catholic politics as such, but religion itself. The most prominent examples of such conservative scruples were Ernst Ludwig von Gerlach and Hans von Kleist, both men formed by the Pietist milieu of old Prussia.

Even if the support for Bismarck's policy had been more secure, it is

50. Anti-clerical stereotypes. Cartoon by Ludwig Stutz from the satirical journal Kladderadatsch, *Berlin, December 1900.*

highly doubtful that he could ever have succeeded in neutralizing Catholic dissent by any of the means available to a constitutional and law-abiding state. Bismarck himself had been in his twenties when the fight over mixed marriages broke out in the Prussian Rhineland in 1837, a struggle that mobilized the Catholic population in the province and enhanced the moral authority of the episcopate. He must also have remembered the vain efforts of the Prussian government to impose the Prussian Union on the 'Old Lutherans' of Silesia – here again was a clear illustration of the futility of applying legal coercion to a confessional minority. And yet Bismarck and his partisans made the old mistake of overrating the power of the state and underestimating the determination of their opponents. In many areas, Catholic clerical personnel simply failed to respond in any way at all to the new laws.[29] The new state 'cultural examinations' for young priests approaching ordination were not attended; the state endorsements required for new ecclesiastical appointments were not sought.

The Prussian authorities, who had rushed these laws through and had not thought very deeply about how to ensure compliance, responded to this civil disobedience (as had their predecessors in the 1830s) by imposing improvised sanctions ranging from fines of varying severity to terms of imprisonment and exile. But these measures had virtually no detectable effect. The church continued to make 'illegal' appointments and the fines levied by the government authorities continued to accumulate. By early 1874, the archbishop of Gnesen-Posen alone had incurred fines totalling 29,700 thalers, more than twice his annual stipend; the figure for his colleague in Cologne was 29,500. When fines remained unpaid, the local authorities confiscated the property of bishops and offered it up at public auction. But this too was counter-productive, because loyal Catholics would rally to manage the auction in such a way as to ensure that the goods were sold at the lowest possible prices and returned to the expropriated clergyman.

Imprisonment was equally futile. As senior ecclesiastical dignitaries, bishops and archbishops were treated with such leniency during their incarceration that they might as well have been in their homes. They were allowed to occupy suites of rooms furnished from the episcopal palace and they dined on food prepared by the palace kitchens. In the case of Johannes von der Marwitz, the elderly bishop of Kulm (West Prussia), the option of imprisonment was even vetoed by the local judiciary on the grounds that the stairs of the local penitentiary were too steep for him to ascend. The authorities treated common parish priests far more harshly, but this too was ineffective, since it merely intensified the solidarity of the faithful with their beleaguered priests and hardened the determination of the latter to resist. After even brief jail terms, priests returned as heroes to their parishes.

The government attempted to resolve this problem in May 1874 by introducing a new batch of regulations known collectively as the Expulsion Law and providing for the exile of insurgent bishops and clergy to remote locations – a favourite was the Baltic island of Rügen. Several hundred priests were rounded up and exiled under these regulations in the four years between 1875 and 1879. But this measure created more problems than it solved. Who was to police the enforcement of the expulsion orders? In theory, this responsibility fell to the district commissioners (*Landräte*), but an official overseeing a population of 50,000 scattered over 200 square kilometres could hardly be expected to keep abreast of developments in every parish. It was not unknown for priests simply to return unnoticed after their expulsions and resume their clerical duties. In one such case an expelled priest worked in his parish for two years before the authorities became aware of his existence; by this time, the expulsion order against him had elapsed.[30] It also proved extremely difficult to replace the displaced priests with politically reliable successors. The individuals appointed by the state to replace dismissed clergymen were an abject failure, since they were despised and vilified by the Catholic populace. In a number of cases, the local authorities found that the only way to ensure compliance was to organize compulsory church parades in army encampments.

Far from neutralizing Catholicism as a political and social force, then, Bismarck's campaign enhanced it. Bismarck had reckoned that the Catholic camp would split under the pressure of the new laws, marginalizing the ultramontanes (exponents of papal authority) and transforming the remainder of the church into a compliant partner of the state. But in fact the opposite happened: the effect of state action was to drive back and marginalize liberal and statist elements within Catholicism. The controversies provoked in many Catholic communities by the declaration of papal infallibility in 1870 were put aside as critics of the doctrine acknowledged that papal absolutism was a lesser evil than the secularizing state. A small contingent of liberal anti-infallibilists, most of them academics, did split from Rome to form 'Old Catholic' congregations – a distant echo of the radical 'German-Catholics' who had congregated under the motto 'away from Rome' in the 1840s – but they never acquired a significant social base.

Perhaps the most conspicuous evidence of Bismarck's failure is simply the spectacular growth of the Centre Party, the party of the Prussian – and many German – Catholics. Although Bismarck did succeed in isolating the Centre Party within the Prussian parliament – at least for a time – he could do nothing to prevent it from increasing its share of German votes in the national elections. Whereas only 23 per cent of Prussian Catholics had voted Centre in 1871, 45 per cent did so in 1874. Thanks in large part to the ravages of Bismarck's *Kulturkampf*, the Centre Party 'peaked early', efficiently colonizing its social milieu, mobilizing Catholics who had hitherto been politically inactive, expanding the frontiers of partisan politics.[31] The other parties would gradually follow suit by mobilizing their own new voters from the non-Catholic parts of the population, but it was not until 1912 that the Centre Party's great leap forward was evened out by improvements in the performance of other parties. Even then, the Centre remained the strongest Reichstag party after the Social Democrats. Since most liberals and conservatives were still wary of dealing with the socialists, this made the Centre the most powerful player on the parliamentary scene – hardly the outcome Bismarck had in mind when he opened hostilities in 1871.

Prussia was no stranger to confessional tensions, but the scope and brutality of Bismarck's anti-Catholic campaign was unprecedented in the history of the state. The controversy over mixed marriages in the later 1830s had been dramatic, partly because of the emotive character of the issue, but it was essentially an institutional conflict between church and state, in which the objective was to stake out the boundaries of authority within an administrative grey zone. By contrast, the *Kulturkampf* was a 'culture war', a struggle in which it seemed that the very identity of the new nation was at stake. That the conflict between state and church should have expanded in this way to embrace the totality of public life was a consequence of the unstable interaction between Prussia's confessional tensions, Bismarck's ruthlessness and the challenges posed by German nationhood. In seeking to drive the Catholic church out of politics, Bismarck had used Prussian instruments to achieve German objectives. 'You may perhaps prove that I erred,' he told the Reichstag in a speech of 1881, 'but never that I lost sight for one moment of the national goal.'[32] Few political conflicts illustrate more clearly than the *Kulturkampf* the volatilizing effect of German unification on Prussian politics.

POLES, JEWS AND OTHER PRUSSIANS

'During the proceedings in this House,' a Polish deputy told the Reichstag in February 1870,

we find ourselves in a curious position when words ring in our ears about the German past, about German mores and customs, about the welfare of the German people. Not that we begrudge the German people their welfare or want to impede their future. But what for you may be a common bond – this past, these mores and customs, this future – is for us more an element of separation *vis-à-vis* yourselves.[33]

The Poles of the Prussian east responded to the political unification of the German states with a sense of foreboding. To be a Polish subject of the Prussian Crown might be a difficult predicament, but to be a Polish German was a contradiction in terms. Subjecthood and nationality were complementary concepts; the Poles might learn to live – at least outwardly – in peace with the Prussian state. They might even come to prize its virtues. But how could they subsist – as Poles – within a German nation? The ascendancy of the nation as a focal point for identity and a rationale for political action was bound to have far-reaching consequences for the Poles of the Prussian lands.

Of the 18.5 million inhabitants of Prussia in 1861, 2.25 million were Poles, concentrated mainly in the provinces of Posen and West Prussia (55 and 32 per cent Polish respectively) and the south-eastern districts of Silesia. Prussian policy regarding this minority, the largest in the Hohenzollern lands, had always been ambivalent, oscillating between tolerance and repression. After 1815, the government accepted the existence of a distinctive Polish nationality and fatherland under the Hohenzollern sceptre, though only on the condition, of course, that the Poles remained loyal Prussian subjects. When the Polish uprising of 1830 raised concerns about the dangers posed by Polish nationalism, the administration switched to cultural repression centred on the imposition of German as the language of education and public communication, but this policy was abandoned in 1840 after the accession of Frederick William IV. The wind changed again in 1846 after an abortive Polish insurrection in the Grand Duchy of Posen. The group behind the uprising was the Posen-city-based 'Union of the Working Classes', whose objective was to break the power of both the Prussian administration *and* the Polish landed nobility. Before the insurrection could get going, however, its prospective leaders were betrayed by anxious Polish noblemen to the Prussian police. A crackdown followed, in the course of which 254 Poles were tried in Berlin for involvement in the conspiracy, provincial towns combed by police units, and suspect press organs gagged or closed down.

This zig-zag course was essentially pragmatic and reactive. The goal was to ensure the political stability of the Polish areas. The cultivation of a distinctively Polish cultural milieu was acceptable, as long as this did not feed into nationalist or secessionist aspirations. However, the situation changed somewhat after the revolutions of 1848. These seemed at first to bring good news for the Poles. Prussian liberal opinion was overwhelmingly pro-Polish. In March 1848, the imprisoned radicals of the 1846 uprising were liberated and paraded through the streets of Berlin to wild cheering. The new 'March' ministry favoured the restoration of Poland as a buffer against potential Russian aggression, and on 2 April, the reconvened Prussian United Diet also passed a motion in favour of Polish restoration. Not for the first, or the last, time, it seemed that the hour of Polish liberty was at hand. Ludwik Mierosławski, a military strategist and one of the leaders of the 1846 uprising, hurried to Posen to assemble a Polish army.[34] In the mainly Polish areas of the duchy, the authority of the Prussian administration faded away as the local nobility took matters into their own hands, recruiting fighters and raising funds for Mierosławski. It was an alarming demonstration of the fragility of Prussian governance on the eastern margins of the kingdom.

At the same time, however, the revolution triggered a process of ethnic polarization in the Grand Duchy of Posen. When the Polish National Committee in Posen refused to admit German members, the latter formed their own German committee, which soon fell under the influence of nationalists. Many Germans in predominantly Polish areas fled to solidly German districts where the Prussian local administration was still functioning. On 9 April, activists in Bromberg founded the Netze District Central Citizens' Committee for the Promotion of Prussian and German Interests in the Grand Duchy of Posen – the juxtaposition of 'Prussian' and 'German' was telling, to say the least.[35] In May, after various efforts at compromise had collapsed, the Prussian army entered the duchy and crushed Mierosławski's army in a series of bloody military engagements. Prussian officials returned to their posts. The revolutionary National Assembly in Berlin continued to argue for a policy of Polish national equality under Prussian rule, but it was dissolved in the *coup d'état* of November 1848.

The new Prussian constitution of 1848–50 contained no reference to the idea of Polish minority rights and no indication that Posen or any other Polish district enjoyed special status. To senior administrators, the idea that the Prussian Crown might secure Polish loyalties by a policy of leniency now seemed passé. The Poles, it was argued, were beyond such appeals: 'they cannot be won over by any concessions,' an interior ministry report observed in November 1849.[36] Since the conciliation of the Polish national movement in Posen was an impossibility, the Prussian government was left with no option but to 'confine it energetically to the subordinate position it deserves'.[37] The term 'Germanization' (*Germanisierung*) began to appear with increasing frequency in official documents.

Yet the Prussian government showed little interest in adopting the idea of 'Germanization' as the basis for concrete policy measures. Calls from Posnanian Germans for government assistance to the German minority went unanswered – Minister-President Otto von Manteuffel took the view that if the German element was unable to subsist without state intervention, then it had no future. The authorities kept a close watch on nationalist activity, but the Poles continued to enjoy the civil liberties vouchsafed under the Prussian constitution, including the right to mount election campaigns on behalf of Polish deputies to the Landtag. Moreover, the Prussian judiciary in Posen was scrupulous in defending the status of Polish as the language of internal administration and elementary schooling.[38]

In the 1860s there were periodic calls for government Germanization measures, but the government remained reluctant to act, partly because it believed that market forces would ultimately favour German settlement and partly – in the years 1866–9 – because Bismarck was keen to appease the Polish clergy in order not to alienate the German Catholics of the southern states and jeopardize unification. So determined was Bismarck to maintain good relations with the Polish hierarchy during these years that he sacked the provincial president, Carl von Horn, in 1869 after a dispute between the latter and Archbishop Ledóchowski of Posen-Gnesen.[39]

The accomplishment of German political unification brought a paradigm shift in the government's handling of the Polish question. The Prussian authorities in the east were deeply alarmed during the summer of 1870 by the wave of undisguised partisanship for France. Polish recruits were urged to desert their Prussian regiments (a call that virtually none of them followed) and there were angry demonstrations at the news of Prussian-German victories. The situation in Posen appeared so volatile during the hostilities with France that reserve troop contingents were quartered on the province to keep order.[40] This rebellious behaviour triggered outbursts of vengeful fury from Bismarck. 'From the Russian border to the Adriatic Sea,' he told a Prussian cabinet meeting in the autumn of 1871, 'we are confronted with the combined propaganda of Slavs, ultramontanes and reactionaries, and it is necessary openly to defend our national interests and our language against such hostile activities.'[41] Hyperbolic to the point of paranoia, this imagined scenario of Slavic-Roman encirclement revealed the depth of Bismarck's anxieties for the new Prussian-German nation-state. Here again was that paradoxical sense of fragility and beleagueredness that had dogged the Prussian state at every phase of its aggrandizement.

Bismarck's first target was the Polish clergy whose interests he had earlier so assiduously defended. The chief objective of the Schools Inspection Act of 11 March 1872 was to replace the ecclesiastical dignitaries who had traditionally overseen the inspection of the 2,480 Catholic schools in the province with professional full-time inspectors in the pay of the state. Poland thus became the launching pad for Prussia's *Kulturkampf* against the Catholic church, and the old Prussian policy of pragmatic collaboration with the hierarchy was cast aside. The effect, predictably enough, was to reinforce the clergy's leadership in the Polish national struggle. In many areas, the efforts of the Prussian authorities to enforce *Kulturkampf* legislation against local Polish clergy resulted in direct action. Communities gathered to defend their priests physically against arrest. The 'state priests' sent to replace imprisoned or deported clergymen were shunned or even beaten by their congregations. Father Moerke, a German priest assigned by the authorities to the parish of Powidz in 1877, found his church silent and empty – his parishioners preferred to attend the masses of a Polish priest in a nearby village. Even Moerke's death in 1882 did not dispel the stigma – the villagers dug up his coffin and plunged it into a lake.[42]

In 1872-3 a volley of royal instructions issued from Berlin restricting the use of languages other than German in the schools of the eastern provinces. Among the collateral victims of this policy were the Prussian Lithuanians, who had never given any cause for offence, and the Polish-speaking East-Prussian Masurians, who were neither Catholics nor enthusiasts of Polish restoration.[43] A statute of 1876 established German as the sole language of official business for all Prussian government agencies and political bodies; other vernaculars could still be used in a range of parochial institutions, but this was to be phased out over a maximum of twenty years. Across the Polish areas, the lower clergy played a crucial role in coordinating protests against the new language policy. Parish priests assisted in the posting and collection of petitions – some bearing as many as 300,000 signatures – denouncing the Prussian authorities.[44]

From this point onwards, Germanization would remain the principle underpinning the rhetoric and much of the action of successive Prussian administrations in the Polish areas. In one of the most notorious manifestations of the new hard-line approach, the Prussian government expelled 32,000 non-naturalized Poles and Jews from Berlin and the eastern provinces in 1885, though they had done nothing to breach German or Prussian law. In 1886, alarmed by the increasing emigration of Germans from the depressed agrarian east to the rapidly industrializing western regions, the conservative-national liberal majority in the Prussian Landtag approved the foundation of a Royal Prussian Colonization Commission. With its headquarters in Posen City and a capital of 100 million marks, the commission's purpose was to purchase failing Polish estates, subdivide them and hand them out to incoming German farmers. Bismarck – along with many of the conservatives – had initially been opposed to subdivision because he deemed it inimical to the interests of the Junker class, but the colonization programme could succeed only with the backing of the National Liberals, who insisted on parcellation.

As Bismarck's compromise over colonization policy revealed, Prussian policy in the Polish regions in the late 1880s had to take account of a wide spectrum of domestic political pressures. This trend deepened during the 1890s, when a number of powerful lobby groups emerged with a special interest in the Polish question. Of these, the most important were the Pan-German League (*Alldeutscher Verband*), founded in 1891 as the voice of German ultra-nationalist opinion and the Society for the Support of the Germans in the Eastern Marches (known from 1899 as the *Ostmarkenverein*), whose very name was a mission statement. These organizations soon made their presence felt in the sphere of Polish policy. The Pan-Germans cut their teeth in 1894 with a vociferous public campaign against Bismarck's successor, Chancellor Leo von Caprivi, who was criticized for slackening the pace of Germanization in the Polish areas. The Eastern Marches Society also propagandized energetically through its journal, *Die Ostmark*, organizing public meetings and lobbying friendly parliamentarians. Such organizations occupied a curious place between the state and civil society. They were, in one sense, independent entities funded by donations, membership fees and the sale of publications. But there were also links to government agencies. The founder of the Pan-Germans, Alfred Hugenberg, had come to Posen as a local official with the Royal Colonization Commission. The membership of the Eastern Marches Society, numbering some 20,000 by 1900, included a substantial contingent of minor state officials and school teachers. These people would have left any organization whose objectives conflicted with the interests of the state, but any doubts on this score were laid to rest in 1895 when the Prussian minister of the interior publicly endorsed the 'defensive' work of the Eastern Marches Society during a political debate in the Landtag.

Despite differences within the agrarian-conservative-nationalist milieu over individual issues (such as the increasing use of Polish seasonal labour on the great estates), Germanization remained the operative principle in government policy. In 1900, new measures were introduced under Chancellor Bernhard von Bülow to further prune back the use of Polish. Religious instruction, the traditional safe haven for Polish-language schooling, was henceforth to be administered in German at all levels above elementary. In 1904, the Prussian Landtag passed a law permitting county officials to withhold building permits in situations where granting them would obstruct the colonization programme – the idea was to prevent Poles from buying and subdividing German farms and selling them on to Polish smallholders. There was also state financial aid for the Mittelstandskasse, a bank that specialized in easing the debt burden of German farmers. These actions were flanked by discriminatory recruitment practices in the local and provincial administration – of 3,995 new personnel hired by the Posnanian post and railway authority during the years 1907–9, only 795 were Poles, the rest were Germans. Polish place names began to be erased from the maps (though they remained vivid in Polish popular memory).[45] The high point (or low point) of the 'Germanization' programme was the anti-Polish expropriation law of 20 March 1908, which permitted the forcible removal of Polish landowners (with financial compensation) for the purposes of German colonization. The conservatives agonized over expropriation, and one can readily see why, but in the end they supported it, having decided that the ethnic struggle between Germans and Slavs overrode the sanctity of legitimate property title.

The Germanization programme was an exercise in futility. It failed to prevent Polish population growth in the eastern areas from outstripping the German. The parcellation of German farms continued, financed in part by energetic Polish banks that skilfully exploited loopholes in the Prussian regulations. The attempt to convert schools to the exclusive use of German had to be abandoned after repeated school strikes and sustained civil disobedience. The expropriation law never fulfilled its fearsome promise. No sooner was it enshrined in law but its teeth were filed down by internal guidelines exempting vast areas of Polish land – for pragmatic and political reasons – from expropriation. Not until October 1912 did the Prussian government announce its intention to execute an actual expropriation. But even then the area involved was small (only 1,700 hectares encompassing four economically insignificant landholdings) and the public backlash in the Polish areas so intense that the administration resolved to avoid any further expropriations.[46]

The real significance of the Germanization programme thus lies less in its negligible impact on the ethnic boundaries in East Elbia than in what it tells us about the changing political climate in Prussia. The traditional view of the Prussian monarchy had been that the Poles were – like the German-speaking Brandenburgers and Pomeranians and the Lithuanians of East Prussia – Christian subjects of the Prussian Crown. But from the 1870s onwards, Prussian administrators departed from this standpoint. In doing so, they followed the promptings of organizations outside the state whose arguments and propaganda were saturated with the rhetoric of German ultra-nationalism. There was a negative circularity in this relationship: ever uncertain of the depth of its public support, the state endorsed the work of the nationalist lobbies, who in turn derived much of their authority from the endorsement – implicit or explicit – of the state.

In the process the state placed at risk the principle of its historical existence, namely the presumption that the identity of Prussia proceeded from the dominion of a dynasty whose sun shone (albeit with varying warmth) on all subjects. Throughout the early to mid nineteenth century, Prussian administrations had recognized in German nationalism a powerful solvent of the dynastic principle. Yet by the turn of the century, the ascendancy of the national paradigm was incontestable. Nationalist historians busied themselves rewriting the history of Prussia as the eastward expansion of Germanic dominion and Chancellor Bernhard von Bülow (a Mecklenburger, not a native Prussian) did not scruple to stand before the Prussian Landtag and justify anti-Polish measures on the grounds that Prussia was and always would be a German 'national state'.[47]

The Prussian Jews also felt the impact of these developments. There was, of course, no question in the Jewish case of forcing the pace of cultural assimilation (a goal the great majority of Prussian Jews had already enthusiastically embraced) or of repressing ambitions for secession or political independence. What mattered most to the Jewish communities of nineteenth-century Germany was the removal of their ancient legal disabilities. This had already been achieved on the eve of political unification: the Confederal Law (valid throughout the North German Confederation) of 3 July 1869 explicitly stated that all curtailments of civil and citizenship rights that derived from differences of creed were henceforth abolished. It seemed that the long journey to legal emancipation that had begun with the Hardenberg edict of March 1812 was at last complete.

One important doubt remained. The Prussian government continued to discriminate against Jewish applicants to public office. Jews found it extremely difficult to achieve promotion into the upper ranks of the judiciary, for example, despite the disproportionate presence of Jews among lawyers, court clerks and assistant judges and the strong performance of

Jewish candidates in the key state examinations. The same applied to most branches of the senior civil service, as well as other important state-funded institutions of cultural significance such as primary schools, the secondary Gymnasien and the universities. Between 1885 and the outbreak of the First World War, moreover, no Jew was promoted to reserve officer status in Prussia, nor in the other German states whose military contingents were subordinate to the Prussian army (Bavaria retained a measure of military autonomy and operated a more open promotions policy).[48]

This discrimination by the state authority was all the more conspicuous for the fact that it represented something of an anomaly within the Prussian political landscape. Jews had no difficulty in being elected to important political and administrative posts in many large Prussian cities, where as high taxpayers they benefited from restrictive franchises. Jews held a substantial proportion (as many as a quarter) of council seats in the city of Breslau and could hold any position in the city administration except those of mayor and deputy, which were in the gift of the central state authorities in Berlin.[49] In Königsberg, Jewish residents flourished in an urban environment marked by easy inter-communal relations and 'cultural pluralism'. In many of the larger Prussian cities, Jews became core constituents of the urban *Bürgertum*, participating fully in its political and cultural life.[50]

The inequitable handling of appointments in the state sector generated a deep sense of grievance among politically aware and active Jews in Prussia.[51] The process of emancipation had always been intimately bound up with the state. To be emancipated was to 'enter into the life of the state', as Christian Wilhelm von Dohm had put it in his influential tract of 1781. Moreover, the constitutional position was clear: imperial law stipulated that any discrimination on faith grounds was illegal. The Prussian constitution stated (art. 12) that all Prussians were equal before the law and (art. 4) that public offices were equally accessible to all equally qualified persons. Only in the case of public offices involving religious observance was it admissible to favour Christian candidates. The surest way for the Jewish minority to safeguard its rights was thus to hold the state authority to the letter and spirit of its own law.[52]

Pressed by left-liberal parliamentary deputies to give an account of themselves, Prussian ministers either denied that such discrimination took place, or sought to justify it. They argued, for example, that the government must take into account the mood of the population when making sensitive public appointments. In a Landtag debate over judicial appointments in 1901, the Prussian minister of justice, Karl Heinrich von Schönstedt, declared that he could not 'when appointing notaries, simply treat Jewish advocates on the same basis as Christian ones, since the broadest strata of the population are not willing to have their affairs managed by Jewish notaries'.[53] The Prussian minister of war, von Heeringen, made a veiled appeal to the same logic when he replied to a Reichstag enquiry of February 1910 concerning the exclusion of Jewish volunteers from reserve officer promotions. In appointing a commanding officer, he declared, the army must look to more than simply 'ability, knowledge and character'. Other 'imponderable' factors were also in play:

> The entire personality of the man concerned, the way he stands in front of the troops, must inspire respect. Now far be it from me to claim [...] that this is missing in our Jewish fellow citizens. But on the other hand, we cannot deny that a different view prevails among the lower orders.[54]

This readiness to accommodate 'public opinion' also left its mark in other areas. In the early 1880s, for example, the Prussian ministry of the interior intervened in support of anti-Semitic student associations, undercutting the predominantly liberal university administrations that were trying to suppress them.[55] At around the same time, the Prussian administration also began to tighten its policy on the naturalization of foreign Jews: this was the background to the extraordinary expulsion of over 30,000 non-naturalized Poles and Jews in 1885.

Under pressure from anti-Semitic agitation and petitions, the Prussian government even began during the 1890s to prevent Jewish citizens from adopting Christian family names. Anti-Semites objected to Jewish name-changing on the racist grounds that it created confusion about who was Jewish and who was not. The Prussian state authorities (especially the conservative minister of the interior Botho von Eulenburg) adopted the anti-Semitic viewpoint, departing from established policy to discriminate specifically against Jewish applicants.[56] The same logic was at work in the 'Jew Count' (*Judenzählung*) ordered by the Prussian ministry of war in October 1916 with a view to establishing how many Jews were in active service on the front line.[57] National anti-Semitic organizations such as the *Reichshammerbund* (founded in 1912) had long been propagating the claim that the German Jews were war profiteers who were not pulling their weight in the defence of the fatherland. From the outbreak of the war and particularly from the end of 1915, they bombarded the Prussian ministry of war with anonymous denunciations and complaints.

Having for some time disregarded these protests, the Prussian minister of war, Wild von Hohenborn, decided to mount a statistical survey of Jews in the armed forces. In a decree of 11 October 1916 announcing the survey, the minister referred to allegations that the majority of Jewish servicemen had managed to avoid combat by securing posts well behind the front line. Although the results confirmed that Jews were in fact well represented in front-line units, the decree dismayed Jewish contemporaries, especially those whose relatives or comrades were at that moment fighting in the German trenches. It was, as one Jewish writer recalled at the end of the war, 'the most indelibly shameful insult that has dishonoured our community since its emancipation'.[58]

There were, of course, limits to the state's tolerance of anti-Semitism. In 1900, an anti-Jewish riot broke out in the West Prussian town of Konitz after the discovery of a macabrely dismembered corpse near the house of a Jewish butcher. Anti-Semitic journalists (mainly from Berlin) lost no time in levelling charges of 'ritual murder' against the butcher, and they were followed in this by a number of credulous townsfolk, most of them Poles. However, none of the Prussian judges or investigating police involved in the case ever placed any credence in the allegation, and the authorities lost no time in suppressing the unrest and punishing the main offenders.[59] Emancipation was treated as an accomplished fact by official Prussia and no serious attention was ever given to the idea – much urged by the anti-Semites – of returning to the era of legal discrimination. Jews continued to play prominent roles in Prussian public life, as parliamentarians, journalists, entrepreneurs, theatre directors, municipal officials, as personal associates of the Emperor and even as ministers and members of the upper house of the Prussian Landtag.

Yet the Jews were surely right to view with alarm the state's reluctance to enforce more energetically the letter of the constitution. It was one thing for the traditional Protestant agrarian oligarchies to cling to their accustomed share of government patronage (which of course they did); it was another somewhat more ominous thing for the state authorities to invoke the 'mood of the population' as grounds for departing from constitutional practice or the principle of equitable administration. In doing so, they allowed the anti-Semites to set the terms of the debate. There was an irony here, because whereas the Jews were among the foremost friends of the state, the anti-Semites were without question among its most implacable enemies. For them, the very word 'state' possessed connotations of artificiality and machine-like impersonality, in contrast to the organic, natural attributes associated with the *Volk*. The only acceptable form of state organization was that which demoted the apparatus of the state to an instrument for the self-empowerment of the *Volk* – an ethnic, not a political, entity.[60] Herein lies the parallel with Polish policy. Poles and Jews were fundamentally different social groups in almost every conceivable way, but they both presented the conservative elites that ran Prussia with policy domains in which the political logic of the modern state, conceived as a zone of undifferentiated legal authority, conflicted with the ethnic logic of the nation. In both cases, it was the idea of the (Prussian) state that gave way and the ideology of the (German) nation that prevailed.

PRUSSIAN KING AND GERMAN KAISER

The creation of the German Empire confronted the Hohenzollern dynasty with a complex task of adjustment. The King of Prussia was now also the German Kaiser. What exactly this would mean in practice remained unclear during the early years after unification. The new German constitution had little to say about the role of the Kaiser. The liberal nationalist Frankfurt constitution of 1848 had included a section entitled 'The head of the Reich', which dealt exclusively with the imperial office. There was no such section in the German constitution of 1871. The powers of the Emperor were set out in section IV under the modest rubric 'the presidency of the Federal Council'. These and other passages in the document made it clear that the Kaiser was no more than one German prince among others, a *primus inter pares*, whose powers derived from his special place within the federal body rather than from any claim to direct dominion over the territory of the Reich. It followed that his official designation was not 'Emperor of Germany', as Kaiser

William I would personally have preferred, but 'German Emperor'. There were distant echoes here of the limited sovereignty implied in the eighteenth-century title 'King *in* Prussia'; then as now, allowance had to be made for the other sovereigns whose sphere of authority overlapped with that of the new office.

In the relationship between chancellor and Emperor-king, it was generally Bismarck who had the upper hand. William I did assert himself on occasions, and he was no 'shadow figure', but he could generally be pressed, bullied, blackmailed or cajoled into agreement with Bismarck on matters of importance. William I had not wanted the war against Austria and he disapproved of the chancellor's political campaign against the Catholics. When there were disagreements, Bismarck could unleash the full force of his personality, hammering his arguments home with tears, rages and threats of resignation. It was these scenes, which the Kaiser found almost intolerable, that moved him to make the famous observation: 'It is hard being Emperor under Bismarck.' There was no false modesty in the Emperor's observation, on another occasion, that 'he is more important than I.'[61]

The effect of Bismarck's dominance, both as a political manager and as a national figurehead, was to retard the expansion of the Prussian throne into its imperial role. William I was a hugely respectable and widely revered man, a figure with the gravitas and whiskers of a biblical patriarch. But he was in his seventies when the Reich was proclaimed and essentially remained a Prussian king until his death at the age of ninety in 1888. He rarely spoke in public and seldom journeyed outside the territory of his kingdom. He retained the thrifty habits of an East-Elbian Junker: he resisted the installation of hot-water baths in the Berlin palace on the grounds of cost, for example, preferring to bathe once a week in a watertight leather bag slung from a frame that had to be carted over from a nearby hotel. He marked the labels on liquor bottles to prevent tippling on the sly by the servants at court. Old uniforms were made to do long service. After signing state papers, William would wipe the wet nib of his pen on the dark blue sleeve of his jacket. He made a point of eschewing carriages with rubber tyres on the grounds that they were an unnecessary luxury. There was an element of self-conscious performance in all of this – the king aspired to be the personification of Prussian simplicity, self-discipline and thrift. Every day he would appear punctually at the corner window of his study to oversee the changing of the guard – this reinvention of an old Prussian tradition became one of the great tourist attractions of Berlin.[62]

William I's son and successor, Frederick III, was a charismatic man with strong ties to the German liberal movement. He was also respected for the important command role he had played in the wars of unification. Given the chance, he might well have become a genuinely national-imperial monarch. But by the time Frederick came to the throne in March 1888, he was already dying of throat cancer and had only three months to live. He remained bedridden for much of his reign, reduced by his condition to communicating in scribbled notes with his family and staff.

In 1888, then, when William II came to the throne, the office of emperor was like a house in which most of the rooms had never been occupied. His arrival inaugurated a style revolution in the management of the German imperial monarchy. From the very beginning, William II saw himself as a public figure. He was fastidiously attentive to his outward appearance, rapidly alternating uniforms and outfits to match specific occasions, training his famous moustaches to trembling stiffness with a special patented wax and affecting a grave official countenance during public ceremonies. The obsession with outward presentation extended to close management of the Empress, the former Princess Auguste-Viktoria of Schleswig-Holstein-Sonderburg-Augustenburg. William not only provided designs for her clothes, her distinctive jewels and extravagant hats, but also pressured her to maintain her hourglass waist by means of dieting, drugs and corsetry.[63] He was the first German monarch to live and work in close proximity – one might even say symbiosis – with photographers and cameramen. They filmed him during public appearances and on family occasions, they filmed him on manoeuvres and riding to the hunt; they even followed him on to the royal yacht. Contemporary films of this Kaiser, of which there are many, show him always surrounded by the winding cranks of the movie cameras.

William II was, in other words, a media monarch, perhaps the first European monarch truly to deserve this epithet. More than any of his predecessors or, indeed, than any of his contemporary colleagues, he courted the attention of the public. The aim was not simply to draw attention to himself, though there is no doubt that this Emperor was a deeply narcissistic individual, but to fulfil the national and imperial

51. Dressed in the relatively austere uniform of the II Guards Regiment, Kaiser William II walks with his family in the grounds of Sans Souci. Painting by Wilhelm Friedrich Georg Pape, 1891.

promise of his office. He promoted the German navy, the genuinely national alternative to the Prussian-dominated army, lending his support to fund-raising campaigns and presiding at the massive naval reviews that were held annually at Kiel. He attempted, with mixed results, to establish a national cult around the figure of his grandfather William the Great, the founder of the Empire. He travelled across the Empire, opening hospitals, christening ships, visiting factories and observing parades. And, most of all, he gave speeches.

No Hohenzollern monarch had ever spoken as often and as directly to so many large gatherings of his subjects as William II. He treated the Germans to a virtually uninterrupted flow of public utterances. During the six-year period from January 1897 until December 1902, for example, he made at least 233 visits to at least 123 German towns and cities, in most of which he gave addresses that were subsequently published and discussed in the regional and national press. William's speeches, at least until 1908, were not set-pieces prepared for him by professional writers. The men of the civil cabinet busied themselves researching and writing up texts for specific places and occasions, sometimes pasting a final printed version to a wooden reading-board that was passed to the Emperor when the moment arrived, but their work was largely in vain – William preferred to speak without assistance. By contrast with his father, who as crown prince had always written out his texts beforehand and then 'changed them over and over again', William only rarely prepared his speeches in advance.[64] They were consciously performed as impromptu, unmediated acts of communication.

The Kaiser's most flamboyant performances were like nineteenth-century history paintings – charged with heavy-handed symbolic imagery, in which tempests alternated with shafts of redeeming light where all about was dark, and sublime figures (often members of his own dynasty) floated above the petty conflicts of the day. The aim was to 'charismatize' the monarchy and invoke the kind of transcendent, sovereign vantage point from which an emperor should reign over his people. A central theme was the historical continuity of the Hohenzollern dynasty and its Prusso-German mission.[65] There was an emphasis on the imperial monarchy as the ultimate guarantor of the unity of the Empire, the point at which 'historical, confessional and economic oppositions may be reconciled'.[66] Lastly, the providential dimension of monarchy was a leitmotif that ran through all the speeches of his reign. God had established him in this exalted office in order to fulfil God's plan for the German nation. During a very characteristic address delivered in the Rathaus at Memel in September 1907, he urged his audience to remember that 'the hand of divine providence' was at work in the great historical achievements of the German people: 'and if our Lord God did not have in store for us some great destiny in the world, then he wouldn't have bestowed such magnificent traits and abilities upon our people.'[67]

The public resonance of William's speeches was mixed. One central difficulty was that the people who heard his words and those who read them were not the same people. Live audiences were easily impressed. But words that seemed appropriate, or even rousing, before a rustical assembly of Junkers in Brandenburg might appear less so when they appeared in the broadsheets of Munich and Stuttgart. Early in 1891, William told a gathering of Rhenish industrialists in Düsseldorf that 'the Reich has but one leader and I am he.' The remark was intended as a stab at Bismarck, who had begun after his retirement to snipe at the Kaiser in the press and was known to be popular among Rhenish industrial circles, but it also caused unintended offence to those in non-Prussian Germany who saw it as a slight to the federal princes. After all, they too were 'rulers in the Reich'.[68]

The fact was that William II's public office was an awkward composite of distinct identities. When he spoke each year to the annual dinner of the Brandenburg Diet, an occasion he was especially fond of, he was in the habit of styling himself 'Margrave' in order to invoke the unique historical ties between his dynasty and its home province.[69] It was a harmless if somewhat self-dramatizing gesture that went down well with the conservative backwoodsmen of the Brandenburg Diet, but it was deeply unpalatable fare to the south Germans who pored over the published texts of such speeches in the daily press on the following day. The Emperor's close friend and adviser Philipp zu Eulenburg, who was posted as the Prussian envoy in Munich, explained the problem in a letter of March 1892:

The great eloquence and the manner and style of Your Majesty exert a captivating influence upon listeners and audience – as the mood among the Brandenburgers after Your Majesty's speech has once again proven. But in the hands of the German professor, a cool assessment of the content gives a different picture ... Here in Bavaria, people are '*beside themselves*' when Your Majesty speaks as 'Margrave', and 'the Margrave's Words' are printed in the *Reich*sanzeiger [*Imperial* Gazette] – as words, so to speak, of the *emperor*. In the Imperial Gazette, members of the empire expect to hear *imperial words* – they don't care for Frederick the Great (who referred to Bavaria, as they know only too well, as 'a paradise inhabited by animals' and so forth); and they don't care for Rossbach and Leuten.'[70]

The relationship between the imperial crown and the Bavarian state was a persistent source of tension. In November 1891, during a visit to Munich, William II was asked to make an entry in the official visitors' book of the city. For reasons that remain unclear, he chose to inscribe the text '*suprema lex regis voluntas*' (the will of the king is the highest law). The choice of citation may well have been linked with a conversation the Kaiser was having at the time when he was asked to sign the book, but it soon acquired an unexpected notoriety. Once again, it was Eulenburg who pointed out the blunder:

It is not for me to ask why Your Majesty wrote these words, but I would be committing a cowardly injustice if I did not write of the ill effects that this text has had in south Germany, where Your Majesty has stationed me to keep watch. [...] People here discern in it [the assertion of] a kind of personal imperial will over and above the Bavarian will. All parties, without exception, were offended by the words of Your Majesty, and the remark seemed perfectly made to be exploited against Your Majesty in the most disgraceful way.[71]

When south German cartoonists sought to disparage the Kaiser's imperial pretensions, they almost invariably did so by drawing him as an emphatically and incorrigibly Prussian figure. A wonderful drawing for *Simplicissimus* of 1909 by the Munich-based cartoonist Olaf Gulbransson shows William II in conversation with the Bavarian regent at the annual imperial manoeuvres. The setting was in itself charged with significance, because the relationship between the Prussian-imperial and the Bavarian army was a highly sensitive issue in Munich. The caption reads: 'His Majesty explains enemy positions to Prince Ludwig of Bavaria.' The stereotypical Prusso-Bavarian contrasts are exquisitely captured in the postures and clothing of the two figures. While William stands ramrod-straight in his immaculate uniform and spiked helmet, in cavalry boots that gleam like columns of polished ebony, Prince Ludwig resembles a human bean-bag. Loose trousers crumple shapelessly down his legs and a whiskery face peers bewilderedly from behind a pince-nez. Everything that is erect and dominant in the Prussian is cosily flaccid in the Bavarian.[72]

William II was, it must be said, singularly ill-suited to the communicative tasks of his office. He found it impossible to express himself in the sober measured diction that the politically informed public clearly expected of him. The texts of his speeches made easy targets for ridicule. They appeared excessive, pompous, megalomaniacal. They 'overshot the target', as one senior government figure observed.[73] Images and phrases from his speeches were often picked up and turned against him in the satirical press. Neither William I nor Bismarck had ever been ridiculed with such intensity (though closer parallels can be found in contraband depictions of Frederick William IV around the time of the 1848 revolutions). The legal sanctions against *lèse-majesté*, such as the confiscation of journal numbers or the prosecution and imprisonment of authors and editors, were extensively applied, but they were counterproductive, since they generally had the effect of boosting circulation figures and transforming persecuted journalists into national celebrities.[74] Efforts to control the form in which the Emperor's remarks reached the broader public proved futile.[75] William II travelled so frequently and spoke in such a great variety of places and contexts that it

52. 'Imperial Manoeuvres'.
Caricature by Olaf Gulbransson
from Simplicissimus,
20 September 1909.

was virtually impossible to control the diffusion of information about his utterances. The Kaiser's infamous 'Huns Speech' in Bremerhaven on 27 July 1900 was a case in point. On this occasion, ugly sound bites from a tasteless improvised speech to troops preparing to embark for China made it into print despite the best efforts of the officials present, stirring uproar in press and parliament.[76] The Kaiser – like many a modern celebrity – had learned how to court, but not how to control the media.

The imperial office lacked, as we have seen, a secure foundation in the German constitution. It also lacked a political tradition. There was, most strikingly, no imperial coronation. William II recognized this deficit. He saw more clearly than his predecessors how completely the Prussian Crown had failed to establish itself as a point of reference in the public life of the German Empire. He came to the throne determined to fill out the imperial dimension of his office. He travelled constantly among the German states; he glorified his grandfather as the warrior-saint who had built a new dwelling for the German people, and he instigated new public holidays and memorial observances to shroud, as it were, the constitutional and cultural nakedness of the Prussian throne in the mantle of a national history. He projected himself to the German public as the personification of the 'imperial idea'. In this unceasing effort to create the imperial crown as a political and symbolic reality in the minds of Germans, the speeches played a crucial role. They were instruments of 'rhetorical mobilization' that secured for the Kaiser-king a unique prominence in German public life.[77] For William personally, they offered compensation for the situation of political constraint and disempowerment in which he so often found himself. Indeed, they were, as Walther Rathenau, author of one of the most insightful reflections on this monarch, observed in 1919, the single most effective instrument of his imperial sovereignty.[78]

How successful William was in achieving his objective is another question. On the one hand, the more striking indiscretions provoked waves of hostile published comment. As the most visible (or audible) sign of the sovereign's independence, they became the primary focal point for the political critique of 'personal rule'.[79] Over the longer term, their effect was a gradual erosion of the political status of pronouncements from the throne. It became increasingly common, especially after 1908, for the government to disassociate itself entirely from unwelcome speeches on the grounds that these were not binding programmatic utterances, but simply personal expressions of opinion by the monarch, a disclaimer implying that the political views of the Emperor were of no wider political consequence.[80] As the Viennese correspondent of the *Frankfurter Zeitung* observed in 1910, a comparison between William II and Emperor Francis Joseph of Austria-Hungary revealed how counter-productive was William's over-use of the public word: the Habsburg dynast, it was noted, was a 'silent emperor' who always distinguished between his private person and his public office and never used the public forum to make personal utterances of any kind, and yet 'anyone who tries in Austria to talk about their emperor as we hear [ours] discussed at every table in Germany will soon be in serious trouble.'[81]

It is, on the other hand, notoriously difficult to get the measure of public opinion, and we should be wary of any judgement that relies exclusively on newspaper commentaries – 'published opinion' and 'public opinion' are not the same thing. The Emperor may have lost 'the aura of the sovereign who is above criticism,' wrote one foreign observer in the autumn of 1908, when William II was engulfed in a scandal over tactless utterances published in the London *Daily Telegraph*. 'But with all the personal magnetism that he possesses, he will always retain an immense ascendancy in the eyes of the mass of his subjects.'[82] William's invocations of divine providence were the laughing stock of the quality papers, but they struck a sympathetic chord with the more plebeian theological tastes of many humbler Germans. By the same token, his outspoken denunciations of avant-garde art appeared ludicrous and retrograde to the cultural intelligentsia, but made sense to those more numerous cultural consumers who believed that art ought to provide escapism and edification.[83] In Bavaria, the ceremonies of the 'imperial cult' (parades, unveilings and the jubilee celebrations of 1913) attracted the mass attendance not only of the middle classes, but also of peasants and tradesmen.[84] Even within the Social Democratic milieu of the industrial regions, there appears to have been a gulf between the critical perspective of the SPD elite and that of the mass of SPD supporters, among whom the Emperor was perceived as the embodiment of a 'patriarchal-providential principle'.[85] The conversations recorded by police informers in the taverns of Hamburg's working-class districts registered some disparaging, but also many supportive and even affectionate comments about 'our William'.[86] Substantial (if not precisely quantifiable) reserves of imperial-royalist capital did accumulate in German society. It would take the social transformations and political upheavals of a world war to consume them.

SOLDIERS AND CIVILIANS

On 16 October 1906, a down-and-out drifter by the name of Friedrich Wilhelm Voigt pulled off an extraordinary heist in Berlin. Voigt had spent much of his life in prison. Having left school at the age of fourteen following a conviction for theft, he had taken an apprenticeship with his father, a cobbler in Tilsit on the eastern margins of the Prussian state. Between 1864 and 1891, he was convicted on six occasions for theft, robbery and forgery, for which he spent a total of twenty-nine years behind bars. In February 1906, after serving a fifteen-year sentence for robbery, he was a free man once again. Having been refused a residence permit by the Berlin police authorities, he settled illegally in a tenement near the Schlesischer Bahnhof railway station, where he found a place as a 'night-lodger', sleeping in a bed that was occupied during the daylight hours by a factory worker on night-shift.

During the second week of October 1906, Voigt assembled the uniform of a captain of the I Foot Guards Regiment from garments and equipment purchased in second-hand shops across Potsdam and Berlin. On the morning of 16 October, he collected his uniform from where he had deposited it in the left-luggage store at Beusselstrasse station and walked to the Jungfernheide Park to change clothes. Attired as a Prussian captain, he headed downtown by S-Bahn. At around midday, when the guards were changing across the city, Voigt stopped a detachment of four soldiers and a non-commissioned officer who were on their way back to barracks from doing guard duty at the military swimming baths on Plötzensee. The NCO ordered his men to stand to attention while Voigt informed them that he was taking command under the authority of a cabinet order from the king. Having dismissed the NCO, Voigt collected a further six guardsmen returning from duty at a nearby rifle range and led 'his' troops to Putlitzstrasse station, where they all caught a train to Köpenick. On the way he treated them to beer from a station kiosk.

Arriving at the council chambers, Voigt placed guards at the main entrances and made his way with some troops to a suite of administrative offices where he ordered the arrest of the senior city secretary, Rosenkranz, and the mayor, Dr Georg Langerhans. Langerhans, who was himself a lieutenant in the reserve, leapt to his feet at the sight of Voigt's epaulettes and made no attempt to resist when he was told he was to be escorted under guard to Berlin. The council police inspector was found snoring in his office – it was a warm autumn afternoon in this quiet suburban district – and Voigt treated him to a stern reprimand. The municipal cashier von Wildberg was ordered to open the cashbox and transfer the entire contents – 4,000 marks and 70 pfennig – to Voigt, who presented him with a receipt for the sequestered sum. Voigt ordered a detachment of his guards to escort the arrested officials to Berlin by rail and report to the military post at the Neue Wache in Unter den Linden. Minutes later, he was seen leaving the building in the direction of Köpenick station, where he disappeared from view. He later revealed that he spent the next hour getting back to Berlin, shedding his military clothes and settling himself in a city café with a view of the Neue Wache. From here he was able to watch the confusion unfold as the guards arrived with their bewildered prisoners. On 1 December 1906, after spending six weeks at large, he was arrested and sentenced to four years of imprisonment.

Voigt's exploit generated huge contemporary interest. Within days it was being lampooned on the stage of the Metropol theatre. There was extensive international press coverage. The story of the conman in captain's uniform who walked away with the Köpenick council cashbox under his arm soon established itself as one of the most beloved and enduring fables of modern Prussia. It was dramatized for the stage in numerous versions, the most famous being Carl Zuckmayr's wonderful *Hauptmann von Köpenick* of 1931, and later adapted for the screen in a sparkling and atmospheric film starring the amiable Heinz Rühmann in the eponymous role. Among those who profited from the story's popularity was the perpetrator himself. Voigt was freed from Tegel prison after serving less than half of his sentence, thanks to a royal pardon from William II. Within four days of his release, he was making public appearances in the Passagenpanoptikum, a gallery of urban amusements on the corner of Friedrich and Behrensstrasse in the centre of Berlin. Having been forbidden to make further such appearances by the Prussian authorities, he mounted a highly successful tour to Dresden, Vienna and Budapest, where he was already a celebrity. Over the next two years, Voigt appeared in nightclubs and restaurants and at fairs, where he retold his story and signed postcards bearing his photograph as the Captain of Köpenick. In 1910, there were further tours in Germany, Britain, America and Canada. Such was his notoriety that he was modelled in wax for Madame Tussaud's gallery in London. From the sales of his memoirs, *How I Became the Captain of Köpenick*, published in Leipzig in 1909, Voigt acquired sufficient means to purchase a house in Luxembourg, where he settled permanently in 1910. He remained in Luxembourg throughout the First World War and died in 1922.[87]

At one level, of course, this was a parable about the power of a Prussian uniform. Voigt himself was an unimpressive figure whose appearance bore all the marks of a life spent in poverty and confinement – a police report based on witness accounts described the hoaxer as 'thin', 'pale', 'elderly', 'stooped', 'bent sideways' and 'bow-legged'. It was, as one journalist remarked, the uniform rather than its weather-beaten inhabitant that carried off the crime. Seen in this light, Voigt's tale evokes a social setting marked by a servile respect for military authority. This message was not lost on contemporaries: French journalists saw in it further evidence of the blind and mechanical obedience for which the Prussians were famed; *The Times* commented smugly that this was the kind of thing that could happen only in Germany.[88] By this reading, the captain's story was a concentrated exposé of Prussia's militarism.

But the fascination of the episode surely lies in its ambivalence. Voigt's exploit began with obedience, but it ended with laughter.[89] No sooner had he walked off with the cash, but his crime was a media event. The papers in and around Berlin described it as an 'unheard-of trickster's exploit', 'a robber's tale as adventurous and romantic as any novel' and conceded that it was impossible to reflect on it without smiling; Voigt was described as 'cheeky', 'brazen', 'clever' and 'ingenious'. The Social Democrat newspaper *Vorwärts!* reported that the 'hero's deed' was the talk of the town; in restaurants, in the streetcars and trains the 'heroic exploit' was discussed: 'It's not that one expresses indignation over the robbery of the Köpenick municipal treasury – instead the tone is mocking, sarcastic; everywhere a certain gleefulness over the ingenious prank at Köpenick refuses to be suppressed.'[90] Quick-witted entrepreneurs published mass-produced 'sympathy postcards' with before-and-after depictions of Voigt as cobbler and captain. Purchasers were informed that a portion of the income generated by their sale would go to a local society for the care of prisoners or even to Voigt himself.[91] It was precisely the comedic, subversive element of the story that Voigt so skilfully exploited in his memoirs and theatrical performances. As a media event, the captain's exploit was nothing short of a disaster for the Prussian military. It was, as the socialist journalist and historian Franz Mehring put it, a 'second Jena'.[92]

The roots of this laughter are not difficult to discern. The butt of the joke was Prussian 'militarism'. But what exactly did this term mean? The word first passed into general circulation as a liberal anti-absolutist slogan during the constitutional struggle of the early 1860s and it never lost these liberal connotations. In the south German states, the term 'militarism' was widely used in the later 1860s, almost always with an anti-Prussian charge.[93] 'Militarism' meant the Prussian system of universal conscription (as opposed to the arrangement still operating in the south, where wealthy subjects could purchase exemption from service), or the payment of matricular contributions for the upkeep of the national army, or the assertion more generally of Prussian hegemony over the southern states. For left-liberals, militarism could mean high taxes and potentially unchecked state expenditure. For some national liberals, anti-militarism captured echoes of the militia romanticism that had driven the reforms of the Napoleonic era. For the Marxist analysts of the Social Democratic movement, militarism was an expression of the violence and repression latent in capitalism. Precisely because it channelled and focused multiple preoccupations in changing combinations, 'militarism' became one of the foremost 'semantic rallying-points' in modern German political culture.[94] In whatever sense it was used, it drew attention to the structural connections between the military and the wider social and political system in which it was embedded.

The army was without a doubt one of the central institutions of Prussian life after 1871. Its presence was felt in everyday life to an extent that would be unimaginable today. The army, whose public standing had been low for much of the nineteenth century, emerged from the wars of unification in a nimbus of glory. Its role in the foundation of the new Germany was commemorated throughout the imperial era in the annual Sedan Day festivals that recalled the victory over France. The military establishment acquired a new kind of public resonance. Its prestige found expression in the imposing buildings that sprang up in garrison towns to accommodate serving troops and regimental administrations. There was an elaborate culture of military display in the form of parades, marching bands and manoeuvres. Military men took pride of place in virtually every official public festivity.[95] And the proliferation of military imagery and symbols infiltrated the sphere of private life: the photograph in uniform was a prized possession, especially for recruits from poor rural families where photographs were still a costly rarity; the uniform was worn with pride, even on holiday; military insignia and medals were treasured as mementos of deceased male relatives. The Prussian Reserve officer commissions – there were some 120,000 by 1914 – were a hotly sought-after status symbol in bourgeois society (hence the efforts of former Jewish volunteers to secure access to the corps). School children in garrison towns sang martial songs and marched in their playgrounds. Huge numbers of former servicemen joined the rapidly growing veterans' associations and military clubs; by 1913, the Kyffhäuser League, the central organization of veterans' clubs in Germany, counted some 2.9 million members.[96]

In other words, the military wove itself more deeply into the fabric of everyday life after 1871. Assessing the precise significance of this fact is far from straightforward. According to one influential view, the militarization of Prussian-imperial society widened the gap between Germany and the western European states, stifling the critical and liberal energies of civil society, perpetuating a hierarchical approach to social relations and inculcating millions of Germans with political views that were reactionary, chauvinistic and ultra-nationalist.[97] But was the Prussian experience really so unusual? Prussia was not alone in seeing an expansion of military cultures during the last four decades before the First World War. In France, too, veterans and servicemen flocked to join military clubs and associations – in numbers comparable with Prussia-Germany. A comparison of the militarization of national commemorations in France and Prussia-Germany after 1871 reveals close parallels.[98]

Even in Britain, a predominantly naval power that prided itself on the emphatically civilian quality of its political culture, the National Service League attracted some 100,000 members, including 177 members of the House of Commons. The league's propaganda combined a paranoid perspective on questions of national security with racist presumptions about the superiority of the British race.[99] In Britain, as in Germany, the late Victorian era saw a massive unfolding of imperial ceremonial. The 'civility' and anti-militarism of British society were perhaps more a matter of self-perception than a faithful representation of reality.[100] It is also worth noting that the German peace movement developed on a scale unparalleled elsewhere. On Sunday 20 August 1911, 100,000 people gathered at a peace rally in Berlin to protest against the brinkmanship of the great powers over the Moroccan Crisis. There was a wave of similar protests in Halle, Elberfeld, Barmen, Jena, Essen and other German towns throughout the late summer, culminating in a mammoth peace rally in Berlin on 3 September, when 250,000 people thronged to the Treptow Park. The movement subsided somewhat in 1912–13, but at the end of July 1914, when war was clearly imminent, there were once again large peace rallies in Düsseldorf and Berlin. The response of the German public to the news of war was not, as used to be claimed, one of universal enthusiasm. On the contrary: the mood in the early days of August 1914 was muted, ambivalent and in some places fearful.[101]

'Militarism' was, moreover, a diffuse and internally fissured phenomenon. A distinction has to be drawn between the essentially aristocratic and conservative ethos of the Prussian officer corps and the very different identities and attachments involved in the 'militarism of the little people'.

The legendary corporate arrogance of the Prussian officer caste and its disdain for civilian values and norms were essentially a distillation of the old spirit of East-Elbian noble corporate exclusiveness admixed with the defensiveness and paranoia of a social group determined not to relinquish its traditional pre-eminence. By contrast, the ethos of many veterans' clubs was plebeian and egalitarian. A study of soldiers from the annexed Prussian provinces of Hessen-Nassau who joined military clubs over the period 1871–1914 has shown that many of these were landless rural labourers, craftsmen and poor smallholders. They did not join out of enthusiasm for military service, but because membership provided a way of asserting their value, status and entitlements *vis-à-vis* the self-sufficient large-holding peasants who dominated their communities. Membership of the veterans' club was thus a 'vehicle of participation'. Viewed 'from below', what mattered about the military was not the imposition of deference *between* ranks, but the equality among men who served together.[102]

It was, in any case, the German navy, rather than the Prussian army, that captured popular enthusiasm for German national aggrandizement. Through his promotion of a massive naval construction programme from the late 1890s, Kaiser William II made his bid to establish himself as a genuinely national and German imperial ruler. The German naval programme soon attracted huge public support. By 1914, the German Fleet Association (*Deutscher Flottenverein*) counted over 1 million members, the great majority of them middle and lower-middle class. The navy was perceived as a genuinely national service, free of particularist territorial ties, with a relatively meritocratic approach to recruitment and promotions. The wave of technological innovations that transformed fleet-building around the turn of the century also attracted interest; ships were exciting because they were at the cutting-edge of what German science and industry could achieve. The fleet also carried the promise of a more expansive German global policy under the banner of *Weltpolitik*.

The army, by contrast, bore the burden of its association with the particularist power structure of Prussia. The most radical popular militarist organization of the pre-war years, the Defence Club (*Wehrverein*), whose membership numbered around 100,000 by the summer of 1914, was actually highly critical of the 'conservative' militarism of the Prussian elite, which they saw as reactionary, lethargic, narrow-minded and crippled by otiose class distinctions. They had a point: until 1913, parts of the Prussian military command opposed army expansion on the grounds that this would dilute the aristocratic *esprit de corps* of the officer caste by flooding the upper ranks with middle-class aspirants.[103]

ARMY AND STATE

The failure to integrate authority over civilian and military affairs had been one of the defining flaws of the Prussian constitution of 1848–50. The 1848 revolutions, as we have seen, constitutionalized Prussian politics without demilitarizing the Prussian monarchy. This was a flaw that the new German Empire inherited from the old Prussian state. The question of control over military spending remained unresolved. The constitution of 1871 stipulated on one hand (art. 63) that 'the Emperor determines the effective strength, the division and the arrangement of the contingents of the Reich army', and on the other (art. 60) that 'the effective strength of the army in peace will be determined by legislation of the Reichstag.'[104] The indeterminacy of these arrangements gave rise to periodic conflicts between the executive and the legislature. Of the four Reichstag dissolutions decreed during the life of the Empire (1878, 1887, 1893, 1907), three occurred for reasons related to the control of military expenditure.[105]

The Prussian army remained a praetorian guard under the personal command of the king, largely shielded from parliamentary scrutiny. The executive organs of the German military in turn remained embedded in the sovereign institutions of the old Prussian state. There was, for example, no imperial minister of war, just a Prussian one with responsibility for imperial military affairs. The Prussian minister of war was appointed by the Emperor (in his capacity as King of Prussia) and swore an oath of loyalty to the Prussian, but not the imperial, constitution. He was responsible to the Kaiser in most matters, but answerable in budgetary questions to the Reichstag. Yet he appeared before this body not as Prussian minister of war (for this post was formally quite unconnected to the imperial legislature) but in his complementary role as a Prussian plenipotentiary to the Federal Council.

As for the organs that administered the army in peacetime and at war, these were completely independent from the structures of civil authority. The military cabinet, the body responsible for personnel decisions (appointments and promotions), formally separated itself from the Prussian ministry of war in 1883, as did the Great General Staff, which was entrusted in the event of war with overall control of the operations of the field army.[106] Both henceforth reported directly to the monarch himself. Rather than establishing authoritative organs of central military governance, William II further fragmented the command structure by creating, just a few weeks after his accession, a new military establishment known by the grandiloquent title 'Headquarters of His Majesty the Kaiser and King'.[107] He also stepped up the number of military and naval command posts that reported directly to the Emperor.[108] This was all part of a conscious strategy to create an environment that would permit the untrammelled exercise of the monarchical command function.[109] The Prussian-German military system thus remained a foreign body within the German constitution, institutionally sealed off from the organs of civil governance and ultimately responsible only to the Emperor himself, who came to be known from around 1900 in general parlance as the 'supreme warlord'.[110] The result was a perennial uncertainty about the demarcation between civil and military authority. This was Prussia's most fateful legacy to the new Germany.

Nowhere before 1914 were the potentialities of this 'avoided decision' at the heart of the Empire's political fabric more disturbingly revealed than in the war of 1904–7 in German South-West Africa (modern Namibia), where an insurrection broke out in January 1904. By the middle of the month, groups of armed Herero had encircled Okahandja, a township in the centre-west of the colony, plundering farms and police stations, killing a number of settlers and cutting the telegraph and railway links to Windhoek, the administrative capital. The man charged with maintaining order in the colony was Governor Theodor Gotthilf von Leutwein, a native of Strümpfelbronn in the Grand Duchy of Baden who had been a serving soldier in the colony since 1893 and had held the post of governor since 1898. Finding himself unable to contain the uprising with the small local militia (there were fewer than 800 troops in a colony one and a half times the size of the German Empire), Leutwein requested that reinforcements be sent urgently from Berlin and that an experienced commander be despatched to take control of military operations.[111] The Kaiser responded by sending Lieutenant-General Lothar von Trotha, descendant of a Prussian military family from Magdeburg, who had already held a number of overseas postings.

Although both men were career officers, they occupied quite different positions within the Prussian-German political structure. As governor, Leutwein was the senior civilian authority in the colony and reported to the Colonial Department of the Prussian Foreign Office, which in turn reported to the imperial chancellor and Prussian minister-president, Bernhard von Bülow. Trotha entered the colony in a purely military role: he was not directly answerable to the political authorities, but only to the General Staff, which reported directly to the Kaiser. In other words, Leutwein and Trotha were locked into two quite separate chains of command. The two men personified the civil–military fault-line that ran through the Prussian constitution.

The governor and the general soon found themselves at loggerheads over how to handle the insurgency. Leutwein's intention had always been to manoeuvre the Herero by military means into a position where a negotiated surrender would be possible. His efforts and those of his subordinates focused on weakening the uprising by isolating the most determined element and negotiating separate settlements with other Herero groups. But General Trotha pursued a different approach. Having tried without success to encircle and destroy a large mass of Herero in a pitched battle at the Waterberg on 11–12 August 1904, he switched to a policy of genocide. On 2 October, the general had an official proclamation posted throughout the colony and read to the troops under German command. Composed in the pompous Wild West German of a Karl May novel, it closed with an unequivocal threat:

The people of the Herero must leave the country. If the people does not do this, I will force it to with the Big Pipe [artillery]. Within the German borders every male Herero who is found with or without a weapon, with or without cattle, will be shot. I will take no more children or women. Instead I will drive them back to their people or order them to be fired upon. These are my words to the People of the Herero. [Signed:] The great general of the Mighty German Kaiser[112]

This was not just an exercise in psychological warfare. In a letter composed two days later for his superiors on the Prussian General Staff, Trotha explained his actions. The 'nation of the Herero', he declared, were to be 'annihilated as such', or failing that, 'removed from the territory'. Since a victory through straightforward military engagements appeared impossible, Trotha proposed instead to execute all captured Herero males and drive the women and children back into the desert area of the colony, where their death by thirst, starvation or disease was a virtual certainty. There was no point, he argued, in making exceptions for Herero women and children, since these would simply infect German troops with their diseases and increase the burden on water and food supplies. This insurrection, Trotha concluded, 'is and remains the beginning of a racial struggle . . .'[113]

In a letter addressed to the Colonial Department of the Prussian Foreign Office at the end of October – in other words, to the *civilian* colonial authority in Berlin, Governor Leutwein defended his own very different view of the situation. As he saw it, Trotha had worsened the conflict in the colony by undermining the efforts of Leutwein's subordinates to negotiate an end to the fighting. Had these initiatives been followed up, Leutwein argued, the insurgency might well already have been resolved. At the centre of the crisis was a problem of demarcation. In adopting an avowed policy of indiscriminate murder and displacement, Trotha had exceeded his competence as military commander.

I take the view that my rights as governor have been compromised. For the question of whether a people is to be destroyed or hunted across the borders is not a military question, but a political and economic one.[114]

In an exasperated telegram of 23 October 1904, Leutwein asked for 'clarification of how much political power and responsibility still rest in the hands of the Governor'.[115]

The chancellor and Prussian minister-president, Bernhard von Bülow, shared Leutwein's misgivings about Trotha's extremism. The 'comprehensive and planned extirpation' of the Herero, Bülow informed the German Emperor, would be contrary to Christian and humanitarian principle, economically devastating and damaging to Germany's international reputation. Yet although he was the most senior political figure in Prussia and the Empire, he had no authority over General Trotha or his superiors on the Prussian General Staff, and thus no means of resolving the crisis in the colony through direct intervention. Only in the person of the Kaiser did the civilian and military chains of command converge. In order to achieve his objectives, Bülow had thus to manoeuvre the Emperor into countermanding Trotha's shooting order of 2 October. This was duly done, after a tug of war with the General Staff over various technical details, and a new imperial order was sent out to the colony on 8 December 1904. For the Herero, it was too late. By the time the order to stop shootings and forced displacements arrived, a substantial part of the indigenous population had already perished, most of them in the waterless areas of the Omaheke on the eastern side of the colony.[116]

The constitutional chasm between the civil and the (Prussian) military authority structures remained open throughout the life of the German Empire. It exacerbated the situation in Alsace-Lorraine, where civil administrators and corps commanders clashed over various issues, most famously the Zabern incident of October 1913, when insulting remarks by a young officer set off a train of minor clashes with the local population that culminated in the illegal arrest of some twenty citizens. The military had clearly overstepped the boundaries of their competence and there were loud protests from the civil authorities. But the Kaiser took the view that the prestige of 'his' army was at stake and openly supported the soldiers against the civilians. There was a national uproar over the case. Only with great difficulty did the chancellor succeed in persuading the Emperor to take disciplinary action against the main military culprits.[117]

Was there a specifically Prussian dimension to the war that broke out in August 1914? A war on two fronts, encirclement by a coalition of European powers – these had traditionally been Prussian, rather than Saxon, Badensian or Bavarian nightmares. Of all the nineteenth-century German states, only Prussia had to meet the challenge of exposed frontiers adjoining the territories of great powers in east and west. In this sense, the Schlieffen Plan, with its carefully weighted western and eastern spearheads, was an intrinsically Prussian device. To many contemporaries, moreover, it seemed obvious that the mobilization of 1914 belonged within a sequence of earlier Prussian 'appointments with destiny': 1870, 1813, 1756. Reference to these precedents cropped up everywhere in the public discussion that greeted the news of war in 1914. These invocations of continuity concealed, of course, the fact that the constellation of 1914 was born out of the fundamental changes wrought by German unification. This was a war of the German Empire, not of the Prussian state. When contemporaries invoked the 'memory' of earlier Prussian wars, they were in fact projecting the nationalist preoccupations of 1914 on to the Prussian past: 1813 was (falsely) remembered as a national German uprising against the French; Frederick the Great's pre-emptive strike of 1756 was refashioned into a 'German, even Pan-German' feat of arms.[118]

There was nothing especially novel about this conflation of the Prussian with the German past – the century since the Napoleonic Wars had witnessed the gradual nationalization of Prussia's most prestigious territorial symbols, from the Iron Cross to Frederick the Great and Queen Luise. Seen from this perspective, the history of Brandenburg-Prussia was merely an episode in a grander German story, whose early chapters recalled the antique cadences of the Song of the Nibelungs and the twisted oaks of the Teutoburg forest, where Hermann the Cheruskian had once defeated the armies of Rome. It is a telling detail that the first German victory in the east, the envelopment and destruction of the Russian 2nd Army on 26–31 August, was not named after one of the obscure East Prussian locales – Grünfliess, Omulefofen, Kurken – around which it actually took place but after Tannenberg, some thirty kilometres away to the west. The name was deliberately chosen in order to represent the battle as Germany's answer to the defeat inflicted by the Polish and Lithuanian armies on the knights of the Teutonic Order at the 'first' battle of Tannenberg in 1410, an event that predated the existence of the Prussian kingdom and called to mind the era of medieval eastern Germanic colonization.

Far from consolidating a distinctive Prussian state identity, the experience of war had a corrosive effect, accentuating the primacy of the German national struggle, while at the same time exacerbating anti-Prussian sentiments in the most recently annexed provinces. The war toughened the sinews of the imperial executive, creating new and powerful trans-regional authorities and accelerating economic integration. It also heightened awareness of the nation as a community of solidarity by creating new relationships of interdependence: the damage and dislocation inflicted on East Prussia, for example, during the brief Russian occupation prompted a massive wave of charitable donations from across the Empire. Billeting, military service and the growth in nationally organized forms of relief and social provision all helped to deepen identification with the imagined community of all Germans. Even in Masuria, where attachments to the Hohenzollern state had traditionally been strong, 'the last traces of the pre-national Prussian identity fell prey to an all-German patriotism.'[119]

On the other hand, the war stimulated regionalist resentments, even among serving troops. The monitoring of letters from front-line soldiers revealed that denigration of 'the Prussians' was common among Rhenish, Hanoverian, Hessian and even Silesian troop units. The same applied to an even greater degree to Bavarian troops – their despair at the duration and course of the war found expression in frequent outbursts of rage against the Prussians, whose arrogance and 'megalomania' were supposedly prolonging the war. A Bavarian police observer summarized the attitude of Bavarian soldiers returning from the front on leave: 'After the war, we'll talk French, but better French than Prussian, we're sick and tired of that...' Other reports from 1917 warned of intensified 'hatred of Prussia' within the civilian population of the south.[120]

The most important Prussian legacy to wartime Germany was constitutional in character. The problem of the German military constitution became even more acute after the outbreak of war. On the day of mobilization, the Prussian Law of Siege of 4 June 1851 came into effect for the entire Empire. Under this antique statute, the twenty-four army corps districts were placed under the authority of their respective deputy commanding generals, who were invested with near-dictatorial powers. The parallelism of civilian and military chains of command that had sown tension in Alsace-Lorraine before 1914 and delivered such mayhem in South-West Africa was now extended to the Empire as a whole. The results were inefficiency, wastage and disorder as the 'twenty-odd shadow governments' fought it out with the civil administrations across Germany (except in Bavaria, where the district commands were subject to the authority of the Bavarian ministry of war).[121]

At the apex of the German state, too, the military leadership exploited the Prussian defects in the system to usurp the powers of the civilian administration. The key figures behind the challenge were two archetypal products of the Prussian military establishment. Paul von Hindenburg und Beneckendorff (born in 1847) hailed from a Junker officer family in the province of Posen and had attended the cadet schools at Wahlstatt and Berlin. Erich Ludendorff (born in 1865) was the son of an estate owner in the same province who had been trained in the Royal Prussian *Cadetten-Haus* at Plön, Holstein and the cadet school at Gross-Lichterfelde near Berlin. Ludendorff was a jumpy, nervous workaholic prone to violent mood swings. Hindenburg, by contrast, was a towering, charismatic figure with bristling moustaches and an almost rectangular head; he radiated calm and confidence at all times. Ludendorff was the more brilliant tactician and strategist, but Hindenburg was the more gifted communicator. It was a supremely effective wartime partnership.[122] Hindenburg had already retired from the army at the age of sixty-four in 1911, but he was recalled when war broke out and sent to East Prussia to command the German 8th Army against the Russians. After a brief period of service in Belgium, Ludendorff was sent to East Prussia to work with Hindenburg as his chief of staff. After two major victories over the Russian 2nd and 1st Armies at the battles of Tannenberg and the Masurian Lakes (26–30 August and 6–15 September 1914), Hindenburg was appointed supreme commander of German troops on the eastern front.

By the winter of 1914, a rift had opened within the German military command. Erich von Falkenhayn, Chief of the General Staff and a favourite of the Emperor, argued that the key to ultimate success lay on the western front and was determined to commit the bulk of German resources to that sector. By contrast, Hindenburg and Ludendorff, emboldened by the scale of their success against the Russians, believed that the key to a German victory lay in the complete destruction of the Russian forces in the east. On 11 January 1915, Hindenburg – in a move unprecedented in the history of the Prussian army – threatened to resign unless Falkenhayn were dismissed. The resignation was refused and Falkenhayn remained in post, but the two eastern commanders gradually undermined his authority, pressuring William II into allowing a restructuring of the eastern command that substantially diminished the position of the staff chief. In the summer of 1916, William finally bowed to the inevitable, dismissed Falkenhayn, and appointed Hindenburg Chief of the General Staff, with Ludendorff as his quartermaster general.

There was a popular dimension to this ascendancy of the military leadership. A cult unfolded around the thick-set general; his likeness, with the unmistakable rectangular head, was endlessly reproduced and exhibited in public spaces. 'Hindenburg statues', wooden colossi erected in town squares and studded with devotional nails purchased with donations to the Red Cross, sprang up across Germany. Hindenburg seemed to answer the longing felt in some quarters during the war for a Führer whose authority and power over friend and foe alike would be absolute and undiluted. In the words of one prominent industrialist, what Germany needed in her darkest hour was 'the strong man, who alone can save us from the abyss'.[123] That neither William II nor Chancellor Bethmann Hollweg qualified for this role went without saying.

Having acquired the most powerful military post in the Empire by means of blackmail and insubordination, Hindenburg and Ludendorff now proceeded to undermine the authority of the civil leadership. One by one, they forced the Kaiser to dismiss ministers and senior aides who appeared antipathetic to their objectives. Early in July 1917, when they learned that the chancellor was in the process of preparing a franchise reform for Prussia, the two men travelled by train to Berlin to demand Bethmann Hollweg's dismissal. At first the Emperor held firm: Bethmann remained in office and the Prussian franchise reforms were duly announced on 11 July. On the following day, in yet another spasm of insubordination, Hindenburg and Ludendorff telephoned their resignations to Berlin, insisting that they could no longer work with the chancellor. To save the Kaiser further agonizing, Bethmann resigned two days later. His departure marked a fundamental break in the political history of the Empire. Henceforth, the Emperor was largely at the mercy of the 'Siamese twins'. The military command intervened extensively in civilian life, introducing new labour regulations and mobilizing the economy for total warfare. Germany remained under what was effectively a military dictatorship until the last days of the war.

A KING DEPARTS, THE STATE REMAINS

The last days of the Prussian monarchy were attended by bathos rather than tragedy. William II had been shielded by his entourage from the worst news about the collapse of the German offensive of 1918. He was all the more shocked to learn from Ludendorff himself on 29 September that defeat was inevitable and imminent. William's future as sovereign was now in question. During the last weeks of the war, the issue was increasingly widely discussed, especially after the censorship regulations were relaxed in mid-October. It acquired a heightened immediacy from the wording of the American note to the German government of 14 October, in which President Wilson referred to 'the destruction of

53. *'Buy War Bonds! Times are Hard, but Victory is Certain!' Poster designed by Bruno Paul, 1917.*

every arbitrary power anywhere that can [. . .] disturb the peace of the world', and added ominously that 'the power which has hitherto controlled the German nation is of the sort here described. It is within the choice of the German nation to alter it.'[124] Many Germans inferred from this communication that only wholesale removal of the Prussian-German monarchy would satisfy the Americans. There was a swelling chorus of calls for the Emperor's abdication, and questions arose as to whether the monarch would be safe in the city of Berlin. On 29 October, William left the capital for the general headquarters at Spa. There were people close to him who argued that this was the only way to avoid abdication, and even that his presence at headquarters might revive German morale at the front and thus trigger a reversal of German fortunes.[125] In reality, however, like the fateful flight to Varennes of the captive King Louis XVI, the move to Spa dealt a drastic blow to William's prestige and that of his office.

During the last week of his reign, an atmosphere of unreality permeated the royal-imperial entourage. Far-fetched plans received serious attention, including one proposal that William should redeem the dignity of the throne by sacrificing himself in a suicidal attack on enemy lines.

The king spoke of marching back into Berlin at the head of 'his army'. But the military informed him that the army was no longer his to command. He then toyed with the various permutations of abdication – perhaps he could abdicate as Kaiser, but stay on as King of Prussia? But with revolution spreading across the cities of Germany, there was no mileage in this quixotic attempt to disentangle the two offices that had become so hopelessly muddled since the proclamation of the Empire. Political events soon outpaced and pre-empted the anguished deliberations at Spa. At two o'clock on the afternoon of 9 November, just as he was about to sign a statement abdicating the imperial, but not the Prussian throne, news reached the headquarters that the new imperial chancellor, Max von Baden, had already announced the Emperor's abdication of both thrones one hour before, and that government was now in the hands of the Social Democrat Philipp Scheidemann. After some hours spent absorbing the impact of this momentous news, William boarded the royal train for Germany without having signed an instrument of abdication (he eventually did so in respect of both thrones on 28 November). When it became clear that a return to Germany was out of the question, the royal train changed course for Holland. Upon hearing that parts of the railway to the border had fallen under the control of 'revolutionaries', the royal party shifted to a small convoy of automobiles. In the early hours of 10 November 1918, William crossed the Dutch border and left his country for ever.

There is – if one takes the long view – something poignant in this sober Dutch conclusion to the story of the Hohenzollern monarchy. Elector John Sigismund's conversion to Calvinism in 1613 had been a homage to the robust political and military culture of the Dutch Republic. It was here that the young Frederick William found a safe refuge during the darkest years of the Thirty Years War, and it was from the Calvinist ruling House of Orange that he chose his wife. In later years, the Great Elector sought to remodel his patrimony in the image of the Republic. The dynastic link between the two houses was periodically renewed, notably in 1767 when William V of Orange married Princess Wilhelmina of Prussia, niece of Frederick the Great and sister of Frederick William II. The close family connection served as a pretext for Prussia's Dutch intervention of 1787, when Frederick William II led a small invasion force into the Netherlands to secure the authority of the House of Orange against the machinations of the French-backed 'Patriot

Party'. In 1830–31, the Prussians supported the Dutch king (without success) in his bid to prevent the secession of Belgium from the United Netherlands. And finally, at the end of the First World War, the last of the Prussian kings sought and received asylum in the Netherlands.

It was a matter of life or death for the Kaiser-king, who was by now the most wanted man in Europe. But Queen Wilhelmina of the Netherlands steadfastly refused to give way to Allied demands that the Kaiser be extradited for trial as a war criminal (a procedure that might well have ended with the monarch's execution by hanging). After a brief interim as the house-guests of a Dutch nobleman, William, his wife and what remained of their entourage established themselves at Doorn, in a graceful country residence. 'Huis Doorn' was nationalized by the Dutch government after the end of the Second World War and can be visited today. It still conveys the intense, unreal atmosphere of a lilliputian realm where the titles and rituals of the extinct Prussian-German monarchy were punctiliously observed in rooms cluttered with royal-imperial memorabilia, salvaged furniture, family portraits and cards from well-wishers. Here William II spent the remainder of his life (he died on 4 June 1941) sawing wood with his one good arm, reading, writing, talking and drinking tea.

'As a Prussian, I feel betrayed and sold out!' declared the Conservative leader Ernst von Heydebrand und der Lasa before the lower house of the Prussian Landtag in December 1917. He was referring to the fact that the newly appointed chancellor and minister-president of Prussia, Count Georg von Hertling, was a Bavarian, while his deputy, Friedrich Payer, was a left-liberal from Württemberg. The imperial state secretaries who now routinely attended meetings of the Prussian ministry of state were a further sign of Prussia's dwindling autonomy within the German system. 'What is this Prussia of ours coming to?'[126] These were the words of a man who knew that his era was coming to a close. The three-class franchise, the life-support machine of conservative hegemony, was already on notice. Those other props of the conservative system – the House of Lords, the royal court and the system of patronage that went with it – were all swept away in the defeat and revolution of 1918–19. The conservative-agrarian establishment, a network connecting the world of the rural estate with that of the officers' mess and the ministerial corridor, forfeited its formal anchorage in the structures of the state.

Something was coming to an end. It was not the world, of course, nor was it Prussia; it was a particular Prussian world, or rather the world of Prussian particularism. 'Old Prussia' had long been on the defensive. Faced with the threat of change, its champions had always insisted on the uniqueness of its ethos and institutions. But their advocacy for Prussia had always been partial: they spoke for the Protestant Prussia of the rural estates, not for the Catholic and socialist Prussia of the industrial towns. They saw the quintessence of Prussian identity in the collective ethos of a specific class and the deferential solidarities of an idealized East-Elbia.

But the conservatives did not monopolize allegiance to Prussia, though they might sometimes have felt that they did. There had always been an alternative tradition – not particularist but universalist in temperament – attached not to the unique personality of a specific historically 'grown' community, but to the state as an impersonal, trans-historical instrument of change. This was the Prussia celebrated in the first great blooming of the 'Prussian school' whose histories proliferated after unification. In the grand narratives of the 'Borussian' historians, the state held pride of place. It was the compact Protestant answer to the diffuse structures of the Holy Roman Empire. But it was also an antidote to the fog and narrowness of the province and a counterweight to the authority of those who ruled the roost there. Whereas historical narration in Victorian Britain carried the imprint of the Whig teleology, according to which all history was the rise of civil society as the carrier of liberty *vis-à-vis* the monarchical state, in Prussia the polarities of the argument were reversed. Here it was the state that rose, gradually unfolding its rational order in place of the arbitrary personalized regimes of the old grandees.

This celebration of the state as the carrier of progress was no nineteenth-century invention – it can be traced back, for example, to the treatises and narratives of the Hobbesian political theorist and sometime Brandenburg court historiographer Samuel Pufendorf. But the idea of the state acquired an intense charisma at the time of the Stein-Hardenberg reforms, when it became possible to speak of merging the life of the state with that of the people, of developing the state as an instrument of emancipation, enlightenment and citizenship. And no one, as we have seen, sang the song of the state more sweetly than Hegel, the Swabian philosopher who lived and taught in Berlin from October 1818 until his death in 1831, and once commented that the featureless sands of Brandenburg were a more congenial setting for philosophical speculations than the crowded romantic landscape of his homeland. By the 1820s, Hegel, now something of an academic celebrity, was teaching generations of Berlin students that the reconciliation of the particular and the universal – that Holy Grail of German political culture – had been achieved in the reformed Prussian state of his own time.[127]

The influence of this exalted conception of the state was felt so widely that it bestowed a distinctive flavour on Prussian political and social thought. In his *Proletariat and Society* (1848), Lorenz Stein, one of Hegel's most gifted pupils, observed that Prussia, unlike either France or Britain, possessed a state that was sufficiently independent and authoritative to intervene in the interest-conflicts of civil society, thereby preventing revolution and safeguarding all the members of society from the 'dictatorship' of any one interest. It was thus incumbent upon Prussia to fulfil its mission as a 'monarchy of social reform'. A closely affiliated position was that of the influential conservative 'state socialist' Carl Rodbertus, who argued in the 1830s and 1840s that a society based upon the property principle alone would always exclude the propertyless from true membership – only a collectivized authoritarian state could weld the members of society into an inclusive and meaningful whole.[128] Rodbertus's arguments influenced in turn the thinking of Hermann Wagener, editor of the ultra-conservative *Neue Preussische Zeitung* (known as the *Kreuzzeitung* because it bore a large black iron cross on its banner). Even that most romantic of conservatives, Ludwig von Gerlach, viewed the state as the only institution capable of bestowing a sense of purpose and identity upon the masses of the population.[129]

For many protagonists of this tradition, it appeared self-evident that the state must take a more or less limited responsibility for the material welfare of the governed. Among the most influential later nineteenth-century readers of Lorenz Stein was the historian Gustav Schmoller, who coined the term 'social policy' (*Sozialpolitik*) to convey the right and obligation of the state to intervene in support of the most vulnerable members of society; to leave society to regulate its own affairs, Schmoller argued, was to invite chaos.[130] Schmoller was closely associated with the economist and 'state socialist' Adolph Wagner, who took up a professorial chair at the University of Berlin in 1870. Wagner, a keen student of Rodbertus's writings, was among the founding members of the Association for Social Policy founded in 1872, an important early forum for debate on the social obligations of the state. Wagner and Schmoller exemplified the outlook of the 'young historical school' that flourished in the soil of the Hegelian-Prussian tradition.[131] Their belief in the redemptive social mission of the state resonated widely in a political environment troubled by the pains of the recession that set in from 1873 and looking for alternatives to a liberal doctrine of laissez-faire that appeared to have exhausted its credibility. So strong was the intellectual pull of social policy that it attracted a highly diverse constituency, including National Liberals, Centre Party leaders, state socialists and conservative figures close to Bismarck, including the *Kreuzzeitung* editor Hermann Wagener, who advised Bismarck on social matters in the 1860s and 1870s.[132]

The scene was thus set long in advance for the pioneering Bismarckian social legislation of the 1880s. The medical insurance law of 15 June 1883 created a network of local insurance providers who dispensed funds from income generated by a combination of worker and employer contributions. The accident insurance law of 1884 made arrangements for the administration of insurance in cases of illness and work-related injury. The last of the three foundational pillars of German social legislation came in 1889, with the age and invalidity insurance law. These provisions were quantitatively small by present-day standards, the payments involved extremely modest, and the scope of the new provisions far from comprehensive – the law of 1883, for example, did not apply to rural workers. At no point did the social legislation of the Empire come close to reversing the trend towards increased economic inequality in Prussian or German society. It is clear, moreover, that Bismarck's motives were narrowly manipulative and pragmatic. His chief concern was to win the working classes back to the Prussian-German 'social monarchy' and thereby cripple the growing Social Democratic movement.

But to personalize the issue is to miss the point. Bismarck's support for social insurance was, after all, merely one articulation of a broader 'discourse coalition' with deep cultural and historical roots. In this congenial ideological setting, the provisions available under the state insurance laws swiftly expanded, to the point where they did begin to have an appreciable impact on the welfare of workers, and perhaps even, as Bismarck had hoped, a mollifying effect on their politics.[133] The momentum of reform continued into the early 1890s, when the new administration under William II and Chancellor Caprivi enacted labour laws that brought progress in the areas of industrial safety, working conditions, youth protection and arbitration. The principle they embodied, namely that 'entrepreneurial forces must respect the state-endorsed interests of all groups', remained a dominant theme in imperial and Prussian social policy during the following decades.[134]

By the eve of the First World War, the Prussian state was big. Between the 1880s and 1913, it expanded to encompass over 1 million employees. According to an assessment published in 1913, the Prussian ministry of public works was 'the largest employer in the world'. The Prussian railways administration alone employed 310,000 workers and the state-controlled mining sector a further 180,000. Across all sectors, the Prussian state offered cutting-edge social services, including unemployment and accident insurance and medical protection schemes. In a speech of 1904, the Prussian minister of public works, Hermann Friedrich von Budde, a former cadet and staff officer, declared before the Prussian Chamber of Deputies that a large part of his work was devoted to the welfare of his public workers. The ultimate purpose of Prussia's public sector employers, he added, was 'to solve the social question by means of social provision [Fürsorge]'.[135] Here was a Prussia that might survive the débâcle of the Hohenzollern monarchy with its legitimacy intact.

17

Endings

REVOLUTION IN PRUSSIA

At the end of October 1918, sailors in Kiel harbour (Schleswig-Holstein) mutinied when they were ordered to put to sea for a futile attack on the British Grand Fleet. As the sailors took control of the naval base, the commander, Prince Heinrich of Prussia, was forced to flee in disguise. A wave of strikes and military rebellions spread across the country, engulfing all the major cities. The revolution quickly acquired its own novel political organizations – 'councils' elected locally by workers and servicemen across the country to articulate the demands of those broad sectors of the population that had withdrawn their allegiance from the monarchical system and its doomed war effort. This was not, as one contemporary observer noted, an upheaval of the French type, in which the capital city visits revolution upon the provinces; it was more like a Viking invasion spreading inwards 'like a patch of oil' from the coast.[1] One after another, the local and provincial Prussian administrations capitulated without complaint to the insurgents.

At around two o'clock in the afternoon on Saturday 9 November, Philipp Scheidemann, speaking for the Social Democrats who had just formed a provisional national government, announced to cheering crowds from the balcony of the Reichstag building in Berlin that 'the old rotten order, the monarchy, has collapsed. Long live the new! Long live the German Republic!' When the art critic and diarist Harry Kessler entered the Reichstag building at ten o'clock in the evening of 9 November, he found 'a colourful hubbub'; sailors, armed civilians, women, soldiers thronged up and down the stairways. Groups of soldiers and sailors, some standing, some lying on the thick red carpet, others stretched out asleep on the benches that lined the walls, were scattered round the great hall. It was, Kessler recalled, like a film scene from the Russian Revolution.[2] Here, as in all revolutions, the mobilized public demonstrated its prowess by the festive usurpation of formerly privileged space. The Prussian civil servant Herbert du Mesnil, a descendant of Prussian Huguenot colonists, experienced a similar sense of displacement on the evening of 8 November, when a band of insurgents invaded his club in Koblenz. Their leader, a soldier on horseback, clattered around the finely appointed ground-floor rooms of the club, while the diners, most of them officers of Prussian reserve regiments stationed in the town, looked on in astonishment.[3]

It seemed unlikely at first that the state of Prussia would survive the upheaval. The Hohenzollern Crown was no longer there to provide the diverse lands of the Prussian patrimony with a unifying focal point. In the Rhineland, moreover, there were calls in the Catholic press for separation from Berlin.[4] In December 1918, a manifesto demanding territorial autonomy issued by the German-Hanoverian party attracted 600,000 signatures.[5] In the eastern provinces, Polish demands for a national restoration erupted on Boxing Day 1918 in an insurrection against the German authorities across the province of Posen and the fighting there soon escalated into a full-scale guerrilla campaign.[6] There were good reasons, moreover, to suppose that the new Germany might be better off without Prussia. Even after the territorial annexations imposed by the Treaty of Versailles,[7] Prussia remained by far the largest German state. The memory of Prussian dominance within the old Empire suggested that the state's disproportionate size might prove a burden upon the new German Republic. A report prepared by the Reich Interior Ministry under the direction of the liberal constitutional lawyer Hugo Preuss in December 1918 observed that it made no sense to retain the existing state boundaries within Germany, because these bore no relation to geography or convenience and were 'merely the coincidental constructions of a purely dynastic policy'. The report concluded that the end of Prussian hegemony over Germany must mean the dismemberment of Prussia.[8]

Yet the Prussian state survived. The moderate Social Democratic leadership clung to a policy of continuity and stability. This meant, among other things, putting aside their doctrinal commitment to a unitary republican state and preserving the still functioning structures of

620

the Prussian administration. On 12 November 1918, the revolutionary Executive Council of the Workers' and Soldiers' Council of Greater Berlin issued an order to the effect that all administrative offices at communal, provincial and state level were to continue operating. On the following day, the council issued a manifesto under the rubric 'To the Prussian People!' announcing that the new authorities intended to transform the 'thoroughly reactionary Prussia of the past' into a 'completely democratic people's republic'. And on 14 November, a coalition Prussian government was formed, comprising representatives of the SPD and the left-wing socialist Independent SPD (USPD). Civil servants facilitated this transition at the local level by assuring the workers' and soldiers' councils that their loyalty was not to the defunct monarchy, but to the Prussian state now under revolutionary custodianship.[9]

The national revolutionary leadership had no principled objection to the continued existence of the Prussian state.[10] There was little support for Preuss's proposal that Prussia be dismembered to make way for a more strictly centralized national structure. Unsurprisingly perhaps, the SPD and USPD ministers who now exercised joint control over Prussia soon acquired a sense of ownership over the state and became strong opponents of centralization. Even the national Council of People's Representatives rejected Preuss's view (with the exception of the leader and later president Friedrich Ebert, a native of Baden).[11] Social Democrats also saw Prussian unity as the best antidote to separatist strivings in the Rhineland. They feared that secession from Prussia would ultimately mean secession from Germany itself. In view of French designs in the west and Polish annexationist objectives in the east, they argued, autonomist experiments would only play into the hands of Germany's enemies. Germany's security and cohesion as a federal state therefore depended on the integrity of Prussia. This break with the unitarist tradition of the German left removed one of the main threats to the state's existence.

None of this meant that Prussia could resume the hegemonial position it had occupied within the old Empire. To be sure, the Prussian administration was still the largest in Germany; the Prussian school system remained the model for all the German states, and the Prussian police force was, after the Reichswehr, the most important power instrument in the Weimar Republic. National legislation could not be implemented without the collaboration of the Prussian state, provincial and local bureaucracies.[12] But Prussia no longer possessed the means to wield direct influence over the other German states. There was now a national German executive entirely separate from the Prussian government; the personal union between German chancellor and Prussian minister-president, so crucial to the wielding of Prussian influence in the imperial era, became a thing of the past. For the first time, moreover, Germany possessed a genuinely national army (subject to the limitations imposed by the Versailles Treaty) with a ministerial executive independent of Prussian control. The fiscal dualism of the old Empire, in which the member states held exclusive control of direct taxation and financed the Reich through a system of matricular contributions, was also done away with. What emerged in its place was a centralized administration in which taxing authority was concentrated in the Reich government and revenues were directed to the states in accordance with their needs. Prussia, along with all the other German states, thus forfeited its fiscal autonomy.[13]

During the winter of 1918, the revolutionary movement remained unstable and internally divided. There were essentially three main political camps on the left: the largest was the Majority SPD, comprising the bulk of the wartime Social Democratic Party and its mass membership. To their immediate left was the Independent SPD (USPD), the radical leftist wing of the old SPD that had split with the mother party in 1917 in protest over the moderate reformism of its leadership. On the extreme left were the Spartakists who founded the Communist Party in December 1918. Their objective was all-out class war and the creation of a German Soviet system on the Bolshevik model. In the early weeks of the revolution, the SPD and USPD worked closely together to stabilize the new order. Both the national and the Prussian governments were run by SPD/USPD coalitions. But cooperation proved difficult in practice, partly because the USPD was a highly unstable formation whose political identity was still in flux. Within weeks of the revolution, the SPD/USPD partnership was tested to breaking point by disputes over the future status of the Prussian-German army.

The terms of the relationship between the provisional socialist leadership and the military command had been set on the very first day of the new republic. On the evening of 9 November, Friedrich Ebert, chairman of the Council of People's Representatives made a telephone call to First Quartermaster-General Wilhelm Groener (Ludendorff had been sacked by the Kaiser on 26 October), in which the two men agreed to cooperate in restoring order in Germany. Groener undertook to effect a smooth and swift demobilization. In return, he demanded Ebert's assurance that the government would secure supply sources, assist the army in maintaining discipline, prevent disruption of the railway network, and generally respect the autonomy of the military command. Groener also made it clear that the army's chief objective was to prevent a Bolshevik revolution in Germany and that he expected Ebert to support him in this.

The Ebert–Groener pact was an ambivalent achievement. It secured for the socialist republican authority the means to enforce order and protect itself against further upheavals. This was a major step forward for an executive structure that had no meaningful armed force of its own and no constitutional foundation for its authority, save the right of usurpation bestowed by the revolution itself. Seen in this light, the Ebert–Groener pact was shrewd, pragmatic and in any case necessary, since there was no plausible alternative. Yet there was also something ominous in the army's setting of political conditions even for the fulfilment of urgent tasks within its own remit, such as demobilization. What mattered here was not the substance of Groener's demands, which were reasonable enough, but the army's formal arrogation of the right to treat with the civilian authority on an equal footing.[14]

There was deep distrust between the army and the leftist elements in the revolutionary movement, despite Ebert's well-intentioned efforts to build bridges between the military command and the revolutionary soldiers' councils. On 8 December, when General Lequis arrived at the outskirts of Berlin with ten divisions of troops, the executive committee (the national executive of the soldiers' and sailors' councils) and the Independent Socialist ministers within the provisional government refused to allow the general to enter the capital. Ebert managed with some difficulty to persuade them to open the city to Lequis, the majority of whose men were Berliners desperate to return to their homes.[15] There was further tension on 16 December, when the first national congress of Workers' and Soldiers' Councils passed a resolution demanding the revolutionization of the military: Hindenburg was to be dismissed as chief of staff, the old Prussian cadet school system closed down and all marks of rank abolished. Officers were henceforth to be elected by their troops and a people's militia (*Volkswehr*) established alongside the regular army. Hindenburg rejected these proposals outright and ordered Groener to inform Ebert that the agreement between them would be null and void if there were any attempt to translate them into practice. When Ebert told a joint meeting of the cabinet and the Executive Council[16] that the proposals of 16 December would not be implemented, there was consternation among the Independents, who at once began to mobilize their radical following across Berlin.

The political climate was now exceptionally volatile. Relations between the SPD and the Independents were very tense. Berlin was thronging with armed workers and units of radicalized soldiers – the most boisterous of these was the People's Naval Division, whose headquarters were the Royal Stables, an imposing neo-baroque building on the eastern side of Palace Square. There was talk on the extreme left of an armed uprising. At a general meeting of the Independent Social Democrats of Greater Berlin, the Spartakist leader and ideologue Rosa Luxemburg attacked the compromise policy of the Independents and demanded that they withdraw their allegiance from the Ebert government. There was no point, she declared, in debating with 'Junkers and bourgeois' over whether one should introduce socialism:

Socialism does not mean getting together in a parliament and passing laws, socialism means for us overthrowing the ruling classes with all the brutality [loud laughter] that the proletariat is capable of deploying in its struggle.[17]

The flashpoint for an open conflict came on 23 December. On this day, after reports of looting and vandalism by 'red sailors', the provisional government ordered the People's Naval Division to leave the Royal Stables and quit the capital. Instead of complying, the sailors seized and mistreated the Berlin city commandant Otto Wels, surrounded the chancellery building (seat of the SPD/USPD government), occupied the central telephone exchange, and cut off the lines connecting the chancellery with the outside world. Using a secret chancellery hotline to the Military Supreme Command in Kassel, Ebert requested military assistance. General Lequis was called in from Potsdam to restore order. His performance was not confidence-inspiring: on the morning of Christmas Day 1918, his troops drove the 'red sailors' away from the chancellery and bombarded the Royal Stables for two hours. It was enough to secure a surrender by the rebellious sailors, but word had got around and an angry (and partly armed) crowd of Spartakists, Independents and leftist fellow travellers soon gathered around the troops, who promptly withdrew from the scene.

The débâcle of Christmas Day 1918 had a polarizing effect on the political climate. It encouraged the extreme left to believe that a more resolute strike would suffice to break the authority of the Ebert–Scheidemann regime. It also ruined the prospects for further collaboration between the SPD and the Independents, who left the provisional national government on 29 December. Their Prussian colleagues withdrew from the Prussian coalition cabinet on 3 January. The majority SPD now ruled alone in the state.[18] Groener responded to the growing tension by calling for the formation of volunteer units, or *Freikorps*, a term that recalled the stirring myths of 1813. One of these had already formed in Westphalia under General Ludwig Maercker, and others soon followed: the Freikorps Reinhard, under the former Guards officer Colonel Wilhelm Reinhard, was created on Boxing Day; another Freikorps assembled at Potsdam under Major Stephani, composed of demobilized officers and men from the I Regiment of Foot Guards and the Imperial Potsdam Regiment. Freikorps recruits were driven by an unsteady mix of ultra-nationalism, a desire to make good the humiliation at the German defeat, hatred of the left and visceral fear of a Bolshevik uprising. All these units were placed under the general command of the Silesian career officer General Walther Freiherr von Lüttwitz.

To ensure harmonious relations between the military and the civilian authority, Ebert appointed the SPD man Gustav Noske to head the ministry of military affairs. Noske, the son of a weaver and an industrial worker from the city of Brandenburg, had worked as an apprentice basket weaver before joining the SPD and achieving distinction within the party for his services to socialist journalism. In 1906, he had joined the SPD parliamentary fraction in the Reichstag, where he was associated with the right-wing SPD leadership group around Ebert. Noske had long been known for his friendly attitude to the military; he joined the provisional government on 29 December, after the departure of the USPD coalition partners. When asked to oversee the provisional government's campaign against the leftist revolutionaries in Berlin, Noske is said to have replied: 'Fine. Someone has to be the bloodhound, and I am not afraid of taking the responsibility.'[19]

The next uprising was not long in coming. On 4 January, the Berlin provisional government ordered the dismissal of Emil Eichhorn, the commissary police chief of Berlin, a left-wing Independent who had refused to support the government during the 'Christmas Battles'. Eichhorn refused to resign, choosing instead to distribute arms from the police arsenal to left-radical troops and to barricade himself in the police presidency. Without authorization from the USPD leadership, the police chief ordered a general insurrection, a call that was answered with gusto by the extreme left. On 5 and 6 January, the Communists mounted their first concerted attempt to seize power in Berlin, pillaging arsenals, arming bands of radical workers and occupying key buildings and positions in the city. Once again, the SPD provisional government called in troops to bring an end to the unrest.

For some days the city was transformed into a lurid and dangerous jungle, a dadaist nightmare. There was shooting at every corner and it was seldom clear who was shooting at whom. Neighbouring streets were occupied by opposing forces, there were desperate struggles on roofs and in cellars, machine-guns positioned anywhere suddenly struck up fire and then fell silent, squares and streets that had just now been quiet were suddenly filled with running, fleeing pedestrians, groaning wounded and the bodies of the dead.[20]

On 7 January, Harry Kessel witnessed a battle scene on the Hafenplatz in Berlin: government troops were trying to take control of the railway administration headquarters, which had been occupied by leftists. The rattling of small arms and machine-gun fire was deafening. In the heat of the battle an elevated train filled with urban commuters trundled across the viaduct that spanned the square, seemingly oblivious to the firefight raging below. 'The screaming is continuous,' Kessel noted. 'The whole of Berlin is a bubbling witches' cauldron where forces and ideas are stirred up together.'[21] On 15 January, after an extensive manhunt, the Communist leaders Rosa Luxemburg and Karl Liebknecht were found, arrested and subsequently beaten to death by members of a cavalry guards division stationed at the Hotel Eden in central Berlin.

The Communists now seethed with an implacable hatred of the Social Democrats. In March 1919, they called a general strike and fighting once again broke out in Berlin. Some 15,000 armed Communists and fellow travellers seized control of police stations and rail terminals. Determined to break the power of the extreme left at all costs, Gustav Noske brought in 40,000 government and Freikorps troops, who used machine guns, field artillery, mortars, flame-throwers and even aerial strafing and bombardment to put down the rebellion. When the fighting in Berlin came to an end on 16 March, 1,200 people were dead. The violent suppression of the January and March uprisings and the murder of its intellectual leaders dealt the extreme left a blow that it was never prepared to forgive. In their eyes, the Social Democrats had betrayed the German worker to sign a 'devil's pact' with Prussian militarism.[22]

No one gave clearer visual expression to this view of events than the Berlin artist George Grosz. Grosz, an early participant in the Berlin Dadaist movement, had been exempted from military service on psychological grounds and had spent the later years of the war in Berlin. In December 1918 he was one of the first wave of Communist Party members, receiving his card personally from the hands of Rosa Luxemburg. He spent the days of the March uprising hiding in the Berlin apartment of his future mother-in-law. In a remarkable polemical drawing published at the beginning of April 1919, Grosz depicted a street littered with blood-stained bodies, one disembowelled. Protruding diagonally into the lower right-hand of the picture frame is a swollen corpse, its trousers pulled down to reveal mutilated genitalia. Standing in the centre foreground, with the heel of his boot pressing on the belly of one of the dead, is the travesty of a Prussian officer, his monocle screwed tightly into his face, his teeth bared in a cramped grimace, his posture ramrod-straight. In his right hand he carries a blood-smeared sword, in his left a raised champagne flute. The caption reads: 'Cheers Noske! The proletariat is disarmed!'[23]

Even for those who did not share Grosz's Spartakist commitment, *Prost Noske!* captured something disturbing about the events of early 1919. The extreme violence of the repressions was in itself disquieting. The Freikorps units brought a new brand of politically motivated terrorist ultra-violence to their counter-insurgency operations in the city, hunting out hidden and fleeing leftists and subjecting them to brutal mistreatment and summary executions. The Berlin press reported executions of thirty prisoners at a time by makeshift Freikorps tribunals, and Harry Kessler observed ruefully that a hitherto unknown spirit of 'blood vengeance' had entered the city of Berlin. Here – though not only here[24] – could be seen the brutalizing effects of the war and the ensuing defeat, the anti-civilian ethos of the military, and the profoundly unsettling ideological impact of Russia's October Revolution of 1917.

Another ominous feature of the conflicts of 1919 was the deepening

54. 'Cheers Noske! The proletariat is disarmed!' Drawing for the leftist satirical journal Die Pleite *by George Grosz, April 1919.*

dependence of the new political leadership on a military establishment whose enthusiasm for the emerging German Republic was questionable, to say the least. Exactly how questionable became clear in January 1920, when a number of senior officers refused outright to implement the military stipulations of the Versailles Treaty. Heading the rebellion was none other than General Walther Freiherr von Lüttwitz, who had commanded the troops engaged in the repressions of January and March in Berlin. When Army Minister Noske ordered him to disband the elite Marine Brigade under Captain Hermann Ehrhardt, Lüttwitz refused outright, called for new elections and demanded that he be placed in command of the entire German army. Here was yet another example of that spirit of egotistical insubordination that had been gaining ground within the old-Prussian military leadership since Hindenburg and Ludendorff had held the government to ransom during the First World War.

On 10 March 1920, Lüttwitz was finally dismissed from active service; two days later he launched a putsch against the government in collaboration with the conservative ultra-nationalist activist Wolfgang Kapp, a political intriguer who had been involved in the fall of Chancellor Bethmann Hollweg in 1917. The aim was to unseat the republican government and establish an autocratic military regime. On 13 March, Lüttwitz and the Ehrhardt Brigade took control of the capital, forcing the government to flee, first to Dresden and then to Stuttgart. Kapp appointed himself Reich chancellor and minister-president of Prussia and Lüttwitz minister of the army and supreme commander of the armed forces. It looked for a moment as if the history of the young republic was already at an end. In the event, the Kapp–Lüttwitz putsch collapsed after only four days – it had been poorly planned and the would-be dictators had no means of dealing with an SPD-sponsored general strike that paralysed German industry and parts of the civil service. Kapp announced his 'resignation' on 17 March and quickly slipped off to Sweden; Lüttwitz resigned on the same evening and later resurfaced in Austria.

The problem of the army and its relationship with the republican authority did not disappear after the failure of the Kapp–Lüttwitz putsch. The chief of the army command from March 1920 was Hans von Seeckt, a Prussian career staff officer from Schleswig-Holstein, who initially refused to oppose Kapp and Lüttwitz, but ostentatiously sided with the government once they had failed. Under his shrewd leadership, the military command focused on building German military strength within the narrow parameters imposed by Versailles and abstained from conspicuous political interventions. Yet the army remained in many respects a foreign body within the fabric of the republic. Its loyalty was not to the existing political authority, but 'to that permanent and imperishable entity', the German Reich.[25] In an essay published in 1928, Seeckt set out his views on the status of the military within a republican state. He acknowledged that the 'supreme leadership of the state' must control the army, but also insisted that 'the army has the right to demand that its share in the life and the being of the state be given full consideration' – whatever *that* meant!

Seeckt's expansive conception of the army's status found expression in his claim that 'in domestic and foreign policy the military interests represented in the army must be given full consideration' and that the 'particular way of life' of the military must be respected. Even more telling was his observation that the army was subordinate only 'to the state as a whole' and not 'to separate parts of the state organization'. The question of who or what exactly embodied the totality of the state remained unresolved, though it is tempting to read these words as encoded articulations of a crypto-monarchism in which allegiance was ultimately focused not on the state, but on the empty throne of the departed Emperor-king. This was, in other words, an army whose legitimacy derived from something outside the existing political order and whose commitment to upholding that order remained conditional.[26] Here was a potentially troublesome legacy of the Prussian constitutional tradition, in which the army had sworn its fealty to the monarch and led an existence apart from the structures of civil authority.

DEMOCRATIC PRUSSIA

It was as if reality had been turned inside out. The Prussian state had passed through the looking glass of defeat and revolution to emerge with the polarities of its political system in reverse. This was a mirror-world in which Social Democrat ministers despatched troops to put down strikes by leftist workers. A new political elite emerged; former apprentice locksmiths, office clerks and basket-weavers sat behind Prussian ministerial desks. In the new Prussia, according to the Prussian constitution of 30 November 1920, sovereignty rested with 'the entirety of the people'. The Prussian parliament was no longer convened and dissolved by a higher authority, but summoned itself under rules set out in the constitution. By contrast with the Weimar (national) constitution, which concentrated formidable powers in the person of the Reich president, the Prussian system made do without a president. It was in this sense a more thoroughly democratic and less authoritarian system than the Weimar Republic itself. Throughout the years 1920–32 (with a few very brief interruptions), an SPD-led republican coalition consisting of Social Democrats, Centre Party deputies, left-liberals (DDP) and – later – right-liberals (DVP) governed with a majority in the Prussian Landtag. Prussia became the 'rock of democracy' in Germany and the chief bastion of political stability within the Weimar Republic. Whereas Weimar politics at the national level were marked by extremism, conflict and the rapid alternation of governments, the Prussian grand coalition held firm and steered a steady course of moderate reform. Whereas the German national parliaments of the Weimar era were periodically cut short by political crises and dissolutions, every one of their Prussian counterparts (except the last) was allowed to live out its full natural lifespan.

Presiding over this surprisingly stable political system was Prussia's 'red Tsar', Minister-President Otto Braun. The son of a railway clerk in Königsberg, Braun had been trained in his youth as a lithographer, joined the SPD at the age of sixteen in 1888 and soon became well known as a leader of the socialist movement among rural East Prussian labourers. He became a member of the party's executive council in 1911 and joined the small contingent of SPD deputies in the lower house of the old Prussian Landtag two years later. His sobriety, pragmatism and moderation helped to create a framework for harmonious government in Germany's largest federal territory. Like many other Social Democrats of his generation, Braun professed a deep attachment to Prussia and a respect for the intrinsic virtue and authority of the Prussian state – an attitude shared to some extent by all the coalition partners. Even the Centre Party made its peace with the state that had once so energetically persecuted Catholics; the high point of their rapprochement was the concordat agreed between the Prussian state and the Vatican on 14 June 1929.[27] In 1932, Braun could look back with a certain satisfaction on what had been achieved since the end of the First World War. 'In twelve years,' he declared in an article for the SPD newspaper *Volksbanner* in 1932, 'Prussia, once the state of the crassest class domination and political deprivation of the working classes, the state of the centuries-old feudal Junker caste hegemony, has been transformed into a republican people's state.'[28]

But how deep was the transformation? How profoundly did the new political elite penetrate the fabric of the old Prussian state? The answer depends upon where one looks. If we focus on the judiciary, the achievement of the new power-holders looks unimpressive. There were certainly piecemeal improvements in discrete areas – prison reform, industrial arbitration and administrative rationalization – but little was done to consolidate a pro-republican ethos among the upper ranks of the judicial bureaucracy and particularly among the judges, who tended to remain sceptical of the legitimacy of the new order. Many judges mourned the loss of king and crown – in a famous outburst of 1919, the head of the League of German Judges declared that 'all majesty lies prostrate, including the majesty of the law.' It was common knowledge that many judges were biased against left-wing political offenders and prone to look more leniently on the crimes of right-wing extremists.[29] The key impediment to radical action by the state in this area was a deeply embedded respect – especially among the liberal and Centre Party coalition partners – for the functional and personal independence of the judge. The autonomy of the judge – his freedom from political reprisals and manipulation – was seen as crucial to the integrity of the judicial process. Once this principle was enshrined in the Prussian constitution of 1920, a thorough-going purge of anti-republican elements in the judiciary became impossible. Changes to the appointments procedures for new judges promised future improvement, as did the setting of a compulsory retirement age, but the system inaugurated in 1920 did not last long enough to allow these adjustments to take effect. A senator of the Supreme Court in Berlin estimated in 1932 that perhaps 5 per cent of the judges sitting on the Prussian bench could be described as supporters of the republic.

The SPD-led government also inherited a civil service that had been socialized, schooled, recruited and trained in the imperial era and whose allegiance to the republic was correspondingly weak. Just how weak was revealed in March 1920, when many provincial and district governors continued working in their offices during the Kapp–Lüttwitz putsch and thus implicitly accepted the authority of the would-be usurpers. The situation was most acute in the province of East Prussia, where the entire senior bureaucracy recognized the Kapp–Lüttwitz 'government'.[30]

The first office-holder to tackle this problem with the required energy was the new Social Democrat Interior Minister Carl Severing, a former locksmith from Bielefeld, who had risen through the ranks of the SPD as a journalist-editor and sometime Reichstag deputy. Under the 'Severing system', grossly compromised individuals were dismissed and representatives of the governing parties vetted all new appointees to 'political' (i.e. senior) civil service posts. It was not long before this practice had a marked effect on the political complexion of the senior echelons. By 1929, 291 of the 540 political civil servants in Prussia were members of the solidly republican coalition parties SPD, Centre and DDP. Nine of the eleven provincial governors and 21 of the 32 district governors belonged to the coalition parties. The social composition of the political elite was transformed in the process: whereas eleven out of twelve provincial governors had been noblemen in 1918, only two of the men who served in this post over the years 1920–32 were of noble descent. That this transition could be effected without disrupting the operations of the state was a remarkable achievement.

Policing was another area of crucial importance. The Prussian police force was far and away the largest in the country. Here too, there were nagging doubts about political loyalty, especially after the Kapp–Lüttwitz putsch, when the Prussian police administration failed unequivocally to declare its allegiance to the government. On 30 March 1920, only two weeks after the collapse of the putsch, Otto Braun announced that he intended to institute a 'root and branch transformation' of the Prussian security organs.[31] Personnel reform in this area was not particularly problematic, since control over appointments lay entirely in the hands of the interior ministry, which, with one brief break, remained under SPD control until 1932. Responsibility for overseeing personnel policy fell to the decidedly republican head of the police department (from 1923) Wilhelm Abegg, who saw to it that adherents of the republican parties were appointed to all key posts. By the late 1920s, the upper echelons of the police force had been comprehensively republicanized – of thirty Prussian police presidents on 1 January 1928, fifteen were Social Democrats, five belonged to the Centre, four were German Democrats (DDP) and three were members of the German People's Party; the remaining three declared no political affiliation. It was official policy throughout the police service to base recruitment not only upon mental and physical aptitude, but also upon the candidate's having a record of 'past behaviour guaranteeing that they would work in a positive sense for the state'.[32]

Yet doubts remained about the political reliability of the police force. The great majority of officers and men were former military men who brought military manners and attitudes with them into the service. Among senior police cadres, there was still a strong old-Prussian reserve officer element with informal links to various right-wing organizations. The mood in most police units was anti-Communist and conservative, rather than specifically republican. They saw the enemies of the state on the left – including the left wing of the SPD, the party of government! – rather than among the extremists on the right, whom they viewed with indulgence if not sympathy. A police officer who openly proclaimed his pro-republican allegiance was likely to remain an outsider. The Centre Party functionary Marcus Heimannsberg was a man of modest social origin who rose swiftly through the ranks under the protection of SPD Interior Minister Carl Severing. But he was widely resented among his fellow senior officers as a political appointment and remained socially isolated. Others who were less protected suffered the discrimination of their colleagues and risked being passed over for promotion. In many locations, policemen of known republican sentiment were ostracized from the gregarious – and professionally important – after-hours sociability of the regulars' table at the local pub.[33]

Ultimately, the record of the Prussian state government has to be judged in the light of what was realistically possible in the circumstances. A purge of the old judiciary would have run against the ideological grain of the Centre and liberal parties, as well as the right wing of the SPD, all of whom held dear the principle of the *Rechtsstaat* in which the judge enjoys immunity from political interference. It is certainly true that some right-wing Prussian judges handed down biased verdicts in political cases, but the importance of these verdicts was diminished by the frequency of amnesties for political offenders and has probably been exaggerated in the literature on 'political justice' in the Weimar Republic.[34] It is clear that in the longer term, the new retirement age and the new state guidelines for judicial appointments would have facilitated the formation of a comprehensively republican judiciary. As far as the civil service is concerned, an all-out purge of government personnel was out of the question, given the shortage of qualified republican substitutes and the moderate outlook of the Prussian coalition. In the case of the police, installing a pro-republican leadership cadre while retaining the services of the bulk of officers and men from the old regime looked like the best way to ensure the stability and effectiveness of the service, especially in the unstable early years. The coalition governments thus opted to pursue a policy of gradual republicanization. What they could not know was that the German Republic would be extinguished before there was time for this programme to fulfil its potential.

The real threat to Prussia's existence did not in any case stem from the state civil service, but from powerful interests outside the state that remained dedicated to the downfall of the republic. The threat of a Spartakist uprising was neutralized in 1919–20, but the extreme left continued to attract significant electoral support – indeed the Communists were the only party whose tally of votes increased with every single Prussian election, from 7.4 per cent in 1921 to 13.2 per cent in 1933.

Less ideologically homogeneous but equally radical and determined and far more numerous were the forces mustered on the right. It is one of the salient features of Weimar politics in Prussia (as in Germany more generally) that the 'conservative interest', for lack of a better term, never accommodated itself to the political culture of the new republic. The post-war years saw the emergence of a large, fragmented and radicalized right-wing opposition that refused to accept the legitimacy of the new order.

The most important organizational focal point for right-wing politics in Weimar Prussia before 1930 was the German Nationalist Party, or DNVP. Founded on 29 November 1918, the DNVP was in formal terms a successor organization to the Prussian conservative parties of the pre-war era; the first DNVP programme was published on 24 November 1918 in the *Kreuzzeitung*, the conservative organ founded in Berlin during the 1848 revolutions. Taken as a whole, however, the DNVP represented a new force in Prussian politics. East-Elbian agrarians were no longer so dominant within its social constituency, since the party also catered to a large contingent of urban white-collar employees, ranging from clerks, secretaries and office assistants to middle and upper management. Of the forty-nine DNVP deputies elected to the Prussian Constituent Assembly on 26 January 1919, only fourteen had served in the Prussian Landtag before 1918. The party was a rainbow coalition of interests ranging from pragmatic moderate conservatives (a minority), to enthusiasts of a monarchist restoration, ultra-nationalists, 'conservative revolutionaries' and exponents of a racist *völkisch* radicalism. In this sense the party occupied an uncomfortable position somewhere between the 'old' Prussian conservatism and the extremist organizations of the German 'new right'.[35]

The politico-cultural matrix of the old East-Elbian provincial conservatism no longer existed. It had been in flux since the 1890s; after 1918, it dissolved entirely. First there was the damage inflicted on conservative networks by the revolution of 1918–19. Virtually the entire apparatus of privilege that had sustained the agrarian political lobby was swept away. The abolition of the three-class franchise destroyed at one stroke the electoral basis for conservative political hegemony, while the abdication of the crown and the proclamation of a republic decapitated the old system of privilege and patronage that had secured for the agrarian nobility an unparalleled leverage on public office. Even at regional and local level, the recruitment policies of the new SPD-led government soon began to change the scene, as provincial governors and district commissioners of the old school made way for republican successors.

All this came at a time of unprecedented economic disruption. The removal of restrictions on strikes and collective bargaining by farm labourers and the repeal of the old Servants' Law raised the pressure on wages across the farming sector. Tax reforms dismantled the fiscal exemptions that had always been a structural feature of Prussian agriculture. The new republic was also far less receptive to the protectionist arguments of the farmers than its imperial predecessors; grain tariffs were lowered to facilitate industrial exports and there was a dramatic rise in food imports, even after the reintroduction of a reduced tariff in 1925. Under the impact of rising taxes and interest rates, galloping debt, wage pressures and the misallocation of capital during the inflation, many food producers – especially among the larger estates – went into bankruptcy.[36] These pressures did not let up after the currency stabilization of 1924. On the contrary, the later years of the Weimar Republic were a period of unpredictable price fluctuations, depression and crisis for the agricultural sector.[37]

There was also a religious dimension to the dissolution of what remained of the old conservative milieu. For the Protestants of the Church of the Prussian Union who comprised the majority of the population in the East-Elbian provinces, the loss of the king was a more than merely political event. The Unionist Church had always been a specifically royal institution: the King of Prussia was *ex officio* supreme bishop of the Union, with extensive patronage powers and a prominent place in the liturgical life of the congregation. William II in particular had taken his ecclesiastical-executive role very seriously indeed.[38] The termination of the monarchy as an institution thus brought a measure of institutional disorientation to Prussia's Protestants, heightened by the loss (to Prussia and Germany) of substantial Protestant areas in West Prussia and the former province of Posen, and by the openly secular and anti-Christian demeanour of some prominent republican political figures.[39] That the Catholic Centre Party had managed to secure an influential place at the heart of the new system was a further irritant.

Many Prussian Protestants responded to these developments by turning their backs on the republic and voting in great numbers for the

DNVP, which, despite early overtures to the Catholic electorate, remained an overwhelmingly Protestant party. 'Our special difficulty,' one senior clergyman observed in September 1930, 'lies in the fact that the most loyal members of our church are opposed to the existing form of government.'[40] There were signs of an accelerating fragmentation and radicalization of religious rhetoric and belief. It became fashionable after 1918 to rationalize the legitimacy of the evangelical church through an appeal to its national and ethnic-German vocation. The Union for German Church, founded in 1921 by Joachim Kurd Niedlich, a Protestant teacher at the French Gymnasium in Berlin, was one of many *völkisch-religious* groups founded in the early years of the Weimar Republic. Niedlich became well known as the exponent of a racist Christian creed rooted in the notion that Jesus had been a heroic fighter and Godseeker of Nordic lineage. In 1925, the Union merged with the newly founded German Christians' Union. Their joint programme included calls for a German national church, a 'German Bible' reflecting the German moral character, and the promotion of racial hygiene in Germany.[41]

The influence of ultra-nationalist and ethnocentric thinking was not confined to the margins of church life. After 1918, the care for the German Protestant communities marooned in territories transferred to the new Polish Republic took on symbolic importance. Protestants, especially in the truncated state of Prussia, equated the predicament of their church with the condition of the German people as a whole. '*Volk* and Fatherland' was the official theme of the second German Protestant Church Congress held in Königsberg in 1927.

Closely linked with this shift in emphasis was an increasingly strident strain of anti-Semitism. A publication of 1927 by the Union for German Church declared that Christ, as the divine transfiguration of Siegfried, would eventually 'break the neck of the Jewish-satanic snake with his iron fist'.[42] During the 1920s, there was agitation by a range of Christian groups to end official collections for the mission to the Jews, and in March 1930, the General Synod of the Old Prussian Union voted to cease defining the mission as an official beneficiary of church funding.[43] Dismayed by this decision, the president of the Berlin mission composed a circular letter to the consistories and provincial church councils of the Prussian state church warning against the insidious influence of anti-Semitism and observing that the number of clergymen within the Prussian Union who had 'succumbed' to anti-Semitism was 'astonishingly and terrifyingly high'.[44] High-ranking academics at the Prussian theological faculties were among those who saw in the Jewish minority a menace to German *Volkstum*, and a survey of Protestant Sunday papers in the years from 1918 to 1933 reveals the strength of ultra-nationalist and anti-Jewish sentiment in Protestant circles.[45] It was in part as a consequence of these processes of reorientation and radicalization that the National Socialists found it so easy to establish themselves within the East-Elbian Protestant milieu.[46]

And what of the old Prussian elite, the Junkers, who had once ruled the roost in East-Elbia? This was the social group most exposed to the transformations unleashed by defeat and revolution. For the older generation of the Prussian military nobility, defeat and revolution brought a traumatic sense of loss. On 21 December 1918, General von Tschirschky, commander of the III Guards Regiment of Uhlans and a former wing-adjutant to the Emperor, ordered his regiment to form up for a final parade in Potsdam. 'There he stood, the wine-loving old warrior, with his smart Emperor Wilhelm moustaches and a stentorian voice that thundered across the whole of Bornstedt Field – and the tears poured down over his rough cheeks.'[47] Ceremonies of this type – and there were many such – were self-consciously historical rituals of renunciation and withdrawal, acknowledgements that the old world was passing. Siegfried Count Eulenburg, the last commander of the I Footguards, gave expression to this sense of closure in a 'leave-taking ceremony' orchestrated in the winter of 1918 in the 'deathly stillness' of the Garrison Church in Potsdam. There was a shared awareness, one participant recalled, that 'the old order had collapsed and no longer had a future'.[48]

But these elegant performances did not typify the general mood within the Prussian noble families. Although some noblemen (especially of the older generation) accepted the verdict of events in a spirit of fatalism and withdrawal, others (especially of the younger generation) displayed a determination to remain the masters of the moment and to reconquer their ancestral leadership positions. In many areas of East Elbia, the nobility, operating through the agencies of the Agrarian League, was astonishingly successful in infiltrating local revolutionary organizations and orienting the politics of rural organizations away from leftist redistributive goals towards the agrarian bloc politics of the old regime. Noblemen dominated the Homeland League East Prussia, for example, an agrarian group that expounded ultra-nationalist and anti-democratic political objectives.[49] Many younger noblemen – especially from the lesser families – played a prominent role in the formation of the Freikorps that crushed the extreme left during the early months of the Republic. These men experienced the ultra-violence of the Freikorps as liberation, an intoxicating release from the sense of loss and precipitous decline that attended the events of 1918–19. The memoirs of noble Freikorps activists published during the early years of the republic reveal the total abandonment of traditional chivalric codes and the adoption of a brutal, uninhibited, anti-republican, hypermasculine warrior persona ready to deal out murderous and indiscriminate violence against an ideologically defined enemy.[50]

The extinction of the Prussian monarchy was an existential shock for the East-Elbian nobility – more perhaps than for any other social group. 'I feel as if I can no longer live without our Kaiser and king,' wrote the magnate Dietlof Count Arnim-Boitzenburg, the last president of the Prussian upper house, in January 1919.[51] But the attitude of most nobles to the exiled king – and his family – remained ambivalent. For many representatives of the Prussian nobility, the ignominious circumstances of the monarch's departure, and particularly his failure to preserve the prestige of his crown by sacrificing himself in battle, impeded any genuine identification with the last occupant of the Prussian throne. Monarchism thus never developed into an ideological formation capable of providing the conservative nobility as a whole with a coherent and stable political standpoint. Noblemen, especially of the younger generation, drifted away from the personal, flesh-and-blood monarchism of their fathers and forebears towards the diffuse idea of a 'leader of the people', whose charisma and natural authority would fill the vacuum created by the departure of the king.[52] We find a characteristic articulation of this longing in the diary jottings of Count Andreas von Bernstorff-Wedendorf, descendant of a line of distinguished servants of the Prussian throne: 'Only a dictator can help us now, one who will sweep an iron broom through this whole international parasitic scum. If only we had, like the Italians, a Mussolini!'[53] In short, within the Prussian nobility, as across the East-Elbian conservative milieu, the Weimar years witnessed a drastic radicalization of political expectations.

By the late 1920s, the experience of repeated crises had fragmented the agrarian political landscape, generating a profusion of special interest groups and movements of increasingly radical protest. The chief beneficiaries of this volatility were the Nazis, whose 1930 party programme promised to place the entire rural sector on a privileged footing through a regime of tariffs and price controls. Farmers who were disillusioned by the DNVP's failure to secure benefits for the rural sector now deserted the party in search of a more radical alternative – in all, one-third of the voters who had supported the DNVP in the national elections of 1928 switched to the Nazis in the elections of 1930.[54] The efforts of the Nationalist leadership to win back the renegades by hardening the party's anti-republican course were in vain. Among those who were drawn to the National Socialist movement were numerous members of the East-Elbian nobility. A particularly striking case is that of the Wedel family, an old Pomeranian military lineage whose forebears had fought with distinction in every Prussian war since the foundation of the kingdom. No fewer than seventy-seven Wedels joined the NSDAP – the largest contingent from any German noble family.[55]

Nowhere was popular electoral support for the Nazis greater than in the Masurian areas of southern East Prussia, where the summer election campaign of 1932 brought forth the bizarre spectacle of National Socialist political rallies in Polish. In July 1932, 70.6 per cent of voters in the Masurian district of Lyck supported the Nazis, a higher figure than anywhere else in the Reich. The percentages for nearby Neidenburg and Johannisburg were only fractionally lower. In the March elections of 1933, Masuria once again led the Reich in its support for the Nazis, with 81 per cent in Neidenburg, 80.38 per cent in Lyck and 76.6 per cent in Ortelsburg, where Frederick William III had once paused with Queen Luise during their flight from the French.[56]

PRUSSIA DISSOLVED

The German national elections of September 1930 brought the first major electoral breakthrough for the National Socialists. In the previous elections of May 1928, they had been a splinter party with just 2.6 per cent of the votes (under the current constitution of the Federal Republic of Germany, they would not have qualified for entry into parliament at all) and had the Reichstag of 1928 been allowed to live out its natural lifetime, this would have remained unchanged until 1932. But in September 1930, thanks to a Reichstag dissolution conducted on the authority of the Reich President, Paul von Hindenburg, the Nazis were returned with 18.3 per cent. The number of Nazi voters rose from 810,000 to 6.4 million, the number of their deputies from twelve to 107. This was the greatest gain ever to be made by any party in German history from one Reichstag election to the next. It completely transformed the landscape of German politics.

The Prussian administration was shielded from this upheaval by the fact that there was no election in the state that year. The Prussian Landtag of 1928 remained in session and was allowed, like all its predecessors, to live out its four-year term. Within the state legislature, the Nazis remained a small splinter party. But there were many auguries of danger. Most importantly, it now became impossible for the Prussian state administration and the German national government to collaborate in addressing the threat posed by the extreme right. Under the SPD-led national government of Hermann Müller (1928–30), the German and the Prussian administrations had agreed on the need to counter the threat posed by the National Socialist movement. The means of doing so were provided by the Weimar constitution, which expressly forbade public servants to engage in political activity of any kind of behalf of a group deemed to be anti-constitutional. On 25 May 1930, the Prussian government issued an order making it illegal for Prussian civil servants to be members of the NSDAP or the Communist Party (KPD). Braun urged his colleagues in the national government to follow suit with a federal prohibition. The SPD Reich Interior Minister Carl Severing agreed and preparations were put in train to have the Nazis banned as an anti-constitutional organization. Had this measure succeeded, it would have enabled the cabinet to prevent the infiltration of government bodies (including the German army) by card-carrying National Socialists. Action could also have been taken against the Thuringian state government, where the appointment of the National Socialist Heinrich Frick to the interior ministry had opened the door to a rapid infiltration of the bureaucracy by Nazis.[57]

Things changed after the September elections. Heinrich Brüning, Müller's successor as chancellor, dropped the idea of a ban, stating publicly that it would be fatal to make the mistake of regarding the NSDAP as a threat comparable to the Communist Party. He continued to play down the threat posed by the Nazis, even after the discovery in 1931 of a cache of documents belonging to an SA leader that contained plans for a violent overthrow of the Weimar regime and lists of death sentences to be carried out thereafter. Brüning's long-term aim was to replace the Weimar constitution with something closer to the old imperial one. This goal could be achieved only if the left were disabled and pushed out of politics. Brüning planned to dislodge the SPD from their Prussian stronghold by merging the office of Prussian minister-president with that of Reich chancellor – a return to the Bismarckian model of 1871. At the same time, Brüning aimed to exclude the Social Democrats from the exercise of political power altogether through the creation of an integrated right-wing power bloc that would incorporate the Nazis in a subordinate role.

In pursuit of this objective, the Brüning administration directly obstructed the efforts of the Prussian government to neutralize the Nazi movement. In December 1931, Albert Grzesinski, police president of Berlin, a former interior minister of Prussia, and one of the most energetic defenders of democracy against extremism, persuaded Otto Braun to have Adolf Hitler arrested. But Brüning refused to allow the arrest to go ahead. The Prussians were informed that if they attempted to deport Hitler, Reich President Hindenburg would countermand the order using an emergency decree that had already been drawn up for the purpose. On 2 March 1932, Prussian Minister-President Otto Braun sent Heinrich Brüning a 200-page dossier analysing in detail the activities of the NSDAP and demonstrating that the party was a seditious organization dedicated to undermining the constitution and overthrowing the republic. Accompanying the dossier was a letter informing the chancellor that a Prussia-wide prohibition of the SA was imminent. Only now, under pressure, did Brüning respond by urging Hindenburg to support nation-wide action against the Nazis. The result was the emergency decree of 13 April 1932 banning all National Socialist paramilitary organizations throughout the Reich.

This was a victory of sorts. In a limited way, the Prussian state was fulfilling its promise as the bulwark of democracy in the Weimar Republic. But the position of the republican coalition remained extremely fragile. It seemed reasonable to assume that the millions who had voted Nazi in the national elections of September 1930 might well do so again at the next Prussian election of 1932. The size of the problem was made clear in February 1931, when a loose alliance of right-wing parties – including the DNVP and the Nazis – secured the introduction of a plebiscite proposing the dissolution of the Prussian Landtag. When the plebiscite went to the polls in August 1931, it received the support of no fewer than 9.8 million Prussians, with a marked concentration in the agrarian eastern provinces – not enough to secure dissolution, but worrying none the less.[58] In many areas new recruits were still streaming to the Nazi Storm Troopers, despite the government ban on their activities – in Upper and Lower Silesia, the numbers of (now clandestine) SA members jumped from 17,500 in December 1931 to 34,500 in July 1932.[59] Street violence remained a problem, as Nazis, Communists, police and men of the Reichsbanner, a republican militia, slugged it out on the streets with blackjacks, brass knuckles and firearms.[60]

By the spring of 1932, as preparations got under way for the next state elections, it was clear that the result would leave the Prussian government without a democratic majority. The Prussian elections of 24 April 1932 confirmed the worst fears of the beleaguered republicans. In an election marked by an exceptionally high rate of participation (81 per cent), the Nazis weighed in with 36.3 per cent of the popular vote. The main victim of this success was the DNVP (whose share shrank to 6.9 per cent) and the liberal DDP and DVP, which collapsed into splinter parties controlling 1.5 per cent each. The Communists registered their best result to date, with 12.8 per cent. A curious interregnum thus ensued: under the revised procedural regulations of the Prussian Landtag, the right-wing anti-republican opposition could not accede to power because it was incapable of mustering a majority – a coalition with the Communists was out of the question. So the SPD-led government coalition under Otto Braun remained nominally in office, though it was unable to command a majority and was thus dependent on its emergency powers. On 14 July 1932, the annual state budget had to be passed by emergency decree. Democratic Prussia had lost its mandate.

At the national level, too, there were ominous political developments with far-reaching consequences for the state of Prussia. By the spring of 1932, the conservatives in President Hindenburg's entourage – and the president himself – had lost faith in Brüning. He had made no progress against the Social Democrats in Prussia. He had also done nothing to integrate the right into a conservative bloc capable of driving the left out of politics. In the presidential elections of 10 April 1932, to Hindenburg's profound consternation, the right-wing parties all put forward their own candidates, leaving the Centre Party and the Social Democrats to vote the 84-year-old incumbent back into office. Hindenburg, once a celebrated figurehead of the nationalist right, had become the candidate of socialists and Catholics.[61] Nothing could better have demonstrated the failure of Brüning's plans to prepare the way for a conservative restoration. Hindenburg was thus in an ill humour when his attention was drawn to legislation under preparation by the Brüning government to partition a number of financially unviable East-Elbian estates and parcel them out as smallholdings for the unemployed. For Hindenburg, himself a landowner with numerous close connections in the Junker milieu, this amounted to agrarian Bolshevism.[62] Brüning had no majority in the Reichstag and he had forfeited the support of the President. On 30 May 1932, he drew the consequences and resigned.

Brüning's departure removed the last semblance of a functioning Weimar democracy. What replaced him was a junta of ultra-conservatives determined to dismantle the republican system without delay. Hindenburg appointed the new chancellor, Franz von Papen, on 1 June 1932. Papen was a Westphalian nobleman and landowner, an old friend of the president, and a man of truly reactionary instincts. The most influential figure in the cabinet was the Reichswehr minister Kurt von Schleicher, a seasoned intriguer who had persuaded the President to appoint Papen. Another key player was Reich Interior Minister Friedrich von Gayl. Gayl, Papen and Schleicher disagreed on a number of tactical issues, but they were all enthusiastic exponents of a conservative 'new state' that would do away with political parties and cut back the powers of elected assemblies at every level. They also agreed that the time had come to roll back the republican system.

The first step was to appease the Nazis and win them over to collaboration on terms acceptable to the conservatives. Hitler had long been calling for a further Reichstag dissolution and on 4 June, only three days after his appointment, Chancellor von Papen secured a decree of dissolution from the President. Eight days later, he suspended the nation-wide ban on the SS and SA in return for a promise from Hitler that the Nazi Reichstag fraction would not oppose his continuation in office or vote down his emergency decrees.[63] The 'integration of the right' had begun.

Prussia was next on the list. Kurt von Schleicher, the most influential figure in the camarilla around Reich President Paul von Hindenburg, had long been in favour of using presidential emergency powers to do away with the Prussian government by transferring its responsibilities to the national executive.[64] In a cabinet meeting of 11 July 1932, the new interior minister, Wilhelm Freiherr von Gayl, called for what he described as a 'final solution' of the Prussian problem:

The young, ever larger and more inclusive circles of the Adolf Hitler movement must, in order to render the forces of the nation useful to the reconstruction of the people, free itself from the chains that were laid upon it by Brüning and Severing and must be supported in the victorious struggle against international Communism. [. . .] In order to free the way for [this] task and in order to strike a blow against the Socialist-Catholic coalition in Prussia, the dualism between the Reich and Prussia must be eliminated once and for all through the removal of the Prussian government.[65]

Since Gayl had already agreed these points in separate meetings with Papen and Schleicher, his proposals went uncontested. Five days later, on 16 July, Papen informed his cabinet colleagues that he had a 'blank cheque' from the Reich President to proceed against Prussia.[66]

While the plans of the presidential clique matured, the Nazis were making the fullest use of the opportunities created by Papen's suspension of the ban against the SS and the SA. From 12 June, Nazi Storm Troops swarmed back on to the streets in search of a final reckoning with the Communists. There was a wave of street violence. The mayhem reached a high point in Altona, a busy harbour and manufacturing town adjoining Hamburg, but situated within the Prussian province of Holstein. Here, on the 'Bloody Sunday' of 17 July 1932, the Nazis mounted a provocative procession through the working-class (and largely Communist) quarter of the town. In the mêlée that followed, eighteen were killed – most by police gunfire – and over 100 wounded. Papen and his colleagues saw their moment. Arguing that the Prussian government had failed in its duty to impose law and order within its territory – a fantastically cynical charge, given that it was Papen himself who had suspended the ban on the paramilitary organizations – the chancellor secured from Hindenburg an emergency decree on 20 July 1932 deposing the government of Minister-President Otto Braun and replacing the Prussian ministers with 'commissary' agents of the national executive.[67] Albert Grzesinski, his deputy president of police in Berlin, Bernhard Weiss, and

Marcus Heimannsberg, the Centre Party man who had risen through the ranks to a senior post in the service, were all imprisoned and then released when they undertook to withdraw peacefully from their official duties. A state of emergency was declared in Berlin.

The SPD leadership responded with profound passivity and resignation to this utterly illegal manoeuvre. It had been known for some weeks that an action of this kind was being prepared, but no attempt was made to plan or organize resistance. In December 1931, the Social Democrats had formed a defence organization called the Iron Front, consisting of a militia called the *Reichsbanner*, various union organizations and a network of workers' sporting clubs, but it was not mobilized or even placed on alert. Even after the events of 17 July in Altona, when the SPD in Berlin learned that a coup was imminent, nothing was done. On the contrary, at a meeting held on the day after 'Bloody Sunday', the party leadership agreed not to issue a call for a general strike and not to authorize armed resistance. This was encouraging, to say the least, for Papen and his co-conspirators, who could now be fairly sure that the coup would pass without serious opposition.

The reasons for this regrettable lethargy are easy enough to discern. The Prussian Social Democrats and their coalition allies were already demoralized by their failure to assemble a majority in the Landtag after the state elections of April 1932. As principled democrats, they felt politically undermined by the verdict of the electorate. For a legally minded man such as Otto Braun, the move from officialdom into insurgency did not come naturally: 'I have been a democrat for forty years,' he told his secretary, 'and I am not about to become a guerrilla chief.'[68] Braun and many of his associates thought the centralization of the Reich and the partitioning of Prussia were inevitable in the long run – did this perhaps disincline them to take a stand over the issue of state rights, however appalled they might be by the political machinations behind the coup?[69] The balance of forces was in any case stacked against the Prussian government. The call for a general strike – the weapon that had brought down Kapp and Lüttwitz in 1920 – would have been futile, given the high level of unemployment in 1932.

There had always been friction between the Prussian ministries and the army ministry in Berlin, and it was clear that the Reichswehr leadership did not oppose the foreclosure of Prussia. Resisting the coup might thus mean a fight between the Prussian police and the German army, and it was uncertain how police units would react. The Nazis had been quite successful in some areas in infiltrating police social networks – it was forbidden under the decree of 25 June 1930 for policemen to be active National Socialists, but the Nazis got around this by placing activists within the Association of Former Police Officers, a body of conservative outlook that was receptive to the Nazi critique of the republic and maintained multifarious links with the men still in active service.[70] Had they been raised, the 200,000 paramilitaries of the republican Reichsbanner would have faced Nazi and conservative militia forces numbering over 700,000. Finally, there was the fact that the Social Democratic Minister-President Otto Braun was ill, not to mention physically and emotionally exhausted.

Instead, the Prussian coalition leaders looked to the German constitutional court in Leipzig, which they presumed would declare the coup illegal, and to the forthcoming national elections, which they believed would punish the conservatives around Papen for their wanton destruction of a respected republican institution. Both hopes were disappointed. In the national elections of 31 July 1932, the Nazis emerged as the strongest party in Germany, with 37.4 per cent of all votes cast. It was the party's greatest ever performance in a free election. In a mealy-mouthed verdict, the Constitutional Court rejected the charge that the Prussian authorities had been negligent in pursuing their duties, but failed to deliver the outright condemnation of the coup that the democrats so desperately needed. The moment for a last-ditch defence of the republic had passed. 'You only have to bare your teeth at the reds and they knuckle under,' the Nazi propaganda chief Josef Goebbels gloated in his diary entry for 20 July. On the following day he added: 'The Reds are finished. [They] have missed their big chance. It will never come again.'[71]

The putsch against Prussia ushered in the terminal phase of the Weimar Republic. Papen, Schleicher and the 'cabinet of barons', a team of conservative technocrats of noble lineage who were virtually unknown to the wider German public, began to tighten the screws. *Vorwärts!*, the moderate daily paper of the SPD, was banned twice, and official warnings were issued to the left-liberal *Berliner Volkszeitung*.[72] There was also a small but significant adjustment to Prussian judicial practice. In the province of Hanover and the Cologne court district, the guillotine was still used for judicial executions. However, as Reich

Commissioner for Prussia, Papen ordered on 5 October 1932 that the use of the guillotine – a device bearing the imprint of the French Revolution – be discontinued. In its place, state executioners were to use the older, Germanic and 'Prussian' hand-held axe. Here was a clear signal of Papen's intention to 'roll back' the French Revolution, of which the Social Democrats were the ideological heirs, and annul its historical consequences.[73] Small wonder that some among the Nazi leadership feared the Papen government would 'do too much and leave nothing over for us'.[74]

Papen's days in government were already numbered. During the chancellorship of Heinrich Brüning, the SPD had tolerated the chancellor in order to secure the system against a Nazi challenge. But after the coup against Prussia, Papen forfeited any hope of further support from the Social Democrats. Frustrated by the intrigues of Papen and his collaborators, the Nazis, too, returned to open opposition. There was now no prospect that the Chancellor would be able to muster a majority within the new parliament. As soon as it met on 12 September 1932, the new Reichstag passed a vote of no confidence. The motion had the support of 512 deputies. Only forty-two deputies supported Papen. There were five abstentions. It was hardly a workable parliamentary base.

There were now two possibilities. The Papen government could once again dissolve the Reichstag and announce new elections. Then, at least, they would have three months' time – sixty days until the election and thirty more until the new Reichstag met. Ninety days of reprieve, before the process restarted itself. German democracy had been reduced to this, the machine-like repetition of the electoral reflex at the heart of the republic, a rhythmic spasm that would eventually tear the system apart. But there was an alternative, namely the dissolution of the Reichstag *without* elections. There was even a precedent for this course of action in Prussian history: Bismarck's open break with the Prussian parliament during the constitutional crisis in 1862. At that time Bismarck had succeeded in overcoming a deadlock between government and parliament by breaking the constitution and ruling without the legislature. This alternative was open to Papen and Hindenburg. Reich President Hindenburg was old enough – he was born in 1846 (!) – to have lived as a young adult through the crisis of the 1860s. He was also a man of Bismarck's own class and social background whose family must have followed these events with intense interest.

Papen considered the option of a Bismarckian coup d'état, but turned it down. It was clear that a coup would bring grave risks; it might even provoke civil war – this possibility was discussed in the national cabinet. There was also uncertainty about the attitude of the Reichswehr, whose political spokesman, Kurt von Schleicher, was fast emerging as the chancellor's rival. Papen thus opted to call yet another election for 6 November 1932. But the results of this contest, in which the Nazis shed a few percentage points but remained the strongest party, made it clear that a new Reichstag would be no more willing to tolerate Papen as chancellor than the old one had been. It was certain that the new Reichstag would use its first session to pass a vote of no confidence. Papen had to go. He was replaced on 1 December 1932 by his former friend Kurt von Schleicher. Schleicher's first achievement as Chancellor was to get the Reichstag to agree not to meet until after Christmas. Elections during the Christmas season, and for the third time in one year, would have been too much for the German *Volk* to bear. The Reichstag's Council of Elders agreed that parliament would not meet again until 31 January 1933.

By the time it did so, Franz von Papen had persuaded his old friend Hindenburg to appoint Hitler Reich chancellor. After extensive negotiations behind the scenes, Papen was able to make Hindenburg an offer he couldn't refuse. Hitler had agreed that if he were to be appointed chancellor, he would take only two National Socialists into the cabinet. The other seven ministers would be conservatives, and Papen himself would be vice-chancellor. Hemmed in thus, Hitler would be forced to take account of the conservative camarilla.[75] 'Within two months,' Papen crowed, 'we will have pushed Hitler so far into a corner that he'll squeak.'[76]

And so it was that Hitler, as Alan Bullock put it many years ago, was 'jobbed into office by a backstairs intrigue'.[77] The Nazi seizure of power had not ended. On the contrary, it had just begun. But the Nazis had a few important cards in their hands. Thanks to Papen's putsch of 20 July 1932, the elected state government of Prussia had been replaced by a Reich Commissariat for Prussia. This meant, among other things, that Hermann Goering could occupy a ministerial post without portfolio in the national cabinet and at the same time function as commissarial Prussian minister of the interior, a post that placed him in charge of Germany's largest police force. During the spring of 1933,

Goering would make ruthless and effective use of his Prussian policing powers. In this way – and not only in this way – the extravagant manoeuvres of the conservatives around the President before January 1933 helped to smooth the way towards a National Socialist monopoly of power.

Threads of the Prussian legacy were thickly woven into the skein of intrigues that brought the Nazis to power. We see them in the attitude of the army, which stood aloof from the republic after 1930, assessing the situation as it unfolded and playing its own game. We see them in the susceptibility of President Hindenburg to the arguments of the East-Elbian landed interest. Chancellors Brüning and Schleicher both lost credit with the President as soon as they began to support land reform initiatives involving the partitioning of bankrupt East-Elbian estates. The still vivid memory of conservative hegemony in the old state of Prussia breathed life into the political fantasies of the reactionaries who helped to disable the republic.[78] The corporate arrogance of the Prussian nobility and its presumption of a right to lead were also in evidence, nowhere more clearly than in Franz von Papen's boast that he and his cabinet of barons had 'engaged' Hitler, as if the Nazi leader were a part-time gardener or a passing minstrel. For Hindenburg, too, a sense of the vast difference in station and dignity between himself, a field marshal of the Prussian army, and Hitler, the Austrian corporal, made it difficult to see who Hitler really was, to apprehend the threat that he represented, and to understand how easily he would dissolve convention and order in politics.

But the democrats and republicans of the state government were also Prussians, albeit from a very different social world. The energetic Albert Grzesinski hailed from Tollense near Treptow in Pomerania. Born the illegitimate son of a Berlin housemaid, he completed his training as a panel-beater in Berlin, before making a career as a trade union official and political activist. After the revolution, Grzesinski could have taken office in the national German government – he was offered the army ministry in 1920 – but he chose instead to serve the Prussian state, both as police president in Berlin (1925–6 and 1930–32) and as interior minister (1926–30). In both roles he pursued a robustly republican personnel policy. In 1927 he oversaw the drafting of laws eliminating the special police jurisdiction of the rural estate districts. In removing this last vestige of Junker feudal privilege, Grzesinski closed a fissure in the administrative fabric of the state, completed the work of the Prussian reformers of the Napoleonic era and earned the lasting hatred of the right. As a robust anti-Nazi, Grzesinski also attracted the intense loathing of the Goebbels press, which repeatedly (and erroneously) denounced him as a 'Jew in a Jewish Republic'.[79] In December 1931 he worked on a deportation order expelling Hitler from Prussia, only to find it blocked by the national government under Brüning. In a widely noticed speech in Leipzig at the beginning of 1932, Grzesinski declared it 'lamentable' that 'the foreigner Hitler' should be allowed to negotiate with the Reich government, 'instead of being chased away with a dog whip'. Hitler did not forget or forgive these words and Grzesinski wisely fled Germany in 1933, first for France and later for New York, where he earned his living once again as a panel-beater.[80] Here was a career driven by a deep commitment, not only to democracy as such, but to the specific historical calling of the Prussian state and its institutions.

The same can be said for the man who served at the helm of the Prussian state until 1932, Minister-President Otto Braun. The son of a low-ranking Königsberg railway employee, Braun joined the Social Democratic Party in 1888, when it was still illegal in Bismarck's Prussia. He won notice and respect for his work among landless rural East-Elbian labourers and the sharpness of his editorial pen. He had held a seat in the old Prussian Landtag, one of a small band of Social Democrat deputies who managed to squeeze through the barriers of the three-class franchise. As a champion of the rural proletariat, Braun was the antitype of the old-Prussian agrarian elite whose political hegemony he helped to overthrow in 1918–19. Yet he was as emphatically and unmistakably Prussian as they. His endless appetite for work, his fastidious attention to detail, his dislike of posturing, and his profound sense of the nobility of state service were all attributes from the conventional catalogue of Prussian virtues. Even his authoritarian style of management, which earned him the nickname 'the red tsar of Prussia', could be construed as an ancestral Prussian trait. 'A Social Democrat like Otto Braun,' the conservative journalist Wilhelm Stapel observed in 1932, 'is, for all the anti-Prussianism of his party, more a Prussian than a German. His demeanour in office is that of the Junker who leaves an ungrateful king to his own devices and "grows his own cabbage".'[81] Braun even became a passionate hunter, a pastime he shared with Reich President Paul von

55. *Otto Braun, Prussian minister-president. Portrait by Max Liebermann, 1932.*

Hindenburg. The two men hunted in adjacent areas during the season and developed a comfortable personal intimacy that allowed them to exchange views on the key political issues of the day.[82] Here again was evidence of the curious affinity between the Social Democratic Party elite and the Prussian state that had once been its nemesis. It is striking that SPD leaders of this era found it far easier to handle the responsibilities and risks of state power in Prussia than they did in the German Reich.

We might thus say that on 20 July 1932, the day of the putsch, the old Prussia destroyed the new. Or, to put it more precisely, particularist, agrarian Prussia laid an axe to the universalist, state-centred Prussia of the Weimar coalition. Traditional society, one might argue, prevailed at last over the modernizing state; the descendants of von der Marwitz triumphed over the spirit of Hegel. But this metaphorical antinomy, though it certainly captures part of the meaning of what happened in the summer of 1932, is perhaps too neat. The men of the putsch against Prussia were hardly Junkers of the classic type. Papen was a Westphalian Catholic, Friedrich von Gayl a Rhinelander – both were, in this sense, 'marginal Prussians'.[83] Even Kurt von Schleicher, though the son of a Silesian officer, was an untypical figure, a political intriguer from outside the provincial landowning elite; his politics, a hybrid blend of authoritarian corporatism and constitutionalism, remain difficult to pigeonhole.[84] All three men pursued a politics of the nation, not of the Prussian state and certainly not of the Prussian province.

Hindenburg, the man at the centre of events in 1932, is a complex case. As an East-Elbian estate-owner and celebrated commanding officer, Hindenburg appeared to embody the Prussian tradition. But his life was formed by the forces that unified the German Reich. He was nineteen when he fought at Königgrätz during the Austrian war of 1866. He hailed from the province of Posen, an area of heightened nationalist antagonism between Germans and Poles. Having returned from retirement at the beginning of the First World War, he used his role at the apex of the German forces on the eastern front to challenge and hollow out the authority of the Prussian-German civilian executive. He blackmailed the Kaiser, to whom he professed the deepest personal loyalty, into compliance with his projects, which included the catastrophic policy of unconditional submarine warfare – a provocative and futile campaign that brought the United States into the war and doomed Germany to defeat at the hands of her enemies. One by one, he picked off the Kaiser's closest allies – including Chancellor Theobald von Bethmann Hollweg – and drove them out of politics. This was not the one-off conscientious objection of a Seydlitz or a Yorck – it was systematic insubordination born of vast ambition and an utter disregard of any interest or authority outside the military hierarchy that he himself dominated. At the same time, Hindenburg deliberately cultivated the national obsession with his own person, projecting the image of an indomitable Germanic warrior that overshadowed the increasingly marginal figure of the Emperor-king.

Although Hindenburg was among those who urged William II to abdicate and flee to Holland in November 1918, he subsequently shrouded himself in the mantle of a principled monarchism. Later again (on ascending to the office of Reich president in 1925 and on his reappointment in 1932), he put aside his monarchist convictions to swear a solemn oath to the republican constitution of the German Empire. In the last days of September 1918, Hindenburg urgently pressed the German civilian government to initiate ceasefire negotiations, yet he later disassociated himself entirely from the resulting peace, leaving the civilians to carry the responsibility and the opprobrium. On 17 June 1919, when the government of Friedrich Ebert was deliberating over whether to accept the terms of the Versailles Treaty, Hindenburg conceded in writing that further military resistance would be hopeless. Yet only a week later, when President Ebert called the Supreme Command for a clear formal decision in support of acceptance, the field marshal contrived to be absent from the telephone room during the call, leaving his colleague Wilhelm Groener to play the 'bête noire' (as Hindenburg himself put it).[85] Hindenburg went even further: in perhaps the most mythopoeic moment of a myth-saturated career, he claimed in November 1919 before the commission investigating the causes of the German defeat that the German armies in the field had not been vanquished by the enemy powers, but by a cowardly 'stab in the back' from the home front – this conceit would haunt the republic throughout its short life, tainting the new political elite with intimations of treachery and betrayal of the nation.

As Reich president after 1925, Hindenburg developed – despite all the social distance between them – an unlikely friendship with the conscientious Social Democratic Prussian Minister-President Otto Braun. In 1932, when Hindenburg stood for re-election to the presidency, Braun endorsed the old man warmly as 'the embodiment of calm and consistency, of manly loyalty and devotion to duty for the whole people'.[86] Yet in 1932, presented with the schemes of the conservative camarilla, Hindenburg abandoned his erstwhile friend without, as it seems, the slightest compunction, withdrawing from his solemn constitutional oaths of 1925 and 1932 to make common cause with the sworn enemies of the republic. And then, having publicly declared that he would never consent to appoint Hitler to any post more elevated than minister of postal services, Hindenburg levered the Austrian Nazi leader into the German chancellery in January 1933. The field marshal had a high opinion of himself and he doubtless sincerely believed that he personified a Prussian 'tradition' of selfless service. But he was not, in truth, a man of tradition. He was not in any deterministic sense a product of the old Prussia, but rather of the flexible power politics that fashioned the new Germany. As a military commander and later as Germany's head of state, Hindenburg broke virtually every bond he entered into. He was not the man of dogged, faithful service, but the man of image, manipulation and betrayal.

PRUSSIA AND THE THIRD REICH

On 21 March 1933, the Garrison Church at Potsdam provided the setting for a ceremony marking the inauguration of the 'new Germany' under Adolf Hitler. The occasion was the opening of the new Reichstag following the national elections of 5 March 1933. It was a festivity that would usually have been conducted in the Reichstag building itself. But on 27 February the Dutch leftist Marinus van der Lubbe had torched the building, reducing the main chamber to a blackened ruin. Built by Frederick William I in 1735, the Garrison Church was an eloquent memorial to Prussia's military history. Mounted on the church tower was a weather vane bearing the initials FWR and the iron silhouette of a Prussian eagle aspiring towards a gilded sun. Trumpets, flags and cannon, rather than angels or biblical figures, decorated the stone of the chancel. The tombs of the 'soldier king' Frederick William I and his illustrious son Frederick the Great lay side by side in the crypt.[87] Josef Goebbels, the Nazi propaganda chief, saw immediately the symbolic potential of this historic setting and he took personal control of the preparations, planning the event in painstaking detail as a propaganda spectacle. After all, as he noted in a diary entry of 15 March 1933, this was the moment when the 'new state' inaugurated by Hitler's appointment to the chancellorship would 'present itself symbolically for the first time'.[88]

The 'Day of Potsdam', as it has come to be known, was a concentrated act of political communication. It offered the image of a synthesis, even a mystical union, between the old Prussia and the new Germany.[89] Veterans of the Wars of Unification were ferried to the town to take part in the festivities. The flags of the most venerable Prussian regiments – including the renowned IX Infantry, whose recruits were traditionally sworn in under the vaults of the Garrison Church – were placed on prominent display. The streets of the city were decked with German imperial, Prussian and swastika flags. The red, black and gold tricolour of the Weimar Republic was nowhere to be seen. Even the date was significant. Goebbels had chosen 21 March not only because it was officially the first day of spring, but also because it was the anniversary of the opening of the first German Reichstag after the proclamation of the German Reich in January 1871. At the centre of the proceedings

56. The Day of Potsdam, 21 March 1933. Hitler and Hindenburg shake hands in front of the Garrison Church in Potsdam.

was Reich President Hindenburg. Decked out in full uniform, glittering with medals of every shape and size, and clutching his field marshal's baton in his right hand, Hindenburg processed at a stately pace through the streets of the old town past ranks of Reichswehr men and brown-shirted paramilitaries with their arms raised in salute. As he took up his prominent seat before the altar, he turned to acknowledge with a solemn flourish of his marshal's baton the empty throne of the former king and Emperor William II, now in Dutch exile. This exercise in humbug was devised in part for the benefit of the two Hohenzollern princes in attendance, one in the traditional uniform of the Death's Head Hussars, the other in the brown outfit of an SA man.

In his speech to the assembled guests, Hindenburg expressed the hope that 'the ancient spirit of this place of renown' would enthuse a new generation of Germans. Prussia had earned greatness through 'never-failing courage and love of fatherland'; might the same apply to the new Germany. In his reply from the reader's lectern, Hitler – wearing a dark tailored lounge suit rather than his party uniform – expressed his profound veneration for Hindenburg and gave thanks for the 'Providence' that had placed this indomitable warlord at the head of the movement for Germany's renewal. He closed with words that summed up the propagandistic function of the ceremony: 'As we stand in this space that is holy to every German, may Providence bestow upon us that courage and that steadfastness that we feel as we struggle for the freedom and greatness of our people at the foot of the tombs of the greatest of kings.'[90] Having shaken hands before the congregation, the two men laid wreaths on the tombs of the Prussian kings, while a battery of Reichswehr guns outside the church fired a salute and the choir within belted out the 'Leuten Chorale'. There followed a military review through the streets of the city. Goebbels recalled the moment in an effusive diary entry:

The Reich President stands on a raised platform, the Field Marshal's baton in his hand, and greets Army, SA, SS and Stahlhelm as they march past him. He stands and waves. Over the whole scene shines the eternal sun, and God's hand stands invisibly bestowing his blessing over the grey city of Prussian greatness and duty.[91]

The celebration of 'Prussiandom' was a consistent strand of National Socialist ideology and propaganda. The right-wing ideologue and inventor of the idea of the 'Third Reich', Arthur Moeller van der Bruck, had prophesied in 1923 that the new Germany would be a synthesis of the 'manly' spirit of Prussia with the 'feminine' soul of the German nation.[92] In *Mein Kampf*, published two years later, Adolf Hitler found warm words for the old Prussian state. It was the 'germ cell of the German Empire', which owed its very existence to the 'resplendent heroism' and 'death-defying courage of its soldiers'; its history demonstrated 'with marvellous sharpness that not material qualities but ideal virtues alone make possible the formation of a state'.[93] 'Our ears still ring,' wrote the Nazi Baltic-German ideologue Alfred Rosenberg in 1930, 'with the trumpets of Fehrbellin and the voice of the Great Elector, whose deed spelt the beginning of Germany's resurrection, salvation and rebirth.' Whatever one might criticize in Prussia, he added, 'the decisive salvation of Germanic substance will remain forever *its* deed of renown; without it there would be no German culture, and no trace of a German people.'[94]

No one trumpeted the Prussian theme more consistently than Josef Goebbels, who first became aware of its propaganda potential during a visit to Sans Souci in September 1926. Prussia thereafter remained one of the stock themes of the Goebbels publicity machine. 'National Socialism,' he claimed in an election speech of April 1932, 'can justly lay claim to Prussiandom. All over Germany, wherever we National Socialists stand, we are the Prussians. The idea we carry is Prussian. The symbols for which we fight are filled with the spirit of Prussia, and the objectives we hope to achieve are a renewed form of the ideals for which Frederick William I, the Great Frederick and Bismarck once strove.'[95]

The continuity between the Prussian past and the National Socialist present was asserted at many levels in the cultural policy of the regime after 1933. A famous political poster depicted Hitler as the latest in a succession of German statesmen extending from Frederick the Great via Bismarck to Hindenburg. Shortly after the 'Day of Potsdam', Hitler and Goebbels reinforced public awareness of these themes with the 'Days of Tannenberg', a propaganda spectacle centred on the inauguration of a vast national monument on 27 August 1933. Consisting of a circle of vast towers joined by massive walls, the Tannenberg monument recalled both the defeat of the German Order at the hands of a Muscovite army in 1410 and the victory of 1914 by which the Germans took 'revenge' on their erstwhile Russian foes. It also served to project the (utterly unhistorical) idea that East Prussia had always been the bastion of 'Germandom' against the Slavic east. As the 'Victor of Tannenberg', the 87-year-old Hindenburg was once again wheeled out to perform the liturgical honours for a now irreversibly Nazified Germany. When he died almost a year later, his body – along with that of his wife – was entombed in one of the towers of the monument. In accordance with the dead man's wish that he should be buried 'under a single slab of East Prussian stone' the entrance to his tomb was surmounted with a huge lintel of solid granite, the 'Hindenburg Stone'. This stone had been unearthed near Cojehnen in the flatlands of northern East Prussia, and was well known to German geologists as one of the largest monoliths in the region. Working to tight deadlines, a team of stonemasons and mining specialists cleared the earth from around the granite mass, cut it with explosive charges and power tools into a vast oblong and transported it to the monument on a purpose-built railway.[96]

57. The 'Hindenburg stone': workers rest after excavating earth from under the monolith, photograph, c.1930s

The official architecture of the Third Reich invoked a distinctively Prussian cultural heritage. We see it in the three '*Ordensburgen*' constructed during the Third Reich at Crössinsee, Vogelsang and Sonthofen for the elite schooling of future party cadres. With their soaring towers and frowning eaves, these monumental structures recalled the castles of the German Order that had once conquered the 'German east' and established itself in the Baltic principality of Prussia. Another very different Prussian architectural legacy lived on in the neo-classical public buildings commissioned by the regime as part of the National Socialist reshaping of German urban space. Hitler's favourite architect, Paul Ludwig Troost, was a disciple of Schinkel (1781–1841), the canonical exponent of the 'Prussian building style'. Troost's House of German Art, constructed in 1933–7 on the Ludwigsplatz in central Munich, was widely seen as a twentieth-century gloss on the austere neo-classicism of Schinkel's Old Museum in Berlin.

Albert Speer, a party member from 1931 who became Hitler's court architect after Troost's early death in 1934, was likewise an admirer of Schinkel. Speer hailed from a family with a long architectural tradition – his grandfather had studied under Schinkel at the Berlin Academy of

58. Hindenburg's coffin is carried into his mausoleum under the battlements of the Tannenberg monument; photograph, Matthias Bräunlich, 1935

Building, and his most important teacher at the Technical University Berlin-Charlottenburg was Heinrich Tessenow, who was well known for having converted Schinkel's Neue Wache on Unter den Linden into a memorial for the fallen of the First World War. The façade and courts of Speer's New Reich chancellery, commissioned by Hitler at the beginning of 1938 and completed after twelve months of frenzied construction on 12 January 1939, made numerous conscious references to Schinkel's most famous buildings. The continuity message was driven home in a sumptuous official volume published in 1943 under the auspices of the Reich Chamber of Architects. Entitled *Karl Friedrich Schinkel: The Forerunner of the New German Architectural Ideology*, the book expressly set out to locate the achievements of Nazi building within the Prussian neo-classicist tradition.[97]

Prussian subjects also featured prominently in the ideologically harmonized cinematic output of the German film studios after the Nazi seizure of power. Drawing on trends established during the Weimar Republic, Goebbels deployed Prussian themes as instruments of ideological mobilization.[98] The escapism and nostalgia of earlier productions made way for dramas with an unmistakable contemporary resonance. *The Old and the Young King*, for example, released in 1935, offered a grotesquely distorted account of the breakdown in the relationship between the future Frederick the Great and his father Frederick William I. The intrigues of British diplomacy were blamed for the misunderstanding between father and son, and there is a scene where the prince's French books are piled up and burnt on the order of his father – a contemporary reference that audiences could not have failed to recognize. The execution of Katte is presented as the legitimate expression of a sovereign will. The dialogue included such gems of anachronism as the following: 'I want to make Prussia healthy. And anyone who tries to stop me is a scoundrel' (Frederick William); and 'The king does not commit murder. His will is law. And whatever does not submit to him must be annihilated' (an officer commenting on Katte's sentence).[99]

Other major productions dwelt on anecdotal scenes from the life of Frederick the Great, or on dramatic plots set in the context of an historic crisis, such as the Seven Years War or the aftermath of the defeat at the hands of Napoleon in 1806–7. A favoured theme – especially during the war years – was the dramatic interplay between the perfidy of betrayal (of one's country or one's leader) and the redemption that comes with self-sacrifice in the name of the greater good.[100] Nowhere was this theme more trenchantly presented than in the last major film production of the Third Reich, *Kolberg*. This was an epic period drama set in the eponymous fortress, where Gneisenau and Schill collaborated with the civil authorities in the town to hold the numerically superior French at bay. Against all odds – and contrary to the historical record – the French are forced to fall back and the town is unexpectedly saved by a peace treaty. Here was the image of Prussia as a kingdom of the pure will, holding out by courage and fortitude alone. The film's purpose was obvious enough; it was a call to mobilize every last resource against the enemies who were closing in around Germany. It was, as the director Veit Harlan put it, a 'symbol of the present' that should give viewers strength 'for today, for the time of our own struggle'. Whether this objective was achieved may be doubted: there were very few functioning cinemas by the time the film was available for general release. Where the film did find an audience, the response was one of resignation and gloom. Amid the ruins and chaos of spring 1945, there were very few Germans who could still believe that Germany might be rescued by the efforts of a band of patriots.

It would be a mistake to see all this purely as cynical manipulation. Goebbels had a remarkable propensity to believe his own lies. And

Hitler's subjective identification with Frederick the Great was so intense that the only decoration in the Reich Chancellery bunker, in which Hitler spent the last days of his life sixteen metres below the streets of Berlin, was Graff's portrait of Frederick the Great. Throughout the war years, Hitler repeatedly compared himself to Frederick, the man to whose 'heroism' Prussia owed its historical ascendancy.[101] 'From this picture,' he told the tank commander Guderian at the end of February 1945, 'I always draw new strength when the bad news threatens to crush me.' In the unreal, detached atmosphere of the bunker, it was easy to imagine that the history of Prussia was re-enacting itself in the epic drama of the Third Reich. Goebbels bolstered Hitler's morale during the early months of 1945 with readings from Carlyle's *Life of Frederick the Great*, especially those passages that described how in the darkest hour of the Seven Years War, when all seemed lost, Prussia was saved from destruction by the death of Tsarina Elisabeth in February 1762.[102] Hitler drew on the same historical themes when he spent four days in early April 1945 trying to stiffen Mussolini's resolve. The monologues he delivered at the war-weary *Duce* included long disquisitions on the history of Prussia.[103] So tight was the grip of this historical romance on the mind of Goebbels that the propaganda minister responded with elation and a sense of triumph to the news of the death of President Franklin Roosevelt on 12 April 1945. He believed 1945 was to be the *annus mirabilis* of the Third Reich. He ordered that champagne be served in his office and immediately put a call through to Hitler's apartment: 'My Führer, I congratulate you. Roosevelt is dead! Fate has struck down your greatest enemy. God has not abandoned us.'[104]

None of this should be read as evidence of the continuing vitality of the 'Prussian tradition'. Those who seek to legitimate a claim to power in the present often have recourse to the idea of tradition. They decorate themselves with its cultural authority. But the encounter between the self-proclaimed inheritors of tradition and the historical record rarely takes place on equal terms. The National Socialist reading of the Prussian past was opportunistic, distorted and selective. The entire historical career of the Prussian state was shoehorned into the paradigm of a national German history conceived in racist terms. The Nazis admired the military state-building of the 'soldier king' but had little sympathy for or understanding of the Pietist spirituality that provided an ethical framework for all the king's endeavours and left such a deep imprint on his reign – hence, for example, the almost complete evacuation of Christianity from the ceremony in the Garrison Church in March 1933. The Frederick the Great of National Socialist propaganda was a heavily truncated version of the original – the monarch's insistence on French as the medium of civilized discourse, his disdain for German culture and his ambiguous sexuality were simply airbrushed away. There was little interest in the other Hohenzollern monarchs, with the exception of Wilhelm I, founder of the German Empire of 1871. Frederick William II and Frederick William IV, the sensitive and artistically gifted 'romantic on the throne' disappeared almost entirely from view.

Two periods were singled out for their mythopoeic power: the Seven Years War and the Wars of Liberation, but there was no interest in the Prussian enlightenment. The Nazis prized the Prussian reformer Stein for his nationalist commitment; Hardenberg, by contrast, the Francophile *Realpolitiker* and emancipator of the Prussian Jews, languished in obscurity. There was some enthusiasm for Fichte and Schleiermacher, but little official interest in Hegel, whose emphasis on the transcendent dignity of the state was uncongenial to the *völkisch* racism of the National Socialists. In short, Nazi-Prussia was a glittering fetish assembled from fragments of a legendary past. It was a manufactured memory, a talismanic adornment to the pretensions of the regime.

In any case, none of this official enthusiasm for 'Prussiandom' (*Preussentum*) could revive the fortunes of the real Prussia. In 1933, the Prussian Landtag was dissolved after new elections had failed to yield a Nazi absolute majority. The Law on the Reorganization of the Reich of January 1934 placed regional governments and the new imperial commissars under the direct authority of the Reich ministry of the interior. The Prussian ministries were gradually merged with their Reich counterparts (with the exception, for technical reasons, of finance) and plans were drawn up (though they remained unrealized in 1945) to partition the state into its constituent provinces. Prussia was still an official designation and a name on the map, indeed it was the only German state not to be formally absorbed into the Reich. But it ceased de facto to exist as a state of any kind. There was no inconsistency here with the regime's official celebrations of the Prussian legacy. The diffuse abstraction 'Prussiandom' did not denote a specific form of state, or a particular social constellation, but a disembodied catalogue of virtues, a 'spirit' that transcended history and would thrive at least as well in the

'Führer-democracy' of the Third Reich as it had under the absolutist rule of Frederick the Great. Hermann Goering, who replaced Papen as commissary minister-president of Prussia in April 1933, invoked this distinction when he addressed the Prussian Council of State in June 1934. 'The concept of the Prussian state', he declared, had been 'subsumed into the Reich'. 'What remains is the eternal spirit of Prussiandom.'[105]

Much to the disgust of some of the traditionalist noble families, the new regime made no attempt to restore the old monarchy after 1933. Throughout the 1920s, there had been frequent contacts between the ex-royal and imperial entourage at Doorn and a loose network of (mainly Prussian) conservative and monarchist groups in the German Republic. The late 1920s brought closer informal ties with the Nazi movement: William II's eldest son, August William, joined the SA in 1928, an act for which he had the former Emperor's permission. The ex-Emperor's second wife, Princess Hermine von Schönaich-Carolath, had friends among the high-ranking party members and even participated in the Nuremberg Rally of 1929. The collapse of the conservative block and the success of the Nazis in the German elections of 1930 encouraged the restorationists at Doorn to put out formal feelers to the Hitler movement. Their fruit was a meeting at Doorn between William and Hermann Goering in January 1931. No minutes survive of this meeting, but it would seem that Goering spoke positively of the prospect of William's returning to Germany.[106]

But despite these friendly signals – there were encouraging noises from Hitler and a second meeting with Goering in the summer of 1932 – the idea was unceremoniously dropped after the seizure of power. Hitler had encouraged the Kaiser's hopes only because he wanted to strengthen his credentials as the legitimate successor to Prussia-Germany's monarchical tradition. The moment of truth came on 27 January 1934, when Hitler ordered the breaking up of celebrations in honour of the Kaiser's seventy-fifth birthday. The fate of the restoration movement was sealed a few days later by new legislation outlawing all monarchist organizations. The royal SA-man Prince August William was placed under house arrest during the Röhm Putsch and thereafter ordered to refrain from political utterances of any kind. Gradually, the regime erased the memory of monarchy in Prussia and Germany, prohibiting the display of imperial images and memorabilia, while paying the former royal family a substantial retainer to ensure that it caused no trouble.[107] Among those who strongly objected was Count Ewald von Kleist-Wendisch-Tychow, regional chief of the Corporation of the German Nobility (*Deutsche Adelsgenossenschaft*) in Eastern Pomerania. In January 1937 he dissolved his section of the corporation, declaring that the regime's refusal to restore the Prussian-German Crown was 'not compatible with the traditions and honour of the nobility'.[108]

Characterizing the relationship between the Hitler regime and the Prussian traditional and functional elites is difficult. There has to date been no systematic study of attitudes and conduct within the German regional nobilities throughout the life of the Third Reich. But one thing is clear: the conventional picture of the landed nobility haughtily withdrawing to the splendid isolation of their estates and waiting for the Nazi storm to pass is misleading. There was hardly a single East-Elbian noble family that did not have at least one party member. The ancient lineage of the Schwerins supplied no fewer than fifty-two members, the Hardenbergs twenty-seven, the Tresckows thirty, the Schulenburgs forty-one, of whom seventeen had already joined the party before 1933. Many nobles were attracted to the NSDAP because they saw an alliance with the Hitler movement as the key to securing their traditional social leadership role on new terms.[109] But others joined because they found the party's ideology and ambience congenial – the attitudinal gap between noble circles and the National Socialist movement was narrower than has often been supposed.

There was also broad support within the Prussian nobility for the foreign policy objectives of the new regime – especially revision of the Versailles Treaty and the retrieval of lands transferred to the Poles. The paucity of Prussians within the leadership echelons of the NSDAP initially had an off-putting effect on some families – according to one assessment there were only seventeen Prussians among the 500 top Nazi cadres in 1933.[110] But as the focus of the party's activity – and its electoral base – shifted northwards, these misgivings often faded. Fritz-Dietlof Count von der Schulenburg was initially suspicious of the NSDAP because he saw it as an essentially south-German movement, but he later embraced it as 'a new form of Prussiandom' – here again that usefully obfuscating abstraction.[111]

The officer corps of the Reichswehr, in which the sons of Junker families still formed a substantial group, was initially sceptical of the Nazi movement but shifted after the March elections of 1933 towards a policy of alliance with the new leadership. Many senior officers were reassured by Hitler's reprisals against the brownshirts in the Röhm Putsch of 31 June 1934. The commencement of the rearmament programme and the remilitarization of the Rhineland in March 1935 also helped to cement relations. A characteristic example of this transition was the inspector of weapons training in Berlin, Lieutenant-General Johannes Blaskowitz, who hailed from Peterswalde in East Prussia and had been educated in the cadet schools of Köslin and Berlin-Lichterfelde. In 1932, Blaskowitz had warned his regiment during an exercise that 'if the Nazis make any false moves, [we] will proceed against them with maximum force, and [we] will not shrink even from the bloodiest conflict.'[112] By the spring of 1935, however, he was speaking a different language. In a speech for the opening of a monument to the fallen of the First World War, Blaskowitz, the son of a Pietist East Prussian pastor, hailed Adolf Hitler as the man sent by God in Germany's hour of need: 'God's help gave us our Leader, who has gathered all the forces of national life into one powerful movement [. . .] and who has yesterday restored the military sovereignty of the German people and thereby fulfilled the testament of our dead heroes.'[113]

Prussians were, needless to say, deeply implicated in the atrocities committed by the SS and Security Police and by the German Wehrmacht, whose claim to a 'clean' wartime record has been comprehensively exploded. But being Prussian was not by any means a precondition for enthusiastic service in the regime's cause. Bavarians, Saxons and Württembergers also served with zeal and distinction in all branches of the regime's activity. The battalion of policemen whose mass shootings of Jewish men, women and children are so harrowingly documented in Christopher Browning's *Ordinary Men* were not Prussians, but natives of traditionally liberal, bourgeois, Anglophile Hamburg.[114] The Austrians, those historical and cultural antipodes of the Prussians, were strikingly over-represented in the upper echelons of the Nazi machinery of mass murder – Odilo Globocnik, overseer of the death camps, Hans Rauter, the SS and police official who deported 100,000 Dutch Jews to the East, Franz Stangl, the commandant of Sobibor (later transferred to Treblinka) and the notorious Adolf Eichmann were just a few of the more prominent Austrians implicated in the Holocaust.[115] Such observations do nothing whatsoever to diminish the role played by Prussians in the criminal activities of the Third Reich, but they do undermine the

59. The deportation of Jews from Memel, in what had once been Prussian Lithuania. In their campaign to murder German and European Jewry, the Nazi regime destroyed one highly distinctive strand of the Prussian heritage.

view that Prussian values or habits of mind were in themselves a special qualification for zealous service.

Prussians – and especially representatives of the traditional Prussian elites – also figured prominently within the ranks of the German national conservative resistance. Many of the old Pomeranian Pietist families – among them the Thaddens, Kleists and Bismarcks – supported the Confessing Church that emerged to resist the regime's attempt to re-sculpt German Christianity.[116] The active military resistance was, to be sure, never large enough to account for more than a very small fraction of men under arms. Yet it is significant that of the conspirators of 20 July 1944, two-thirds came from the Prussian milieu, and many from old and distinguished military families. Among those arrested immediately after the failed attempt on Hitler's life was the former deputy police president of Berlin, Fritz-Dietlof von der Schulenburg, descendant of a family whose sons had served for centuries as officers of the Brandenburg-Prussian army. Another was the jurist and officer Peter Count Yorck von Wartenburg, a direct descendant of the Yorck who had walked across to the Russians at Tauroggen in December 1812. Field-Marshal Erwin von Witzleben, another prominent Prussian conspirator, was the scion of an old East-Elbian military family who had been chosen by the conspirators to take over the supreme command of the Wehrmacht after the assassination of Hitler. He was arrested on 21 July and subjected to weeks of torture and humiliations at the hands of the Gestapo. On 7 August 1944, still bearing the marks of his ill-treatment, he was brought before the People's Court, where he stood holding up his beltless trousers and enduring the insults of Roland Freisler, Hitler's hanging judge. He was executed by guillotine on the following day.[117]

No single unit of the German Wehrmacht was more deeply implicated in resistance activity than the Potsdam IX Infantry Regiment, a Prussian traditional regiment (it was the official successor to the I Prussian Foot Guards) with strong ties to the Potsdam Garrison Church. This was the regiment of Major-General Henning von Tresckow, who in March 1943 smuggled a package of explosives on to a plane carrying Hitler back to Berlin (the parcel failed to explode and was retrieved without incident at the other end). After collaborating closely with Stauffenberg and the other military conspirators, Tresckow blew himself up with a hand grenade on 21 July 1944. Captain Axel Freiherr von dem Bussche of the IX Regiment undertook to strap explosives to his body and destroy Hitler in a suicide bombing during a demonstration of new uniforms in 1943, but was refused leave to attend by his commanding officer on the eastern front. Lieutenant Ewald von Kleist-Schmenzin agreed to take von dem Bussche's place, but the planned demonstration was cancelled and the opportunity never arose. Other IX Regiment officers directly involved in the July plot included the son of former Chief of Staff Ludwig Freiherr von Hammerstein-Equord, Captain Hans Fritzsche of the Potsdam Reserve and Lieutenant Georg Sigismund von Oppen, whose family ran an estate in Altfriedland, fifty kilometres to the east of Berlin. Hammerstein-Equord, Oppen and Fritzsche returned to regimental headquarters in time to escape notice and survived the reprisals that followed the assassination attempt, largely because Fritz-Dietlof von der Schulenburg refused even under torture to reveal their names to the Gestapo. Several other members of the regiment were executed or committed suicide during the wave of reprisals that followed the collapse of the July plot.[118]

The motives for resistance varied. Many of the key figures had passed through a phase of infatuation with the Hitler movement and some had even become implicated in its crimes. Some were disgusted at the mass murder of Jews, Poles and Russians, others had religious reservations; some sought the restoration of the monarchy, though not necessarily of William II, whose flight to Holland had neither been forgotten nor forgiven. Prussian themes insinuated themselves into the resistance at many levels. The Kreisau Circle, for example, a network of mainly conservative civilian and military resisters centred on the Moltke estate at Kreisau in Silesia, were sceptical of the virtues of democracy (which, as they saw it, had failed to protect Germany against the advent of Hitler) and looked to the unelected upper chamber of the old Prussian Landtag as the model for an authoritarian alternative to modern parliamentary politics.[119] Many of the resisters clung to the idea of Prussia as a vanished better world whose traditions were being perverted by the taskmasters of the Third Reich. 'True Prussiandom can never be separated from the concept of freedom,' Henning von Tresckow told a family gathering when his two sons were confirmed at the Garrison Church in the spring of 1943. Uncoupled from the imperatives of 'freedom', 'understanding' and 'compassion', he warned, the Prussian ideals of self-discipline and the fulfilment of duty would degenerate into 'spiritless soldiery and narrow bigotry'.[120]

The historical imagination of the Prussian elite resistance was anchored in the mythical memory of the wars of liberation. The figure of Yorck, who risked the charge of betrayal and treason to walk across the snow to the Russians at Tauroggen, was a recurring example.[121] When Carl Goerdeler, perhaps the most senior civilian associate of the military resistance, composed a memorandum urging the army to rise up against Hitler in the summer of 1940, he ended the document with an extended quotation from Baron Stein's letter of 12 October 1808 urging Frederick William III to show his hand against Napoleon: 'If nothing but misfortune and suffering can be expected, then it is better to take a decision that is honourable and noble and offers comfort and solace, should things end badly.'[122] In later years he compared the defeats of North Africa and Stalingrad to the salutary disasters at Jena and Auerstädt.[123] A particularly striking example comes from an exchange between the resister Rudolf von Gersdorff, author of an aborted suicide bombing of Hitler in the spring of 1943, and Field Marshal Erich von

Manstein. When Manstein reproached Gersdorff for his seditious views, reminding him that Prussian field marshals did not mutiny, Gersdorff cited Yorck's defection at Tauroggen.[124]

For the resisters Prussia became a virtual homeland, the focal point for a patriotism that could find no referent in the Third Reich. The charisma of this mythical Prussia was not lost upon the non-Prussians who moved within resistance circles. The Social Democrat Julius Leber, an Alsatian who grew up in Lübeck and was executed on 5 January 1945 for his part in the conspiracy against Hitler, was among those who looked back in admiration at the years when Stein, Gneisenau and Scharnhorst re-established the state 'in the citizen's consciousness of freedom'.[125] There was an energetic polarity between the Prussia of Nazi propaganda and that of the civilian and military resistance. Goebbels used Prussian themes to drive home the primacy of loyalty, obedience and will as indispensable aids in Germany's epic struggle against her enemies. The resisters, by contrast, insisted that these secondary Prussian virtues became worthless as soon as they were severed from their ethical and religious roots. For the Nazis, Yorck was the symbol of an oppressed Germany rising up against foreign 'tyranny' – for the resisters he represented a transcendent sense of duty that might even, under certain circumstances, articulate itself in an act of treason. We naturally look more kindly on one of these Prussia-myths than on the other. Yet both were selective, talismanic and instrumental. Precisely because it had become so abstract, so etiolated, 'Prussiandom' was up for grabs. It was not an identity, nor even a memory. It had become a catalogue of disembodied mythical attributes whose historical and ethical significance was, and would remain, in contention.

THE EXORCISTS

In the end, it was the Nazi view of Prussia that prevailed. The western allies needed no persuading that Nazism was merely the latest manifestation of Prussianism. They could draw on an intellectually formidable tradition of anti-Prussianism that dated back to the outbreak of the First World War. In August 1914, Ramsay Muir, a distinguished liberal activist and holder of the chair of modern history at the University of Manchester, published a widely read study that claimed to examine the 'historical background' of the current conflict. 'It is the result,' Muir wrote, 'of a poison which has been working in the European system for more than two centuries, and the chief source of this poison is Prussia.'[126] In another study published early in the war, William Harbutt Dawson, a social liberal publicist and one of the most influential commentators on German history and politics in early twentieth-century Britain, pointed to the militarizing influence of the 'Prussian spirit' within the otherwise benign German nation: 'this spirit has ever been a hard and immalleable element in the life of Germany; it is still the knot in the oak, the nodule in the softer clay.'[127]

Common to many analyses was the notion that there were in fact two Germanies, the liberal, congenial and pacific Germany of the south and west and the reactionary, militaristic Germany of the north-east.[128] The tensions between the two, it was argued, remained unresolved within the Empire founded by Bismarck in 1871. One of the most sophisticated and influential early analysts of this problem was the American sociologist Thorstein Veblen. In a study of German industrial society published in 1915 and re-issued in 1939, Veblen argued that a lopsided process of modernization had distorted German political culture. 'Modernism' had transformed the sphere of industrial organization, but had failed to effect 'an equally secure and disturbing lodgement in the tissues of the body politic'. The reason for this, Veblen diagnosed, lay in the survival of an essentially pre-modern Prussian 'territorial state'. The history of this state, he suggested, amounted to a career of more or less uninterrupted aggressive war-making. The consequence was a political culture of extreme servility, for 'the pursuit of war, being an exercise in the following of one's leader and execution of arbitrary orders, induces an animus of enthusiastic subservience and unquestioning obedience to authority.' In such a system, the loyal support of popular sentiment could be maintained only by 'unremitting habituation [and] discipline sagaciously and relentlessly directed to this end', and 'by a system of bureaucratic surveillance and unremitting interference in the private life of subjects'.[129]

Veblen's account was light on empirical data and supporting evidence, but it was not without theoretical sophistication. It aimed not only to describe but also to explain the supposed deformations of Prussian-German political culture. It was supported, moreover, by an implicit conception of the 'modern' in the light of which Prussia could be deemed archaic, anachronistic, only partially modernized. It is striking how

671

much of the substance of the 'special path' thesis that would rise to prominence in German historical writing of the late 1960s and 1970s is already anticipated in Veblen's account. This was no accident – Ralf Dahrendorf, whose synoptic study *Society and Democracy in Germany* (1968) was one of the foundational texts of the critical school, drew heavily on the American sociologist's work.[130]

Even the rather cruder accounts that passed for historical analyses of modern Germany during the Second World War often preserved a sense of historical perspective, rather than settling for generalizations about German 'national character'. Since the seventeenth century, one writer observed in 1941, the 'old German spirit of conquest' had been 'deliberately developed more and more and along the lines of that mentality which is known as "Prussianism"'. The history of Prussia had been 'an almost uninterrupted period of forcible expansion, under the iron rule of militarism and absolutist officialism'. Under a harsh regime of compulsory education, in which teachers were recruited from the ranks of former non-commissioned officers, the young were instilled with 'the typical Prussian obedience'. The rigours of school life were succeeded by a prolonged period in barracks or on active military service. It was here that 'the German mind received its last coat of varnish. Anything that had not been done by the schools was achieved in the army.'[131]

In the minds of many contemporaries, the link between 'Prussianism' and Nazism was obvious. The German émigré Edgar Stern-Rubarth described Hitler – notwithstanding the dictator's Austrian birth – as 'the Arch-Prussian' and declared that 'the whole structure of his dreamed-of Reich' was based not only on the material achievements of the Prussian state, but 'even more on the philosophical foundations of Prussianism'.[132] In a study of German industrial planning published in 1943, Joseph Borkin, an American official who later helped to prepare the case against the giant chemicals combine I. G. Farben at Nuremberg, observed that the political evolution of the Germans had long been retarded by a ruling class of Prussian Junkers who had 'never been unsaddled by social change' and concluded that the Prussian 'Weltanschauung of political and economic world hegemony is the well-spring from which both Hohenzollern imperialism and National Socialism flow'. Like many such accounts, this book drew on a tradition of German critical commentary on Prussian history and German political culture more generally.[133]

It would be difficult to overstate the hold of this scenario of power-lust, servility and political archaism over the imaginations of the policy-makers most concerned with Germany's post-war fate. In a speech of December 1939, Foreign Secretary Anthony Eden observed that 'Hitler is not so unique as all that. He is merely the latest expression of the Prussian spirit of military domination.' The *Daily Telegraph* published a discussion of the speech under the headline 'Hitler's Rule is in the Tradition of Prussian Tyranny' and there were positive comments throughout the tabloid press.[134] On the day of the German invasion of the Soviet Union in 1941, Winston Churchill spoke memorably of the 'hideous onslaught' of the Nazi 'war machine with its clanking, heel-clicking dandified Prussian officers' and 'the dull, drilled docile brutish masses of the Hun soldiers plodding on like a swarm of crawling locusts'.[135] In an article for the *Daily Herald* in November 1941, Ernest Bevin, minister of labour in Churchill's War Cabinet, declared that German preparation for the current war had begun long before the advent of Hitler. Even if one 'got rid of Hitler, Goering and others', Bevin warned, the German problem would remain unsolved. 'It was Prussian militarism, with its terrible philosophy, that had to be got rid of from Europe for all time.'[136] It followed that the defeat of the Nazi regime itself would not suffice to bring the war to a satisfactory close.

In a paper presented to cabinet in the summer of 1943, Labour leader and Deputy Prime Minister Clement Attlee warned passionately against the notion that it might be possible, in the aftermath of the regime's collapse, to do business with some kind of German successor government drawn from the traditional elites of German society. The 'real aggressive element' in German society, he argued, was the Prussian Junker class, and the chief danger lay in the possibility that this class, which had allied itself with the masters of heavy industry in Westphalia, might depose the Nazi leadership and present itself to the Allies as a successor government prepared to settle peace terms. The error of 1918 had been to allow these elements to remain as a bulwark against Bolshevism. This must not happen again. Only the 'liquidation of the Junkers as a class', Attlee argued, would 'eradicate the Prussian virus'.[137]

For President Roosevelt too, the assumption that Prussia was historically the source of German militarism and aggression played a central role in his conception of policy *vis-à-vis* Germany. 'This is one thing that I want to make perfectly clear,' he told Congress on 17 September

1943. 'When Hitler and the Nazis go out, the Prussian military clique must go with them. The war-breeding gangs of militarists must be rooted out of Germany [...] if we are to have any real assurance of future peace.'[138] The memory of 1918, when Woodrow Wilson had refused to parley with 'the military masters and the monarchical autocrats of Germany' was still vivid.[139] Yet the military system that had sustained the German war effort in 1914–18 had survived the privations inflicted by the Peace of Versailles to mount a renewed campaign of conquest only two decades later. For Roosevelt (as for Attlee), it followed that the traditional Prussian military authorities were no less of a threat to peace than the Nazis. There could thus be no negotiated armistice with the military command, even in the event that the Nazi regime were to be deposed from within or to collapse. In this way, the idea of 'Prussianism' made an important contribution to the policy of unconditional surrender adopted by the Allies at the Casablanca conference of January 1943.[140]

Among the Allies, only the Soviets remained aware of the tension between Prussian tradition and the National Socialist regime. While the July plot of 1944 evoked little positive comment among western politicians, the Soviet official media found words of praise for the conspirators.[141] Soviet propaganda, by contrast with that of the western powers, consistently exploited Prussian themes – the National Committee for a Free Germany, established as a propaganda vehicle in 1943 and composed of captured German officers, appealed explicitly to the memory of the Prussian reformers, above all Gneisenau, Stein and Clausewitz, all of whom had resigned their Prussian commissions during the French occupation and joined the army of the Tsar. Yorck, the man who ignored the command of his sovereign to walk across the ice to the Russians in 1812, naturally held pride of place.[142]

This was all eyewash, of course, yet it also reflected a specifically Russian perspective on Prussia's history. The history of relations between the two states was no chronicle of unremitting mutual hatred. Stalin's hero Peter the Great had been a warm admirer of the Prussia of the Great Elector, whose administrative innovations served as models for his own reforms. Russia and Prussia had cooperated closely in the partitioning of Poland and the Russian alliance was crucial to Prussia's recovery against Napoleon after 1812. Relations remained warm after the Napoleonic Wars, when the diplomatic bond of the Holy Alliance was reinforced by the marriage of Frederick William III's daughter Charlotte to Tsar Nicholas I. The Russians backed Austria in the dualist struggles of 1848–50, but favoured Prussia with a policy of benevolent neutrality during the war of 1866. The assistance rendered to the beleaguered Bolsheviks in 1917–18 and the close military collaboration between Reichswehr and Red Army during the Weimar years were more recent reminders of this long history of interaction and cooperation.

Yet none of this could preserve Prussia from dissolution at the hands of the victorious Allies. By the autumn of 1945, there was a consensus among the various British organs involved in the administration of occupied Germany that (in a tellingly redundant formulation) 'this moribund corpse of Prussia' must be 'finally killed'.[143] Its continued existence would constitute a 'dangerous anachronism'.[144] By the summer of 1946, this was a matter of firm policy for the British administration in Germany. A memorandum of 8 August 1946 by the British member of the Allied Control Authority in Berlin put the case against Prussia succinctly:

I need not point out that Prussia has been a menace to European security for the last two hundred years. The survival of the Prussian State, even if only in name, would provide a basis for any irredentist claims which the German people may later seek to put forward, would strengthen German militarist ambitions, and would encourage the revival of an authoritarian, centralised Germany which in the interests of all it is vital to prevent.[145]

The American and French delegations broadly supported this view; only the Soviets dragged their feet, mainly because Stalin still hoped to use Prussia as the hub of a unified Germany over which the Soviet Union might eventually be able to secure control. But by early February 1947, they too had fallen into step and the way was open for the legal termination of the Prussian state.

In the meanwhile, the extirpation of Prussia as a social milieu was already well advanced. The Central Committee of the German Communist Party in the Soviet zone of occupation announced in August 1945 that the 'feudal estate-owners and the Junker caste' had always been 'the bearers of militarism and chauvinism' (a formulation that would find its way into the text of Law No. 46 of the Allied Control Council). The removal of their 'socio-economic power' was thus the first and fundamental precondition for the 'extirpation of Prussian militarism'. There followed a wave of expropriations. No account was taken of the political orientation of the owners, or of their role in resistance activity. Among those whose estates were confiscated was Ulrich-Wilhelm Count Schwerin von Schwanenfeld, who had been executed on 21 August 1944 for his role in the July conspiracy.[146]

These transformations took place against the background of the greatest wave of migrations in the history of German settlement in Europe. During the last months of the war, millions of Prussians fled westwards from the eastern provinces to escape the advancing Red Army. Of those who remained, some committed suicide, others were killed or died of starvation, cold or illness. Germans were expelled from East Prussia, West Prussia, eastern Pomerania and Silesia, and tens of thousands perished in the process. The emigrations and resettlements continued into the 1950s and 1960s. The looting or burning of the great East-Elbian houses signalled the end not only of a socio-economic elite but also of a distinctive culture and way of life. Finckenstein, with its Napoleonic memorabilia, Beynuhnen with its collection of antiques, Waldburg with its rococo library, Blumberg and Gross Wohnsdorff with their memories of the liberal ministers von Schön and von Schroetter were among the many country seats to be plundered and gutted by an enemy bent on erasing every last trace of German settlement.[147] So it was that the Prussians, or at least their mid-twentieth-century descendants, came to pay a heavy price for the war of extermination that Hitler's Germany unleashed on Eastern Europe.

The scouring of Prussia from the collective awareness of the German population began before the end of the war with a massive aerial attack on the city of Potsdam. As a heritage site with little strategic or industrial significance, Potsdam was very low on the list of Allied targets and had been spared significant bombardment during the war. Late in the evening of Saturday 14 April 1945, however, 491 planes of British Bomber Command dropped their payloads over the city, transforming it into a sea of fire. Almost half the historical buildings of the old centre were obliterated in a bombing that lasted for only half an hour. When the fires had been extinguished and the smoke had cleared, the scorched 57-metre tower of the Garrison Church stood as the dominant landmark in a cityscape of ruins. Of the fabled carillon, famous for its automated renditions of the 'Leuthen Chorale', there remained only a lump of metal. The scouring continued after 1945, as entire districts of the old city were cleared to make way for socialist reconstruction. The

60. *East Berlin, 1950: five years after the end of the Second World War, the upper torso and head of a fallen statue of Kaiser William I rest near a chunk of his horse*

imperatives of post-war city planning were reinforced by the anti-Prussian iconoclasm of the Communist authorities.[148]

Nowhere was the rupture with the past more comprehensive than in East Prussia. The north-eastern part of the province, including Königsberg, fell to Soviet Russia as war booty. On 4 July 1946, the city was renamed Kaliningrad, after one of Stalin's most faithful henchmen, and the sovietized district around it became the Kaliningradskaya oblast. The city had been bitterly fought over during the last months of the war and during the early post-war years it remained a lunar landscape of ruins. 'What a city!' one Soviet Russian visitor declared in 1951. 'The tram leads us through the humped, narrow streets of erstwhile Königsberg. "Erstwhile" because Königsberg truly is an erstwhile city. It doesn't exist. For kilometres in every direction, an unforgettable landscape of ruins. The old Königsberg is a dead city.'[149] Most of the historical buildings in the old centre were stripped and torn down in an attempt to erase memories of its history. In some streets, only the Latin letters inscribed on the steel manhole covers of the city's late-nineteenth-century sewerage system survived to remind the passerby of an older history.

61. The capture of Königsberg by Soviet troops, 1945

Around the devastation, a new Soviet city took shape, monotonous and provincial, cut off from the world by a military exclusion zone.

In the western zones of occupation too, the work of erasure proceeded apace. French policy-makers and commentators spoke in the early post-war years of the need for wholesale '*déprussification*'.[150] The bronze relief panels on the base of the Victory Column, raised in 1873 in celebration of the triumphs of Prussian arms over the Danes, the Austrians and the French in the Wars of German Unification, were removed

62. *Workers bury the statues of Hohenzollern ancestors in the Bellevue Palace gardens, 1954*

by the French occupation authorities and shipped to Paris. They were handed back to Berlin only on the occasion of the city's 750th-anniversary celebrations in 1986. An even more emblematic fate awaited the colossal figures representing historic rulers from the House of Hohenzollern that had once lined the Siegesallee. These objects – bombastic masses of carved white stone – were transferred by the Nazi authorities to the Grosse Sternallee, one of the axes of the future Reich capital planned by Albert Speer, Hitler's Chief Inspector of Buildings. Here they spent the war draped in camouflage netting. In 1947, they were torn down on the orders of the Allied Control Council in Berlin. In 1954 they were secretly buried in the sandy soil of Brandenburg, almost as if this were necessary to prevent the Germans from re-grouping for battle around their ancestral Prussian totems.[151]

These impulses were carried over into the sphere of Allied re-education policy in the occupied zones. Here, the objective was to eliminate Prussia as a 'mental construct', to 'deprussianize' the German imagination. What exactly this would mean in practice was never agreed among the Allies or concretely defined by any of the zonal administrations, but the idea was influential none the less. Prussia was de-emphasized in the teaching of German history. In the French zone in particular, traditional textbooks charting a teleological nationalist narrative culminating in the formation of the Bismarckian Empire of 1871 made way for narratives focused on Germany's pre-national history and its manifold ties with the rest of Europe (especially France). The chronicle of battles and diplomacy that was the staple of the old Prussocentric history made way for the study of regions and cultures. Where references to Prussia were unavoidable, they were given a markedly negative spin. In the new textbooks of the French zone, Prussia figured as a voracious, reactionary power that had thwarted the beneficent effects of the French Revolution and destroyed the roots of enlightenment and democracy in Germany. Bismarck in particular emerged from this process of re-orientation with his reputation in ruins.[152] Frederick the Great, too, retreated from his privileged position in public memory, despite the best efforts of the conservative historian Gerhard Ritter to rehabilitate him as an enlightened ruler.[153] Allied policies were successful precisely because they harmonized with homegrown German (especially Catholic Rhenish and South German) traditions of antipathy to Prussia.

These endeavours were reinforced, moreover, by the global geopolitical imperatives that governed German politics after the establishment of two separate states in 1949. The German Federal and the German Democratic Republics now lay on either side of the Iron Curtain that divided the capitalist and Communist worlds. While Konrad Adenauer, the first Chancellor of the Federal Republic, pursued a policy of unconditional commitment to the West, the Communist eastern neighbour became a political dependency of Moscow, a 'homunculus from the Soviet test-tube'. Under the pressure of this partition, which came to seem a permanent feature of the post-war world, the Prussian past retreated to the horizons of public memory. Berlin meanwhile, islanded deep within the eastern republic, acquired a new and charismatic identity. In 1949, when the Soviets blocked supplies to the western-occupied zones of the city, the Allies broke the siege with a massive airlift. Across the western world there was a surge of solidarity with the beleaguered outpost. It was a crucial first step towards the rehabilitation of western Germany as a member of the international community. The city's prominence was further heightened by the erection of the Berlin Wall in August 1961, a spectacular monument to the polarities of the Cold War. In the 1960s and 1970s, West Berlin evolved into a showcase of western liberty and consumerism, a vibrant walled enclave of neon go-go bars, high culture and political ferment. It no longer belonged to Prussia, nor even to Germany, but to the western world – a condition memorably encapsulated in President John F. Kennedy's declaration during a visit to the city on 26 June 1963 that he, too, was 'ein Berliner'.

BACK TO BRANDENBURG

In a sparkling essay of 1894, the celebrated Prussian novelist Theodor Fontane, then an elderly man, recalled the occasion of his first literary composition. The reminiscence took him back six decades to the year 1833, when he had been a fourteen-year-old schoolboy lodging with an uncle in Berlin. It was a warm Sunday afternoon in August. Fontane decided to put off his school homework, a German composition 'on a self-chosen theme', and visit family friends in the village of Löwenbruch, some five kilometres to the south of Berlin. By three in the afternoon he had reached the Halle Gate on the city boundary. From there the road led south across the broad Teltow plateau through Kreuzberg and Tempelhof to Grossbeeren. As he reached the outskirts of Grossbeeren, Fontane sat down at the foot of a poplar tree to rest. It was nearly evening and wisps of mist hung over the newly ploughed fields. Further down the road he could make out the raised ground of the Grossbeeren cemetery and the village church tower glowing in the rays of the sinking sun.

As he sat watching this peaceful scene, Fontane fell to pondering on the events that had transpired in this very spot almost exactly twenty years before, at the height of the wars against Napoleon. It was here that General Bülow with his Prussians, most of them men of the Landwehr, had attacked the French and Saxon forces under General Oudinot, denying them access to Berlin and turning the tide of the 1813 summer campaign. Fontane had only a sketchy schoolboy knowledge of the battle, but what he remembered was enough to embellish the landscape before him with vibrant *tableaux vivants* from the past. Urged by his commanding officer to retreat behind the capital city and await the French advance, Bülow had refused, saying that 'he would rather see the bones of his militiamen whiten before than behind Berlin'. To the right of where Fontane was sitting was a low hill where a windmill turned; it was here that the Prince of Hessen-Homburg, 'like his ancestor before him at Fehrbellin', had led a few battalions of Havelland militia-men against the French positions. Even more vivid than all of this was a story his mother had often retold from his earliest childhood, a 'small event' that had passed into family lore. Emilie Labry (later Fontane) was a daughter of the Francophone Huguenot colony in Berlin. On 24 August 1813, at the age of fifteen, she was among the women and girls who came out from the city to tend to the wounded still lying in the field on the morrow of the battle. The first man she happened upon was a mortally wounded Frenchman with 'scarcely a breath left in his body'. Hearing himself addressed in his native language, he sat up 'as if trans-figured', grasping her beaker of wine in one hand and her wrist with the other. But before he could raise the wine to his lips, he was dead. As he lay that night under his blankets in Löwenbruch, Fontane knew that he had found his theme. The topic of his school composition would be the battle of Grossbeeren.[154]

Was this passage about Prussia, or was it about Brandenburg? Fontane invoked a recognizably Prussian historical narrative (though only in fragments), but the immediacy of the recollection derives from the inti-macy of the local setting: ploughed fields, a poplar tree, a low hill, a church tower glowing in the rays of the setting sun. It was the landscape of Brandenburg that opened the portals of memory into the Prussian past. An intense awareness of place was one of the signal features of Fontane's work as a writer. Indeed, the walk to Grossbeeren in 1833 was the prototype – he subsequently claimed – for the provincial excursion narrative he would later establish as a literary genre. Fontane is now best known for his novels – sharply observed dramas of nineteenth-century society – but his most famous and best-loved work during his lifetime was the four-volume homage to his native province known as *Walks Through the Mark Brandenburg*.

The *Walks* are a work unlike any other. Fontane made notes during a long sequence of meandering excursions across the Mark and interwove these with material drawn from inscriptions and local archives. The wandering began in the summer of 1859, with two trips to the Ruppin and Spreewald districts, and continued throughout the 1860s. Initially published as articles in various newspapers, the essays were subsequently revised, compiled by district and published from the early 1860s as bound volumes. Readers encountered an unfamiliar mix of topograph-ical observations, inscriptions, inventories and architectural sketches, romantic episodes from the past and scraps of unofficial memory gleaned from conversations with cab-drivers, inn-keepers, landowners, servants, village mayors and agricultural labourers. Passages of blank descriptive prose and wry vignettes of small-town life are interspersed with meditative scenes – a graveyard, a still lake enclosed by frowning trees, a ruined wall drowning in grass, children running in the stubble of a freshly mown field. Nostalgia and melancholy, those markers of modern literary sensibility, pervade the whole. Fontane's Brandenburg is a memoryscape that shimmers between past and present.

Perhaps the most remarkable thing about the *Walks* is their emphatically provincial focus. There seemed to many contemporaries, as Fontane well knew, something preposterous about devoting four volumes of historical travelogue to prosaic, featureless, backwoods Brandenburg. But he knew what he was doing. 'Even in the sand of the Mark,' he told a friend in 1863, 'the springs of life have flowed and still flow everywhere and every square foot of ground has its story and is telling it, too – but one has to be willing to listen to these often quiet voices.'[155] His aim was not to survey the *grand récit* of Prussian history, but to 're-animate locality', as he put it in a letter of October 1861.[156] In order to do this he had to work against the grain, uncovering the 'hidden beauties' of his native country, teasing out the nuances of its understated topography, gradually pulling Brandenburg from under the political identity of Prussia. The Mark had to be detached from Prussia's history in order to appear in its individuality.[157] Prussian history is present in the *Walks*, but it seems remote, like the rumour of a distant battlefield. It is the Brandenburgers, with their peppery wit and the spare cadences of their speech, who have the last word.

The *Walks* did not escape the strictures of historical pedants, but they were hugely popular with the broader public and have been widely imitated since. Their success draws our attention to the abiding strength of provincial attachments in the Prussian lands. Prussia remained, at the end of its life as in the beginning, a composite of provinces whose identity was substantially independent of their membership within the Prussian polity. This was most obviously the case for the more recently acquired provinces. The relationship between the Rhine province and Berlin remained a 'marriage of convenience', despite the relatively pragmatic and flexible governance of successive Prussian administrations.[158] In Westphalia, which was not, strictly speaking, a single historical entity but a jigsaw of culturally diverse lands, the later nineteenth century witnessed an intensified sense of regional belonging, heightened by confessional polarities. In Catholic areas of Westphalia such as the bishopric of Paderborn there was little enthusiasm for Prussia's war against France in 1870; volunteers were thin on the ground and many conscripts fled to Holland to avoid service.[159] It is thus misleading to speak of the 'assimilation' of the Rhineland provinces after 1815; what happened was rather that the western territories joined the Prussian amalgam, forcing the state to constitute itself anew. Paradoxically (and not only in the Rhineland), the introduction of Prussian governance, with its provincial presidencies and provincial diets, actually reinforced the sense of a distinctive provincial identity.[160]

These effects were intensified by Prussia's territorial expansion in the aftermath of the Austrian war. Many in the conquered provinces resented the high-handed annexations of 1866. The problem was particularly pronounced in Hanover, where the ancient dynasty of the Guelphs was deposed and its landed wealth sequestered by the Bismarck administration, an act of robbery and *lèse-majesté* that stuck in many conservative throats.[161] These concerns found expression in the German-Hanoverian Party, which advocated a Guelph restoration, but also pursued broader conservative-regionalist objectives. Guelphist Hanoverians might eventually become enthusiastic Germans, but they would never become wholeheartedly Prussian. To be sure, the Guelph regionalists were opposed within Hanover by the province's powerful National Liberal movement, which strongly supported the new Bismarckian state. But the National Liberals, as their name suggests, were enthusiasts of Germany, rather than of Prussia. They hailed Bismarck as the instrument of a German, rather than a specifically Prussian, mission.

Prussia's last great phase of expansion happened to coincide with an intensification of regionalist sentiment across Germany. Archaeological and historical associations run by local worthies dedicated themselves to laying bare the linguistic, cultural and political history of the many German 'landscapes'. In Schleswig-Holstein, this trend was intensified by the Prussian annexation of 1866. There was a burgeoning of regionalist loyalties, not only among the Danish-speaking 'Prussians' of north Schleswig, who remained unreconciled to the new order and seceded when they had the chance in 1919, but also among those ethnic Germans who were attached to the idea of Schleswig-Holstein as an autonomous state. Most of the deputies who represented the duchies in the constituent Reichstag of the North German Confederation in 1867 were supporters of regional autonomy. These aspirations acquired a certain academic credibility by the efforts of the Schleswig-Holstein-Lauenburg Society for Patriotic History, whose lectures and publications emphasized regionalist themes.[162]

The point should not be overstated. Regionalist sentiments posed no direct threat to Prussian authority. The Schleswig-Holsteiners may have grumbled, but they continued to pay their taxes and perform their military service. Yet the strength of provincial identities is significant. Their importance lay less in their subversive political potential than in the synergies that could develop between regional and national attachments. The folksy modern ideology of *Heimat* (homeland) blended seamlessly into cultural or ethnic concepts of a composite German nationhood, bypassing the imposed, supposedly inorganic structures of the Prussian state.[163] Prussia, as an identity, was thus eroded simultaneously from above (by nationalism) and below (by the regionalist revival). Only in the Mark Brandenburg (and to a lesser extent in Pomerania) did a regionalist identity evolve that fed directly into an allegiance to Prussia and its German mission (though not necessarily to Berlin, which some saw as an alien urban growth on the agrarian landscape of the Mark).

Yet even here, as the example of Fontane suggests, the rediscovery of the province and its claims on the sentiments of its inhabitants could entail a turning away from Prussia. Fontane, often regarded as an apologist for 'Prussiandom', was in fact deeply ambivalent towards the Prussian state and could on occasion be fiercely critical.[164] 'Prussia was a lie,' he declared in the opening sentence of a scathing essay he published during the revolutions of 1848. 'The Prussia of today has no history.'[165] Fontane was among those who argued – not only in 1848 but also after the foundation of the Second Empire in 1871 – that the unification of Germany must necessarily bring about the demise of Prussia.[166] It went without saying that the Brandenburg whose particular history and character he had so painstakingly documented would survive the demolition of the monarchical state that had sprung up on its soil.

The strength of provincial attachments and the corresponding feebleness of Prussia as a locus of collective identity has remained one of the most striking features of the state's afterlife since 1947. It is remarkable, for example, how inconspicuous Prussia has been in the official rhetoric of the organizations formed in West Germany after the Second World War to represent the interests of the 10 million expellees who were forced to leave the East-Elbian provinces at the end of the Second World War. The refugees defined themselves, by and large, not as Prussians, but as East Prussians, Upper or Lower Silesians, Pomeranians; there were also organizations representing the Masurians from the Polish-speaking southern districts of East Prussia, the Salzburgers of Prussian Lithuania (descendants of the communities of Protestant refugees from Salzburg who were resettled to the Prussian east in the early 1730s) and various other sub-regional groups. But there has been little evidence of a shared 'Prussian' identity and surprisingly little collaboration and exchange between the different groups. In this sense the expellee movement has tended to reflect the composite, highly regionalized character of the old Prussian state.

To be sure, Prussia was the subject of great public interest in both the post-war Germanies. The official historians of the German Democratic Republic (GDR) soon abandoned the leftist anti-Prussianism of the older Communist cadres and adopted the military reformers of the Napoleonic era as the fathers of the new paramilitary People's Police founded in 1952. In 1953, the authorities used the occasion of the 140th anniversary of the wars against Napoleon to launch a propaganda campaign in which the events of 1813 were reframed to serve the interests of the Communist polity. The theme of 'Russo-German friendship' naturally loomed large and 1813 now figured as a 'people's uprising' against tyranny and monarchy.[167] The creation of the prestigious Order of Scharnhorst in 1966 for operatives of the National People's Army, television serials on Scharnhorst and Clausewitz in the late 1970s, the appearance of Ingrid Mittenzwei's pathbreaking bestseller *Frederick II of Prussia* in 1979 and the relocation of Christian Daniel Rauch's splendid equestrian statue of the king to a prominent position on Unter den Linden were just some of the milestones in the evolution of an increasingly sympathetic and differentiated approach to the history of the Prussian state. The aim – at least of the state authorities – was to deepen the public identity of the GDR by annexing to it a version of the history and traditions of Prussia. It was partly in answer to these developments that the authorities in West Berlin and their backers in the Federal Republic supported the immense Prussia exhibition that opened in West Berlin's Gropius Building in 1981. And yet, for all the controversy and genuine public interest on both sides of the German–German border, these remained top-down initiatives, driven by the imperatives of 'political education' and 'social paedagogy'. They were about the identities of states, not of the people who live in them.

But while the emotional resonance of Prussia has faded, attachments to Brandenburg remain strong. After 1945, the GDR authorities made a concerted effort to erase the regional identities that pre-existed the socialist state. The five *Länder* in the eastern zone (including Brandenburg) were abolished in 1952 and replaced with fourteen completely new 'districts' (*Bezirke*). The aim was not merely to expedite the centralization of the East German administration, but also 'to create new popular allegiances', to supersede the traditional regional identifications with 'new, socialist identities'.[168] Yet the extirpation of regional identities proved extraordinarily difficult. Regional fairs, music, cuisine and literary cultures flourished, despite the ambivalence and intermittent hostility of the central administration. Official efforts to encourage emotional attachments to the newly minted 'socialist homelands' of the 1952 districts generated only superficial acknowledgement from the majority of East Germans.

How hardy the traditional affiliations were became clear in 1990, when the districts were abandoned and the old *Länder* reinstated. The county of Perleberg in the Prignitz to the north-east of Berlin had been part of the Mark Brandenburg since the fourteenth century. In 1952, it was enlarged to encompass three Mecklenburg villages and incorporated into the district of Schwerin (a name traditionally associated not with Brandenburg, but with its northern neighbour, the Duchy of Mecklenburg-Schwerin). In 1990, after forty years in Mecklenburg exile, the people of the county of Perleberg took the opportunity to assert their attachment to Brandenburg. Seventy-eight point five per cent of Perleberg voters opted to return and the county was duly transferred to Brandenburg administration. This caused consternation, however, among the inhabitants of the Mecklenburg villages that had been merged into Perleberg county in 1952. The men and women of Dambeck and Brunow loudly demanded a retransfer to their ancestral Mecklenburg. Late in 1991, after protests and negotiations, their wish was granted. Now everybody was happy. Everybody, that is, except the people of Klüss, population *c.* 150, whose village was officially attached to Brunow but actually lay right on the old border with Brandenburg. Since the eighteenth century, Klüss had depended for its livelihood upon cross-border transactions (including a lucrative smuggling trade), and its residents were reluctant to cut their traditional ties with the Mark.[169]

In the end, there was only Brandenburg.

Notes

Introduction

1. Control Council Law No. 46, 25 February 1947, *Official Gazette of the Control Council for Germany*, No. 14, Berlin, 31 March 1947.
2. Speech to Parliament, 21 September 1943, Winston S. Churchill, *The Second World War*, vol. 5, *Closing the Ring* (6 vols., London, 1952), p. 491.
3. Ludwig Dehio, *Gleichgewicht oder Hegemonie. Betrachtungen über ein Grundproblem der neueren Staatengeschichte* (Krefeld, 1948), p. 223; id., 'Der Zusammenhang der preussisch-deutschen Geschichte, 1640–1945', in Karl Forster (ed.), *Gibt es ein deutsches Geschichtsbild?* (Würzburg, 1961), pp. 65–90, here p. 83. On Dehio and the debate over Prussian-German continuity, see Thomas Beckers, *Abkehr von Preussen. Ludwig Dehio und die deutsche Geschichtswissenschaft nach 1945* (Aichach, 2001), esp. pp. 51–9; Stefan Berger, *The Search for Normality. National Identity and Historical Consciousness in Germany since 1800* (Providence, RI and Oxford, 1997), pp. 56–71; Jürgen Mirow, *Das alte Preussen im deutschen Geschichtsbild seit der Reichsgründung* (Berlin, 1981), pp. 255–60.
4. On the critical school in general, see Berger, *Search for Normality*, pp. 65–71. On the German *Sonderweg*: Jürgen Kocka, 'German History before Hitler: The Debate about the German *Sonderweg*', *Journal of Contemporary History*, 23 (1988), pp. 3–16. For a critical view: David Blackbourn and Geoff Eley, *The Peculiarities of German History. Bourgeois Society and Politics in Nineteenth-century Germany* (Oxford, 1984). For a recent discussion of the case for Prussian peculiarity, see Hartwin Spenkuch, 'Vergleichsweise besonders? Politisches System und Strukturen Preussens als Kern des "deutschen Sonderwegs"', *Geschichte und Gesellschaft*, 29 (2003), pp. 262–93.
5. For examples of this literature, see Hans-Joachim Schoeps, *Preussen. Geschichte eines Staates* (Frankfurt/Berlin, 1966; repr. 1981); Sebastian Haffner, *Preussen ohne Legende* (Hamburg, 1978); Gerd Heinrich, *Geschichte Preussens. Staat und Dynastie* (Frankfurt, 1981). Commenting on this tendency: Ingrid Mittenzwei, 'Die zwei Gesichter Preussens' in *Forum 19* (1978); repr. in *Deutschland-Archiv*, 16 (1983), pp. 214–18; Hans-Ulrich Wehler, *Preussen ist wieder chic. Politik und Polemik in zwanzig Essays* (Frankfurt/Main, 1983), esp. ch. 1; Otto Büsch (ed.), *Das Preussenbild in der Geschichte. Protokoll eines Symposions* (Berlin, 1981).
6. See especially (with literature) Manfred Schlenke, 'Von der Schwierigkeit, Preussen auszustellen. Rückschau auf die Preussen-Ausstellung, Berlin 1981', in id. (ed.), *Preussen. Politik, Kultur, Gesellschaft* (2 vols., Hamburg, 1986), vol. 1, pp. 12–34. On the debate triggered by the exhibition, see Barbara Vogel, 'Bemerkungen zur Aktualität der preussischen Geschichte', *Archiv für Sozialgeschichte*, 25 (1985), pp. 467–507; T. C. W. Blanning, 'The Death and Transfiguration of Prussia', *Historical Journal*, 29 (1986), pp. 433–59.
7. The organizational hub of the present-day conservative Prussophiles is the Preussische Gesellschaft. The society publishes a journal (*Preussische Nachrichten von Staats- und*

Gelehrten-Sachen), for which it claims a readership of 10,000; its website can be consulted at *http://www.preussen.org/page/frame.html*. The society's following spans a wide range of right-of-centre positions, from authoritarian neo-liberals to Prussian federal autonomists, ultra-conservative monarchists and right-wing extremists.

8. The remains of Frederick the Great had been transferred to Hohenzollern-Hechingen towards the end of the Second World War to prevent their disinterment by the approaching Russians. They were repatriated in 1991 in conformity with the king's testament, which had stipulated that he should be buried with his greyhounds on one of the terraces of Sans Souci. The presence of the then Chancellor Helmut Kohl at the re-interment ceremony was particularly controversial. On the city palace initiatives, see 'Wir brauchen zentrale Akteure', *Süddeutsche Zeitung*, 10 January 2002, p. 17; Peter Conradi, 'Das Neue darf nicht verboten werden', *Süddeutsche Zeitung*, 8 March 2002, p. 13; Joseph Paul Kleihues, 'Respekt vor dem Kollegen Schlüter', *Die Welt*, 30 January 2002, p. 20. For details of the campaign to restore the palace, see *http://www.berliner-stadtschloss.de/index1.htm* and *http://www.stadtschloss-berlin.de/*.

9. Hans-Ulrich Wehler, 'Preussen vergiftet uns. Ein Glück, dass es vorbei ist!', *Frankfurter Allgemeine Zeitung*, 23 February 2002, p. 41; cf. Tilman Mayer, 'Ja zur Renaissance'. Was Preussen aus sich machen kann', *Frankfurter Allgemeine Zeitung*, 27 February 2002, p. 49; see also Florian Giese, 'Preussens Sendung und Gysis Mission' in *Die Zeit*, September 2002, accessed online at *http://www.zeit.de/archiv/2002/09/200209 preussen.xml*.

10. See, for example, Linda Colley, *Britons. Forging the Nation* (New Haven, CT, 1992) and, more generally, James C. Scott, *Seeing Like a State. How Certain Schemes to Improve the Human Condition Have Failed* (New Haven, CT, 1998), esp. pp. 11, 76–83, 183. On the debate over the 'constructed' character of nationalism, see Oliver Zimmer and Len Scales (eds.), *Power and the Nation in European History* (Cambridge, 2005).

11. Voltaire to Nicolas Claude Theriot, au Chêne, 26 October [1757], in Theodor Bestermann (ed.), *Voltaire's Correspondence*, trans. Julius R. Ruff (51 vols., Geneva, 1958), vol. 32, p. 135.

1 The Hohenzollerns of Brandenburg

1. 'Regio est plana, nemorosa tamen, & ut plurimus paludosa . . .', Nicolaus Leuthinger, *Topographia prior Marchiae regionumque vicinarum . . .* (Frankfurt/Oder, 1598), reprinted in J. G. Kraus (ed.), *Scriptorum de rebus marchiae brandenburgensis maxime celebrium . . .* (Frankfurt, 1729), p. 117. For other examples, see Zacharias Garcaeus, *Successiones familiarum et Res gestae illustrissimum praesidium Marchiae Brandenburgensis ab anno DCCCCXXVII ad annum MDLXXXII*, reprinted in ibid., pp. 6–7.

2. William Howitt, *The Rural and Domestic Life of Germany* (London, 1842), p. 429.

3. Tom Scott, *Society and Economy in Germany, 1300–1600* (London, 2002), pp. 24, 119.

4. Dirk Redies, 'Zur Geschichte des Eisenhüttenwerkes Peitz', in Museumsverband des Landes Brandenburg (ed.), *Ortstermine. Stationen Brandenburg-Preussens auf dem Weg in die moderne Welt* (Berlin, 2001), Part 2, pp. 4–16.

5. F. W. A. Bratring, *Statistisch-Topographische Beschreibung der gesamten Mark Brandenburg* (Berlin, 1804), repr. edn by Otto Büsch and Gerd Heinrich (2 vols., Berlin, 1968), vol. 1, pp. 28, 30, vol. 2, p. 1108. Bratring gives figures, but these derive from a later period when improvements had been made to many parts of the Mark and are in any case of dubious accuracy.

6. William W. Hagen, *Ordinary Prussians. Brandenburg Junkers and Villagers, 1500–1840* (Cambridge, 2002), p. 44.

7. On the 'holiness' of the 'Reich', see Hans Hattenhauer, 'Über die Heiligkeit des Heiligen Römischen Reiches', in Wilhelm Brauneder (ed.), *Heiliges Römisches Reich und moderne Staatlichkeit* (Frankfurt/Main, 1993), pp. 125–46. On the multivalence of the term, see Georg Schmidt, *Geschichte des alten Reiches, Staat und Nation in der frühen Neuzeit 1495–1806* (Munich, 1999), p. 10.

8. Only in the years 1742–5, under exceptional circumstances, did the imperial title pass to a member of the Bavarian Wittelsbach dynasty.

9. On dynastic partitions, see Paula Sutter Fichtner, *Protestantism and Primogeniture in Early Modern Germany* (New Haven, CT, 1989), esp. pp. 4–21; Geoffrey Parker, *The Thirty Years' War* (London, 1984), p. 15.

10. Elizabeth's dramatic departure had less to do with the fear of religious persecution than with the extramarital liaisons for which Luther had reproached Joachim I in a series of published open letters. Manfred Rudersdorf and Anton Schindling, 'Kurbrandenburg', in Anton Schindling and Walter Ziegler (eds.), *Die Territorien des Reiches im Zeitalter der Reformation und Konfessionalisierung. Land und Konfession 1500–1650* (6 vols., Münster, 1990), vol. 2, *Der Nordosten*, pp. 34–67, here p. 40.

11. Axel Gotthard, 'Zwischen Luthertum und Calvinismus (1598–1640)', in Frank-Lothar Kroll (ed.), *Preussens Herrscher. Von den ersten Hohenzollern bis Wilhelm II* (Munich, 2000), pp. 74–94, here p. 75; Otto Hintze, *Die Hohenzollern und ihr Werk. Fünfhundert Jahre Vaterländischer Geschichte* (7th edn, Berlin, 1916), p. 153.

12. Walter Mehring, *Die Geschichte Preussens* (Berlin, 1981), p. 37.

13. For a discussion of the inheritance law involved in this claim, see Heinz Ollmann-Kösling, *Der Erbfolgestreit um Jülich-Kleve (1609–1614). Ein Vorspiel zum Dreissigjährigen Krieg* (Regensburg, 1996), pp. 52–4.

14. For an overview with literature, see Rudolf Endres, *Adel in der frühen Neuzeit* (Munich, 1993), esp. pp. 23–30, 83–92.

15. Peter-Michael Hahn, 'Landesstaat und Ständetum im Kurfürstentum Brandenburg während des 16. und 17. Jahrhunderts', in Peter Baumgart (ed.), *Ständetum und Staatsbildung in Brandenburg-Preussen. Ergebnisse einer international Fachtagung* (Berlin, 1983), pp. 41–79, here p. 42.

16. This account is based on the text of the Geheimratsordnung of 13 December 1604, transcribed in Siegfried Isaacsohn, *Geschichte des preussischen Beamtenthums vom Anfang des 15. Jahrhunderts bis auf die Gegenwart* (3 vols., Berlin, 1874–84), vol. 2, pp. 24–8.

17. Ibid., p. 28; Johannes Schultze, *Die Mark Brandenburg* (4 vols., Berlin, 1961–69), vol. 4, p. 188; Hintze, *Die Hohenzollern*, pp. 154–5.

18. Gotthard, 'Zwischen Luthertum und Calvinismus', in Kroll (ed.), *Preussens Herrscher*, pp. 85–7; Schultze, *Die Mark Brandenburg*, vol. 4, pp. 176–9.

19. Hintze, *Die Hohenzollern*, p. 162. Alison D. Anderson, *On the Verge of War. International Relations and the Jülich-Kleve Succession Crisis (1609–1614)* (Boston, 1999), pp. 18–40.

20. Parker, *Thirty Years' War*, pp. 28–37; Schultze, *Die Mark Brandenburg*, vol. 4, p. 185.

21. Gotthard, 'Zwischen Luthertum und Calvinismus', p. 84.

22. Friedrich Schiller, *The History of the Thirty Years War in Germany*, trans. Capt. Blacquiere (2 vols., London, 1799), vol. 1, p. 93.

23. Cited in Gotthard, 'Zwischen Luthertum und Calvinismus', p. 84.

2 Devastation

1. There is a vast literature in English on the genesis and course of the Thirty Years War. Geoffrey Parker, *The Thirty Years' War* (London, 1988) remains the standard general account; Ronald G. Asch, *The Thirty Years War: The Holy Roman Empire and Europe, 1618–1648* (London, 1997) provides a useful recent introduction to the issues; a general history is currently in preparation by Peter H. Wilson. Sigfrid Henry Steinberg, *The 'Thirty Years War' and the Conflict for European Hegemony, 1600–1660* (London, 1966) and Georges Pagès, *The Thirty Years War, 1618–1648*, trans. David Maland and John Hooper (London, 1970) are older works that stress the primacy of European over infra-German confessional issues.

2. Frederick II, *Mémoires pour servir à l'Histoire de la Maison de Brandebourg* (2 vols., London, 1767), vol. 1, p. 51.

3. From notes recorded by Count Adam von Schwarzenberg, cited in J. W. C. Cosmar, *Beiträge zur Untersuchung der gegen den Kurbrandenburgischen Geheimen Rath Grafen Adam zu Schwarzenberg erhobenen Beschuldigungen. Zur Berichtigung der Geschichte unserer Kurfürsten Georg Wilhelm und Friedrich Wilhelm* (Berlin, 1828), p. 48.

4. Count Schwarzenberg to Chancellor Pruckmann, 22 July 1626, reporting remarks by the Elector, cited in Johann Gustav Droysen, *Geschichte der preussischen Politik* (14 vols., Berlin, 1855–6), vol. 3, part I, *Der Staat des Grossen Kurfürsten*, p. 41; Cosmar, *Beiträge*, p. 50.

5. Catholic possessions were calculated according to the status quo at the time of the Peace of Passau (1552). For an English translation of the Edict of Restitution, see E. Reich (ed.), *Select Documents* (London, 1905), pp. 234–5.

6. On Swedish objectives and involvement in the war, see Michael Roberts, *Gustavus Adolphus: A History of Sweden 1611–1632* (2 vols., London, 1953–8), vol. 1, pp. 220–28, vol. 2, pp. 619–73.

7. Cited in L. Hüttl, *Friedrich Wilhelm von Brandenburg, der Grosse Kurfürst* (Munich, 1981), p. 39.

8. Frederick II, *Mémoires*, p. 73.

9. W. Lahne, *Magdeburgs Zerstörung in der zeitgenössischen Publizistik* (Magdeburg, 1931), esp. pp. 7–24; 110–47.

10. Roberts, *Gustavus Adolphus*, vol. 2, pp. 508–13.

11. Hintze, *Die Hohenzollern*, p. 176.

12. Frederick II, *Mémoires*, p. 51; J. A. R. Marriott and C. Grant Robertson, *The Evolution of Prussia. The Making of an Empire* (Oxford, 1917), p. 74; Gotthard, 'Zwischen Luthertum und Calvinismus', pp. 87–94.

13. Droysen, *Der Staat des Grossen Kurfürsten*, p. 38.

14. Roberts, *Gustavus Adolphus*, vol. 1, pp. 174–81.

15. Droysen, *Der Staat des Grossen Kurfürsten*, p. 31.

16. Christoph Fürbringer, *Necessitas und Libertas. Staatsbildung und Landstände im 17. Jahrhundert in Brandenburg* (Frankfurt/Main, 1985), p. 34.

17. Hahn, 'Landesstaat und Ständetum', p. 59.

18. Droysen, *Der Staat des Grossen Kurfürsten*, p. 118.

19. Fürbringer, *Necessitas und Libertas*, p. 54.

20. Ibid., pp. 54–7.

21. Otto Meinardus (ed.), *Protokolle und Relationen des Brandenburgischen Geheimen Rates aus der Zeit des Kurfürsten Friedrich Wilhelm* (4 vols., Leipzig, 1889–1919), vol. 1 (= vol. 41 of the series *Publicationen aus den K. Preussischen Staatsarchiven*), p. xxxiv.

22. Ibid., p. xxxv; August von Haeften (ed.), *Ständische Verhandlungen*, vol. 1: Kleve-Mark (Berlin, 1869) (= vol. 5 of the series *Urkunden und Acktenstücke zur Geschichte des Kurfürsten Friedrich Wilhelm von Brandenburg*; henceforth UuA), pp. 58–82.

23. Fritz Schröer, *Das Havelland im dreissigjährigen Krieg. Ein Beitrag zur Geschichte der Mark Brandenburg* (Cologne, 1966), p. 32.

24. Ibid., p. 37.

25. Geoff Mortimer, *Eyewitness Accounts of the Thirty Years' War 1618–1648* (Houndmills, 2002), p. 12.

26. On contributions, see ibid., pp. 47–50, 89–92; Parker, *Thirty Years' War*, pp. 197, 204.

27. Schröer, *Havelland*, p. 48.

28. Ibid., p. 34.

29. B. Seiffert (ed.), 'Zum dreissigjährigen Krieg: Eigenhändige Aufzeichnungen von Stadtschreibern und Ratsherren der Stadt Strausberg', *Jahresbericht des Königlichen Wilhelm-Gymnasiums zu Krotoschin*, 48 (1902), Supplement, pp. 1–47, cited in Mortimer, *Eyewitness Accounts*, p. 91.

30. Herman von Petersdorff, 'Beiträge zur Wirtschafts- Steuer- und Heeresgeschichte der Mark im dreissig-Jährigen Kriege', *Forschungen zur Brandenburgischen und Preussischen Geschichte* (henceforth FBPG), 2 (1889), pp. 1–73, here pp. 70–73.

31. Robert Ergang, *The Myth of the All-Destructive Fury of the Thirty Years' War* (Pocono Pines, Pa, 1956); Steinberg, *The Thirty Years' War*, pp. 2–3, 91. Revisionist analysis: Ronald G. Asch, ' "Wo der Soldat hinkömbt, da ist alles sein": Military Violence and Atrocities in the Thirty Years War Re-examined', *German History*, 18 (2000), pp. 291–309.

32. Philip Vincent, *The Lamentations of Germany* (London, 1638).

33. On the relationship between narrative and experienced trauma in the Thirty Years War, see Bernd Roeck, 'Der dreissigjährige Krieg und die Menschen im Reich. Überlegungen zu den Formen psychischer Krisenbewältigung in der ersten Hälfte des siebzehnten Jahrhund-erts', in Bernhard R. Kroener and Ralf Pröve (eds.), *Krieg und Frieden. Militär und Gesellschaft in der frühen Neuzeit* (Paderborn, 1996), pp. 265–79; Geoffrey Mortimer, 'Individual Experience and Perception of the Thirty Years War in Eyewitness Personal Accounts', *German History*, 20 (2002), pp. 141–60.

34. Report of the outdwellers (*Kiezer*) of Plaue, 12 January 1639, cited in Schröer, *Havelland*, p. 94.

35. B. Elsler (ed.), *Peter Thiele's Aufzeichnung von den Schicksalen der Stadt Beelitz im Dreissigjährigen Kriege* (Beelitz, 1931), p. 12.

36. Ibid., p. 13.

37. Ibid., pp. 12, 15.

38. Georg Grüneberg, *Die Prignitz und ihre städtische Bevölkerung im 17. Jahrhundert* (Lenzen, 1999), pp. 75–6.

39. Meinardus (ed.), *Protokolle und Relationen*, vol. 1, p. 13.

40. Address by Schwarzenberg to various commanders of the Brandenburg regiments, Cölln, 22 February/1 March 1639, cited in Otto Meinardus, 'Schwarzenberg und die brandenbur-gische Kriegführung in den Jahren 1638–1640', *FBPG*, 12/2 (1899), pp. 87–139, here pp. 127–8.

41. Meinardus (ed.), *Protokolle und Relationen*, vol. 1, p. 181, doc. no. 203, 12 March 1641.

42. Mortimer, *Eyewitness Accounts*, pp. 45–58, 174–8.

43. M. S. Anderson, *War and Society in Europe of the Old Regime 1618–1789* (Phoenix Mill, 1998), pp. 64–6.

44. Werner Vogel (ed.), *Prignitz-Kataster 1686–1687* (Cologne, Vienna, 1985), p. 1. The standard work on mortalities is still Günther Franz, *Der dreissigjährige Krieg und das deutsche Volk* (3rd edn, Stuttgart, 1961), pp. 17–21. Franz occupies a complex position in the historiography, mainly because of his outspoken adherence to the National Socialist regime. The traces of this commitment can still be discerned – despite some careful editing of the more egregious passages – in the post-war editions of his work. In the 1960s, Franz's calculations were vehemently rejected by Saul Steinberg, who argued that they were based on reports that exaggerated mortalities or vacancies in order to evade taxation. Steinberg came to the provocative – and bizarre – conclusion that 'in 1648, Germany was neither better nor worse off than in 1609' (Steinberg, *The Thirty Years War*, p. 3); this view was taken up by Hans-Ulrich Wehler in p. 54 of the first volume of his *Deutsche Gesellschaftsge-schichte* (5 vols., Munich, 1987–2003). However, recent studies have tended to endorse Franz's findings. The sources are especially full and reliable for Brandenburg. See J. C. Thiebault, 'The Demography of the Thirty Years War Revisited: Günther Franz and his Critics', *German History*, 15 (1997), pp. 1–21.

45. Lieselott Enders, *Die Uckermark. Geschichte einer kurmärkischen Landschaft vom 12. bis zum 18. Jahrhundert* (Weimar, 1992), p. 527.

46. See, for example, A. Kuhn, 'Über das Verhältniss Märkischer Sagen und Gebräuche zur altdeutschen Mythologie', *Märkische Forschungen*, 1 (1841), pp. 115–46.

47. Samuel Pufendorf, *Elements of Universal Jurisprudence in Two Books* (1660), Book 2, Observation 5, in Craig L. Carr (ed.), *The Political Writings of Samuel Pufendorf*, trans. Michael J. Seidler (New York, 1994), p. 87.

48. Samuel Pufendorf, *On the Law of Nature and Nations in Eight Books* (1672), Book 7, ch. 4, in ibid., p. 220.

49. Ibid., p. 221.

50. Samuel Pufendorf, *De rebus gestis Friderici Wilhelmi Magni Electoris Brandenburgici commentatiorum*, book XIX (Berlin, 1695).

51. Johann Gustav Droysen, 'Zur Kritik Pufendorfs', in id., *Abhandlungen zur neueren Geschichte* (Leipzig, 1876), pp. 309–86, here p. 314.

3 An Extraordinary Light in Germany

1. Ferdinand Hirsch, 'Die Armee des Grossen Kürfürsten und ihre Unterhaltung während der Jahre 1660–1666', *Historische Zeitschrift*, 17 (1885), pp. 229–75.

2. Helmut Börsch-Supan, 'Zeitgenössische Bildnisse des Grossen Kurfürsten', in Gerd Heinrich (ed.), *Ein Sonderbares Licht in Teutschland. Beiträge zur Geschichte des Grossen Kurfürsten von Brandenburg (1640–1688)* (Berlin, 1990), pp. 151–66.

3. Otto Meinardus, 'Beiträge zur Geschichte des Grossen Kurfürsten', *FBPG*, 16/2 (1903), pp. 173–99, here p. 176.

4. On the influence of neo-stoicism on the political thought and action of Elector Frederick William and of early modern sovereigns more generally, see esp. Gerhard Oestreich, *Neostoicism and the Early Modern State*, ed. B. Oestreich and H. G. Koenigsberger, trans. D. McLintock (Cambridge, 1982).

5. Derek McKay, *The Great Elector, Frederick William of Brandenburg-Prussia* (Harlow, 2001), pp. 170–71.

6. Cited from an edict of 1686 in Martin Philippson, *Der Grosse Kurfürst Friedrich Wilhelm von Brandenburg* (3 vols., Berlin, 1897–1903), vol. 3, p. 91.

7. On the naval and colonial plans of the Elector, see Ernst Opgenoorth, *Friedrich Wilhelm der Grosse Kurfürst von Brandenburg* (2 vols., Göttingen, 1971–8), vol. 2, pp. 305–11; E. Schmitt, 'The Brandenburg Overseas Trading Companies in the 17th Century', in Leonard Blussé and Femme Gaastra (eds.), *Companies and Trade. Essays on European Trading Companies During the Ancien Regime* (Leiden, 1981), pp. 159–76; Hüttl, *Friedrich Wilhelm*, pp. 445–6; Heinz Duchhardt, 'Afrika und die deutschen Kolonialprojekte der 2. Hälfte des 17. Jahrhunderts', *Archiv für Kulturgeschichte*, 68 (1986), pp. 119–33; a useful historiographical discussion is Klaus-Jürgen Matz, 'Das Kolonialexperiment des Grossen Kurfürsten in der Geschichtsschreibung des 19. und 20. Jahrhunderts', in Heinrich (ed.), *Ein Sonderbares Licht*, pp. 191–202.

8. Albert Waddington, *Le Grand Électeur Frédéric Guillaume de Brandenbourg: sa politique extérieure, 1640–1688* (2 vols., Paris, 1905–8), vol. 1, p. 43; comments by Götze and Leuchtmar, Stettin, 23 April 1643, in Bernhard Erdmannsdörffer (ed.), *Politische Verhandlungen*, (4 vols., Berlin, 1864–84), vol. 1 (= UuA, vol. 1), pp. 596–7.

9. Lisola to Walderode, Berlin, 30 November 1663, in Alfred Pribram (ed.), *Urkunden und Aktenstücke zur Geschichte des Kurfürsten Friedrich Wilhelm von Brandenburg*, vol. 14 (Berlin, 1890), pp. 171–2.

10. Hermann von Petersdorff, *Der Grosse Kurfürst* (Gotha, 1926), p. 40.

11. McKay, *Great Elector*, p. 21; Philippson, *Der Grosse Kurfürst*, vol. 1, pp. 41–2.

12. Margrave Ernest to Frederick William, Cölln, 18 May 1641, in Erdmannsdörffer (ed.), *Politische Verhandlungen*, vol. 1, pp. 451–2.

13. Privy councillors to Frederick William, 6 September 1642 and report on the Margrave's death by Dr Johannes Magirius, 26 September 1642, in Erdmannsdörffer (ed.), *Politische Verhandlungen*, vol. 1, pp. 499–502, 503–5.

14. Alexandra Richie, *Faust's Metropolis. A History of Berlin* (London, 1998), pp. 44–5.

15. Philippson, *Der Grosse Kurfürst*, vol. 1, pp. 56–8.

16. Hirsch, 'Die Armee des grossen Kurfürsten', pp. 229–75; Waddington, *Grand Électeur*, vol. 1, p. 89; McKay, *Great Elector*, pp. 173–5.

17. Curt Jany, 'Lehndienst und Landfolge unter dem Grossen Kurfürsten', *FBPG*, 8 (1895), pp. 419–67.

18. For an analysis of the battle (with diagrams), see Robert I. Frost, *The Northern Wars 1558–1721* (Harlow, 2000), pp. 173–6.

19. Frederick William to Otto von Schwerin, Schweinfurt, 10 February 1675, in Ferdinand Hirsch (ed.), *Politische Verhandlungen* (Berlin 1864–1930) vol. 11 (= UuA, vol. 18), pp. 824–5; Jany, 'Lehndienst und Landfolge unter dem Grossen Kurfürsten', in FBPG, 10 (1898), pp. 1–30, here p. 7.

20. Droysen, *Der Staat des Grossen Kurfürsten*, p. 351.

21. *Diarium Europeaeum XXXII*, cited in Jany, 'Lehndienst und Landfolge', p. 7.

22. Pufendorf, *Rebus gestis*, Book VI, § 36–9; Leopold von Orlich, *Friedrich Wilhelm der Grosse Kurfürst. Nach bisher noch unbekannten Original-Handschriften* (Berlin, 1836), pp. 79–81; the Elector's account is reprinted in the Appendix, pp. 139–42.

23. Cited in Peter Burke, *The Fabrication of Louis XIV* (New Haven, CT, 1992), p. 152.

24. Frederick William, Political Testament of 1667 in Richard Dietrich (ed.), *Die politischen Testamente der Hohenzollern* (Cologne, 1986), pp. 179–204, here pp. 191–2.

25. Heinz Duchhardt and Bogdan Wachowiak, *Um die Soveränität des Herzogthums Preussen: Der Vertrag von Wehlau, 1657* (Hanover, 1998); for contemporary Polish perspectives on the treaty, see Barbara Szymczak, *Stosunki Rzeczypospolitej z Brandenburgią i Prusami Książęcymi w latach 1648–1658 w opinii i działaniach szlachty koronnej* (Warsaw, 2002), esp. pp. 229–58.

26. Comment to Louis XIV by the Austrian envoy in Paris, cited in Orlich, *Friedrich Wilhelm*, p. 158.

27. Cited from Count Raimondo Montecuccoli's *Treatise on War* (1680), in Johannes Kunisch, 'Kurfürst Friedrich Wilhelm und die Grossen Mächte' in Heinrich (ed.), *Ein Sonderbares Licht*, pp. 9–32, here pp. 30–31.

28. Memoir by Count Waldeck in Bernhard Erdmannsdörffer, *Graf Georg Friedrich von Waldeck. Ein preussischer Staatsmann im siebzehnten Jahrhundert* (Berlin, 1869), pp. 361–2, also pp. 354–5.

29. W. Troost, 'William III, Brandenburg, and the construction of the anti-French coalition, 1672–88', in Jonathan I. Israel, *The Anglo-Dutch Moment: Essay on the Glorious Revolution and Its World Impact* (Cambridge, 1991), pp. 299–334, here p. 322.

30. Philippson, *Der Grosse Kurfürst*, vol. 3, pp. 252–3.

31. Peter Baumgart, 'Der Grosse Kurfürst. Staatsdenken und Staatsarbeit eines europäischen Dynasten', in Heinrich (ed.), *Ein Sonderbares Licht*, pp. 33–57, here p. 45.

32. Dietrich (ed.), *Die politischen Testamente*, p. 191.

33. For an account of the oath ceremony on which the present description is based, see Bruno Gloger, *Friedrich Wilhelm, Kurfürst von Brandenburg. Biografie* (Berlin, 1985), pp. 152–4.

34. André Holenstein, *Die Huldigung der Untertanen. Rechtskultur und Herrschaftsordnung (800–1800)*, (Stuttgart and New York, 1991), pp. 512–3.

35. This interpretation of the raised fingers is widely documented for the German territories from the early fifteenth century, but the practice is far older; see ibid. pp. 57–8; an illustration in Gloger, *Friedrich Wilhelm* (p. 153) shows the deputies raising their hands in the traditional salute. The quotation is from the text of an oath sworn by the subjects of a rural lordship in the Brandenburg province of Prignitz, cited in Hagen, *Ordinary Prussians*, p. 79.

36. F. L. Carsten, *The Origins of the Junkers* (Aldershot, 1989), p. 17.

37. On the seventeenth-century crisis in governance generally, see Trevor Aston (ed.), *Crisis in Europe, 1560–1660* (New York, 1966); Geoffrey Parker and Lesley M. Smith, *The General Crisis of the Seventeenth Century* (London, 1978); Theodor K. Rabb, *The Struggle for Stability in Early Modern Europe* (New York, 1975).

38. Frederick William to supreme councillors of Ducal Prussia, Kleve, 18 September 1648, in Erdmannsdörffer (ed.), *Politische Verhandlungen*, vol. 1, pp. 281–2.

39. Fürbringer, *Necessitas und Libertas*, p. 59; for examples of this mode of argument, see supreme councillors of Ducal Prussia to Frederick William, Königsberg, 12 September 1648, in ibid., pp. 292–3.

40. Resolution of the Estates of the county of Mark, Emmerich, 22 March 1641 in Haeften (ed.), *Ständische Verhandlungen*, vol. 1; pp. 140–45, here p. 142.

41. See, for example, Frederick William to the Cities of Wesel, Calcar, Düsseldorf, Xanten and Rees, Küstrin, 15 May 1643, and Kleve Estates to Dutch Estates General, Kleve, 2 April 1647, in ibid., pp. 205, 331–4.

42. Helmuth Croon, *Stände und Steuern in Jülich-Berg im 17. und vornehmlich im 18. Jahrhundert* (Bonn, 1929), p. 250; examples: Estates of county of Mark to protesting Estates of Kleve, Unna, 10 August 1641; Estates of Mark to Estates of Kleve, Unna, 10 December 1650, in Haeften (ed.), *Ständische Verhandlungen*, vol. 1, pp. 182, 450.

43. Comment by the viceroy of Ducal Prussia, Prince Boguslav Radziwill, cited in McKay, *Great Elector*, p. 135.

44. Comments by the Estates, Königsberg, 24 April 1655, in Kurt Breysig (ed.), *Ständische Verhandlungen* (Berlin, 1894–9), vol. 3: *Preussen*, Part 1 (= UuA, vol. 15), p. 354. On these questions in Ducal Prussia, see Stefan Hartmann, 'Gefährdetes Erbe. Landesdefension und Landesverwaltung in Ostpreussen zur Zeit des Grossen Kurfürsten Friedrich Wilhelm von Brandenburg (1640–1688)', in Heinrich (ed.), *Ein Sonderbares Licht*, pp. 113–36; Hugo Rachel, *Der Grosse Kurfürst und die Ostpreussischen Stände (1640–1688)* (Leipzig, 1905), pp. 299–304.

45. E. Arnold Miller, 'Some Arguments Used by English Pamphleteers, 1697–1700, Concerning a Standing Army', *Journal of Modern History* (henceforth *JMH*) (1946), pp. 306–13, here pp. 309–10; Lois G. Schwoerer, 'The Role of King William III in the Standing Army Controversy – 1697–1699', *Journal of British Studies* (1966), pp. 74–94.

46. David Hayton, 'Moral Reform and Country Politics in the Late Seventeenth-century House of Commons', *Past & Present*, 128 (1990), pp. 48–91, here p. 48.

47. Anon, pamphlet of 1675 entitled 'Letter from a Person of Quality', cited in J. G. A. Pocock, 'Machiavelli, Harrington and English Political Ideologies in the Eighteenth Century', *William and Mary Quarterly*, 22/4 (1965), pp. 549–84, here p. 560.

48. Fürbringer, *Necessitas und Libertas*, p. 60.

49. F. L. Carsten, *Die Entstehung Preussens* (Cologne, 1968), pp. 209–12; Kunisch, 'Kurfürst Friedrich Wilhelm', in Heinrich (ed.), *Ein Sonderbares Licht*, pp. 9–32, here pp. 21–2.

50. Reply of the privy councillors on behalf of the Elector, Cölln [Berlin], 2 December 1650, in Siegfried Isaacsohn (ed.), *Ständische Verhandlungen*, vol. 2 (= UuA, vol. 10) (Berlin, 1880), pp. 193–4.

51. Patent of Contradiction by the Estates of Kleve, Jülich, Berg and Mark, Wesel, 14 July 1651; Union of the Estates of Kleve and Mark, Wesel, 8 August 1651, in Haeften (ed.), *Ständische Verhandlungen*, vol. 1, pp. 509, 525–6. F. L. Carsten, 'The Resistance of Cleves and Mark to the Despotic Policy of the Great Elector', *English Historical Review*, 66 (1951), pp. 219–41, here p. 224; McKay, *Great Elector*, p. 34; Waddington, *Grand Électeur*, vol. 1, pp. 68–9.

52. Karl Spannagel, *Konrad von Burgsdorff. Ein brandenburgischer Kriegs- und Staatsmann aus der Zeit der Kurfürsten Georg Wilhelm und Friedrich Wilhelm* (Berlin, 1903), pp. 265–7.

53. For Kleve taxation figures see Sidney B. Fay, 'The Beginnings of the Standing Army in Prussia', *American Historical Review*, 22 (1916/17), pp. 763–77, here p. 772; McKay, *Great Elector*, p. 132. Report from Johann Moritz: Carsten, 'Resistance of Cleves and Mark', p. 235. On the impact of the Northern wars on conditions in Kleve, see Haeften (ed.), *Ständische Verhandlungen*, vol. 1, pp. 773–93. On the arrest of activists, see Frederick William to Jacob von Spaen, Cölln an der Spree, 3 July 1654, in ibid., pp. 733–4; Carsten, 'Resistance of Cleves and Mark', p. 231.

54. McKay, *Great Elector*, p. 62; Volker Press, 'Vom Ständestaat zum Absolutismus: 50 Thesen zur Entwicklung des Ständewesens in Deutschland', in Baumgart (ed.), *Ständetum und Staatsbildung*, pp. 280–336, here p. 324.

55. Fay, 'Standing Army', p. 772.

56. McKay, *Great Elector*, pp. 136–7; Philippson, *Der Grosse Kurfürst*, vol. 2, p. 165; Otto Nugel, 'Der Schoppenmeister Hieronymus Roth', *FBPG*, 14/2 (1901), pp. 19–105, here p. 32.

57. Roth and Schwerin produced radically divergent accounts of what transpired during the meeting; see Otto von Schwerin to Viceroy and Supreme Councillors of Prussia, Bartenstein, 21 October 1661 and Private Circular of the Alderman Roth [early November 1661], in Kurt Breysig (ed.), *Ständische Verhandlungen, Preussen*, pp. 595, 611, 614–19. For a detailed narrative, see Nugel, 'Hieronymus Roth', pp. 40–44; Andrzej Kamieński, *Polska a Brandenburgia-Prusy w drugiej połowie XVII wieku. Dzieje polityczne* (Poznan, 2002), esp. pp. 61–4. For an account much less sympathetic to Roth, see Droysen, *Der Staat des Grossen Kurfürsten*, vol. 2, pp. 402–3.

58. Cited in Nugel, 'Hieronymus Roth', p. 100.

59. The execution was of Christian Ludwig von Kalckstein, who had served in the Polish army and been exiled to his estates in 1668 for plotting the Elector's assassination. On the Kalckstein affair, see Josef Paczkowski, 'Der Grosse Kurfürst und Christian Ludwig von Kalckstein', *FBPG*, 2 (1889), pp. 407–513 and 3 (1890), pp. 419–63; Petersdorff, *Der Grosse Kurfürst* (Gotha, 1926), pp. 113–16; Droysen, *Der Staat des Grossen Kurfürsten*, vol. 3, pp. 191–212; Opgenoorth, *Friedrich Wilhelm*, vol. 2, pp. 115–18; Kamieński, *Polska a Brandenburgia-Prusy*, pp. 65–71, 177–9.

60. Thus the complaint of a local official cited in McKay, *Great Elector*, p. 144.

61. Dietrich (ed.), *Die politischen Testamente*, p. 185; Erdmannsdörffer, *Waldeck*, p. 45; Rachel, *Der Grosse Kurfürst*, pp. 59–62; Peter Bahl, *Der Hof des Grossen Kirfürsten. Studien zur höheren Amtsträgerschaft Brandenburg-Preussens* (Cologne, 2001), pp. 196–217.

62. McKay, *Great Elector*, p. 114. On the decline in noble financial power and influence, see Frank Göse, *Ritterschaft – Garnison – Residenz. Studien zur Sozialstruktur und politischen Wirksamkeit des brandenburgischen Adels 1648–1763* (Berlin, 2005), pp. 133, 414, 421, 424.

63. On this distinction, applied to a very different German region, see Michaela Hohkamp, *Herrschaft in Herrschaft. Die vorderösterreichische Obervogtei Triberg von 1737 bis 1780* (Göttingen, 1988), esp. p. 15.

64. See, for example, Konrad von Burgsdorff to Privy Councillor Erasmus Seidel, Düsseldorf, 20 February 1647, in Erdmannsdörffer (ed.), *Politische Verhandlungen*, vol. 1, p. 300; Kleve Government to Frederick William, Kleve, 23 November 1650, in Haeften (ed.), *Ständische Verhandlungen*, vol. 1, pp. 440–41; Spannagel, *Burgsdorff*, pp. 257–60.

65. See, for example, Otto von Schwerin to Frederick William, Bartenstein, 30 November 1661, where Schwerin urges the Elector to drop the excise in the face of protest from the Estates, in Breysig (ed.), *Ständische Verhandlungen, Preussen*, pp. 667–9.

66. Protocols of the Privy Council, in Meinardus (ed.), *Protokolle und Relationen*. On traffic in complaints from the Estates see Hahn, 'Landesstaat und Ständetum', p. 52.

67. Peter-Michael Hahn, 'Aristokratisierung und Professionalisierung. Der Aufstieg der Obristen zu einer militärischen und höfischen Elite in Brandenburg-Preussen von 1650–1725', in *FBPG*, 1 (1991), pp. 161–208.

68. Cited in Otto Hötzsch, *Stände und Verwaltung von Kleve und Mark in der Zeit von 1666 bis 1697 (=Urkunden und Aktenstücke zur inneren Politik des Kurfürsten Friedrich Wilhelm von Brandenburg*, Part 2) (Leipzig, 1908), p. 740.

69. See Peter Baumgart, 'Wie absolut war der preussische Absolutismus?', in Manfred Schlenke (ed.), *Preussen. Beiträge zu einer politischen Kultur* (Reinbek, 1981), pp. 103–19.

70. Otto Hötzsch, 'Fürst Moritz von Nassau-Siegen als brandenburgischer Staatsmann (1647 bis 1679)', *FBPG*, 19 (1906), pp. 89–114, here pp. 95–6, 101–2; see also Ernst Opgenoorth, 'Johan Maurits as the Stadtholder of Cleves under the Elector of Brandenburg' in E. van den Boogaart (ed.), *Johan Maurits van Nassau-Siegen, 1604–1679: A Humanist Prince in Europe and Brazil. Essays on the Tercentenary of his Death* (The Hague, 1979), pp. 39–53, here p. 53. On Soest, see Ralf Günther, 'Städtische Autonomie und fürstliche Herrschaft. Politik und Verfassung im frühneuzeitlichen Soest', in Ellen Widder (ed.), *Soest. Geschichte der Stadt. Zwischen Bürgerstolz und Fürstenstaat. Soest in der frühen Neuzeit* (Soest, 1995), pp. 17–123, here pp. 66–71.

71. King Frederick William I attempted to overrule this arrangement but the local election of *Landräte* was restored under Friedrich II; see Baumgart, 'Wie absolut war der preussische Absolutismus?', p. 112.
72. McKay, *Great Elector*, p. 261.
73. This is reported by the British envoy Stepney to Secretary Vernon, Berlin, 19/29 July 1698, PRO SP 90/1, fo. 32.
74. Dietrich (ed.), *Die politischen Testamente*, p. 189.
75. Ibid., p. 190.
76. Ibid., pp. 190, 191.
77. Ibid., p. 187.
78. Ibid., p. 188.
79. Cited in McKay, *The Great Elector*, p. 210. On 'powerlessness' see also Droysen, *Der Staat des grossen Kurfürsten*, vol. 2, p. 370, Philippson, *Der Grosse Kurfürst*, vol. 2, p. 238; Waddington, *Histoire de Prusse* (2 vols., Paris, 1922), vol. 1, p. 484.

4 Majesty

1. For descriptions and analyses of the coronation, see Peter Baumgart, 'Die preussische Königskrönung von 1701, das Reich und die europäische Politik', in Oswald Hauser (ed.), *Preussen, Europa und das Reich* (Cologne and Vienna, 1987), pp. 65–86; Heinz Duchhardt, 'Das preussische Königtum von 1701 und der Kaiser', in Heinz Duchhardt and Manfred Schlenke (eds.), *Festschrift für Eberhard Kessel* (Munich, 1982), pp. 89–101; Heinz Duchhardt, 'Die preussische Königskrönung von 1701. Ein europäisches Modell?' in id. (ed.), *Herrscherweihe und Königskrönung im Frühneuzeitlichen Europa* (Wiesbaden, 1983), pp. 82–95; Iselin Gundermann, 'Die Salbung König Friedrichs I. in Königsberg', *Jahrbuch für Berlin-Brandenburgische Kirchengeschichte*, 63 (2001), pp. 72–88.
2. Johann Christian Lünig, *Theatrum ceremoniale historico-politicum oder historisch- und politischer Schau-Platz aller Ceremonien* etc. (2 vols., Leipzig, 1719–20), vol. 2, pp. 100, 96.
3. George Stepney to James Vernon, 19/29 July 1698, PRO SP 90/1, fo. 32.
4. Burke, *Fabrication of Louis XIV*, pp. 23, 25, 29, 76, 153, 175, 181, 185, 189.
5. Lord Raby to Charles Hedges, Berlin, 14 July 1703, PRO SP 90/2, fo. 39.
6. Ibid., 30 June 1703, PRO SP 90/2, fo. 21.
7. Lord Raby to Secretary Harley, 10 February 1705, PRO SP 90/3, fo. 195.
8. The later seventeenth century saw a proliferation of new foundations of this type, of which the most important models for Frederick III/I were the Académie des Sciences in Paris (1666), the Royal Society in London (1673) and the Paris Academy (1700). Leibniz was a member of both the Royal Society and the Paris Academy. See R. J. W. Evans, 'Learned Societies in Germany in the Seventeenth Century', *European Studies Review*, 7 (1977), pp. 129–51.
9. The classic study of the academy and its history is Adolf Harnack's monumental *Geschichte der Königlich Preussischen Akademie der Wissenschaften zu Berlin* (3 vols., Berlin, 1900).
10. Frederick II, 'Mémoires pour servir à l'histoire de la maison de Brandebourg', in J. D. E. Preuss (ed.), *Oeuvres de Frédéric II, Roi de Prusse* (33 vols., Berlin, 1846–57), vol. 1, pp. 1–202, here pp. 122–3.
11. Christian Wolff, *Vernünfftige Gedancken von dem Gesellschafftlichen Leben der Menschen und insonderheit dem gemeinen Wesen zur Beförderung der Glückseligkeit des menschlichen Geschlechts* (Frankfurt, 1721), p. 466. On the importance of display and 'reputation' for the contemporary legitimation of monarchy, see Jörg Jochen Berns, 'Der nackte Monarch und die nackte Wahrheit', in A. Buck, G. Kauffmann, B. L. Spahr et al. (eds.), *Europäische Hofkultur im 16. und 17. Jahrhundert* (Hamburg, 1981); Andreas Gestrich, 'Höfisches Zeremoniell und sinnliches Volk: Die Rechtfertigung des Hofzeremoniells im 17. und frühen 18. Jahrhundert', in Jörg Jochen Berns and Thomas Rahn (eds.), *Zeremoniell als höfische Ästhetik in Spätmittelalter und früher Neuzeit* (Tübingen, 1995),

pp. 57–73; Andreas Gestrich, *Absolutismus und Öffentlichkeit: Politische Kommunikation in Deutschland zu Beginn des 18. Jahrhunderts* (Göttingen, 1994).

12. Linda and Marsha Frey, *Frederick I: The Man and His Times* (Boulder, CO, 1984), p. 225. According to the British ambassador, over 20,000 foreign visitors attended the queen's funeral in June 1705; Lord Raby to Secretary Harley, PRO SP 90/3, fo. 333.

13. See A. Winterling, *Der Hof der Kurfürsten von Köln 1688–1794: Eine Fallstudie zur Bedeutung 'absolutistischer' Hofhaltung* (Bonn, 1986), pp. 153–5.

14. David E. Barclay, *Frederick William IV and the Prussian Monarchy 1840–1861* (Oxford, 1995), pp. 73–4, 287–8.

15. Schultze, *Die Mark Brandenburg*, vol. 4, *Von der Reformation bis zum Westfälischen Frieden (1535–1648)*, pp. 206–7; Gotthard, 'Zwischen Luthertum und Calvinismus', p. 93. On the later marginalization of the consort, see Thomas Biskup, 'The Hidden Queen: Elisabeth Christine of Prussia and Hohenzollern Queenship in the Eighteenth Century', in Clarissa Campbell-Orr (ed.), *Queenship in Europe 1660–1815. The Role of the Consort* (Cambridge, 2004), pp. 300–332.

16. Frey and Frey, *Frederick I*, pp. 35–6.

17. Carl Hinrichs, *Friedrich Wilhelm I. König in Preussen. Eine Biographie* (Hamburg, 1941), pp. 146–7; Baumgart, 'Die preussische Königskrönung' in Hauser (ed.) *Preussen*, pp. 65–86.

18. Wolfgang Neugebauer, 'Friedrich III/I (1688–1713)', in Kroll, *Preussens Herrscher*, pp. 113–33, here p. 129.

19. Cited in Frey and Frey, *Frederick I*, p. 247.

20. Hans-Joachim Neumann, *Friedrich Wilhelm I. Leben und Leiden des Soldatenkönigs* (Berlin, 1993), pp. 51–5.

21. Will Breton to Earl of Strafford, Berlin, 28 February 1713, PRO SP 90/6; Carl Hinrichs, 'Der Regierungsantritt Friedrich Wilhelms I', in id., *Preussen als historisches Problem*, ed. Gerhard Oestreich (Berlin, 1964), pp. 91–137, here p. 106.

22. Whitworth to Lord Townshend, 15 August 1716, PRO SP 90/7, fo. 9.

23. Report dated 2 October 1728, in Richard Wolff, *Vom Berliner Hofe zur Zeit Friedrich Wilhems I. Berichte des Braunschweiger Gesandten in Berlin, 1728–1733 (=Schriften des Vereins für die Geschichte Berlins)* (Berlin, 1914), pp. 20–21.

24. This verse (in my translation) and all details on Gundling's life are taken from Martin Sabrow, *Herr und Hanswurst. Das tragische Schicksal des Hofgelehrten Jacob Paul von Gundling* (Munich, 2001), esp. pp. 62–7, 80–81, 150–51.

25. Gustav Schmoller, 'Eine Schilderung Berlin aus dem Jahre 1723', *FBPG*, 4 (1891), pp. 213–16. The author of this account is Field Marshal Count von Flemming, who spent the months of May and June 1723 in Berlin.

26. I owe this typology to Jonathan Steinberg, who employed it in lectures for the Part Two Cambridge Tripos Paper 'The Struggle for Mastery in Germany 1740–1914' that he and Tim Blanning ran together during the 1970s and 1980s. I am one of many historians of Germany now working in Britain who benefited from this inspirational course.

27. Wolfgang Neugebauer, 'Zur neueren Deutung der preussischen Verwaltung im 17. und 18. Jahrhundert in vergleichender Sicht', in Otto Büsch and Wolfgang Neugebauer (eds.), *Moderne preussische Geschichte 1648–1947. Eine Anthologie* (3 vols., Berlin, 1981), vol. 2, pp. 541–97, here p. 559.

28. Reinhold Dorwart, *The Administrative Reforms of Frederick William I of Prussia* (Cambridge, Mass., 1953), p. 118. For an overview of the 'Knyphausen Reorganisation', see Kurt Breysig (ed.), *Urkunden und Aktenstücke zur Geschichte der Inneren Politik des Kurfürsten Friedrich Wilhelm von Brandenburg*, Part 1, *Geschichte der brandenburgischen Finanzen in der Zeit von 1660 bis 1697* vol. 1, *Die Centralstellen der Kammerverwaltung* (Leipzig, 1895), pp. 106–50.

29. The royal domains had previously been administered by a range of provincial authorities. The new central organ was called the *Hofrentei*, later known as the *Generaldomänenkasse*. Richard Dietrich, 'Die Anfänge des preussischen Staatsgedankens in politischen Testa-

menten der Hohenzollern', in Friedrich Benninghoven and Cécile Lowenthal-Hensel (eds.), *Neue Forschungen zur Brandenburg-Preussischen Geschichte* (=Veröffentlichungen aus den Archiven Preussischen Kulturbesitz, 14; Cologne 1979), pp. 1–60, here p. 12.

30. Cited in Andreas Kossert, *Masuren. Ostpreussens vergessener Süden* (Berlin, 2001), p. 86.

31. Hinrichs, *Friedrich Wilhelm I*, pp. 454–7, 464–8, 473–87; Frey and Frey, *Frederick I*, pp. 89–90; Rodney Gotthelf, 'Frederick William I and Prussian Absolutism, 1713–1740', in Philip G. Dwyer (ed.), *The Rise of Prussia 1700–1830* (Harlow, 2000), pp. 47–67, here pp. 50–51; Fritz Terveen, *Gesamtstaat und Retablissement. Der Wiederaufbau des nördlichen Ostpreussen unter Friedrich Wilhelm I (1714–1740)* (Göttingen, 1954), pp. 17–21.

32. Hans Haussherr, *Verwaltungseinheit und Ressorttrennung. Vom Ende des 17. bis zum Beginn des 19. Jahrhunderts* (Berlin, 1953), esp. ch. 1: 'Friedrich Wilhelm I und die Begründung des Generaldirektoriums in Preussen', pp. 1–30.

33. Ibid.; Hinrichs, 'Die preussische Staatsverwaltung in den Anfängen Friedrich Wilhelms I.', in id., *Preussen als historisches Problem*, pp. 138–60, here p. 149; Hinrichs, *Friedrich Wilhelm I*, pp. 609–21 (on Frederick William's collegial restructuring of the General War Commissariat); Dorwart, *Administrative Reforms*, pp. 138–44.

34. Gotthelf, 'Frederick William I', pp. 58–9.

35. Reinhold August Dorwart, *The Prussian Welfare State before 1740* (Cambridge, Mass., 1971), p. 16; cf. Gerhard Oestreich, *Friedrich Wilhelm I. Preussischer Absolutismus, Merkantilismus, Militarismus* (Göttingen, 1977), pp. 65–70, which stresses the unsystematic character of economic policy under Frederick William I.

36. Kossert, *Masuren*, pp. 88–91.

37. Peter Baumgart, 'Der Adel Brandenburg-Preussens im Urteil der Hohenzollern des 18. Jahrhunderts', in Rudolf Endres (ed.), *Adel in der Frühneuzeit. Ein regionaler Vergleich* (Cologne and Vienna, 1991), pp. 141–61, here pp. 150–51.

38. Oestreich, *Friedrich Wilhelm I*, pp. 62, 65.

39. Gustav Schmoller, 'Das Brandenburg-preussische Innungswesen von 1604–1806, hauptsächlich die Reform unter Friedrich Wilhelm I.', *FBPG*, 1/2 (1888), pp. 1–59.

40. On the prohibition of Polish grain, issued in 1722, see Wilhelm Naudé and Gustav Schmoller (eds.), *Die Getreidehandelspolitik und Kriegsmazinverwaltung Brandenburg-Preussens bis 1740* (Berlin, 1901), pp. 208–9 (introduction by Naudé), and doc. no. 27, p. 373; Lars Atorf, *Der König und das Korn. Die Getreidehandelspolitik als Fundament des Brandenburg-preussischen Aufstiegs zur europäischen Grossmacht* (Berlin, 1999), p. 106.

41. Atorf, *Der König und das Korn*, pp. 113–14.

42. Naudé and Schmoller (eds.), *Getreidehandelspolitik*, p. 292; Atorf, *Der König und das Korn*, pp. 120–33.

43. Cited in F. Schevill, *The Great Elector* (Chicago, 1947), p. 242.

44. See Hugo Rachel, 'Der Merkantilismus in Brandenburg-Preussen', *FBPG*, 40 (1927), pp. 221–66, here pp. 236–7, 243; Otto Hintze, 'Die Hohenzollern und die wirtschaftliche Entwicklung ihres Staates', *Hohenzollern-Jahrbuch*, 20 (1916), pp. 190–202, here p. 197; Oestreich, *Friedrich Wilhelm I*, p. 67.

45. Cited in Baumgart, 'Der Adel Brandenburg-Preussens', p. 147.

46. Haussherr, *Verwaltungseinheit*, p. 11.

47. Frederick William I, Instruction for His Successor (1722), in Dietrich (ed.), *Die politischen Testamente*, pp. 221–43, here p. 229.

48. William Breton to Earl of Strafford, 28 February 1713, PRO, SP 90/6.

49. Hinrichs, *Friedrich Wilhelm I*, p. 364.

50. Oestreich, *Friedrich Wilhelm I*, p. 30.

51. Otto Büsch, *Militärsystem und Sozialleben im alten Preussen* (Berlin, 1962), p. 15.

52. William Breton to Earl of Strafford, 18 May 1713, PRO, SP 90/6, fo. 105.

53. Hartmut Harnisch, 'Preussisches Kantonsystem und ländliche Gesellschaft', in Kroener and Pröve (eds.), *Krieg und Frieden*, pp. 137–65, here p. 148.

54. Max Lehmann, 'Werbung, Wehrpflicht und Beurlaubing im Heere Friedrich Wilhelms I.', *Historische Zeitschrift*, 67 (1891), pp. 254–89; Büsch, *Militärsystem*, p. 13.

55. Carsten, *Origins of the Junkers*, p. 34.

56. Gordon Craig, *The Politics of the Prussian Army, 1640–1945* (London and New York, 1964), p. 11.

57. On the motives for recruitment among noblemen, see Hahn, 'Aristokratisierung und Professionalisierung'; on military service as a noble status symbol, see Göse, *Ritterschaft*, p. 232; citation in Harnisch, 'Preussisches Kantonsystem', p. 147.

58. Büsch, *Militärsystem*, makes this general claim, although the evidence presented in this valuable study suggests a more nuanced conclusion.

59. Harnisch, 'Preussisches Kantonsystem', p. 155.

60. Hagen, *Ordinary Prussians*, pp. 468–9.

61. Büsch, *Militärsystem*, pp. 33–4.

62. Harnisch, 'Preussisches Kantonsystem', pp. 157, 162; Büsch, *Militärsystem*, p. 55.

63. Frederick the Great, *History of My Own Times* (excerpt), in Jay Luvaas (ed. and trans.), *Frederick the Great on the Art of War* (New York, 1966), p. 75. The same arguments are set out in more detail in the Political Testament of 1768, see Dietrich, *Die politischen Testamente*, p. 517.

64. Philippson, *Der Grosse Kurfürst*, vol. 1, p. 20; Political Testament of the Great Elector (1667), in Dietrich, *Die politischen Testamente*, pp. 179–204, here p. 203; McKay, *Great Elector*, pp. 14–15.

65. The remark was addressed to the French envoy Rébenac; cited in McKay, *Great Elector*, p. 238.

66. Ibid., pp. 239–40.

67. Carl Hinrichs, 'Der Konflikt zwischen Friedrich Wilhelm I. und Kronprinz Friedrich', in id., *Preussen als historisches Problem*, pp. 185–202, here, p. 189.

68. Cited in Reinhold Koser, *Friedrich der Grosse als Kronprinz* (Stuttgart, 1886), p. 26.

69. Hinrichs, 'Der Konflikt', p. 191; Carl Hinrichs, *Preussentum und Pietismus. Der Pietismus in Brandenburg-Preussen als religiös-soziale Reformbewegung* (Göttingen, 1971), p. 60.

70. Hinrichs, 'Der Konflikt', p. 193.

71. On the growing alienation between father and son, see Johannes Kunisch, *Friedrich der Grosse. Der König und seine Zeit* (Munich, 2004), pp. 18–28.

72. Karl Ludwig Pöllnitz, *Mémoires pour servir à l'histoire des quatre derniers souverains de la Maison de Brandebourg Royale de Prusse* (2 vols., Berlin, 1791), vol. 2, p. 209. These memoirs are unreliable on many points, but this observation is corroborated by other accounts and accords with what we know of the prince at this time.

73. Kunisch, *Friedrich der Grosse*, pp. 34–5.

74. Theodor Schieder, *Frederick the Great*, trans. Sabina Berkeley and H. M. Scott (Harlow, 2000), p. 25.

75. Ibid., p. 25.

76. Cited in Theodor Fontane, *Wanderungen durch die Mark Brandenburg*, ed. Edgar Gross (2nd edn, 6 vols., Munich, 1963), vol. 2, *Das Oderland*, p. 281; on the Katte story in general, see pp. 267–305.

77. Cited in ibid., pp. 286–7.

78. Kunisch, *Friedrich der Grosse*, pp. 43–4.

79. Schieder, *Frederick the Great*, p. 29; Kunisch, *Friedrich der Grosse*, p. 46.

80. Peter Baumgart, 'Friedrich Wilhelm I (1713–1740)', in Kroll (ed.), *Preussens Herrscher*, pp. 134–59, here p. 158.

81. Hintze, *Die Hohenzollern*, p. 280.

82. Edgar Melton, 'The Prussian Junkers, 1600–1786', in H. M. Scott (ed.), *The European Nobilities in the Seventeenth and Eighteenth Centuries* (2 vols., Harlow, 1995), vol. 2, *Northern Central and Eastern Europe*, pp. 71–109, here p. 92.

83. Rainer Prass, 'Die Brieftasche des Pfarrers. Wege der Übermittlung von Informationen in ländliche Kirchengemeinden des Fürstentums Minden', in Ralf Pröve and Norbert Winnige (eds.), *Wissen ist Macht. Herrschaft und Kommunikation in Brandenburg-Preussen 1600–1850* (Berlin, 2001), pp. 69–82, here pp. 78–9.

84. Wolfgang Neugebauer, *Absolutistischer Staat und Schulwirklichkeit in Brandenburg-Preussen* (Berlin, 1985), pp. 172–3.
85. Rodney Mische Gothelf, 'Absolutism in Action. Frederick William I and the Government of East Prussia, 1709–1730', Ph.D. dissertation, University of St Andrews, St Andrews (1998), p. 180.
86. Ibid., pp. 239–42.
87. Ibid., pp. 234–5.
88. Wolfgang Neugebauer, *Politischer Wandel im Osten. Ost- und Westpreussen von den alten Ständen zum Konstitutionalismus* (Stuttgart, 1992), pp. 65–86.
89. Carsten, *Origins of the Junkers*, p. 41.
90. Peter Baumgart, 'Zur Geschichte der kurmärkischen Stände im 17. und 18. Jahrhundert', in Büsch and Neugebauer (eds.), *Moderne Preussische Geschichte*, vol. 2, pp. 509–40, here p. 529; Melton, 'The Prussian Junkers', pp. 100–101.
91. Fritz Terveen, 'Stellung und Bedeutung des preussischen Etatministeriums zur Zeit Friedrich Wilhelms I. 1713–1740', in *Jahrbuch der Albertus-Universität zu Königsberg/ Preussen*, 6 (1955), pp. 159–79.

5 Protestants

1. Andreas Engel, *Annales Marchiae Brandenburgicae, das ist Ordentliche Verzeichniss vnd beschreibung der fürnemsten . . . Märckischen . . . Historien . . . vom 416 Jahr vor Christi Geburt, bis . . . 1596*, etc. (Frankfurt, 1598).
2. Bodo Nischan, *Prince, People and Confession. The Second Reformation in Brandenburg* (Philadelphia, 1994), pp. 111–43. This account of the Elector's confessional policy is deeply indebted to Nischan's study.
3. Ibid., pp. 186–8. Other useful accounts of the 'Berlin tumult' include: Eberhard Faden, 'Der Berliner Tumult von 1615', in Martin Henning und Heinz Gebhardt (eds.), *Jahrbuch für brandenburgische Landesgeschichte*, 5 (1954), pp. 27–45; Oskar Schwebel, *Geschichte der Stadt Berlin* (Berlin, 1888), pp. 500–513.
4. Cited in Nischan, *Second Reformation*, p. 209.
5. On the importance of emotion as a factor in its own right in power conflicts of this kind, see Ulinka Rublack, 'State-formation, gender and the experience of governance in early modern Württemberg', in id. (ed.), *Gender in Early Modern German History* (Oxford, 2003), pp. 200–217, here p. 214.
6. Bodo Nischan, 'Reformation or Deformation? Lutheran and Reformed Views of Martin Luther in Brandenburg's "Second Reformation"', in id., *Lutherans and Calvinists in the Age of Confessionalism* (Variorum repr., Aldershot, 1999), pp. 203–15, here p. 211. Pistoris citation from id., *Second Reformation*, p. 84.
7. Ibid., p. 217.
8. Droysen, *Geschichte der preussischen Politik*, vol. 4, *Der Staat des Grossen Kurfürsten*, p. 25.
9. Schultze, *Die Mark Brandenburg*, vol. 4, p. 192.
10. Frederick William to supreme councillors of Ducal Prussia (draft in the hand of Chancellor von Götze), Königsberg, 26 April 1642, in Erdmannsdörffer (ed.), *Politische Verhandlungen*, vol. 1, pp. 98–103.
11. Königsberg clergy to the supreme councillors of Ducal Prussia [no date; reply to the Elector's letter of 26 April], in Erdmannsdörffer (ed.), *Politische Verhandlungen*, vol. 1, pp. 98–103. The 'law' invoked here refers to the articles of the Political Testament of Duke Albrecht the Elder, which stipulated that the Lutheran supremacy in the duchy was to remain intact.
12. Klaus Deppermann, 'Die Kirchenpolitik des Grossen Kurfürsten', *Pietismus und Neuzeit*, 6 (1980), pp. 99–114, here pp. 110–12.
13. A useful account of these incidents, based on the observations of a Hessian diplomat at the Berlin court, can be found in Walther Ribbeck, 'Aus Berichten des hessischen Sekretärs

Lincker vom Berliner Hofe während der Jahre 1666–1669', *FBPG*, 12/2 (1899), pp. 141–58.

14. Gerd Heinrich, 'Religionstoleranz in Brandenburg-Preussen. Idee und Wirklichkeit', in Manfred Schlenke (ed.), *Preussen. Politik, Kultur, Gesellschaft* (Reinbek, 1986), pp. 83–102; here p. 83.

15. McKay, *Great Elector*, p. 156, n. 40.

16. See Margrave Ernest to Frederick William, Cölln, 1 July 1641; Frederick William, Resolution, Königsberg, 30 July 1641, in Erdmannsdörffer (ed.), *Politische Verhandlungen*, vol. 1, p. 479.

17. Cited in McKay, *Great Elector*, p. 186.

18. See docs. nos. 121–30 in Selma Stern, *Der preussische Staat und die Juden* (8 vols. in 4 parts, Tübingen, 1962–75), part 1, *Die Zeit des Grossen Kurfürsten und Friedrichs 1.*, vol. 2, pp. 108–16.

19. Cited in Martin Lackner, *Die Kirchenpolitik des Grossen Kurfürsten* (Witten, 1973), p. 300.

20. M. Brecht, 'Philipp Jakob Spener, Sein Programm und dessen Auswirkungen', in id. (ed.), *Geschichte des Pietismus* (4 vols., Göttingen, 1993), vol. 1, *Der Pietismus vom 17. bis zum frühen 18. Jahrhundert*, pp. 278–389, here pp. 333–8; H. Leube, 'Die Geschichte der pietistischen Bewegung in Leipzig', in id., *Orthodoxie und Pietismus. Gesammelte Studien* (Bielefeld, 1975), pp. 153–267.

21. On Pietist-Lutheran conflicts in Hamburg, Giessen, Darmstadt and other cities, see Klaus Deppermann, *Der Hallesche Pietismus und der preussische Staat unter Friedrich III (I)* (Göttingen, 1961), pp. 49–50; Brecht, 'Philipp Jakob Spener', pp. 344–51.

22. Johannes Wallmann, 'Das Collegium Pietatis', in M. Greschat (ed.), *Zur neueren Pietismusforschung* (Darmstadt, 1977), pp. 167–223; Brecht, 'Philipp Jakob Spener', pp. 316–19.

23. Philipp Jakob Spener, *Theologische Bedencken* (4 Parts in 2 vols., Halle, 1712–15), part 3, vol. 2, p. 293.

24. Philipp Jakob Spener, *Letzte Theologische Bedencken* (Halle, 1711), part 3, pp. 296–7, 428, 439–40, 678; citations are from the reprint in Dietrich Blaufuss and P. Schicketanz, *Philipp Jakob Spener Letzte Theologische Bedencken und andere Brieffliche Antworten* (Hildesheim, 1987).

25. Cited in T. Kervorkian, 'Piety Confronts Politics: Philipp Jakob Spener in Dresden 1686–1691', *German History*, 16 (1998), pp. 145–64.

26. Article on Philipp Jakob Spener, Klaus-Gunther Wesseling, *Biographisch-Bibliographisches Kirchenlexikon*, vol. 10 (1995), cols. 909–39, *http://www.bautz.de/bbk1/s/spener—p—j.shtml*; accessed 29 October 2003.

27. R. L. Gawthrop, *Pietism and the Making of Eighteenth-century Prussia* (Cambridge, 1993), p. 122.

28. Philipp Jakob Spener, *Pia Desideria: Oder hertzliches Verlangen nach gottgefälliger Besserung der wahren evangelischen Kirchen*, 2nd edn (Frankfurt/Main, 1680). Citations are from the reprint in E. Beyreuther (ed.), *Speners Schriften*, vol. 1 (Hildesheim, 1979), pp. 123–308; here pp. 267–71.

29. Spener, *Pia Desideria*, pp. 250–52.

30. Ibid., p. 257.

31. Brecht, 'Philipp Jakob Spener', p. 352.

32. Deppermann, *Der Hallesche Pietismus*, p. 172.

33. Ibid., pp. 74, 172; Brecht, 'Philipp Jakob Spener', p. 354.

34. Kurt Aland, 'Der Pietismus und die soziale Frage', in id. (ed.), *Pietismus und moderne Welt* (Witten, 1974), pp. 99–137; here p. 101.

35. Brecht, 'Philipp Jakob Spener', p. 290; Deppermann, *Der Hallesche Pietismus*, pp. 58–61.

36. E. Beyreuther, *Geschichte des Pietismus* (Stuttgart, 1978), p. 155.

37. W. Oschlies, *Die Arbeits- und Berufspädagogik August Hermann Franckes (1663–*

1727). Schule und Leben im Menschenbild des Hauptvertreters des halleschen Pietismus (Witten, 1969), p. 20.

38. On the *Fussstapffen* and other programmatic texts by Francke, see M. Brecht, 'August Hermann Francke und der Hallesche Pietismus', in id. (ed.), *Geschichte des Pietismus*, vol. 2, pp. 440–540; here p. 475.

39. F. Ernest Stoeffler (ed.), *Continental Pietism and Early American Christianity* (Grand Rapids, 1976); Mark A. Noll, 'Evangelikalismus und Fundamentalismus in Nordamerika', in Ulrich Gäbler (ed.), *Der Pietismus im neunzehnten und zwanzigsten Jahrhundert* (Göttingen, 2000), pp. 465–531. On epistolary networks and religious revival, see W. R. Ward, *The Protestant Evangelical Awakening* (Cambridge, 1992), esp. ch. 1.

40. Carl Hinrichs, 'Die universalen Zielsetzungen des Halleschen Pietismus', in id., *Preussentum und Pietismus*, pp. 1–125, esp. pp. 29–47.

41. Martin Brecht, 'August Hermann Francke und der Hallische Pietismus' in id. (ed.) *Der Pietismus vom siebzehnten bis zum frühen achtzehnten Jahrhundert* (*Geschichte des Pietismus*, vol. 1) (Göttingen, 1993), pp. 440–539, here pp. 478, 485.

42. Gawthrop, *Pietism*, pp. 137–49, 211, 213 and passim; by contrast, Mary Fulbrook, *Piety and Politics: Religion and the Rise of Absolutism in England, Württemberg and Prussia* (Cambridge, 1983), pp. 164–7, stresses the utilitarian dimension of the relationship. See also, W. Stolze, 'Friedrich Wilhelm I. und der Pietismus', *Jahrbuch für Brandenburgische Kirchengeschichte*, 5 (1908), pp. 172–205; K. Wolff, 'Ist der Glaube Friedrich Wilhelms I. von A. H. Francke beeinflusst?', *Jahrbuch für Brandenburgische Kirchengeschichte*, 33 (1938), pp. 70–102.

43. Deppermann, *Der Hallesche Pietismus*, p. 168.

44. Schoeps, *Preussen*, p. 47; Gawthrop, *Pietism*, p. 255.

45. Fulbrook, *Piety and Politics*, p. 168. This requirement was extended to include the University of Königsberg in 1736.

46. Hartwig Notbohm, *Das evangelische Kirchen- und Schulwesen in Ostpreussen während der Regierung Friedrichs des Grossen* (Heidelberg, 1959), p. 15.

47. M. Scharfe, *Die Religion des Volkes. Kleine Kultur- und Sozialgeschichte des Pietismus* (Gütersloh, 1980), p. 103; Beyreuther, *Geschichte des Pietismus*, pp. 338–9; Gawthrop, *Pietism*, pp. 215–46.

48. Carl Hinrichs, 'Pietismus und Militarismus im alten Preussen' in id., *Preussentum und Pietismus*, pp. 126–73, here p. 155.

49. Gawthrop, *Pietism*, p. 226; Hinrichs, 'Pietismus und Militarismus', pp. 163–4.

50. Benjamin Marschke, *Absolutely Pietist: Patronage, Factionalism, and State-building in the Early Eighteenth-century Prussian Army Chaplaincy* (Halle, 2005), p. 114. I am very grateful to Dr Marschke for letting me see the manuscript of this work before it went to publication.

51. For an argument along these lines, see Gawthrop, *Pietism*, p. 228.

52. Ibid., pp. 236–7.

53. See A. J. La Vopa, *Grace, Talent, and Merit. Poor Students, Clerical Careers and Professional Ideology in Eighteenth-century Germany* (Cambridge, 1988), pp. 137–64, 386–8.

54. For an outline of the legacy of Pietist innovations in the area of schooling, on which this account is based, see J. Van Horn Melton, *Absolutism and the Eighteenth-century Origins of Compulsory Schooling in Prussia and Austria* (Cambridge, 1988), pp. 23–50.

55. Terveen, *Gesamtstaat und Retablissement*, pp. 86–92. On Friedrich Wilhelm I's concern for the evangelization of the Lithuanians, see Hinrichs, *Preussentum und Pietismus*, p. 174; Notbohm, *Das evangelische Schulwesen*, p. 16.

56. Kurt Forstreuter, 'Die Anfänge der Sprachstatistik in Preussen', in id., *Wirkungen des Preussenlandes* (Cologne, 1981), pp. 312–33.

57. M. Brecht, 'Der Hallische Pietismus in der Mitte des 18. Jahrhunderts – seine Ausstrahlung und sein Niedergang', in id. and Klaus Deppermann (eds.), *Der Pietismus im achtzehnten Jahrhundert* (Göttingen, 1995), pp. 319–57, here p. 323.

58. On the Pietist mission to the Jews, see Christopher Clark, *The Politics of Conversion. Missionary Protestantism and the Jews in Prussia 1728–1941* (Oxford, 1995), pp. 9–82.

59. Scharfe, *Die Religion des Volkes*, p. 148.

60. H. Obst, *Der Berliner Beichtstuhlstreit* (Witten, 1972); Gawthrop, *Pietism*, pp. 124–5; Fulbrook, *Piety and Politics*, pp. 160–62.

61. Marschke, *Absolutely Pietist*.

62. Gawthrop, *Pietism*, pp. 275–6.

63. On the association with hypocrisy, see Johannes Wallmann, 'Was ist der Pietismus?', *Pietismus und Neuzeit*, 20 (1994), pp. 11–27, here pp. 11–12.

64. Brecht, 'Der Hallesche Pietismus', p. 342.

65. Justus Israel Beyer, *Auszüge aus den Berichten des reisenden Mitarbeiters beym jüdischen Institut* (15 vols., Halle, 1777–91), vol. 14, p. 2.

66. See e.g. W. Bienert, *Der Anbruch der christlichen deutschen Neuzeit dargestellt an Wissenschaft und Glauben des Christian Thomasius* (Halle, 1934), p. 151.

67. Martin Schmidt, 'Der Pietismus und das moderne Denken', in Aland (ed.), *Pietismus und Moderne Welt*, pp. 9–74, here pp. 21, 27, 53–61.

68. See e.g. J. Geyer-Kordesch, 'Die Medizin im Spannungsfeld zwischen Aufklärung und Pietismus: Das unbequeme Werk Georg Ernst Stahls und dessen kulturelle Bedeutung', in N. Hinske (ed.), *Halle, Aufklärung und Pietismus* (Heidelberg, 1989).

69. On Kant's ambivalent attitude to the Pietist tradition, see the excellent introduction to Immanuel Kant, *Religion and Rational Theology*, ed. and trans. Allen W. Wood and George di Giovanni (Cambridge, 1996).

70. Richard van Dülmen, *Kultur und Alltag in der frühen Neuzeit* (3 vols., Munich, 1994), vol. 3, *Religion, Magie, Aufklärung 16.–18. Jahrhundert*, pp. 132–4.

71. W. M. Alexander, *Johann Georg Hamann. Philosophy and Faith* (The Hague, 1966), esp. pp. 2–3; I. Berlin, *The Magus of the North. Johann Georg Hamann and the Origins of Modern Irrationalism*, ed. H. Hardy (London, 1993), pp. 5–6, 13–14, 91.

72. L. Dickey, *Hegel. Religion, Economics and the Politics of Spirit* (Cambridge, 1987), esp. pp. 149, 161.

73. This comparison is made in Fulbrook, *Piety and Politics*.

74. Political Testament of 1667, in Dietrich (ed.), *Die Politischen Testamente*, p. 188.

75. Memo from Sebastian Striepe to Frederick William [mid-January 1648], in Erdmannsdörffer (ed.), *Politische Verhandlungen*, vol. 1, pp. 667–73.

76. See, for example, Frederick William to Louis XIV, Kleve, 13 August 1666, in B. Eduard Simson, *Auswärtige Acten. Erster Band (Frankreich)* (Berlin, 1865), pp. 416–17.

77. McKay, *Great Elector*, 154.

78. In a furious note to his ambassador in Berlin, the French king accused Frederick William of preventing by force his subjects 'of the supposed reformed religion' from returning to France in recognition of their 'guilt' and warned that unless he desisted from this outrage 'I [Louis XIV] will be forced to make decisions that he will not like' (Waddington, *Prusse*, vol. 1, p. 561).

79. The Principality of Orange had belonged to William III of Orange, Dutch Stadtholder from 1672 and King of Great Britain from 1689. William III, himself an only child, died childless in 1702. The strongest claimant to the title was thus Frederick I, whose mother, Louise Henrietta of Orange, had been the eldest daughter of William's grandfather, Frederick Henry, Dutch Stadtholder from 1625 to 1647, though here, as in so many such cases, there were disputes about the status of the female line of succession. Louis XIV had annexed the territory in 1682, but the struggle over the inheritance was not resolved until the Peace of Utrecht in 1713.

80. Text of the proclamation in Raby to Hedges, Berlin, 19 January 1704, PRO SP 90/2.

81. Ibid.

6 Powers in the Land

1. Andreas Nachama, *Ersatzbürger und Staatsbildung. Zur Zerstörung des Bürgertums in Brandenburg-Preussen* (Frankfurt/Main, 1984). For another very negative assessment of Silesian town life in particular, see Johannes Ziekursch, *Das Ergebnis der friderizianischen Städteverwaltung und die Städteordnung Steins. Am Beispiel der schlesischen Städte dargestellt* (Jena, 1908), pp. 80, 133, 135 and passim; on urbanization, see Jörn Sieglerschmidt, 'Social and Economic Landscapes', in Sheilagh Ogilvie (ed.), *Germany. A New Social and Economic History* (3 vols., London, 1995–2003), pp. 1–38, here p. 17.

2. Nachama, *Ersatzbürger und Staatsbildung*, pp. 66–7; McKay, *Great Elector*, pp. 162–4.

3. Karin Friedrich, 'The Development of the Prussian Town, 1720–1815', in Dwyer (ed.), *Rise of Prussia*, pp. 129–50, here pp. 136–7.

4. Horst Carl, *Okkupation und Regionalismus. Die preussischen Westprovinzen im Siebenjährigen Krieg* (Mainz, 1993), p. 41; Dieter Stievermann, 'Preussen und die Städte der westfälischen Grafschaft Mark', *Westfälische Forschungen*, 31 (1981), pp. 5–31.

5. Carl, *Okkupation und Regionalismus*, pp. 42–4.

6. Martin Winter, 'Preussisches Kantonsystem und städtische Gesellschaft', in Ralf Pröve and Bernd Kölling (eds.), *Leben und Arbeiten auf märckischem Sand. Wege in die Gesellschaftsgeschichte Brandenburgs 1700–1914* (Bielefeld, 1999), p. 243–65, here p. 262.

7. Olaf Gründel, 'Bürgerrock und Uniform. Die Garnisonstadt Prenzlau 1685–1806', in Museumsverband des Landes Brandenburg (ed.), *Ortstermine. Stationen Brandenburg-Preussens auf den Weg in die moderne Welt* (Berlin, 2001), pp. 6–23, here p. 14.

8. For a study of a Swedish Pomeranian town that highlights this problem, see Stefan Kroll, *Stadtgesellschaft und Krieg. Sozialstruktur, Bevölkerung und Wirtschaft in Stralsund und Stade 1700 bis 1715* (Göttingen, 1997).

9. Ralf Pröve, 'Der Soldat in der "guten Bürgerstube". Das frühneuzeitliche Einquartierungssystem und die sozioökonomischen Folgen', in Kroener and Pröve (eds.), *Krieg und Frieden*, pp. 191–217, here p. 216.

10. Friedrich, 'Prussian Town', p. 139.

11. Martin Winter, 'Preussisches Kantonsystem', p. 249.

12. For a discussion of this practice, see 'Ausführlicher Auszug und Bemerkungen über den militärischen Theil des Werks De la monarchie prussienne sous Frédéric le Grand, p. M. le Comte de Mirabeau 1788', *Neues Militärisches Journal*, 1 (1788), pp. 31–94, here pp. 48–9.

13. For excellent discussions of the 'garrison society' that emerged around this symbiosis, see Beate Engelen, 'Warum heiratet man einen Soldaten? Soldatenfrauen in der ländlichen Gesellschaft Brandenburg-Preussens im 18. Jahrhundert', in Stefan Kroll and Kristiane Krüger (eds.), *Militär und ländliche Gesellschaft in der frühen Neuzeit* (Münster, 2000), pp. 251–74; Beate Engelen, 'Fremde in der Stadt. Die Garnisonsgesellschaft Prenzlaus im 18. Jahrhundert', in Klaus Neitmann, Jürgen Theil and Olaf Grundel (eds.), *Die Herkunft der Brandenburger. Sozial – und Mentalitätsgeschichtliche Beiträge zur Bevölkerung Brandenburgs von hohen Mittelalter bis zum 20. Jahrhundert* (Potsdam, 2001); Ralf Pröve, 'Vom Schmuddelkind zur anerkannten Subdisziplin? Die "neue Militärgeschichte" in der frühen Neuzeit. Entwicklungen, Perspektiven, Probleme', *Geschichte in Wissenschaft und Unterricht*, 51 (2000), pp. 597–613.

14. See Brigitte Meier, 'Städtische Verwaltungsorgane in den brandenburgischen Klein- und Mittelstädten des 18. Jahrhunderts', in Wilfried Ehbrecht (ed.), *Verwaltung und Politik in den Städten Mitteleuropas. Beiträge zu Verfassungsnorm und Verfassungswirklichkeit in altständischer Zeit* (Cologne, 1994), pp. 177–81, here p. 179; Gerd Heinrich, 'Staatsaufsicht und Stadtfreiheit in Brandenburg-Preussen unter dem Absolutismus (1660–1806)', in Wilhelm Rausch (ed.), *Die Städte Mitteleuropas im 17. und 18. Jahrhundert* (Linz, 1981), pp. 155–72, here pp. 167–8.

15. On this new economic elite, see Kurt Schwieger, *Das Bürgertum in Preussen vor der Französischen Revolution* (Kiel, 1971), pp. 167–9, 173, 181.

16. All these examples are drawn from Rolf Straubel, *Kaufleute und Manufakturunter-nehmer. Eine Empirische Untersuchung über die sozialen Träger von Handel und Gross-gewerbe in den mittleren preussischen Provinzen (1763 bis 1815)* (Stuttgart, 1995), pp. 10, 431–3.

17. Rolf Straubel, *Frankfurt (Oder) und Potsdam am Ende des Alten Reiches. Studien zur städtischen Wirtschafts- und Sozialstruktur* (Potsdam, 1995), p. 137; Günther, 'Städtische Autonomie', p. 108.

18. Monika Wienfort, 'Preussisches Bildungsbürgertum auf dem Lande 1820–1850', *FBPG*, 5 (1995), pp. 75–98.

19. Neugebauer, *Absolutistischer Staat*, pp. 545–52. Neugebauer observes that many such initiatives were dependent upon the activism of the founding circle of burghers and tended to decline or collapse once these had died or moved away.

20. Brigitte Meier, 'Die "Sieben Schönheiten" der brandenburgischen Städte', in Pröve and Kölling (eds.), *Leben und Arbeiten*, pp. 220–42, here p. 225.

21. Philip Julius Lieberkühn, *Kleine Schriften nebst dessen Lebensbeschreibung* (Züllichau and Freystadt, 1791), p. 9. On Lieberkühn's work in Neuruppin, see also Brigitte Meier, *Neuruppin 1700 bis 1830. Sozialgeschichte einer kurmärkischen Handwerker- und Garni-sonstadt* (Berlin, 1993).

22. Hanna Schissler, 'The Junkers: Notes on the Social and Historical Significance of the Agrarian Elite in Prussia', in Robert G. Moeller (ed.), *Peasants and Lords in Modern Germany. Recent Studies in Agricultural History* (Boston, 1986), pp. 24–51.

23. Carsten, *Origins of the Junkers*, pp. 1–3.

24. Dietrich, *Die politischen Testamente*, pp. 229–31.

25. Edgar Melton, 'The Prussian Junkers, 1600–1786', in Scott (ed.), *The European Nobil-ities*, vol. 2, *Northern, Central and Eastern Europe*, pp. 71–109, here p. 72.

26. On all these points, see Edgar Melton's excellent discussion in 'The Prussian Junkers', esp. pp. 95–9.

27. C. F. R. von Barsewisch, *Meine Kriegserlebnisse während des Siebenjährigen Krieges 1757–1763. Wortgetreuer Abdruck aus dem Tagebuche des Kgl. Preuss. General-Quartiermeister-Lieutenants* (2nd edn, Berlin, 1863).

28. Craig, *Politics of the Prussian Army*, p. 17.

29. Hanna Schissler, *Preussische Agrargesellschaft im Wandel. Wirtschaftliche, gesellsch-aftliche und politische Transformationsprozesse von 1763 bis 1847* (Göttingen, 1978), p. 217; Johannes Ziekursch, *Hundert Jahre Schlesischer Agrargeschichte* (Breslau, 1915), pp. 23–6; Robert Berdahl, *The Politics of the Prussian Nobility. The Development of a Conservative Ideology 1770–1848* (Princeton, NJ, 1988), pp. 80–85. On the presence of non-noble landowners in the district assemblies (*Kreistage*) of the Mark Brandenburg, see Klaus Vetter, 'Zusammensetzung, Funktion und politische Bedeutung der kurmärkischen Kreistage im 18. Jh', *Jahrbuch für die Geschichte des Feudalismus*, 3 (1979), pp. 393–416; Peter Baumgart, 'Zur Geschichte der kurmärkischen Stände im 17. und 18. Jh', in Dieter Gerhard, *Ständische Vertretungen in Europe im 17. und 18. Jahrhundert* (Göttingen, 1969), pp. 131–61.

30. Gustavo Corni, *Stato assoluto e società agraria in Prussia nell'età di Federico II* (= *Annali dell'Istituto storico italo-germanico*, 4; Bologna, 1982), pp. 283–4, 288, 292, 299–300.

31. Melton, 'Prussian Junkers', pp. 102–3; Schissler, 'Junkers', pp. 24–51; Berdahl, *Politics*, p. 79.

32. Hans-Ulrich Wehler, *Deutsche Gesellschaftsgeschichte* (4 vols., Munich, 1987–2003), vol. 1, *Vom Feudalismus des alten Reiches bis zur defensiven Modernisierung der Reformära 1700–1815*, pp. 74, 82.

33. Hans Rosenberg, *Bureaucracy, Aristocracy & Autocracy. The Prussian Experience, 1660–1815* (Cambridge, MA, 1966), pp. 30, 60.

34. Ibid., p. 49; Hans Rosenberg, 'Die Ausprägung der Junkerherrschaft in Brandenburg-Preussen 1410–1648', in id., *Machteliten und Wirtschaftskonjunkturen* (Göttingen,

1978), pp. 24–82, here p. 82; Francis I. Carsten, *The Origins of Prussia* (Oxford, 1954), p. 277.

35. One of the most trenchant and influential expositions of the *Sonderweg* argument is Hans-Ulrich Wehler, *Das deutsche Kaiserreich 1871–1918* (Göttingen, 1973). For the agrarian dimension of the argument, see esp. pp. 15, 238. Wehler's most important inspiration was the sociologist Max Weber, whose powerful National Liberal critique of the Junker class resonates in Wehler's synthesis: Max Weber, 'Capitalism and Rural Society in Germany' (1906), and 'National Character and the Junkers' (1917), in H. H. Gerth and C. Wright Mills (eds.), *From Max Weber: Essays in Sociology* (Oxford, 1946), pp. 363–95. On the anti-Junker tradition more generally, see Heinz Reif, 'Die Junker', in Etienne François and Hagen Schulze (eds.), *Deutsche Erinnerungsorte* (3 vols., Munich, 2001), vol. 1, pp. 520–36, esp. pp. 526–8.

36. See Jan Peters, Hartmut Harnisch and Lieselott Enders, *Märkische Bauerntagebücher des 18. und 19. Jahrhunderts. Selbstzeugnisse von Milchviehbauern aus Neuholland* (Weimar, 1989), p. 54.

37. Carsten, *Origins of the Junkers*, pp. 12, 54, 56.

38. Hagen, *Ordinary Prussians*, pp. 47, 56.

39. Ibid., pp. 65, 78. For a more concentrated discussion of the same issues, see the classic article by William Hagen, 'Seventeenth-century Crisis in Brandenburg: The Thirty Years' War, the Destabilization of Serfdom, and the Rise of Absolutism', *American Historical Review*, 94 (1989), pp. 302–35; also William W. Hagen, 'Die brandenburgischen und grosspolnischen Bauern im Zeitalter der Gutsherrschaft 1400–1800', in Jan Peters (ed.), *Gutsherrschaftsgesellschaften im europäischen Vergleich* (Berlin, 1997), pp. 17–28, here pp. 22–3.

40. Enders, *Die Uckermark*, p. 462.

41. Hagen, *Ordinary Prussians*, p. 72.

42. 'Bauernunruhen in der Priegnitz', Geheimes Staatsarchiv (hereafter GStA) Berlin-Dahlem, HA I, Rep. 22, Nr. 72a, Fasz. 11.

43. These events are reconstructed in detail in Lieselott Enders's panoramic history of the Uckermark. See Enders, *Die Uckermark*, pp. 394–6.

44. Ibid., p. 396.

45. 'Klagen der Ritterschaft in Priegnitz gegen aufgewiegelte Unterthanen, 1701–1703', in GStA Berlin-Dahlem, HA I, Rep. 22, Nr. 72a, Fasz. 15; 'Beschwerde von Dörfern über die Nöte und Abgaben, 1700–1701'. These documents are discussed in Hagen, *Ordinary Prussians*, p. 85.

46. Enders, *Die Uckermark*, p. 446.

47. Hagen, *Ordinary Prussians*, pp. 89–93.

48. Friedrich Otto von der Gröben to Frederick William, Amt Zechlin, 20 January, 1670, in Breysig (ed.), *Die Centralstellen*, pp. 813–16, here p. 814.

49. Hagen, *Ordinary Prussians*, p. 120.

50. This is one of the central themes of Hagen's *Ordinary Prussians*. For a more concise discussion, see William Hagen, 'The Junkers' Faithless Servants', in Richard J. Evans and W. Robert Lee (eds.), *The German Peasantry* (London, 1986), pp. 71–101; Robert Berdahl, 'Christian Garve on the German Peasantry', *Peasant Studies*, 8 (1979), pp. 86–102; id., *The Politics of the Prussian Nobility*, pp. 47–54.

51. Enders, *Die Uckermark*, p. 467.

52. On this literature, see Wehler, *Deutsche Gesellschaftsgeschichte*, vol. 1, *Vom Feudalismus des Alten Reiches*, p. 82; Berdahl, *Politics of the Prussian Nobility*, pp. 45–6.

53. Veit Valentin, *Geschichte der deutschen Revolution von 1848–49* (2 vols., Berlin, 1931), vol. 2, pp. 234–5.

54. On the evolution of the image of the Junker as a 'site of memory', see Heinz Reif's brilliant essay, 'Die Junker', esp. pp. 521–3.

55. Hagen, *Ordinary Prussians*, pp. 292–7.

56. This case is documented and analysed in Heinrich Kaak, 'Untertanen und Herrschaft

gemeinschaftlich im Konflikt. Der Streit um die Nutzung des Kietzer Sees in der östlichen Kurmark 1792–1797', in Peters, *Gutsherrschaftsgesellschaften*, pp. 323–42.

57. See, for example, the case of Frau von Dossow, who purchased parts of the Zieten estate at Wustrau in county Ruppin in 1756 and managed, through the introduction of modern estate-management techniques to achieve rapid growth in output. Carl Brinkmann, *Wustrau. Wirtschafts- und Verfassungsgeschichte eines brandenburgischen Rittergutes* (Leipzig, 1911), pp. 82–3.

58. Thus Veit Ludwig von Seckendorff's *Teutscher Fürstenstaat*, cited in Johannes Rogalla von Biberstein, *Adelherrschaft und Adelskultur in Deutschland* (Limburg, 1998), p. 356.

59. Ute Frevert, *Women in German History. From Bourgeois Emancipation to Sexual Liberation* (Oxford, 1989), pp. 64–5; Heide Wunder, *He is the Sun, She is the Moon: Women in Early Modern Germany*, trans. Thomas Dunlap (Cambridge, MA, 1998), pp. 202–8.

60. On this phenomenon more generally, see Sheilagh Ogilvie, *A Bitter Living. Women, Markets and Social Capital in Early Modern Germany* (Oxford, 2003), pp. 321–2.

61. Hagen, *Ordinary Prussians*, pp. 167, 368.

62. Ibid., p. 256.

63. Ulrike Gleixner, '*Das Mensch' und 'Der Kerl'. Die Konstruktion von Geschlecht in Unzuchtsverfahren der Frühen Neuzeit (1700–1760)* (Frankfurt, 1994), p. 15.

64. Hagen, *Ordinary Prussians*, p. 499.

65. Gleixner, *Unzuchtsverfahren*, pp. 116, 174.

66. Ibid., p. 172.

67. Hagen, *Ordinary Prussians*, pp. 177, 257, 258.

68. Gleixner, *Unzuchtsverfahren*, pp. 176–210.

69. Frederick II, Political Testament of 1752, in Dietrich, *Die politischen Testamente*, p. 261.

70. On the idea that '*industrie*' was an index of the civilizational achievement of a state, see Florian Schui, 'Early debates about *industrie*: Voltaire and his Contemporaries (*c* 1750–78)', Ph. D. thesis, Cambridge (2005); Hugo Rachel, *Wirtschaftsleben im Zeitalter des Frühkapitalismus* (Berlin, 1931), pp. 130–32; Rolf Straubel, 'Bemerkungen zum Verhältnis von Lokalbehörde und Wirtschaftsentwicklung. Das Berliner Seiden- und Baumwollgewerbe in der 2. Hälfte des 18. Jahrhunderts', *Jahrbuch für Geschichte*, 35 (1987), pp. 119–49, here pp. 125–7.

71. William O. Henderson, *Studies in the Economic Policy of Frederick the Great* (London, 1963), pp. 36, 159–60; Ingrid Mittenzwei, *Preussen nach dem Siebenjährigen Krieg. Auseinandersetzungen zwischen Bürgertum und Staat um die Wirtschaftsgeschichte* (Berlin, 1979), pp. 71–100.

72. Clive Trebilcock, *The Industrialisation of the Continental Powers 1780–1914* (Harlow, 1981), p. 27.

73. Cited in August Schwemann, 'Freiherr von Heinitz als Chef des Salzdepartements (1786–96)', *FBPG*, 7 (1894), pp. 111–59, here p. 112.

74. Ibid., pp. 112–13.

75. Schieder, *Frederick the Great*, p. 209.

76. Honoré-Gabriel Riquetti, Comte de Mirabeau, *De la monarchie Prussienne sous Frédéric le Grand* (8 vols., Paris, 1788), vol. 3, pp. 2, 7–8, 9–15, 17, 18.

77. Ibid., vol. 3, p. 191.

78. Ibid., vol. 3, pp. 175–6, vol. 5, pp. 334–5, 339.

79. Trebilcock, *Industrialisation*, p. 28; Walther Hubatsch, *Friedrich der Grosse und die preussische Verwaltung* (Cologne, 1973), pp. 81–2.

80. Johannes Feig, 'Die Begründung der Luckenwalder Wollenindustrie durch Preussens Könige im achtzehnten Jahrhundert', *FBPG*, 10 (1898), pp. 79–103, here pp. 101–2; the quotation from Schmoller is on p. 103.

81. For a discussion of this problem see Wehler, *Deutsche Gesellschaftsgeschichte*, vol. 1, p. 109.

82. Ingrid Mittenzwei, *Preussen nach dem Siebenjährigen Krieg*, pp. 71–100; Max Bark-hausen, 'Government Control and Free Enterprise in Western Germany and the Low Countries in the Eighteenth Century', in Peter Earle (ed.), *Essays in European Economic History* (Oxford, 1974), pp. 241–57; Stefan Gorissen, 'Gewerbe, Staat und Unternehmer auf dem rechten Rheinufer', in Dietrich Ebeling (ed.), *Aufbruch in eine neue Zeit. Gewerbe, Staat und Unternehmer in den Rheinlanden des 18. Jahrhunderts* (Cologne, 2000), pp. 59–85, esp. pp. 74–6; citation from Wilfried Reininghaus, *Die Stadt Iserlohn und ihre Kaufleute (1700–1815)* (Dortmund, 1995), p. 19.

83. Rolf Straubel, *Kaufleute und Manufakturunternehmer*, pp. 11, 24, 26, 29–30, 32, 95, 97. My outline discussion of the growth of the Prussian manufacturing in this period is deeply indebted to Straubel's outstanding pioneering study. A useful older study of the transition to capitalist forms of production in the manufacturing sector, with statistics for all Prussian provinces (Straubel focuses on the central provinces only) is Karl Heinrich Kaufhold, *Das Gewerbe in Preussen um 1800* (Göttingen, 1978).

84. Straubel, *Kaufleute und Manufakturunternehmer*, pp. 399–400; id., 'Berliner Seiden-und Baumwollgewerbe', pp. 134–5; Mittenzwei, *Preussen nach dem Siebenjährigen Krieg*, pp. 39–50.

85. Straubel, *Kaufleute und Manufakturunternehmer*, pp. 397–8, 408–9; for a positive assessment of the impact of tax commissioners on local, developments, see Heinrich, 'Staatsaufsicht und Stadtfreiheit', in Rausch (ed.), *Städte Mitteleuropas*, pp. 155–72, esp. p. 165.

7 Struggle for Mastery

1. H. M. Scott, 'Prussia's Emergence as a European Great Power, 1740–1763', in Dwyer (ed.), *Rise of Prussia*, pp. 153–76, here p. 161.

2. Frederick II, *De la Littérature Allemande; des defauts qu'on peut lui reprocher; quelles en sont les causes; et par quels moyens on peut les corriger* (Berlin, 1780; repr. Heilbronn, 1883), pp. 4–5, 10.

3. T. C. W. Blanning, *The Culture of Power and the Power of Culture. Old Regime Europe 1660–1789* (Oxford, 2002), p. 84.

4. Frederick II, *The Refutation of Machiavelli's Prince, or Anti-Machiavel*, intro. and trans. Paul Sonnino (Athens, O, 1981), pp. 157–62.

5. Dietrich, *Die politischen Testamente*, pp. 657–9.

6. Wolfgang Pyta, 'Von der Entente Cordiale zur Aufkündigung der Bündnispartnerschaft. Die preussisch-britischen Beziehungen im Siebenjährigen Krieg 1758–1762', *FBPG*, New Series 10 (2000), pp. 1–48, here pp. 41–2.

7. For a discussion of the historical works, see Kunisch, *Friedrich der Grosse*, pp. 102–3, 119, 218–23.

8. Frederick William I, *Instruction for his Successor* (1722); Frederick II, *Political Testament* of 1752, both in Dietrich, *Die politischen Testamente*, pp. 243, 255.

9. Ibid., p. 601.

10. Jacques Brenner (ed.), *Mémoires pour servir à la vie de M. de Voltaire, écrits par lui-même* (Paris, 1965), p. 45.

11. Ibid., p. 43.

12. Kunisch, *Friedrich der Grosse*, p. 60.

13. David Wootton, 'Unhappy Voltaire, or "I shall Never Get Over it as Long as I Live"', *History Workshop Journal*, no. 50 (2000), pp. 137–55.

14. Giles MacDonogh, *Frederick the Great. A Life in Deed and Letters* (London, 1999), pp. 201–4.

15. Paul Noack, *Elisabeth Christine und Friedrich der Grosse. Ein Frauenleben in Preussen* (Stuttgart, 2001).

16. Ibid., p. 142; Biskup, 'Hidden Queen', passim.

17. Noack, *Elisabeth Christine*, pp. 185–6.

18. Frederick to Duhan de Jandun, 19 March 1734, in Preuss (ed.), *Oeuvres de Frédéric II* (31 vols., Berlin, 1851), vol. 17, p. 271.
19. PRO SP 90/2, 90/3, 90/4, 90/5, 90/6, 90/7.
20. Charles Ingrao, *The Habsburg Monarchy 1618–1815* (Cambridge, 1994), p. 152.
21. Frederick William I, 'Last Speech' (28 May 1740), in Dietrich (ed.), *Die politischen Testamente*, p. 246. The speech was minuted by the State and Cabinet Minister Heinrich Count von Podewils.
22. Walter Hubatsch, *Friedrich der Grosse und die preussische Verwaltung* (Cologne, 1973), p. 70.
23. H. M. Scott, 'Prussia's Emergence as a European Great Power, 1740–1763', in Dwyer (ed.), *Rise of Prussia*, pp. 153–76.
24. Schieder, *Frederick the Great*, p. 95; Hubatsch, *Friedrich der Grosse*, p. 70; Kunisch, *Friedrich der Grosse*, p. 167.
25. Schieder, *Frederick the Great*, p. 235.
26. For analyses of the battles of the first two Silesian wars, see David Fraser, *Frederick the Great. King of Prussia* (London, 2000), pp. 91–5, 116–9, 178–84; Christopher Duffy, *Frederick the Great. A Military Life* (London, 1985), pp. 21–75; Dennis Showalter, *The Wars of Frederick the Great* (Harlow, 1996), pp. 38–89.
27. Johannes Kunisch, 'Friedrich II., der Grosse (1740–1786)', in Kroll (ed.), *Preussens Herrscher*, pp. 160–78, here p. 166.
28. T. C. W. Blanning, 'Frederick the Great and Enlightened Absolutism', in H. M. Scott (ed.), *Enlightened Absolutism. Reform and Reformers in Later Eighteenth-century Europe* (London, 1990), pp. 265–88, here p. 281.
29. Kunisch, *Friedrich der Grosse*, p. 332.
30. William J. McGill, 'The Roots of Policy: Kaunitz in Vienna and Versailles 1749–1753', *Journal of Modern History*, 43 (1975), pp. 228–44.
31. Frederick II, *Anti-Machiavel*, pp. 160–62. On the ambiguities of the Anti-Machiavel, see Schieder, *Frederick the Great*, pp. 75–89; Kunisch, *Friedrich der Grosse*, pp. 126–8.
32. Situation paper by Kaunitz, 7 September 1778 in Karl Otmar von Aretin, *Heiliges Römisches Reich 1776–1806. Reichsverfassung und Staatssouveränität* (2 vols., Wiesbaden, 1967), vol. 2, p. 2.
33. On the reasons for this defeat and Frederick's role in it, see Reinhold Koser, 'Bemerkung zur Schlacht von Kolin', in *FBPG*, 11 (1898), pp. 175–200.
34. Scott, 'Prussia's Emergence', p. 175.
35. During the last years of the war, the quality of the Prussian rank and file began to deteriorate under the pressure of the high mortality among infantrymen. Frederick compensated for this to some extent by improving the training and deployment of the Prussian artillery.
36. C. F. R. von Barsewisch, *Meine Kriegserlebnisse während des Siebenjährigen Krieges 1757–1763. Wortgetreuer Abdruck aus dem Tagebuche des Kgl. Preuss. General-Quartiermeister-Lieutenants C. F. R. von Barsewisch* (2nd edn, Berlin, 1863), pp. 75, 77.
37. Helmut Bleckwenn (ed.), *Preussische Soldatenbriefe* (Osnabrück, 1982), p. 18.
38. Franz Reiss to his wife, Lobositz, 6 October 1756, in Bleckwenn (ed.), *Preussische Soldatenbriefe*, p. 29.
39. Barsewisch, *Meine Kriegserlebnisse*, pp. 46–51.
40. [Johann] Wilhelm von Archenholtz, *The history of the Seven Years War in Germany*, trans. F. A. Catty (Frankfurt/Main, 1843), p. 102.
41. Horst Carl, 'Unter fremder Herrschaft. Invasion und Okkupation im Siebenjährigen Krieg', in Kroener and Pröve (eds.), *Krieg und Frieden*, pp. 331–48, here p. 335.
42. Comte de Saint-Germain to M. Paris Du Verney, Mühlhausen, 19 November 1757, cited in Carl, 'Invasion und Okkupation', pp. 331–2.
43. von Archenholtz, *Seven Years War*, p. 92.
44. Horst Carl, 'Invasion und Okkupation', p. 341.
45. The key reference text on the Austro-French background to the diplomatic revolution

is still Max Braubach, *Versailles und Wien von Ludwig XIV bis Kaunitz. Die Vorstadien der diplomatischen Revolution im 18 Jahrhundert* (Bonn, 1952).

46. Michel Antoine, *Louis XV* (Paris, 1989), p. 743.

47. The quotations come from Jean-Louis Soulavie, Charles de Peyssonnel and Louis Philippe Comte de Ségur respectively and are cited in T. C. W. Blanning, *The French Revolutionary Wars, 1787–1802* (London, 1996), p. 23.

48. On the demonization of Marie Antoinette, see the essays in Dena Goodman (ed.), *Marie Antoinette: Writings on the Body of a Queen* (London, 2003).

49. Manfred Hellmann, 'Die Friedenschlüsse von Nystad (1721) und Teschen (1779) als Etappen des Vordringens Russlands nach Europa', *Historisches Jahrbuch*, 97/8 (1978), pp. 270–88. More generally: Walther Mediger, *Moskaus Weg nach Europe. Der Aufstieg Russland zum europäischen Machtstaat im Zeitalter Friedrichs des Grossen* (Brunswick, 1952); for an analysis of the broader consequences of the Seven Years War for the European states system, see H. M. Scott, *The Emergence of the Eastern Powers, 1756–1775* (Cambridge, 2001), esp. pp. 32–67.

50. Cited in Christopher Duffy, *Russia's Military Way to the West: Origins and Nature of Russian Military Power 1700–1800* (London, 1981), p. 74.

51. T. C. W. Blanning, *Joseph II* (London, 1994), passim; Ingrao, *Habsburg Monarchy*, p. 182; Werner Bein, *Schlesien in der habsburgischen Politik. Ein Beitrag zur Entstehung des Dualismus im Alten Reich* (Sigmaringen, 1994), pp. 295–322.

52. Kossert, *Masuren*, p. 93.

53. Frederick II, Political Testament of 1768, in Dietrich, *Die politischen Testamente*, p. 554.

54. Atorf, *Der König und das Korn*, pp. 208–22.

55. Gustav Schmoller and Otto Hintze (eds.), *Die Behördenorganisation und die allgemeine Staatsverwaltung Preussens im 18. Jahrhundert* (15 vols., Berlin, 1894–1936), vol. 7 (1894), no. 9, pp. 21–3 and no. 69, pp. 107–8.

56. Atorf, *Der König und das Korn*, pp. 202–3.

57. Carl, *Okkupation und Regionalismus*, p. 415.

58. Frederick II, Political Testament of 1768, in Dietrich, *Die politischen Testamente*, p. 647.

59. Kunisch, *Friedrich der Grosse*, pp. 244–5.

60. Frederick II, 'Reflections on the Financial Administration of the Prussian Government', in Dietrich, *Die politischen Testamente*, p. 723.

61. H. M. Scott, '1763–1786: The Second Reign of Frederick the Great', in Dwyer (ed.), *Rise of Prussia*, pp. 177–200.

62. Cited in Blanning, *French Revolutionary Wars*, p. 8. On the attribution to Berenhorst, see ibid., p. 32, n. 18.

63. Kunisch, 'Friedrich II.', p. 171.

64. Frederick II, Political Testament of 1752, in Dietrich, *Die politischen Testamente*, pp. 254–461, here pp. 331–3.

65. On the politics of the League of Princes, which began as a small-state alliance against both Prussia and the Habsburgs, see Maiken Umbach, 'The Politics of Sentimentality and the German Fürstenbund, 1779–1785', *Historical Journal*, 41, 3 (1998), pp. 679–704.

66. Karl Otmar von Aretin, *Heiliges Römisches Reich: 1776–1806: Reichsverfassung und Staatssouveränität* (2 vols., Weisbaden, 1967), vol. 1, pp. 19–23; Gabriele Haug-Moritz, *Württembergischer Ständekonflikt und deutscher Dualismus: ein Beitrag zur Geschichte des Reichsverbands in der Mitte des 18. Jahrhunderts* (Stuttgart, 1992), pp. 163–99, 344–5; ead., 'Friedrich der Grosse als "Gegenkaiser": Überlegungen zur preussischen Reichspolitik, 1740–1786', in Haus der Geschichte Baden-Württemberg (ed.), *Vom Fels zum Meer. Preussen und Südwestdeutschland* (Tübingen, 2002), pp. 25–44; Volker Press, 'Friedrich der Grosse als Reichspolitiker', in Heinz Duchhardt (ed.), *Friedrich der Grosse, Franken und das Reich* (Cologne, 1986), pp. 25–56, esp. pp. 42–4.

67. Hans-Martin Blitz, *Aus Liebe zum Vaterland. Die deutsche Nation im 18. Jahrhundert* (Hamburg, 2000), pp. 160–63.

68. Haug-Moritz, *Württembergischer Ständekonflikt*, p. 165.
69. Ramler to Gleim, 11 December 1757, in Carl Schüddekopf (ed.), *Briefwechsel zwischen Gleim und Ramler* (2 vols., Tübingen, 1907), vol. 2, pp. 306–7.
70. Johann Wilhelm Archenholtz, *Geschichte des Siebenjährigen Krieges in Deutschland* (5th edn; 1 vol. in 2 parts, Berlin, 1840), part 2, pp. 165–6.
71. August Friedrich Wilhelm Sack, 'Danck-Predigt über 1. Buch Mose 50 v. 20 wegen des den 6ten May 1757 bey Prag von dem Allmächtigen unsern Könige verliehenen herrlichen Sieges', in id., *Drei Danck-Predigten über die von dem grossen Könige Friedrich II. im Jahre 1757 erfochtenen Siege bei Prag, bei Rossbach und bei Leuthen, in demselben Jahre im Dom zu Berlin gehalten. Zum hundertjährigen Gedächtniss der genannten Schlachten wider herausgegeben* (Berlin, 1857), p. 14.
72. Cited in Blitz, *Aus Liebe zum Vaterland*, p. 179.
73. Schüddekopf (ed.), *Briefwechsel*, pp. 306–7; Blitz, *Aus Liebe zum Vaterland*, pp. 171–86.
74. Thomas Biskup, 'The Politics of Monarchism. Royalty, Loyalty and Patriotism in Later 18th-century Prussia', Ph.D. thesis, Cambridge (2001), p. 55.
75. Thomas Abbt, 'Vom Tode für das Vaterland (1761)' in Franz Brüggemann (ed.), *Der Siebenjährige Krieg im Spiegel der zeitgenössischen Literatur* (Leipzig, 1935), pp. 47–94, here p. 92.
76. Christian Ewald von Kleist, 'Grabschrift auf den Major von Blumenthal, der den 1sten Jan. 1757 bey Ostritz in der Oberlausitz in einem Scharmützel erschossen ward', in id., *Des Herrn Christian Ewald von Kleist sämtliche Werke* (2 parts, Berlin, 1760), part 2, p. 123. This verse is also cited in Abbt's 'Vom Tode'.
77. Johannes Kunisch (ed.), *Aufklärung und Kriegserfahrung. Klassische Zeitzeugen zum Siebenjährigen Krieg* (Frankfurt/Main, 1996), commentary on Abbt, p. 986.
78. Friedrich Nicolai, *Das Leben und die Meinungen des Herrn Magister Sebaldus Nothanker* (Leipzig, 1938), p. 34.
79. Helga Schultz (ed.), *Der Roggenpreis und die Kriege des grossen Königs. Chronik und Rezeptsammlung des Berliner Bäckermeisters Johann Friedrich Heyde 1740 bis 1786* (Berlin, 1988).
80. Carl, *Okkupation und Regionalismus*, pp. 366–7.
81. Abbt, 'Vom Tode', in Brüggemann (ed.), *Der Siebenjährige Krieg*, p. 53.
82. Nicolai, *Sebaldus Nothanker*, p. 34.
83. Johann Wilhelm Ludwig Gleim, 'Siegeslied nach der Schlacht bei Rossbach', in Brüggemann (ed.), *Der Siebenjährige Krieg*, pp. 109–17.
84. Abbt, 'Vom Tode', in Brüggemann (ed.), *Der Siebenjährige Krieg*, p. 66.
85. Johann Wilhelm Ludwig Gleim, 'An die Kriegsmuse nach der Niederlage der Russen bei Zorndorf', in Brüggemann (ed.), *Der Siebenjährige Krieg*, pp. 129–36, here p. 135.
86. Anna Louise Karsch, 'Dem Vater des Vaterlandes Friedrich dem Grossen, bei triumphierender Zurückkunft gesungen im Namen Seiner Bürger. Den 30. März 1763', in C. L. von Klenke (ed.), *Anna Louisa Karschin 1722–1791. Nach der Dichterin Tode nebst ihrem lebenslauff Harausgegeben von Ihrer Tochter* (Berlin, 1792); text downloaded from 'Bibliotheca Augustana' *http://www.fh-augsburg.de/~harsch/germanica/Chronologie/18Jh/Karsch/karintr.html*; last accessed 26 November 2003.
87. Schultz, *Der Roggenpreis*, p. 98; Kunisch, *Friedrich der Grosse*, p. 443.
88. Biskup, *Politics of Monarchism*, p. 42; Kunisch, *Friedrich der Grosse*, p. 446.
89. Biskup, *Politics of Monarchism*, p. 43.
90. Bruno Preisendörfer, *Staatsbildung als Königskunst. Ästhetik und Herrschaft im preussischen Absolutismus* (Berlin, 2000), pp. 83–110, esp. pp. 107–9.
91. Helmut Börsch-Supan, 'Friedrich der Grosse im zeitgenössischen Bildnis', in Oswald Hauser (ed.), *Friedrich der Grosse in seiner Zeit* (Cologne, 1987), pp. 255–70, here pp. 256, 266.
92. Eckhart Hellmuth, 'Die "Wiedergeburt" Friedrichs des Grossen und der "Tod fürs Vaterland". Zum patriotischen Selbstverständnis in Preussen in der zweiten hälfte des 18. Jahrhunderts', *Aufklärung*, 10/2 (1998), pp. 22–54.

93. Friedrich Nicolai, *Anekdoten von König Friedrich dem Zweiten von Preussen* (Berlin and Stettin, 1788–1792; reprint Hildesheim, 1985), pp. i–xvii.

94. On these aspects of anecdote more generally, see Volker Weber, *Anekdote. Die andere Geschichte. Erscheinungsformen der Anekdote in der deutschen Literatur, Geschichtsschreibung und Philosophie* (Tübingen, 1993), pp. 25, 48, 59, 60, 62–5, 66.

95. Carl, 'Invasion und Okkupation', p. 347.

96. Colley, *Britons*, esp. pp. 11–54.

97. Hellmuth, 'Die "Wiedergeburt" ', p. 26.

98. This was a consequence of the annexation of 'Polish Prussia' (formerly 'Royal Prussia'), which placed Frederick in sole possession of the ancient principality of Prussia, and thus did away with the need for the awkward title granted to his ancestor Frederick I.

99. Norman Davies, *God's Playground. A History of Poland* (2 vols., Oxford, 1981), vol. 1, pp. 339–40, 511.

100. Dietrich, *Die politischen Testamente*, pp. 369–75, 654–5. On the historical controversy over whether these reflections constituted 'plans' or unfocused musings, see Dietrich's introduction at pp. 128–47.

101. The city of Elbing had been under Prussian administration since 1660; the lands of Elbing district were acquired under leasehold by Frederick I in 1698–1703. Jerzy Lukowski, *The Partitions of Poland. 1772, 1793, 1795* (Harlow, 1999), pp. 16–17.

102. Cf. Ingrid Mittenzwei, *Friedrich II von Preussen: eine Biographie* (Cologne, 1980), p. 172; Wolfgang Plat, *Deutsche und Polen. Geschichte der deutsch-polnischen Beziehungen* (Cologne, 1980), pp. 85–7; Davies, *God's Playground*, p. 523.

103. Ernst Opgenoorth (ed.), *Handbuch der Geschichte Ost- und Westpreussens. Von der Teilung bis zum Schwedisch-Polnischen Krieg, 1466–1655* (Lüneburg, 1994), p. 22.

104. Davies, *God's Playground*, p. 521.

105. Willi Wojahn, *Der Netzedistrikt und die sozialökonomischen Verhältnisse seiner Bevölkerung um 1773* (Münster, 1996), pp. 16–17.

106. See, for example, Heinz Neumeyer, *Westpreussen. Geschichte und Schicksal* (Munich, 1993).

107. William W. Hagen, *Germans, Poles and Jews. The Nationality Conflict in the Prussian East, 1772–1914* (Chicago, 1980), pp. 39–41, 43. On the contemporary German consensus regarding Polish inferiority, see Jörg Hackmann, *Ostpreussen und Westpreussen in deutscher und polnischer Sicht. Landeshistorie als beziehungsgeschichtliches Problem* (Wiesbaden, 1996), p. 66.

108. Peter Baumgart, 'The Annexation and Integration of Silesia into the Prussian State of Frederick the Great', in Mark Greengrass (ed.), *Conquest and Coalescence. The Shaping of the State in Early Modern Europe* (London, 1991), pp. 155–81, here p. 167; Hubatsch, *Friedrich der Grosse*, p. 77.

109. Hans-Jürgen Bömelburg, *Zwischen polnischer Ständegesellschaft und preussischem Obrigkeitsstaat. Vom Königlichen Preussen zu Westpreussen (1756–1806)* (Munich, 1995), pp. 254–5.

110. Brigitte Poschmann, 'Verfassung, Verwaltung, Recht, Militär im Ermland', in Opgenoorth (ed.), *Geschichte Ost- und Westpreussens*, pp. 39–43, here p. 42.

111. Wojahn, *Netzedistrikt*, p. 25.

112. On taxation rates, see Max Bär, *Westpreussen unter Friedrich dem Grossen* (2 vols., Leipzig, 1909), vol. 2, p. 422, esp. n. 1; Hagen, *Germans, Poles and Jews*, p. 40.

113. Corni, *Stato assoluto*, pp. 304–5.

114. Bär, *Westpreussen*, vol. 2, pp. 465–6; Corni, *Stato assoluto*, p. 305.

115. Bär, *Westpreussen*, vol. 1, pp. 574–81.

116. Bömelburg, *Zwischen polnischer Ständegesellschaft*, pp. 411, 413.

117. August Carl Holsche, *Der Netzedistrikt. Ein Beitrag zur Länder- und Völkerkunde mit statistischen Nachrichten* (Königsberg, 1793), cited in Wojahn, *Netzedistrikt*, p. 29.

118. Neumeyer, *Westpreussen*, pp. 313–14; Bömelburg, *Zwischen polnischer Ständegesellschaft*, p. 367.

119. See Bär, *Westpreussen*, vol. 2, passim.

120. Frederick II, Political Testament of 1752, in Dietrich, *Die politischen Testamente*, p. 283.

121. Cited in Kunisch, *Friedrich der Grosse*, p. 245.

122. Frederick II, Political Testament of 1752, in Dietrich, *Die politischen Testamente*, p. 329.

123. Kunisch, *Friedrich der Grosse*, p. 128.

124. On Wolff's place in the emergence of a stronger state concept in Prussia, see Blanning, *The Culture of Power*, p. 200. Wolff had been banished from Prussia after a quarrel with the Pietists at the University of Halle in 1721. One of the first things Frederick II did after his accession was to recall him. See also Christian Freiherr von Wolff, *Vernünfftige Gedanken von dem gesellschaftlichen Leben der Menschen und insonderheit dem gemeinen Wesen* (Halle, 1756), pp. 212–14, 216–17, 238, 257, 345, 353, 357.

125. Cited in Hubatsch, *Friedrich der Grosse*, p. 75.

126. Ibid., p. 85.

127. Blanning, *The Culture of Power*, p. 92; Hans-Joachim Giersberg, 'Friedrich II und die Architektur', in Hans-Joachim Giersberg and Claudia Meckel (eds.), *Friedrich II und die Kunst* (2 vols., Potsdam, 1986), vol. 2, p. 54; Hans-Joachim Giersberg, *Friedrich II als Bauherr. Studien zur Architektur des 18. Jahrhunderts in Berlin und Potsdam* (Berlin, 1986), p. 23.

128. The opera house was in theory for invited guests only; in reality it was widely patronized by Berliners and visitors to the city, who had merely to tip the doormen to gain entrance. The royal library was likewise open at certain hours of the day to the general public.

129. See Martin Engel, *Das Forum Fridericianum und die monumentalen Residenzplätze des 18. Jahrhunderts*, Ph.D. thesis in art history, Freie Universität Berlin (2001), pp. 302–3. This thesis can be read online through the Darwin digital dissertations website at *http:// www.diss.fu-berlin.de/2004/161/indexe.html#information*; last accessed on 24 February 2005. On the Forum, see also Kunisch, *Friedrich der Grosse*, pp. 258–9, 282.

130. Hubatsch, *Friedrich der Grosse*, p. 233; Reinhart Koselleck, *Preussen zwischen Reform und Revolution. Allgemeines Landrecht, Verwaltung und soziale Bewegung von 1791 bis 1848* (Stuttgart, 1967), pp. 23–149; Hans Hattenhauer, 'Preussen auf dem Weg zum Rechtsstaat', in Jörg Wolff (ed.), *Das Preussische Allgemeine Landrecht: politische, rechtliche und soziale Wechsel- und Fortwirkungen* (Heidelberg, 1995), pp. 49–67.

131. ALR §75, Hans Hattenhauer (ed.), *Allgemeines Landrecht für die preussischen Staaten von 1794* (Frankfurt/Main, 1970).

132. Frederick II, Political Testament of 1752, in Dietrich, *Die politischen Testamente*, p. 381.

133. Kunisch, *Friedrich der Grosse*, pp. 293–9.

134. Frederick II, Political Testament of 1768, in Dietrich, *Die politischen Testamente*, p. 519.

135. Neuchâtel remained a Hohenzollern possession until 1857, when it was ceded to the Swiss state. Wolfgang Stribrny, *Die Könige von Preussen als Fürsten von Neuenburg-Neuchâtel (1707–1848)* (Berlin, 1998), p. 296.

136. Frederick II, Political Testament of 1768, in Dietrich, *Die politischen Testamente*, p. 619.

137. Ibid., pp. 510–11. The 'Rétablissement' of East Prussia was discontinued in 1743; see Notbohm, *Das evangelische Schulwesen*, p. 186.

138. Walter Merteneit, *Die fridericianische Verwaltung in Ostpreussen. Ein Beitrag zur Geschichte der preussischen Staatsbildung* (Heidelberg, 1958), p. 179.

139. Ibid., pp. 183–5.

140. Frederick II, Political Testament of 1752, in Dietrich, *Die politischen Testamente*, pp. 325–7.

8 Dare to Know!

1. Immanuel Kant, 'Beantwortung der Frage: Was ist Aufklärung?', *Berlinische Monats-schrift* (dated 30 September 1784, published in December 1784), reprinted in *Berlinische Monatsschrift (1783–1796)* (Leipzig, 1986), pp. 89–96, here p. 89.

2. Ibid., p. 90.

3. Richard van Dülmen, *The Society of the Enlightenment. The Rise of the Middle Class and Enlightenment Culture in Germany*, trans. Anthony Williams (Oxford, 1992), pp. 47–8. On Kant and the 'language of reason', see Hans Saner, *Kant's Political Thought. Its Origins and Development*, trans. E. B. Ashton (Chicago, 1973), p. 76.

4. Ferdinand Runkel, *Geschichte der Freimaurerei in Deutschland* (3 vols., Berlin, 1931–2), vol. 1, pp. 154–8. On the Freemasons more generally, see Ulrich Im Hof, *The Enlightenment*, trans. William E. Yuill (Oxford, 1994), pp. 139–45.

5. Norbert Schindler, 'Freimaurerkultur im 18. Jahrhundert. Zur sozialen Funktion des Geheimwissens in der entstehenden bürgerlichen Gesellschaft', in Robert Berdahl et al. (eds.), *Klassen und Kultur* (Frankfurt/Main, 1982), pp. 205–62, here p. 208.

6. *Berlinische Monatsschrift*, 2 (1783), p. 516.

7. Friedrich Gedike and J. E. Biester, 'Vorrede', *Berlinische Monatsschrift*, 1 (1783), p. 1.

8. Im Hof, *Enlightenment*, pp. 118–22.

9. Joseph Kohnen, 'Druckerei-, Verlags- und Zeitungswesen in Königsberg zur Zeit Kants und Hamanns. Das Unternehmen Johann Jakob Kanters', in id. (ed.), *Königsberg. Beiträge zu einem besonderen Kapitel der deutschen Geistesgeschichte des 18. Jahrhunderts* (Frankfurt/Main, 1994), pp. 1–30, esp. pp. 9–10, 12–13, 15.

10. Obituary by Leopold Friedrich Günther von Goeckingh (1748–1828), cited in Eberhard Fromm, 'Der poetische Exerziermeister', in *Deutsche Denker*, pp. 58–63, *http://www.luise-berlin.de/bms/bmstext/9804deua.htm*; last accessed 18 December 2003.

11. On 'practitioners of civil society', see Isobel V. Hull, *Sexuality, State and Civil Society in Germany, 1700–1815* (Ithaca, NY, 1996), esp. ch. 5.

12. Horst Möller, *Vernunft und Kritik. Deutsche Aufklärung im 17. und 18. Jahrhundert* (Frankfurt/Main, 1986), pp. 295–6.

13. Kant, 'Was ist Aufklärung?', p. 95.

14. Otto Bardong (ed.), *Friedrich der Grosse* (Darmstadt, 1982), p. 542. This passage is discussed in Blanning, 'Frederick the Great', in Scott (ed.), *Enlightened Absolutism*, pp. 265–88, here p. 282.

15. Mittenzwei, *Friedrich II.*, pp. 44–5.

16. Richard J. Evans, *Rituals of Retribution. Capital Punishment in Germany, 1600–1987* (London, 1997), p. 113.

17. Matthias Schmoeckel, *Humanität und Staatsraison. Die Abschaffung der Folter in Europa und die Entwicklung des gemeinen Strafprozess- und Beweisrechts seit dem hohen Mittelalter* (Cologne, 2000), pp. 19–33.

18. Evans, *Rituals*, p. 122.

19. Blanning, 'Frederick the Great', p. 282.

20. Jonathan I. Israel, *Radical Enlightenment. Philosophy and the Making of Modernity 1650–1750* (Oxford, 2001), pp. 659–63.

21. Kant, 'Was ist Aufklärung?', p. 96. A similar argument is advanced in Kant's essay 'On the Common Saying: "This May Be True in Theory but Does Not Apply in Practice"' (first published in the *Berlinische Monatsschrift*, 1793); see Immanuel Kant, *Political Writings*, ed. Hans Reiss, trans. H. B. Nisbet (2nd edn, Cambridge, 1991), pp. 61–92, here esp. pp. 79, 81, 84–5.

22. Blanning, *The Culture of Power*, pp. 103–82.

23. Möller, *Vernunft und Kritik*, p. 303.

24. This quotation is from the senior Prussian judicial official Leopold von Kircheisen and dates from 1792, six years after Frederick II's death. It is cited from Hull, *Sexuality, State and Civil Society*, p. 215.

25. John Moore, *A View of Society and Manners in France, Switzerland and Germany* (2 vols., 4th edn, Dublin, 1789; first pub. anon., 1779), vol. 2, p. 130, cited in Blanning, 'Frederick the Great', p. 287.

26. Friedrich Nicolai, *Beschreibung der Königlichen Residenzstädte Berlin und Potsdam, aller daselbst befindlicher Markwürdigkeiten und der umliegenden Gegend* (2 vols., Berlin, 1786), vol. 2, pp. 839–40.

27. Hilde Spiel, *Fanny von Arnstein. Daughter of the Enlightenment 1758–1818*, trans. Christine Shuttleworth (Oxford, 1991), pp. 15–16.

28. Stern, *Der preussische Staat*, part 3, vol. 2, *Die Zeit Friedrichs II.* (Tübingen, 1971), passim.

29. Frederick William I, Political Testament of 1722, in Dietrich (ed.), *Die politischen Testamente*, pp. 221–43, here p. 236.

30. Frederick II, Political Testament of 1768, in Dietrich (ed.), *Die politischen Testamente*, pp. 462–697, here p. 507.

31. Mordechai Breuer, 'The Early Modern Period', in Michael A. Meyer and Michael Brenner (eds.), *German-Jewish History in Modern Times* (4 vols., New York, 1996), vol. 1, *Tradition and Enlightenment 1600–1780*, pp. 79–260, here pp. 146–9.

32. Stefi Jersch-Wenzel, 'Minderheiten in der preussischen Gesellschaft', in Büsch and Neugebauer (eds.), *Moderne preussische Geschichte*, vol. 1, part 2, pp. 486–506, here p. 492.

33. Dorwart, *Prussian Welfare State*, p. 129; Stern, *Der preussische Staat*, part 2, *Die Zeit Friedrich Wilhelms I.*, part 2, Akten, doc. nos. 7, 8, 211 and passim.

34. J. H. Callenberg, *Siebente Fortsetzung seines Berichts von einem Versuch, das arme jüdische Volck zur Annehmung der christlichen Wahrheit anzuleiten* (Halle, 1734), pp. 92–3, 126, 142. See also id., *Relation von einer weiteren Bemühung, Jesum Christum als den Heyland des menschlichen Geschlechts dem Jüdischen Volcke bekannt zu machen* (Halle, 1738), pp. 134, 149.

35. Michael Graetz, 'The Jewish Enlightenment', in Meyer and Brenner (eds.), *German-Jewish History*, vol. 1, pp. 261–380, here p. 311.

36. Charlene A. Lea, 'Tolerance Unlimited: The "Noble Jew" on the German and Austrian Stage (1750–1805)', *The German Quarterly*, 64/2 (1991), pp. 167–77.

37. Spiel, *Fanny von Arnstein*, p. 19; David Sorkin, *The Transformation of German Jewry, 1780–1840* (New York, 1987), p. 8 and passim.

38. Cited in Michael Graetz, 'The Jewish Enlightenment', in Meyer and Brenner (eds.), *German-Jewish History*, vol. 1, p. 274.

39. Deborah Hertz, *Jewish High Society in Old-regime Berlin* (New Haven and London, 1988), pp. 95–118; Steven M. Lowenstein, *The Berlin Jewish Community. Enlightenment, Family and Crisis, 1770–1830* (New York, 1994), pp. 104–10.

40. Christian Wilhelm Dohm, *Über die bürgerliche Verbesserung der Juden* (2 vols., Berlin and Stettin, 1781–3), vol. 1, p. 130.

41. Dohm, *Über die bürgerliche Verbesserung*. For commentaries on the book and its context, see esp. R. Liberles, 'The Historical Context of Dohm's Treatise on the Jews', in Friedrich-Naumann-Stiftung (ed.), *Das deutsche Judentum und der Liberalismus – German Jewry and Liberalism* (Königswinter, 1986), pp. 44–69; Horst Möller, 'Aufklärung, Judenemanzipation und Staat. Ursprung und Wirkung von Dohms Schrift über die bürgerliche Verbesserung der Juden', in W. Grab (ed.), *Deutsche Aufklärung und Judenemanzipation. Internationales Symposium anlässlich der 250. Geburtstage Lessings und Mendelssohns* (*Jahrbuch des Instituts für deutsche Geschichte*, Suppl. 3; Tel Aviv, 1980), pp. 119–49.

42. Spiel, *Fanny von Arnstein*, p. 183.

43. Ibid., p. 184.

44. The play is discussed in Michael A. Meyer, 'Becoming German, Remaining Jewish', in Meyer and Brenner (eds.), *German-Jewish History*, vol. 2, pp. 199–250, here pp. 204–6. On anti-Jewish satire more generally, see Charlene A. Lea, *Emancipation, Assimilation and Stereotype. The Image of the Jew in German and Austrian Drama (1800–1850)* (Bonn, 1978); Mark H. Gelber, 'Wandlungen im Bild des "gebildeten Juden" in der

deutschen Literatur', *Jahrbuch des Institut für deutsche Geschichte*, 13 (1984), pp. 165–78.

45. The conversion problem is discussed in Hertz, *Jewish High Society*; see also ead., 'Seductive Conversion in Berlin, 1770–1809', in Todd Endelman (ed.), *Jewish Apostasy in the Modern World* (New York and London, 1990), pp. 48–82; Lowenstein, *The Berlin Jewish Community*, pp. 120–33.

46. Cited in James Sheehan, *German History 1770–1866* (Oxford, 1993), p. 293.

47. As Frederick remained childless, the right of succession passed to his younger brother, August William, who died in 1758, leaving his son as heir to the throne.

48. Kunisch, *Friedrich der Grosse*, p. 285.

49. David E. Barclay, 'Friedrich Wilhelm II (1786–1797)', in Kroll (ed.), *Preussens Herrscher*, pp. 179–96.

50. Thomas P. Saine, *The Problem of Being Modern. Or, the German Pursuit of Enlightenment from Leibniz to the French Revolution* (Detroit, Michigan, 1997), p. 300.

51. Dirk Kemper (ed.), *Missbrauchte Aufklärung? Schriften zum preussischen Religionsedikt vom 9. Juli 1788* (Hildesheim, 1996); Ian Hunter, 'Kant and the Prussian Religious Edict. Metaphysics within the Bounds of Political Reason Alone', Working Paper, Centre of the History of European Discourses, University of Queensland, accessed online at *http://eprint.uq.edu.au/archive/00000396/01/hunterkant.pdf*; last accessed 30 December 2003.

52. See the editor's and translator's commentaries in A. W. Wood and G. Di Giovanni (eds.), *Immanuel Kant: Religion and Rational Theology* (Cambridge, 1996); Saine, *The Problem of Being Modern*, pp. 289–309; Paul Schwartz, *Der erste Kulturkampf in Preussen um Kirche und Schule (1788–1798)*, (Berlin 1925), pp. 93–107; Klaus Epstein, *The Genesis of German Conservatism* (Princeton, NJ, 1966), pp. 360–68.

53. This view of Wöllner is persuasively set out in Michael J. Sauter, 'Visions of the Enlightenment: The Edict on Religion of 1788 and Political Reaction in Eighteenth-century Prussia', Ph.D. thesis, Department of History, University of California, Los Angeles (2002).

54. Kemper, *Missbrauchte Aufklärung?*, p. 227.

55. For an interesting discussion of the edict, which draws useful comparisons with the language of the Prussian Law Code, see Nicholas Hope, *German and Scandinavian Protestantism, 1700 to 1918* (Oxford, 1995), pp. 312–13. On the traces of enlightenment in the edict, see especially Fritz Valjavec, 'Das Woellnersche Religionsedikt und seine geschichtliche Bedeutung', *Historisches Jahrbuch*, 72 (1952), pp. 386–400. On instrumental views of religion, see Epstein, *Genesis*, p. 150.

56. Kurt Nowak, *Geschichte des Christenthums in Deutschland. Religion, Politik und Gesellschaft vom Ende der Aufklärung bis zur Mitte des 20. Jahrhunderts* (Munich, 1995), pp. 15–36.

57. Hunter, 'Kant and the Prussian Religious Edict', p, 7.

58. Ibid. pp. 11–12.

59. Frederick William II, cabinet order of 10 September 1788, cited in Klaus Berndl, 'Neues zur Biographie von Ernst Ferdinand Klein', in Eckhart Hellmuth, Immo Meenken and Michael Trauth (eds.), *Zeitenwende? Preussen um 1800* (Stuttgart, 1999), pp. 139–82, here p. 161, n. 118.

60. Saine, *The Problem of Being Modern*, pp. 294–308.

61. Berndl, 'Ernst Ferdinand Klein', pp. 162–4.

62. Wilhelm Schrader, *Geschichte der Friedrichs-Universität zu Halle* (2 vols., Berlin, 1894), vol. 1, p. 521; Epstein, *Genesis*, pp. 364–7; Berndl, 'Ernst Ferdinand Klein', pp. 167–70.

63. Horst Möller, *Aufklärung in Preussen. Der Verleger, Publizist und Geschichtsschreiber Friedrich Nicolai* (Berlin, 1974), p. 213.

64. Axel Schumann, 'Berliner Presse und Französische Revolution: Das Spektrum der Meinungen unter preussischer Zensur 1789–1806', Ph.D. thesis, Technische Universität, Berlin (2001), accessed online at *http://webdoc.gwdg.de/ebook/p/2003/tu-berlin/schumann axel.pdf*; last accessed 31 December 2003, esp. pp. 227–41.

65. *Journal des Luxus*, 11 (1796), p. 428, cited in Hellmuth, 'Die "Wiedergeburt" ', pp. 21–52, here p. 22.

66. For an excellent survey of social life in Berlin at this time, on which the following two paragraphs are based, see Florian Maurice, *Freimaurerei um 1800. Ignaz Aurelius Fessler und die Reform der Grossloge Royal York in Berlin* (Tübingen, 1997), pp. 129–66.

67. Gerhard Ritter, *Stein. Eine politische Biographie* (Stuttgart, 1958), pp. 29, 31, 34, 37, 39, 40; Guy Stanton Ford, *Stein and the Era of Reform in Prussia, 1807–1815* (2nd edn, Gloucester, MA, 1965), pp. 4–26, 31–2.

68. Ford, *Stein*, pp. 33–4.

69. Ritter, *Stein*, p. 71.

70. Silke Lesemann, 'Prägende Jahre. Hardenbergs Herkunft und Amtstätigkeit in Hannover und Braunschweig (1771–1790)', in Thomas Stamm-Kuhlmann (ed.), *'Freier Gebrauch der Kräfte'. Eine Bestandaufnahme der Hardenberg-Forschung* (Munich, 2001), pp. 11–30, here pp. 11–18.

71. Lesemann, 'Prägende Jahre', pp. 18–25.

72. It had long been agreed that Ansbach and Bayreuth would fall to Prussia upon the death of the reigning Hohenzollern margrave. In 1792, however, under the pressure of events in France and of his own immense debts, he allowed himself to be 'bought out' prematurely by Berlin.

73. Andrea Hofmeister-Hunger, *Pressepolitik und Staatsreform. Die Institutionalisierung staatlicher Öffentlichkeitsarbeit bei Karl August von Hardenberg (1792–1822)* (Göttingen, 1994), pp. 32–47; Rudolf Endres, 'Hardenbergs fränkisches Reformmodell', in Stamm-Kuhlmann (ed.), *Hardenberg-Forschung*, pp. 31–49, here p. 38.

74. Rudolf Endres, 'Hardenbergs fränkisches Reformmodell', pp. 45–6.

75. Rolf Straubel, *Carl August von Struensee. Preussische Wirtschafts- und Finanzpolitik im ministeriellen Kräftespiel (1786–1804/06)* (Potsdam, 1999), pp. 112–17.

76. Manfred Gailus, ' "Moralische Ökonomie" und Rebellion in Preussen vor 1806: Havelberg, Halle und Umgebung', *FBPG* (New Series), 11 (2001), pp. 77–100, esp. pp. 95–7.

77. On the use of the new peripheral Polish provinces of South and New East Prussia as 'laboratories' for administrative reform, see Ingeborg Charlotte Bussenius, *Die Preussische Verwaltung in Süd- und Neuostpreussen 1793–1806* (Heidelberg, 1960), pp. 314–15.

78. Hans Hattenhauer, 'Das ALR im Widerstreit der Politik', in Jörg Wolff (ed.), *Das Preussische Allgemeine Landrecht. Politische, rechtliche und soziale Wechsel- und Fortwirkungen* (Heidelberg, 1995), pp. 31–48, here p. 48.

79. ALR §1 Einleitung. For a discussion of this passage, see Hattenhauer, 'Preussen auf dem Weg' in Wolff (ed.), *Das Preussische Allgemeine Landrecht*, pp. 49–67, here p. 62.

80. ALR §22 Einleitung.

81. Thilo Ramm, 'Die friderizianische Rechtskodifikation und der historische Rechtsvergleich', in Wolff (ed.), *Das Preussische Allgemeine Landrecht*, pp. 1–30, here p. 12.

82. On this see Günther Birtsch, 'Die preussische Sozialverfassung im Spiegel des Allgemeinen Landrechts für die preussischen Staaten von 1794', in Wolff (ed.), *Das Preussische Allgemeine Landrecht*, pp. 133–47, here p. 133. For a discussion of corporatist themes more generally in the code, see Andreas Schwennicke, *Die Entstehung der Einleitung des Preussischen Allgemeinen Landrechts von 1794* (Frankfurt/Main, 1993), pp. 34–43, 70–105.

83. ALR §§ 147, 161–72, 185–7, 227–30, 308, 309. Birtsch, 'Die preussische Sozialverfassung', p. 143. On the ALR as an attempt to marry absolutist with corporatist principles, see Günther Birtsch, 'Gesetzgebung und Representation im späten Absolutismus. Die Mitwirkung der preussischen Provinzialstände bei der Entstehung des Allgemeinen Landrechts', *Historische Zeitschrift*, 202 (1969), pp. 265–94; Koselleck, *Preussen zwischen Reform und Revolution*, pp. 23–149.

84. ALR Einleitung, 'Quelle des Rechts'. On this, see also Monika Wienfort, 'Zwischen Freiheit und Fürsorge. Das Allgemeine Landrecht im. 19. Jahrhundert', in Patrick Bahners

and Gerd Roellecke (eds.), *Preussische Stile. Ein Staat als Kunstück* (Stuttgart, 2001), pp. 294–309.

85. For an argument along these lines, see Detlef Merten, 'Die Rechtsstaatlichkeit im Allgemeinen Landrecht', in Friedrich Ebel (ed.), *Gemeinwohl – Freiheit – Vernunft – Rechtsstaat. 200 Jahre Allgemeines Landrecht für die preussischen Staaten* (Berlin, 1995), pp. 109–38.

86. Heinrich Treitschke, *Deutsche Geschichte im neunzehnten Jahrhundert* (5 vols., Leipzig, 1927), vol. 1, p. 77.

87. Madame de Staël, *De L'Allemagne* (2nd edn, Paris, 1814), pp. 141–2.

9 Hubris and Nemesis: 1789–1806

1. Ernst Wangermann, 'Preussen und die revolutionären Bewegungen in Ungarn und den österreichischen Niederlanden zur Zeit der französischen Revolution', in Otto Büsch and Monika Neugebauer-Wölk (eds.), *Preussen und die revolutionäre Herausforderung seit 1789* (Berlin, 1991), pp. 22–85, here pp. 81, 83.

2. Monika Neugebauer-Wölk, 'Preussen und die Revolution in Lüttich. Zur Politik des Christian Wilhem von Dohm, 1789/90', in Büsch and Neugebauer-Wölk (eds.), *Preussen und die revolutionäre Herausforderung*, pp. 59–76, here p. 63.

3. Wangermann, 'Preussen und die revolutionären Bewegungen', p. 82.

4. Paul W. Schroeder, *The Transformation of European Politics 1763–1848* (Oxford, 1994), pp. 66, 76; Brendan Simms, *The Struggle for Mastery in Germany, 1779–1850* (London, 1998), pp. 56–7.

5. The text of the Declaration can be accessed online at NapoleonSeries.org, Reference Library of Diplomatic Documents, Declaration of Pillnitz, ed. Alex Stavropoulos, *http://www.napoleonseries.org/reference/diplomatic/pillnitz.cfm*; last accessed on 13 January 2004.

6. Ibid.

7. On the impact of Pillnitz, see Gary Savage, 'Favier's Heirs. The French Revolution and the Secret du Roi', *Historical Journal*, 41/1 (1998), pp. 225–58; Gunther E. Rothenberg, 'The Origins, Causes and Extension of the Wars of the French Revolution and Napoleon', *Journal of Interdisciplinary History*, 18/4 (1988), pp. 771–93, esp. pp. 780–81; T. C. W. Blanning, *Origins of the French Revolutionary Wars* (London, 1986), pp. 100–101; Patricia Chastain Howe, 'Charles-François Dumouriez and the Revolutionizing of French Foreign Affairs in 1792', *French Historical Studies*, 14/3 (1986), pp. 367–90, here pp. 372–3.

8. The Proclamation of the Duke of Brunswick, in J. H. Robinson (ed.), *Readings in European History* (2 vols., Boston, 1906), vol. 2, pp. 443–5. This text can also be consulted online at Hanover Historical Texts Project, *http://history.hanover.edu/texts/bruns.htm*; last accessed 13 January 2004. On the background to the Manifesto, see Hildor Arnold Barton, 'The Origins of the Brunswick Manifesto', *French Historical Studies*, 5 (1967), pp. 146–69.

9. Cited in Lukowski, *Partitions*, p. 140.

10. Hertzberg to Lucchesini, cited in ibid., p. 143.

11. For general accounts of the second partition, see Michael G. Müller, *Die Teilungen Polens: 1772, 1793, 1795* (Munich, 1984), esp. pp. 43–50; Lukowski, *Partitions*, pp. 128–58.

12. This medley of quotations is drawn from Heinrich von Sybel, *Geschichte der Revolutionszeit von 1789 bis 1800* (5 vols., Stuttgart, 1898), vol. 3, p. 276; Heinrich von Treitschke, *Deutsche Geschichte im neunzehnten Jahrhundert* (5 vols., Leipzig, 1894), vol. 1, p. 207; Rudolf Ibbeken, *Preussen, Geschichte eines Staates* (Stuttgart, 1970), pp. 106–7; Golo Mann, *Deutsche Geschichte des 19. und 20. Jahrhunderts* (Frankfurt/Main, 1992). These views are discussed and analysed in Philip G. Dwyer, 'The Politics of Prussian Neutrality 1795–1805', *German History*, 12 (1994), pp. 351–73.

13. On the financial crisis, see Aretin, *Reich*, vol. 1, p. 318. On links with the 'peace party',

see Willy Real, 'Die preussischen Staatsfinanzen und die Anbahnung des Sonderfriedens von Basel 1795', *FBPG*, 1 (1991), pp. 53–100.

14. Dwyer, 'Politics', p. 357.

15. Schroeder, *Transformation*, esp. pp. 144–50.

16. See Brendan Simms, *The Impact of Napoleon. Prussian High Politics, Foreign Policy and Executive Reform, 1797–1806* (Cambridge, 1997), pp. 101–5.

17. Aretin, *Reich*, vol. 1, p. 277; Sheehan, *German History*, p. 278; Simms, *Struggle for Mastery*, p. 62.

18. Cited in ibid., pp. 60–61.

19. [S.?] Leszczinski (ed.), *Kriegerleben des Johann von Borcke, weiland Kgl. Preuss. Oberstlieutenants. 1806–1815* (Berlin, 1888), pp. 46–8.

20. Hermann von Boyen, *Denkwürdigkeiten und Erinnerungen* (2 vols.; rev. edn Leipzig, 1899), vol. 1, pp. 171–2, cited in Sheehan, *German History*, p. 234.

21. Cited in Dwyer, 'Politics', p. 361. On the transition from an expedient to a principled neutrality, see pp. 358–67.

22. Simms, *Impact of Napoleon*, pp. 148–56; Dwyer, 'Politics' p. 365.

23. Gregor Schöllgen, 'Sicherheit durch Expansion? Die aussenpolitischen Lageanalysen der Hohenzollern im 17. und 18. Jahrhundert im Lichte des Kontinuitätsproblems in der preussischen und deutschen Geschichte', *Historisches Jahrbuch*, 104 (1984), pp. 22–45.

24. Klaus Zernack, 'Polen in der Geschichte Preussens', in Otto Büsch et al. (eds.), *Handbuch der preussischen Geschichte*, vol. 2, *Das Neunzehnte Jahrhundert und grosse Themen der Geschichte Preussens* (Berlin, 1992), pp. 377–448, here p. 430; id., 'Preussen-Frankreich-Polen. Revolution und Teilung', in Büsch and Neugebauer-Wölk (eds.), *Preussen*, pp. 22–40; William W. Hagen, 'The Partitions of Poland and the Crisis of the Old Regime in Prussia, 1772–1806', *Central European History*, 9 (1976), pp. 115–28.

25. These issues are discussed in Torsten Riotte, 'Hanover in British Policy 1792–1815', Ph.D. thesis, University of Cambridge (2003).

26. This point is made by Reinhold Koser in 'Die preussische Politik, 1786–1806' in id., *Zur preussischen und deutschen Geschichte* (Stuttgart, 1921), pp. 202–68, here pp. 248–9.

27. On the Rumbold crisis, see Simms, *The Impact of Napoleon*, pp. 159–67, 277, 285.

28. Cited in McKay, *Great Elector*, p. 105.

29. Brendan Simms, 'The Road to Jena: Prussian High Politics, 1804–06', *German History*, 12 (1994), pp. 374–94. For a fuller analysis of the role played by adversarial rivalries, see id., *Impact of Napoleon*, esp. pp. 285–91.

30. Haugwitz to Lucchesini, 15 June 1806, cited in Simms, 'The Road to Jena', p. 386.

31. These rivalries are analysed in Simms, ibid.

32. This summary is borrowed from Ford, *Stein*, pp. 105–6.

33. Cited in ibid., p. 106.

34. Hardenberg, memorandum of 18 June 1806, cited in Simms, 'The Road to Jena', pp. 388–9.

35. Thomas Stamm-Kuhlmann, *König in Preussens grosser Zeit. Friedrich Wilhelm III., der Melancholiker auf dem Thron* (Berlin, 1992), pp. 229–31.

36. Frederick William III to Napoleon, Naumburg, 26 September 1806, in Leopold von Ranke (ed.), *Denkwürdigkeiten des Staatskanzlers Fürsten von Hardenberg* (5 vols., Leipzig, 1877), vol. 3, pp. 179–87.

37. Napoleon to Frederick William III, 12 October 1806, in Eckart Klessmann (ed.), *Deutschland unter Napoleon in Augenzeugenberichten* (Munich, 1976), pp. 123–6.

38. For a lucid discussion of military improvements and a comparison with French capabilities, see Dennis Showalter, 'Hubertusberg to Auerstädt: The Prussian Army in Decline?', *German History*, 12 (1994), pp. 308–33.

39. Michel Kérautret, 'Frédéric II et l'opinion française (1800–1870). La compétition posthume avec Napoléon', *Francia*, 28/2 (2001), pp. 65–84, here p. 69.

40. Memoir by the Saxon officer Karl Heinrich von Einsiedel, cited in Klessmann (ed.), *Deutschland unter Napoleon*, pp. 147–8; Karl-Heinz Blaschke, 'Von Jena 1806 nach Wien

1815: Sachsen zwischen Preussen und Napoleon', in Gerd Fesser and Reinhard Jonscher (eds.), *Umbruch im Schatten Napoleons. Die Schlachten von Jena und Auerstedt und ihre Folgen* (Jena, 1998), pp. 143–56.

10 The World the Bureaucrats Made

1. Lady Jackson, *The Diaries and Letters of Sir George Jackson from the Peace of Amiens to the Battle of Talavera* (2 vols., London, 1872), vol. 2, p. 53.
2. Frederick William III, 'Eigenhändiges Konzept des Königs zu dem Publicandum betr. Abstellung verschiedener Missbräuche bei der Armee, Ortelsburg', 1 December 1806, GStA Berlin-Dahlem, HA VI, NL Friedrich Wilhelm III, Nr. 45/1, ff. 13–17.
3. Ibid., f. 17; this aspect of the document is discussed in Stamm-Kuhlmann, *König in Preussens grosser Zeit*, pp. 245–6. On the penalties subsequently imposed on officers found guilty of dereliction of duty, see Craig, *Politics of the Prussian Army*, p. 42. On the king's involvement more generally in military reform, see Alfred Herrmann, 'Friedrich Wilhelm III und sein Anteil an der Heeresreform bis 1813', *Historische Vierteljahrsschrift*, 11 (1908), pp. 484–516.
4. Berdahl, *Politics of the Prussian Nobility*, pp. 107–8; Bernd Münchow-Pohl, *Zwischen Reform und Krieg. Untersuchungen zur Bewusstseinslage in Preussen 1809–1812* (Göttingen, 1987), pp. 94–131, esp. pp. 108–9.
5. The question of whether reform was forced on the Prussian state by the external shock of defeat or rooted in a native reforming tradition has been controversial: for outlines of the debate, see T. C. W. Blanning, 'The French Revolution and the Modernisation of Germany', *Central European History*, 22 (1989), pp. 109–29; Paul Nolte, 'Preussische Reformen und preussische Geschichte: Kritik und Perspektiven der Forschung', *FBPG*, 6 (1996), pp. 83–95. On the defeat as a 'traumatic experience', see Ludger Herrmann, 'Die Schlachten von Jena und Auerstedt und die Genese der politischen Öffentlichkeit in Preussen', in Fesser and Jonscher (eds.), *Umbruch im Schatten Napoleons*, pp. 39–52.
6. J. R. Seeley, *Life and Times of Stein, or Germany and Prussia in the Napoleonic Age* (3 vols., Cambridge, 1878), vol. 1, p. 32.
7. Cited in Stamm-Kuhlmann, *König in Preussens grosser Zeit*, p. 255.
8. 'Nicht dem Purpur, nicht der Krone/ räumt er eitlen Vorzug ein./ Er ist Bürger auf dem Throne,/ und sein Stolz ist's Mensch zu sein' (my trans.). On this poem see Thomas Stamm-Kuhlmann, 'War Friedrich Wilhelm III. von Preussen ein Bürgerkönig?', *Zeitschrift für Historische Forschung*, 16 (1989), pp. 441–60.
9. Cited in ibid.
10. Cited in Joachim Bennewitz, 'Königin Luise in Berlin', *Berlinische Monatsschrift*, 7/2000, pp. 86–92, here p. 86, accessed online at: *http://www.berlinische-monatsschrift.de/ bms/bmstxt00/0007gesa.htm*; last accessed on 21 March 2004.
11. See Rudolf Speth, 'Königin Luise von Preussen – deutscher Nationalmythos im 19. Jahrhundert', in Sabine Berghahn and Sigrid Koch (eds.), *Mythos Diana – von der Princess of Wales zur Queen of Hearts* (Giessen, 1999), pp. 265–85.
12. Cited in Thomas Stamm-Kuhlmann, 'War Friedrich Wilhelm III. von Preussen ein Bürgerkönig?', p. 453.
13. See Philipp Demandt, *Luisenkult. Die Unsterblichkeit der Königin von Preussen* (Cologne, 2003), p. 8.
14. Cited in Paul Bailleu, *Königin Luise. Ein Lebensbild* (Berlin, 1908), p. 258.
15. Stamm-Kuhlmann, *König in Preussens grosser Zeit*, p. 318.
16. Richard J. Evans, *Tales from the German Underworld* (New Haven, CT, 1998), pp. 31–5, 46. On the penal reforms of these years, see Jürgen Regge, 'Das Reformprojekt eines "Allgemeinen Criminalrechts fur die preussischen Staaten" (1799–1806)', in Hans Hattenhauer and Götz Landwehr (eds.), *Das nachfriderizianische Preussen 1786–1806* (Heidelberg, 1988), pp. 189–233.
17. Citation of Frederick William from Rudolf Stadelmann, *Preussens Könige in ihrer*

Tätigkeit für die Landescultur (4 vols., Leipzig, 1878–87, repr. Osnabrück, 1965), vol. 4, pp. 209–10, 213–14; Report of the General Directory, 15 March 1800, cited in Stamm-Kuhlmann, *König in Preussens grosser Zeit*, p. 156.

18. Otto Hintze, 'Preussische Reformbestrebungen vor 1806', *Historische Zeitschrift*, 76 (1896), pp. 413–43; Hartmut Harnisch, 'Die agrarpolitischen Reformmassnahmen der preussischen Staatsführung in dem Jahrzehnt vor 1806–1807', *Jahrbuch für Wirtschaftsgeschichte*, 1977/3, pp. 129–54.

19. Thomas Welskopp, 'Sattelzeitgenossen. Freiherr Karl vom Stein zwischen Bergbauverwaltung und gesellschaftlicher Reform in Preussen', *Historische Zeitschrift*, 271/2 (2000), pp. 347–72.

20. On the 'half-hearted and vacillating' quality of Hardenberg's foreign policy before 1806, see Reinhold Koser, 'Umschau auf dem Gebiete der brandenburg-preussischen Geschichtsforschung', *FBPG*, 1 (1888), pp. 1–56, here p. 50.

21. Hans Schneider, *Der preussische Staatsrat, 1817–1914. Ein Beitrag zur Verfassungs- und Rechtsgeschichte Preussens* (Munich, 1952), pp. 21–2.

22. The argument that the reforms expedited the bureaucratization of the Prussian monarchy stems from Rosenberg, *Bureaucracy*, passim. Rosenberg's wider claim that bureaucratic reform represented a *corporate bid* by the bureaucracy acting as a 'fourth estate' to usurp the authority of the monarch has been cogently critiqued by Simms in *Impact of Napoleon*, pp. 25, 306–12.

23. Ritter, *Stein*, pp. 145–55.

24. Ernst Rudolf Huber, *Heer und Staat in der deutschen Geschichte* (Heidelberg, 1938), pp. 115–23, 312–20.

25. Craig, *Politics of the Prussian Army*, p. 31; Simms, *Impact of Napoleon*, pp. 132, 323.

26. William O. Shanahan, *Prussian Military Reforms (1786–1813)* (New York, 1945), pp. 75–82; Craig, *Politics of the Prussian Army*, pp. 24, 28.

27. Craig, *Politics of the Prussian Army*, pp. 29–32. Frederick William's conversation with his son's tutor, General Johann Heinrich von Minutoli, is cited in Stamm-Kuhlmann, *König in Preussens grosser Zeit*, pp. 340–41. On the king's support for military reform, see Seeley, *Stein*, vol. 2, p. 118.

28. Emil Karl Georg von Conrady, *Leben und Wirken des Generals Carl von Grolman* (3 vols., Berlin, 1894–6), vol. 1, pp. 159–62.

29. Cited in Huber, *Heer und Staat*, p. 128.

30. Showalter, 'Hubertusberg to Auerstädt', p. 315; Manfred Messerschmidt, 'Menschenführung im preussischen Heer von der Reformzeit bis 1914', in Militärgeschichtliches Forschungsamt (ed.), *Menschenführung im Heer* (Herford, 1982), pp. 81–112, esp. pp. 84–5.

31. Peter Paret, 'The Genesis of On War', and Michael Howard, 'The influence of Clausewitz', in Carl von Clausewitz, *On War*, ed. and trans. Michael Howard and Peter Paret (London, 1993), pp. 3–28, 29–49.

32. Cited in Stadelmann, *Preussens Könige*, vol. 4, p. 327.

33. Hagen, *Ordinary Prussians*, p. 598.

34. I am grateful to Sean Eddie, currently preparing a Ph.D. dissertation on the fiscal history of Prussia *c.* 1750–1850, for clarifying this aspect of the agrarian system.

35. Karl Heinrich Kaufhold, 'Die preussische Gewerbepolitik im 19. Jahrhundert (bis zum Erlass der Gewerbeordnung für den norddeutschen Bund 1869) und ihre Spiegelung in der Geschichtsschreibung der bundesrepublik Deutschland', in Bernd Sösemann (ed.), *Gemeingeist und Bürgersinn. Die preussischen Reformen* (Berlin, 1993), pp. 137–60, here p. 141.

36. Hagen, *Ordinary Prussians*, pp. 612, 614; Berdahl, *Politics of the Prussian Nobility*, p. 118.

37. Hartmut Harnisch, 'Vom Oktoberedikt des Jahres 1807 zur Deklaration von 1816. Problematik und Charakter der preussischen Agrarreformgesetzgebung zwischen 1807 und 1816', *Jahrbuch für Wirtschaftsgeschichte* (Sonderband, 1978), pp. 231–93.

38. Contemporary arguments to this effect are surveyed in Georg Friedrich Knapp, *Die Bauernbefreiung und der Ursprung der Landarbeiter in den älteren Theilen Preussens* (2 vols., Leipzig, 1887), vol. 2, p. 213. On Schön's economic liberalism, see Berdahl, *Politics of the Prussian Nobility*, pp. 116–17.

39. Diary of Leopold von Gerlach, 1 May 1816, BA Potsdam, NL von Gerlach, 90 Ge 2, Bl. 9.

40. Ewald Frie, *Friedrich August Ludwig von der Marwitz, 1777–1837. Biographien eines Preussen* (Paderborn, 2001), esp. pp. 333–41.

41. Altenstein, memo for Hardenberg, Riga, 11 September 1807, cited in Clemens Menze, *Die Bildungsreform Wilhelm von Humboldts* (Hanover, 1975), p. 72.

42. Martina Bretz, 'Blick in Preussens Blüte: Wilhelm von Humboldt und die "Bildung der Nation" ', in Bahners and Roellecke (eds.), *Preussische Stile*, pp. 235–48, here p. 230; Tilman Borsche, *Wilhelm von Humboldt* (Munich, 1990), p. 26.

43. Borsche, *Humboldt*, p. 60.

44. Wilhelm von Humboldt, 'Der Königsberger und der litauische Schulplan', in Albert Leitzmann (ed.), *Gesammelte Schriften* (17 vols., Berlin, 1903–36), vol. 13, pp. 259–83, here pp. 260–61.

45. Menze, *Bildungsreform*, pp. 320–21; Borsche, *Humboldt*, pp. 62–5.

46. Koselleck, *Preussen*, p. 194.

47. Hardenberg, memorandum of 5 March 1809, cited in Ernst Klein, *Von der Reform zur Restauration. Finanzpolitik und Reformgesetzgebung des preussischen Staatskanzlers Karl August von Hardenberg* (Berlin, 1965), p. 23.

48. Ilja Mieck, 'Die verschlungenen Wege der Städtereform in Preussen (1806–1856)', in Bernd Sösemann (ed.), *Gemeingeist und Bürgersinn*, pp. 53–83, esp. pp. 82–3.

49. Stefi Jersch-Wenzel, 'Legal Status and Emancipation', in Michael A. Meyer and Michael Brenner (eds.), *German-Jewish History in Modern Times*, vol. 2, *Emancipation and Acculturation: 1780–1871* (New York, 1997), pp. 5–49, here pp. 24–7.

50. Humboldt, Report of 17 July 1809, in Ismar Freund (ed.), *Die Emanzipation der Juden in Preussen unter besonderer Berücksichtigung des Gesetzes vom 11. Marz 1812. Ein Beitrag zur Rechtsgeschichte der Juden in Preussen* (2 vols., Berlin, 1912), vol. 2, pp. 269–82, here p. 276.

51. Citation from *Sulamith* in Bildarchiv preussischer Kulturbesitz (ed.), *Juden in Preussen. Ein Kapitel deutscher Geschichte* (Dortmund, 1981), p. 159.

52. Horst Fischer, *Judentum, Staat und Heer in Preussen im frühen 19. Jahrhundert. Zur Geschichte der staatlichen Judenpolitik* (Tübingen, 1968), pp. 28–9.

53. The text of the edict may be found in Anton Doll, Hans-Josef Schmidt, Manfred Wilmanns, *Der Weg zur Gleichberechtigung der Juden* (=Veröffentlichungen der Landesarchivverwaltung Rheinland-Pfalz, 13, Coblenz, 1979), pp. 45–8.

54. Memorandum of 13 May 1809 by State Councillor Köhler, in Freund, *Emanzipation der Juden in Preussen*, vol. 2, pp. 251–2.

55. For an account that stresses the long-term character of societal and administrative change during the period spanning the decades between *c.* 1780 and *c.* 1847, see Koselleck, *Preussen*. For a similarly long-term view of the reform era in Bavaria, Walter Demel, *Der bayerische Staatsabsolutismus 1806/08–1817. Staats- und Gesellschaftspolitische Motivationen und Hintergründe der Reformära in der ersten Phase des Königreichs Bayern* (München, 1983) addresses this long period of adjustment and accommodation under the rubric 'reform absolutism'. For a discussion of historiographical debate around these questions, see Paul Nolte, 'Vom Paradigma zur Peripherie der historischen Forschung? Geschichten der Verfassungspolitik in der Reformzeit', in Stamm-Kuhlmann, *'Freier Gebrauch der Kräfte'*, pp. 197–216.

56. Internal bureaucratic frictions and strife are a central theme of Barbara Vogel, *Allgemeine Gewerbefreiheit. Die Reformpolitik des preussischen Staatskanzlers Hardenberg (1810–1820)* (Göttingen, 1983), pp. 224–5 and passim.

57. Commentary by Theodor von Schön, cited in Monika Wienfort, *Patrimonialgerichte in*

Preussen. Ländliche Gesellschaft und bürgerliches Recht 1770–1848/49 (Göttingen, 2001), p. 86.

58. On peasant protest as a retardative factor, see Clemens Zimmermann, 'Preussische Agrarreformen in neuer Sicht', in Sösemann (ed.), *Gemeingeist und Bürgersinn*, pp. 128–36, here p. 132.

59. Wienfort, *Patrimonialgerichte*, p. 92.

60. Manfred Botzenhart, 'Landgemeinde und staatsbürgerliche Gleichheit. Die auseinandersetzungen um eine allgemeine Kreis- und Gemeindeordnung während der preussischen Reformzeit', in Sösemann (ed.), *Gemeingeist und Bürgersinn*, pp. 85–105, here pp. 99–100.

61. Wienfort, *Patrimonialgerichte*, p. 94.

62. Botzenhart, 'Landgemeinde und staatsbürgerliche Gleichheit', pp. 104–5.

63. Cited in Klein, *Von der Reform zur Restauration*, pp. 34–52.

64. Edict Concerning the Finances of the State and the New Arrangements Regarding Taxes of 27 October 1810, *Preussische Gesetzsammlung 1810*, p.25.

65. For an analysis of these contrasts, see Paul Nolte, *Staatsbildung als Gesellschaftsreform. Politische Reform in Preussen und den süddeutschen Staaten 1800 bis 1820* (Frankfurt/Main), 1990, p. 124; Horst Moeller, *Fürstenstaat oder Bürgernation. Deutschland 1763–1815* (Berlin, 1998), pp. 620–21.

66. Hagen, *Ordinary Prussians*, pp. 595–6, 632; Helmut Bleiber, 'Die preussischen Agrarreformen in der Geschichtsschreibung der DDR', in Sösemann (ed.), *Gemeingeist und Bürgersinn*, pp. 109–25, here p. 122. For a similarly positive evaluation of the condition of peasants after emancipation in the Marienwerder district, see Horst Mies, *Die preussische Verwaltung des Regierungsbezirks Marienwerder (1830–1870)* (Cologne, 1972), p. 109; Wehler, *Deutsche Gesellschaftsgeschichte*, vol. 1, pp. 409–28.

67. On the limits of what was achieved, see Menze, *Bildungsreform*, pp. 337–468. On Prussian institutions as models, see Hermann Lübbe, 'Wilhelm von Humboldts Bildungsziele im Wandel der Zeit', in Bernfried Schlerath (ed.), *Wilhelm von Humboldt. Vortragszyklus zum 150. Todestag* (Berlin, 1986), pp. 241–58.

68. See Stefan Hartmann, 'Die Bedeutung des Hardenbergschen Edikts von 1812 für den Emanzipationsprozess der preussischen Juden im 19. Jahrhundert', in Sösemann, *Gemeingeist und Bürgersinn*, pp. 247–60.

69. See Wienfort's analysis of the changing function of the patrimonial courts in *Patrimonialgerichte*, passim.

70. Schneider, *Staatsrat*, pp. 47, 50; Paul Haake, 'König Friedrich Wilhelm III., Hardenberg und die preussische Verfassungsfrage', *FBPG*, 26 (1913), pp. 523–73, 28 (1915), pp. 175–220, 29 (1916), pp. 305–69, 30 (1917), pp. 317–65, 32 (1919), pp. 109–80, here 29 (1916), pp. 305–10; id., 'Die Errichtung des preussischen Staatsrats im März 1817', *FBPG*, 27 (1914), pp. 247–65, here pp. 247, 265.

71. Andrea Hofmeister-Hunger, *Pressepolitik*, pp. 195–209.

72. Hermann Granier, 'Ein Reformversuch des preussischen Kanzleistils im Jahre 1800', *FBPG*, 15 (1902), pp. 168–80, esp. pp. 169–70, 179–80.

73. On Stein in particular, see Andrea Hofmeister, 'Presse und Staatsform in der Reformzeit', in Heinz Duchhardt and Karl Teppe (eds.), *Karl vom und zum Stein: Der Akteur, der Autor, seine Wirkungs- und Rezeptionsgeschichte* (Mainz, 2003), pp. 29–48.

74. Matthew Levinger, 'Hardenberg, Wittgenstein and the Constitutional Question in Prussia, 1815–22', *German History*, 8 (1990), pp. 257–77.

11 A Time of Iron

1. Sack to Interior Minister Dohna, Berlin, 15 April 1809, cited in Hermann Granier, *Berichte aus der Berliner Franzosenzeit 1807–1809* (Leipzig, 1913), p. 401.

2. Stamm-Kuhlmann, *König in Preussens grosser Zeit*, p. 299.

3. Münchow-Pohl, *Zwischen Reform und Krieg*, pp. 133–4.

4. Frederick William III, handwritten note of 24 June 1809, cited in Stamm-Kuhlmann, *König in Preussens grosser Zeit*, p. 302.

5. On these incidents, see Münchow-Pohl, *Zwischen Reform und Krieg*, p. 139; Heinz Heitzer, *Insurrectionen zwischen Weser und Elbe. Volksbewegungen gegen die französische Fremdherrschaft im Königreich Westfalen (1806–1813)* (Berlin, 1959), pp. 158–60.

6. Cited in Münchow-Pohl, *Zwischen Reform und Krieg*, p. 140.

7. The following account is largely drawn from Georg Bärsch, *Ferdinand von Schill's Zug und Tod im Jahre 1809. Zur Erinnerung an den Helden und die Kampfgenossen* (Berlin, [1860]).

8. Ibid., p. 25.

9. Klessmann (ed.), *Deutschland unter Napoleon*, p. 358.

10. Police Chief Gruner to Interior Minister Dohna, report of 2 May 1809, cited in Stamm-Kuhlmann, *König in Preussens grosser Zeit*, p. 308.

11. Bärsch, *Schill*, pp. 55, 72, 74, 100–112. On the disposal of Schill's head, see Wolfgang Menzel, *Germany from the Earliest Period with a Supplementary Chapter of Recent Events by Edgar Saltus*, trans. Mrs George Horrocks (4th edn, 3 vols., London, 1848–9; Germ. orig., Zurich, 1824–5), vol 3, p. 273.

12. Cabinet order to von der Goltz, 9 May 1809, cited in Stamm-Kuhlmann, *König in Preussens grosser Zeit*, p. 309.

13. Cited in ibid., p. 306.

14. Blücher to Frederick William, Stargard, 9 October 1809, in Wilhelm Capelle, *Blüchers Briefe* (Leipzig, [1915]), pp. 32–3.

15. The full text of the memorandum of 8 August 1811 is in Georg Heinrich Pertz, *Das Leben des Generalfeldmarschalls General Grafen Neidhardt von Gneisenau* (5 vols., Berlin, 1864–9), vol. 2, pp. 108–42.

16. Heinrich von Kleist, 'Germanien an ihre Kinder' (1809–14; my translation), reprinted with commentary in Helmut Sembdner, 'Kleists Kriegslyrik in unbekannten Fassungen', in id., *In Sachen Kleist. Beiträge zur Forschung* (3rd edn, Munich, 1994), pp. 88–98, accessed online at *http://www.textkritik.de/bka/dokumente/materialien/sembdnerkk.htm*; last accessed on 21 April 2004.

17. Friedrich Ludwig Jahn, *Die deutsche Turnkunst* (2nd edn, Berlin, 1847), pp. vii, 97.

18. Ibid., p. 97.

19. On the egalitarian character of the *Turner* uniform, see George L. Mosse, *The Nationalization of the Masses. Political Symbolism and Mass Movements in Germany from the Napoleonic Wars through the Third Reich* (Ithaca, NY, 1975), p. 28.

20. Cited in Simms, *Struggle for Mastery*, p. 95.

21. Pertz, *Gneisenau*, vol. 2, pp. 121, 137.

22. A brilliant synthesis of the background to the Franco-Russian conflict, with literature, can be found in Schroeder, *Transformation*, pp. 416–26.

23. These quotations all come from Münchow-Pohl, *Zwischen Reform und Krieg*, pp. 352–6.

24. Ompteda to Münster, Berlin, 26 June 1812, in Friedrich von Ompteda, *Politischer Nachlass des hannoverschen Staats- und Cabinetts-Ministers Ludwig v. Ompteda aus den Jahren 1804 bis 1813* (5 vols., Jena, 1862–9), vol. 2, p. 281.

25. Draft report of 12 November 1812, cited in Münchow-Pohl, *Zwischen Reform und Krieg*, pp. 373–4.

26. Cited from a published memoir of 1825 by Johann Theodor Schmidt, in Münchow-Pohl, *Zwischen Reform und Krieg*, p. 377.

27. Report from Schön, 21 December 1812, cited in ibid., p. 378.

28. Stamm-Kuhlmann, *König in Preussens grosser Zeit*, p. 362.

29. Frederick William, notes of 28 December 1812, cited and discussed in ibid., pp. 362–4.

30. Wilhelm von Schramm, *Clausewitz. Leben und Werk* (Esslingen, 1977), pp. 401, 406–8.

31. On the debate over whether there was any form of authorization for Yorck's action, see Theodor Schiemann, 'Zur Würdigung der Konvention von Tauroggen', *Historische*

Zeitschrift, 84 (1900), pp. 210–43, here pp. 210–12. For the details of Yorck's motivation and planning, see Peter Paret, *Yorck and the Era of Prussian Reform 1807–1815* (Princeton, NJ, 1966), esp. pp. 192–4.

32. Yorck to Frederick William, 3 January 1813. The full text is given in Schiemann, 'Würdigung', pp. 229–32, here p. 231.

33. Johann Gustav Droysen, *Das Leben des Feldmarschalls Grafen Yorck von Wartenburg* (3 vols., 7th edn, Berlin, 1875), vol. 1, pp. 209, 215, 226; Paret, *Yorck*, pp. 155–7.

34. Yorck to Bülow, 13 January 1813, cited in Droysen, *Yorck von Wartenburg*, vol. 1, p. 424.

35. Ibid., pp. 426, 428–9, 434, 439–43.

36. Cited in Stamm-Kuhlmann, *König in Preussens grosser Zeit*, p. 369.

37. Cited in ibid., p. 371.

38. The full text of '*An Mein Volk*' can be accessed online at Martin Hentrich, *http://www.davier.de/anmeinvolk.htm*; last accessed on 5 April 2004.

39. Stamm-Kuhlmann, *König in Preussens grosser Zeit*, p. 373.

40. Carl Euler, *Friedrich Ludwig Jahn. Sein Leben und Wirken* (Stuttgart, 1881), pp. 225, 262–80; Thomas Nipperdey, *Deutsche Geschichte, 1800–1860. Bürgerwelt und starker Staat* (Munich, 1983), pp. 83–5; Eckart Klessmann (ed.), *Die Befreiungskriege in Augenzeugenberichten* (Düsseldorf, 1966), p. 41.

41. Leopold von Gerlach, Diary [February/March] 1813, Bundesarchiv Potsdam, 90 Ge 6 Tagebuch Leopold von Gerlach, 1, fo. 42.

42. Schroeder, *Transformation*, p. 457.

43. For an analysis of this phase of the campaign, to which this outline is indebted, see Michael V. Leggiere, *Napoleon and Berlin. The Franco-Prussian War in North Germany, 1813* (Norman, OK, 2002), esp. pp. 256–77.

44. Cited in Klessmann, *Befreiungskriege*, p. 168.

45. Etienne-Jacques-Joseph-Alexandre Macdonald, *Souvenirs du maréchal Macdonald, duc de Tarente* (Paris, 1892), cited in ibid., p. 173.

46. Leggiere, *Napoleon and Berlin*, p. 293.

47. Craig, *Politics of the Prussian Army*, pp. 64–5.

48. For a detailed analysis of the battle, on which this account is based, see Peter Hofschroer, *1815. The Waterloo Campaign. Wellington, His German Allies and the Battles of Ligny and Quatre Bras* (London, 1999); id., *1815. The Waterloo Campaign. The German Victory: From Waterloo to the Fall of Napoleon* (London, 1999), esp. pp. 116–29; David Hamilton-William, *Waterloo. New Perspectives. The Great Battle Reappraised* (London, 1993), pp. 332–53.

49. Hans-Wilhelm Möser, 'Commandement et problèmes de commandement dans l'armée prussienne de Basse-Rhénanie', in Marcel Watelet and Pierre Courreur (eds.), *Waterloo. Lieu de Mémoire européenne: histoires et controverses (1815–2000)* (Louvain-la-Neuve, 2000), pp. 51–7.

50. Cited in Craig, *Politics of the Prussian Army*, p. 62.

51. Dennis Showalter, 'Prussia's Army: Continuity and Change, 1713–1830', in Dwyer (ed.), *Rise of Prussia*, pp. 234–5.

52. Hofschroer, *Waterloo Campaign. The German Victory*, pp. 59–60.

53. Leggiere, *Napoleon and Berlin*, p. 290.

54. Hagen Schulze, *Der Weg zum Nationalstaat. Die deutsche Nationalbewegung vom 18. Jahrhundert bis zur Reichsgründung* (Munich, 1985), pp. 67–8; Ute Frevert, *Die kasernierte Nation. Militärdienst und Zivilgesellschaft in Deutschland* (Munich, 2001), pp. 39–41.

55. Eugen Wolbe, *Geschichte der Juden in Berlin und in der Mark Brandenburg* (Berlin, 1937), p. 238.

56. Cited in Spiel, *Fanny von Arnstein*, p. 276.

57. On the Iron Cross, see Stamm-Kuhlmann, *König in Preussens grosser Zeit*, pp. 389–93.

58. Jean Quataert, *Staging Philanthropy. Patriotic Women and the National Imagination in Dynastic Germany* (Ann Arbor, MI, 2001), p. 30.

59. The text of the document inaugurating the order can be consulted at: 'Preussische Order', *http://www.preussenweb.de/prorden.htm*; last accessed on 10 January 2006.

60. On the gymnasts and masculinity, see David A. McMillan, ' ". . . die höchste und heiligste Pflicht . . ." Das Männlichkeitsideal der deutschen Turnbewegung, 1811–1871', in Thomas Kühne (ed.), *Männergeschichte, Geschlechtergeschichte* (Frankfurt/Main, 1996), pp. 88–100. On Arndt, see Karen Hagemann, 'Der "Bürger" als Nationalkrieger. Entwürfe von Militär, Nation und Männlichkeit in der Zeit der Freiheitskriege', in Karen Hagemann and Ralf Pröve (eds.), *Landsknechte, Soldatenfrauen und Nationalkrieger* (Frankfurt/Main, 1998), pp. 78–89.

61. This is one of the central contentions of Karen Hagemann, *'Männliche Muth und Teutsche Ehre': Nation, Militär und Geschlecht zur Zeit der Antinapoleonischen Kriege Preussens* (Paderborn, 2002). On military service and masculinity, see Frevert, *Die kasernierte Nation*, pp. 43–9; on female participation, pp. 50–62.

62. T. A. H. Schmalz, *Berichtigung einer Stelle in der Bredow-Venturinischen Chronik vom Jahre 1808* (Berlin, 1815). The pamphlet was published on the pretext of correcting an erroneous biographical reference in the Bredow-Venturini almanac.

63. See the article on Schmalz in *Allgemeine Deutsche Biographie*, vol. 31 (Leipzig, 1890), pp. 624–7, here p. 626.

64. 'Es ist kein Krieg, von dem die Kronen wissen;/ Es ist ein Kreuzzug, s'ist ein heil'ger Krieg!', from the poem 'Aufruf' (1813), in T. Körner, *Sämmtliche Werke*, ed. K. Streckfuss (3rd edn, Berlin, 1838), p. 21.

65. George Mosse, *Fallen Soldiers. Reshaping the Memory of the World Wars* (New York, Oxford, 1990), pp. 19–20.

66. Friedrich von Gentz, *Schriften von Friedrich von Gentz. Ein Denkmal*, ed. G. Schlesier (5 vols., Mannheim, 1838–40), vol. 3, pp. 39–40.

67. Nipperdey, *Deutsche Geschichte*, pp. 83–5.

68. George Henry Rose to Castlereagh, Berlin, 6 January 1816, PRO FO 64 101, fo. 8. On 'fermentation within all orders of the state' and insubordination within the regular army after the closure of hostilities in 1815, see also Castlereagh to G. H. Rose, Blickling, 28 December 1815, PRO FO 64 100, fo. 241.

69. See Leopold von Gerlach, 'Familiengeschichte' (written by Leopold von Gerlach in the 1850s and continued by his brother Ludwig after his death in 1859), in Hans-Joachim Schoeps (ed.), *Aus den Jahren preussischer Not und Erneuerung. Tagebücher und Briefe der Gebrüder Gerlach und ihres Kreises 1805–1820* (Berlin, 1963), p. 95.

70. See, for example, Friedrich Keinemann, *Westfalen im Zeitalter der Restauration und der Juli-Revolution 1815–1833. Quellen zur Entwicklung der Wirtschaft, zur materiellen Lage der Bevölkerung und zum Erscheinungsbild der Volksstimmung* (Münster, 1987), esp. pp. 22–3, 31, 94, 95, 100, 273. Also the contemporary account of memorial celebrations compiled on the initiative of Ernst Moritz Arndt by the patriot Karl Heinrich Wilhelm Hoffmann, *Des Teutschen Volkes Feuriger Dank und Ehrentempel* (Offenbach, 1815).

71. On the role of these groups in memorializing the 'generational experience' of 1813–15, see Eckhard Trox, *Militärischer Konservatismus. Kriegervereine und 'Militärpartei' in Preussen zwischen 1815 und 1848/49* (Stuttgart, 1990), esp. pp. 56–7.

72. *Vossische Zeitung*, no. 132 (5 June 1845), no. 147 (27 June 1847).

73. Theodor Fontane, *Meine Kinderjahre. Autobiographischer Roman* (Frankfurt/Main, 1983), pp. 126–30.

74. Schiemann, 'Würdigung . . .', p. 217.

75. On the role of the locality in shaping the memory of war and the interaction between 'national' and 'local' forms of memorialization after the First World War, see A. Prost, 'Mémoires locales et mémoires nationales. Les monuments de 1914–18 en France', *Guerres Mondiales et Conflits Contemporains*, 42 (July 1992), pp. 42–50.

76. Fischer, *Judentum, Staat und Heer*, pp. 33, 38.

77. Moshe Zimmermann, *Hamburgischer Patriotismus und deutscher Nationalismus. Die*

Emanzipation der Juden in Hamburg 1830–1865 (Hamburg, 1979), p. 27; Frevert, *Die kasernierte Nation*, pp. 95–103.

78. See, for example, *Der Orient*, 4 (1843), no. 47, 21 November 1843, pp. 371–2; ibid., no. 48, 28 November 1843, pp. 379, 387; ibid., no. 51, 19 December 1843, p. 403. On responses from the *Allgemeine Zeitung des Judentums* and other liberal journals such as *Aachener Zeitung* and *Vossische Zeitung*, see Fischer, *Judentum, Staat und Heer*, pp. 47–53.

79. See Ziva Amishai-Maisels, 'Innenseiter, Aussenseiter: Moderne Jüdische Künstler im Portrait', in Andreas Nachama, Julius Schoeps, Edward von Voolen (eds.), *Jüdische Lebenswelten. Essays* (Frankfurt/Main, 1991), pp. 165–84, here p. 166.

80. On Oppenheimer's work, see I. Schorsch, 'Art as Social History: Moritz Oppenheimer and the German Jewish Vision of Emancipation', in id., *From Text to Context. The Turn to History in Modern Judaism* (Hanover, NH, 1994), pp. 93–117.

81. Helmut Börsch-Supan and Lucius Griesebach (eds.), *Karl Friedrich Schinkel. Architektur, Malerei, Kunstgewerbe* (Berlin, 1981), p. 143.

82. Mosse, *Fallen Soldiers*, p. 20.

83. Börsch-Supan and Griesebach, *Schinkel*, p. 143.

84. Cited in Jost Hermand, 'Dashed Hopes: On the Painting of the Wars of Liberation', trans. J. D. Steakley, in S. Drescher, D. Sabean and A. Sharlin (eds.) *Political Symbolism in Modern Europe. Essays in Honor of George L. Mosse* (New Brunswick, London, 1982), pp. 216–38; here p. 224. This passage in Friedrich's correspondence with Arndt was seized upon by the investigators of the Royal Prussian Commission of Investigation in Mainz as potentially incriminating evidence during their interrogation of Arndt in 1821. C. Sommerhage, *Caspar David Friedrich. Zum Portrait des Malers als Romantiker* (Paderborn, Munich, Vienna, Zurich, 1993), p. 127.

85. Cited in Reinhart Koselleck, 'Kriegerdenkmale als Identitätsstiftungen der Überlebenden', in Odo Marquard and Karlheinz Stierle (eds.), *Identität* (Munich, 1979), pp. 255–76, here p. 269. The remark is cited from a letter to Stägemann of 30 August 1822, in which Schön goes on to ask: 'If all the king's friends are to get statues, where is the limit?'

86. See, for example, Otto Dann, *Nation und Nationalismus in Deutschland 1770–1990* (Munich, 1993), pp. 86–7; Schulze, *Der Weg zum Nationalstaat*, pp. 63–5; Dieter Langewiesche, ' "Für Volk und Vaterland kräftig zu wirken": Zur politischen und gesellschaftlichen Rolle der Turner zwischen 1811 und 1871', in Ommo Grupe (ed.), *Kulturgut oder Körperkult? Sport und Sportwissenschaft im Wandel* (Tübingen, 1990), pp. 22–61; Dieter Düding, *Organisierter gesellschaftlicher Nationalismus in Deutschland (1808–1847). Bedeutung und Funktion der Turner- und Sängervereine für die deutsche Nationalbewegung* (Munich, 1984), pp. 85–6. My account of the *Turner* movement is much indebted to Düding's excellent analysis of the early nationalist movement.

87. 'Grundsätze und Beschlüsse der Wartburgfeier, den studierenden Brüdern auf anderen Hochschulen zur Annahme, dem gesamten Vaterlande zur Würdigung vorgelegt von den Studierenden in Jena', Principles §3. This document, written at the suggestion of the Jena historian Heinrich Luden in December 1817, is transcribed in H. Ehrenreich, 'Heinrich Luden und sein Einfluss auf die Burschenschaft', in Herman Haupt (ed.), *Quellen und Darstellungen*, (17 vols., Heidelberg, 1910–40), vol. 4 (1913), pp. 48–129 (text on pp. 113–29, quotation from pp. 114, 117).

88. On romanticism and the emergence of an 'art of experience' (*Erlebniskunst*), see Joseph Leo Koerner, *Caspar David Friedrich and the Subject of Landscape* (London, 1990), pp. 13, 109.

89. Nipperdey, *Deutsche Geschichte*, p. 280.

90. Dietmar Klenke, 'Nationalkriegerisches Gemeinschaftsideal als politische Religion. Zum Vereinsnationalismus der Sänger, Schützen und Turner am Vorabend der Einigungskriege', *Historische Zeitschrift*, 260 (1995), pp. 395–448.

91. Leopold von Gerlach, Diary, Breslau, February 1813, Bundesarchiv Potsdam, 90 Ge 6 Tagebuch Leopold von Gerlach, 1, fo. 60.

92. Stein to Count Münster (Hanoverian minister in London), 20 November 1812, cited in John R. Seeley, *The Life and Times of Stein, or: Germany and Prussia in the Napoleonic Age* (3 vols., Cambridge, 1878), vol. 3, p. 17.

93. For examples, see Johann Gustav Droysen, *Vorlesungen über die Freiheitskriege* (Kiel, 1846); Heinrich Sybel, *Die Erhebung Europas gegen Napoleon I* (Munich, 1860). See also Joachim Streisand, 'Wirkungen und Beurteilungen der Befreiungskriege', in Fritz Straube (ed.), *Das Jahr 1813. Studien zur Geschichte und Wirkung der Befreiungskriege* (Berlin [East], 1963), pp. 235–51. On the nationalization of Prussian symbols in the later nineteenth and early twentieth centuries, see Demandt, *Luisenkult*, pp. 379–430; Svenja Goltermann, *Körper der Nation: Habitusformierung und die Politik des Turnens, 1860–1890* (Göttingen, 1998) and Rainer Lübbren, *Swinegel Uhland. Persönlichkeiten im Spiegel von Strassennamen* (Heiloo, 2001), pp. 32–41. As Lübbren points out, more German streets are today named after Friedrich Ludwig Jahn than after any other German historical figure except Schiller. On Jena 1806 as a national symbol, see Jürgen John, 'Jena 1806: Symboldatum der Geschichte des 19. und 20. Jahrhunderts', in Fesser and Jonscher (eds.), *Umbruch im Schatten Napoleons*, pp. 177–95.

12 God's March through History

1. On the Polish-Saxon crisis, see Schroeder, *Transformation*, pp. 523–38; Stamm-Kuhlmann, *König in Preussens grosser Zeit*, pp. 399–401.

2. Michael Rowe, *From Reich to State. The Rhineland in the Revolutionary Age, 1780–1830* (Cambridge, 2003), p. 214.

3. Schroeder, *Transformation*, p. 544.

4. Metternich to Trauttmannsdorff, 18 March 1828, cited in Lawrence J. Baack, *Christian Bernstorff and Prussia. Diplomacy and Reform Conservatism 1818–1832* (New Brunswick, NJ, 1980), p. 126.

5. Wehler, *Deutsche Gesellschaftsgeschichte*, vol. 2, pp. 125–39, here, p. 129.

6. Rolf Dumke, 'Tariffs and Market Structure: the German Zollverein as a Model for Economic Integration', in W. Robert Lee (ed.), *German Industry and Industrialisation* (London, 1991), pp. 77–115, here p. 84.

7. Wolfram Fischer, 'The German Zollverein. A Study in Customs Union', *Kyklos*, 13 (1960), pp. 65–89; William O. Henderson, *The Zollverein* (London, 1968); W. Robert Lee, ' "Relative Backwardness" and Long-run Development. Economic, Demographic and Social Changes', in Philip G. Dwyer (ed.), *Modern Prussian History 1830–1947* (Harlow, 2001), pp. 61–87, here pp. 81–3.

8. The classic study in this tradition is Helmut Böhme, *Deutschlands Weg zur Grossmacht* (Cologne, 1966), see esp. pp. 211–15; id., *Introduction to the Social and Economic History of Germany: Politics and Economic Change in the Nineteenth and Twentieth Centuries*, trans. and ed. W. Robert Lee (Oxford, 1978). For a more recent argument to the effect that the *Zollverein* laid the basis for Prussian industrial superiority and thereby for the Prussian domination of the German nation-state, see Wehler, *Deutsche Gesellschaftsgeschichte*, vol. 2, pp. 134–5, vol. 3, pp. 288–9, 556.

9. For a revisionist analysis of the *Zollverein*'s economic impact, with a survey of recent literature, see Hans-Joachim Voth, 'The Prussian Zollverein and the Bid for Economic Superiority', in Dwyer (ed.), *Modern Prussian History*, pp. 109–25.

10. Baack, *Christian Bernstorff*, p. 337.

11. On the 1830 crisis, see Robert D. Billinger Jr, *Metternich and the Germans. States' Rights and Federal Duties, 1820–1834* (Newark, Del., 1991), pp. 50–109; Jürgen Angelow, *Von Wien nach Königgrätz. Die Sicherheitspolitik des deutschen Bundes im europäischen Gleichgewicht (1815–1866)* (Munich, 1996), pp. 97–106.

12. Cited in Johann Gustav Droysen, 'Zur Geschichte der preussischen Politik in den Jahren 1830–1832', in id., *Abhandlungen zur neueren Geschichte*, pp. 3–131, here p. 50.

13. Ludwig I to Frederick William III, 17 March 1831, in Anton Chroust (ed.), *Gesandt-*

schaftsberichte aus München 1814–1848, Abteilung III., Die Berichte der preussischen Gesandten (5 vols., Munich, 1950) (= *Schriftenreihe zur bayerischen Landesgeschichte*, vol. 40), vol. 2, pp. 196–7, n. 1.

14. Rühle von Lilienstern to Frederick William III, 27 March 1831, cited in Baack, *Christian Bernstorff*, pp. 271–2.

15. Ibid., pp. 284–94.

16. Robert D. Billinger, 'They Sing the Best Songs Badly: Metternich, Frederick William IV and the German Confederation during the War Scare of 1840–41', in Heinrich Rumpler (ed.), *Deutscher Bund und Deutsche Frage 1815–1866* (Vienna, Munich, 1990), pp. 94–113; Angelow, *Von Wien nach Königgrätz*, pp. 114–25.

17. Hess to Metternich, Berlin, 5 February 1841, cited in Billinger, 'They Sing the Best Songs', p. 103.

18. Ibid., 4 March 1841, cited in ibid., pp. 109–10.

19. William Russell to Viscount Palmerston, Berlin, 18 September 1839, in Markus Mösslang, Sabine Freitag and Peter Wende (eds.), *British Envoys to Germany, 1816–1866* (3 vols., Cambridge, 2002–), vol. 2, *1830–1847*, p. 180.

20. William Russell to Viscount Palmerston, Berlin, 3 May 1837, in ibid., p. 160.

21. On the Tsar's involvement in efforts to bind the Prussian monarchy permanently to an absolutist system, see Stamm-Kuhlmann, *König in Preussens grosser Zeit*, p. 557.

22. Winfried Baumgart, *Europäisches Konzert und nationale Bewegung 1830–1878* (= *Handbuch der Geschichte der Internationalen Beziehungen*, vol. 6, Paderborn, 1999), p. 243.

23. My account of these events is indebted to the analysis in George S. Williamson, 'What killed August von Kotzebue?', *Journal of Modern History*, 72 (2000), pp. 890–943. See also Nipperdey, *Deutsche Geschichte*, pp. 281–2.

24. De Wette to Sand's mother, 31 March 1819, cited in Matthew Levinger, *Enlightened Nationalism. The Transformation of Prussian Political Culture 1808–1848* (Oxford, 2000), p. 142.

25. See Edith Ennen, *Ernst Moritz Arndt 1769–1860* (Bonn, 1968), pp. 22–8; Karl Heinz Schäfer, *Ernst Moritz Arndt als politischer Publizist. Studien zur Publizistik, Pressepolitik und kollektivem Bewusstsein im frühen 19. Jahrhundert* (Bonn, 1974), pp. 143, 212–16.

26. Schoeps, *Not und Erneuerung*, pp. 35, 210–11.

27. Thomas Stamm-Kuhlmann, 'Restoration Prussia, 1786–1848', in Dwyer (ed.), *Modern Prussian History*, pp. 43–65; Levinger, *Enlightened Nationalism*, pp. 135–6; Eric Dorn Brose, *The Politics of Technological Change in Prussia. Out of the Shadow of Antiquity* (Princeton, NJ, 1993), pp. 53–6.

28. See for example, Hardenberg to Wittgenstein, Berlin, 4 April 1819, in Hans Branig (ed.), *Briefwechsel des Fürsten Karl August v. Hardenberg mit dem Fürsten Wilhelm Ludwig von Sayn-Wittgenstein, 1806–1822* (= *Veröffentlichungen aus den Archiven Preussischer Kulturbesitz*, vol. 9) (Cologne, 1972), p. 248; Levinger, 'Hardenberg, Wittgenstein and the Constitutional Question'.

29. Cited in Levinger, *Enlightened Nationalism*, p. 151.

30. Jonathan Sperber, *Rhineland Radicals. The Democratic Movement and the Revolution of 1848–1849* (Princeton, NJ, 1991), pp. 39–40.

31. Gustav Croon, *Der Rheinische Provinziallandtag bis zum Jahre 1874. Im Auftrage des Rheinischen Provinzialausschusses* (Düsseldorf, 1918, repr. Bonn, 1974), pp. 30–41.

32. Neugebauer, *Politischer Wandel*, p. 318.

33. Koselleck, *Preussen zwischen Reform und Revolution*; cf. for Bavaria, Demel, *Der bayerische Staatsabsolutismus 1806/08–1817*. On the historiography of reform, see Paul Nolte, 'Vom Paradigma zur Peripherie der historischen Forschung? Geschichten der Verfassungspolitik in der Reformzeit', in Stamm-Kuhlmann, '*Freier Gebrauch der Kräfte*', pp. 197–216.

34. Jörg van Norden, *Kirche und Staat im preussischen Rheinland 1815–1838. Die Genese der Rheinisch-Westfälischen Kirchenordnung vom 5.3.1835* (Cologne, 1991).

35. Dirk Blasius, 'Der Kampf um die Geschworenengerichte im Vormärz', in Hans-Ulrich Wehler (ed.), *Sozialgeschichte heute. Festschrift für Hans Rosenberg zum 70. Geburtstag* (Göttingen, 1974); Christina von Hodenberg, *Die Partei der Unparteiischen. Der Liberalismus der preussischen Richterschaft 1815–1848/49* (Göttingen, 1996), p. 80.

36. Kenneth Barkin, 'Social Control and Volksschule in Vormärz Prussia', *Central European History*, XVI (1983), pp. 31–52.

37. Horace Mann, *Report on an Educational Tour in Germany and Parts of Great Britain and Ireland* (London, 1846), p. 163.

38. Karl-Ernst Jeismann, *Das preussische Gymnasium in Staat und Gesellschaft* (2 vols., Stuttgart, 1996), vol. 2, pp. 114–5.

39. This is one of the central themes of Levinger, *Enlightened Nationalism*.

40. The standard work on Prussian parliamentary politics before 1848 is still the exhaustive study by Herbert Obenaus, *Anfänge des Parlamentarismus in Preussen bis 1848* (Düsseldorf, 1984), pp. 202–9. See also Neugebauer, *Politischer Wandel*, pp. 312–17.

41. Neugebauer, *Politischer Wandel*, pp. 174, 179, citation p. 390.

42. Ibid., pp. 390, 396–7, 399, 401, 404. See also Obenaus, *Anfänge*, pp. 407–10, 583–94.

43. Neugebauer, *Politischer Wandel*, pp. 430–31.

44. Hagen, *Germans, Poles and Jews*, p. 79.

45. Thomas Serrier, *Entre Allemagne et Pologne. Nations et Identités Frontalières, 1848–1914* (Paris, 2002), esp. pp. 37–51.

46. Georg W. Strobel, 'Die liberale deutsche Polenfreundschaft und die Erneuerungsbewegung Deutschlands', in Peter Ehlen (ed.), *Der polnische Freiheitskampf 1830/31* (Munich, 1982), pp. 31–47, here p. 33.

47. All cited material from Hagen, *Germans, Poles and Jews*, pp. 87–91; Irene Berger, *Die preussische Verwaltung des Regierungsbezirks Bromberg (1815–1847)* (Cologne, 1966) p. 71.

48. Alfred Hartlieb von Wallthor, 'Die Eingliederung Westfalens in den preussischen Staat', in Peter Baumgart (ed.), *Expansion und Integration. Zur Eingliederung neugewonnener Gebiete in den preussischen Staat* (Cologne, 1984), pp. 227–54, here p. 251.

49. Croon, *Der Rheinische Provinziallandtag*, p. 116.

50. James M. Brophy, *Joining the Political Nation. Popular Culture and the Public Sphere in the Rhineland, 1800–1850* (forthcoming: Cambridge, 2006). I am grateful to Professor Brophy for permission to cite from the unpublished typescript of this book.

51. Treitschke, *Deutsche Geschichte*, vol. 5, p. 141.

52. Letter from R. Smith to the Committee of the London Society for Promoting Christianity among the Jews, 17 December 1827, in *The Jewish Expositor and Friend of Israel*, 13 (1828), p. 266.

53. Cited in F. Fischer, *Moritz August von Bethmann Hollweg und der Protestantismus* (Berlin, 1937), p. 70.

54. Adalbert von der Recke, *Tagebuch für die Rettungsanstalt zu Düsselthal 1822–1823*, Archiv der Graf-Recke-Stiftung Düsselthal 1822–3, fo. 8 (19 January 1822).

55. Ibid., fo. 29 (3 February 1822).

56. Gerlach, 'Das Königreich Gottes', *Evangelische Kirchenzeitung*, 68 (1861), cols. 438–54, here cols. 438–9.

57. J. von Gerlach (ed.), *Ernst Ludwig von Gerlach. Aufzeichnungen aus seinem Leben und Wirken 1795–1877* (Schwerin, 1903), pp. 132, 149–50.

58. Friedrich Wiegand, 'Eine Schwärmerbewegung in Hinterpommern vor hundert Jahren', *Deutsche Rundschau*, 189 (1921), pp. 323–36, here p. 333.

59. Christopher Clark, 'The Napoleonic Moment in Prussian Church Policy', in David Laven and Lucy Riall (eds.), *Napoleon's Legacy. Problems of Government in Restoration Europe* (Oxford, 2000), pp. 217–35, here p. 223; Christopher Clark, 'Confessional Policy and the Limits of State Action: Frederick William III and the Prussian Church Union 1817–1840', *Historical Journal*, 39 (1996), pp. 985–1004.

60. See for example GStA Berlin-Dahlem, HA I Rep. 76 III, Sekt. 1, Abt. XIIIa, Nr. 5, vol. 1.

61. For a comparative discussion of the Prussian Union and the Concordat, see Clark, 'The Napoleonic Moment', in Laven and Riall (eds.), *Napoleon's Legacy*, pp. 217–35.

62. Helga Franz-Duhme and Ursula Röper-Vogt (eds.), *Schinkels Vorstadtkirchen. Kirchenbau und Gemeindegründung unter Friedrich Wilhelm III. In Berlin* (Berlin, 1991), pp. 30–60.

63. Rulemann Friedrich Eylert, *Charakter-Züge und historische Fragmente aus dem Leben des Königs von Preussen Friedrich Wilhelm III* (3 vols., Magdeburg, 1844–6), vol. 3, p. 304.

64. Frankfurt/Oder government to Rochow, Frankfurt/Oder, 9 June 1836, GStA Berlin-Dahlem, HA I, Rep. 76 III, Sekt. I, Abt. XIIIa, Nr. 5, vol. 2, Bl. 207–8.

65. Huschke, Steffens, Gempler, von Haugwitz, Willisch, Helling, Schleicher, Mühsam, Kaestner, Mage and Borne to Frederick William III, Breslau, 23 June 1830, GStA Berlin-Dahlem, HA I, Rep. 76 III, Sekt. 15, Abt. XVII, Nr. 44, vol. 1. References to previous generations of 'fathers' are common in the Lutheran petition literature.

66. *Neue Würzburger Zeitung*, 22 June 1838, transcribed in GStA Berlin-Dahlem, HA I, Rep. 76 III, Sekt. I, Abt. XIIIa, Nr. 5, vol. 2, Bl. 135.

67. Cited in Stamm-Kuhlmann, *König in Preussens grosser Zeit*, p. 544.

68. Nils Freytag, *Aberglauben im 19. Jahrhundert. Preussen und die Rheinprovinz zwischen Tradition und Moderne (1815–1918)* (Berlin, 2003), pp. 117–18.

69. Christoph Weber, *Aufklärung und Orthodoxie am Mittelrhein 1820–1850* (Munich, 1973), pp. 46–7.

70. Freytag, *Aberglauben*, pp. 322–33.

71. Ibid., pp. 333–44.

72. On Schoenherr, see H. Olshausen, *Leben und Lehre des Königsberger Theosophen Johann Heinrich Schoenherr* (Königsberg, 1834).

73. Pastor Diestel to Königsberg Consistory, 15 October 1835, GStA Berlin-Dahlem, HA I, Rep. 76 III, Sekt. 2, Abt. XVI, Nr. 4, vol. 1.

74. Account based on contemporary press reports in Samuel Laing, *Notes of a Traveller on the Social and Political State of France, Prussia, Switzerland, Italy and Other Parts of Europe during the Present Century* (London, 1854), pp. 109–10.

75. For details on the Schoenherr-Ebel controversy, see the papers assembled in GStA Berlin-Dahlem, HA I, Rep. 76 III, Sekt. 2, Abt. XVI, Nr. 4, vols. 1 and 2. See also P. Konschel, *Der Königsberger Religionsprozess gegen Ebel und Diestel* (Königsberg, 1909) and Ernst Wilhelm Graf von Kanitz, *Aufklärung nach Actenquellen. Über den 1835 bis 1842 zu Königsberg in Preussen geführten Religionsprozess für Welt- und Kirchen-Geschichte* (Basel, 1862).

76. Recommendation from the ministry of finance, 28 November 1816, in Freund, *Die Emanzipation der Juden*, vol. 2, pp. 475–96, here pp. 482–3.

77. Fischer, *Judentum, Staat und Heer*, p. 95.

78. Frederick William III, cabinet order of 14 June 1824, reproduced in *Bildarchiv Preussischer Kulturbesitz, Juden in Preussen: Ein Kapitel deutscher Geschichte* (Dortmund, 1981), p. 195; Nathan Samter, *Judentaufen im 19. Jahrhundert* (Berlin, 1906), p. 37. On Burg generally, see the recent edition of his memoirs: Meno Burg, *Geschichte meines Dienstlebens. Erinnerungen eines jüdischen Majors der preussischen Armee* (Berlin, 1998).

79. On this policy, see Christopher Clark, 'The Limits of the Confessional State: Conversions to Judaism in Prussia 1814–1843', *Past & Present*, 147 (1995), pp. 159–79.

80. Clark, *Politics of Conversion*.

81. Cabinet order from Frederick William III, excerpted in circular to all church superintendents, 18 October 1821, Evangelisches Zentralarchiv, Berlin, 9/37.

82. Friedrich Julius Stahl, *Der christliche Staat und sein Verhältniss zum Deismus und Judenthum. Eine durch die Verhandlungen des vereinigten landtages hervorgerufene Abhandlung* (Berlin, 1847), pp. 7, 27, 31–3. On the debate in the United Diet, see Wanda Kampmann, *Deutsche und Juden. Studien zur Geschichte des deutschen Judentums*

(Heidelberg, 1963), pp. 189–205. On Stahl's political theory more generally, see Willi Füssl, *Professor in der Politik. Friedrich Julius Stahl (1802–1861)* (Göttingen, 1988).

83. 'Ulm, 12. September', *Der Orient*, 3 (1842), pp. 342–3; 'Vorwärts in der Judenemancipation: Ein offenes Sendschreiben', *Der Orient*, 4 (1843), p. 106; 'Tübingen, im Februar', *Der Orient*, 5 (1844), p. 68.

84. Heinrich, *Staat und Dynastie*, p. 316.

85. Thomas Stamm-Kuhlmann, 'Pommern 1815 bis 1875', in Werner Buchholz (ed.), *Deutsche Geschichte im Osten Europas: Pommern* (Berlin, 1999), pp. 366–422, here p. 369; Ilja Mieck, 'Preussen von 1807 bis 1850. Reformen, Restauration und Revolution', in Büsch et al. (eds.), *Handbuch der preussischen Geschichte*, vol. 2, pp. 3–292, here pp. 104–6.

86. Karl Georg Faber, 'Die kommunale Selbstverwaltung in der Rheinprovinz im neunzehnten Jahrhundert', *Rheinische Vierteljahrsblätter*, 30/1 (1965), pp. 132–51.

87. Manfred Jehle (ed.), *Die Juden und die jüdischen Gemeinden Preussens in amtlichen Enquêten des Vormärz* (4 vols., Munich, 1998), vol. 1, pp. 140–41.

88. On the Westphalian reform, see Norbert Wex, *Staatliche Bürokratie und städtische Autonomie. Entstehung, Einführung und Rezeption des Revidierten Städteordnung von 1831 in Westfalen* (Paderborn, 1997).

89. Cited by Theodor Schieder, 'Partikularismus und nationales Bewusstsein im Denken des Vormärz', in Werner Conze (ed.), *Staat und Gesellschaft im deutschen Vormärz 1815–1848* (Stuttgart, 1962), pp. 9–38, here p. 20. On the 'federal' character of the Prussian state, see Abigail Green, 'The Federal Alternative: A New View of Modern German History?' in *Historical Journal* (forthcoming); I am grateful to Dr Green for letting me see a version of this article before publication.

90. Klaus Pabst, 'Die preussischen Wallonen – eine staatstreue Minderheit im Westen', in Hans Henning Hahn and Peter Kunze (eds.), *Nationale Minderheiten und staatliche Minderheitenpolitik in Deutschland im 19. Jahrhundert* (Berlin, 1999), pp. 71–9.

91. Otto Friedrichs, *Das niedere Schulwesen im linksrheinischen Herzogtum Kleve 1614–1816. Ein Beitrag zur Regionalgeschichte der Elementarschulen in Brandenburg-Preussen* (Bielefeld, 2000). On the Kuren, see Andreas Kossert, *Ostpreussen. Geschichte und Mythos* (Berlin, 2005), pp. 190–95.

92. Forstreuter, 'Die Anfänge der Sprachstatistik' in id., *Wirkungen*, pp. 313, 315, 316.

93. Kurt Forstreuter, *Die Deutsche Kulturpolitik im sogenannten Preussisch-Litauen* (Berlin, 1933), p. 341.

94. Samuel Laing, *Notes of a Traveller*, p. 67.

95. For examples of separatist petitions that cite the code, see the transcripts in Johann Gottfried Scheibel, *Actenmässige Geschichte der neuesten Unternehmungen einer Union zwischen der reformirtes und der lutherischen Kirche vorzüglich durch gemeinschaftliche Agende in Deutschland und besonders in dem preussischen Staate* (2 vols., Leipzig, 1834), vol. 2, pp. 95–104, 106–7, 197–208, 211–12. On the code as the core of a unitary identity, see Koselleck, *Preussen Zwischen Reform und Revolution*, pp. 23–51.

96. 'Hier bei uns im Preussenlande / Ist der König Herr; / Durch Gesetz und Ordnungsbande / Stänkert man nicht kreuz und quer.' Cited in Brophy, *Joining the Political Nation*, chap. 2.

97. Rudolf Lange, *Der deutsche Schulgesang seit fünfzig Jahren. Ein Beitrag zur Schulbuchliteratur* (Berlin, 1867), pp. 50–51. After 1945, the '*Preussenlied*' became popular among East Prussian expellee circles in West Germany, though the Prussia they were singing about was not the Kingdom of Prussia, but the lost Baltic Preussenland of the East.

98. Georg Wilhelm Friedrich Hegel, *Elements of the Philosophy of Right*, trans. H. B. Nisbet, ed. Allen W. Wood, §258, p. 279. My understanding of Hegel's theory of the state is indebted to Gareth Stedman Jones's unpublished typescript 'Civilising the People: Hegel'; I am grateful to Professor Stedman Jones for allowing me to see this work before its appearance in print.

99. Ibid., §273, p. 312.

100. Georg Wilhelm Friedrich Hegel, *Die Philosophie des Rechts. Die Mitschriften Wannen-*

mann (Heidelberg, 1817–1818) und Homeyer (Berlin 1818–1819), ed. K.-H. Ilting (Stuttgart, 1983), §70, p. 132.

101. Cited in Horst Althaus, *Hegel. An Intellectual Biography*, trans. Michael Tarsh (Oxford, 2000), p. 186.

102. See the Introduction by Gareth Stedman Jones to Karl Marx and Friedrich Engels, *The Communist Manifesto* (London, 2002), pp. 74–82.

103. Cited in Althaus, *Hegel*, p. 159.

104. On the sundering of Hegelianism into separate traditions of left and right, see John Edward Toews, *Hegelianism. The Path Toward Dialectical Humanism, 1805–1841* (Cambridge, 1985), pp. 71–140.

105. Cited in Althaus, *Hegel*, p. 161.

106. George G. Iggers, *The German Conception of History. The National Tradition of Historical Thought from Herder to the Present* (Middletown, CT, 1968), pp. 82, 88–9.

107. Cited in Sheehan, *German History*, p. 568.

13 Escalation

1. Christopher Bayly, *The Birth of the Modern World 1780–1914* (Oxford, 2004), p. 147.

2. William Russell to Viscount Palmerston, Berlin, 18 June 1840, in Mösslang, Freitag and Wende (eds.), *British Envoys*, vol. 2, *1830–1847*, p. 184.

3. Walter Bussmann, *Zwischen Preussen und Deutschland. Friedrich Wilhelm IV. Eine Biographie* (Berlin, 1990), pp. 50–51, 94–6; Dirk Blasius, *Friedrich Wilhelm IV, 1795–1861. Psychopathologie und Geschichte* (Göttingen, 1992), pp, 14–17, 55; David E. Barclay, *Friedrich Wilhelm IV and the Prussian Monarchy 1840–1861* (Oxford, 1995), pp. 29–30, 32–5.

4. Bussmann, *Zwischen Preussen und Deutschland*, pp. 130–52.

5. Bärbel Holtz et al. (eds.), *Die Protokolle des preussischen Staatsministeriums, 1817–1934/38* (12 vols., Hildesheim, 1999–2004), vol. 3, *9. Juni 1840 bis 14. März 1848*, p. 15 (introduction by Holtz).

6. Robert Blake, 'The Origins of the Jerusalem Bishopric', in Adolf M. Birke and Kurt Kluxen (eds.), *Kirche, Staat und Gesellschaft. Ein deutsch-englischer Vergleich* (Munich, 1984), pp. 87–97; Bussmann, *Friedrich Wilhelm*, pp. 153–73; Barclay, *Frederick William IV*, pp. 84–92.

7. Frank-Lothar Kroll, 'Monarchie und Gottesgnadentum in Preussen 1840–1861', in id, *Das geistige Preussen. Zur Ideengeschichte eines Staadtes* (Paderborn, 2001), pp. 55–74. See also 'Politische Romantik und Romantische Politik bei Friedrich Wilhelm IV' in the same volume, pp. 75–86.

8. Leopold von Gerlach, Diary, Frankfurt, 3 June 1842, Bundesarchiv Potsdam, 90 Ge 6 Tagebuch Leopold von Gerlach, Bd 1842–6, fo. 21.

9. Treitschke, *Deutsche Geschichte*, vol. 5, p. 138.

10. Neugebauer, *Politischer Wandel*, pp. 446–9.

11. Hagen, *Germans, Poles and Jews*, pp. 91–2.

12. Holtz et al. (eds.), *Protokolle*, vol. 3 (introduction), p. 17.

13. Treitschke, *Deutsche Geschichte*, vol. 5, pp. 154–6.

14. Barclay, *Friedrich Wilhelm IV*, pp. 54–5.

15. Obenaus, *Anfänge*, pp. 532–3; Neugebauer, *Politischer Wandel*, p. 450.

16. The full text of the Political Testament of 1808 is in Heinrich Scheel and Doris Schmidt (eds.), *Das Reformministerium Stein. Akten zur Verfassungs- und Verwaltungsgeschichte aus den Jahren 1807/08* (3 vols., Berlin, 1966–8), vol. 3, pp. 1136–8.

17. Neugebauer, *Politischer Wandel*, pp. 257–8, 329, 372.

18. Theodor von Schön, *Woher und Wohin? oder der preussische Landtag im Jahre 1840. Ausschliesslich für den Verfasser, in wenigen Exemplaren abgedruckt* (Königsberg, 1840), reprinted in Hans Fenske (ed.), *Vormärz und Revolution 1840–1848* (Darmstadt, 1976), pp. 34–40, here pp. 36–7.

19. The following account of the controversy over Schön is based primarily on Treitschke, *Deutsche Geschichte*, vol. 5, pp. 158–67. See also Hans Rothfels, *Theodor von Schön, Friedrich Wilhelm IV und die Revolution von 1848* (Halle, 1937), pp. 107–23.

20. Sheehan, *German History*, p. 625.

21. Karl Obermann, 'Die Volksbewegung in Deutschland von 1844 bis 1846', *Zeitschrift für Geschichte*, 5/3 (1957), pp. 503–25; James Sheehan, *German Liberalism in the Nineteenth Century* (Chicago, 1978), pp. 12–14.

22. Nipperdey, *Deutsche Geschichte*, p. 398; Dirk Blasius, 'Der Kampf um das Geschworenengericht in Vormärz', in Hans-Ulrich Wehler (ed.), *Sozialgeschichte heute. Festschrift für Hans Rosenberg* (Göttingen, 1974), pp. 148–61.

23. Sperber, *Rhineland Radicals*, p. 104.

24. Hagen, *Germans, Poles and Jews*, p. 93.

25. R. Arnold, 'Aufzeichnungen des Grafen Carl v. Voss-Buch über das Berliner Politische Wochenblatt', *Historische Zeitschrift*, 106 (1911), pp. 325–40, esp. pp. 334–9; Berdahl, *Politics of the Prussian Nobility*, pp. 158–81, 246–63; Epstein, *German Conservatism*, p. 66; Fritz Valjavec, *Die Entstehung der politischen Strömungen in Deutschland, 1770–1815* (Munich, 1951), pp. 310, 322, 414.

26. Bärbel Holtz, 'Wider Ostrakismos und moderne Konstitutionstheorien. Die preussische Regierung im Vormärz zur Verfassungsfrage', in ead. and Hartin Spenkuch (eds.), *Preussens Weg in die politische Moderne. Verfassung – Verwaltung – politische Kultur zwischen Reform und Reformblockade* (Berlin, 2001), pp. 101–39; ead., 'Der vormärzliche Regierungsstil von Friedrich Wilhelm IV.', *FBPG*, 12 (2002), pp. 75–113.

27. Leopold von Gerlach, Diary, Sans Souci, 28, 29 October 1843, Bundesarchiv Potsdam, 90 Ge 6 Tagebuch Leopold von Gerlach, Bd 1842–6, fos. 98–101.

28. See the reports reproduced in Jehle (ed.), *Die Juden und die jüdischen Gemeinden Preussens*, esp. vol. 1, pp. 81 (Königsberg), 84–5 (Danzig), 97 (Gumbinnen), 118 (Marienwerder), 139 (Stettin), 147 (Köslin), 174 (Stralsund), 260 (Bromberg), 271 (Province of Silesia), 275 (Breslau), 283 (Liegnitz), 441 (Minden), 457 (Cologne), 477 (Düsseldorf), 497 (Coblenz). The Cologne government's call for full emancipation is at p. 446. On the role of local administrators as co-determiners of policy in general, see Berger, *Die preussische Verwaltung*, p. 260.

29. '. . . Das von den Extremen unserer Zeit / Ein närrisches Gemisch ist . . .' cited from Heinrich Heine's satirical poem 'Der neue Alexander', in Heinrich Heine, *Sämtliche Schriften*, ed. Klaus Briegleb (6 vols., Munich, 1968–76), vol. 4, p. 458.

30. David Friedrich Strauss, *Der Romantiker auf dem Thron der Cäsaren, oder Julian der Abtrünnige. Ein Vortrag* (Mannheim, 1847), esp. p. 52.

31. On the character of and reaction to these calendars, see Brophy, *Joining the Political Nation*, chap. 1.

32. Freytag, *Aberglauben*, pp. 179–82.

33. Brophy, *Joining the Political Nation*; Ann Mary Townsend, *Forbidden Laughter. Popular Humour and the Limits of Repression in Nineteenth-century Prussia* (Ann Arbor, MI, 1992), pp. 24–5, 27, 48–9, 93, 137.

34. James M. Brophy, 'Carnival and Citizenship: the Politics of Carnival Culture in the Prussian Rhineland, 1823–1848', *Journal of Social History*, 30 (1997), pp. 873–904; id., 'The Politicization of Traditional Festivals in Germany, 1815–1848', in Karin Friedrich (ed.), *Festival Culture in Germany and Europe from the Sixteenth to the Twentieth Century* (Lampeter, 2000), pp. 73–106.

35. Sperber, *Rhineland Radicals*, pp. 98–100.

36. These examples come from Barclay, *Friedrich Wilhelm IV*, p. 113.

37. Ibid., p. 118; Townsend, *Forbidden Laughter*, pp. 162–70.

38. Treitschke, *Deutsche Geschichte*, vol. 5, pp. 267–70.

39. 'Hatt' wohl je ein Mensch so'n Pech / Wie der Bürgermeister Tschech, / Dass er diesen dicken Mann / Auf zwei Schritt nicht treffen kann!', cited in Brophy, *Joining the Political*

Nation, chap. 1. On the political significance of the *Tschechlieder*, see also Treitschke, *Deutsche Geschichte*, vol. 5, pp. 268–70.

40. Anon., 'Das Blutgericht (1844)', song of the weavers in Peterswaldau and Langenbielau, reproduced in Lutz Kroneberg and Rolf Schloesser (eds.), *Weber-Revolte 1844. Der schlesische Weberaufstand im Spiegel der zeitgenössischen Publizistik und Literatur* (Cologne, 1979), pp. 469–72.

41. My account of the events is based largely on the contemporary report by Wilhelm Wolff, 'Das Elend und der Aufruhr in Schlesien 1844', written in June 1844 and published in December of the same year in the *Deutsches Bürgerbuch für 1845*. The essay is reprinted in Kroneberg and Schloesser (eds.), *Weber-Revolte*, pp. 241–64.

42. Cited in Sheehan, *German History*, p. 646.

43. Wehler, *Deutsche Gesellschaftsgeschichte*, vol. 2, p. 288; Sperber, *Rhineland Radicals*, p. 35.

44. 'Erfahrungen eines jungen Schweizers im Vogtlande', in Bettina von Arnim, *Politische Schriften*, ed. Wolfgang Bunzel (Frankfurt Main, 1995), pp. 329–68, see also pp. 1039–40.

45. Heinrich Grunholzer, Appendix to Bettina von Arnim, *Dies Buch gehört dem König* (1843), excerpted in Kroneberg and Schloesser (eds.), *Weber-Revolte*, pp. 40–53. Grunholzer's narrative was commissioned by Arnim, who used it to flesh out the claims made in her own introductory essay, a plea to the king to step up social provision in the Kingdom of Prussia.

46. Friedrich Wilhelm Wolff, 'Die Kasematten von Breslau', in Franz Mehring (ed.), *Gesammelte Schriften von Wilhelm Wolff* (Berlin, 1909), pp. 49–56.

47. Cited in Sheehan, *German History*, p. 645.

48. Alexander Schneer, *Über die Not der Leinen-Arbeiter in Schlesien und die Mittel ihr abzuhelfen* (Berlin, 1844).

49. For an argument supporting the Malthusian thesis for Bavaria, see William Robert Lee, *Population Growth, Economic Development and Social Change in Bavaria 1750–1850* (New York, 1977), p. 376.

50. Manfred Gailus, 'Food Riots in Germany in the Late 1840s', *Past & Present*, 145 (1994), pp. 157–93, here p. 163.

51. E. P. Thompson, 'The Moral Economy of the English Crowd in the Eighteenth Century', *Past & Present*, 5 (1971), pp. 76–136; Hans-Gerhard Husung, *Protest und Repression im Vormärz* (Göttingen, 1983), pp. 244–7; Gailus, 'Food Riots', pp. 159–60.

52. Hermann Beck, 'Conservatives and the Social Question in Nineteenth-century Prussia', in Larry Eugene Jones and James Retallack (eds.), *Between Reform, Reaction and Resistance: Studies in the History of German Conservatism from 1789 to 1945* (Providence, RI, 1993), pp. 61–94; id., 'State and Society in pre-March Prussia: the Weavers' Uprising, the Bureaucracy and the Association for the Welfare of Workers', *Central European History*, 25 (1992), pp. 303–31; id., *The Origins of the Authoritarian Welfare State in Prussia. Conservatives, Bureaucracy and the Social Question, 1815–70* (Ann Arbor, MI, 1995); Wolfgang Schwentker, 'Victor Aimé Huber and the Emergence of Social Conservatism', in Jones and Retallack (eds.), *Between Reform, Reaction and Resistance*, pp. 95–121.

53. Kroneberg and Schloesser (eds.), *Weber-Revolte*, pp. 24–5.

54. Karl Marx, 'Kritische Randglossen zu dem Artikel "Der König von Preussen und die Sozialreform" ', *Vorwärts!*, 10 August 1844, excerpted in Kroneberg and Schloesser (eds.), *Weber-Revolte*, pp. 227–8.

55. On the link between the State Indebtedness Law, Prussia's financial needs and constitutional reform, see Niall Ferguson, *The World's Banker. The History of the House of Rothschild* (London, 1998), p. 133.

56. Brose, *Technological Change in Prussia*, pp. 223–4, 235–9; Barclay, *Friedrich Wilhelm IV*, p. 120.

57. Geoffrey Wawro, *The Austro-Prussian War. Austria's War with Prussia and Italy in 1866* (Cambridge, 1996), p. 31.

58. [Agnes von Gerlach] (ed.), *Denkwürdigkeiten aus dem Leben Leopolds von Gerlach, nach seinen Aufzeichnungen* (2 vols., Berlin, 1891–2), vol. 1, p. 99. See also Berdahl, *Politics of the Prussian Nobility*, pp. 324–5.

59. Obenaus, *Anfänge*, pp. 556–63; Friedrich Keinemann, *Preussen auf dem Wege zur Revolution: Die Provinziallandtags- und Verfassungspolitik Friedrich Wilhelms IV. Von der Thronbesteigung bis zum Erlass des Patents vom 3. Februar 1847. Ein Beitrag zur Vorgeschichte der Revolution von 1848* (Hamm, 1975), pp. 45–51; Barclay, *Friedrich Wilhelm IV*, p. 121; Berdahl, *Politics of the Prussian Nobility*, pp. 325–6.

60. Wehler, *Deutsche Gesellschaftsgeschichte*, vol. 2, p. 615. On the politics of railway-building, see Brose, *Technological Change in Prussia*, chap. 7.

61. Simms, *Struggle for Mastery*, pp. 169–70.

62. Eduard Bleich (ed.), *Der erste vereinigte Landtag in Berlin 1847* (4 vols., Berlin, 1847, repr. Vaduz-Liechtenstein, 1977), vol. 1, pp. 3–10.

63. Berdahl, *Politics of the Prussian Nobility*, p. 336.

64. For the text of the speech, see Bleich (ed.), *Der erste vereinigte Landtag*, vol. 1, pp. 22, 25–6.

65. Obenaus, *Anfänge*, pp. 704–5; Ernst Rudolf Huber, *Deutsche Verfassungsgeschichte seit 1789* (7 vols., Stuttgart, 1957–82), vol. 2, *Der Kampf um Einheit und Freiheit. 1830 bis 1850*, p. 494.

66. On the use of the term 'conservative' in the 1840s, see Rudolf Vierhaus, 'Konservatismus', in Otto Brunner, Werner Conze, Reinhard Koselleck (eds.), *Geschichtliche Grundbegriffe. Historisches Lexikon zu politisch-sozialer Sprache in Deutschland* (Stuttgart, 1972), pp. 531–65, esp. pp. 540–51; Alfred von Martin, 'Weltanschauliche Motive im altkonservativen Denken', in Gerd-Klaus Kaltenbrunner, *Rekonstruktion des Konservatismus* (Freiburg, 1972), pp. 139–80.

67. Gerlach, *Denkwürdigkeiten*, vol. 1, p. 118.

68. Diary entries of 22 June 1836, 21 January 1836, 17 June 1837, 14 November 1839, 26 December 1841, Karl Varnhagen von Ense, *Aus dem Nachlass Varnhagen's von Ense. Tagebücher von K. A. Varnhagen von Ense* (14 vols., Leipzig, 1861–70), vol. 1 (1861), pp. 5, 34–5, 151–3, 384–5.

69. Diary entry of 27 August 1837, in ibid., pp. 58–9.

70. Freytag, *Aberglauben*, pp. 151–2.

71. Friedrich Engels to Wilhelm Graeber, 13 November 1839, in *Marx and Engels Collected Works* (50 vols., London, 1975–2004), vol. 2, pp. 476–81, here p. 481.

72. Engels discusses this practice in Engels to Graeber, 29 October 1839, in ibid., p. 476.

73. Brophy, *Joining the Political Nation*; id., 'Violence between Civilians and State Authorities in the Prussian Rhineland, 1830–1848', *German History*, 22 (2004), pp. 1–35.

74. Alf Lüdtke, *Police and State in Prussia 1815–1850*, trans. Pete Burgess (Cambridge, 1989), pp. 72, 73.

75. Evans, *Rituals of Retribution*, pp. 228–9.

76. Cited in Simms, *Struggle for Mastery*, p. 199.

14 Splendour and Misery of the Prussian Revolution

1. *Vossische Zeitung* (*Extrablatt*), 28 February 1848, accessed online at *http://www.zlb.de/projekte/1848/vorgeschichte—image.htm*; last accessed 11 June 2004.

2. Karl August Varnhagen von Ense, 'Darstellung des Jahres 1848' (written in the autumn of 1848), in Konrad Feilchenfeld (ed.), *Karl August Varnhagen von Ense. Tageblätter* (5 vols., Frankfurt/Main, 1994), vol. 4, *Biographien, Aufsätze, Skizzen, Fragmente*, pp. 685–734, here p. 724.

3. Wolfram Siemann, 'Public Meeting Democracy in 1848', in Dieter Dowe, Heinz-Gerhard Haupt, Dieter Langewiesche and Jonathan Sperber (eds.), *Europe in 1848. Revolution and Reform* (New York, 2001), pp. 767–76; Schulze, *Der Weg zum Nationalstaat*,

pp. 3–48; my account of the March Days in Berlin is indebted to Schulze's evocative chronicle of the early revolution.

4. Alessandro Manzoni, *The Betrothed*, trans. Archibald Colquhoun (orig. 1827, London, 1956), pp. 188–9.

5. See the description of events in Palace Square on 15 March in Karl Ludwig von Prittwitz, *Berlin 1848. Das Erinnerungswerk des Generalleutnants Karl Ludwig von Prittwitz und andere Quellen zur Berliner Märzrevolution und zur Geschichte Preussens um die Mitte des 19. Jahrhunderts*, ed. Gerd Heinrich (Berlin, 1985), pp. 71–3.

6. Karl August Varnhagen von Ense, diary entry, 15 March 1848, in Feilchenfeld (ed.), *Varnhagen von Ense*, vol. 5, *Tageblätter*, pp. 429–30.

7. Prittwitz, *Berlin 1848*, p. 116.

8. Cited in ibid., p. 120

9. Ibid., pp. 129–30.

10. Varnhagen, *Tageblätter*, 18 March 1848, p. 433.

11. Cited in Prittwitz, *Berlin 1848*, p. 174.

12. Ibid., p. 232.

13. Text of the address given in ibid., p. 259.

14. For divergent accounts of the role of the military and Frederick William IV in the withdrawal from Berlin, see Felix Rachfahl, *Deutschland, König Friedrich Wilhelm IV. und die Berliner Märzrevolution von 1848* (Halle, 1901); Friedrich Thimme, 'König Friedrich Wilhelm IV., General von Prittwitz und die Berliner Märzrevolution', *FBPG*, 16 (1903), pp. 201–38; Friedrich Meinecke, 'Friedrich Wilhelm IV. und Deutschland', *Historische Zeitschrift*, 89 (1902), pp. 17–53, here pp. 47–9.

15. Heinrich, *Geschichte Preussens*, p. 364.

16. David Blackbourn, *History of Germany 780–1918. The Long Nineteenth Century* (2nd edn, Oxford, 2003), p. 107.

17. Ralf Rogge, 'Umriss des Revolutionsgeschehens 1848/49 in Solingen', in Wilfried Reininghaus (ed.), *Die Revolution 1848/49 in Westfalen und Lippe* (Münster, 1999), pp. 319–44, here pp. 322–3.

18. Manfred Beine, 'Sozialer protest und kurzzeitige Politisierung', in Reininghaus (ed.), *Die Revolution*, pp. 171–215, here p. 172.

19. Theodore S. Hamerow, *Restoration, Revolution, Reaction. Economics and Politics in Germany 1815–1871* (Princeton, NJ, 1958), pp. 103–6.

20. Christof Dipper, 'Rural Revolutionary Movements. Germany, France, Italy', in Dowe et al., (eds.), *Europe in 1848*, pp. 416–42, here p. 421.

21. Manfred Gailus, 'The Revolution of 1848 as Politics of the Streets', in Dowe et al., (eds.), *Europe in 1848*, pp. 778–96, here p. 781.

22. Eyewitness report by Berlin Mayor Krausnick, cited in Prittwitz, *Berlin 1848*, pp. 229–30; Barclay, *Friedrich Wilhelm IV*, p. 145.

23. The king's ride through Berlin is described in Karl Haenchen (ed.), *Revolutionsbriefe 1848: Ungedrucktes aus dem Nachlass König Friedrich Wilhelms IV. von Preussen* (Leipzig, 1930), pp. 53–4 (account by August von Schöler); Adolf Wolff, *Revolutions-Chronik. Darstellung der Berliner Bewegungen im Jahre 1848 nach politischen, socialen und literarischen Beziehungen* (3 vols., Berlin, 1851, 1852, 1854), vol. 1, pp. 294–9.

24. Cited in Prittwitz, *Berlin 1848*, pp. 440–41.

25. Otto von Bismarck, *Gedanken und Erinnerungen* (Stuttgart and Berlin, 1928), p. 58.

26. On military conspiracies at this time, see Manfred Kliem, *Genesis der Führungskräfte der feudal-militaristischen Konterrevolution 1848 in Preussen* (Berlin, 1966).

27. On the National Assembly, see Hans Mähl, *Die Überleitung Preussens in das konstitutionelle System durch den zweiten Vereinigten Landtag* (Munich, 1909), pp. 123–227; Wolfram Siemann, *Die deutsche Revolution von 1848/49* (Frankfurt/Main, 1985), p. 87; Manfred Botzenhart, *Deutscher Parlamentarismus in der Revolutionszeit 1848–1850* (Düsseldorf, 1977), pp. 132–41, 441–53.

28. Frederick William IV to ministry of state, Berlin, 4 June 1848, in Erich Brandenburg (ed.), *König Friedrich Wilhelms IV. Briefwechsel mit Ludolf Camphausen* (Berlin, 1906), pp. 144–7.

29. Barclay, *Friedrich Wilhelm IV*, p. 164.

30. Rüdiger Hachtmann, *Berlin 1848. Eine Politik- und Gesellschaftsgeschichte der Revolution* (Bonn, 1997), pp. 561–6, citation, p. 562.

31. Botzenhart, *Parlamentarismus*, pp. 538–41; Huber, *Verfassungsgeschichte* (8 vols., Stuttgart, 1957–90), vol. 2, pp. 730–32.

32. Gerlach to Brandenburg, 2 November 1848, cited in Barclay, *Friedrich Wilhelm IV*, p. 179.

33. Hachtmann, *Berlin 1848*, pp. 749–52; Botzenhart, *Parlamentarismus*, pp. 545–50; Barclay, *Friedrich Wilhelm IV*, pp. 179–81; Sabrina Müller, *Soldaten in den deutschen Revolutionen von 1848/49* (Paderborn, 1999), p. 299.

34. Sperber, *Rhineland Radicals*, pp. 314–36.

35. Reinhard Vogelsang, 'Minden-Ravensberg im Vormärz und in der Revolution von 1848/49; in Reininghaus (ed.), *Die Revolution*, pp. 141–69, here p. 154.

36. Sperber, *Rhineland Radicals*, pp. 360–86.

37. Barclay, *Friedrich Wilhelm IV*, esp. 138–84. The same general case is made in Bussmann, *Friedrich Wilhelm IV*, passim; cf. Blasius, *Friedrich Wilhelm IV*.

38. Wolfgang Schwentker, *Konservative Vereine und Revolution in Preussen, 1848/49. Die Konstituierung des Konservativismus als Partei* (Düsseldorf, 1988), pp. 142, 156–74, 176, 336–8.

39. Trox, *Militärischer Konservativismus*, pp. 207–9.

40. Müller, *Soldaten in der deutschen Revolution*, pp. 124 and passim.

41. Trox, *Militärischer Konservativismus*, pp. 162–4 and passim.

42. Müller, *Soldaten in der deutschen Revolution*, pp. 81, 83, 85, 299, 300.

43. Albert Förderer, *Erinnerungen aus Rastatt 1849* (Lahr, 1899), p. 104, cited in Müller, *Soldaten in der deutschen Revolution*, p. 310.

44. On the Prussian focus of 'liberal geopolitics', see Simms, *Struggle for Mastery*, pp. 168–94; Harald Müller, 'Zu den aussenpolitischen Zielvorstellungen der gemässigten Liberalen am Vorabend und im Verlauf der bürgerlich-demokratischen Revolution von 1848/49 am Beispiel der "Deutschen Zeitung" ', in Helmut Bleiber (ed.), *Bourgeoisie und bürgerliche Umwälzung in Deutschland, 1789–1871* (Berlin, 1977), pp. 229–66, citation p. 233, n. 45; id., 'Der Blick über die deutschen Grenzen. Zu den Forderungen der bürgerlichen Opposition in Preussen nach aussenpolitischer Einflussnahme am Vorabend und während des ersten preussischen vereinigten Landtags von 1847', *Jahrbuch für Geschichte*, 32 (1985), pp. 203–38.

45. Text in Wilhelm Angerstein, *Die Berliner Märzereignisse im Jahre 1848* (Leipzig, 1865), p. 65.

46. Frederick William, cabinet order, 21 March 1848, transcribed in Prittwitz, *Berlin 1848*, p. 392. For a detailed description of the ride through Berlin, see Schulze, *Der Weg zum Nationalstaat*, p. 47.

47. Frederick William IV, 'An Mein Volk und an die deutsche Nation', transcribed in Prittwitz, *Berlin 1848*, p. 392.

48. For a full account of the cathedral festival, see Thomas Parent, *Die Hohenzollern in Köln* (Cologne, 1981), pp. 50–61.

49. Frederick William IV to Metternich, 7 March 1842, cited in Barclay, *Friedrich Wilhelm IV*, p. 188.

50. Frederick William IV to Friedrich Christoph Dahlmann, 24 April 1848, in Anton Springer, *Friedrich Christoph Dahlmann* (2 vols., Leipzig, 1870, 1872), vol. 2, pp. 226–8.

51. Frederick William IV to Stolberg, 3 May 1848, in Otto Graf zu Stolberg-Wernigerode, *Anton Graf zu Stolberg-Wernigerode: Ein Freund und Ratgeber König Friedrich Wilhelms IV.* (Munich, 1926), p. 117.

52. Frederick William IV to Frederick August II of Saxony, 5 May 1848, in Hellmut

Kretzschmar, 'König Friedrich Wilhelms IV. Briefe an König Friedrich August II. von Sachsen', *Preussische Jahrbücher*, 227 (1932), pp. 28–50, 142–53, 245–63, here p. 46; Barclay, *Friedrich Wilhelm IV*, p. 190.

53. Baumgart, *Europäisches Konzert*, pp. 324–5; Werner Mosse, *The European Powers and the German Question, 1848–1871: with special Reference to England and Russia* (Cambridge, 1958), pp. 18–19.

54. Cited in Bussmann, *Friedrich Wilhelm IV*, p. 319.

55. Roy A. Austensen, 'The Making of Austria's Prussian Policy, 1848–1851', *Historical Journal*, 27 (1984), pp. 861–76, here p. 872.

56. Karl Marx and Friedrich Engels, 'Review: May–October 1850', *Neue Rheinische Zeitung. Politisch-ökonomische Revue* (London, 1 November 1850), accessed online at *http://www.marxists.org/archive/marx/works/1850/11/01.htm*; last accessed on 23 June 2004.

57. Ibid.

58. Heinrich von Sybel, *Die Begründing des Deutschen Reiches durch Wilhelm I.* (6 vols., 3rd pop. edn, Munich and Berlin, 1913), vol. 2, pp. 48–9.

59. Bismarck, *Gedanken und Erinnerungen*, p. 95.

60. Cited in Felix Gilbert, *Johann Gustav Droysen und die preussisch-deutsche Frage* (Munich and Berlin, 1931), p. 122.

61. Johann Gustav Droysen, 'Zur Charakteristik der europäischen Krisis', Minerva (1854), reprinted in id., *Politische Schriften*, ed. Felix Gilbert (Munich and Berlin, 1933), pp. 302–42, here p. 341. The word 'Forward' is a reference to Blücher, who was affectionately known as 'Marshal Forward'.

62. On the operations of the three-class system in Prussia, with a full analysis of voting patterns over its lifetime, see Thomas Kühne, *Handbuch der Wahlen zum preussischen Abgeordnetenhaus 1867–1918. Wahlergebnisse, Wahlbündnisse und Wahlkandidaten* (Düsseldorf, 1994).

63. Eberhard Naujoks, *Die parlamentarische Entstehung des Reichspressegesetzes in der Bismarckzeit (1848/74)* (Düsseldorf, 1975); Wolfram Siemann, *Gesellschaft im Aufbruch 1849–1871* (Frankfurt/Main, 1990), pp. 42, 65–7.

64. Cf. G. R. Elton, *The Tudor Revolution in Government. Administrative Changes in the Reign of Henry VIII* (Cambridge, 1969), which deals of course with a very different subject matter, but speaks of a period 'when the needs of good government prevailed over the demands of free government' and 'order and peace seemed more important than principles and rights' (p. 1) and perceives in administrative innovation a process of 'controlled upheaval' (p. 427).

65. A useful comparative survey of constitutional innovation across Europe is Martin Kisch and Pierangelo Schiera (eds.), *Verfassungswandel um 1848 im europäischen Vergleich* (Berlin, 2001); see esp. the introductory essay by Kisch, 'Verfassungswandel um 1848 – Aspekte der Rezeption und des Vergleichs zwischen den europäischen Staaten', pp. 31–62.

66. Barclay, *Friedrich Wilhelm IV*, p. 183.

67. H. Wegge, *Die Stellung der Öffentlichkeit zur oktroyierten Verfassung und die preussische Parteibildung 1848/49* (Berlin, 1932), pp. 45–8; quotation p. 48.

68. Barclay, *Friedrich Wilhem IV*, p. 221.

69. Günther Grünthal, *Parlamentarismus in Preussen 1848/49–1857/58: Preussischer Konstitutionalismus – Parlament und Regierung in der Reaktionsära* (Düsseldorf, 1982), p. 185.

70. Ibid., p. 392.

71. William J. Orr, 'The Prussian Ultra Right and the Advent of Constitutionalism in Prussia', *Canadian Journal of History*, 11 (1976), pp. 295–310, here p. 307; Heinrich Heffter, 'Der Nachmärzliberalismus: Die Reaktion der fünfziger Jahre', in Hans-Ulrich Wehler (ed.), *Moderne deutsche Sozialgeschichte* (Cologne, 1966), pp. 177–96, here pp. 181–3; Hans Rosenberg, 'Die Pseudodemokratisierung der Rittergutsbesitzerklasse', in id., *Machteliten und Wirtschaftskonjunkturen. Studien zur neueren deutschen Sozial- und Wirtschaftsgeschichte* (Göttingen, 1978), p. 94.

72. For an excellent comparative discussion of conservative-liberal modernization in Prussia and Austria, see Arthur Schlegelmilch, 'Das Projekt der konservativ-liberalen Modernisierung und die Einführung konstitutioneller Systeme in Preussen und Österreich, 1848/49', in Kisch and Schiera (eds.), *Verfassungswandel*, pp. 155–77.

73. James Brophy, *Capitalism, Politics and Railroads in Prussia, 1830–1870* (Columbus, OH, 1998), pp. 165–75.

74. Grünthal, *Parlamentarismus*, pp. 281–6.

75. William I to Otto von Manteuffel, director in the interior ministry under Camphausen, 7 April 1848, cited in Karl-Heinz Börner, *Wilhelm I Deutscher Kaiser und König von Preussen. Eine Biographie* (Berlin, 1984), p. 81.

76. Grünthal, *Parlamentarismus*, p. 476.

77. Charles Tilly, 'The Political Economy of Public Finance and the Industrialization of Prussia 1815–1866', *Journal of Economic History*, 26 (1966), pp. 484–97, here p. 490.

78. Ibid., p. 494.

79. Ibid., p. 492.

80. Brophy, *Capitalism, Politics and Railroads*, p. 58.

81. Grünthal, *Parlamentarismus*, p. 476.

82. H. Winkel, *Die deutsche Nationalökonomie im 19. Jahrhundert* (Darmstadt, 1977), pp. 86–7, 95. On this view as an instance of the German engagement with 'Smithianism', see E. Rothschild, ' "Smithianismus" and Enlightenment in Nineteenth-century Europe', King's College Cambridge: Centre for History and Economics, October 1998.

83. David Hansemann, cited in Brophy, *Capitalism, Politics and Railroads*, p. 50.

84. Brophy, *Capitalism, Politics and Railroads*, pp. 50, 56, 58. Von der Heydt's policy of nationalization was reversed in the 1860s.

85. James Brophy, 'The Political Calculus of Capital: Banking and the Business Class in Prussia, 1848–1856', *Central European History*, 25 (1992), pp. 149–76; id., 'The Juste Milieu: Businessmen and the Prussian State during the New Era and the Constitutional Conflict', in Holtz and Spenkuch (eds.), *Preussens Weg*, pp. 193–224.

86. On the Techen scandal, see Barclay, *Friedrich Wilhelm IV*, pp. 252–5.

87. D. Fischer, *Handbuch der politischen Presse in Deutschland, 1480–1980. Synopse rechtlicher, struktureller und wirtschaftlicher Grundlagen der Tendenzpublizistik im Kommunikationsfeld* (Düsseldorf, 1981), pp. 60–61, 65; Kurt Koszyk, *Deutsche Presse im 19. Jahrhundert* (Berlin, 1966), p. 123; F. Schneider, *Pressefreiheit und politische Öffentlichkeit* (Neuwied, 1966), p. 310.

88. Kurt Wappler, *Regierung und Presse in Preussen. Geschichte der amtlichen Pressestellen, 1848–62* (Leipzig, 1935), p. 94.

89. R. Kohnen, *Pressepolitik des deutschen Bundes. Methoden staatlicher Pressepolitik nach der Revolution von 1848* (Tübingen, 1995), p. 174.

90. Wappler, *Regierung und Presse*, pp. 3–4.

91. Ibid., pp. 16–17.

92. Barclay, *Friedrich Wilhelm IV*, p. 262.

93. Wappler, *Regierung und Presse*, p. 5.

94. Manteuffel to Rochow, 3 July 1851, cited in Wappler, *Regierung und Presse*, p. 91. On the transition from censorship to news management in the lesser German states, see Abigail Green, *Fatherlands. Statebuilding and Nationhood in Nineteenth-century Germany* (Cambridge, 2001), pp. 148–88.

15 Four Wars

1. *The Times*, 23 October 1860, cited in Raymond James Sontag, *Germany and England. Background of Conflict 1848–1898* (New York, 1938, reprint, 1969), p. 33.

2. Ernst Portner, *Die Einigung Italiens im Urteil liberaler deutscher Zeitgenossen* (Bonn, 1959), pp. 65, 119–22, 172–8; Angelow, *Von Wien nach Königgrätz*, pp. 190–200.

3. Mosse, *The European Great Powers*, pp. 49–77.

4. See, with literature, Dierk Walter, *Preussische Heeresreformen 1807–1870. Militärische Innovation und der Mythos der "Roonschen Reform"* (Paderborn, 2003).

5. English reprint in Helmut Böhme (ed.), *The Foundation of the German Empire. Select Documents*, trans. Agatha Ramm (Oxford, 1971), pp. 93–5.

6. Börner, *Wilhelm I*, pp. 17, 21.

7. Crown Prince William to General O. von Natzmer, Berlin, 20 May 1849, in Ernst Berner (ed.), *Kaiser Wilhelm des Grossen Briefe, Reden und Schriften* (2 vols., Berlin, 1906), vol. 1, pp. 202–3. Citation from May 1850 in Börner, *Wilhelm I*, p. 115. On William's nationalism generally, see pp. 96–101.

8. Craig, *Politics of the Prussian Army*, pp. 136–79. For a powerful revisionist account of the military reforms, which explodes many longstanding myths (among others, the view that the mobilization of 1859 was an utter fiasco) see Walter, *Heeresreformen*.

9. On Manteuffel, see Otto Pflanze, *Bismarck and the Development of Germany* (2nd edn, 3 vols., Princeton, NJ, 1990), vol. 1, *The Period of Unification, 1815–1871*, pp. 171–3, 182–3, 208; Ritter, *Staatskunst*, vol. 1, pp. 174–6, 231–4; Craig, *Politics of the Prussian Army*, pp. 149–50, 232–5.

10. Craig, *Politics of the Prussian Army*, pp. 151–7.

11. Sheehan, *German History*, p. 879.

12. For a discussion of this letter, see Lothar Gall, *The White Revolutionary*, trans. J. A. Underwood (2 vols., London, 1986), vol. 1, p. 16.

13. Ibid., vol. 1, pp. 3–34; cf. Ernst Engelberg, *Bismarck. Urpreusse und Reichsgründer* (2 vols., Berlin, 1998), vol. 1, pp. 39–40, which makes the point that the Mencken connection in no way undermined the status pretensions of the Bismarcks and finds little trace of a 'self-consciously bourgeois' mentality among the Bismarck ancestors.

14. Cited in Gall, *White Revolutionary*, vol. 1, p. 57.

15. Letter to his cousin, 13 February 1847, cited in ibid., pp. 18–19.

16. Cited in Pflanze, *The Period of Unification*, p. 82.

17. Allen Mitchell, 'Bonapartism as a Model for Bismarckian Politics', *Journal of Modern History*, 49 (1977), pp. 181–99.

18. Bismarck to Crown Prince Frederick, 13 October 1862, in Kaiser Friedrich III, *Tagebücher von 1848–1866*, ed. H. O. Meisner (Leipzig, 1929), p. 505.

19. Craig, *Politics of the Prussian Army*, p. 167.

20. After the German-Danish war of 1848 had ended in the stalemate of Malmö, the issue was settled (or so everyone thought) by a series of international treaties signed in 1851 and 1852. These acknowledged the right of Frederick VII's prospective successor, Crown Prince Christian of Glücksburg, to reign as sovereign over the Kingdom of Denmark and the duchies; in return, the Danes had to promise not to annex Schleswig or tamper with the constitutional status of the duchies without first consulting the (largely German) Estates of the two disputed principalities.

21. For a full analysis of Bismarck's reasoning, see Pflanze, *Bismarck*, vol. 1, pp. 237–67. For a useful overview of the run-up to the war, see Dennis Showalter, *The Wars of German Unification* (London, 2004), pp. 117–22; Craig, *Politics of the Prussian Army*, pp. 180–84.

22. Showalter, *Wars of German Unification*, p. 126.

23. Wolfgang Förster (ed.), *Prinz Friedrich Karl von Preussen, Denkwürdigkeiten aus seinem Leben* (2 vols., Stuttgart, 1910), vol. 1, pp. 307–9.

24. Albrecht von Roon, *Denkwürdigkeiten*, (5th edn, 3 vols., Berlin, 1905), vol. 2, pp. 244–6.

25. Pflanze, *Bismarck*, vol. 1, pp. 271–9.

26. Siemann, *Gesellschaft im Aufbruch*, pp. 99–123; Wehler, *Deutsche Gesellschaftsgeschichte*, vol. 3, *Von der 'Deutschen Doppelrevolution' bis zum Beginn des Ersten Weltkrieges 1849–1914*, pp. 66–97.

27. Pflanze, *Bismarck*, vol. 1, p. 290.

28. Bismarck to Baron Karl von Werther, Berlin, 6 August 1864, in Böhme (ed.), *Foundation of the German Empire*, pp. 128–9.

29. Cited in Mosse, *European Powers*, p. 133.

30. On this meeting, see Pflanze, *Bismarck*, vol. 1, p. 292; Ernst Engelberg, *Bismarck*, p. 570. Bismarck did not, as has often been claimed, adduce the need to defeat the liberals as a reason for going to war. This argument was put forward by another participant in the conference and explicitly rejected by Bismarck.

31. Heinrich von Srbik, 'Der Geheimvertrag Österreichs und Frankreichs vom 12. Juni 1866', *Historisches Jahrbuch*, 57 (1937), pp. 454–507; Gerhard Ritter, 'Bismarck und die Rheinpolitik Napoleons III.', *Rheinische Vierteljahrsblätter*, 15–16 (1950–51), pp. 339–70; E. Ann Pottinger, *Napoleon III and the German Crisis. 1856–1866* (Cambridge, MA, 1966), pp. 24–150; Pflanze, *Bismarck*, vol. 1, pp. 302–3.

32. On the Russian perspective, see Dietrich Beyrau, *Russische Orientpolitik und die Entstehung des deutschen Kaiserreichs 1866–1870/71* (Wiesbaden, 1974); id., 'Russische Interessenzonen und europäisches Gleichgewicht 1860–1870', in Eberhard Kolb (ed.), *Europa vor dem Krieg von 1870* (Munich, 1987), pp. 67–76; id., 'Der deutsche Komplex. Russland zur Zeit der Reichsgründung', in Eberhard Kolb (ed.), *Europa und die Reichsgründung. Preussen-Deutschland in der Sicht der grossen europäischen Mächte 1860–1880* (= Historische Zeitschrift, Beiheft New Series, vol. 6; Munich, 1980), pp. 63–108.

33. On the run-up to the war of 1866, see Showalter, *Wars of German Unification*, pp. 132–59; Sheehan, *German History*, pp. 899–908; Pflanze, *Bismarck*, vol. 1, pp. 292–315.

34. Frank J. Coppa, *The Origins of the Italian Wars of Independence* (London, 1992), pp. 122, 125.

35. Walter, *Heeresreformen*.

36. On this point see Voth, 'The Prussian Zollverein', pp. 122–4.

37. Showalter, *Wars of German Unification*, p. 168.

38. Wawro, *Austro-Prussian War*, pp. 130–35, 145–7.

39. Ibid., p. 134.

40. Communiqué to von der Goltz, Berlin, 30 March 1866, in Herman von Petersdorff et al. (eds.), *Bismarck: Die gesammelten Werke* (15 vols., Berlin 1923–33), vol. 5, p. 429.

41. Cited in Koppel S. Pinson, *Modern Germany* (New York, 1955), pp. 139–40. On Siemens, see Jürgen Kocka, *Unternehmerverwaltung und Angestelltenschaft am Beispiel Siemens, 1847–1914. Zum Verhältnis von Kapitalismus und Bürokratie in der deutschen Industrialisierung* (Stuttgart, 1969), pp. 52–3.

42. Rudolf Stadelmann, *Moltke und der Staat* (Krefeld, 1950), p. 73; Sheehan, *German Liberalism*, pp. 109–18.

43. For an English translation of the text of William I's Landtag speech of 5 August 1866 proposing the indemnity bill, see Theodor Hamerow, *The Age of Bismarck. Documents and Interpretations* (New York, 1973), pp. 80–82.

44. Pflanze, *Bismarck*, vol. 1, p. 335.

45. Hagen Schulze, 'Preussen von 1850 bis 1871. Verfassungsstaat und Reichsgründung', in Büsch et al. (eds.), *Handbuch der preussischen Geschichte*, vol. 2, pp. 293–374.

46. Conversation reported by Gelzer to Grand Duke Frederick, Berlin, 20 August 1866, in Hermann Oncken (ed.), *Grossherzog Friedrich I von Baden und die deutsche Politik von 1854 bis 1871: Briefwechsel, Denkschriften, Tagebücher* (2 vols., Stuttgart, 1927), vol. 2, pp. 23–5, here p. 25.

47. Ibid., p. 25.

48. Katherine Lerman, *Bismarck* (Harlow, 2004), p. 145.

49. David Wetzel, *A Duel of Giants. Bismarck, Napoleon III and the Origins of the Franco-Prussian War* (Madison, WI, 2001), p. 93.

50. On Bismarck's planning, see Jochen Dittrich, *Bismarck, Frankreich und die spanische Thronkandidatur der Hohenzollern* (Munich, 1962); Eberhard Kolb, *Der Kriegsausbruch 1870* (Göttingen, 1970); Josef Becker, 'Zum Problem der Bismarckschen Politik in der spanischen Thronfrage', *Historische Zeitschrift*, 212 (1971), pp. 529–605 and id., 'Von Bismarcks "spanischer Diversion" zur "Emser Legende" des Reichsgründers', in Johannes Burkhardt et al. (eds.), *Lange und Kurze Wege in den Ersten Weltkrieg. Vier Augsburger Beiträge zur Kriegsursachenforschung* (Munich, 1996), pp. 87–113. Becker makes the

case for a planned preventive war; the contrary position is set out in Eberhard Kolb, 'Mächtepolitik und Kriegsrisiko am Vorabend des Krieges von 1870: Anstelle eines Nachwortes', in id. (ed.), *Europa vor dem Krieg von 1870. Mächtekonstellation, Konfliktfelder, Kriegsausbruch* (Munich, 1987), pp. 203–9.

51. Martin Schulze Wessel, *Russlands Blick nach Preussen, Die polnische Frage in der Diplomatie und der politischen Öffentlichkeit des Zarenreiches und des Sowjetstaates 1697–1947* (Stuttgart, 1995), pp. 131–2; Barbara Jelavich, 'Russland und die Einigung Deutschlands unter preussischer Führung', *Geschichte in Wissenschaft und Unterricht*, 19 (1968), pp. 521–38; Klaus Meyer, 'Russland und die Gründing des deutschen Reiches', *Jahrbuch für die Geschichte Mittel-und Ostdeutschlands*, 22 (1973), pp. 176–95.

52. Cited in William Flardle Moneypenny George Earl Buckle, *The Life of Benjamin Disraeli, Earl of Beaconsfield* (new and revised edn, 2 vols. New York, 1920), vol. 2, pp. 473–4.

53. Cited in J.-P. Bled, *Franz Joseph* (Oxford, 1994), p. 178. See also Steven Beller, *Francis Joseph* (Harlow, 1996), pp. 107–10.

54. Claude Digeon, *La Crise allemande dans la pensée française 1870–1914* (Paris, 1959), pp. 535–42.

55. Volker Ullrich, *Otto von Bismarck* (Hamburg, 1998), p. 93.

56. Cited in Eckhard Buddruss, 'Die Deutschlandpolitik der Französischen Revolution zwischen Tradition und revolutionärem Bruch', in Karl Otmar von Aretin and Karl Härter (eds.), *Revolution und Konservatives Beharren. Das Alte Reich und die Französische Revolution* (Mainz, 1990), pp. 145–52, here p. 147; Simms, *Struggle for Mastery*, pp. 44–5.

57. Martin Schulze Wessel, 'Die Epochen der russisch-preussischen Beziehungen', in Neugebauer (ed.), *Handbuch der preussischen Geschichte*, vol. 3, p. 713.

58. Paul W. Schroeder, 'Lost intermediaries'; Rainer Lahme, *Deutsche Aussenpolitik 1890–1894: von der Gleichgewichtspolitik Bismarcks zur Allianzstrategie Caprivis* (Göttingen, 1990), pp. 488–90 and passim; Wolfgang Canis, *Von Bismarck zur Weltpolitik. Deutsche Aussenpolitik 1890–1902* (Berlin, 1997), pp. 400–401 and passim.

16 Merged into Germany

1. For text of the Reich constitution of 1871 and useful commentary, see E. M. Hucko (ed.), *The Democratic Tradition. Four German Constitutions* (Leamington Spa, Hamburg, New York, 1987), p. 121. All quotations are from this translation. The full German text can be found at *http://www.deutsche-schutzgebiete.de/verfassung—deutsches—reich.htm*; last accessed on 1 September 2004.

2. Under article 3. On definitions of citizenship more generally, see Andreas Fahrmeir, *Citizens and Aliens. Foreigners and the Law in Britain and the German States, 1789–1870* (New York, 2000), esp. pp. 39–43, 232–6.

3. Reich constitution of 1871, art. 6, in Hucko (ed.), *Democratic Tradition*, p. 123.

4. Michael Stürmer, 'Eine politische Kultur – oder zwei? Betrachtungen zur Regierungsweise des Kaiserreichs', in Oswald Hauser (ed.), *Zur Problematik Preussen und das Reich* (Cologne, 1984), pp. 35–48, here pp. 39–40.

5. Friedrich-Christian Stahl, 'Preussische Armee und Reichsheer 1871–1914', in Hauser (ed.), *Preussen und das Reich*, pp. 181–246, here p. 234.

6. Thomas Kühne, *Dreiklassenwahlrecht und Wahlkultur in Preussen 1867–1914. Landtagwahlen zwischen korporativer Tradition und politischem Massenmarkt* (Düsseldorf, 1994), pp. 57–8.

7. On the *Herrenhaus* and its role in the Prussian social and political system, the standard work is now Hartwin Spenkuch, *Das Preussische Herrenhaus. Adel und Bürgertum in der Ersten Kammer des Landtags 1854–1918* (Düsseldorf, 1998). On the 'ballast' function of the house, see p. 552.

8. Kühne, *Dreiklassenwahlrecht*, pp. 59, 62, 71–3, 79–80.

9. Bernhard von Bülow, *Memoirs*, trans. F. A. Voigt (4 vols., London and New York,

1931–2), vol. 1 pp. 233–4, 291; H. Horn, *Der Kampf um den Bau des Mittellandkanals. Eine politologische Untersuchung über die Rolle eines wirtschaftlichen Interessenverbandes im Preussen Wilhelms II* (Cologne and Opladen, 1964), pp. 40–43.

10. Lothar Gall, 'Zwischen Preussen und dem Reich: Bismarck als Reichskanzler und Preussischer Minister-Präsident', in Hauser (ed.), *Preussen und das Reich*, pp. 155–64. On Prussia's 'braking role' more generally, see Hagen Schulze, 'Preussen von 1850 bis 1871' in Büsch et al. (eds.), *Handbuch der preussischen Geschichte*, vol. 2, pp. 293–373, here pp. 367–70; Spenkuch, 'Vergleichsweise besonders?', passim.

11. Simone Lässig, 'Wahlrechtsreform in den deutschen Einzelstaaten. Indikatoren für Modernisierungstendenzen und Reformfähigkeit im Kaiserreich', in id. et al. (eds.), *Modernisierung und Region im wilhelminischen Deutschland* (Bielefeld, 1995), pp. 127–69.

12. Helmut Croon, 'Die Anfänge der Parlamentarisierung im Reich und die Auswirkungen auf Preussen', in Hauser (ed.), *Preussen und das Reich*, pp. 105–54, here p. 108.

13. On the east–west divide within Prussian political culture, see Heinz Reif, 'Der katholische Adel Westfalens und die Spaltung des Adelskonservatismus in Preussen während des 19. Jahrhunderts', in Karl Teppe (ed.), *Westfalen und Preussen* (Paderborn, 1991), pp. 107–24.

14. Shelley Baranowski, 'East Elbian Landed Elites and Germany's Turn to Fascism: The Sonderweg revisited', in *European History Quarterly* (1996), pp. 209–40; Ilona Buchsteiner, 'Pommerscher Adel im Wandel des 19. Jahrhunderts', *Geschichte und Gesellschaft*, 25 (1999), pp. 343–74.

15. James Sheehan, 'Liberalism and the City in Nineteenth-century Germany', *Past & Present*, 51 (1971), pp. 116–37; Dieter Langewiesche, 'German Liberalism in the Second Empire', in Konrad Jarausch and Larry Eugene Jones (eds.), *In Search of Liberal Germany. Studies in the History of German Liberalism from 1789 to the Present* (New York, 1990), pp. 217–35, esp. pp. 230–33.

16. Bernhard von Bülow to Philipp zu Eulenburg, Bucharest, 9 January 1893, in John Röhl (ed.), *Philipp Eulenburgs Politische Korrespondenz* (3 vols., Boppard am Rhein, 1976–83), vol. 2, pp. 1000–1001.

17. Wolfgang Mommsen, 'Culture and Politics in the German Empire', in id., *Imperial Germany 1867–1918. Politics, Culture and Society in an Authoritarian State*, trans. Richard Deveson (London, 1995), pp. 119–40, here pp. 129–30.

18. Cited in Rudolf Braun and David Guggerli, *Macht des Tanzes – Tanz der Mächtigen. Hoffeste und Herrschaftszeremoniell 1550–1914* (Munich, 1993), p. 318.

19. Bernd Nicolai, 'Architecture and Urban Development', in Gert Streidt and Peter Feierabend (eds.), *Prussia. Art and Architecture* (Cologne, 1999), pp. 416–55.

20. Margrit Bröhan, *Walter Leistikow, Maler der Berliner Landschaft* (Berlin, 1988).

21. Examples of buildings that engage with the 'Prussian style' are Messel's Wertheim department store (1896–8) and State Insurance Office (1903–4), and Behrens's AEG small engine factory (1910–13) and AEG turbine plant (1909), all in Berlin.

22. Margaret Lavinia Anderson, *Windthorst. A Political Biography* (Oxford, 1981), esp. pp. 130–200; David Blackbourn, *Marpingen: Apparitions of the Virgin Mary in Bismarckian Germany, 1871–1887* (Oxford, 1993), pp. 106–20; Ronald J. Ross, *The Failure of Bismarck's Kulturkampf. Catholicism and State Power in Imperial Germany, 1871–1887* (Washington, 1998), pp. 49, 95–157.

23. Cited and discussed in Pflanze, *Bismarck*, vol. 1, p. 368, and vol. 2, p. 188.

24. Christa Stache, *Bürgerlicher Liberalismus und katholischer Konservatismus in Bayern 1867–1871: kulturkämpferische Auseinandersetzungen vor dem Hintergrund von nationaler Einigung und wirtschaftlich-sozialem Wandel* (Frankfurt, 1981), pp. 66–108.

25. Lerman, *Bismarck*, p. 176.

26. Michael Gross, *The War Against Catholicism. Liberalism and the Anti-Catholic Imagination in Nineteenth-century Germany* (Ann Arbor, MI, 2004); Roisín Healy, *The Jesuit Spectre in Imperial Germany* (Leiden, 2003).

27. Pflanze, *Bismarck*, vol. 2, p. 205.
28. Gordon Craig, *Germany 1866–1945* (Oxford, 1981), p. 71.
29. The examples that follow are taken from Ross, *Failure*, pp. 53–74, 95–101.
30. Günther Dettmer, *Die Ost- und Westpreussischen Verwaltungsbehörden im Kultur-kampf* (Heidelberg, 1958), p. 117.
31. Jonathan Sperber, *The Kaiser's Voters. Electors and Elections in Imperial Germany* (Cambridge, 1997); Margaret Lavinia Anderson, *Practicing Democracy. Elections and Political Culture in Imperial Germany* (Princeton, NJ, 2000), pp. 69–151.
32. Reichstag speech of 24 February 1881, in H. von Petersdorff (ed.), *Bismarck. Die gesammelten Werke* (15 vols., Berlin, 1924–35), vol. 12, *Reden, 1878–1885*, ed. Wilhelm Schüssler, pp. 188–95, here p. 195.
33. Speech of 24 February 1870 by Deputy Kantak of Inowracław-Mogilno (Province of Posen), *Stenographische Berichte über die Verhandlungen des Reichstages des Norddeutschen Bundes*, vol. 1 (1870), p. 74.
34. Hagen, *Germans, Poles and Jews*, p. 106.
35. Klaus Helmut Rehfeld, *Die preussische Verwaltung des Regierungsbezirks Bromberg (1848–1871)* (Heidelberg, 1968), p. 25. On inter-ethnic tensions, see Kasimierz Wajda, 'The Poles and the Germans in West Prussia province in the 19th and the beginning of the 20th century', in Jan Sziling and Mieczysław Wojciechowski (eds.), *Neighbourhood Dilemmas. The Poles, the Germans and the Jews in Pomerania along the Vistula River in the 19th and the 20th century* (Toruń, 2002), pp. 9–19.
36. Siegfried Baske, *Praxis und Prinzipien der preussischen Polenpolitik vom Beginn der Reaktionszeit bis zur Gründung des deutschen Reiches* (Berlin, 1963), p. 209.
37. Hagen, *Germans, Poles and Jews*, p. 121; Baske, *Praxis*, p. 78.
38. Baske, *Praxis*, pp. 186–8.
39. Ibid., pp. 123, 224; Manfred Laubert, *Die preussische Polenpolitik von 1772–1914* (3rd edn, Cracow, 1944), pp. 131–2.
40. Report of 16 August 1870, cited in Pflanze, *Bismarck*, vol. 2, p. 108.
41. Bismarck to cabinet meeting of 1 November 1871 in Adelheid Constabel (ed.), *Die Vorgeschichte des Kulturkampfes* (Berlin, 1956), pp. 136–41.
42. Lech Trzeciakowski, *The Kulturkampf in Prussian Poland*, trans. Katarzyna Kretkowska (Boulder, CO, 1990), pp. 88–95.
43. Kossert, *Masuren*, pp. 196–205. On the Lithuanians, see Forstreuter, 'Die Anfänge der Sprachstatistik' and id., 'Deutsche Kulturpolitik im sogenannten Preussisch-Litauen', in id., *Wirkungen*, pp. 312–33 and 334–44.
44. Pflanze, *Bismarck*, vol. 2, p. 111; Hagen, *Germans, Poles and Jews*, pp. 128–30, 145.
45. Serrier, *Entre Allemagne et Pologne*, p. 286.
46. Hagen, *Germans, Poles and Jews*, pp. 180–207.
47. On historians, see Michael Burleigh, *Germany Turns Eastwards. A Study of Ostforschung in the Third Reich* (Cambridge, 1988), pp. 4–7; Wolfgang Wippermann, *Der deutsche "Drang nach Osten". Ideologie und Wirklichkeit eines politischen Schlagwortes* (Darmstadt, 1981).
48. Werner T. Angress, 'Prussia's Army and the Jewish Reserve Officer Controversy Before World War I', *Leo Baeck Institute Yearbook*, 17 (1972), pp. 19–42; Norbert Kampe, 'Jüdische Professoren im deutschen Kaiserreich', in Rainer Erb and Michael Schmidt (eds.), *Antisemitismus und jüdische Geschichte. Studien zu Ehren von Herbert A. Strauss* (Berlin, 1987), pp. 185–211.
49. Till van Rahden, 'Mingling, Marrying and Distancing. Jewish Integration in Wilhelmine Breslau and its Erosion in Early Weimar Germany', in Wolfgang Benz, Arnold Paucker and Peter Pulzer (eds.), *Jüdisches Leben in der Weimarer Republik – Jews in the Weimar Republic* (Tübingen, 1988), pp. 193–216; id., *Juden und andere Breslauer. Die Beziehungen zwischen Juden, Protestanten und Katholiken in einer deutschen Grossstadt, 1860–1925* (Göttingen, 2000).
50. Stephanie Schueler-Springorum, *Die jüdische Minderheit in Königsberg/Pr. 1871–1945*

(Göttingen, 1996), p. 192. See also the essays in Andreas Gotzmann, Rainer Liedtke and Till van Rahden (eds.), *Juden, Bürger, Deutsche: Zur Geschichte von Vielfalt und Differenz 1800–1933* (Tübingen, 2001).

51. Moritz Lazarus, 'Wie wir Staatsbürger wurden', *Im Deutschen Reich*, 3 (1897), pp. 239–47, here p. 246; Reinhard Rürup, 'The Tortuous and Thorny Path to Legal Equality. "Jew Laws" and Emancipatory Legislation in Germany from the Late Eighteenth Century', *Leo Baeck Institute Yearbook*, 31 (1986), pp. 3–33. On 'state citizenship', see esp. anon., 'Der Centralverein deutscher Staatsbürger jüdischen Glaubens am Schlusse seines ersten Lustrums', *Im Deutschen Reich*, 4 (1898), pp. 1–6; anon., 'Die Bestrebungen und Ziele des Centralvereins', *Im Deutschen Reich*, 1 (1895), pp. 142–58; anon., 'Unsere Stellung', *Im Deutschen Reich*, 1 (1895), pp. 5–6.

52. Christopher Clark, 'The Jews and the German State in the Wilhelmine Era', in Michael Brenner, Rainer Liedtke and David Rechter (eds.), *Two Nations. British and German Jews in Comparative Perspective* (Tübingen, 1999), pp. 163–84.

53. Ernst Hamburger, *Juden im öffentlichen Leben Deutschlands* (Tübingen, 1968), p. 47; anon., 'Justizminister a.D. Schönstedt', *Im Deutschen Reich*, 11 (1905), pp. 623–6.

54. Heeringen, Reichstag speech of 10 February 1910, cited in Angress, 'Prussia's Army', p. 35.

55. Norbert Kampe, *Studenten und 'Judenfrage' im deutschen Kaiserreich. Die Entstehung einer akademischen Trägerschicht des Antisemitismus* (Göttingen, 1988), pp. 34–7.

56. Dietz Bering, *The Stigma of Names. Anti-Semitism in German Daily Life, 1812–1933* (Oxford, 1992), esp. pp. 87–118.

57. Werner T. Angress, 'The German Army's Judenzählung of 1916. Genesis – Consequences – Significance', *Leo Baeck Institute Yearbook*, 23 (1978), pp. 117–37.

58. Werner Jochmann, 'Die Ausbreitung des Antisemitismus', in Werner E. Mosse and Arnold Paucker (eds.), *Deutsches Judentum in Krieg und Revolution, 1916–1923* (Tübingen, 1971), pp. 409–510, here pp. 411–13. The text of the Judenzählung decree is in Werner T. Angress, 'Das deutsche Militär und die Juden im Ersten Weltkrieg', *Militärgeschichtliche Mitteilungen*, 19 (1976), pp. 77–146; Helmut Berding, *Moderner Antisemitismus in Deutschland* (Frankfurt/Main, 1988), p. 169. The comment is from R. Lewin, 'Der Krieg als jüdisches Erlebnis', in *Monatsschrift für Geschichte und Wissenschaft des Judentums*, 63 (1919), pp. 1–14.

59. Helmut Walser Smith, *The Butcher's Tale. Murder and Antisemitism in a German Town* (New York, 2002), esp. pp. 180–84; Christoph Nonn, *Eine Stadt sucht einen Mörder: Gerücht, Gewalt und Antisemitismus im Kaiserreich* (Göttingen, 2002), pp. 169–87.

60. Christoph Cobet, *Der Wortschatz des Antisemitismus in der Bismarckzeit* (Munich, 1973), p. 49.

61. Quotations from Michael Stürmer, *Das Ruhelose Reich* (Berlin, 1983), p. 238. On Bismarck's dominance over William I, see Börner, *Wilhelm I*, pp. 182–5, 218–20.

62. Börner, *Wilhelm I*, pp. 239, 265; Franz Herre, *Kaiser Wilhelm I. Der letzte Preusse* (Cologne, 1980), pp. 439–40, 487.

63. Christopher Clark, *Kaiser Wilhelm II* (Harlow, 2000), p. 161.

64. Thomas Kohut, *Wilhelm II and the Germans. A Study in Leadership* (New York and Oxford, 1991), pp. 235–8. On the management of speeches by the civil cabinet, see Eisenhardt to Valentini, 11 August 1910, pencilled comment, GStA Berlin-Dahlem, HA I, Rep. 89, Nr. 678. On Frederick's speeches as crown prince, Empress Frederick to Queen Victoria, September 1891, in Frederick E. G. Ponsonby (ed.), *Letters of the Empress Frederick* (London, 1928), pp. 427–9.

65. Thomas Kohut, *Wilhelm II and the Germans: A Study in Leadership* (New York, 1991), p. 138. On 'charismatization', see Isobel V. Hull, 'Der kaiserliche Hof als Herrschaftsinstrument', in Hans Wilderotter and Klaus D. Pohl (eds.), *Der Letzte Kaiser. Wilhelm II im Exil* (Berlin, 1991), pp. 26–7.

66. See e.g. speech given at gala reception in Münster, 31 August 1907, based on notes written by William himself, GStA Berlin-Dahlem, HA I, Rep. 89, Nr. 673, folder 28.

67. Stenogram of a speech given at Memel, 23 September 1907, GStA Berlin-Dahlem, HA I, Rep. 89, Nr. 673, folder 30.

68. Pflanze, *Bismarck*, vol. 3, *The Period of Fortification, 1880–1898* (Princeton, NJ, 1990), p. 394; Count Waldersee, Diary entry 21 April 1891, in Meisner (ed.), *Denkwürdigkeiten des General-Feldmarschalls Alfred Grafen von Waldersee* (3 vols., Stuttgart and Berlin, 1923–5), vol. 2, p. 206. On particularist responses, see Röhl (ed.), *Politische Korrespondenz*, vol. 1, p. 679, n. 2.

69. See e.g. William's speeches to the diet of 24 February 1892 and 24 February 1894, in Louis Elkind (ed.), *The German Emperor's Speeches. Being a Selection from the Speeches, Edicts, Letters and Telegrams of the Emperor William II* (London, 1904), pp. 292, 295.

70. Eulenburg to William II, Munich, 10 March 1892, in Röhl (ed.), *Politische Korrespondenz*, vol. 2, p. 798, emphases in original.

71. Eulenburg to William II, Berlin, 28 November 1891, in Röhl (ed.), *Politische Korrespondenz*, vol. 1, p. 730.

72. Olaf Gulbransson, 'Kaisermanöver', *Simplicissimus*, 20 September 1909. This image is discussed in Jost Rebentisch, *Die Vielen Gesichter des Kaisers. Wilhelm II. in der deutschen und britischen Karikatur (1888–1918)* (Berlin, 2000), pp. 86, 299.

73. Holstein to Eulenburg, 27 February 1892, in Röhl (ed.), *Politische Korrespondenz*, vol. 2, p. 780.

74. Helga Abret and Aldo Keel, *Die Majestätsbeleidigungsaffäre des 'Simplicissimus'-Verlegers Albert Langen. Briefe und Dokumente zu Exil und Begnadigung, 1898–1903* (Frankfurt/Main, 1985), esp. pp. 40–1.

75. Consistorial councillor Blau to Lucanus (chief of civil cabinet), Wernigerode, 4 April 1906, GStA Berlin-Dahlem, HA I, Rep. 89, Nr. 672, folder 17; Carl von Wedel, Diary entries of 20, 22 April 1891, in id. (ed.), *Zwischen Kaiser und Kanzler. Aufzeichnungen des Generaladjutanten Grafen Carl von Wedel aus den Jahren 1890–1894* (Leipzig, [1943]), pp. 176–7.

76. Bernd Sösemann, 'Die sogenannte Hunnenrede Wilhelms II. Textkritische und interpretatorische Bemerkungen zur Ansprache des Kaisers vom 27. Juli 1900 in Bremerhaven', *Historische Zeitschrift*, 222 (1976), pp. 342–58; Clark, *Kaiser Wilhelm II*, pp. 169–71.

77. Bernd Sösemann, ' "Pardon wird nicht gegeben; Gefangene nicht gemacht". Zeugnisse und Wirkungen einer rhetorischen Mobilmachung', in John Röhl (ed.), *Der Ort Kaiser Wilhelms II. in der deutschen Geschichte* (Munich, 1991), pp. 79–94, here p. 88.

78. Walther Rathenau, *Der Kaiser. Eine Betrachtung* (Berlin, 1919), pp. 28–9.

79. Isobel Hull, 'Persönliches Regiment', in Röhl (ed.), *Der Ort*, pp. 3–24.

80. See, for example, *Norddeutsche Allgemeine Zeitung*, 30 August 1910 (cutting in GStA Berlin-Dahlem HA I, Rep. 89, Nr. 678, folder 43).

81. 'Der schweigende Kaiser', *Frankfurter Zeitung*, 14 September 1910.

82. Gevers to Dutch ministry of foreign affairs, Berlin, 12 November 1908, *Algemeen Rijksarchief Den Haag*, 2.05.19, Bestanddeel 20.

83. Willibald Guttsmann, *Art for the Workers. Ideology and the Visual Arts in Weimar Germany* (Manchester, 1997).

84. Werner K. Blessing, 'The Cult of Monarchy, Political Loyalty and the Workers' Movement in Imperial Germany', *Journal of Contemporary History*, 13 (1978), pp. 357–73, here pp. 366–9.

85. See M. Cattaruzza, 'Das Kaiserbild in der Arbeiterschaft am Beispiel der Werftarbeiter in Hamburg und Stettin', in Röhl (ed.), *Der Ort*, pp. 131–44.

86. Richard J. Evans (ed.), *Kneipengespräche im Kaiserreich. Stimmungsberichte der Hamburger Politischen Polizei 1892–1914* (Reinbek, 1989), pp. 328, 329, 330.

87. F. Wilhelm Voigt, *Wie ich Hauptmann von Köpenick wurde: Mein Lebensbild* (Leipzig and Berlin, 1909). On the details of this case, see esp. pp. 107–27; Wolfgang Heidelmeyer, *Der Fall Köpenick. Akten und zeitgenössische Dokumente zur Historie einer preussischen Moritat* (Frankfurt/Main, 1967); Winfried Löschburg, *Ohne Glanz und Gloria. Die*

Geschichte des Hauptmanns von Köpenick (Berlin, 1998). Much useful material is compiled on *http://www.koepenickia.de/index.htm*; last accessed 16 September 2004.

88. *Vorwärts!*, 18, 19, 20, 21, 23, 28 October 1906.

89. Nicholas Stargardt, *The German Idea of Militarism. Radical and Socialist Critics, 1866–1914* (Cambridge, 1994), p. 3.

90. *Vorwärts!* 19 October 1906.

91. Philipp Müller, ' "Ganz Berlin ist Hintertreppe". Sensationen des Verbrechens und die Umwälzung der Presselandschaft im wilhelminischen Berlin (1890–1914)', Ph.D. dissertation, European University Institute, Florence (2004), pp. 341–53.

92. Franz Mehring, 'Das Zweite Jena', *Neue Zeit* (Berlin), 25 January 1906, pp. 81–4.

93. Stache, *Bürgerlicher Liberalismus*, pp. 91–2.

94. Werner Conze, Michael Geyer and Reinhard Stumpf, 'Militarismus', in Otto Brunner et al. (eds.), *Geschichtliche Grundbegriffe. Historisches Lexikon zur politisch-sozialen Sprache in Deutschland* (8 vols., Stuttgart, 1972–97), vol. 4, pp. 1–47; Bernd Ulrich, Jakob Vogel and Benjamin Ziemann (eds.), *Untertan in Uniform. Military und Militarismus im Kaiserreiche 1871–1914* (Frankfurt/Main, 2001), p. 12; Stargardt, *German Idea*, pp. 24–5.

95. For an example of how military traditions and rituals infiltrated public ceremonial, see Klaus Tenfelde, *Ein Jahrhundertfest. Das Krupp-Jubiläum in Essen 1912* (Essen, 2004).

96. Dieter Düding, 'Die Kriegervereine im wilhelminischen Reich und ihr Beitrag zur Militarisierung der deutschen Gesellschaft', in Jost Dulffer and Karl Holl (eds.), *Bereit zum Krieg. Kriegsmentalität im wilhelminischen Deutschland 1890–1914* (Göttingen, 1986), pp. 99–212; Thomas Rohkrämer, *Der Gesinnungsmilitarismus der 'kleinen Leute'. Die Kriegervereine im deutschen Kaiserreich 1871–1914* (Munich, 1990); id., 'Der Gesinnungsmilitarismus der "kleinen Leute" im deutschen Kaiserreich', in Wolfram Wette (ed.), *Der Krieg des kleinen Mannes* (Munich, 1992), pp. 95–109.

97. Wehler, *Deutsche Gesellschaftsgeschichte*, vol. 3, pp. 880–85.

98. Jakob Vogel, *Nationen im Gleichschritt. Der Kult der 'Nation in Waffen' in Deutschland und Frankreich, 1871–1914* (Göttingen, 1997).

99. Anne Summers, 'Militarism in Britain before the Great War', *History Workshop Journal*, 2 (1976), pp. 104–23; John M. Mackenzie (ed.), *Popular Imperialism and the Military, 1850–1950* (Manchester, 1992).

100. Ulrich, Vogel and Ziemann, *Untertan in Uniform*, p. 21.

101. Stargardt, *German Idea*, pp. 132–3, 142; Jeffrey Verhey, *The Spirit of 1914. Militarism, Myth and Mobilisation in Germany* (New York, 2000).

102. Robert von Friedeburg, 'Klassen-, Geschlechter- oder Nationalidentität? Handwerker und Tagelöhner in den Kriegervereinen der neupreussischen Provinz Hessen-Nassau 1890–1914', in Ute Frevert (ed.), *Militär und Gesellschaft im 19. und 20. Jahrhundert* (Stuttgart, 1997), pp. 229–44.

103. Roger Chickering, 'Der "Deutsche Wehrverein" und die Reform der deutschen Armee 1912–1914', *Militärgeschichtliche Mitteilungen*, 25 (1979), pp. 7–33; Stig Förster, *Der doppelte Militarismus. Die deutsche Heeresrüstungspolitik zwischen Status-quo-Sicherung und Aggression 1890–1913* (Stuttgart, 1985), pp. 208–96; Volker Berghahn, *Germany and the Approach of War in 1914* (London, 1973), esp. pp. 5–24.

104. Hucko (ed.), *Democratic Tradition*, pp. 139, 141.

105. On army expenditure as a 'structural weakness' in the constitutional system of the Empire, see Huber, *Verfassungsgeschichte*, vol. 4, *Struktur und Krisen des Kaiserreichs*, pp. 545–9; Dieter C. Umbach, *Parlamentsauflösung in Deutschland. Verfassungsgeschichte und Verfassungsprozess* (Berlin, 1989), pp. 221, 1227–9; John Iliffe, *Tanganyika Under German Rule, 1905–1912* (Cambridge, 1969), p. 42.

106. Stahl, 'Preussische Armee', in Hauser (ed.), *Preussen und das Reich*, pp. 181–246.

107. Wilhelm Deist, 'Kaiser Wilhelm II in the context of his military and naval entourage', in John C. G. Röhl and Nicholas Sombart (eds.), *Kaiser Wilhelm II. New Interpretations* (Cambridge, 1982), pp. 169–92, here pp. 182–3.

108. Wilhelm Deist, 'Kaiser Wilhelm II als Oberster Kriegsherr', in Röhl (ed.), *Der Ort*, p. 30; id., 'Entourage' in Röhl and Sombart (eds.), *Wilhelm II*, pp. 176–8.

109. Huber, *Heer und Staat* (2nd edn, Hamburg, 1938), p. 358.

110. Deist, 'Oberster Kriegsherr', in Röhl (ed.), *Der Ort*, pp. 25–42, here p. 26. On the military dimension of William's sovereignty more generally, see Elisabeth Fehrenbach, *Wandlungen des Kaisergedankens 1871–1918* (Munich, 1969), pp. 122–4, 170–72.

111. Leutwein to General Staff, Okahandja, 25 April 1904, Reichskolonialamt: 'Akten betreffend den Aufstand der Hereros im Jahre 1904, Bd. 4, 16 April 1904–4. Juni 1904', Bundesarchiv Berlin, R1001/2114, Bl. 52. I am very grateful to Marcus Clausius for making available to me his transcriptions of correspondence regarding SWA from the Bundesarchiv Berlin.

112. Proclamation, Colonial Troop Command, Osombo-Windhoek, 2 October 1904, copy held in Reichskanzlei, 'Differenzen zwischen Generalleutnant v. Trotha und Gouverneur Leutwein bezügl. der Aufstände in Dtsch. Süwestafrika im Jahre 1904', Bundesarchiv Berlin, R1001/2089, Bl. 7.

113. Trotha to Chief of the General Staff, Okatarobaka, 4 October 1904 in ibid., Bl. 5–6. For an even more extreme formulation of his objectives, see Trotha to Leutwein, Windhoek, 5 November 1904 (copy), in ibid., Bl. 100–102: 'I know enough tribes in Africa. They are all the same in that they will only bow to violence. To apply this violence with blatant terrorism and even with cruelty was and is my policy. I annihilate the insurgent tribes with streams of blood and streams of money. Only on this foundation can something enduring take root' (!).

114. Leutwein to Foreign Office Colonial Department, Windhoek, 28 October 1904 in ibid., Bl. 21–2.

115. Leutwein to Foreign Office, Windhoek, 23 October 1904, excerpted in ibid.

116. Telegram (in cipher) to Trotha, Berlin, 8 December 1904, in ibid., Bl. 48. The disputes over the content of the telegram are documented in Bl. 14–20. Exact numbers of the dead are difficult to establish, since the estimates of the Herero population before the conflict vary from 35,000 to 80,000. A headcount in the colony in 1905 produced a total of 24,000 Herero inhabitants. It is thought that several thousand escaped across the borders and did not return. The rest, perhaps as few as 6,000, perhaps as many as 45,000 or 50,000, were dead. Some had been killed in fighting, shot as they approached German encampments to surrender, or captured and executed after formulaic trials by military field tribunals; thousands more – men, women and children – had died of thirst, hunger or disease while searching for water in the desert areas into which they had been displaced. Casualties on the German side were 1,282 – the majority from illnesses contracted during the campaign. On the Herero war, see esp. Jan Bart Gewald, *Towards Redemption. A Socio-political History of the Herero of Namibia between 1890 and 1923* (Leiden, 1996); Horst Drechsler, *Südwestafrika unter deutscher Kolonialherrschaft: Der Kampf der Herero und Nama gegen den deutschen Imperialismus* (Berlin [GDR], 1966); Helmut Bley, *South-West Africa under German Rule 1894–1914*, trans. Hugh Ridley (London, 1971); Jürgen Zimmerer and Joachim Zeller (eds.), *Völkermord in Deutsch-Südwestafrika. Der Kolonialkrieg (1904–1908) in Namibia und seine Folgen* (Berlin, 2003), esp. the essays by Zimmerer, Zeller and Caspar W. Erichsen.

117. Hans-Günter Zmarzlik, *Bethmann Hollweg als Reichskanzler, 1908–1914. Studien zu Möglichkeiten und Grenzen seiner innerpolitischen Machtstellung* (Düsseldorf, 1957), pp. 103–29; David Schoenbaum, *Zabern 1913. Consensus Politics in Imperial Germany* (London, 1982), pp. 87–105, 118–19, 148–9; Konrad Jarausch, *Enigmatic Chancellor. Bethmann Hollweg and the Hubris of Imperial Germany* (Madison, WI, 1966), p. 101; Lamar Cecil, *Wilhelm II* (2 vols., Chapel Hill, NC, 1989 and 1996), vol. 2, *Emperor and Exile: 1900–1941*, pp. 189–92.

118. Johannes Burkhardt, 'Kriegsgrund Geschichte? 1870, 1813, 1756 – historische Argumente und Orientierungen bei Ausbruch des Ersten Weltkrieges', in id. et al. (eds.), *Lange und Kurze Wege*, pp. 9–86, here pp. 19, 36, 37, 56, 57, 60–61, 63.

119. Kossert, *Masuren*, p. 241.

120. Benjamin Ziemann, *Front und Heimat. Ländliche Kriegserfahrungen im südlichen Bayern 1914–1923* (Essen, 1997), pp. 265–74.

121. Gerald D. Feldman, *Army, Industry and Labor in Germany, 1914–1918* (Princeton, NJ, 1966), pp. 31–3; the reference to 'shadow governments' is from Crown Prince Rupprecht von Bayern, *In Treue fest. Mein Kriegstagebuch* (3 vols., Munich, 1929), vol. 1, p. 457, cited in ibid., p. 32.

122. For a narrative overview of the partnership, see John Lee, *The Warlords. Hindenburg and Ludendorff* (London, 2005).

123. Cited from a speech by the industrialist Duisberg in Treutler to Bethmann Hollweg, 6 February 1916, GStA Berlin-Dahlem, HA I, Rep. 92, Valentini, No. 2. On the Hindenburg cult, see Roger Chickering, *Imperial Germany and the Great War 1914–1918* (Cambridge, 1988), p. 74; Matthew Stibbe, 'Vampire of the Continent. German Anglophobia during the First World War, 1914–1918', Ph.D. thesis, University of Sussex (1997), p. 100.

124. Lansing to Oederlin, Washington, 14 October 1918, in US Department of State (ed.), Papers Relating to the Foreign Relations of the United States (suppl. I, vol. 1, 1918), p. 359.

125. Cecil, *Wilhelm II*, vol. 2, p. 286.

126. Ernst von Heydebrand und der Lasa, speech to Landtag of 5 December 1917, cited in Croon, 'Die Anfänge des Parlamentarisierung', p. 124.

127. Toews, *Hegelianism*, p. 62.

128. Hermann Beck, *The Origins of the Authoritarian Welfare State in Prussia. Conservatives, Bureaucracy and the Social Question, 1815–1870* (Providence, RI, 1993), pp. 93–100.

129. On Wagener and Gerlach, see Hans-Julius Schoeps, *Das andere Preussen. Konservative Gestalten und Probleme im Zeitalter Friedrich Wilhelms IV.* (3rd edn, Berlin, 1966), pp. 203–28.

130. On the links between Stein and Schmoller, see Giles Pope, 'The Political Ideas of Lorenz Stein and their Influence on Rudolf Gneist and Gustav Schmoller', D. Phil. thesis, Oxford University (1985); Karl Heinz Metz, 'Preussen als Modell einer Idee der Sozialpolitik. Das soziale Königtum', in Bahners and Roellecke (eds.), *Preussische Stile*, pp. 355–63, here p. 358.

131. James J. Sheehan, *The Career of Lujo Brentano: A Study of Liberalism and Social Reform in Imperial Germany* (Chicago, 1966), pp. 48–52, 80–84.

132. Erik Grimmer-Solem, *The Rise of Historical Economics and Social Reform in Germany 1864–1894* (Oxford, 2003), esp. pp. 108–18.

133. Hans-Peter Ullmann, 'Industrielle Interessen und die Entstehung der deutschen Sozialversicherung', *Historische Zeitschrift*, 229 (1979), pp. 574–610; Gerhard Ritter, 'Die Sozialdemokratie im Deutschen Kaiserreich in sozialgeschichtlicher Perspektive', *Historische Zeitschrift*, 249 (1989), pp. 295–362; Wehler, *Deutsche Gesellschaftsgeschichte*, vol. 3, pp. 907–15.

134. Gerhard Ritter, *Arbeiter im Deutschen Kaiserreich, 1871 bis 1914* (Bonn, 1992), esp. p. 383; J. Frerich and M. Frey, *Handbuch der Geschichte der Sozialpolitik in Deutschland*, vol. 1, *Von der vorindustriellen Zeit bis zum Ende des Dritten Reiches* (3 vols., Munich, 1993), pp. 130–32, 141–2.

135. Andreas Kunz, 'The State as Employer in Germany, 1880–1918: From Paternalism to Public Policy', in W. Robert Lee and Eve Rosenhaft (eds.), *State, Society and Social Change in Germany, 1880–1914* (Oxford, 1990), pp. 37–63, here pp. 40–41.

17 Endings

1. Harry Count Kessler, Diary entry, Magdeburg, 7 November 1918, in id., *Tagebücher 1918–1937*, ed. Wolfgang Pfeiffer-Belli (Frankfurt/Main, 1961), p. 18.

2. Ibid., p. 24.

3. Jürgen Kloosterhuis (ed.), *Preussisch Dienen und Geniessen. Die Lebenszeiterzählung des Ministerialrats Dr Herbert du Mesnil (1857–1947)* (Cologne, 1998), p. 350.

4. *Bocholter Volksblatt*, 14 November 1918, cited in Hugo Stehkamper, 'Westfalen und die Rheinisch-Westfälische Republik 1918/19. Zenturmnskiskussionen über einen bundesstaatlichen Zusammenschluss der beiden preussischen Westprovinzen', in Karl Dietrich Bracher, Paul Mikat, Konrad Repgen, Martin Schumacher and Hans-Peter Schwarz (eds.), *Staat und Parteien. Festschrift für Rudolf Morsey* (Berlin, 1992), pp. 579–634.

5. Edgar Hartwig, 'Welfen, 1866–1933', in Dieter Fricke (ed.), *Lexikon zur Parteiengeschichte* (4 vols., Leipzig, Cologne, 1983–6), vol. 4, pp. 487–9.

6. Peter Leśniewski, 'Three Insurrections: Upper Silesia 1919–21', in Peter Stachura (ed.), *Poland between the Wars, 1918–1939* (Houndsmills, 1998), pp. 13–42.

7. Prussia lost about 16 per cent of its surface area as a consequence of the territorial adjustments that followed the defeat of 1918. These encompassed the Memel area (Lithuania), the land removed from West Prussia to form the Free City of Danzig, the bulk of the old provinces of West Prussia and Posen, as well as small sections of Pomerania and East Prussia (to Poland), North Schleswig with the islands of Alsen and Röm (to Denmark), Eupen and Malmédy (to Belgium), a part of the Saar region (placed under international administration, with coal mines under French control), the Hultschin district of Upper Silesia (to Czechoslovakia) and parts of Upper Silesia (to Poland, following local plebiscites). In all, Prussia's territorial losses amounted to 56,058 square kilometres; the total on 1 November 1918 was 348,780 square kilometres.

8. Cited in Horst Möller, 'Preussen von 1918 bis 1947: Weimarer Republik, Preussen und der Nationalsozialismus', in Wolfgang Neugebauer (ed.), *Handbuch der preussischen Geschichte*, vol. 3, *Vom Kaiserreich zum 20. Jahrhundert und Grosse Themen der Geschichte Preussens* (Berlin, 2001), pp. 149–301, here p. 193.

9. Gisbert Knopp, *Die preussische Verwaltung des Regierungsbezirks Düsseldorf in den Jahren 1899–1919* (Cologne, 1974), p. 344.

10. Möller, 'Preussen', pp. 177–9; Henry Friedlander, *The German Revolution of 1918* (New York, 1992), pp. 242, 244.

11. Heinrich August Winkler, *Weimar 1918–1933. Die Geschichte der ersten deutschen Demokratie* (Munich, 1993), p. 66.

12. Hagen Schulze, 'Democratic Prussia in Weimar Germany, 1919–33', in Dwyer (ed.), *Modern Prussian History*, pp. 211–29, here p. 213.

13. Gerald D. Feldman, *The Great Disorder. Politics, Economics and Society in the German Inflation 1914–1924* (Oxford, 1997), pp. 134, 161.

14. In a classic study of German civil–military relations after the First World War, John Wheeler Bennett argued that the Ebert–Groener pact sealed the fate of the Weimar Republic; most other historians have taken a more moderate view. See John Wheeler Bennett, *The Nemesis of Power. The German Army and Politics 1918–1945* (London, 1953), p. 21; cf. Craig, *Prussian Army*, p. 348; Wehler, *Deutsche Gesellschaftsgeschichte*, vol. 4, *Vom Beginn des Ersten Weltkriegs bis zur Gründung der beiden deutschen Staaten* (Munich, 2003), pp. 69–72.

15. Craig, *Politics of the Prussian Army*, p. 351.

16. The cabinet, or Council of People's Representatives, refers to the new SPD/USPD government that succeeded the old Prussian-German executive. The Executive Council, elected on 10 November, represented the diffuse interests gathered in the Soldiers' and Workers' Councils movement in Berlin. The relationship between the two bodies was a matter of contention during the early months of the republic.

17. This speech was reprinted in *Die Freiheit* (Berlin), 16 and 17 December 1918. The text may also be consulted at *http://www.marxists.org/deutsch/archiv/luxemburg/1918/12/uspdgb.htm*; last accessed 26 October 2004.

18. Möller, 'Preussen', pp. 188–9.

19. Susanne Miller, *Die Bürde der Macht. Die deutsche Sozialdemokratie 1918–1920* (Düsseldorf, 1979), p. 226.

20. Hagen Schulze, *Weimar. Deutschland 1917–1933* (Berlin, 1982), p. 180.

21. Diary entries of 7 January and 6 January in Kessler, *Tagebücher*, pp. 97, 95.

22. Annemarie Lange, *Berlin in der Weimarer Republik* (Berlin/GDR, 1987), pp. 47, 198–9.

23. This image was published in the third edition of *Die Pleite* (Bankruptcy), a journal produced by the leftist Malik Verlag, later one of the foremost publishing houses for Communist intellectuals in the Weimar Republic.

24. There were further repressions in Halle, Magdeburg, Mühlheim, Düsseldorf, Dresden, Leipzig and Munich. The repressions in Munich, where the Communists actually succeeded briefly in seizing power and proclaiming a 'Soviet Republic of Bavaria', were exceptionally brutal.

25. Craig, *Prussian Army*, p. 388.

26. Hans von Seeckt, 'Heer im Staat' in id., *Gedanken eines Soldaten* (Berlin, 1929), pp. 101–16, here p. 115.

27. On the 'Prussian *étatisme*' of the coalition parties, see Dietrich Orlow, *Weimar Prussia, 1918–1925. The Unlikely Rock of Democracy* (Pittsburgh, 1986), pp. 247, 249; Hagen Schulze, *Otto Braun oder Preussens demokratische Sendung* (Frankfurt/Main, 1977), pp. 316–23 and passim; Winkler, *Weimar*, pp. 66–7. On the Catholics, see Möller, 'Preussen', p. 237.

28. Cited in Schulze, 'Democratic Prussia' in Dwyer (ed), *Modern Prussian History*, pp. 211–29, here p. 214.

29. Heinrich Hannover and Christine Hannover-Druck, *Politische Justiz 1918–1933* (Bornheim-Merten, 1987), pp. 25–7 and passim.

30. Peter Lessmann, *Die preussische Schutzpolizei in der Weimarer Republik. Streifendienst und Strassenkampf* (Düsseldorf, 1989), p. 82.

31. Ibid., p. 88.

32. Hsi-Huey Liang, *The Berlin Police Force in the Weimar Republic* (Berkeley, 1970), pp. 73–81; Schulze, 'Democratic Prussia', p. 215.

33. Lessmann, *Schutzpolizei*, pp. 211–14; Christoph Graf, *Politische Polizei zwischen Demokratie und Diktatur* (Berlin, 1983), pp. 43–8; Eric D. Kohler, 'The Crisis in the Prussian Schutzpolizei 1930–32', in George Mosse (ed.), *Police Forces in History* (London, 1975), pp. 131–50.

34. Henning Grunwald, 'Political Trial Lawyers in the Weimar Republic', Ph.D. thesis, University of Cambridge (2002).

35. Orlow, *Weimar Prussia*, pp. 16–7. On the 'old' and the 'new' right, see Hans Christof Kraus, 'Altkonservativismus und moderne politische Rechte. Zum Problem der Kontinuität rechter politischer Strömungen in Deutschland', in Thomas Nipperdey et al. (eds.), *Weltbürgerkrieg der Ideologien. Antworten an Ernst Nolte* (Berlin, 1993), pp. 99–121. On right-wing enthusiasm for the idea of a radical 'conservative revolution' that would break the boundaries of the traditional Prussian conservatism, see Jeffrey Herf, *Reactionary Modernism. Technology, Culture and Politics in Weimar and the Third Reich* (Cambridge, 1984), esp. pp. 18–48; Armin Mohler, *Die konservative Revolution in Deutschland, 1918–1932* (Darmstadt, 1972); George Mosse, 'The Corporate State and the Conservative Revolution' in id., *Germans and Jews: the Right, the Left and the Search for a "Third Force" in Pre-Nazi Germany* (New York, 1970), pp. 116–43.

36. On the agrarian sector after 1918, see Shelley Baranowski, 'Agrarian transformation and right radicalism: economics and politics in rural Prussia', in Dwyer (ed.), *Modern Prussian History*, pp. 146–65; id., *The Sanctity of Rural Life. Nobility, Protestantism and Nazism in Weimar Prussia* (New York, 1995), pp. 128–44.

37. On Weimar agriculture and politics, see Wolfram Pyta, *Dorfgemeinschaft und Parteipolitik 1918–1933: Die Verschränkung von Milieu und Parteien in den protestantischen Landgebieten Deutschlands in der Weimarer Republik* (Düsseldorf, 1996); Dieter Gessner, *Agrarverbände in der Weimarer Republik. Wirtschaftliche und soziale Voraussetzungen agrarkonservativer Politik vor 1933* (Düsseldorf, 1976); id., 'The Dilemma of German Agriculture during the Weimar Republic', in Richard Bessel and Edward J. Feuchtwanger

(eds.), *Social Change and Political Development in Weimar Germany* (London, 1981), pp. 134–54; John E. Farquharson, *The Plough and the Swastika. The NSDAP and Agriculture in Germany 1918–1945* (London, 1976), pp. 25–42; Robert G. Moeller, 'Economic Dimensions of Peasant Protest in the Transition from the Kaiserreich to Weimar', in id. (ed.), *Peasants and Lords*, pp. 140–67.

38. See Klaus Erich Pollmann, 'Wilhelm II und der Protestantismus', in Stefan Samerski (ed.), *Wilhelm II. und die Religion. Facetten einer Persönlichkeit und ihres Umfelds* (Berlin, 2001), pp. 91–104.

39. Nicholas Hope, 'Prussian Protestantism', in Dwyer, *Modern Prussian History*, pp. 188–208. The standard works on the Union in this period are Daniel R. Borg, *The Old Prussian Church and the Weimar Republic. A Study in Political Adjustment 1917–1927* (Hanover and London, 1984) and Kurt Nowak, *Evangelische Kirche und Weimarer Republik: zum politischen Weg des deutschen Protestantismus zwischen 1918 und 1932* (Göttingen, 1981).

40. Comment by General-Superintendent Walter Kähler, cited in Baranowski, *Sanctity of Rural Life*, p. 96.

41. For a survey of these groups, see Friedrich Wilhelm Kantzenbach, *Der Weg der evangelischen Kirche vom 19. bis zum 20. Jahrhundert* (Gütersloh, 1968), esp. pp. 176–8.

42. Cited in Doris L. Bergen, *Twisted Cross. The German Christian Movement in the Third Reich* (Chapel Hill, WI, 1996), p. 28.

43. Clark, *Politics of Conversion*, pp. 286–7.

44. Committee of the Berlin Society for the Promotion of Christianity Among the Jews to all Consistories and Provincial Church Councils, 5 December 1930, Evangelisches Zentralarchiv Berlin, 7/3648.

45. Richard Gutteridge, *Open Thy Mouth for the Dumb! The German Evangelical Church and the Jews* (Oxford, 1976), p. 42. On the conference of 1927 and the development of *völkisch* religion, see Kurt Scholder, *The Churches and the Third Reich, 1. Preliminary History and the Time of Illusions 1918–1934*, trans. J. Bowden (London, 1987), pp. 99–119. The outstanding study on 'German Christianity' is Bergen, *Twisted Cross*. On Protestant academics, see Marijke Smid, 'Protestantismus und Antisemitismus 1930–1933', in Jochen-Christoph Kaiser und Martin Greschat (eds.), *Der Holocaust und die Protestanten* (Frankfurt/Main, 1988), pp. 38–72, esp. pp. 50–55; Hans-Ulrich Thamer, 'Protestantismus und "Judenfrage" in der Geschichte des Dritten Reiches', in ibid., pp. 216–40. On the Protestant press, see Ino Arndt, 'Die Judenfrage im Lichte der evangelischen Sonntagsblätter 1918–1933', Ph.D. thesis, University of Tübingen (1960).

46. See Manfred Gailus, *Protestantismus und Nationalsozialismus. Studien zur Durchdringung des protestantischen Sozialmilieus in Berlin* (Cologne, 2001); id., 'Deutsche, Christen, Olias, Olias! Wie Nationalsozialisten die Kirchengemeinde Alt-Schöneberg eroberten', in id. (ed.), *Kirchgemeinden im Nationalsozialismus: sieben Beispiele aus Berlin* (Berlin, 1990), pp. 211–46.

47. Stephan Malinowski, *Vom König zum Führer: Sozialer Niedergang und politische Radikalisierung im deutschen Adel zwischen Kaiserreich und NS-Staat* (Berlin, 2003), p. 208.

48. Cited in ibid., p. 221.

49. Kossert, *Ostpreussen*, p. 267.

50. Malinowski, *Vom König zum Führer*, pp. 212–28; see also Klaus Theweleit, *Mannerrhantasien* (Hamburg, 1980) – a surprising number of the ego-narratives analysed by Theweleit stem from noblemen. On the penetration of the agrarian milieu, see Baranowski, *Sanctity of Rural Life*, pp. 145–76.

51. Malinowski, *Vom König zum Führer*, p. 239.

52. On the strength of the 'Führer' idea among Prussian nobles, see ibid., pp. 246, 247, 251, 253, 257–9.

53. Diary entries of June 1926 and March 1928, cited in Eckart Conze, *Von deutschem Adel. Die Grafen von Bernstoff im zwanzigsten Jahrhundert* (Munich, 2000), pp. 164, 166.

54. Jürgen W. Falter, *Hitlers Wähler* (Munich, 1991), pp. 110–23.

55. Marcus Funck, 'The Meaning of Dying: East-Elbian Noble Families as "Warrior-Tribes" in the Nineteenth and Twentieth Centuries', trans. Gary Shockey, in Greg Eghigian and Matthew Paul Berg, *Sacrifice and National Belonging in Twentieth-century Germany* (Arlington, TX, 2002), pp. 26–63, here p. 53. On Nazi votes in East-Elbia as a whole, see Falter, *Hitlers Wähler*, pp. 154–63.

56. Kossert, *Ostpreussen*, p. 266.

57. Gotthard Jasper, *Die gescheiterte Zähmung. Wege zur Machtergreifung Hitlers 1930–1934* (Frankfurt/Main, 1986), pp. 55–87; Schulze, 'Democratic Prussia', pp. 224–5.

58. Lessmann, *Schutzpolizei*, p. 285.

59. Richard Bessel, *Political Violence and the Rise of Nazism. The Storm Troopers in Eastern Germany (1925–1934)* (London, 1984), pp. 29–31; Ulrich Herbert, *Best: Biographische Studien über Radikalismus, Weltanschauung und Vernunft 1903–1989* (Bonn, 1996), pp. 249–51.

60. On the scale of violence in this period and its effects on the political climate; see Richard J. Evans, *The Coming of the Third Reich* (London, 2003), pp. 269–75.

61. Heinrich August Winkler, *Der Weg in die Katastrophe. Arbeiter und Arbeiterbewegungen in der Weimarer Republik 1930 bis 1933* (Bonn, 1987), p. 514.

62. Karl Dietrich Bracher, *Die Auflösung der Weimarer Republik: Eine Studie zum Problem des Machtverfalls in der Demokratie* (Villingen, 1960), pp. 511–17.

63. Under the terms of the Weimar constitution, the Reichstag was not obliged to accept indefinitely an unpopular emergency decree. After a certain period, the decree could be thrown out by a majority vote against it.

64. Hagen Schulze, *Otto Braun oder Preussens demokratische Sendung. Eine Biographie* (Frankfurt/Main, 1981), pp. 623, 627.

65. Citation from Schulze, 'Democratic Prussia'. On Gayl's role, see also Horst Möller, *Weimar. Die unvollendete Demokratie* (Munich, 1997), p. 304; Martin Broszat, *Die Machtergreifung. Der Aufstieg der NSDAP und die Zerstörung der Weimarer Republik* (Munich, 1984), pp. 145–56; Schulze, *Otto Braun*, pp. 735–44.

66. Möller, 'Weimar', p. 304.

67. On the dissolution, see Möller, *Weimar*, pp. 57–78; Bracher, *Die Auflösung der Weimarer Republik*, pp. 491–526; Rudolf Morsey, 'Zur Geschichte des "Preussenschlags"', *Vierteljahrshefte für Zeitgeschichte*, 9 (1961), pp. 430–39; Andreas Dorpalen, *Hindenburg and the Weimar Republic* (Princeton, NJ, 1964), pp. 341–7.

68. Cited in Heinrich, *Geschichte Preussens*, p. 496; cf. Otto Braun, *Von Weimar zu Hitler* (2nd edn, New York, 1940), pp. 409–11.

69. Kloosterhuis (ed.), *Preussisch Dienen und Geniessen*, p. 433; Schulze, *Otto Braun*, pp. 584–60, 689–71.

70. Lessmann, *Schutzpolizei*, pp. 302–18.

71. Josef Goebbels, *Vom Kaiserhof zur Reichskanzlei. Eine historische Darstellung in Tagebuchblättern (Vom 1. Januar 1932 bis zum 1. Mai 1933)*, pp. 131, 132–3.

72. Evans, *Coming of the Third Reich*, p. 284.

73. Evans, *Rituals of Retribution*, pp. 613–14.

74. Goebbels, Diary entry of 22 July 1932, in id., *Vom Kaiserhof zur Reichskanzlei*, p. 133.

75. Papen's plan was not as stupid as it now looks. He had planned that soon after its formation, the new cabinet would place an enabling law (*Ermächtigungsgesetz*) before the Reichstag. This was a law which gave the government the power to initiate legislation for a certain period of time. With Hitler's help, Papen believed there would be no problem raising the two-thirds majority needed to get the law through the Reichstag. The deadlock between cabinet and Reichstag could at last be broken. And since laws would be passed by a vote *within* the cabinet, the conservative majority provided a guarantee that the Nazis would be held in check by their conservative colleagues. Papen did not foresee the radicalization that followed the Reichstag fire and the role of the Nazi political machine in intimidating and marginalizing conservative, nationalist political leaders.

76. Ewald von Kleist-Schmenzin, 'Die letzte Möglichkeit', *Politische Studien*, 10 (1959), pp. 89–92, here p. 92.

77. Allan Bullock, *A Study in Tyranny* (rev. edn, London, 1964), p. 253.

78. Spenkuch, *Herrenhaus*, pp. 561–2.

79. Dietz Bering, ' "Geboren im Hause Cohn". Namenpolemik gegen den preussischen Innenminister Albert Grzesinski', in Dietz Bering and Friedhelm Debus (eds.), *Fremdes und Fremdheit in Eigennamen* (Heidelberg, 1990), pp. 16–52.

80. For Grzesinski's own account of his life, see Eberhard Kolb (ed.), *Albert Grzesinski. Im Kampf um die deutsche Republik. Erinnerungen eines Sozialdemokraten* (Munich, 2001). The most recent biography is Thomas Albrecht, *Für eine Wehrhafte Demokratie. Albert Grzesinski und die preussische Politik in der Weimarer Republik* (Bonn, 1999).

81. Cited in Heinrich, *Geschichte Preussens*, p. 497.

82. Schulze, *Otto Braun*, pp. 488–98.

83. 'Marginal Prussians' (*Randpreussen*) is the term coined by Gerd Heinrich to describe the conspirators of 1932; see *Geschichte Preussens*, p. 495.

84. On Schleicher and his motivations, see Henry Ashby Turner, Jr, *Hitler's Thirty Days to Power. January 1933* (London, 1996), pp. 19–21; Theodor Eschenburg, 'Die Rolle der Persönlichkeit in der Krise der Weimarer Republik: Hindenburg, Brüning, Groener, Schleicher', *Vierteljahrshefte für Zeitgeschichte*, 9 (1961), pp. 1–29. For a dissenting view that emphasizes Schleicher's democratic and constitutional commitments, see Wolfram Pyta, 'Konstitutionelle Demokratie statt monarchischer Restauration: Die verfassungspolitische Konzeption Schleichers in der Weimarer Staatskrise', *Vierteljahrshefte für Zeitgeschichte*, 47 (1999), pp. 417–41.

85. On this episode, see Craig, *Politics of the Prussian Army*, p. 372; cf. John Wheeler-Bennett, *Hindenburg: the Wooden Titan* (London, 1967), pp. 220–21.

86. *Vorwarts!*, 10 March 1932, cited in Winkler, *Der Weg*, p. 514; Evans, *Coming of the Third Reich*, p. 279.

87. Frederick William I had initially planned that he and his wife would be entombed together in the crypt of the Garrison Church. But upon her death in 1757, his queen, Sophie Dorothea, was in fact interred in Berlin Cathedral. The space beside the king thus remained empty until it was occupied by the remains of his son on 18 August 1786.

88. Elke Fröhlich (ed.), *Die Tagebücher von Joseph Goebbels. Sämtliche Fragmente*, Part 1, *Aufzeichnungen, 1924–1941*, vol. 2 (4 vols., Munich, 1987), pp. 393–4.

89. Brendan Simms, 'Prussia, Prussianism and National Socialism', in Dwyer (ed.), *Modern Prussian History*, pp. 253–73.

90. Werner Freitag, 'Nationale Mythen und kirchliches Heil: Der "Tag von Potsdam" ', in *Westfälische Forschungen*, 41 (1991), pp. 379–430.

91. Goebbels, Diary entry of 21 March 1933, in *Vom Kaiserhof*, pp. 285–6.

92. Fritz Stern, *The Politics of Cultural Despair: a Study in the Rise of the Germanic Ideology* (Berkeley, 1974), pp. 211–13.

93. Adolf Hitler, *Mein Kampf*, trans. Ralph Manheim (London, 1992; reprint of the orig. edn of 1943), pp. 139, 141. The Prussian theme recurs in Hitler's 'Second Book', a text he composed in 1928 as an appendix to the foreign political section of *Mein Kampf*, but never published; see Manfred Schlenke, 'Das "preussische Beispiel" in Propaganda und Politik des Nationalsozialismus', *Aus Politik und Zeitgeschichte. Beilage zur Wochenzeitung Das Parlament*, 27 (1968), pp. 15–27, here p. 16.

94. Alfred Rosenberg, *Der Mythus des 20. Jahrhunderts* (Munich, 1930), p. 198.

95. Cited in Schlenke, 'Das "preussische Beispiel" ', p. 17.

96. For a detailed contemporary account of the excavation of the 'Hindenburg Stone' with numerous photographs, see Alfred Postelmann, 'Der "Hindenburgstein" für das Reichsehrenmal Tannenberg', *Zeitschrift für Geschiebeforschung und Flachlandsgeologie*, 12 (1936), pp. 1–32, quotation p. 1. This article can be viewed online at *http://www.rapakivi.de/posthi/anfang.htm*.

97. Josef Schmid, *Karl Friedrich Schinkel. Der Vorläufer neuer deutscher Baugesinnung* (Leipzig, 1943).

98. On nationalist themes in cinematic depictions of Prussia during the Weimar Republic, see Helmut Regel, 'Die Fridericus-Filme der Weimarer Republik', in Axel Marquardt and Hans Rathsack (eds.), *Preussen im Film. Eine Retrospective der Stiftung Deutsche Kinemathek* (Hamburg, 1981), pp. 124–34.

99. Friedrich P. Kahlenberg, 'Preussen als Filmsujet in der Propagandasprache der NS-Zeit', in Marquardt and Rathsack (eds.), *Preussen im Film*, pp. 135–77, 256–7.

100. Examples are: *Der höhere Befehl* (1935), *Kadetten* (1941), *Kameraden* (1941), *Der grosse König* (1942), *Affäre Roedern* (1944) and *Kolberg* (1945).

101. Ian Kershaw, *Hitler. Nemesis 1936–1945* (London, 2000), p. 277.

102. Cited in Schlenke, 'Das "preussische Beispiel" ', p. 23.

103. Kershaw, *Hitler. Nemesis*, p. 581.

104. Cited in Schlenke, 'Das "preussische Beispiel" ', p. 23.

105. 'Aus der Rede des Ministerpräsidenten Göring vor dem preussischen Staatsrat vom 18. Juni 1934 über Preussen und die Reichseinheit', in Herbert Michaelis and Ernst Schraepler (eds.), *Ursachen und Folgen. Vom deutschen Zusammenbruch 1918 und 1945 bis zur staatlichen Neuordnung Deutschlands in der Gegenwart*, vol. 9, *Das Dritte Reich. Die Zertrümmerung des Parteienstaats und die Grundlegung der Diktatur* (29 vols., Berlin, 1958), pp. 122–4, here p. 122.

106. Sigurd von Ilsemann, *Der Kaiser in Holland. Aufzeichnungen des letzten Flügeladjutanten Kaiser Wilhelm II.*, ed. by Harald von Königswald (2 vols., Munich, 1968), vol. 2, p. 154.

107. Clark, *Kaiser Wilhelm II*, p. 251.

108. Georg H. Kleine, 'Adelsgenossenschaft und Nationalsozialismus', *Vierteljahrshefte für Zeitgeschichte*, 26 (1978), pp. 100–143, here p. 125; Stephan Malinowski, ' "Führertum" und "neuer Adel". Die Deutsche Adelsgenossenschaft und der Deutsche Herrenklub in der Weimarer Republik', in Heinz Reif (ed.), *Adel und Bürgertum in Deutschland. Entwicklungslinien und Wendepunkte im 20. Jahrhundert* (2 vols., Berlin, 2001), vol. 2, pp. 173–211.

109. Malinowski, *Vom König zum Führer*, pp. 476–500; Heinz Reif, *Adel im 19. und 20. Jahrhundert* (Munich, 1999), pp. 54–5, 115–18.

110. Christian Count Krockow, *Warnung vor Preussen* (Berlin, 1981), p. 8.

111. Ulrich Heinemann, *Ein konservativer Rebell. Fritz-Dietlof Graf von der Schulenburg und der 20. Juli* (Berlin, 1990), pp. 25, 27–34.

112. Letter of Captain Stieff (an officer serving with Blaskowitz) to his wife, Truppenübungsplatz Ohrdruf, 21 August 1932, in Horst Mühleisen (ed.), *Hellmuth Stieff, Briefe* (Berlin, 1991), letter no. 36, p. 71.

113. Speech by Johannes Blaskowitz for the opening of the Memorial for the Fallen of the World War in Bommelsen, Sunday 17 March 1935 (copy), BA-MA Freiburg, MSg 1/1814. Blaskowitz is referring to Hitler's remilitarization of the Rhineland in March 1935.

114. Christopher Browning, *Ordinary Men. Reserve Police Battalion 101 and the Final Solution* (New York, 1992).

115. Simon Wiesenthal has estimated that Austrians were responsible for the deaths of some 3 million of the 6 million Jews murdered by the Nazis and their auxiliaries. See Andreas Maislinger, ' "Vergangenheitsbewältigung" in der Bundesrepublik Deutschland, der DDR und Österreich. Psychologisch-Pädagogische Massnahmen im Vergleich', in Uwe Backes, Eckhard Jesse and Rainer Zitelmann (eds.), *Die Schatten der Vergangenheit. Impulse zur Historisierung des Nationalsozialismus* (Berlin, 1990), pp. 479–96, here p. 482.

116. Eckart Conze, 'Adel und Adeligkeit im Widerstand des 20. Juli 1944', in Reif (ed.), *Adel und Bürgertum*, vol. 2, pp. 269–95; Baranowski, *Sanctity of Rural Life*, p. 183.

117. Hitler reintroduced the guillotine in 1936 in order to speed up the execution process.

118. Members of the IX Potsdam Infantry Regiment executed for their role in resistance activity after 20 July 1944 include: Colonel Hans-Ottfried von Linstow, Colonel Alexis Freiherr von Roenne, Lieutenant-Colonel Hasso von Boehmer. Lieutenant-Colonel Alex-

ander von Voss committed suicide on 8 November. Lieutenant-General Hans Count von Sponeck, a suspect on account of his insubordinate behaviour during the Kerch Peninsula campaign in 1941–2, was also executed by firing squad on 23 July 1944, although he was not involved in the July plot. On the place of the IX Potsdam Infantry in the German Resistance, see Ekkehard Klausa, 'Preussische Soldatentradition und Widerstand', in Jürgen Schmädeke and Peter Steinbach (eds.), *Der Widerstand gegen den Nationalsozialismus. Die deutsche Gesellschaft und der Widerstand gegen Hitler* (Munich, 1985), pp. 533–45.

119. Spenkuch, *Herrenhaus*, p. 562.

120. Cited in Bodo Scheurig, *Henning von Tresckow. Ein Preusse gegen Hitler. Biographie* (Frankfurt, 1990), p. 147. See also Ger van Roon, *Neuordnung im Widerstand. Der Kreisauer Kreis innerhalb der deutschen Widerstandsbewegung* (Munich, 1967); Wolfgang Wippermann, 'Nationalsozialismus und Preussentum', in *Aus Politik und Zeitgeschichte. Beilage zur Wochenzeitung das Parlament*, 52–3 (1981), pp. 13–22, here p. 17.

121. Annedore Leber, *Conscience in Revolt. Sixty-four Stories of Resistance in Germany 1933–45*, trans. Rosemary O'Neill (Boulder, CO., 1994), p. 161.

122. Gerhard Ritter, *Carl Goerdeler und die deutsche Widerstandsbewegung* (3rd edn, Stuttgart, 1956), p. 274; Eberhard Zeller, *The Flame of Freedom. The German Struggle against Hitler*, trans. R. P. Heller and D. R. Masters (Boulder, CO, 1994), pp. 50–51, 127.

123. Ritter, *Carl Goerdeler*, p. 352.

124. Christian Schneider, 'Denkmal Manstein. Psychogramm eines Befehlshabers', in Hannes Heer and Klaus Neumann (eds.), *Vernichtungskrieg. Verbrechen der Wehrmacht 1941–1944* (Hamburg, 1995), pp. 402–17.

125. Julius Leber, *Ein Mann geht seinen Weg* (Berlin, 1952), p. 173.

126. Ramsay Muir, *Britain's Case Against Germany. An Examination of the Historical Background of the German Action in 1914* (Manchester, 1914), p. 3.

127. See the nuanced discussion in Stefan Berger, 'William Harbutt Dawson: The Career and Politics of an Historian of Germany', *English Historical Review*, 116 (2001), pp. 76–113.

128. S. D. Stirk, *The Prussian Spirit. A Survey of German Literature and Politics 1914–1940* (Port Washington, NY, 1941), p. 16.

129. Thorstein Veblen, *Imperial Germany and the Industrial Revolution* (2nd edn, London, 1939), pp. 66, 70, 78, 80.

130. Ralf Dahrendorf, *Society and Democracy in Germany* (London, 1968), esp. pp. 55–6.

131. Verrina (pseud.), *The German Mentality* (2nd edn, London, 1946), pp. 10, 14.

132. Edgar Stern-Rubarth, *Exit Prussia. A Plan for Europe* (London, 1940), p. 47.

133. Joseph Borkin and Charles Welsh, *Germany's Master Plan. The Story of Industrial Offensive* (London, New York, [1943]), p. 31.

134. Cited in Stirk, *Prussian Spirit*, p. 18.

135. Cited in Lothar Kettenacker, 'Preussen in der alliierten Kriegszielplanung. 1939–1947', in L. Kettenacker, M. Schlenke and H. Seier (eds.), *Studien zur Geschichte Englands und der deutsch-britischen Beziehungen. Festschrift für Paul Kluke* (Munich, 1981), pp. 312–40, here p. 323.

136. Cited in T. D. Burridge, *British Labour and Hitler's War* (London, 1976), p. 60.

137. Burridge, *British Labour*, p. 94; see also Attlee's report as chair of the APW on 11 July 1944, PRO CAB 86/67, fo. 256.

138. Anne Armstrong, *Unconditional Surrender. The Impact of the Casablanca Policy upon World War II* (Westport, CT, 1961), pp. 20–21.

139. Cited in J. A. Thompson, *Woodrow Wilson* (Harlow, 2002), pp. 176–7.

140. Kettenacker, 'Preussen in der alliierten Kriegszielplanung'.

141. Martin Schulze-Wessel, *Russlands Blick auf Preussen. Die polnische Frage in der Diplomatie und der politischen Öffentlichkeit des Zahrenreiches und des Sowjetstaates, 1697–1947* (Stuttgart, 1995), p. 345.

142. Gerd R. Ueberschär (ed.), *Das Nationalkommittee Freies Deutschland und der Bund*

deutscher Offiziere (Frankfurt, 1995), pp. 268, 272; Schulze-Wessel, *Russlands Blick auf Preussen*, pp. 334, 373.

143. Memorandum by C. E. Steel, Political Division, Control Commission for Germany (British Element) Advance HQ BAOR, 11 October 1945, PRO FO 1049/226.

144. Memorandum of 27 September 1945, HQ IA&C Division C. C. for Germany, BAOR, PRO 1049/595.

145. Allied Control Council Coordinating Committee, Abolition of the State of Prussia, Memorandum by the British Member, 8 August 1946, PRO FO 631/2454, p. 1.

146. Arnd Bauerkämper, 'Der verlorene Antifaschismus. Die Enteignung der Gutsbesitzer und der Umgang mit dem 20. Juli 1944 bei der Bodenreform in der sowjetischen Besatzungszone', *Zeitschift für Geschichtswissenschaft*, 42 (1994), pp. 623–34; id., 'Die Bodenreform in der Provinz Mark Brandenburg', in Werner Stang (ed.), *Brandenburg im Jahr 1945* (Potsdam, 1995), pp. 265–96.

147. For a panoramic account of the fate of the East-Elbian noble families and their estates, see Walter Görlitz, *Die Junker. Adel und Bauer im deutschen Osten. Geschichtliche Bilanz von 7 Jahrhunderten* (Glücksburg, 1957), pp. 410–24.

148. Heiger Ostertag, 'Vom strategischen Bombenkrieg zum sozialistischen Bildersturm. Die Zerstörung Potsdams 1945 und das Schicksal seiner historischen Gebäude nach dem Kriege', in Bernhard R. Kroener (ed.), *Potsdam: Staat, Armee, Residenz in der preussischdeutschen Militärgeschichte* (Berlin, 1993), pp. 487–99; Andreas Kitschke, *Die Potsdamer Garnisonkirche* (Potsdam, 1991), p. 98; Olaf Groehler, 'Der Luftkrieg gegen Brandenburg in den letzten Kriegsmonaten', in Stang (ed.), *Brandenburg*, pp. 9–37.

149. Cited in Kossert, *Ostpreussen*, p. 341.

150. Henning Köhler, *Das Ende Preussens in französischer Sicht* (Berlin, 1982), pp. 13, 18, 20, 23, 25, 29, 40, 43, 47, 75, 96.

151. Uta Lehnert, *Der Kaiser und die Siegesallee: réclame royale* (Berlin, 1998), pp. 337–40.

152. On these trends in Allied education policy, see Riccarda Torriani, 'Nazis into Germans: Re-education and Democratisation in the British and French Occupation Zones, 1945–1949', Ph.D. thesis, Cambridge (2005). I am grateful to Dr Torriani for letting me see a copy of her manuscript before its completion. On Bismarck, see esp. Lothar Machtan, 'Bismarck', in François and Schulze (eds.), *Deutsche Erinnerungsorte*, vol. 2, pp. 620–35, here p. 101.

153. Franz-Lothar Kroll, 'Friedrich der Grosse', in François and Schulze (eds.), *Deutsche Erinnerungsorte*, vol. 2, pp. 86–104, here p. 634.

154. Theodor Fontane, 'Mein Erstling: Das Schlachtfeld von Gross-Beeren', in Kurt Schreinert and Jutta Neuendorf-Fürstenau (eds.), *Meine Kinderjahre* (= *Sämtliche Werke*, vol. XIV) (Munich, 1961), pp. 189–91.

155. Theodor Fontane to Heinrich von Mühler, Berlin, 2 December 1863, in Otto Drude et al. (eds.), *Theodor Fontane. Briefe* (5 vols., Munich, 1976–94), vol. 2, pp. 110–11.

156. Cited in Kenneth Attwood, *Fontane und das Preussentum* (Berlin, 1970), p. 146.

157. Gordon A. Craig, *Theodor Fontane. Literature and History in the Bismarck Reich* (New York, 1999), p. 50.

158. Rüdiger Schütz, 'Zur Eingliederung der Rheinlande', in Peter Baumgart (ed.), *Expansion und Integration. Zur Eingliederung neugewonnener Gebiete in den preussischen Staat* (Cologne, 1984), pp. 195–226, here p. 225.

159. Kurt Jürgensen, 'Die Eingliederung Westfalens in den preussischen Staat', in Baumgart (ed.), *Expansion*, pp. 227–54, here p. 250.

160. Walter Geschler, *Das Preussische Oberpräsidium der Provinz Jülich-Kleve-Berg in Köln 1816–1822* (Cologne, 1967), pp. 200–201; Oswald Hauser, *Preussische Staatsräson und nationaler Gedanke. Auf Grund unveröffentlichter Akten aus dem Schleswig-Holsteinischen Landesarchiv* (Neumünster, 1960); Arnold Brecht, *Federalism and Regionalism in Germany. The Division of Prussia* (New York, 1945).

161. See Hans-Georg Aschoff, 'Die welfische Bewegung und die Deutsch-Hannoversche

Partei zwischen 1866 und 1914', *Niedersächsisches Jahrbuch für Landesgeschichte*, 53 (1981), pp. 41–64.

162. Kurt Jürgensen, 'Die Eingliederung der Herzogtümer Schleswig, Holstein und Lauenburg in das preussische Königreich', in Baumgart (ed.), *Expansion*, pp. 327–56, here pp. 350–52.

163. Georg Kunz, *Verortete Geschichte. Regionales Geschichtsbewusstsein in den deutschen Historischen Vereinen des 19. Jahrhunderts* (Göttingen, 2000), pp. 312–22. On the interchangeability of local, regional and national concepts of *Heimat*, see Alon Confino, 'Federalism and the Heimat Idea in Nineteenth-century Germany', in Maiken Umbach (ed.), *German Federalism* (London, 2002), pp. 70–90.

164. Attwood, *Fontane und das Preussentum*, pp. 15–30. A nuanced monographic study is Gerhard Friedrich, *Fontanes preussische Welt. Armee – Dynastie – Staat* (Herford, 1988).

165. This essay (and two others on the same theme published in 1848) can be found in Albrecht Gaertner (ed.), *Theodor Fontane. Aus meiner Werkstatt. Unbekanntes und Unveröffentlichtes* (Berlin, 1950), pp. 8–15.

166. Attwood, *Fontane und das Preussentum*, pp. 166–7.

167. Andreas Dorpalen, 'The German Struggle Against Napoleon: The East German View', *Journal of Modern History*, 41 (1969), pp. 485–516.

168. See Jan Palmowski, 'Regional Identities and the Limits of Democratic Centralism in the GDR', in *Journal of Contemporary History* (forthcoming). My thanks to Jan Palmowski for allowing me to see this fascinating piece before its appearance in print.

169. Ibid. On Klüss, see also the informative notes in Karl-Heinz Steinbruch, 'Gemeinde Brunow. History of the Villages of Gemeinde Brunow', at *http://www.thies-site.com/loc/brunow/steinbruch—history—kluess-en.htm*; last accessed 23 December 2004.

Index

often forgotten, Clark argues, is that it had also been an exemplar of the European humanistic tradition, boasting a formidable government administration, an incorruptible civil service, and religious tolerance. Clark demonstrates how a state deemed the bane of twentieth-century Europe has played an incalculable role in Western civilization's fortunes. *Iron Kingdom* is a definitive, gripping account of Prussia's fascinating, influential, and critical role in modern times.

CHRISTOPHER CLARK is Reader in Modern European History at St. Catharine's College, University of Cambridge. He is the author of *Politics of Conversion: Missionary Protestantism and the Jews in Prussia 1728–1941* and *Kaiser Wilhelm II*, and the coeditor of *Culture Wars: Catholic-Secular Conflict in Nineteenth-Century Europe*.